A COMPLETE GUIDE

BIRDS

OF BRITISH COLUMBIA
AND THE PACIFIC NORTHWEST

Richard Cannings,

Tom Aversa,

and Hal Opperman

HERITAGE

VICTORIA · VANCOUVER · CALGARY

Heritage House Publishing Company Ltd.
heritagehouse.ca

LIBRARY AND ARCHIVES CANADA CATALOGUING IN PUBLICATION

Published simultaneously in the U.S. by the Seattle Audubon Society and University of
Washington Press under the title *Birds of the Pacific Northwest: A Photographic Guide.*

Cannings, Richard J. (Richard James) author
    Birds of British Columbia and the Pacific Northwest : a complete guide /
Richard Cannings, Tom Aversa, Hal Opperman.

Issued in print and electronic formats. ISBN 978-1-927527-56-6 (paperback).
—ISBN 978-1-927527-57-3 (html).—ISBN 978-1-927527-58-0 (pdf)

    1. Birds—British Columbia—Identification. 2. Bird watching—British Columbia.
3. Birds—Northwest, Pacific—Identification. 4. Bird watching—Northwest, Pacific.
I. Opperman, Hal N., author II. Aversa, Tom, 1957–, author III. Title.

QL685.5.B7C367 2016   578.09711   C2013-908567-X   C2013-908568-8

Edited by Karla Decker and Renate Preuss
Proofread by Renate Preuss
Cover and interior book design by Jacqui Thomas
Cover photos: Townsend's Warbler, by Glenn Bartley (*front*), and Northern Pygmy-Owl,
by Glenn Bartley (*back*)

This book was produced using FSC®-certified, acid-free paper, processed chlorine free and
printed with vegetable-based inks.

We acknowledge the financial support of the Government of Canada through the Canada
Book Fund and the Canada Council for the Arts, and the Province of British Columbia
through the British Columbia Arts Council and the Book Publishing Tax Credit.

 The Canada Council | Le Conseil des Arts
for the Arts | du Canada
 BRITISH COLUMBIA
ARTS COUNCIL

20 19 18 17 16   1 2 3 4 5

Printed in Canada

For my father, Salvatore, who set many wonderful examples for his children, but none as important as demonstrating that persistence is critical in achieving any difficult goal. —**TOM AVERSA**

In memory of Jamie Smith, who studied and loved the birds of this region and worked diligently to protect their world. —**RICHARD CANNINGS**

For my mentors in natural history and the art of living in the landscape: Paul H. Shepard, Jr. (1925–1996), Mildred E. Mathias (1906–1995), Clinton H. Conaway (1923–2002). —**HAL OPPERMAN**

Contents

AUTHORS' PREFACE

The first glimmer of a desire to produce what became this book goes back a dozen years, as Tom and Hal co-authored a pair of pocket-sized field guides for the Puget Sound and Willamette Valley regions, published by the R.W. Morse Company. These books were well received. Nonetheless, we asked ourselves, wasn't there also room for a book for birders looking to move beyond the localized, beginner-oriented level? In our thinking, such a work would include more than just the commonest species; would devote more attention to field-identification criteria, behavior, and ecology; would have more photos; and would cover the entire Pacific Northwest. In 2005, when Dick joined Tom and Hal to co-author the third of these little guides (*Birds of Southwestern British Columbia*, published by Heritage House), the idea for a comprehensive Pacific Northwest book not only took root but slowly began to leaf out. Our team was complete.

Our working concept was to fill a niche between, on one hand, the scientifically intensive state and provincial "Birds of..." tomes, which provide exhaustive detail on status, distribution, and biology but offer few images of birds and next to nothing on identification; and on the other hand, the widely used North American field guides, which are well illustrated but generally limit information to the essentials of field identification, and depict range and seasonal movements only at a broad continental scale. In our book, discussion of status, distribution, subspecies, and habitats would be closely tailored to the Pacific Northwest, and photographs would be taken within the region, by regional photographers, to the extent possible.

We adopted the definition of the Pacific Northwest almost universally favored by ecologists and wildlife biologists (see the essay beginning on page 9). Politically, however, the term leads to confusion, because from a Canadian perspective this is, after all, the southwest. It might help to recall that, at one time, the region was a single territory claimed by both Great Britain and the United States, jointly administered by these two powers until divided at the present international boundary in 1846. Known to the British as the Columbia District and to Americans as the Oregon Country, this territory had exactly the same terrestrial limits as the Pacific Northwest of our book. The northern limit at 54°40′N marks the old colonial boundary with Russian America (today Alaska); and the southern limit at 42°N is the old colonial boundary with Spanish California. The eastern boundary —a political one back then—is the Continental Divide, just as it is for our book.

Early in the project we had to determine which birds would be given full species accounts. It is difficult to know precisely how many species have been recorded at least once somewhere in the Pacific Northwest, but the total number certainly approaches 600.

We decided to limit our focus to only those species that reliably occur annually. This enabled us to better treat the regulars while leaving most vagrants and megararities to the all-encompassing North American guides. We defined criteria for annual occurrence as any species that had one or more credible records in at least nine of the ten years from 1999–2008 in any one of four entities—Washington, or Oregon, or our part of British Columbia, or Idaho taken together with the bordering parts of Montana and Wyoming west of the Continental Divide; or had accrued over 20 records in the Pacific Northwest as a whole during the same period. This gave us a total of 412 species to be treated in the book.

By 2008 we had developed a formal publication proposal, and in early 2010 this proposal was accepted by the Seattle Audubon Society. Heritage House, a noted publisher of non-fiction titles on topics of the Canadian West, signed on as co-publisher for the Canadian edition in 2012, and in early 2016 the University of Washington Press joined Seattle Audubon as co-pubisher of the US edition. We are proud that our book will appear in the distinguished series of regional natural history titles Seattle Audubon has published since 1942, and that it will join the natural history lists at Heritage House and University of Washington Press. We could not have been better served.

During the years that the project advanced, writing of accounts, creation of range maps, and the review and revision of both was a rolling collaborative process among the three of us, as was building a short-list of photographs and determining the final selections. Regional photographers offered many incredible images, allowing us to depict the most representative plumages. When photos could not be found from within the region, birds of the same subspecies photographed in nearby states/provinces were given precedence. Whenever we could, we chose images of birds in action rather than in "standard" pure-profile views as long as photographic quality and clarity of the field marks were not compromised.

This book would never have been possible without the aid and encouragement of friends and colleagues at every stage, and it is our great pleasure to thank them collectively here. Nonetheless, full responsibility for any errors or other shortcomings lies with the authors, not with those who have so generously assisted us.

First and foremost, we acknowledge our deep indebtedness to three experts in the birdlife of parts of the Pacific Northwest less familiar to us than our home territories of British Columbia and Washington. Hendrik Herlyn of Oregon, Shirley Sturts of Idaho, and Dan Casey of Montana took on the task of reviewing all of the species accounts and maps. In turn, they consulted many others about finer points of current status and distribution for individual species or localities within their states. The book has benefitted from their intervention in countless ways.

No group of contributors has done more to ensure the appeal and usefulness of the book than our photographers. Gregg Thompson, an unflagging supporter from the beginning, is our source for an astonishing 160 images. Ten other photographers have provided from 20 to over 70 images apiece. In descending order, these are Greg Gillson, Laure Wilson Neish, Ryan Shaw, Darren Clark, Doug Schurman, Ralph Hocken, Gerald Romanchuk, Doug Brown, Keith Carlson, and Dennis Paulson. More than a hundred others answered the call with fewer but no less impressive photographs. Thanks to each and every one of you.

We are grateful to the many birders and biologists, too numerous to name, who shared their knowledge in response to specific questions. It is a particular joy to thank the many birding companions with whom we have explored the spectacular habitats and rich birdlife of this vast region, and learned so much.

The Seattle Audubon Society's Publications Committee, chaired by Connie Sidles, established the platform upon which this enterprise is built and has continuously provided valuable advice and other support, both moral and material. We are fortunate indeed to have worked with Rodger Touchie, President of Heritage House, who served as administrative coordinator of the co-publication project and whose expert staff, under the leadership of Senior Editor Lara Kordic, oversaw the editorial, design, and production aspects of the book. Bob Berman, Andrew Couturier, Donald Gunn, Cindy Lippincott, Lorie Ransom, Terry Rich, Anderson Sandes, and Andrew Valleley also made essential contributions.

As we write these words, the book you are now holding in your hands is about to go off to the printer. We hope it brings you some good measure of the same satisfaction and understanding that creating it has brought us.

Tom Aversa
Dick Cannings
Hal Opperman
March 2016

THE PACIFIC NORTHWEST
Geography, Climate, Ecology

The physiography of the Pacific Northwest is, at its simplest, a series of north–south trending mountain ranges separated by valleys, basins, and plateaus, bounded on the west by the Pacific Ocean and on the east by the Rocky Mountains. To the north lie the great boreal forests and to the south are the southwestern deserts. Within these boundaries is a region of tremendous geographic, climatic, and biological diversity.

Almost all the region's land was formed through a series of collisions between North America and various island arcs in the Pacific as the continent drifted westward starting about 180 million years ago. These collisions added land mass to North America, pushed up the Rockies and other mountain ranges, and provided the magma for intense plutonic and volcanic activity that shaped both mountains and plateaus. The pattern of landforms that resulted—the mountain ranges, valleys, and plateaus—is largely what governs the pattern of bird distribution in the region today.

The rivers of the Pacific Northwest are dominated by two massive systems. The Columbia River, including its main tributaries the Kootenay and the Snake, drains 258,000 sq mi (668,000 km²) to the Pacific Ocean west of Portland, from across the full breadth of the region and four-fifths of its length. The Fraser River drains 84,942 sq mi (220,000 km²) in central British Columbia to its mouth at Vancouver. The Salish Sea—the great inland sea embracing the Strait of Georgia, Puget Sound, and the Strait of Juan de Fuca—receives not only the outflow of the Fraser but also that of many smaller rivers, principally the Skagit. Other rivers drain the coastal ranges directly to the ocean. Some mid-sized rivers in this category are worthy of note, including the Dean, Klinaklini, and Homathko in British Columbia, the Chehalis in Washington, and the Umpqua and Rogue in Oregon.

It is not a simple accident that this region is called the Pacific Northwest, for it is the Pacific Ocean that shapes much of its climate and ecosystems. From November through March a seemingly endless series of storms sweep off the Pacific and onto the coast. These cyclones are born in a low-pressure center known as the Aleutian Low that sits just south of the Alaska Peninsula in winter, and bring mild temperatures and heavy rain to the open coast. Henderson Lake, on the west coast of Vancouver Island, is the wettest place in North America with a mean annual precipitation of 272 in/690 cm. As the storms move farther east they are forced to climb the coastal ranges, where winter precipitation falls primarily as snow. These mountains are the snowiest place on earth; the world record for annual snowfall is held by Mount Baker, Washington, which reported 95 ft/29 m of snow in the winter of 1998–1999.

As the airstreams pass over the crest of the Coast Mountains of British Columbia and the Cascade Range, they descend to valleys and plateaus east of the mountains, depleted of their moisture. These areas are the driest parts of the region with mean annual precipitation under 8 in/20 cm in places. Less dramatic rain shadows are found in the lee of the outer coastal mountains on Vancouver Island, the Olympic Peninsula, and the Oregon coast, resulting in drier areas on southeastern Vancouver Island, the Gulf and San Juan Islands, and the Willamette Valley. East of the Coast Mountains and Cascade Range the dry airstreams pick up moisture again, particularly in the forested parts of British Columbia, and precipitation increases on the western flanks of interior ranges such as the Cariboo, Monashee, and Selkirk Mountains.

Two other sources of air masses influence the region, at times dramatically. In winter, Arctic air often spills through passes in the Rocky Mountains and flows over the plateaus and into the valleys in the eastern part of the Pacific Northwest. This cold, dry air brings low temperatures and clear skies to interior locations, but the barrier of mountain ranges and the eastward movement of warm Pacific air along the coast protect most coastal locations from its influence. In summer, hot, dry air often moves northward from high-pressure centers over the southwestern desert into eastern portions of the region, bringing daily highs of over 100°F/38°C for periods of days or even weeks.

In general, the annual temperature regimes of coastal locations result in mild winters and cool summers, while locations east of the main coastal mountain ranges experience cold winters and hot summers.

THREE ECOREGIONS are recognized in the Pacific Northwest, encompassing the wet forests of the maritime climate regime on the Pacific slope; the coniferous forests of the continental climate regime of the interior mountains; and the arid grasslands of the southern interior. Each is home to a distinctive community of flora and fauna, ecologically interrelated with its physical environment.

Marine West Coast Forest Ecoregion

This ecoregion extends from southern coastal Alaska to northwestern California, eastward to the crest and upper east slopes of the Cascades and British Columbia Coast Range to the point where prevailing Pacific winds have lost most of their moisture. Climate is generally mild except in winter at the highest elevations. Precipitation is abundant, rising in proportion to elevation and proximity to the ocean, dropping in the western lowlands sheltered by the coastal mountains from the prevailing moisture-laden Pacific winds.

The Marine West Coast Forest ecoregion is composed of one oceanic and four terrestrial subregions.

1) PACIFIC OCEAN. The Pacific Ocean is here treated as an integral part of the Pacific Northwest, to a limit of 200 nautical miles/370 km offshore. The coastal currents are highly productive due to upwelling caused by prevailing winds and strong tidal currents around islands, nurturing substantial seabird breeding colonies. The rich waters also attract marine species that do not breed in the area, particularly along the edges of the continental shelf and various subsurface banks, mounts, and trenches. Black-footed Albatrosses even fly to the Pacific Northwest coast to gather

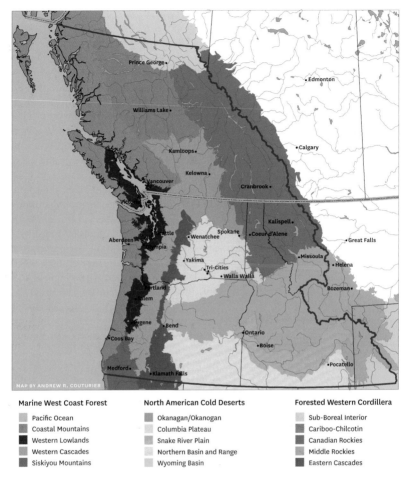

MAP BY ANDREW R. COUTURIER

Marine West Coast Forest	North American Cold Deserts	Forested Western Cordillera
Pacific Ocean	Okanagan/Okanogan	Sub-Boreal Interior
Coastal Mountains	Columbia Plateau	Cariboo-Chilcotin
Western Lowlands	Snake River Plain	Canadian Rockies
Western Cascades	Northern Basin and Range	Middle Rockies
Siskiyou Mountains	Wyoming Basin	Eastern Cascades

food to feed their chicks on Midway Island. Great migrations of species that breed in the southern hemisphere such as Pink-footed, Buller's, and Sooty Shearwaters move up and down the coast annually, joined by species that mostly nest north of the region such as Northern Fulmar, jaegers, Black-legged Kittiwake, Sabine's Gull, and Arctic Tern.

2) COASTAL MOUNTAINS. Starting from the northwest corner of the region, the outermost flank of mountains consists of two large island masses—Haida Gwaii and Vancouver Island—that dominate the outer British Columbia coast. Just south of Vancouver Island across the Strait of Juan de Fuca, the Olympic Mountains are the westernmost range in Washington. Peaks of Vancouver Island and the Olympics reach above 7,000 ft/2,100 m, with subalpine meadows and alpine parkland at high elevations. The terrain is steep, the outer coastline generally rocky. Headlands, sea-stacks, and small islands along the coast are often the sites of important breeding colonies of seabirds such as Fork-tailed and Leach's Storm-Petrels, cormorants, Glaucous-winged and Western Gulls, Common Murre, Ancient Murrelet, Cassin's and Rhinoceros Auklets, and Tufted Puffin. Black Oystercatchers breed on rocky shorelines, joined in winter by Black Turnstones, Surfbirds, and Rock Sandpipers.

The Willapa Hills in southern Washington, and the Oregon Coast Range, complete the coastal ramparts. These much lower hills, rarely exceeding 2,500 ft/750 m, are often fronted by coastal plains with grasslands, freshwater ponds and marshes, dunes, and broad beaches. Snowy Plovers breed in small numbers in coastal dune habitats, and many other shorebirds use the open beaches in migration and winter. Numerous major estuaries along this portion of the coast provide essential feeding grounds for migrant shorebirds such as Black-bellied Plovers, Western and Least Sandpipers, and Short-billed Dowitchers. In winter, hundreds of thousands of dabbling ducks forage on estuarine mudflats, while diving ducks and other waterbirds feed in protected estuarine waters. Most of the inhabitants of the Coastal Mountains subregion live along this part of the coast. Aberdeen/Hoquiam and Coos Bay/North Bend, each with a population of around 25,000, are by far the largest communities.

The inner British Columbia coast—east of Haida Gwaii and Vancouver Island—is characterized by deep and long fjords that were carved by massive glaciers during the Pleistocene. There are few beaches in that part of the region; the mountains plunge directly and deeply into the ocean. Above and around the fjords is the granitic massif of the Coast Mountains of British Columbia, bounded on the south by the Fraser River. These mountains offer some of the most rugged, inaccessible terrain in the region, with permanent ice fields and summits reaching 11,000–13,000 ft/3,400–4,000 m. Subalpine meadows and alpine tundra above timberline are home to Willow, Rock, and White-tailed Ptarmigans.

The forests of the Coastal Mountains subregion are among the most biologically productive areas on earth. In consequence they have been relentlessly logged for the last century and a half, although extensive tracts with stands of ancient trees the height of modern skyscrapers have been preserved. Dominant tree species are western hemlock, Sitka spruce, western redcedar, and Pacific silver fir in the north, with grand fir and Douglas-fir increasing in importance from Vancouver Island south. Bigleaf maple is a dominant species along stream courses, and red alder is an important successional species after disturbance; southward, Oregon ash becomes increasingly common.

Low- to mid-elevation forest-breeding avifauna includes characteristic species such as Sooty Grouse, Marbled Murrelet, Band-tailed Pigeon, Northern Pygmy-Owl, Barred and Northern Saw-whet Owls, Vaux's Swift, Rufous Hummingbird, Red-breasted Sapsucker, Hairy Woodpecker, Northern Flicker, Western Wood-Pewee, Olive-sided, Hammond's, and Pacific-slope Flycatchers, Hutton's and Warbling Vireos, Gray and Steller's Jays, Common Raven, Chestnut-backed Chickadee, Red-breasted Nuthatch, Brown Creeper, Pacific Wren, American Dipper, Golden-crowned Kinglet, Swainson's, Hermit, and Varied Thrushes, "Audubon's" (Yellow-rumped), Black-throated Gray, and Wilson's Warblers, Song Sparrow, "Oregon" (Dark-eyed) Junco, Western Tanager, Purple Finch, Red Crossbill, and Pine Siskin. Hermit Warbler breeds commonly in Oregon but becomes quickly outnumbered by Townsend's Warbler northward into Washington, where the two interbreed. The subalpine and alpine zones host breeding Horned Lark, American Pipit, and Gray-crowned Rosy-Finch.

3) WESTERN LOWLANDS. Lying between the coastal ranges and the Cascades at an elevation ranging from sea level to about 1,000 ft/300 m, this subregion is home to the Pacific Northwest's busiest seaports; to its three largest metropolitan areas (Vancouver, Seattle, Portland); and to the majority of the combined population of British Columbia, Washington, and Oregon. In the north, it occupies the glacial basin of the Salish Sea (Georgia Depression/Puget Trough), from southeastern Vancouver Island and the British Columbia Lower Mainland to the drainage plain of southern Puget Sound. Subject to intense development, these plains and foothills have been largely denuded of the once ubiquitous damp conifer forests, but where these persist, birdlife is pretty much the same as at lower elevations of the Coastal Mountains. The deltas and estuaries of several rivers, most importantly the Fraser and the Skagit, provide habitat for large numbers of resident and migrant birds.

The lowlands farther south, drained principally by the Columbia River and tributaries, attain their greatest extent along the Willamette River in Oregon. A broad, level plain rising from nearly sea level at the Columbia confluence (Portland) to an elevation of 400 ft/120 m at the southern end (Eugene/Springfield), the Willamette Valley is now mostly given over to agriculture, including wineries, but many marshes and other wetlands provide vital bird habitat. Endemic subspecies of Horned Lark and Vesper Sparrow carry on in declining numbers in hayfields, pastures, and grass-seed farms.

Broadleaf riparian woods line ponds and watercourses throughout the subregion. Riparian, mixed-forest, and shrubby habitats in lowlands and foothills attract Rufous Hummingbird, Downy Woodpecker, Hutton's Vireo, "California" (Western) Scrub-Jay (Oregon north to Puget Sound), Bushtit, Bewick's Wren, Swainson's Thrush, Cedar Waxwing, Orange-crowned, Black-throated Gray, and Wilson's Warblers, Spotted Towhee, Song and White-crowned Sparrows, Black-headed Grosbeak, and Purple Finch, among many other species. Anna's Hummingbirds are common in parks and gardens where feeders keep them through the winter. Pacific madrone (*Arbutus*) and Garry (Oregon white) oak are important tree species in drier sites, the latter forming savanna habitats in localized prairies—but many of the open habitats are dominated by Scotch broom, Himalayan and evergreen blackberries, and other invasive plants. The Columbia bottomlands, now largely diked, support vast numbers of migratory and wintering waterfowl and Sandhill Cranes. Wrentits skulk in thicket habitats south from the Columbia, extending up river valleys to higher elevations in the Cascade foothills.

4) WESTERN CASCADES. The division between the coastal forests and the arid interior runs along the Cascade Range, extending from the Fraser River in southern British Columbia to northern California. Its snow- and ice-clad volcanoes reach above 12,000–14,000 ft/3,700–4,300 m. The western and upper eastern slopes sustain damp, marine-influenced conifer forests, in stark contrast to the dry forests of the lower eastern slopes and foothills that belong to the Forested Western Cordillera ecoregion.

This subregion has few year-round human inhabitants, and most of the land is publicly owned. The northern Washington Cascades—characterized by steep-sided, glacier-carved valleys—have been little disturbed, especially at higher elevations. The terrain of the southern Washington and Oregon Cascades is less forbidding, and logging is more extensive there. Forest composition is generally similar to that of the coastal mountains, and similarly stratified by elevation, slope, aspect, and precipitation. Sitka spruce disappears south of Puget Sound; ponderosa pine and other drought-tolerant conifers mix in with Douglas-fir at lower elevations in Oregon. Some reservoirs and many smaller natural lakes occur throughout. Wet meadows, bogs, and swamps are found at higher elevations, and subalpine parkland, alpine meadows, snowfields, and permanent glaciers still higher up.

Low- to mid-elevation forest-breeding avifauna differs little from that of the coastal ranges and lowlands foothills, including characteristic species such as Sooty Grouse, Band-tailed Pigeon, Barred Owl, Red-breasted Sapsucker, Hammond's and Pacific-slope Flycatchers, Steller's Jay, Chestnut-backed Chickadee, Pacific Wren, American Dipper, Golden-crowned Kinglet, Varied Thrush, Townsend's Warbler, and Dark-eyed Junco. The subalpine and alpine zones host breeding White-tailed Ptarmigan (absent from Oregon), Horned Lark, Mountain Bluebird, American Pipit, and Gray-crowned Rosy-Finch.

5) SISKIYOU MOUNTAINS. Part of a complex of ranges extending south through the Klamath River drainage basin in California, Oregon's Siskiyou Mountains form a wedge between the Cascades and the Coast Range, broadening southward from its northern tip just south of the Willamette Valley and nearly reaching the coast and the Cascade crest at the California line. Highly dissected and geologically complex, the Siskiyous range in elevation from 600 ft/180 m to escarpments over 7,400 ft/2,200 m. The rocks that compose them—non-volcanic in origin—are the oldest in Oregon.

Biogeographically transitional between the coastal Pacific Northwest, the Cascades (both slopes), and Mediterranean California, this subregion sustains a unique diversity of plant and animal species. The mild climate and coniferous rainforest of the adjacent Coast Range and Cascades contrast markedly with the low precipitation and hot summers of the valleys of the Rogue/Illinois Rivers in the Siskiyous. Dry interior slopes grow to forests of conifers mixed with broadleaf species such as tanoak, California black oak, and Pacific madrone. Oak Titmouse, Blue-gray Gnatcatcher, and California Towhee reach the Pacific Northwest in the Siskiyous. Tricolored Blackbirds nest locally in the Rogue Valley. Black Phoebe has been gradually pushing north from its Siskiyous stronghold for decades. Spotted Owl populations, plummeting farther north, are still relatively stable here.

The Siskiyou Mountains subregion has a more resilient economy than its neighbors. Tourism, recreation, and small-scale manufacturing supplement grazing, dairying, orchards, vineyards, nurseries, and the forest products industry. Population, concentrated along Interstate 5, is increasing. Medford (75,000 inhabitants) is the largest city in southwestern Oregon.

Forested Western Cordillera Ecoregion

This ecoregion is characterized by high mountains and vast forested plateaus. Lodgepole pine, Engelmann spruce, and subalpine fir are the prevalent conifer forest components. Of the five subregions the northernmost is transitional to the cold boreal zone, whereas the other four are transitional to the interior hot desert zone they frame.

1) SUB-BOREAL INTERIOR. The southern quarter of this subregion—the part included in our book—lies mostly in the low, rather flat Fraser Basin, characterized by forests of white spruce and subalpine fir accompanied by Douglas-fir toward the south and lodgepole pine toward the north. Stands of paper birch and quaking aspen occur throughout. The area has an abundance of wetland types, including sphagnum bogs. The section of the Rocky Mountains that forms the eastern edge is lower and less rugged than the peaks along the crest to the north and south. Forests of subalpine fir, Engelmann spruce, and lodgepole pine cover the slopes up to subalpine parkland and patches of tundra at the rounded summits. Warm summers are succeeded by Arctic air masses in winter. Precipitation is moderate year-round.

The Sub-Boreal Interior is the Pacific Northwest's center of abundance for breeding Northern Waterthrush and American Redstart. Yellow-bellied Flycatcher, Magnolia Warbler, and White-throated Sparrow breed here; Ovenbird and other "eastern" songbirds are increasing.

The limited economy of this lightly populated subregion is based on logging, mining, and grazing. Prince George (75,000 inhabitants) is by far the largest city.

2) CARIBOO–CHILCOTIN. The heart of the Cariboo–Chilcotin subregion is the broad, rolling Fraser Plateau, a system of mountains, plateaus, and basins flanked on the southwest by the higher Chilcotin Ranges. The climate is continental. The Coastal Mountains cast a strong rain shadow over the southern half, favoring the growth of dry forests dominated by lodgepole pine. The Cariboo Basin along the Fraser River in the southeast—the lowest, driest, hottest part—has Douglas-fir forest and shrub-steppe communities. Less sheltered from Pacific moisture, the cooler northern half of the subregion is typified by white spruce/subalpine fir forests.

Solitary Sandpipers and Greater Yellowlegs nest in sedge marshes in this northern half, and Yellow Rails are local breeders in those habitats as well. Marshy ponds, bogs, and other wetlands common across the Cariboo and Chilcotin Plateaus support a high diversity of breeding ducks, grebes, and other waterbirds, along with Sandhill Crane, gulls, Black Tern, and Rusty Blackbird. Smaller mountain lakes have breeding Common and Barrow's Goldeneyes. Grasslands support Sharp-tailed Grouse, Long-billed Curlew, Horned Lark, Vesper Sparrow, and Western Meadowlark, but generally lack the species associated with arid shrub-steppe landscapes of the hot desert zone farther south.

The region is sparsely populated; Williams Lake (11,000 inhabitants) is the largest community. Economic activity centers around forest products, mining, and grazing.

3) CANADIAN ROCKIES. The subregion consists of a series of parallel northwest–southeast trending mountain ranges and trenches known collectively as the Columbia Mountains, gaining elevation progressively from west to east and lapping over the Rocky Mountain spine onto the high eastern slopes in Alberta and Montana. From the northeastern corner of the book's coverage area, this mountain/valley system extends along the Rocky Mountain Trench in British

Columbia through the Kootenays and the Idaho Panhandle to the North Fork of the Clearwater River, the Flathead River drainage basin of northwestern Montana, and the Pend Oreille River watershed in northeastern Washington. Subsidiary ranges include the Selkirk, Purcell, Cabinet, and northern Bitterroot Mountains.

The lowlands have dry, warm summers and cold winters—a climate regime that sustains grasslands and mid-elevation forests of Douglas-fir with some ponderosa pine. These forests are a center of abundance for species such as Black-backed Woodpecker (particularly in burned areas), Least Flycatcher, Cassin's Vireo, Western Tanager, and Townsend's Warbler. Higher slopes, under maritime influence, receive ample precipitation, fostering a unique interior rainforest highly diverse in tree species composition but generally resembling a coastal forest type, dominated by western hemlock, grand fir, and western redcedar. Most of the breeding bird species of these higher, wetter forests are the same as those of the coastal mountains.

Several large glacial lakes (Pend Oreille, Coeur d'Alene, Priest, Flathead) and reservoirs (e.g., Revelstoke, Kinbasket, Kootenay, Boundary Lakes), and many small lakes and marshes, host nesting and migrating waterfowl. Remarkable concentrations of Ospreys breed locally in the southern part of the subregion. Blue Jays now nest regularly on the western flanks of the Rockies and are apparently spreading westward valley by valley.

Treeline occurs at about 7,000–8,000 ft/2,100–2,400 m and is often characterized by open woodlands of subalpine larch and whitebark pine above the lodgepole pine, subalpine fir, and Engelmann spruce forests. Alpine tundra habitats—common on high snow- and ice-crowned peaks—are home to White-tailed Ptarmigan (and Willow Ptarmigan in the north), Horned Lark, American Pipit, and Gray-crowned Rosy-Finch. Prominent summits attain elevations from around 10,000 ft/3,000 m (Montana) up to 13,000 ft/4,000 m (Mt. Robson in British Columbia).

Poised in lowland valleys at the very edge of the subregion, two large cities serve as gateways: Coeur d'Alene, Idaho, and Missoula, Montana, both with more than 100,000 metro-area residents. The mountainous heart is far less densely populated. The largest cities are Cranbrook, British Columbia, in the East Kootenay (population 19,000) and Kalispell, Montana, in the Flathead Basin (population 20,000).

Grazing, haying, and forest products remain economically significant throughout. Agriculture is more extensive and diversified in the south, including cereal crops, orchards, and a nascent viticulture industry (five wineries in the Kootenays). Tourism and recreational activities, including wildlife viewing, are much more highly developed in the south than in the north.

4) MIDDLE ROCKIES. The Middle Rockies subregion reaches from the Clark Fork Valley of Montana southward along the main Rocky Mountain chain to northwestern Wyoming. A large section of it, including southwestern Montana and the Yellowstone Plateau down to the Great Plains margin, lies across the Continental Divide in the Missouri River watershed. Although technically not part of the Pacific Northwest, this eastern section has the same birds and forest composition as the western section.

Middle Rockies forests, under little maritime influence, are drier and have a lower diversity of conifer types than those of the Canadian Rockies. Lodgepole pine is typical, with Douglas-fir in moister situations; subalpine fir and Engelmann spruce appear at upper elevations, where precipitation is greater. High ridges and peaks have alpine vegetation. Many of Wyoming's highest peaks (above 9,000 ft/2,700 m) are in this subregion. Streams are numerous, sometimes bordered by broadleaf trees, at other times meandering through wide, flat, open valleys with grasses and low, shrubby growth. Aspen stands, mountain big sagebrush, and meadows thrive on high plateaus and slopes. Yellowstone Lake is the most magnificent of the numerous lakes, usually smallish, that dot the landscape. The Middle Rockies subregion supports a breeding avifauna similar to that of the Canadian Rockies, with a few notable absences (Black Swift, Chestnut-backed and Boreal Chickadees) and additions (Broad-tailed Hummingbird, Prairie Falcon, Cordilleran Flycatcher, Canyon Wren, Green-tailed Towhee, Black Rosy-Finch).

Two mountain formations stretching westward from Montana across central Idaho and north-central Oregon—each composed of several ranges—are part of this subregion. The Idaho Batholith extends southward from the North Fork Clearwater River to the northern edge of the Snake River Plain, brushing the border of southwestern Montana on the east. The western end abuts the Blue Mountains, which continue westward from west-central Idaho and the southeastern corner of Washington to the Deschutes River drainage at the base of the Cascades in northern Oregon.

These mountains have a complex and varied geological history. Typically they are rounded and unimposing, reaching about 6,000–7,000 ft/1,800–2,100 m above sea level and forested to the top, but some clusters of towering, sheer-faced, barren peaks in northeastern Oregon and central Idaho rise well above timberline to 9,000–12,000 ft/2,700–3,700 m. Climate, topography, flora, and fauna are similar to those of the Middle Rockies *sensu stricto*. Shrub-steppe at the margins, in the baking summer heat of the arid Columbia Plateau, Harney Basin, and Snake River Plain, yields to forested slopes with the familiar altitudinal gradient of conifer types, from Douglas-fir, grand fir, and ponderosa pine in the lower, drier, hotter zone to Engelmann spruce and subalpine fir in the cooler, moister zone higher up. Winters are cold throughout.

Like the other mountain subregions, the Middle Rockies are virtually unpopulated. Mining, grazing, and logging anchor the legacy economy, along with limited haying, dairying, and dryland wheat cultivation. Tourism and recreation are highly developed and account for an increasingly significant share of regional income. Missoula, Bozeman, Boise, and Bend, stationed around the periphery, have metropolitan-area populations of 100,000–200,000 and diversified economies.

5) EASTERN CASCADES. The Eastern Cascades subregion takes in the dry forests of the rain-shadowed eastern slopes of the Cascade Range down to the edge of the arid, treeless habitats of the interior. This is a zone of hot summers and cold winters with a pronounced altitudinal moisture gradient. Its northern limit is Sawtooth Ridge in Washington, where it meets the Okanogan subregion north of Lake Chelan; southward, the subregion extends through Oregon to the Modoc Plateau of California. The northern portion (adjacent to the Columbia Plateau and Blue Mountains) drains to the Columbia, largely via the Yakima, Wenatchee, Chelan/Stehekin, and Klickitat Rivers in Washington and the Deschutes River in Oregon, whereas the southern portion (south of Bend, adjacent to the Northern Basin and Range subregion) lies mostly in the Klamath River drainage basin.

Forests of the northern portion are composed principally of ponderosa pine, Douglas-fir, and western larch, with grand fir at mid-elevations, cottonwoods in riparian corridors, and aspen groves in openings. Forests are drier and more open at lower elevations, with a grass-and-shrub understory. Garry oak is increasingly important from the Yakima River south. Stimulated by higher moisture passing through the Columbia Gorge from the coast, oak woodlands are highly developed along the interior Cascade slopes for a considerable distance north and south of the river. Lake Chelan is the only large water body. Small lakes, wet meadows, and marshes occur locally, e.g., below Mt. Adams in southern Washington (Conboy Lake NWR, Trout Lake).

Typical birds of these riparian, dry-forest, and edge habitats include Ruffed and Sooty Grouse, Western Screech-Owl, Spotted Owl, Common Poorwill, Calliope Hummingbird, Lewis's, Hairy, and White-headed Woodpeckers, Williamson's (western larches) and Red-naped Sapsuckers, Western Wood-Pewee, Olive-sided, Gray (ponderosa pines with grassy understory), Dusky, and Ash-throated (oaks) Flycatchers, Eastern Kingbird, Cassin's Vireo, Mountain Chickadee, all three nuthatches, House Wren, American Dipper, Western and Mountain Bluebirds, Townsend's Solitaire, Veery, Gray Catbird, Nashville, MacGillivray's, "Audubon's" (Yellow-rumped), and Townsend's Warblers, Yellow-breasted Chat, Chipping Sparrow, Western Tanager, Black-headed Grosbeak, Lazuli Bunting, Bullock's Oriole, and Cassin's Finch.

Much of the southern portion is a high plateau (elevation 4,000 ft/1,200 m) with volcanic soils sustaining conifer forests largely of ponderosa and lodgepole pines, and white fir at higher elevations. Numerous basins cradle some of the most important interior wetlands in the Pacific Northwest, protected in a complex of wildlife refuges on both sides of the California line—among others, Upper Klamath Lake (Oregon's largest lake) and the Klamath Marsh. However, management of these areas is plagued by competing priorities among various interests for scarce water rights.

Great numbers of migrating waterfowl use these wetlands, as do Sandhill Cranes and shorebirds. Nesting birds include Eared, Western, and Clark's Grebes, American White Pelican, American and Least Bitterns, Great and Snowy Egrets, Black-crowned Night-Heron, White-faced Ibis, Yellow Rail, Sandhill Crane, Ring-billed and California Gulls, Caspian and Forster's Terns, and Tricolored Blackbird. The network of streams feeding the Klamath River provides some riparian habitat. Highland sites, extending east to the Warner Mountains at the limits of the interior high deserts, grow to shrub-steppe, juniper woodlands, and ponderosa pine. Riparian and woodland birds of this southern portion include the majority of those of the northern portion, with the addition of Pinyon Jay and Green-tailed Towhee. Wrentits have expanded their range eastward from the Siskiyou Mountains subregion as far as Klamath Falls.

Lumber production, grazing, and recreation provide the economic base of much of the region, with irrigated agriculture for orchards, croplands, and haying important locally, mostly in the south. Bend, the largest city in eastern Oregon (metro-area population 170,000), is strategically situated at the juncture of the Eastern Cascades, Middle

Rockies (Blue Mountains), and Northern Basin and Range subregions. The Cascades slopes are lightly populated. The largest communities are Wenatchee in the north and Klamath Falls in the south, with 33,000 and 21,000 inhabitants, respectively.

North American Cold Deserts Ecoregion

This ecoregion includes the vast intermontane arid grasslands in the rain shadow of the Cascade Range, north through the Okanagan Valley to the dry grasslands along the Thompson and Fraser Rivers in the southern interior of British Columbia. Bunchgrass species dominate the native ground cover at low elevations, almost always in association with dryland shrubs such as big sagebrush, antelope bitterbrush, greasewood, and common rabbitbrush. Invasive cheatgrass infests disturbed habitats, particularly where overgrazing has occurred. In the southern part of the region, juniper and mountain-mahogany species are a common component of this shrubland as well.

There are five well-marked subregions.

1) OKANAGAN/OKANOGAN. British Columbia and Washington share this subregion and the river it is named for. The spelling changes, however, at the international boundary—Okanagan in Canada, Okanogan in the United States. Lying between the Coastal Mountains and Western Cascades subregions on the west and the Canadian Rockies subregion on the east, the Okanagan/Okanogan subregion is a transition zone of relatively cool, moist, forested plateaus and warm, dry, river-bottom grasslands, subject to winter influxes of frigid air from the north and incursions of searing summer heat from the Columbia Plateau subregion that borders it to the south.

The subregion is formed of three main upland sections. The Thompson Plateau occupies most of the British Columbia portion, carved through in the north by the basin of the Thompson River, a tributary of the Fraser. The Okanagan/Okanogan River flows south from the northeastern corner of the subregion in British Columbia to merge into the Columbia River in Washington. The deep river basin divides the eastern side of the subregion, the Okanagan/Okanogan Highlands, from its western side, composed of the Thompson Plateau and the third upland section—the leeward face of the Cascades in Washington and far southern British Columbia. The Cascade slopes drain to the Columbia via the Methow and the Similkameen, a tributary of the Okanogan. East of the Okanagan/Okanogan River, the Sanpoil, Kettle, Colville, and Spokane Rivers also flow to the Columbia.

The low river basins, hot and very dry, were originally grown to grasslands. In the Okanagan/Okanogan Basin this native vegetation is still comparatively intact in Washington but has largely been appropriated for agriculture in British Columbia. In much of the Thompson Basin, overgrazing has encouraged replacement of grasses by sagebrush. Parklands with shrub-steppe and stands of ponderosa pine and Douglas-fir are typical of the somewhat cooler, moister, higher valleys. Farther up the slopes, these same drought-tolerant conifers form closed-canopy forests, succeeded higher still by lodgepole pine. Engelmann spruce and subalpine fir appear in the subalpine zone, and subalpine meadows and alpine tundra at the highest elevations. The Thompson Plateau has extensive grasslands in its drier southern part; the moister northern part has wetlands and small lakes. The glacially rounded ridges and broad valleys of the Okanagan/Okanogan Highlands are also comparatively moist. The Washington section, more extensive and more accessible than its British Columbia counterpart, offers many wetlands and small lakes in a grassland/conifer-forest mosaic.

Grassland bird species of the Okanagan/Okanogan are similar to those of the Columbia Plateau, although many occur in smaller numbers and more locally. Dry-forest species are mostly the same as those of similar ponderosa-pine and Douglas-fir habitats of the Eastern Cascades subregion—e.g., Mourning Dove, Flammulated Owl, Calliope Hummingbird, Black-backed and White-headed Woodpeckers, White-breasted and Pygmy Nuthatches, Western Bluebird, and Cassin's Finch. Upper-elevation forests resemble those of the Canadian Rockies, with bird species such as "Franklin's" (Spruce) Grouse, Great Gray and Boreal Owls, American Three-toed Woodpecker, Boreal Chickadee, Gray-crowned Rosy-Finch, Pine Grosbeak, and White-winged Crossbill.

The Okanagan is the most populated subregion of interior British Columbia and home to its two largest population centers, Kelowna (117,000 inhabitants) on the shores of Okanagan Lake and Kamloops (86,000 inhabitants) in the Thompson Basin. The appealing climate and well-developed cultural and recreational resources draw retirees and vacationers alike, augmenting the traditional regional economy based on forest products, ranching, and mining. Okanagan wines have achieved distinction in recent years, and vineyards are gaining acreage over orchards in the agricultural sector.

By contrast, the Washington Okanogan is very thinly populated and relies for income primarily on timber harvest, livestock raising, a few orchards, and forage crops. Recreational opportunities, while abundant and prized, are commercially underdeveloped. Spokane, the metropolis of the Inland Northwest (537,000 inhabitants in the metro area), is sited at an intersection of the Canadian Rockies and Columbia Plateau at the southeastern corner of the Okanogan, drawing from and serving all three of these subregions and beyond with its robust, diverse economy of manufacturing, technology industries, health sciences, commerce, and finance.

2) COLUMBIA PLATEAU. The Columbia Plateau occupies the greater part of eastern Washington as well as smaller areas in Oregon and Idaho. Its limits are marked by the lower forest line of the surrounding subregions—Okanogan on the north, Canadian Rockies on the east, Middle Rockies (Blue Mountains) on the south, and Eastern Cascades on the west. Composed of thick layers of basalt from Miocene lava flows, the plateau declines from about 2,500 ft/760 m elevation in the northeast to about 100 ft/30 m above sea level along the Columbia in the southwest.

A deep, rich topsoil of loess (silt blown in from prehistoric alluvial plains) blankets some parts of the region, most spectacularly in the rolling Palouse Prairies of southeastern Washington and adjacent Idaho. Other areas were stripped to bare rock by a series of massive floods during the most recent ice age, forming the Channeled Scablands with their distinctive coulees and potholes. Summers are extremely hot and dry in the lower basin, slightly milder and damper higher on the plateau. Winters are cold, snowfall light.

The native flora of the Columbia Plateau is mostly grassland where moisture and soil conditions are favorable, and shrub-steppe in drier, thin-soiled areas. Trees and shrubs grow along drainages and on the slopes of a few isolated mountains rising above the basalt floor. Although the original plant communities survive more or less intact in many places—especially those with the poorest soils—to a great extent they have been replaced by irrigated agriculture. Long reaches behind the Columbia and Snake River dams are now reservoirs. Natural basins, formerly dry, have been repurposed to store large volumes of water for irrigation (e.g., Banks Lake, Potholes Reservoir, Scooteney Reservoir). Irrigation runoff has created many small lakes and wetlands, and allows some formerly intermittent streams to flow year-round. Natural lakes and wetlands of various types, often ephemeral, exist from pre-irrigation times. All of these wetlands and water bodies provide important bird habitat.

Characteristic breeding species of grassland, shrub-steppe, agricultural, and riparian habitats include Gray Partridge, Northern Harrier, Swainson's and Ferruginous Hawks, Long-billed Curlew, Barn, Great Horned, Burrowing, Long-eared, and Short-eared Owls, Common Nighthawk, Black-chinned Hummingbird, American Kestrel, Say's Phoebe, Western and Eastern Kingbirds, Loggerhead Shrike, Black-billed Magpie, Horned Lark, Northern Rough-winged, Bank, and Barn Swallows, Mountain Bluebird, Sage Thrasher, Yellow Warbler, Brewer's, Vesper, Lark, Sagebrush, Grasshopper, and Savannah Sparrows, Western Meadowlark, and Bullock's Oriole. Breeders closely associated with wet habitats include many dabbling ducks, Barrow's Goldeneye, Ruddy Duck, grebes, American White Pelican, herons and egrets, rails, Black-necked Stilt, American Avocet, Wilson's Snipe, Wilson's Phalarope, California and Ring-billed Gulls, Marsh Wren, and Red-winged, Tricolored (uncommon), and Yellow-headed Blackbirds.

Particularly associated with cliffs and canyons are Chukar, Golden Eagle, Rock Pigeon, White-throated Swift, Prairie Falcon, Common Raven, Violet-green and Cliff Swallows, and Rock and Canyon Wrens. Migration brings Sandhill Cranes and a great diversity of waterfowl, shorebirds, and passerines. Many waterfowl winter on Columbia River reservoirs. Other notable winter residents are Herring Gull, Rough-legged Hawk, Snowy Owl, Gyrfalcon, Northern Shrike, American Tree Sparrow, and Gray-crowned Rosy-Finch.

Economically and culturally the subregion turns toward Spokane, Washington's second-largest city, located on its eastern edge at a corner of the Okanogan subregion (see above); and also southward toward the Tri-Cities of Richland, Kennewick, and Pasco (metropolitan area population 273,000) at the confluence of the Columbia, Yakima, and Snake Rivers. Among the numerous smaller cities, Yakima and Walla Walla are important regional market centers. Agriculture is the dominant economic activity, led by grain production—irrigated where feasible, or dry, as in the Palouse Prairies and the upper part of the Columbia Plateau in Oregon. Some land is given over to hayfields, pastures, orchards, and the growing of hops, potatoes, vegetables, and berries, notably in the Yakima Valley. Viticulture is thriving, with many wineries of repute in the Yakima, Walla Walla, and Columbia Valleys.

3) SNAKE RIVER PLAIN. The Snake River Plain follows the looping course of the river from near Yellowstone Park across southern Idaho into Oregon, framed on the north by the lower slopes of the Middle Rockies and on the south by uplands of the Northern Basin and Range ecoregion. Elevation ranges from 2,100 ft/640 m in the west (Ontario, Oregon) to over 5,000 ft/1,500 m in the east (St. Anthony, Idaho). The original land cover is mainly shrub-steppe, with small areas of wetland vegetation locally.

Climate and land use are similar to those of the Columbia Plateau, although the growing season is significantly shorter at higher elevations of the upper valley. The Snake and its tributaries have been impounded behind dams in many places. Areas with good soil and flat terrain are farmed intensively, producing irrigated potatoes, sugar beets, vegetables, melons, mint, and hay, complemented by dairy and livestock-feeding operations, grain crops, orchards, and a small but growing wine industry. Some natural grasslands and wetlands remain. Much of the subregion, unsuitable for farming, is arid sagebrush/bunchgrass rangeland open to cattle grazing.

Habitat for habitat, the list of breeding birds of the Snake River Plain is generally much the same as that of the Columbia Plateau, augmented by several different or more abundant species—among others, Greater Sage-Grouse, Snowy and Cattle Egrets, White-faced Ibis, Sandhill Crane, Willet, Franklin's Gull, Black Tern, Yellow-billed Cuckoo (rare), Western Screech-Owl, Bobolink, and Common and Great-tailed Grackles. Post-breeding irruptions of Lark Bunting occur every few years. The valley is an important staging area and migration route for waterbirds and shorebirds. Snow Geese pass through the upper valley by the tens of thousands in spring, along with smaller numbers of Ross's. Isolated stands of trees in open country act as migrant traps, regularly attracting passerine rarities. Black Rosy-Finches winter all across southern Idaho, usually in mixed flocks with Gray-crowned.

The subregion is home to Idaho's largest cities and to three-quarters of the population of the state. The small section in Oregon is of a piece with the fertile plain at the junction of several rivers in the lower Snake Valley in Idaho, known in both states as the Treasure Valley. This district has some of the Pacific Northwest's most productive agricultural land and is the location of Boise, the Idaho state capital.

4) NORTHERN BASIN AND RANGE. This broad subregion spans Oregon and Idaho from the Cascades to the Rockies, reaching south from the Blue Mountains and the Snake River Plain into northern Nevada and adjoining bits of California and Utah, at an elevation of 4,000 ft/1,200 m or greater nearly throughout. The climate is semi-arid to arid, with cold winters; summers bring warm days and cool evenings. The western two-thirds of the Oregon portion, and the southeastern corner of the Idaho portion, drain to interior basins with no outlets—the northernmost extensions of the hydrographic Great Basin. The remainder of the subregion, in both states, is in the Snake River (Columbia) watershed.

The core of the interior basin area of Oregon is a high-desert plain grown to shrub-steppe, with junipers on the uplands. Lakes, marshes, and other wetlands in the bottoms—shrunken remainders of large Pleistocene lakes—vary in depth and extent in response to annual precipitation swings. Summer Lake, Lake Abert, the

Warner Lakes, and the lakes and marshes of the Malheur-Harney Basin, along with many smaller sites, are of great importance for wetland birds.

Breeders, to cite only a representative few, include Gadwall, Mallard, Cinnamon and Blue-winged Teals, Northern Pintail, Redhead, Eared, Western, and Clark's Grebes, American White Pelican, Snowy Egret, White-faced Ibis, Sandhill Crane, Black-necked Stilt, American Avocet, Wilson's Phalarope, Franklin's Gull, and Caspian, Black, and Forster's Terns. Wetlands are also heavily used by migrating, staging, and sometimes wintering waterfowl, cranes, and shorebirds. Grasslands support breeding Ferruginous Hawk, Willet, Great Horned, Burrowing, and Short-eared Owls, Common Nighthawk, and largely the same guild of shrub-steppe passerines as the Columbia Plateau and Snake River Plain. Southeastern Oregon sagebrush lands are the Pacific Northwest stronghold for Greater Sage-Grouse. Mountains and canyons host Chukar, Black-throated Gray Warbler, and Green-tailed Towhee. Passerine migrants gather at desert oases.

Steens Mountain (elevation 9,700 ft/3,000 m) is the grandest of several high mountains rising from the plains, unforested above the juniper zone and offering limited alpine habitat along summit ridges—the only place in Oregon where Black Rosy-Finch nests regularly. In the rain shadow of Steens, more than 5,000 ft/1,500 m below its sheer eastern front, is the Alvord Desert, a barren playa in one of the most arid parts of the basin country. Other arid valleys in former lake bottoms are vegetated with alkali-tolerant grasses and shrubs such as saltgrass, budsage, and greasewood. Southeastern Oregon is the Pacific Northwest center of abundance for Black-throated Sparrow, and these are its preferred habitats. Snowy Plover nests locally on alkali flats, usually near a lake.

The Snake-drained part of the subregion in southeastern Oregon and southwestern Idaho is mostly shrub-steppe rangeland dissected by deep canyons, with juniper woodlands along ridges and aspen, mountain-mahogany, and sparse conifer forest of ponderosa pine and Douglas-fir upslope. On the whole, birdlife here is similar to that of shrub-steppe habitats in adjacent areas.

In southeastern Idaho, shrub-steppe-covered hills climb almost from the banks of the Snake into mountains, with some juniper woodlands at lower elevations. Higher-elevation mountainous terrain supports aspen groves, shrubs, Douglas-fir, and lodgepole pine; shrub-steppe and some cropland, both irrigated and dry, are found in the valleys. These same habitats carry over into the Great Salt Lake watershed in the south. Avian specialties of this part of Idaho include Sharp-tailed Grouse, Broad-tailed Hummingbird, Plumbeous Vireo, Pinyon Jay, "Woodhouse's" (Western) Scrub-Jay, Juniper Titmouse, Blue-gray Gnatcatcher, Virginia's Warbler, and "South Hills" (Red) Crossbill.

The Northern Basin and Range subregion is virtually uninhabited. Burns (population 2,800) and Preston (population 5,200) are its largest towns in Oregon and Idaho, respectively, although several cities along the Snake in Idaho lie close to the northern edge (notably Pocatello). Grazing, agriculture, and tourism/recreation are the principal economic activities.

5) WYOMING BASIN. This subregion occupies most of the unforested area of central and southwestern Wyoming. The Pacific Northwest portion consists of the upper

Green River Valley, lying between the Wind River and Wyoming Ranges in the Colorado River watershed, and a small section extending into the Great Salt Lake watershed at the extreme southeastern corner of Idaho. The floor elevation is about 6,000–7,000 ft/1,800–2,100 m above sea level. The climate is dry and continental with warm summers and cold winters. Vegetation is mostly shrub-steppe; juniper and mountain-mahogany appear on mid-elevation slopes. Wetlands occur locally. Especially important for birds are the marshlands and wet meadows along the Bear River at Cokeville Meadows NWR in Wyoming, and the grasslands, sedge meadows, bulrush marsh, and open water of Bear Lake NWR in the adjacent corner of Idaho.

Breeding waterbirds at Bear Lake include Trumpeter Swan, White-faced Ibis, Sandhill Crane, and Franklin's Gull, among many other species; Cokeville has the largest breeding population of American Bittern in Wyoming. Both refuges are important stopovers for migrating waterfowl, cranes, and shorebirds. Farther east, a tree-shaded campground along the Green River below Fontenelle Dam is a famous passerine migrant trap in the midst of a wide-open landscape. A distinctive Wyoming addition to the grasslands avifauna of the Pacific Northwest is Mountain Plover, irregular here in summer at the western limit of its breeding range.

The Pacific Northwest portion of the Wyoming Basin subregion has no towns of any size. Rangeland grazing, some irrigated hayfields, and wildlife-oriented recreation provide the economic base.

USERS' GUIDE

Bird Names

Species are presented in the taxonomic sequence of the *Check-list of North American Birds* of the American Ornithologists' Union (revised 2015), occasionally with a few minor liberties to allow similar species to be placed on facing pages for ease of comparison. Common (English) and scientific (Latin) names of species appear in a bar of a different color for each family. Family names are placed in the footer.

Subspecies (distinctive populations within a species) have a third component of the scientific name. For example, Yellow-rumped Warbler (*Setophaga coronata*) has several geographic subspecies, including *Setophaga coronata auduboni*. Frequently the first two names (genus and species) are abbreviated to their initials, and only the subspecies name is spelled out. Common names of subspecies are given in quotation marks, to distinguish them from full species. *S.c. auduboni*, for example, is known as "Audubon's" Warbler. Names of other forms not recognized as species also appear in quotation marks. These include the names of several former species that have fairly recently been split into two or more separate species but that are still useful as collective names or because of their familiarity: "Blue" Grouse (now split into Dusky Grouse and Sooty Grouse), "Xantus's" Murrelet (now Scripps's and Guadalupe Murrelets), "Western" Flycatcher (Pacific-slope and Cordilleran), "Solitary" Vireo (Blue-headed, Plumbeous, and Cassin's), and "Plain" Titmouse (Oak and Juniper).

Descriptions

Length is given for all species, bill tip to tail tip. Additionally, wingspan is given for larger species. Distinctive identification field marks are indicated in **bold typeface**. The basic description applies to birds in any plumage. Notable variations in plumage by season, age, sex, subspecies, or morph are described separately. Photos show adults unless the captions indicate otherwise.

- *Breeding (or "alternate")* – plumage held during the breeding season
- *Non-breeding (or "basic")* – duller plumage held after the breeding plumage is molted
- *Juvenile* – refers to a bird wearing its first (or "juvenal") plumage after leaving the nest—depending on the family, this may be held only briefly (songbirds), or throughout the first year of life (hawks)
- *First-year* – refers to a bird that has undergone one or more additional molts beyond juvenal plumage but is less than one year old
- *Subadult* – refers to a bird that is older than one year but has not yet achieved full adult plumage—a process which, depending on the family, may move through a series of plumage stages over two or more years.

Parts of a Bird

Accurately describing the appearance of a bird requires a specialized vocabulary. The principal structural and plumage terms used in this book are indicated on the two drawings that follow. These are also defined in the glossary (pp. 27–31), along with many other technical terms related to avian biology, behavior, and habitat.

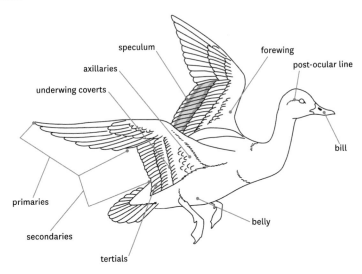

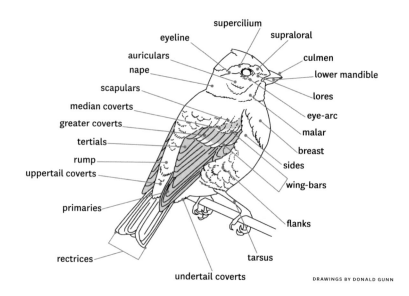

supercilium
eyeline
supraloral
auriculars
culmen
nape
lower mandible
scapulars
lores
median coverts
greater coverts
eye-arc
tertials
malar
rump
breast
uppertail coverts
sides
wing-bars
primaries
flanks
rectrices
tarsus
undertail coverts

DRAWINGS BY DONALD GUNN

Status & Distribution

Months are abbreviated to the first three letters (Jan, Feb, Mar, etc.). Pacific Northwest is abbreviated (PNW). United States is abbreviated (US); Canada and all other countries are spelled out. The six states and province wholly or partially within the Pacific Northwest are abbreviated: British Columbia (BC), Idaho (ID), Montana (MT), Oregon (OR), Washington (WA), Wyoming (WY). All other states and provinces are spelled out. Other abbreviated names are National Forest (NF), National Park (NP), National Wildlife Refuge (NWR), and Provincial Park (PP).

We use the following terms, adopted from the American Birding Association, to indicate the relative abundance of a species, and the likelihood of observing it, at a given place and season:

- *Common* – occurs in moderate to large numbers; easily found in appropriate habitat
- *Fairly Common* – occurs in small to moderate numbers; usually easy to find in appropriate habitat
- *Uncommon* – occurs in small numbers; usually—but not always—found with some effort in appropriate habitat
- *Rare* – occurs annually in very small numbers. Not to be expected on any given day, but may be found with extended effort
- *Casual* – occurs less than annually, but there tends to be a pattern over time at the right time of year in appropriate habitat
- *Accidental* – represents an exceptional occurrence that might not be repeated again for decades. Very few records
- *Irregular* – numbers highly variable year to year; may irrupt into a region in small or even large numbers one year, while in another it may be absent altogether.

Range Maps

Species are generally only mapped in a specific area if they reach a status of rare or better at that location and season. A major exception to this occurs when a species barely reaches rare status across the entire PNW and is considered only casual in any one state, province, or other broad subregion. Migration ranges of these rare species are mapped to indicate areas where they are most likely to occur even if they have not been recorded there annually.

Seasonal range is represented by the following colors:

- **Red** – *breeding season*; where a species breeds during the spring/summer months, but migrates elsewhere for winter
- **Blue** – *non-breeding season*; where a species winters or spends the majority of the non-breeding season, but breeds elsewhere
- **Purple** – *year-round*; where a species both breeds and winters. A few species colored purple (such as Common Loon and most pelagic species) may not breed in these areas despite occurring commonly through the summer months
- **Yellow** – *migration*; indicates presence while in transit between summer and winter range, usually during spring and fall migration periods. Small numbers of individuals of a migratory species may occasionally remain in yellow areas during summer or winter, instead of just passing through.

GLOSSARY OF TECHNICAL TERMS

Accipiters – hawks in the genus *Accipiter*, identified by long tails and fairly short, rounded wings

Aerie – cliffside nest (usually of a raptor)

Alcid – any member of the family Alcidae (auks)

Allopatric – said of species that live in different geographic areas from each other

Altricial – hatched in a helpless, immobile state

Auriculars – feathers comprising the ear coverts (located behind and below the eye)

Axillaries – "armpit" feathers

Belly – underparts posterior to the breast and between the flanks

Breast – underparts between the belly and the throat

Brood parasitism – reproductive strategy involving laying eggs in nests of other bird species

Buteos – hawks in the genus *Buteo*, identified by broad wings and fairly short tails

Carpal bar – dark band across the leading edge of the upperwing from the tertials to the "wrist"

Carpal patch – patch of dark feathers on the underwing at the "wrist"

Cline – gradual change of characteristics within a species or other taxonomic entity across its geographic range

Clutch – set of eggs produced in one laying period

Conspecific – of the same species

Corvid – any member of the family Corvidae (crows and jays)

Crest (location) – term frequently used in this book without specific context, to denote the crest of the Cascades/BC Coast Range

Crest (plumage term) – elongated feathers on the top of the head

Culmen – dorsal ridge of the bill

Dabbler, dabbling duck – duck in the genus *Anas* that feeds primarily at or near the water surface

Dihedral – position of wings when held angled upwards from the horizontal in soaring flight

Dorsal – pertaining to the upperparts; includes the crown, nape, back, scapulars, rump, and the upper surface of the tail and wings

Double-brood – to raise two broods during a breeding season

Ear coverts – small feathers behind the eye that cover the ear openings, also known as auriculars

Eastside – in this book, the area of the Pacific Northwest lying east of the Cascades/ BC Coast Range crest; also called "interior"

Ecoregion – geographic area containing a distinct group of species, natural communities, and environmental conditions

Ecotone – transition zone between two plant communities

Emberizid – any member of the family Emberizidae (New World sparrows)

Eye-arc – small, curved area of light-colored feathers (usually white) either above or below the eye

Eye-comb – bare, fleshy skin above the eye on some species of the family Phasianidae (partridges and grouse)

Eyeline – dark line of feathers extending from the base of the bill through the lores and continuing behind the eye

Flanks – underparts on either side of the belly, ventral to the folded flight feathers

Flight feathers – thick-shafted feathers of the wing (remiges) and tail (rectrices) that provide lift and maneuverability

Foot-trembling – feeding method involving vibrating a foot to stir up invertebrate prey

Forewing – combined upperwing coverts on the proximal section of the wing

Gadfly petrel – any species in the seabird genus *Pterodroma*, known for their arcing, stiff-winged flight

Gape – edge of the bill where the upper and lower mandibles meet

Gorget – brightly colored (often iridescent) throat, chin, and upper-breast feathers of a male hummingbird

Gular pouch – expandable throat area, often with bare skin

Hover-gleaning – plucking food from twigs or leaves while airborne

Interior – in this book, the area of the Pacific Northwest lying east of the Cascades/BC Coast Range crest; also called "eastside"

Irruption – periodic, irregular movement of above average numbers of birds into an area

Juvenal – plumage worn by a bird when it leaves the nest; often of short duration, but molt sequences vary

Juvenile – bird in its juvenal plumage

Kettle – flock of birds circling in flight on rising columns of air called thermals

Kleptoparasitize – to steal food from another bird

Leading edge (wing) – in flight, the front edge of the wing (nearest the head)

Lek – traditional display site where males gather and establish symbolic territories to compete for breeding access to females

Leucistic – abnormal plumage condition due to a lack of melanin, resulting in white feathers

Long-call – extended, repetitive call; most frequently used to describe the complex trumpeting call (often given in an aggressive context) by gulls and similar species

Lores – small area between the eye and the bill

Malar – line of contrastingly colored feathers extending back and downward from the lower mandible; sometimes termed submoustachial stripe

Mandible – upper mandible and lower mandible are the two halves of a bird's bill

Mantle – dorsal body feathers from the nape to the rump, often defined as including the scapulars

Mast – hard fruits produced by certain species of forest trees, including larger seeds and nuts

Mimic-thrush – any member of the family Mimidae (mockingbirds and thrashers)

Morph – consistent, identifiable form maintained across age, sex, or seasonal variation within a polymorphic species

Nape – back of the neck

Pacific slope – in this book, the area of the Pacific Northwest lying west of the Cascades/BC Coast Range crest; also called "westside"

Patagial bar – dark mark across all or part of the proximal half of the leading edge of the underwing

Peeps – informal name for the smallest sandpipers (length 5–7 in/13–18 cm) of the genus *Calidris*

Pelagic – pertaining to the open ocean; far offshore, out of sight of land

Polyandry, polygamy, polygyny – breeding systems in which females may mate with more than one male (polyandry); males with more than one female (polygyny); or both (polygamy)

Polymorphic – said of a species showing a discontinuous genetic variation that results in two or more different forms within the species; in this book, applies to plumage variation

Polytypic – said of a species that consists of two or more identifiable subspecies

Post-ocular line – dark plumage marking extending rearward from the eye

Precocial – hatched in a relatively mature, mobile state, usually with eyes open and the ability to walk, swim, and peck at food

Primaries – outermost flight feathers of the wing; attached to the "hand"

Primary projection – amount by which the primaries extend beyond the tertial tips on the folded wing

Rectrices – flight feathers of the tail

Remiges – flight feathers of the wing (primaries, secondaries, tertials)

Riparian – pertaining to, or situated along, the banks of a stream, river, lake, or other freshwater body

Rump – part of a bird's body on the lower back just above the tail, often defined as including the uppertail coverts

Scapulars – feathers overlapping the folded wing dorsal to the coverts; often considered part of the mantle

Secondaries – flight feathers of the wing proximal to the primaries; attached to the "forearm"

Secondary coverts – three overlapping tracts of upperwing feathers (lesser, median, and greater coverts) that cover the bases of the secondaries/tertials

Shorebird – any member of the families Recurvirostridae (stilts and avocets), Haematopodidae (oystercatchers), Charadriidae (plovers), or Scolopacidae (sandpipers, snipes, and phalaropes)

Speculum – patch on the dorsal surface of a duck's wing formed by the contrastingly colored (often iridescent) secondaries

Sides – underparts of a bird on either side of the breast

Subadult – bird beyond its first year that has not yet attained full adult plumage

Supercilium – stripe of contrastingly colored feathers above the eye extending from the lores toward the rear of the head; sometimes called "eyebrow"

Supraloral – feather tract above the lores at the anterior end of the supercilium

Sympatric – said of species that live in the same geographic area as each other

Tarsus (plural tarsi) – fused bone above the toes unique to birds (also called tarsometatarsus); unfeathered in most birds

Tertials – inner flight feathers of the wing; attached to the "upper arm" or humerus

Trailing edge (wing) – in flight, the rear edge of the wing (nearest the tail)

Underparts – ventral plumage

Undertail coverts – ventral feathers covering the bases of the rectrices

Underwing – ventral surface of the wing, visible when the wing is spread as in flight

Underwing coverts – several tracts of underwing feathers covering the bases of the flight feathers

Upperparts – dorsal plumage

Uppertail coverts – dorsal feathers covering the bases of the rectrices

Upperwing – dorsal surface of the wing

Upperwing coverts – several layered tracts of upperwing feathers covering the bases of the primaries (primary coverts) and secondaries/tertials (lesser, median, and greater coverts)

Vagrant – a bird found far outside the typical range of its species

Vent – undertail orifice that allows the passage of waste

Ventral – pertaining to the underparts of a bird; includes the throat, breast, sides, flanks, belly, and the undersurface of the tail and wings

Vermiculated – marked by a pattern of densely packed, thin, wavy, alternating light-and-dark lines

Westside – in this book, the area of the Pacific Northwest lying west of the Cascades/BC Coast Range crest; also called "Pacific slope"

Wing-bars – pale tips on the upperwing coverts, forming one or two bars across the folded wing

Wing linings – combined underwing coverts and axillaries

SPECIES ACCOUNTS

WA (Thurston County)—May · KEN ARCHER

BC (Victoria)—Apr · TED ARDLEY

Juvenile · BC (Penticton)—Oct · LAURE W. NEISH

Greater White-fronted Goose
Anser albifrons

DESCRIPTION 29 in/74 cm, wingspan 54 in/137 cm. Mostly grayish, dorsal feathers edged whitish; white rump, belly, undertail. **Dark tail with white tip**. Size varies with sex, age, range. "Tule" subspecies larger; browner head, neck. **Adult:** White line between flank, folded wing. **Front of face white**, variable black belly barring; pinkish bill, **yellow-orange legs**. **Juvenile:** Lacks white face, flank line, belly patches; dull-yellow bill, legs.

SIMILAR SPECIES Canada, Cackling Geese (pp. 38–41) have white cheek, dark bill, legs; black tail lacks white tip. Barnyard geese heavier; fat rear end.

STATUS & DISTRIBUTION Nearly Holarctic breeder; in New World, most winter central California, Mexico, Mississippi Valley, Gulf Coast. In PNW, common BC/WA late Apr–May, mostly from outer coast; uncommon late Aug–early Nov (common Sep–Oct Kootenay Valley near Creston). From Dec–Mar, uncommon west of Cascades/BC Coast Range, Klamath Basin; rare farther east until migrants arrive Columbia Plateau (late Feb). Casual Jun–Jul, primarily BC. "Tule" (*A.a. elgasi*) breeds Cook Inlet (Alaska); most winter California (rare WA, ID, uncommon south-central OR).

HABITAT ASSOCIATIONS Nests on tundra, taiga; winters in agricultural fields, wetlands ("Tule" favors marshes). Migrants mostly fly along outer coast.

BEHAVIOR & FEEDING Gregarious; often with other geese. Aquatic or terrestrial, forages primarily on waste grains; also roots, tubers, grasses; grazes in fields or tips up for aquatic plants. Some migrants fly non-stop from Alaska to Klamath Basin, move overland near Columbia River.

VOCALIZATIONS High-pitched, rising yelp, more complex than region's other geese.

Family Anatidae—GEESE, SWANS, AND DUCKS **33**

Blue morph · *California—Nov* · BENJAMIN KNOOT

Juvenile Blue morph · *BC (Richmond)—Nov* · RAYMOND NG

WA (Skagit County)—Nov · NICK DEAN

Juveniles · *WA (Snohomish County)—Dec* · RYAN MERRILL

Snow Goose
Chen caerulescens

DESCRIPTION 29 in/74 cm, wingspan 54 in/137 cm. **White with black wingtips**, pinkish legs, **pink bill with blackish "grinning patch."** Distant flying flocks appear as undulating, irregular wavy lines. *Juvenile:* Dusky upperparts, grayish legs; whiter plumage with progressing season. *Blue Morph:* Adult **gray with white head, front of neck**, variably whitish belly; juvenile dusky grayish throughout, including bill.

SIMILAR SPECIES Swans larger without black wingtips. Ross's Goose (p. 35) smaller, with stubby bill; lacks grinning patch. Juvenile Greater White-fronted Goose (p. 33) brown with yellowish bill.

STATUS & DISTRIBUTION Breeds on Arctic tundra, northeastern Russia east to Greenland, winters very locally from southwestern BC, Atlantic states south to Mexico. In PNW, migrants common locally Feb–May, late Sep–Nov. Most (~800,000) take inland route through western MT, southeastern OR (stage Harney Basin). Smaller Wrangel Island, Siberia, population (~150,000) flies mostly west of Cascades; about half winter in PNW riverine lowlands (predominantly Fraser Delta to Snohomish Valley), half in California (stage in Klamath Basin); uncommon/rare Dec–Jan elsewhere in PNW. Casual Jun–Aug throughout. Blue morph rare in PNW.

HABITAT ASSOCIATIONS Aquatic, terrestrial. Nests coastal Arctic tundra, winters agricultural fields, tidal wetlands, extensive inland marshes.

BEHAVIOR & FEEDING Highly gregarious; flocks number into thousands with populations increasing exponentially for decades. Individuals sometimes mix with Cackling, Canada Geese. Forages on land, also shallow water; eats grasses, shoots, waste grain. Pairs mate for life; family groups remain together to next nesting season.

VOCALIZATIONS Highly vocal; constant high-pitched, raucous barking *huowk kwouk*.

White and Blue morphs · *California—Apr*
PETER J. THIEMANN

California—Mar · GREG GILLSON

Ross's Goose
Chen rossii

DESCRIPTION 22 in/56 cm, wingspan 45 in/114 cm. Immaculate **white with black wingtips**, pinkish legs, **short pink bill with warty blue base**. *Juvenile:* Dusky dorsally from crown to wingtips. *Blue Morph:* Dark gray with white face, belly; juvenile has grayish bill, legs, lacks white face.

SIMILAR SPECIES Swans much larger without black wingtips. Snow Goose (p. 34) larger, has long bill with black "grinning patch." Emperor Goose (p. 36) larger, stockier; white extends down back of neck.

STATUS & DISTRIBUTION Breeds on central Canadian Low Arctic tundra, fewer Hudson Bay, northeastern Alaska; most winter central California; smaller numbers to Gulf Coast, northern Mexico. Populations once reduced to a few thousand, now number in hundreds of thousands. Large numbers stage just east of PNW at Freezeout Lake (MT) in Apr. In PNW, common migrant principally across eastern OR, staging Feb–May in Klamath, Harney Basins; a few winter there. Peripheral migrants rare but widespread (Mar–May, Oct–Nov; more frequent during spring). Blue morph recorded only casually.

HABITAT ASSOCIATIONS Nests on grassy Arctic tundra amid dwarf willow patches, often on islands in shallow lakes; winters agricultural fields, wet meadows, shallow lakes, wetlands.

BEHAVIOR & FEEDING Gregarious; colonial nester, often mixing with Snow Geese. Short bill adapted for grazing on grasses, sedges; also waste grains, seeds, legumes; wetlands used more for roosting. Individuals or small flocks often mixed with other geese in region, usually Snow or Cackling Geese.

VOCALIZATIONS High-pitched, barked *keeek keek*, uttered less frequently than Snow Goose; also yelps, honks.

*Family Anatidae—*GEESE, SWANS, AND DUCKS **35**

Juvenile · OR (Washington County)—Oct · GREG GILLSON

WA (Thurston County)—Jun · KEITH BRADY

Emperor Goose
Chen canagica

DESCRIPTION 26 in/66 cm, wingspan 47 in/119 cm. Stocky, compact, short necked; bluish gray including undertail, prominent black-and-white feather edging; **white tail.** Yellowish feet, legs; **small pink bill.** *Adult:* **Head, back of neck white**; underparts black to chin; **bright yellow-orange legs.** *Juvenile:* Dark head, neck, but shows varying amounts of white with progressing season; legs dull yellow.

SIMILAR SPECIES Greater White-fronted Goose (p. 33), Ross's Goose (p. 35), Snow Goose (p. 34) have white undertail in all plumages. Snow has larger bill. Blue-morph Snow, Ross's adults have dark napes.

STATUS & DISTRIBUTION Breeds in High Arctic coastal salt-marsh habitats in western Alaska (Kotzebue Sound to St. Lawrence, Nunivak Islands), west to Siberia; winters mostly to Aleutians, also Kamchatka Peninsula, Kodiak Island, rarely south along coast to California. In PNW, rare Oct–May, mostly near tidewater: Haida Gwaii, Vancouver Island, Salish Sea, WA/OR outer coast, lower Columbia River, Willamette Valley. Only a few records east of Cascades (ID, OR).

HABITAT ASSOCIATIONS Breeds in tidal marshland; stages in estuaries, lagoons; winters in intertidal zone. In PNW, uses tidal marsh, rocky shoreline, agricultural habitats.

BEHAVIOR & FEEDING Gregarious; stragglers in PNW flock with Cackling or Snow Geese. Preferred diet includes intertidal invertebrates (mostly bivalves), eelgrass, tubers, grasses, other plant materials. Monogamous pair nests on ground, remains together until death of either individual.

VOCALIZATIONS Loud, hoarse, double-noted *kla kla* in flight. Generally quiet for a goose.

Juvenile · BC (Oyster River)—Nov · JUKKA JANTUNEN

"Gray-bellied" · WA (King County)—Apr · CAMDEN HACKWORTH

"Black" · BC (Victoria)—Apr · GERALD ROMANCHUK

Brant
Branta bernicla

DESCRIPTION 23 in/58 cm, wingspan 43 in/109 cm. Stocky, short necked, **mostly blackish; small black bill**; black legs; white rump, undertail; flanks barred, whitish; **white neck-ring**. "Gray-bellied" subspecies grayish white (versus dark) belly, incomplete neck-ring. *Juvenile:* Lacks neck-ring in fall; duller with white-tipped upperwing coverts.

SIMILAR SPECIES Cackling, Canada Geese (pp. 38–41) have white cheek patch; all but *B.h. minima* larger with longer bill. Juvenile Emperor Goose (p. 36) shows dark undertail.

STATUS & DISTRIBUTION Holarctic breeder on high-latitude coastal tundra, winters mostly to temperate zone. Two subspecies in PNW: widespread "Black" Brant (*B.b. orientalis*) breeds eastern Russia to northwestern Canada, winters coastally to Baja California, northwestern Mexico; "Gray-bellied" Brant (*B.b. nigricans*) breeds Melville, Prince Patrick Islands, winters Salish Sea (mostly Padilla, Bellingham Bays). In PNW, both subspecies locally common along coastlines Nov–May; numbers (*orientalis*) increase beginning Feb; a few summer. Casual inland except rare Willamette Valley, accidental MT/WY.

HABITAT ASSOCIATIONS Nests on Arctic tundra. Away from nesting areas generally restricted to protected marine waters; prefers gravel bottom. Forages in intertidal zone, rarely upland fields.

BEHAVIOR & FEEDING Flies low over ocean in ragged lines. Highly gregarious; shares habitats with other species but usually remains in segregated flocks. Grazes tidal flats for leafy marine vegetation (eelgrass, sea lettuce), more grasses, forbs in Arctic. Wades, upends, follows advancing, receding tides to correct water depth. In PNW, stragglers rarely graze upland fields with other geese. Pairs mate for life; family groups remain together through migration.

VOCALIZATIONS Quietly murmured, nasal *rrok rronk*.

"Aleutian" · BC (Haida Gwaii)—Nov · JUKKA JANTUNEN

"Ridgway's" (right); "Lesser" Canada Goose (left)
Yukon Territory—Sep · JUKKA JANTUNEN

"Ridgway's" · WA (Thurston County)—Mar · DOUG SCHURMAN

Cackling Goose
Branta hutchinsii

DESCRIPTION 30 in/76 cm, wingspan 49 in/124 cm (averages). Comparatively small, **long winged**. Grayish brown with **black legs**, tail; white rump, undertail; **stubby black bill**. Neck, **head black with white cheek**. *Juvenile:* Smaller through summer with subdued plumage. Three subspecies regular in PNW. Much individual variation in plumage characteristics such as breast color, neck collar; many birds not safely identifiable to subspecies in field. "Ridgway's" smallest; shows **tiny bill**, rich **bronzy-brown breast**, short neck, prominent white edging on upperparts, sometimes with narrow white collar. "Aleutian" lighter breast, relatively **broad white neck collar**; steep forehead imparts somewhat blocky head shape. "Taverner's" largest subspecies; **gray breast, stout bill**; neck collar rare.

SIMILAR SPECIES Brant (p. 37), Greater White-fronted Goose (p. 33) lack white cheek patch; latter shows pale bill, pinkish/orangish legs. Canada Goose (p. 40–41) longer necked with longer, narrower bill; most subspecies larger. "Western" (*B.c. moffiti*) very large, with pale breast. "Lesser" (*B.c. parvipes*) overlaps in size with shorter-billed "Taverner's" Cackling, often difficult to separate. "Dusky" (*B.c. occidentalis*), "Vancouver" (*B.c. fulva*) dark breasted like "Ridgway's" Cackling, but much larger. All PNW subspecies of Canada Goose call with honks, not yelps.

STATUS & DISTRIBUTION Nests Alaska to Baffin Island, winters south to central California, northern Mexico, mostly in West. In PNW, locally common Oct–May in lowlands west of Cascades/BC Coast Range, uncommon to rare east of crest (absent at higher elevations). Major wintering concentrations southwestern WA/northwestern OR at Columbia/Willamette confluence (Ridgefield NWR, Sauvie Island), spreading northward in recent years. Massive migratory movement along outer coast late Apr–May. "Ridgway's" (*B.h. minima*) breeds western Alaska, migrates across northeast Pacific to southwestern WA, OR (Willamette Valley), Central Valley of California. "Taverner's" (*B.h. taverneri*) breeds northwestern, northern Alaska, perhaps east to Northwest Territories (Mackenzie Delta), winters Central Valley of California, more recently growing numbers north to southwestern BC;

"Ridgway's" · BC (Parksville)—Oct · MIKE YIP

"Taverner's" · WA (Thurston County)—Apr · JON. ANDERSON

"Taverner's" · WA (Yakima County)—Oct · DENNY GRANSTRAND

"Ridgway's"

"Taverner's"

"Aleutian"

most Cacklers found in interior PNW are this subspecies. Formerly endangered "Aleutian" (*B.h. leucopareia*) breeds on a few Aleutian Islands, winters mostly Central Valley of California, fewer to northwestern OR (Tillamook County); migrants uncommon southwestern WA (Willapa NWR); some may winter.

HABITAT ASSOCIATIONS Breeds on coastal tundra; uses ponds, lakes, marshes, grassy fields, estuaries, rivers in other seasons. Migrants fly along outer coast, sometimes up to 30 mi/50 km offshore.

BEHAVIOR & FEEDING Highly gregarious, strongly migratory; flocks into tens of thousands. Forages primarily on grasses; also waste grains, tubers, in fields or shallow water. Individuals or small groups flock with other geese.

VOCALIZATIONS High-pitched squeaky yelps.

"Dusky" · WA (Grays Harbor County)—Feb · DENNIS PAULSON

"Lesser" · OR (Washington County)—Apr · GREG GILLSON

"Western" · WA (King County)—Mar · NETTA SMITH

Canada Goose
Branta canadensis

"Western"

DESCRIPTION 40 in/102 cm, wingspan 56 in/142 cm (averages). Mostly grayish brown with **black legs**, tail; white rump, undertail; **long, relatively slender bill. Black head, neck, with white cheek.** Generally lacks neck collar. *Juvenile:* Smaller through summer with subdued plumage. Four subspecies regular in PNW. Much individual variation in plumage characteristics such as breast color, neck collar; many birds not safely identifiable to subspecies in field. "Western" largest; **light breasted**, long necked; forehead slopes into long bill; white upper breast contrasts abruptly with black neck. "Lesser" smallest; breast variably brownish gray; rarely shows white neck collar. **Dark-breasted** "Dusky," "Vancouver," functionally impossible to separate with confidence in field; intermediate in size between "Western," "Lesser."

SIMILAR SPECIES Cackling Goose (p. 38–39) has shorter bill, squeaky yelp-like call; proportionately longer wings evident in flight. Most (but not all) subspecies much smaller, often show white neck collar. "Ridgway's" (*B.h. minima*) far smaller with tiny, stubby bill. "Aleutian" (*B.h. leucopareia*) smaller, usually shows broad white neck collar. "Taverner's" (*B.h. taverneri*) usually lacks neck collar; averages smaller than "Lesser" Canada Goose; difficult to separate, but "Taverner's" shorter neck, bulbous-based bill noticeable in direct comparison. See also under Cackling Goose.

STATUS & DISTRIBUTION Widespread throughout Canada, US; northern breeders winter south to northern Mexico. "Western" (*B.c. moffitti*) native to interior of continent east of Cascades; in PNW, also introduced westside last century, now locally common resident throughout, vacating frozen, snowbound terrain in winter. "Dusky" (*B.c. occidentalis*) breeds southern Alaska; most winter Oct–May southwestern WA, western OR (especially lower Columbia River floodplain, Willamette

"Dusky" / "Vancouver" · BC (Haida Gwaii)—Oct · JUKKA JANTUNEN

"Western" · WA (Asotin County)—Feb · KEITH CARLSON

"Vancouver" · Alaska—Apr · BOB ARMSTRONG

"Dusky"

"Vancouver"

"Lesser"

Valley). "Vancouver" (*B.c. fulva*) nearly indistinguishable visually from "Dusky" but genetically distinct, resident southeastern Alaska to northern coastal BC; some hints of southward post-breeding dispersal as far as Willamette Valley, but documentation slim. "Lesser" (*B.c. parvipes*) breeds on tundra/taiga Alaska/ western Canada, winters discontinuously to central California, Texas; in PNW, locally common Oct–Apr eastside lowlands, uncommon westside, but status obscured by confusion with "Taverner's" Cackling Goose.

HABITAT ASSOCIATIONS Aquatic or terrestrial habitats, including farmland, ponds, lakes, wetlands, estuaries, rivers; for "Western," also lawns, golf courses, parks.

BEHAVIOR & FEEDING Gregarious, mixing with Cackling Geese. Forages on grains, grasses, plant materials in fields or by upending in shallow water. Migrants fly in V-shaped formations. Begins nesting (usually on ground) by Mar; male aggressively defends nest against intruders while female provides nest care.

VOCALIZATIONS Honks; highly vocal, particularly in flight.

WA (Snohomish County)—Dec · GREGG THOMPSON

ID (Jefferson County)—Apr · DARREN CLARK

Juveniles · BC (Oyama)—Feb · BOB LALONDE

Trumpeter Swan
Cygnus buccinator

DESCRIPTION 57 in/145 cm, wingspan 87 in/220 cm. Long necked, plumage entirely white; black bill with straight culmen, reddish cutting edge. Dark bare skin of **bill base extends to eye in broad triangle**; V-shaped edge across forehead. Weighs up to 29 lb/13 kg; on average, heaviest North American bird. *Juvenile:* **Dingy-gray plumage** (mostly retained through spring); dusky-pinkish bill.

SIMILAR SPECIES Tundra Swan (p. 43) smaller, face/bill pattern differs; gives yelping call. Mute Swan (p. 44) has black knob on orange bill. Snow Goose (p. 34), American White Pelican (p. 118) wingtips black; pelican's bill pouched.

STATUS & DISTRIBUTION Breeds south-central Alaska, scattered south to Nevada, east to Great Lakes. Formerly close to extinction; range rapidly expanding, in part due to introductions. Alaska birds winter in PNW, predominantly near coast, BC to northwestern OR. Other populations resident or winter farther east. In PNW, nests locally in southeastern BC (Kootenays), eastern WA (Turnbull NWR), southeastern OR, southeastern ID, northwestern MT, western WY. Migrants concentrate Nov–Apr in lowlands—southwestern BC, western WA, fewer elsewhere. Most along major rivers, reservoirs (before freeze-up).

HABITAT ASSOCIATIONS Nests shallow ponds, marshes with emergent vegetation; winters on ice-free waters. In PNW, uses estuaries, ponds, rivers close to agricultural fields for feeding.

BEHAVIOR & FEEDING Gregarious; often flocks with Tundra Swans. Forages primarily on root crops, grains, tubers, grasses, other plant materials, grazing or upending while swimming. Both sexes build nest, incubate, care for young; preferred site mammal lodge, small island.

VOCALIZATIONS Low-pitched, trumpet-like; calls infrequently.

"Bewick's" Swan · WA (King County)—Nov · GREGG THOMPSON

Juvenile · WA (King County)—Feb · RYAN MERRILL

WA (King County)—Jan · NICK DEAN

WA (Skagit County)—Jan · TOM KOGUT

Tundra Swan
Cygnus columbianus

DESCRIPTION 52 in/132 cm, wingspan 71 in/180 cm. Long necked, plumage entirely white; black bill slightly concave in profile. Variable **yellow spot on lores** gives impression that bill tapers to thin horizontal **line at eye**; edge of bill rounded across forehead. *Juvenile:* Dingy gray; **adult plumage attained before spring**; bill mostly pink. "Bewick's" Swan often appears thicker necked; yellow spot looks fleshy, extends halfway down bill toward nares, may connect across forehead.

SIMILAR SPECIES See under Trumpeter Swan (p. 42). Whooper Swan (not shown, casual Nov–Mar in PNW) larger than "Bewick's" Swan; forehead flatter, with more extensive yellow on bill always connecting across top, extending forward in point beyond nares.

STATUS & DISTRIBUTION New World subspecies (*C.c. columbianus*) breeds Arctic tundra; most winter BC to Arizona, also Middle Atlantic coast. In PNW, migrants widespread (mid-Oct–Dec, Feb–May); coastal breeders west of Cascades/BC Coast Range, interior breeders east—thousands sometimes reported at stopovers. Notable winter concentrations BC (Fraser Lowlands, Thompson River, Okanagan Valley), WA (Skagit Flats, Ridgefield NWR), OR (Willamette Valley, Klamath Basin). Eurasian subspecies "Bewick's" Swan (*C.c. bewickii*) casual migrant, winter visitor in PNW.

HABITAT ASSOCIATIONS Breeds at tundra ponds, lakes, mostly near deltas; shallow water bodies with pondweed in migration. Winters in estuaries, wetlands, often near agricultural fields.

BEHAVIOR & FEEDING Gregarious; often flocks with Trumpeter Swans. Primarily herbivorous, foraging on seeds, grains, tubers, grasses by grazing or upending; also eats mollusks. Pair shares nesting duties, usually produces three young.

VOCALIZATIONS Somewhat gooselike *klow wow*, reminiscent of small dog barking.

Mute Swan
Cygnus olor

DESCRIPTION 58 in/147 cm, wingspan 80 in/204 cm. Long necked, **plumage entirely white**; **orange-red bill, black knob** at base. While swimming, neck held in graceful S-shape, wings often raised. *Juvenile:* Two color morphs: grayish brown, white; slate-gray bill (tan in white morph), without knob, becomes pink over winter as knob grows; adult plumage attained before spring.

SIMILAR SPECIES Trumpeter, Tundra Swans (pp. 42–43) generally hold neck straight while swimming; adults with black bills, typically held horizontally. Snow Goose (p. 34), American White Pelican (p. 118) with black wingtips.

STATUS & DISTRIBUTION Introduced from Old World; feral populations well established along coast from southern Maine to Carolinas, Great Lakes, southwestern BC. In PNW, established only in BC (metropolitan Vancouver, southeastern Vancouver Island). Strays rare elsewhere in region; controlled in many areas by lethal removal.

HABITAT ASSOCIATIONS Generally aquatic habitats: estuaries, marshes, coastal ponds, municipal ponds, tidal rivers.

BEHAVIOR & FEEDING Less gregarious than other PNW swans; in winter, may aggregate in marine habitats. Herbivorous; forages while swimming or upends for submerged plants, tubers. Rarely mixes with native swans grazing agricultural fields. Wings make loud whooshing sound in flight, audible at great distance. Mates for life; in PNW, nests Apr–Jul; both sexes gather cattails, grasses, other materials to form shoreline nest in female's natal territory, defending it aggressively. Prone to overgrazing aquatic ecosystems; displaces native waterfowl.

VOCALIZATIONS Grunts, muffled whistles, hisses, crane-like bugle.

Male · BC (Delta)—Apr · GERALD ROMANCHUK

Male · WA (King County)—Feb · GREGG THOMPSON

Female · WA (King County)—Feb · GREGG THOMPSON

Summer Male · WA (Pierce County)—Jun · JOHN RIEGSECKER

Wood Duck
Aix sponsa

DESCRIPTION 17 in/43 cm, wingspan 28 in/71 cm. Unique, short-necked duck with **long, broad tail**, swept-back crest, white belly, dark-blue speculum bordered at rear by white. *Male:* Spectacularly **multicolored**. Green head, white partial neck collar, scarlet eye-ring, bill base. Dull in summer, retaining neck collar, red bill. *Female:* Brownish with broad **teardrop-shaped eye-ring**.

SIMILAR SPECIES Mandarin Duck (not shown; introduced from Asia, rare in PNW) similar, but male has white face, orange "side-whiskers"; female has smaller crest, eye-ring.

STATUS & DISTRIBUTION Widespread breeder across North America south to Texas, Cuba; winters ice-free parts of breeding range, a few to Mexico. In PNW, fairly common breeder south from south-central BC (except southeastern OR), with fewer at higher elevations. Uncommon, more local Nov–Jan; withdraws from interior BC. Populations depressed a century ago, now recovered thanks to managed harvest, nest boxes, forest regrowth.

HABITAT ASSOCIATIONS Riparian woodlands, wooded swamps, sloughs, small ponds, wastewater treatment impoundments; open lakeshores; coastal bays less frequently.

BEHAVIOR & FEEDING Takes hazelnuts, acorns, other mast; waste grain; fruits, seeds, vegetative parts of various aquatic, terrestrial plants; invertebrates more often summer. Forages preferably in water. Disperses late Jul–Sep; more prone to flock Oct–Jan, with up to 200 recorded at favorite PNW roost sites. Breeds in cavities, often using abandoned Pileated Woodpecker nest or provided nest box; fairly agile among tree branches, where frequently observed.

VOCALIZATIONS Male gives thin, high whistles, also *jib jib jib*; female piercing *ooo eeek* when alarmed.

Family Anatidae—GEESE, SWANS, AND DUCKS **45**

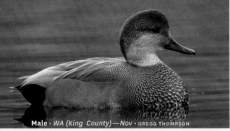
Male · WA (King County)—Nov · GREGG THOMPSON

Male · WA (King County)—Nov · BOB KOTHENBEUTEL

Female · OR (Harney County)—May · MATT T. LEE

Gadwall
Anas strepera

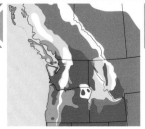

DESCRIPTION 20 in/51 cm, wingspan 34 in/86 cm. Rather plain dabbling duck; thin bill, white belly, steep forehead, **white patch in speculum**. *Male:* Variegated gray; brown back plumes, silvery tertials; **puffy head shape**, dark bill; **black rump, undertail**; dull as female in summer. *Female:* Mottled brown; bill has yellowish-orange sides.

SIMILAR SPECIES Female Mallard (p. 47) more bulky, speculum blue-and-white; wigeons (pp. 48–49) have small blue-gray bill.

STATUS & DISTRIBUTION Holarctic. In North America, expanding from historic core Prairie Potholes breeding range, now widespread Alaska to New Brunswick, south to California, Virginia. Winters southern coastal Alaska, BC, Colorado, east to southern New England, south through Mexico. In PNW, fairly common breeder in lowlands, originally mostly east of Cascades/BC Coast Range; increasing dramatically post-1960s in Willamette Valley, Puget Trough, Fraser Delta; more recently, expansion has continued to WA outer coast; still scarce southern OR. Winters throughout; retreats southward to ice-free waters on eastside.

HABITAT ASSOCIATIONS Prefers fresh water; ponds, marshes, sloughs, sewage ponds, rarely brackish estuaries. Spread into urban lakes facilitated by introduced invasive water milfoil.

BEHAVIOR & FEEDING Dabbles or upends, often in deeper water than other surface ducks; occasionally grazes on land. Forages mostly on plant materials, more invertebrates during nesting season. Often flocks with other dabblers; frequently steals pondweed from diving coots. Pairs form mostly by winter. Female nests on ground, later than Mallards, usually laying smaller clutches.

VOCALIZATIONS Male gives low-pitched nasal *reb reb*, most frequent Jan–May; also squeaked whistles. Female gives nasal quack.

Male · OR (Washington County)—Jan · GREG GILLSON

Male · BC (Penticton)—Nov · LAURE W. NEISH

Female · WA (Kitsap County)—Feb · JAMES HALSCH

Mallard
Anas platyrhynchos

DESCRIPTION 23 in/58 cm, wingspan 35 in/89 cm. Heavy-bodied dabbling duck; orange legs; **blue speculum bordered front and rear with white.** *Male:* Iridescent-**green head**, gray sides with darker back, chestnut breast, white neck-ring, yellow bill; in summer, dull as female; greenish-yellow bill. *Female:* Mottled brown; **orange bill with dark blotches.**

SIMILAR SPECIES Other dabbling ducks in PNW smaller, lack white-bordered blue speculum.

STATUS & DISTRIBUTION Holarctic, ranging from subarctic to subtropics. Most common dabbler in North America, having extended range eastward across continent from original Prairie Potholes nesting locations in 20th century. Winters along coasts south from Alaska, Greenland, across interior US to Mexico. Most numerous resident duck in PNW, numbers augmented Sep–Mar by northern migrants; less common in mountains from subalpine-fir to mountain-hemlock zones.

HABITAT ASSOCIATIONS Any fresh- or saltwater habitat including wet meadows, flooded fields, city parks; less common in coastal habitats than pintail or wigeon.

BEHAVIOR & FEEDING Dabbles or upends, feeding near surface, rarely dives; takes plant material, a few invertebrates. Grazes on land for waste grain, grass, invertebrates; often habituates to humans in urban areas. Gregarious, flocking with other ducks. Flight strong, able to spring vertically from water. Pair formation, courtship begin in fall; nests Mar–May, usually on ground, sometimes fairly distant from water. Females lead ducklings to water to forage. Males gather for post-breeding flight-feather molt in secretive locations, as other ducks.

VOCALIZATIONS Female quacks; male offers single whistle while courting, rapid grating *rab rab rab* in aggression.

Female · WA (Snohomish County)—Dec · GREGG THOMPSON

Male · WA (Pierce County)—Feb · RYAN SHAW

Eurasian Wigeon
Anas penelope

DESCRIPTION 20 in/50 cm, wingspan 33 in/84 cm. Short-necked, white-bellied dabbling duck; bluish-gray bill, fairly long, pointed tail. **White forewing patch**, gray axillaries visible in flight. *Male:* **Russet-red head**, creamy-yellow forehead; **gray sides**, back; white flanks, black undertail. Immatures, summer males much duller. *Female:* **Warm brown, including head** blending into breast; smaller forewing patch.

SIMILAR SPECIES American Wigeon (p. 49) male has brownish sides, gray head, white forehead, green behind eye; female, gray head contrasts with brown breast. In flight both sexes show white (versus gray) axillaries. Mixed-plumaged hybrids (males) regularly identified. Gadwall (p. 46) shows white speculum, not forewing; female, yellowish bill.

STATUS & DISTRIBUTION Not known to breed in North America. Nests from Iceland east to Siberia; winters Iceland, Britain, south to tropics; fewer to temperate New World. In PNW, associates closely with American Wigeons. Casual Jun–early Sep; uncommon late Sep–May with peak in Feb. Most abundant northwestern WA, southwestern BC lowland deltas; North American high counts of several hundreds from Samish Flats (WA); fewer south on Pacific Slope to OR. Rare but increasingly reported east of Cascades/BC Coast Range; uncommon Mar–Apr northwestern MT, northern ID.

HABITAT ASSOCIATIONS Lowlands, often near coast; freshwater bodies, bays, estuaries, flooded agricultural fields, park lawns.

BEHAVIOR & FEEDING Gregarious. In PNW, usually found within large American Wigeon flocks, foraging for plant material by grazing, skimming, rarely upending for pondweed, marine grasses, preferring leafy plant parts.

VOCALIZATIONS Male, whistled *wheehr* higher, more strident than American Wigeon; female, growled quack.

Male · OR (Washington County)—Feb · GREG GILLSON

Male · BC (Penticton)—Jan · LAURE W. NEISH

Female · WA (Asotin County)—Dec · MICHAEL WOODRUFF

American Wigeon
Anas americana

DESCRIPTION 20 in/51 cm, wingspan 34 in/86 cm. Short-necked, white-bellied dabbling duck. Bluish-gray bill, fairly long, pointed tail, **white forewing patch**. Bright-**white axillaries** contrast with gray underwing in flight. *Male:* Gray head, **green behind eye**, buff forehead variably extending to throat; **brownish** back, **sides**; white flanks, black undertail. *Female:* Black-peppered gray head contrasts with brown breast; smaller forewing patch. Immatures (both sexes), summer males resemble females.

SIMILAR SPECIES Eurasian Wigeon (p. 48) shows gray (versus white) axillaries in flight; male: gray sides, reddish head, yellowish forehead; female: warm-brown head, breast. Intermediate-plumaged male hybrids frequent. Gadwall (p. 46) shows white speculum, not forewing; female shows yellowish bill.

STATUS & DISTRIBUTION Range primarily Western. Breeds across boreal zone, tundra, Great Basin, Prairie Pothole Region, disjunctly to central California. Winters coastal BC, Massachusetts, to West Indies, Panama. In PNW, common Aug–May, highest densities northwestern WA, southwestern BC deltas Feb–Apr. Rare breeder on Pacific Slope; uncommon east of crest, concentrated central interior BC (Cariboo–Chilcotin), south-central, southeastern OR. Abundant migrant eastern interior.

HABITAT ASSOCIATIONS Nests open woodlands, brushy prairie, adjacent to freshwater wetland; winters lowlands with freshwater bodies, flooded fields, bays, estuaries, lawns, golf courses.

BEHAVIOR & FEEDING Highly gregarious. Forages for plants, preferring leafy parts; grazes in tight flocks; skims for pondweed, marine grasses. Like Gadwall, steals plant material brought up by other water birds. Relatively small clutch; male may help attend brood.

VOCALIZATIONS Male, whistled, lispy *wee whe whir*; female, growled quack.

Male · BC (Parksville)—Feb · RALPH HOCKEN

Female · BC (Victoria)—Mar · TERRY THORMIN

Northern Pintail
Anas acuta

DESCRIPTION 22 in/56 cm (male 27 in/69 cm), wingspan 35 in/89 cm. Slender, **long-necked** dabbling duck. Long, **thin gray bill**; green **speculum bordered buff at front, white at rear.** *Male:* Grayish, brown head, long **needle-like tail**, white on breast extending in thin line up side of neck; dull as female in summer. *Female:* Mottled gray brown, shorter pointed tail.

SIMILAR SPECIES Male unmistakable. Female slender, longer necked than other dabblers; Mallard (p. 47), Gadwall (p. 46) have yellowish bills.

STATUS & DISTRIBUTION Holarctic, highly migratory; most abundant duck of Pacific flyway. Breeds from Arctic south to southern California, Great Lakes, Caspian Sea; winters coastal BC, Massachusetts, Britain south to tropics. In PNW, common, widespread migrant throughout. East of Cascades/BC Coast Range, fairly common breeder, uncommon Nov–Feb. Rare, local breeder on westside (e.g., Haida Gwaii, Fraser Lowlands, Puget Trough, Willamette Valley), common Aug–Apr; most numerous along outer coast, where up to one million move through annually.

HABITAT ASSOCIATIONS Fresh water, salt water. Most frequent in lowlands, but occurs to moderate elevation. Ponds, lakes, estuaries, marshes, tidal flats, flooded fields.

BEHAVIOR & FEEDING Dabbles, upends, skims surface; also grazes with wigeons, Mallards in flooded fields, foraging mainly for waste grain, other plant materials; pre-nesting females increase invertebrate intake. Gregarious, flocks with other ducks, often makes long flights from feeding sites to night roost. Pair formation begins in fall. Nests early, on ground; lays smaller clutches than other dabblers.

VOCALIZATIONS Male gives whistled *toop toop*, wheezy *zweea*; female, *kuk*.

Female · OR (Washington County)—Sep · GREG GILLSON

"Eurasian" Male · WA (Skagit County)—Mar · MARV BREECE

Female · BC (Burnaby)—Mar · GREGG THOMPSON

Male · BC (Burnaby)—Mar · PAUL KUSMIN

Green-winged Teal
Anas crecca

DESCRIPTION 13.5 in/34 cm, wingspan 23 in/59 cm. Smallest dabbling duck in PNW; **short dark bill**, green-and-black speculum. *Male:* Grayish; **chestnut-and-green head**, yellow undertail; vertical white bar on side. Like female in summer. *Female:* Mottled brown; **dark eyeline**. "Eurasian" Teal male shows horizontal (versus vertical) white bar on side, brighter-yellow facial outline, but female virtually indistinguishable.

SIMILAR SPECIES Smaller, shorter billed than other dabblers; other female teals (pp. 52–53) show less-pronounced eyeline, blue forewing patch in flight.

STATUS & DISTRIBUTION New World subspecies (*A.c. carolinensis*) breeds Arctic south to central California, Colorado, Great Lakes; winters Aleutians, Connecticut, south to Caribbean, Mexico. In PNW, uncommon east but common west of Cascades/BC Coast Range Nov–Mar. Widespread eastside breeder (common BC; fairly common ID, northwestern MT, western WY; uncommon OR, WA) but rare west of crest (e.g., Haida Gwaii, southern Vancouver Island, northern Puget Sound, Columbia River bottomlands). Old World form "Eurasian" Teal (*A.c. crecca/nimia*) rare Oct–May, mostly west of Cascades/BC Coast Range; intergrades with New World form reported frequently.

HABITAT ASSOCIATIONS Lowlands; fewer breed in mountains. Nests at wooded boreal, sedge-lined ponds, wetlands; winters at marshes, estuaries, flooded fields. Migrants sometimes fly offshore.

BEHAVIOR & FEEDING Dabbles in shallows, infrequently upends; walks about, straining wet mud. Takes seeds, other vegetation, aquatic organisms. Flies swiftly in tight units; flocks often large. Mixes with other ducks. Courting begins in fall. Ground nester; produces smaller clutches than most dabblers.

VOCALIZATIONS Male highly vocal, gives ringing whistle; female, nasal quack.

Male · WA (Grant County)—Apr · GREGG THOMPSON

Female · WA (Clark County)—Apr · KEN ARCHER

Blue-winged Teal
Anas discors

DESCRIPTION 16 in/41 cm, wingspan 25 in/63 cm. **Small** dabbling duck. Long, **dark bill**; green speculum, **powder-blue forewing patch** visible in flight. *Male:* Black-spotted brown sides, white flank patch; gray head, **bold white crescent behind bill**; dull as female in summer. *Female:* Mottled brownish with diffuse **pale area behind bill**; dark eyeline.

SIMILAR SPECIES Cinnamon Teal (p. 53) male reddish with red eye; female warmer brown, plainer face, lacks strong eyeline; juvenile extremely similar but shows longer, more spatulate bill. Blue-winged, Cinnamon occasionally hybridize; males with mixed plumage characteristics regularly reported. Green-winged Teal (p. 51) smaller, bill shorter; lacks forewing patch.

STATUS & DISTRIBUTION Breeds Alaska to Labrador, south in Midwest to Texas; winters coastal California, Carolinas south to Brazil. In PNW, fairly common breeder east of Cascades/BC Coast Range throughout interior, although uncommon OR. Uncommon-to-rare westside breeder, but migrants fairly common May–early Jun: highest densities southwestern BC (Fraser Lowlands, southeastern Vancouver Island), northwestern WA (northern Puget Trough). Departs PNW Oct, returns late Apr–May; casual in winter.

HABITAT ASSOCIATIONS Prefers shallow fresh water, mostly lowlands, rarely to mid-elevation; uses small ponds, mud flats, sewage ponds, marshes, coastal ponds; less regularly, flooded fields.

BEHAVIOR & FEEDING Dabbles, rarely upends, taking more invertebrates than other surface ducks (particularly breeding females). Also eats waste grains, rice, other plant materials. Agile flyer. Often flocks with other teals. Breeds later than most dabblers.

VOCALIZATIONS Females give high-pitched quack; males, thin *tsee* whistle.

Male · OR (Washington County)—May · GREG GILLSON

Female · OR (Washington County)—Aug · GREG GILLSON

Male · BC (Victoria)—May · TED ARDLEY

Cinnamon Teal
Anas cyanoptera

DESCRIPTION 16.5 in/42 cm, wingspan 25 in/63 cm. **Small** dabbling duck. **Dark shoveler-like bill**; green speculum, powder-**blue forewing patch** visible in flight. *Male:* **Chestnut red** with red eye; dull as female in summer. *Female:* Mottled **warm brown** with plain face, tends to lack strong eyeline.

SIMILAR SPECIES Blue-winged Teal (p. 52) male has brown sides, white face crescent; female more gray brown; strong eye-line, pale at base of bill; juvenile extremely similar but bill smaller, less spatulate. Green-winged Teal (p. 51) smaller, bill shorter; lacks forewing patch. Northern Shoveler (p. 54) bulkier, shows larger yellowish bill.

STATUS & DISTRIBUTION Breeds western North America from BC, southern Saskatchewan to Mexico; most winter south from California, southern Texas, to Guatemala. Also resident South America. In PNW, fairly common breeder Mar–Oct east of Cascades/BC Coast Range, fewer west; highest nesting densities southern OR (Malheur NWR, Klamath Basin, Summer Lake), central interior BC (Cariboo–Chilcotin). Rare but increasing Nov–Feb, mostly southwestern WA (Ridgefield NWR), western OR (Fern Ridge Reservoir); casual east of crest.

HABITAT ASSOCIATIONS Mostly low-elevation freshwater wetlands. Prefers alkaline marshes with emergent vegetation; also uses sewage ponds, less frequently flooded fields.

BEHAVIOR & FEEDING Dabbles in pairs in shallows, straining for seeds, rice, other plant materials. Takes more invertebrates than most dabblers, particularly Apr–Jul. Agile in flight, flocking with other teals. Arrives, nests before Blue-winged Teal in PNW; interbreeding occurs rarely but regularly.

VOCALIZATIONS Quiet for duck; female gives high-pitched quack; male chatters.

Female · OR (Linn County)—Nov · MATT T. LEE

Male · BC (Victoria)—Apr · RALPH HOCKEN

Male · WA (Pierce County)—Apr · JOHN RIEGSECKER

Northern Shoveler
Anas clypeata

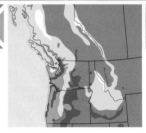

DESCRIPTION 19 in/48 cm, wingspan 30 in/76 cm. Fairly small dabbling duck. **Large, long spatulate bill**, orange legs, green speculum, powder-**blue forewing patch** visible in flight. *Male:* White breast, **rust-brown belly**, sides; iridescent-green head, yellow eye, black bill. Like female in summer but retains yellow eye. *Female:* Mottled brown with dark eye, dusky-orange bill.

SIMILAR SPECIES Female Cinnamon Teal (p. 53), Blue-winged Teal (p. 52) smaller with darker, smaller bills.

STATUS & DISTRIBUTION Holarctic breeder northern temperate, boreal zones; winters southern BC, Great Britain south to tropics. In PNW, locally common in lowlands; most breed east of Cascades/BC Coast Range, fewer west; migrants swell numbers Mar–Apr, Aug–Sep. Remains fairly common west Oct–Feb; can be locally common east prior to freeze-up, e.g., Umatilla NWR (OR/WA); Moses, Coulee Lakes (WA).

HABITAT ASSOCIATIONS Prefers shallow freshwater ponds, marshes, flooded fields, less frequently saline wetlands, tidal marshland; often abundant at sewage lagoons. Migrants seen annually flying up to 55 mi/90 km offshore.

BEHAVIOR & FEEDING Dabbles while swimming, often encircling plankton in tight, pinwheeling group. Sweeps bill side to side, straining plant, animal material by means of lamellae (transverse bill ridges); occasionally upends to strain mud. Usually in single-species flocks, but mixes with other ducks. Breeding phenology late compared to other dabblers—pairs form winter into spring, egg laying continues to late Jun, dependent young seen through Sep. Male summer molt begins while still paired.

VOCALIZATIONS Male nasal *paaay*; low *thuk tuk tuk* while courting. Female quacks hoarsely.

Male · WA (King County)—Jan · BOB KOTHENBEUTEL

Female · BC (Penticton)—Feb · LAURE W. NEISH

Canvasback
Aythya valisineria

DESCRIPTION 20 in/51 cm, wingspan 30 in/76 cm. Sleek, elegant, long-necked diving duck. **Sloping forehead**; long, dark bill; **whitish-gray wings, back**. *Male:* **Chestnut-reddish head**; black bib, rump, undertail; red eye. Like female in summer. *Female:* Duller overall; brown head, neck, bib.

SIMILAR SPECIES Redhead (p. 56) back darker gray, bill bluish with black tip; round headed, lacks sloping forehead.

STATUS & DISTRIBUTION Breeds in interior, central Alaska to Colorado, Minnesota; winters from southwestern BC, Massachusetts down coasts, across southern US to Mexico. In PNW, fairly common but local Oct–Apr, mostly large rivers, Klamath Basin, Okanagan Valley, southern coastal BC. Migrant peaks late Feb–Mar (Apr northwestern MT), Oct–Nov. Breeds east of Cascades/BC Coast Range—common BC (Cariboo–Chilcotin), south-central OR (Klamath Basin), uncommon to rare elsewhere; a few linger west of crest through summer.

HABITAT ASSOCIATIONS Lowlands; some breed to mid-elevation (mostly BC). Nests on fresh water with emergent vegetation, deepwater marshes, alkaline lakes, bays of large lakes, open boreal-zone marsh. Migrants, winter birds use estuaries, coastal bays, sewage ponds, lakes, major rivers.

BEHAVIOR & FEEDING Dives primarily for plants; prefers buds, other submergent plant material. Also takes invertebrates. Gregarious, often in large single-species flocks or with other *Aythya*. Courts less on wintering ground than most ducks; pair formation occurs in spring. Females build bulky ground nest, often victim of nest parasitism by Redhead, Ruddy Duck, or conspecific (up to 80 percent of nests). Males remain with female into incubation.

VOCALIZATIONS Female raspy guttural grunts; courting male gives eerie, trisyllabic hooting.

Female · BC (Penticton)—Feb · LAURE W. NEISH   Male · WA (Lincoln County)—May · JON ISACOFF

Redhead
Aythya americana

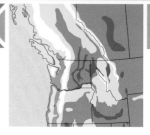

DESCRIPTION 19 in/48 cm, wingspan 30 in/76 cm. **Round-headed** diving duck; rounded back, gray speculum. Large bill with concave culmen, **pale ring near black tip**. *Male:* **Red head**, gray back; black bib, rump, undertail; yellow eye, bluish bill. Plumage, bare parts turn duller in summer. *Female:* Plain **tawny brownish**; pale eye-ring, grayish bill.

SIMILAR SPECIES Canvasback (p. 55) has longer neck, sloping forehead, whitish-gray wings. Scaup females (pp. 58–59) show white patch near bill base, appear less tawny. Female Ring-necked Duck (p. 57) has peaked head shape.

STATUS & DISTRIBUTION Breeds disjunctly from central Alaska, central BC to South Dakota, Texas, Mexico; winters east to Massachusetts, south to Mexico, majority to Gulf Coast. In PNW, widespread, locally common resident east of Cascades/BC Coast Range; less frequent, more local Nov–Feb, in large flocks—e.g., Okanagan (BC), Flathead Lake (MT). Uncommon to rare west of crest, mostly Oct–May, rare breeder (e.g., Ridgefield NWR).

HABITAT ASSOCIATIONS Throughout lowlands; migrants rarely to mid-elevation. Breeds in extensive marshes, small ponds with emergent vegetation, ephemeral wetlands; uses lakes, estuaries, sewage ponds in winter, migration. In PNW, winters on deeper lakes, major rivers in interior.

BEHAVIOR & FEEDING Dives mostly in shallows for plant materials, some invertebrates; also dabbles. Gregarious; winter flocks reach tens of thousands (far smaller in PNW); often with other *Aythya* or dabblers. Tends toward brood parasitism, often laying in conspecific or other species' nests.

VOCALIZATIONS Male call wheezy *weee oh*. Female nasal *gurr*, quacked alarm note, low *kuk kuk kuk*.

Ring-necked Duck
Aythya collaris

DESCRIPTION 17 in/43 cm, wingspan 25 in/64 cm. Compact diving duck with **peaked head**; gray bill with **whitish ring near black tip**; grayish wing in flight. *Male:* Purplish-iridescent head; **black back**, breast; vertical **white mark on gray side in front of wing**; color pattern duller in summer. *Female:* Brownish with white eye-ring, diffuse pale area near bill.

SIMILAR SPECIES Lesser Scaup (p. 59) head less angular; lacks whitish bill ring; male has gray back; female, bold white patch near bill base. Both Tufted Duck (p. 60), Redhead (p. 56) have round head shape.

STATUS & DISTRIBUTION Breeds western Alaska to Labrador, south disjunctly to Arizona; winters southwestern BC to Yucatan, Caribbean. In PNW, uncommon breeder across interior to moderate elevation, rare west of Cascades/BC Coast Range; common in migration (Feb–May, late Aug–Oct); common winter but more localized (nearly absent western WY).

HABITAT ASSOCIATIONS Prefers fresh water, mostly lowlands; breeds on wooded ponds, boggy meadows, marshes, acidic bogs; at other seasons, also frequents lakes, sewage lagoons, flooded fields; rarely coastal bays, brackish sloughs.

BEHAVIOR & FEEDING Mostly dives but also dabbles, predominantly in shallows for aquatic plants, invertebrates. Gregarious; winter flocks into thousands (usually smaller in PNW), single-species or mixed with other *Aythya* or dabblers. Ability to spring directly off water into flight enables it to use small, tree-lined ponds year-round. Highly migratory. Pairs form in spring, nest in flooded emergent vegetation. Male sometimes mates with second female.

VOCALIZATIONS Male *woww* during display; female growls softly.

Female (*left*) and Male · WA (Pacific County)—May · KEITH CARLSON

Greater Scaup
Aythya marila

DESCRIPTION 19 in/48 cm, wingspan 29 in/74 cm. **Round-headed** diving duck. Yellowish eye; long, wide bluish-gray bill with broad black tip; in flight, white **wing stripe extends into primaries**. *Male:* Head iridescence usually greenish; **grayish back**; black bib, rump, undertail; white sides; duller in summer, first-year plumages. *Female:* Brownish; **white patch at bill base**, another **often over ear**.

SIMILAR SPECIES Lesser Scaup (p. 59) crown peaks behind eye; thinner neck, smaller black bill tip, white wing stripe only in secondaries, male head usually glosses purplish. Ring-necked Duck (p. 57), Tufted Duck (p. 60) males have black backs; latter female shows tuft.

STATUS & DISTRIBUTION Holarctic breeder in treeless north, winters to temperate zone, mostly coastally. In PNW, common westside lowlands Oct–May; non-breeders uncommon Jun–Aug, mostly on outer BC, WA coasts. East of Cascades/BC Coast Range, common Oct–May primarily on major rivers, larger lakes, but rare ID, western WY; non-breeders casual Jun–Aug (but annual in tiny numbers on WA Columbia Plateau).

HABITAT ASSOCIATIONS Breeds on tundra, predominantly near shallow lakes, large ponds. At other seasons, mostly lowland waters such as marine bays, sheltered harbors, estuaries, freshwater ponds, lakes, sewage ponds, Columbia Plateau reservoirs.

BEHAVIOR & FEEDING Feeds in nutrient-rich waters, diving for mollusks, other invertebrates, plant material dependent on availability. Highly gregarious; flocks tightly, often with other *Aythya*. Pairs form late winter/spring, break up during incubation; post-breeding male flocks may move great distances to molting lakes.

VOCALIZATIONS Male displays with whistled *wek wek whew*. Female gives raspy grunts when disturbed.

Male · Alberta—May · GERALD ROMANCHUK

Male · WA (King County)—Feb · GREGG THOMPSON

Female · BC (Burnaby)—Mar · GREGG THOMPSON

Lesser Scaup
Aythya affinis

DESCRIPTION 17 in/43 cm, wingspan 26 in/66 cm. Thin-necked diving duck; **peaked crown**, yellowish eye, moderately narrow bluish-gray bill with black tip; in flight, **white wing stripe extends only to secondaries**. *Male:* Head iridescence usually purplish; **grayish back**, black bib, rump, undertail; whitish sides; duller in summer, first-year plumages. *Female:* Brownish; **white patch at bill base**.

SIMILAR SPECIES Greater Scaup (p. 58) crown round, neck thicker, black bill tip larger, wing stripe extends into primaries; male head usually appears greenish, female often shows pale auricular area. Ring-necked Duck (p. 57), Tufted Duck (p. 60) males have black backs; former shows contrasting white mark on side.

STATUS & DISTRIBUTION Breeds central Alaska to Colorado, Quebec; winters southern BC, New England, south as far as Colombia. In PNW, common Oct–Apr with notable concentrations WA (Columbia Plateau, Whidbey Island), BC (Boundary Bay); uncommon outer coast; few remain after fall migration in southeastern BC, nearly absent western WY, southeastern OR. Common breeder Jun–Sep east of Cascades/BC Coast Range, majority in north; uncommon west of crest, mainly northern Puget Trough.

HABITAT ASSOCIATIONS Lowlands to mid-elevation. Prefers open marsh, sewage ponds, seasonal wetlands for breeding; uses lakes, estuaries, rivers in other seasons.

BEHAVIOR & FEEDING Dives mostly for invertebrates, some plant materials. Highly gregarious, flocks tightly, often with other *Aythya*; breeds late—pairs form Apr–May, break up well along in incubation; broods fledge Jul–Aug. May use upland nest sites.

VOCALIZATIONS Relatively quiet. Whistled *whew* from male; female, *purr* calls.

First-year Male · WA (King County)—Feb · COLLIN VASSALLO

Male · BC (Victoria)—Mar · MIKE YIP

Male · BC (Richmond)—Feb · RAYMOND NG

Female · England—May · NICK STACEY

Tufted Duck
Aythya fuligula

DESCRIPTION 18.5 in/47 cm, wingspan 28 in/70 cm. **Round-headed** diving duck with variable **tuft at rear of crown**; yellowish eye; gray bill with black tip; white wing stripe visible in flight. *Male:* Purplish-iridescent head **with long shaggy tuft**, white sides, **black back**, breast; duller with shorter tuft during first year, summer. *Female:* **Short tuft**; dark brown replaces black areas of male; some show white near bill base.

SIMILAR SPECIES Other *Aythya* lack tuft. Greater Scaup (p. 58) female has bold white patch near bill base; Ring-necked Duck (p. 57) has peaked head, whitish bill ring.

STATUS & DISTRIBUTION Palearctic. Breeds Iceland east to Siberia, winters to northern Africa, Middle East, southern, eastern Asia. Rare in North America, mainly along Atlantic, Pacific Coasts. In PNW, rare Oct–May (increasing in spring migration); casual Jun–Sep. Annual on Pacific slope; much less frequent interior BC, WA, OR, mostly on major rivers; accidental ID, northwestern MT, western WY. Hybrids with scaups show mixed characteristics, including short tuft.

HABITAT ASSOCIATIONS Prefers fresh water, lowlands; breeds on lakes fringed with emergent vegetation; at other seasons, sewage lagoons, rivers, flooded fields, coastal bays, ponds in city parks.

BEHAVIOR & FEEDING Dives for aquatic plants, invertebrates; sometimes upends or dabbles in shallows; patters along water to take flight. Highly gregarious; in PNW, almost always recorded as lone individuals within flocks of other *Aythya*. Semi-colonial nester; pair formation occurs in winter.

VOCALIZATIONS Male whistles in display; female, soft growl. Quiet in PNW.

Female · WA (Pierce County)—Nov · DOUG SCHURMAN

Male · Alaska—Jun · GREGG THOMPSON

First-winter Male · Ontario—Feb · GREG SCHNEIDER

King Eider
Somateria spectabilis

DESCRIPTION 23 in/58 cm, wingspan 36 in/93 cm. Bulky, block-headed diving duck with fairly small bill. *Male:* Adult has black back; **white breast**, wing, flank patches; black line divides greenish face from **blue crown**, nape; **orange bill with large swelling** at base. Dull in summer, retaining orange bill; in first winter, brownish with white breast; subadults transition over three years. *Female:* **Rich brownish**, hint of male facial line, vague eye-ring, dark bill.

SIMILAR SPECIES Male unmistakable; female browner than scoters (pp. 62–64), thicker-necked, more robust than dabbling ducks; female Mallard (p. 47) has boldly white-bordered blue speculum, orange bill.

STATUS & DISTRIBUTION Holarctic. In North America, High Arctic breeder central Alaska to Greenland; winters regularly along coasts to Aleutians, Massachusetts; casual south to California, Florida. In PNW, individuals found barely annually in BC, WA, OR combined, most Oct–May but many long staying, casually through summer flightless molt.

HABITAT ASSOCIATIONS Nests in various tundra habitats, coastal or near inland ponds; migrates to openings in sea ice, coastal bays, fjords, estuaries.

BEHAVIOR & FEEDING Most winter near southern edge of sea ice. During migration, highly gregarious; flocks reach thousands, often concentrating at openings in sea ice, diving up to 130 ft/40 m to bottom for mollusks, other invertebrates, plant material; on breeding grounds, forages in shallows ponds. Pairs form spring, nest soon after reaching tundra. In PNW, usually associates with scoters in protected marine habitats.

VOCALIZATIONS Male dove-like *brew brooo* in courtship; female low growls, seldom heard south of Arctic.

Male · *WA (Kitsap County)—Feb* · JOHN RIEGSECKER

WA (Grays Harbor County)—Apr · KEITH CARLSON

Female · *California—Jan* · LAURE W. NEISH

First-winter Male · *BC (Comox)—Nov* · JUKKA JANTUNEN

Surf Scoter
Melanitta perspicillata

DESCRIPTION 20 in/51 cm, wingspan 30 in/76 cm. Diving duck with large **bulging bill**, sloping forehead, white eye. *Male:* Black with **white patches on forehead, nape**, sides of fleshy **red-and-yellow bill**; first winter, brownish; dark eye, pale belly, lacks white head markings; transitions through second spring to adult plumage. *Female:* Smaller, brownish black, **whitish patches on cheeks, near bill base**.

SIMILAR SPECIES Black Scoter (p. 64) smaller, thinner bill; ventrally pale primaries contrast in flight; female's entire lower face whitish. White-winged Scoter (p. 63) shows white speculum. Harlequin Duck (p. 65) smaller; petite bill, steep forehead.

STATUS & DISTRIBUTION Nests western Alaska to central Quebec, south to central BC; winters along coastlines south to Baja California, Georgia. In PNW, common coastally Aug–May; non-breeders also locally common Jun–Jul. Established as rare breeder south to Cariboo–Chilcotin in recent work for BC Breeding Bird Atlas. Uncommon-to-rare (BC, WA) inland migrant, most frequent Oct–Nov, also May in BC; winters casually central WA, ID.

HABITAT ASSOCIATIONS Breeds on shallow tundra, boreal-zone lakes; at other seasons, uses shallow coastal bays, estuaries, breakwaters; rarely lakes, rivers.

BEHAVIOR & FEEDING Highly gregarious, flocking with other scoters, often over mussel beds. Dives nearly exclusively for mollusks Jul–Apr; spring flocks of tens of thousands follow West Coast herring spawns northward for eggs. Feeds on aquatic invertebrates while nesting. Broader wings than most divers enable agile takeoffs. Nests on forested lakes. Males depart quickly, but pair bond may continue beyond nesting.

VOCALIZATIONS Seldom heard in PNW. Male whistles, gurgles; female croaks.

WA (Whatcom County)—Apr · DOUGLAS L. BROWN

Female · WA (Clallam County)—Nov · DOUG SCHURMAN

Male · BC (White Rock)—Dec · MIKE D. BAILEY

White-winged Scoter
Melanitta fusca

DESCRIPTION 22 in/56 cm, wingspan 35 in/89 cm. Bulky diving duck, **white speculum** visible in flight, often obscured at rest. *Male:* Black with white eye, **white comma mark behind eye**, reddish bill with dark basal knob; first winter browner, lacks comma. *Female:* Dark brown with dark eye, whitish patches on cheeks, near bill base; immature has pale belly.

SIMILAR SPECIES Other scoters lack white speculum; Surf's (p. 62) bulging bill extends farther onto face; Black (p. 64) smaller, female's entire lower face whitish. Pigeon Guillemot (p. 204) petite with thin bill, white patch at front of wing.

STATUS & DISTRIBUTION Holarctic. In North America, breeds Alaska to southern BC, Hudson Bay; winters to temperate zone. In PNW, rare breeder east of BC Coast Range northward from Douglas Lake, also Haida Gwaii. Common along coasts late Jul–May, predominantly northern Salish Sea; non-breeders rare Jun. Most frequent migrant scoter across inland PNW, uncommon Oct–Nov (also May in BC) on lakes, rivers; rarely winters (central WA to northwestern MT).

HABITAT ASSOCIATIONS Nests near large freshwater or brackish coniferous-zone lakes; at other seasons, mostly marine, often farther offshore than other scoters.

BEHAVIOR & FEEDING Dives to bottom mostly for mollusks, crustaceans; in fresh water, various invertebrates. Gregarious; flies in low lines over water with heavy flight; may flock with other scoter species. Most pairs form during migration. Often nests ~1,000 ft/300 m from water, preferring dense ground vegetation, island sites.

VOCALIZATIONS Male whistle, female croak, but seldom heard.

Female · BC (Qualicum)—Mar · MIKE YIP

Male · BC (Qualicum Beach)—Feb · RALPH HOCKEN

BC (Haida Gwaii)—Oct · JUKKA JANTUNEN

Black Scoter
Melanitta americana

DESCRIPTION 19 in/43 cm, wingspan 29 in/73 cm. Stocky, **round-headed** diving duck; fairly **thin black bill** held parallel to water; undersides of flight feathers flash silvery gray in flight. *Male:* Black with fleshy **yellowish knob** at bill base; first-winter browner; lacks yellow knob, which develops through second spring. *Female:* Dark brown with **entire lower face light gray**; immature with paler belly.

SIMILAR SPECIES Other scoters larger, bills held angled downward. White-winged (p. 63) shows white speculum, immature male Surf (p. 62,) sloping head profile, larger bill; females of both have two small, whitish face patches. Ruddy Duck (p. 73) smaller with broad bill, longer tail.

STATUS & DISTRIBUTION Recently split from Common Scoter of Eurasia. Two disjunct breeding populations (central Alaska, northern Quebec) winter coastally, south to US Gulf Coast, Baja California. Most western breeders winter coastal Alaska, many fewer farther south. In PNW, locally common Oct–Apr at traditional sites, particularly Haida Gwaii, southeastern Vancouver Island; mostly uncommon elsewhere along Pacific coast, Salish Sea; rare May–Sep. Casual inland (most Oct–Nov) on lakes, impoundments.

HABITAT ASSOCIATIONS Nests on tundra, taiga lakes; at other seasons, prefers sheltered marine waters near headlands with gravelly bottoms.

BEHAVIOR & FEEDING Dives primarily for mollusks, some crustaceans, plant materials; in fresh water, also larval insects. Gregarious; flocks with other scoters, Harlequin Ducks, but often in segregated group. Courtship, pair formation probably occurs during winter. Nests on ground at potholes, small shallow lakes.

VOCALIZATIONS Most vocal scoter. Male gives forlorn-sounding whistles; female, low growls.

Harlequin Duck
Histrionicus histrionicus

DESCRIPTION 16 in/41 cm, wingspan 26 in/66 cm. Compact, short-necked diving duck; steep forehead, grayish **stubby bill**. *Male:* Darkly **multicolored**; slate blue with rusty sides, bold **white marks on head, sides, back**; brown in summer, partially retains white markings. *Female:* Brown with lighter belly; white spots on cheek, near bill base.

SIMILAR SPECIES Female scoters (pp. 62–64) larger with heavier bill, sloping forehead; female Bufflehead (p. 67) smaller with white wing patch, single oval face patch.

STATUS & DISTRIBUTION Breeds from northeastern Russia, Alaska, Yukon south to OR, WY, on Atlantic side Quebec to Iceland; winters coastally south to Korea, northern California, Maryland. In PNW, widespread but uncommon local breeder in forested mountains (to sea level in BC), but absent OR/WA/ID Blue Mountains, eastern slope OR Cascades south from Mt. Hood. Winters to coasts (where present year-round); fairly common in protected waters, generally uncommon along outer coast. Migrants rare on large rivers, interior lakes where recorded casually Dec–Feb.

HABITAT ASSOCIATIONS Breeds on fast-flowing streams; winters to rocky marine shorelines.

BEHAVIOR & FEEDING Dives, dabbles near surface for animal material (mollusks, crustaceans, sea worms, fish from sea; insects, fish eggs in streams). Gregarious in winter, usually in small flocks but may concentrate at herring spawns. Pairs move up nesting streams early spring. Females may share care of mixed broods. Males depart during incubation, greatly outnumber females at coast Jun–Aug; durable monogamous pair bonds re-established on wintering territory.

VOCALIZATIONS Male has high mouse-like whistle; female, nasal *ek ek ek ek*.

Spring Female · *Alaska—Jun* · GREGG THOMPSON

Winter Female · *BC (White Rock)—Feb* · MIKE D. BAILEY

Spring Male · *Alaska—Jun* · GREGG THOMPSON

Winter Male · *BC (White Rock)—Mar* · MIKE D. BAILEY

Long-tailed Duck
Clangula hyemalis

DESCRIPTION 16 in/41 cm (male 21 in/53 cm), wingspan 28 in/71 cm. Short-necked, **stubby-billed** diving duck; white belly, **blackish wings**. Highly variable due to three annual molts; intermediate (supplemental) plumage Jul–Sep. *Male:* Elegant; **long, pointed tail**, dark bill with pink band. Oct–Apr, mostly white with black breast, back, neck patch; May–Jun, black with rufous tertials, white face. *Female:* Grayish bill. Oct–Apr, **dark upperparts with whitish face**; May–Jun, brownish, loses white face.

SIMILAR SPECIES Northern Pintail (p. 50) male has brown face, green speculum. Auks (pp. 198–209) have shorter necks.

STATUS & DISTRIBUTION Circumpolar breeder on Arctic tundra, winters to temperate zone. In PNW, Oct–May locally common BC/northern WA marine waters; uncommon–rare southern WA/OR, rare southern Puget Sound. Sometimes migrates north into Jun, south into Dec; rare Jun–Sep (mostly BC). Rare but increasing inland in recent years, mostly Oct–Mar; casual Apr–Sep.

HABITAT ASSOCIATIONS Breeds in sedge-dominated Arctic wetlands; at other seasons, deeper coastal waters, usually near spits, headlands; rare on fresh water in PNW (major rivers, lakes, sewage ponds).

BEHAVIOR & FEEDING Dives for mollusks, other marine organisms, often to great depths; takes some plant material; at breeding ponds, also insects. Concentrates at herring spawns in BC during spring migration, eating roe. Highly gregarious, although flocks reach thousands only in BC, much smaller south to OR. Courtship begins in winter, pairs form by spring.

VOCALIZATIONS Male highly vocal with loud multisyllabic yodels; female gives soft grunts, barks.

Male · BC (Victoria)—Apr · GERALD ROMANCHUK

Female · WA (King County)—Feb · LEE BARNES

WA (King County)—Dec · GREGG THOMPSON

Bufflehead
Bucephala albeola

DESCRIPTION 13.5 in/34 cm, wingspan 20 in/51 cm. Plump **little diving duck**. Gray bill, white belly; white wing patches visible in flight. *Male:* White with black back, iridescent-greenish **puffy head with white patch at back**; female-like in summer, first-year plumages. *Female:* Smaller; dull grayish with **white oval cheek patch**; wing patch limited to speculum.

SIMILAR SPECIES Goldeneyes (pp. 68–69) larger; facial patch of male in front of eye. Hooded Merganser (p. 72) male has rusty sides with black bars. Ruddy Duck (p. 73) cheek patch extends to larger bill.

STATUS & DISTRIBUTION Nests interior of continent from central Alaska to western Quebec, disjunctly south to Colorado, northern California; winters from coastal Alaska, Maritimes, to northern Mexico. In PNW, common Oct–May; east of Cascades/BC Coast Range, common breeder May–Aug in BC, becoming less common, local southward into OR Cascades. Non-breeders uncommon Jun–Sep throughout region.

HABITAT ASSOCIATIONS Breeds at low to middle elevations in aspen parklands, open forest near wetlands, ponds, lakes, rivers. At other seasons uses sheltered marine waters, freshwater bodies, flooded fields, sewage lagoons.

BEHAVIOR & FEEDING Dives in shallow water for aquatic invertebrates, some seeds; patters along surface before flying. Usually in small parties, but large flocks occur at stopovers, favored sites. Breeds in cavities, frequently using abandoned flicker nest, also nest boxes; pair bond can persist long-term, but males leave family to molt.

VOCALIZATIONS Fairly quiet outside of breeding. Females utter *cuk cuk cuk*. Males chatter, growl during head-bobbing display.

Female · BC (Burnaby)—Mar · MIKE D. BAILEY

Male · BC (Qualicum Beach)—Feb · RALPH HOCKEN

Common Goldeneye
Bucephala clangula

DESCRIPTION 18 in/46 cm, wingspan 27 in/69 cm. Plump, short-necked diver. Yellowish iris, short sloping bill, **puffy head peaked in middle**, white wing patch. *Male:* White with black back, wings; **mostly white scapulars**, iridescent-greenish head, **round white loral patch**. Summer, first-winter plumages female-like but head darker. *Female:* Grayish with brown head, blackish bill (pale tipped Nov–May).

SIMILAR SPECIES Barrow's Goldeneye (p. 69) head peaked over steep forehead, smaller bill; male head purplish, loral patch crescent shaped, less white in scapulars; female bill mostly yellow (versus mostly black), but black in both species Jun–Oct. See under Bufflehead (p. 67).

STATUS & DISTRIBUTION Holarctic breeder across northern forest zones, winters south through temperate zone. In PNW, widespread, common Nov–Apr; breeds May–Aug (common northwestern MT, uncommon/rare interior BC, ID, extreme northeastern WA, casual southwestern BC). Understanding of breeding distribution complicated by identification difficulties with female goldeneyes; Barrow's far more numerous in most of PNW. Non-breeders rare May–Oct, often on sewage ponds.

HABITAT ASSOCIATIONS Mostly lowlands; some breed on clear, forested mid-elevation lakes, ponds with few invertebrate-eating fish present. Migrates, winters to intertidal marine habitats; also rivers, ice-free ponds, lakes.

BEHAVIOR & FEEDING Dives principally for animal material, some plants; on breeding ponds, migration, takes aquatic invertebrates, fish roe; on coasts, eats mollusks, other marine organisms. Flocks outside nesting season. Wings whistle loudly in flight. Pairs form through winter; males display frequently. Nests in trees, usually woodpecker holes, nest boxes; rarely rock cavity.

VOCALIZATIONS Quiet; male *peent*, female croak.

Summer Female and young · *WA (Okanogan County)—Jun* · RYAN SHAW

Winter Female · *BC (Qualicum Beach)—Apr* · RALPH HOCKEN

Male · *WA (King County)—Feb* · GREGG THOMPSON

Barrow's Goldeneye
Bucephala islandica

DESCRIPTION 18 in/46 cm, wingspan 28 in/71 cm. Plump, short-necked diving duck with stubby bill, white wing patch, yellowish iris, **puffy head peaked above steep forehead**. *Male:* Head iridescent purplish with **white crescent-shaped loral patch**. Mostly white; **black back extends across most of scapulars** downward in spur at bend of wing; summer, first-winter plumages like female. *Female:* Grayish with dark-brown head; bill bright orange yellow Nov–May, blackish Jun–Oct.

SIMILAR SPECIES See under Common Goldeneye (p. 68), Bufflehead (p. 67).

STATUS & DISTRIBUTION Breeds central Alaska disjunctly to Colorado, also northeastern Quebec, Iceland; winters mostly coastally, south to California, Long Island. In PNW, locally common Oct–Apr along coast, uncommonly rivers, rarer on lakes—numbers boosted during migration; rare western OR. Common breeder May–Aug interior BC on small mountain/plateau lakes, fairly common locally farther south (absent from some mountains); rare to coastal BC. Greatly outnumbers Common Goldeneye as breeder in PNW, except northwestern MT.

HABITAT ASSOCIATIONS Breeds up to alpine on freshwater ponds, lakes with few invertebrate-eating fish. Winters, migrates along coasts, also major rivers, lakes.

BEHAVIOR & FEEDING Dives for aquatic invertebrates, fewer plants. Often near pilings or rocky shores, mussel beds; spring flocks concentrate at herring spawn, stage on rivers, sewage ponds until breeding ponds thaw. Lays eggs in tree cavity by forested lake (rock crevices around unforested central WA lakes; grassland, alpine situations in BC); males highly territorial in spring.

VOCALIZATIONS Quiet; male grunts, female emits *cuk uck cuck.*

Female · BC (Parksville)—Jan · RALPH HOCKEN

Male · OR (Washington County)—Jan · GREG GILLSON

Common Merganser
Mergus merganser

DESCRIPTION 25 in/63 cm, wingspan 35 in/89 cm. Sleek, robust white-bellied diving duck; thin **reddish serrated bill**. Large white wing patches visible in flight. In first winter, shows white linear patch from under eye to bill. *Male:* **White** with dark wings, back; **dark-green rounded head**; first-winter, adult summer/fall plumages female-like. *Female:* Gray; sharply contrasting brown head with raggedy crest, white chin; wing patches limited to speculum.

SIMILAR SPECIES Red-breasted Merganser (p. 71) female very similar but less bulky, crest shaggier; lacks distinct white throat, sharp division between grayish body, brown head; bill thinner at base. Female Hooded Merganser (p. 72) smaller; bill not reddish.

STATUS & DISTRIBUTION Holarctic. Breeds in forest zones from northern treeline south to Arizona, Pennsylvania, central Europe, India; winters Alaska, Iceland south through temperate zone. In PNW, widespread, common breeder sea level to middle elevations, but absent most of Columbia Plateau, southeastern OR/southwestern ID deserts; winters throughout in ice-free waters.

HABITAT ASSOCIATIONS Nests along forested banks of rivers, lakes; also uses estuaries, brackish river mouths.

BEHAVIOR & FEEDING Dives in clear water for fish, other vertebrates/invertebrates, reaching depths of 115 ft/35 m. Fast, agile flier, cold tolerant; early-spring, late-fall migrant. Highly gregarious; hundreds flock Aug–Dec on rivers, estuaries, where pair formation begins. Nests in tree cavities, cliff crevices. Loosely colonial. Sometimes practices brood parasitism, with "dumping" of eggs into one cavity by multiple females resulting in broods of over 20.

VOCALIZATIONS Guttural croaks in alarm; courting male emits bell-like notes, twangs.

Male · WA (Whatcom County)—Jan · DOUGLAS L. BROWN

Female · WA (Pierce County)—Feb · RYAN SHAW

Red-breasted Merganser
Mergus serrator

DESCRIPTION 23 in/58 cm, wingspan 30 in/76 cm. Slim, long-necked, white-bellied diving duck. Long, thin, **reddish serrated bill**; **shaggy crest**. Large white wing patches visible in flight. In first winter, diffuse buff linear patch under eye to bill. *Male:* Elegant; green head, dark back, **brownish breast**, white neck-ring, gray sides; in summer, female-like but with white forewing. *Female:* Grayish; grades gradually to brown head; wing patches limited to speculum.

SIMILAR SPECIES Common Merganser (p. 70) female similar but bulkier with smaller crest, white throat; abrupt line between gray body, brown head; thicker bill. Hooded Merganser (p. 72) smaller, bill not reddish.

STATUS & DISTRIBUTION Holarctic breeder in tundra, boreal zones although absent most of BC; winters coastally (Aleutians, Labrador to subtropics in North America). In PNW, common coastally Oct–Apr, uncommon/rare May–Sep; breeds only Haida Gwaii. Inland generally rare Oct–May but uncommon on some major rivers, lakes, impoundments—e.g., Osoyoos Lake (BC), Banks Lake (WA), Upper Klamath Lake (OR), Flathead Lake (MT); casual at favored sites Jun–Sep.

HABITAT ASSOCIATIONS Nests freshwater, saltwater wetlands; at other seasons uses bays, estuaries, rocky coasts, less frequently fresh water.

BEHAVIOR & FEEDING Forages by diving, mostly for fish, other animal prey; gregarious year-round, herding schools of fish cooperatively. Requires running takeoff but gains speed quickly; among fastest-flying ducks. Courtship increases in spring; arrives for breeding paired; nests on ground near water in dense cover, sometimes colonially, preferring island sites.

VOCALIZATIONS Gruff croaks; courting male gives cat-like *meow*.

Family Anatidae—GEESE, SWANS, AND DUCKS **71**

Female · WA (King County)—Feb · GREGG THOMPSON

Male · BC (Penticton)—Oct · LAURE W. NEISH

Hooded Merganser
Lophodytes cucullatus

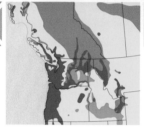

DESCRIPTION 16 in/41 cm, wingspan 24 in/61 cm. Long-tailed diving duck; **narrow serrated bill**, puffy crest, white belly. Small white wing patches visible in flight. *Male:* Striking; blackish above, including bill; yellow iris; white ornamental back plumes, fan-shaped white crest; **rusty sides**, two black vertical foreside bars. Female-like in summer/first-year plumages, except iris yellow, crest shows varying amounts of white. *Female:* Brownish; **dark bill** with yellowish edge.

SIMILAR SPECIES Other mergansers (pp. 70–71) larger with reddish bills. Bufflehead (p. 67) smaller; female shows small cheek patch, male with white sides.

STATUS & DISTRIBUTION Breeds southeastern Alaska to OR, southeastern ID, also eastern Alberta to Nova Scotia, southeastern states; winters south to California, Texas. In PNW, fairly common breeder May–Aug, except western WY, treeless areas of eastern OR, ID; rare BC Coast Range. Common, widespread Sep–Apr; southbound migrants boost numbers Nov–Dec.

HABITAT ASSOCIATIONS Fish-rich, low- to mid-elevation sites; breeds in forested wetlands with emergent vegetation, also sluggish forested streams. At other seasons uses sheltered fresh water, estuaries, bays, sewage ponds.

BEHAVIOR & FEEDING Forages by diving for fish, aquatic insects, crustaceans, frogs. Usually forms small parties post-breeding, often larger concentrations at favorable sites, especially late fall/early winter. Allows close approach before pattering along surface with rapid wingbeats, lands at full speed, skidding to stop. Pairs form in fall. Nests in tree cavities, nest boxes; hybridizes rarely with other cavity-nesting ducks.

VOCALIZATIONS Male gives frog-like croak; female, growled *greep* in alarm.

Summer Male · WA (Okanogan County)—Jun · DOUGLAS L. BROWN

Female · WA (Douglas County)—Jul · GREGG THOMPSON

Winter Male · OR (Washington County)—Jan · RICHARD GRIFFIN

Ruddy Duck
Oxyura jamaicensis

DESCRIPTION 15 in/38 cm, wingspan 19 in/48 cm. Compact, short-necked, **broad-billed** diving duck. Long, stiff tail often cocked upward. *Male:* Temporal pattern of plumages reverse of other ducks. Breeding plumage (held Apr–Sep) bright **reddish brown with white cheek**; black crown, nape; powder-blue bill. Dull brown Oct–Mar; retains face pattern; immature resembles female. *Female:* Brownish; **cheek crossed by horizontal dark line**.

SIMILAR SPECIES Female Bufflehead (p. 67) bill, cheek patch smaller. Female Black Scoter (p. 64) has longer neck, smaller bill.

STATUS & DISTRIBUTION Nests mostly western North America from Prairie Provinces to Mexico, disjunctly elsewhere on continent, Greater Antilles; winters southwestern BC to New England, Honduras; also resident western South America. In PNW, east of Cascades/BC Coast Range, common breeder May–Sep, more local Oct–Apr in large flocks (rare BC). West of crest, fairly common Sep–May except rare north coastal BC; increasing but still uncommon breeder Willamette Valley, Puget Trough. Migrants swell numbers Sep–Nov, Mar–May throughout region.

HABITAT ASSOCIATIONS Breeds on lowland marshes, ponds with emergent vegetation; at other seasons larger open lakes, protected coastal bays; year-round on sewage ponds.

BEHAVIOR & FEEDING Dives, skims for animal or plant materials. Gregarious; flocks often into thousands. Rides low in water, clumsy on land. Often polygynous, but weak pair bond may form on breeding grounds. Pugnacious male chases competitors, displays with raised tail, rapid head pumping, producing bubbles by slapping bill on water.

VOCALIZATIONS Displaying male emits stuttered *tic tic tic tic* series.

WA (Mason County)—Jul · BOB KOTHENBEUTEL

Mountain Quail
Oreortyx pictus

DESCRIPTION 11 in/28 cm, wingspan 16 in/41 cm. **Large**, strikingly marked quail; **upright stance**. Gray-brown back; chestnut throat bordered in white; gray breast, chestnut **flanks prominently barred white. Straight twin head plumes** (longer in male).

SIMILAR SPECIES California Quail (p. 75) smaller with forward-curved topknot, horizontal rather than vertical barring on flanks. Chukar (p. 78) larger with red legs, bill; white throat, lighter-gray back. Barring on sides more extensive; lacks head plumes.

STATUS & DISTRIBUTION Ranges in West from WA, western ID to northern Baja California. In PNW, originally native to OR, south-central, southeastern WA, central ID; now rare, declining in severely shrunken interior range, but uncommon to locally fairly common in Coast Range, Siskiyou Mountains of OR; also long-established introduced population in southwestern Puget Trough of WA (Kitsap Peninsula, Mason County).

HABITAT ASSOCIATIONS Variety of sites with shrubby cover such as riparian edges, open forest, regenerating clear-cuts, Scotch-broom-dominated wasteland; from sea level, foothills to steep, rugged mountain terrain. Shuns development, but may visit feeders in rural settings.

BEHAVIOR & FEEDING Secretive, difficult to observe. Flies short distances but usually runs from intruders with characteristic upright posture. Forages on ground, in shrubs, trees for seeds, berries, other plant matter, some insects. Nests on ground, well concealed. Young feed on their own within day of hatching but remain in family groups. Flocks outside nesting season.

VOCALIZATIONS Calls include male's loud, far-carrying *quee ark* given in breeding season from stump, rock, other exposed perch.

California Quail
Callipepla californica

DESCRIPTION 10 in/25 cm, wingspan 14 in/36 cm. Grayish brown with gray breast; **scaled belly, nape**; white streaks on sides. *Male:* **Black cheeks, throat, bordered by white**; yellowish forehead, white eyebrow, brown crown, **forward-drooping black topknot, rusty belly patch**. *Female:* Plain head, smaller topknot, no belly patch.

SIMILAR SPECIES Mountain Quail (p. 74) larger with long, straight head plumes, plain belly, bold white bars on sides. Gambel's Quail (p. 76) lighter coloration, unscaled belly.

STATUS & DISTRIBUTION Native to Pacific Coast, northern Great Basin, from southern OR through Baja California; introduced north to BC, east to MT. In PNW, common OR except northern Coast Range, western Cascades; fairly common western WA lowlands from Puget Trough south to Vancouver; widespread, common eastern WA, western ID; uncommon, local northwestern MT (especially Bitterroot Valley). In BC, locally fairly common southeastern Vancouver Island, Gulf Islands, southern interior (common Okanagan Valley).

HABITAT ASSOCIATIONS Open habitats, edges, e.g., small-scale agricultural fields, pastures, weedy fencerows; farmsteads, towns, gardens, parks; rangelands, ravines; chaparral, oak grasslands, shrub steppe; ponderosa pine forest. Avoids wet, closed forests, higher elevations.

BEHAVIOR & FEEDING Like other New World quails, spends most of life on ground, raises large brood of precocial young. Numerous families band together after nesting, forage communally; coveys post sentries to warn of threats. Diet predominantly plant material.

VOCALIZATIONS *Chi CA go* assembly call given by both sexes. Other vocalizations include sharp *chip* alarm call, male's loud *cow* in breeding season, various contact notes within flocks.

Male · *Arizona—Jul* · PAUL KUSMIN

Female · *Arizona—Jul* · PAUL KUSMIN

Gambel's Quail
Callipepla gambelii

DESCRIPTION 10 in/25 cm, wingspan 14 in/36 cm. Olive-brown back, chestnut sides with white streaks, light-gray breast, **pale-yellowish belly**. *Male:* **Black face, throat, bordered by white**; white eyebrow, chestnut crown, **forward-drooping black topknot, black belly patch**. *Female:* Browner (less gray), plain head, smaller topknot, no belly patch.

SIMILAR SPECIES California Quail (p. 75) very similar but darker, with scaling on belly, nape; male has rusty (not black) belly patch. See also Mountain Quail (p. 74). In PNW, established range of Gambel's Quail does not overlap those of other quail species, but recently released birds might occasionally be found anywhere.

STATUS & DISTRIBUTION Native to deserts of southwestern US, northwestern Mexico. Introduced population established since 1921 in vicinity of Salmon, ID.

HABITAT ASSOCIATIONS Shrubby growth (mesquite, in much of native range), bramble tangles, brush piles along stream bottoms, washes, in open country. Dense thickets thought to allow survival in ID range, protecting against overgrazing by cattle, deep winter snow.

BEHAVIOR & FEEDING As with other New World quails, mostly vegetal diet. Usually runs from danger; rarely flies more than a few hundred yards (meters). Pairs nest on ground, raise large broods, rejoin multifamily winter coveys when young aged about 12 weeks.

VOCALIZATIONS Resemble those of California Quail. Male's *cow* advertising call delivered from top of post, shrub. Assembly call, given by both sexes, usually with syllable repeated at end: *chi CA go go*. Other contact, alarm calls.

Male · *Kansas—Jun* · RICK FRIDELL

Female · *Texas—Jan* · MIKE DANZENBAKER

Northern Bobwhite
Colinus virginianus

DESCRIPTION 10 in/25 cm, wingspan 13 in/33 cm. Upperparts **brown** with fine black-and-buffy accents; **white breast, belly, barred black**. *Male:* Chestnut crown, **white eyebrow**, lores, bordered above by black; **white chin, throat**, set off by dark eyeline, white-spotted dark neck. Short crest (often flattened). *Female:* Markings more subtle; **buffy replaces white on head**.

SIMILAR SPECIES Other quails in PNW (pp. 74–76) have head plumes. Ruffed Grouse (p. 82) much larger, longer tailed, feathered legs.

STATUS & DISTRIBUTION Native from central Great Plains, lower Great Lakes, southern New England, south through southeastern states, eastern Mexico, to Guatemala. Repeatedly introduced in much of PNW for 150 years, resulting in numerous self-sustaining populations in OR, WA, BC, ID. Almost all died out by 1990s; last long-established population hangs on at Ft. Lewis, WA, south of Puget Sound. Informal, small-scale releases continue; single birds, family groups frequently reported in PNW, but transient.

HABITAT ASSOCIATIONS In native range, broad array of open settings, including small farms, grasslands, brushy rangelands, broadleaf/pine forests, edges, clearings. Remaining WA population on dry prairies with scattered oaks, conifers.

BEHAVIOR & FEEDING Typical for New World quail. Feeds on or from ground, mostly on leafy vegetation, berries, seeds, some arthropods (especially young birds). Runs when disturbed; undertakes low flights for short distances. Nests on ground. In normal range, may raise more than one brood.

VOCALIZATIONS Familiar whistled *bob white* call in breeding season, almost exclusively by males. Many other types of calls for communication within flocks.

OR (Sherman County)—May · GREG GILLSON

Chukar
Alectoris chukar

DESCRIPTION 14 in/36 cm, wingspan 21 in/53 cm. Colorful partridge. Brownish-gray upperparts, gray breast, buff belly. Buffy **flanks strongly barred** black-and-chestnut. **Black eyeline continues around whitish throat. Red legs, bill.** *Juvenile:* Smaller, brownish, head not strongly marked; light barring on sides.

SIMILAR SPECIES Red legs, bill, distinctive. Gray Partridge (p. 79) somewhat smaller, plain cinnamon head, rufous-on-gray flank barring; juvenile similar but plainer. Quails (pp. 74–77) much smaller; most have head plumes.

STATUS & DISTRIBUTION Native to mountains from Balkans, Middle East, to northeastern China. Introduced as game bird, successfully established in rocky, arid terrain of Intermountain West from Great Basin to Columbia Plateau. In PNW, common eastern OR, southwestern–central ID, eastern WA, locally south-central BC.

HABITAT ASSOCIATIONS Open rangeland, canyons, talus slopes, shrub steppe; disturbed grasslands dominated by invasive, non-native cheatgrass. In hottest months stays close to water source. Attracted to ranches, feedlots in winter.

BEHAVIOR & FEEDING Like most other terrestrial gallinaceous (chicken-like) birds. Usually runs rather than flying. If flushed, explosive takeoff, rapid ascent, long glides to safety. Nests on ground, well hidden among rocks, vegetation; 10–20 eggs, precocial young. Diet leaves, seeds, fruit, some insects; may glean in grain fields in winter. Forms coveys in winter, but disperses to pioneer new territories more readily than other gallinaceous birds in PNW.

VOCALIZATIONS Raucous, far-carrying location call (both sexes): low *chuk chuk chuk* building to louder, two-syllable *ka chuk ka chuk ka chuk*, full *chuk ar chuk ar* crescendo. Many other vocalizations.

Gray Partridge
Perdix perdix

DESCRIPTION 13 in/33 cm, wingspan 19 in/48 cm. Overall muted, grayish plumage; upperparts browner, chestnut bars on flanks; **cinnamon-colored head. Rufous tail** readily shown, especially in flight. *Male:* **Dark belly patch.** *Female:* Cinnamon of head paler, less extensive; belly patch smaller or absent. *Juvenile:* Brownish mottling, no strong markings.

SIMILAR SPECIES Quails (pp. 74–77) smaller; most have head plumes. Chukar (p. 78) slightly larger, dark bars on light flanks, boldly patterned head, red bill, legs; juvenile has more-pronounced flank barring.

STATUS & DISTRIBUTION Native to Eurasia, widely introduced elsewhere for hunting. Core North American range prairies, plains, farmlands from Illinois, Minnesota to WY, Alberta, east of Rockies; also Great Basin, Columbia Plateau in Intermountain West. In PNW, uncommon to locally common at low-to-middle elevations in north-central/northeastern OR, central/southeastern WA, south-central BC (Okanagan Valley), northwestern MT, most of ID, adjacent southwestern WY.

HABITAT ASSOCIATIONS Grasslands, rangeland, meadows, pastures, crop fields (in PNW, especially dryland wheat), sagebrush, ponderosa pine forest; forages in open but also requires nesting/roosting cover (trees, shrubs, undisturbed grasses/forbs).

BEHAVIOR & FEEDING Similar to other open-country game birds: ground dwelling, large clutch, precocial young, forms post-breeding coveys. Diet mainly vegetation, some insects in summer (crucial for growing young); waste grain important in winter. Numbers fluctuate with weather patterns—high brood mortality in damp springs, starvation in winters of deep snow.

VOCALIZATIONS Male's loud, repeated *kee aah* call in spring likened to rusty gate. *Kut kut kut* alarm call, other intra-flock notes.

Female · WA (Mason County)—Dec · JOHN RIEGSECKER   Male · BC (Boundary Bay)—Feb · GREGG THOMPSON

Ring-necked Pheasant
Phasianus colchicus

DESCRIPTION 33 in/84 cm (male), 23 in/58 cm (female), wingspan 28–34 in/71–86 cm. Large game fowl with **long, pointed tail**, often cocked upward. *Male:* Bronze-toned, showy. **Iridescent-green head** with small ear tufts, **red skin on face**; white neck-ring, wine-purple breast, orangish flanks, gray rump. Many races, intergrades, with sometimes striking differences in male plumage. *Female:* Subdued, **mottled-brown plumage**; 35–40 percent **smaller** than male by weight, tail shorter.

SIMILAR SPECIES Male unmistakable. Sharp-tailed Grouse (p. 87) smaller, shorter tailed, legs feathered; Greater Sage-Grouse (p. 81) has black belly.

STATUS & DISTRIBUTION Native of Asia, widely introduced elsewhere. In North America, found principally from Maritimes, Middle Atlantic states, across southern Great Lakes, Midwest to southern Alberta, eastern New Mexico, patchily west of Rockies. In PNW, common ID, eastern OR, eastern WA, south-central BC (Okanagan Valley), northwestern MT; uncommon in lowlands west of Cascades, declining due to land-use changes.

HABITAT ASSOCIATIONS Agricultural landscapes with nearby uncultivated land, brush, woodlots for nesting, shelter. Absent from closed forest.

BEHAVIOR & FEEDING Runs fast; flies fast but not far. Eats all types of plant matter; also insects, especially in nesting season. Male defends harem of several females; after copulation, females disperse to nest. Nests mostly on ground, average 9–10 eggs. Young precocial, independent of female by 11 weeks. May form flocks in winter; females more gregarious than males.

VOCALIZATIONS Male territorial crowing loud, grating *krrok ook* accompanied by wing beating. Many other sounds (both sexes), including harsh alarm call, soft clucking.

Male · ID (Clark County)—Apr · NETTA SMITH

Female · ID (Fremont County)—Mar · DARREN CLARK

Male · ID (Fremont County)—Mar · DARREN CLARK

Greater Sage-Grouse
Centrocercus urophasianus

DESCRIPTION 28 in/71 cm (male), 22 in/56 cm (female), wingspan 33–38 in/84–97 cm. **Hefty** grayish-brown game bird with short, feathered legs, long, pointed tail feathers, **black belly, white underwing** coverts. *Male:* Black throat, bib; **white-feathered breast** forming loose-skinned ruff; 60–90 percent larger than female by weight.

SIMILAR SPECIES Female Ring-necked Pheasant (p. 80) more slender with buffy belly, grayish underwing, long, unfeathered legs. Other "chickens" in habitat smaller.

STATUS & DISTRIBUTION Northern Great Plains, Great Basin, Columbia Plateau; historic numbers and range much reduced due to habitat alteration. In PNW, now found in southeastern OR, central/southern ID, western WY; two vestigial populations in central WA; extirpated from south-central BC.

HABITAT ASSOCIATIONS Shrub–steppe communities with sagebrush component. May forage in adjacent meadows, crop fields, damp swales, riparian zones.

BEHAVIOR & FEEDING Ground dwelling; strong flier, but prefers to walk. Eats sagebrush year-round, also forbs, insects in breeding season. In late winter/spring, both sexes gather at leks for mating. Displaying males fan tail, unfold wings against sides; extend yellow eye-combs, black filoplumes from back of neck; expand ruff; inflate two yellow air sacs on breast (see Vocalizations). Female chooses one male to mate with; afterward, nests (usually under sagebrush), lays 6–9 eggs, raises brood alone. Young precocial, fly at two weeks, disperse at 10–12 weeks. All ages gather in mixed-sex winter flocks.

VOCALIZATIONS Various contact, warning calls. Displaying male produces series of gulping, plopping sounds accompanied by brushing of wings against body.

Gray morph · *WA (Okanogan County)—Dec* · GREGG THOMPSON

Rufous morph · *MT (Flathead County)—May* · KEN ARCHER

Ruffed Grouse
Bonasa umbellus

DESCRIPTION 18 in/46 cm, wingspan 22 in/56 cm. Grayish brown with black-and-white mottling, **barred flanks**. Half-feathered tarsus. **Small crest**; black neck feathers form ruff when raised. **Black subterminal band on tail** (visible when spread). Two morphs, best separated by upper surface of tail: alternating black-and-rust bands in rufous morph, black-and-gray in gray morph.

SIMILAR SPECIES No other chicken-like bird in PNW has broad black band near tip of tail. See smaller Northern Bobwhite (p. 77), Willow Ptarmigan (p. 84); similar-sized Sharp-tailed Grouse (p. 87), female "Franklin's" Grouse (p. 83); larger Dusky Grouse (p. 88), Sooty Grouse (p. 89).

STATUS & DISTRIBUTION Ranges across continent's northern forest zones. In PNW, resident throughout except Haida Gwaii, San Juan Islands of WA; rare northern mainland coast of BC. Gray morph more prevalent in interior, rufous morph toward coast. Both show cline in coloration—darkest, warmest-toned birds along coast; palest, grayest in southeastern ID, western WY.

HABITAT ASSOCIATIONS Low-elevation open woodland, mixed forest, up to alpine. Favors stream bottoms, brushy edges, second-growth broadleaf woods, aspen groves, mountain meadows; sometimes denser conifer forest in winter.

BEHAVIOR & FEEDING Male attracts females by beating wings from log or other ground perch to produce muffled, accelerating "drumming" sound. Female nests on ground, typically 10–12 eggs, raises precocial young alone. Largely solitary after families disperse, but may form loose flocks. Winter diet buds, twigs; rest of year forages on forest floor, in clearings for leaves, fruits, seeds, also invertebrates (especially chicks).

VOCALIZATIONS Clucks; other contact, warning notes.

Male · MT (Beaverhead County)—May · MICHAEL WOODRUFF   Female · MT (Glacier NP)—Sep · DOUGLAS L. BROWN

"Franklin's" (Spruce) Grouse
Falcipennis canadensis franklinii

DESCRIPTION 16 in/41 cm, wingspan 22 in/56 cm. Medium-sized forest grouse, legs feathered to base of toes. *Male:* **Scarlet eye-combs.** Slate-gray upperparts; black neck, upper breast; **prominent white markings** on black lower breast, flanks, belly. **Tail uniformly black, uppertail coverts tipped white.** *Female:* Barred black with varying proportion of gray brown (gray morph), warm golden brown (rufous morph).

SIMILAR SPECIES Ruffed Grouse (p. 82) has crest, black subterminal tail band. Ptarmigans (pp. 84–86) have white wings in all plumages. Dusky Grouse (p. 88), Sooty Grouse (p. 89) larger, underparts not heavily marked; males have inflatable neck sacs; male Sooty has gray terminal tail band.

STATUS & DISTRIBUTION "Franklin's" only subspecies of Spruce Grouse in PNW; formerly recognized as separate species, may be again. Spruce Grouse as whole ranges across continent in boreal forest zones; "Franklin's" from southeastern Alaska, west-central Alberta, south in mountains of interior BC, interior WA, northeastern OR, central ID, northwestern MT. Uncommon to fairly common, but unobtrusive, often difficult to find.

HABITAT ASSOCIATIONS Subalpine conifer forests, especially those with strong spruce component.

BEHAVIOR & FEEDING Unwary, approachable. Feeds on buds, needles of Engelmann spruce, other conifers; seasonally, fruit of understory plants such as huckleberries; hatchlings eat arthropods. In display flight, male launches from branch, tail spread, brings wings together above back to produce loud whip-crack sound twice while fluttering to ground. Female rears precocial young alone. Ground nest, 4–9 eggs typical.

VOCALIZATIONS Female's high-pitched territorial song delivered from tree in spring. Various other calls.

Summer Female · *Manitoba—Jun* · NETTA SMITH

Winter · *Alaska—Feb* · RON HORN

Summer Male · *Manitoba—Jun* · DEBRA HERST

Willow Ptarmigan
Lagopus lagopus

DESCRIPTION 14 in/36 cm, wingspan 23 in/58 cm. Small mountain grouse, scarlet eye-combs (paler in female), legs feathered to toe tips. In all plumages, **white wings, black tail** (often concealed). Head, body **all-white in winter**. Beginning Apr, molts progressively to summer plumage, back to winter white by Nov. *Summer male:* Rich **reddish-brown head, neck**, sides; finely barred back; belly extensively white. *Summer female:* Black-white-brownish mottling; limited white on belly.

SIMILAR SPECIES Rock Ptarmigan (p. 85) smaller billed; summer male brown to grayish brown (not reddish); winter male has black eyeline; females very difficult to separate. White-tailed Ptarmigan (p. 86) has white tail in all plumages. Among grouse, only ptarmigans have white wings.

STATUS & DISTRIBUTION Circumpolar. Ranges across northern Eurasia, Arctic North America, south through Alaska to south-central BC, west-central Alberta. In PNW, locally common in mountains of mainland western BC south to about Whistler; rare west side of Coast Ranges, northern Rockies, Chilcotin Range. Population cyclical, peaking about every 10 years.

HABITAT ASSOCIATIONS Moist subalpine/alpine tundra, meadows, birch/willow scrub; moves down to subalpine forest in winter.

BEHAVIOR & FEEDING Tame; prefers walking to flight. Vegetal diet, some insects. Largely monogamous; only grouse with full male participation in brood rearing. In courtship, male prances before female, combs erect; drags wingtips on ground, flicks tail feathers; pair signals mating assent with head wagging. Nests on ground; young precocial. May form large, single-sex winter flocks.

VOCALIZATIONS Many, including clucks, territorial rattle call. Loud male display vocalizations reminiscent of cartoon characters' speech.

Summer Male · *Alaska—Jun* · DOUG BACKLUND

Winter Male · *Alaska—Jun* · KEITH BRADY

Summer female · *Alaska—Jun* · ZAK POHLEN

Rock Ptarmigan
Lagopus muta

DESCRIPTION 14 in/36 cm, wingspan 23 in/58 cm. Small alpine grouse, scarlet eye-combs (smaller, paler in female), legs feathered to toe tips. In all plumages, **white wings, black tail** (often concealed). Head, body **white in winter** (by Nov). *Male:* **Black eyeline in winter**. Beginning Apr, **buffy wash** on underparts; otherwise holds white winter plumage through mating season (Jun). Summer plumage finely vermiculated **grayish brown** with largely **white flanks, belly**. *Summer female:* Medium brown with fine black, white markings, beginning Apr.

SIMILAR SPECIES See under Willow Ptarmigan (p. 84).

STATUS & DISTRIBUTION Eurasia, North America, on Arctic tundra; farther south, disjunctly on high mountain summits. In PNW, rare, local, little-known resident on mountaintops of western mainland BC; rarely descends to lower elevations in winter.

HABITAT ASSOCIATIONS Open tundra at or above timberline. Occupies higher, drier, more sparsely vegetated mountain slopes than Willow Ptarmigan, less rocky areas than White-tailed Ptarmigan (p. 86).

BEHAVIOR & FEEDING Spends most of time on ground, although strong flier. Diet buds, shoots in winter, other plant material rest of year, especially of heather family; larvae for young chicks. Mostly monogamous. Males establish territories, attract females. Elaborate mating ritual follows male flight display. Ground nest, completely exposed; average 7–9 eggs. Male not usually involved in brood rearing. Gregarious, non-territorial outside breeding season.

VOCALIZATIONS Many, varied, including frog-like croaks, cricket-like chirps, growls, rattles, clicks. In display, male flies up, floats to ground on bowed wings, eye-combs raised, tail spread, delivering loud, staccato "song" that continues after landing.

Summer Female · WA (Pierce County)—Aug · GREGG THOMPSON

Summer Male · Alberta—Jun · JON TIMMER

Winter · BC (North Vancouver)—Feb · LIRON GERSTMAN

White-tailed Ptarmigan
Lagopus leucura

DESCRIPTION 12 in/31 cm, wingspan 21 in/53 cm.
Smallest ptarmigan. Scarlet eye-combs (smaller, pink in females), legs feathered to toe tips. In all plumages, **white wings, white tail** (often hidden). **All-white in winter.** Beginning Apr, molts progressively to summer plumage, then back to white by Nov. *Summer Male:* Upperparts marbled brownish with some white; underparts white with large **black spots on flanks, breast.** *Summer Female:* Mottled light grayish brown, buffy; finely barred black.

SIMILAR SPECIES See Willow Ptarmigan (p. 84), Rock Ptarmigan (p. 85). When visible, white tail diagnostic. White wings separate ptarmigans from other grouse.

STATUS & DISTRIBUTION Alpine zone of mountains of Yukon, southern Alaska, BC, discontinuously to New Mexico. In PNW, fairly common resident mainland BC, Vancouver Island, WA Cascades; uncommon northwestern MT (Glacier NP); rare, perhaps not annual, Idaho Panhandle, northeastern WA.

HABITAT ASSOCIATIONS Spectrum of alpine habitats; most common on dry, stony ground with dwarf vegetation, also found in lush meadows along snowmelt streams. Usually moves below timberline in winter, especially into sheltered willow, birch, alder thickets.

BEHAVIOR & FEEDING Rarely flies. Crouches when threatened, remains still, difficult to detect. Eats buds, twigs, needles, flowers, fruits, seeds, insects, depending on season; willow preferred when available. Mostly monogamous. Territorial male spreads tail, raises eye-combs, struts before female with wingtips dragging. Ground nest, mean clutch 5–6 eggs. Chicks precocial, reared by female. Forms sex-segregated winter flocks.

VOCALIZATIONS Various clucks, other sounds; male gives loud, territorial *kik kik kik kik EEYA* call.

Sharp-tailed Grouse
Tympanuchus phasianellus

DESCRIPTION 17 in/43 cm, wingspan 24 in/61 cm. Legs short, feathered. Upperparts grayish brown with brown, black, buffy mottling. Graduated, **pointed tail; long, white undertail coverts**. Wing feathers finely spotted white. **White underparts with dark-brown V-shaped markings**. Small crest, yellow eye-combs (enlarged in breeding male). Male's inflatable violet neck sacs visible in display.

SIMILAR SPECIES Colloquial names—spike-tail, speckle-belly, white-breasted grouse—capture key differences from other chicken-like birds. See Ruffed Grouse (p. 82), Greater Sage-Grouse (p. 81), female Ring-necked Pheasant (p. 80).

STATUS & DISTRIBUTION Historic range Hudson Bay, Great Lakes, upper Midwest to central Alaska, south to northern Oklahoma, northern New Mexico, northern California; range now drastically contracted, fragmented, especially southern, western portions (including PNW). Extirpated OR, reintroduced Wallowa County; uncommon southeastern ID, rare, local southwestern ID; casual extreme western WY; extirpated northwestern MT; several small, isolated populations northcentral WA; uncommon, local central BC.

HABITAT ASSOCIATIONS Shrub-steppe, grasslands, may use adjacent cropland. In winter, riparian trees (willow, birch, alder), shrubs, often distant from breeding areas.

BEHAVIOR & FEEDING Mostly terrestrial; forages in shrubs, trees when snow covers ground. Diet wide range of plant matter (insects for young). Gathers at leks ("dancing grounds") for mating. In courtship, males spread wings, stomp feet, vocalize, rub tail feathers together to produce clicking sound. Dominant males mate with numerous females. No permanent pair bond; females raise young alone. Nest on ground, under vegetation; 10–12 eggs, chicks precocial.

VOCALIZATIONS Clucks when taking flight. Dancing male gives cork-popping sound.

Female · WA (Okanogan County)—Jun · DOUGLAS L. BROWN

Male · Alberta—Jun · JON TIMMER

Dusky Grouse
Dendragapus obscurus

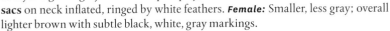

DESCRIPTION 20 in/51 cm, wingspan 26 in/66 cm. Large grouse, **yellow eye-combs** (smaller, duller in female; red, enlarged in displaying male), feathered legs. Finely vermiculated **grayish-brown upperparts.** *Male:* **Plain slate-gray underparts; black tail**, tip sometimes narrowly fringed in gray. In courtship display, **wine-red air sacs** on neck inflated, ringed by white feathers. *Female:* Smaller, less gray; overall lighter brown with subtle black, white, gray markings.

SIMILAR SPECIES Sooty Grouse (p. 89) male darker with yellow air sacs, wide gray tail band; female slightly darker, difficult to separate. "Franklin's" Grouse (p. 83) smaller, shorter tailed, shorter necked, with red eye-combs; female underparts boldly barred; male has black throat, white-spotted underparts. Ruffed Grouse (p. 82) smaller, crested; black tail band.

STATUS & DISTRIBUTION Intermountain West from Yukon to New Mexico, east of coastal mountains, Great Basin. In PNW, uncommon resident east of Cascades/ Coast Ranges in BC; fairly common north-central, northeastern, southeastern WA, northeastern OR; uncommon to locally fairly common ID, northwestern MT; common western WY.

HABITAT ASSOCIATIONS Shrub-steppe, grasslands; open dry conifer, mixed forest, aspen groves, up to subalpine; alpine meadows. Migrates locally to dense conifer forest in winter.

BEHAVIOR & FEEDING Terrestrial summer/fall, eats mostly plant material (insects for young). Arboreal in winter, lives on conifer needles, buds. Males territorial, promiscuous. Females depart after copulation, nest on ground, average 4–9 eggs; tend precocial young alone.

VOCALIZATIONS Clucks, other calls. Male song five soft, low-pitched hoots delivered from ground or low perch; also single *ooop*, audible at greater distance.

Male · BC (Burnaby)—Apr · BRIAN STECH

Female · WA (Snohomish County)—Jun · GEORGE PAGOS

Sooty Grouse
Dendragapus fuliginosus

DESCRIPTION 20 in/50 cm, wingspan 26 in/65 cm. Large grouse, **yellow eye-combs** (smaller, duller in female; red, enlarged in displaying male), legs feathered. *Male:* **Upperparts dark gray, brown; underparts plain** deep gray; **tail black** with prominent **gray terminal band**. In courtship display, **yellow air sacs** on neck inflated, narrowly bordered by white feathers. *Female:* Smaller, overall more brownish than gray, brown-black-gray-white mottling; lower breast, belly plain gray.

SIMILAR SPECIES See under Dusky Grouse (p. 88).

STATUS & DISTRIBUTION Pacific slope from coastal ranges/Cascades to sea level, southeastern Alaska to northern California; also Sierra Nevada. Fairly common in PNW, including larger coastal islands. Former "Blue" Grouse species recently split into Dusky, Sooty, which hybridize in narrow contact zone along eastern slope of Cascades/Coast Ranges in BC, WA. Sooty replaces Dusky in Cascades southward from Yakima River.

HABITAT ASSOCIATIONS Coastal subspecies in wet conifer forest from sea level across crest of Cascades/BC Coast Range; interior subspecies in dry, open montane forest of eastern Cascades in southern WA, OR, up to subalpine. Some populations migrate locally to denser conifer forest in winter.

BEHAVIOR & FEEDING Diet, reproductive behaviors generally similar to Dusky Grouse. Both species usually walk or run but can fly fast for short distances. Both essentially solitary, although may flock casually.

VOCALIZATIONS Various calls, both sexes. Male song, usually given from high in tree, series of six low-pitched hoots—louder than Dusky, audible up to 1,600 ft/500 m. Singing male notoriously hard to locate.

Male · WA (Skamania County)—Oct · ROGER WINDEMUTH

Female · MT (Flathead County)—Oct · KURT LINDSAY

Wild Turkey
Meleagris gallopavo

DESCRIPTION 47 in/119 cm (male), 36 in/91 cm (female), wingspan 50–61 in/127–155 cm. **Large**, heavy gallinaceous bird. Long bare legs, long tail. **Head, upper neck largely featherless**, hence seem small; blue gray with pink wattles (red, enlarged in breeding male). **Dark, iridescent body feathering**. Lower back, tail feathers tipped white or buffy in some populations, chestnut in others. *Male:* Larger, darker; black-tipped back, breast feathers. Spurred legs; long, **dark "beard"** hangs down from upper breast. *Female:* Smaller, duller, more reddish brown than black. Some have short beard.

SIMILAR SPECIES Turkey Vulture (p. 129) also large, dark, bare headed, tree roosting, gregarious, but easily ruled out by other traits.

STATUS & DISTRIBUTION Ancestral range New England, lower Midwest, south to Florida, Texas, Arizona, Mexico; introduced elsewhere, including PNW. Uncommon to locally common in southeastern, south-central BC (Kootenays, Kettle Valley); many parts of WA; western, north-central, northeastern OR; ID (mostly western half); northwestern MT. Domesticated worldwide.

HABITAT ASSOCIATIONS Needs balance between trees, open land (fields, stream corridors, clearings). Moves between summer, winter ranges, often considerable distance.

BEHAVIOR & FEEDING Ground dwelling but roosts in trees. Strong flier for short distances. Eats seeds, fruits, nuts, buds, grasses, forbs, roots, some invertebrates. Highly gregarious; single-sex flocks. Male gobbles to attract female, then struts about, tail fanned, head back, breast puffed out, spread wingtips touching ground. Female nests on ground (9–12 eggs), raises precocial young alone.

VOCALIZATIONS Familiar male gobble sets off chorus of gobbling from other males in earshot. Many other calls.

Breeding · *Alaska—Jun* · GREGG THOMPSON

Non-breeding · *OR (Lincoln County)—Dec* · GREG GILLSON

Breeding · *OR (Lincoln County)—Jul* · GREG GILLSON

Red-throated Loon
Gavia stellata

DESCRIPTION 24 in/61 cm, wingspan 36 in/91 cm. Smallest loon, **finely built, thin bill** upcurved at tip, **held tilted upward.** *Breeding:* **Dark back**, gray head, **red throat patch.** *Non-breeding:* Appears **pale**; white throat, neck; medium-gray crown, back of neck. *Juvenile:* Browner; dusky cheek, neck.

SIMILAR SPECIES Pacific Loon (p. 92) larger, bill held level; sharp contrast between upperparts, underparts. Other loons (pp. 93–94) much larger with larger trailing feet obvious in flight. Red-necked Grebe (p. 95) has longer neck, white wing patches.

STATUS & DISTRIBUTION Holarctic breeder, winters along temperate-zone coasts. In PNW, common coastally Oct–May; small numbers nest along BC coast, mostly Vancouver Island, Haida Gwaii. Abundant migrant, more numerous spring (Mar–May). Some linger Jun–Sep south along coast to OR. Very rare inland Sep–Nov (WA, ID, casual northwestern MT); casual Dec–May on major rivers (lakes in BC).

HABITAT ASSOCIATIONS Nests on small ponds near coast; outside of breeding, uses inshore marine habitats, rarely brackish rivers. Concentrations occur at shallow, protected prime feeding locales—e.g., Deception Pass (WA), Fraser Delta.

BEHAVIOR & FEEDING Feeds mostly on marine fish, even while breeding on fresh water. Maneuverable; able to fly from small ponds or land, due to proportionately longer wings than other loons. Coastal migrant counts in spring exceed a thousand per hour. Courtship includes penguin-like postures; pair shares nesting duties. Most likely loon found on shore when not breeding.

VOCALIZATIONS Wails, mews, yelps near nest, also calls at other seasons; quack-like *gah gah gah* in flight.

Non-breeding · *WA (Jefferson County)—Feb* · JOSEPH V. HIGBEE

Molting Juvenile · *WA (Cowlitz County)—Mar* · RYAN SHAW

Breeding · *Alaska—Jun* · GREGG THOMPSON

Pacific Loon
Gavia pacifica

DESCRIPTION 26 in/66 cm, wingspan 36 in/91 cm. Fairly small with **evenly rounded head**, slender dark bill, held horizontal. *Breeding:* Prominent **checkered scapular patches**, pale **gray nape**, dark throat patch. *Non-breeding:* Dark **hindneck sharply contrasts** in even line with clean white foreneck; may show chinstrap. *Juvenile:* Pale-edged back feathers.

SIMILAR SPECIES Common Loon (p. 93), Yellow-billed Loon (p. 94) larger; Red-throated Loon (p. 91) bill tilts upward. Slightly larger Arctic Loon (not shown; casual in PNW) nearly identical but shows white flanks, heavier bill; nape darker gray in breeding plumage. Grebes (pp. 95–100) have white wing patches, different shape.

STATUS & DISTRIBUTION Breeds from northeastern Siberia across northern Canada to Baffin Island, possibly Greenland; winters along Pacific Coast, Kodiak Island to southern Baja California; rare inland, East Coast. In PNW, common Oct–early Jun inshore along coasts, including Salish Sea; abundant in migration, particularly May. Good numbers linger Jun–Sep. Uncommon inland Oct–Nov; fewer winter; rare as spring transient.

HABITAT ASSOCIATIONS Nests taiga, tundra ponds. Migrates coastally, often farther offshore in deeper water than other loons; feeds near upwellings, convergences. Winters protected bays, estuaries; good concentrations in Strait of Georgia.

BEHAVIOR & FEEDING Feeds on small fish, aquatic invertebrates; takes freshwater fish from breeding ponds. In marine waters, usually found in small-to-large flocks rather than singly, unlike other loons. Counts of coastal migrants in spring may approach 10,000 per hour.

VOCALIZATIONS Yodels near nest, also grunts, croaks; seldom heard during non-breeding periods.

Non-breeding · WA (Whatcom County)—Mar · GREGG THOMPSON

Breeding · WA (Grays Harbor County)—Apr · GREGG THOMPSON

California—Oct · GLEN TEPKE

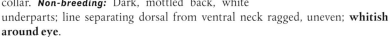

Common Loon
Gavia immer

DESCRIPTION 33 in/84cm, wingspan 51 in/130 cm. Large loon, **thick dagger-like bill**, steep forehead. Size variable; males larger, central Canadian breeders smaller. *Breeding:* Black head, bill; **checkered back**; striped patch on neck sides surmounts black collar. *Non-breeding:* Dark, mottled back, white underparts; line separating dorsal from ventral neck ragged, uneven; **whitish around eye**.

SIMILAR SPECIES Pacific Loon (p. 92) smaller with slender bill, rounded head, pale nape; in winter, even line separates dark dorsal from white ventral neck. Yellow-billed Loon (p. 94) all-yellow bill with straight (versus slightly convex) culmen. Non-breeding plumage paler; in breeding plumage, striped neck patch oval-shaped (versus wider toward nape).

STATUS & DISTRIBUTION Breeds Alaska across Canada to Iceland—north to tundra edge, south to northern US; winters south to subtropics, mostly along coasts. In PNW, nests May–Aug, widely BC, northwestern MT; locally, sparingly WA, ID, western WY (one record Lane County, OR); a few non-breeders summer inland, many more on coast. Sep–Apr, common along coast, fairly common inland.

HABITAT ASSOCIATIONS Nests on fish-rich lakes with clear water, stretches of undisturbed shoreline. Coastally, prefers inshore marine waters <65 ft/20 m deep.

BEHAVIOR & FEEDING Catches fish underwater. Migrates high over land or water, mostly Mar–Jun, Sep–Nov; may concentrate at stopovers. Rarely on land except for nesting; often uses island nest sites, particularly in BC. Pairs form on territory; female usually lays two eggs; male shares all duties.

VOCALIZATIONS Loud wails, yodeling, mostly on breeding grounds, also in migration.

Breeding · *BC (Lillooet)—Oct* · IAN ROUTLEY

Juvenile · *WA (Pacific County)—Jan* · RYAN SHAW

Yellow-billed Loon
Gavia adamsii

DESCRIPTION 35 in/89 cm, wingspan 55 in/140 cm. Largest loon on average; thick neck, steep forehead; thick dagger-like **yellowish bill held angled upward**. As with Common Loon, large trailing feet evident in flight. **Breeding:** Plumage retained to at least Oct. Head, collar black; checkered back; striped **oval-shaped patch** on neck sides. **Non-breeding: Pale head, neck**; back mottled brownish, underparts white; straw-colored bill. **Juvenile:** Back with light feather edging.

SIMILAR SPECIES Common Loon (p. 93) averages smaller with rounder head, bill held horizontal, upper mandible has dark convex culmen; breeding neck patch wider toward rear. Pacific Loon (p. 92), Red-throated Loon (p. 91) smaller with slender bills, smaller feet.

STATUS & DISTRIBUTION Holarctic breeder on remote tundra north of treeline; winters Scandinavia, Japan, Alaska south to OR, casually to Baja California. In PNW, uncommon principally Nov–Apr along BC coast (locally common Hecate Strait), progressively rarer farther south through OR. Most recorded Salish Sea, Haida Gwaii; non-breeders summer regularly at latter location. Casual inland; reports increasing in recent years (Oct–Jun).

HABITAT ASSOCIATIONS Tundra breeder, mostly on clear, low-lying larger ponds, lakes. Winters in shallow marine waters, rarely lakes, reservoirs, major rivers. Migrants sometimes pelagic.

BEHAVIOR & FEEDING Catches fish, some invertebrates underwater. Awkward on land, only comes ashore to nest. Flight-feather molt may render flightless while wintering. Female lays one or two eggs Jun–Jul. Pair builds raised nest mound on ground near water, shares duties.

VOCALIZATIONS Wails, yodeling lower pitched than Common Loon, seldom heard in PNW.

Non-breeding · BC (White Rock)—Dec · MIKE D. BAILEY

Breeding · BC (Penticton)—Jul · LAURE W. NEISH

Red-necked Grebe
Podiceps grisegena

DESCRIPTION 19 in/48cm, wingspan 27 in/69 cm. **Sturdy**, grayish; dark eye. Flat-topped triangular head, thick neck, **long yellowish bill**. In flight, white leading edge, secondary patch visible on wing. *Breeding:* Black crown, reddish-brown neck, **whitish cheeks**, throat. *Non-breeding:* Subdued colors; dingy-gray neck, **pale ear patch**. Like smaller grebes, chicks show light stripes throughout plumage.

SIMILAR SPECIES Eared Grebe (p. 97), Horned Grebe (p. 96), Pied-billed Grebe (p. 100) much smaller with shorter bills. Western Grebe (p. 98), Clark's Grebe (p. 99) larger, more gracile with thin necks, clean black-and-white plumage. Loons (pp. 91–94) sit lower in water.

STATUS & DISTRIBUTION Holarctic; most breed from 45th parallel to northern treeline, winter along coasts south to central California, North Carolina, Adriatic, Caspian Seas, eastern China. In PNW, fairly common late July–Apr west of Cascades/BC Coast Range, especially Salish Sea (Fraser Delta, central Puget Sound). East of crest, breeds south to central WA, northwestern MT, disjunctly to central ID, western WY, south-central OR (Upper Klamath Lake). Most leave interior Nov–Mar; small numbers winter on large ice-free lakes.

HABITAT ASSOCIATIONS Nests clear, deep lakes with marshy edges; at other seasons, prefers marine habitats. Migrants, rarely wintering birds, use large lakes, major rivers.

BEHAVIOR & FEEDING Captures fish, invertebrates, rarely amphibians, by diving. Flocks loosely away from nest. Non-colonial breeder; performs elaborate courtship displays. Like other grebes, pair builds floating nest, shares duties, carries young on back.

VOCALIZATIONS When breeding, loud braying squeals, also purrs, rattling; quiet at other seasons.

Non-breeding · *OR (Washington County)—Nov* · GREG GILLSON

Breeding · *BC (Deep Bay)—Apr* · RALPH HOCKEN

Horned Grebe
Podiceps auritus

DESCRIPTION 13 in/33cm, wingspan 22 in/55 cm. Red eye; **short stout bill**; somewhat flat head. **Rides low in water.** *Breeding:* Gray back, **reddish neck**, gold feather "horns" from eye to rear of crown. *Non-breeding:* Blackish crown, back, hindneck; **whitish throat, cheek**, foreneck. Chicks show light stripes throughout plumage, like other small grebes.

SIMILAR SPECIES Eared Grebe (p. 97) slighter; slender bill with thinner tip, rump held higher in water; top of head peaks behind eye; black neck in breeding plumage, grayish cheek in non-breeding. Western Grebe (p. 98) larger with long neck, long, greenish-yellow bill. Non-breeding Red-necked Grebe (p. 95) larger with longer neck, longer yellow bill; appears dingy gray.

STATUS & DISTRIBUTION Holarctic, breeding mostly north of 50th parallel, wintering south to Baja California, Florida, Mediterranean, Caspian Seas, Korea, mostly along coasts. In PNW, common Aug–Apr west of Cascades/BC Coast Range; locally common Sep–Apr inland on large ice-free lakes, major rivers. Breeds central, southern BC, irregularly south to northwestern MT, interior OR; old records exist for ID, WA. Some non-breeders summer throughout.

HABITAT ASSOCIATIONS Nests marshes, small, shallow ponds with emergent vegetation; at other times widespread on sheltered marine waters, larger lakes, major rivers.

BEHAVIOR & FEEDING Dives for small fish; invertebrates skimmed from surface or plucked from air during summer. In migration forms flocks; may dive synchronously for schooling fish. Mostly non-colonial; monogamous pair builds floating nest attached to vegetation, shares all nesting duties.

VOCALIZATIONS When breeding, repeated nasal, descending *we ARRR*, harsh rattles, chitters, trills; otherwise quiet.

Non-breeding · OR (Washington County)—Dec
GREG GILLSON

Breeding · ID (Owyhee County)—May · DAVE LAWRENCE

Eared Grebe
Podiceps nigricollis

DESCRIPTION 12 in/30 cm, wingspan 19 in/48 cm. Red eye; **slender**, thin-tipped **bill**; head appears fluffy, peaks above eye. Rides high in water, **rump held up**. *Breeding:* Dark back, **black neck**, head, with frazzled yellowish feather "ears" behind eye. *Non-breeding:* Dull colored; grayish cheek, dusky neck. *Juvenile:* Like non-breeding, browner, buff nape. Chicks striped like other small grebes.

SIMILAR SPECIES Horned Grebe (p. 96) bulkier, stouter bill, crown appears flatter; blackish hindneck; front of neck, cheek white in non-breeding; reddish neck in breeding. Red-necked Grebe (p. 95) much larger; longer, yellowish bill. Pied-billed Grebe (p. 100) shows thick bill.

STATUS & DISTRIBUTION Circumpolar. Breeds across Eurasia, North America, mainly between 30°–55°N, also locally East Africa; most move south (in North America, as far as El Salvador) or to coasts for winter. In PNW, common breeder May–Aug east of Cascades/BC Coast Range; migrants stage inland—e.g., WA (Coulee Lakes), OR (Lake, Crook Counties); may winter if water ice free (casual BC). West of crest, uncommon Aug–Apr; a few non-breeders often summer.

HABITAT ASSOCIATIONS Nests shallow ponds, prefers alkaline or saline conditions; migrants use inshore marine waters, sewage lagoons, lakes, major rivers. Avoids higher elevations in PNW.

BEHAVIOR & FEEDING Feeds on invertebrates, mostly brine shrimp; skims or picks flies from surface; also dives, takes some fish. Forms huge staging flocks at stopovers. Builds floating nest attached to vegetation. Colonial breeder; chicks ride on adult's back.

VOCALIZATIONS When breeding, whistled *ooo ecch*, other trills; quiet other seasons.

Courtship · *California—Mar* · BOB KOTHENBEUTEL

ID (Nez Perce County)—Oct · KEITH CARLSON

Western Grebe
Aechmophorus occidentalis

DESCRIPTION 25 in/64cm, wingspan 27 in/69 cm. Lean, **long necked**; long thin **greenish-yellow bill**. Red eye. Grayish back, sides; white underparts, throat. White foreneck sharply demarcated from black hindneck. *Breeding:* **Eye within black cap**. *Non-breeding:* Grayish-white plumage surrounds eye.

SIMILAR SPECIES Clark's Grebe (p. 99) lighter-gray sides, whiter flanks, black area of hindneck thinner, white face encompasses eye; yellow-orange bill (reddish at lower base). Horned Grebe (p. 96) smaller, short necked.

STATUS & DISTRIBUTION Breeds interior West from southern BC to Manitoba, western Minnesota, south to southern California, Mexican Plateau; winters mostly West Coast, fewer on inland lakes, rarely to Gulf Coast. In PNW, locally common breeder Mar–Aug interior OR, southern ID, western WY; fewer sites central, eastern WA, northern ID, northwestern MT, south-central, southeastern BC; uncommon west of Cascade crest, nesting regularly only at Fern Ridge Reservoir (OR). From Aug–May, common on westside, concentrating BC (Strait of Georgia), WA (central Puget Sound); uncommon in interior lowlands. Wintering populations declining in recent years.

HABITAT ASSOCIATIONS Nests on vegetated lakes, deep marshes with open water; at other seasons, sheltered marine habitats, major rivers, larger lakes.

BEHAVIOR & FEEDING Forages by diving, nearly exclusively for fish. Colonial breeder; often forms large flocks at other seasons. Elaborate courtship display includes pairs running synchronously across water. Pair fashions floating nest of heaped plant materials attached to emergent vegetation. Like other grebes, carries young on back.

VOCALIZATIONS Most frequently, loud harsh two-note *creeed creet*, common near nest, also given throughout year.

Courtship · OR (Klamath County)—May · PETER J. THIEMANN   OR (Harney County)—Jul · DENNIS PAULSON

Clark's Grebe
Aechmophorus clarkii

DESCRIPTION 25 in/63cm, wingspan 27 in/69 cm. Lean, **long necked**; long thin **yellow-orange bill**, base reddish ventrally. White throat, cheeks, foreneck sharply demarcated from black hindneck. **White extends above red eye to lore**. Light-gray sides; white of belly continues diffusely into flanks. **Breeding:** White below dark cap completely surrounds eye. **Non-breeding:** Plumage behind eye grayish white.

SIMILAR SPECIES Confusingly similar Western Grebe (p. 98) with sides, flanks darker gray; black cap surrounds eye, black area of hindneck wider; greenish-yellow bill without any trace of reddish. Horned Grebe (p. 96) smaller, short necked with short bill.

STATUS & DISTRIBUTION Fairly common local breeder in interior West from Prairie Provinces south to California, southern states, disjunctly Mexican Plateau; winters mostly Pacific Coast, fewer inland. In PNW, fairly common breeder Apr–Aug south-central OR–southeastern ID; fewer sites central WA, rare south-central, southeastern BC (Shuswap, Duck Lakes), possibly northwestern MT. Widespread migrant; rarely lingers to freeze-up. On westside, uncommon Aug–Apr, mostly coastal; wintering increasing in recent years. A few non-breeders remain May–Jul (has nested Fern Ridge Reservoir, OR).

HABITAT ASSOCIATIONS Nests on large, open lakes with emergent vegetation; at other seasons, sheltered marine habitats, major rivers, lakes.

BEHAVIOR & FEEDING Captures fish by diving. Gregarious at all seasons, almost always closely associated with Western Grebe. Colonial breeder; elaborate courtship similar to Western Grebe. Pair shares nesting duties.

VOCALIZATIONS Most frequent call high, screeched one-note *cweeea*, mostly near nest.

Family Podicipedidae—GREBES **99**

Chick · BC (Burnaby)—Aug · ALICE SUN

Non-breeding · WA (Asotin County)—Dec · KEITH CARLSON

Breeding · BC (Victoria)—Mar · TED ARDLEY

Pied-billed Grebe
Podilymbus podiceps

DESCRIPTION 12 in/30cm, wingspan 20 in/51 cm. **Plain brownish, short necked**; pale **thick short bill**, white undertail, whitish eye-ring. *Breeding:* Black throat, **white bill with black ring**, dark forehead. *Non-breeding:* Bill becomes plain, horn colored. *Juvenile:* Chicks show light stripes throughout plumage, retained (as for other small grebes) on head, neck until adult sized.

SIMILAR SPECIES Horned Grebe (p. 96), Eared Grebe (p. 97), Red-necked Grebe (p. 95) have thinner bills, brightly colored breeding plumage. Non-breeding Horned shows contrasting black-and-white plumage. Red-necked larger, longer billed.

STATUS & DISTRIBUTION Widespread in New World, breeds north to Prairie Provinces, south to Patagonia; high-latitude breeders move toward equator to escape freeze-up. In PNW, fairly common resident Pacific-slope lowlands but uncommon near outer coast, fewer at higher elevations. Increases Aug–Oct as migrants appear, remain to winter. Locally common breeder inland; arrives Mar–Apr, most leave by Dec; uncommon in winter in major valleys where suitable waters remain ice free.

HABITAT ASSOCIATIONS Freshwater marshes, lakes, ponds with emergent vegetation; rarely marine estuaries in winter; may nest in city parks, suburbs.

BEHAVIOR & FEEDING Opportunistic feeder, catching fish, frogs, invertebrates underwater. When submerging, dives or sinks like submarine. Seldom seen flying, migrates by night. Rarely flocks, but concentrates at preferred habitats during stopovers. Highly territorial monogamous pair builds floating nest attached to vegetation, shares all duties. Young ride on adult back, like other grebes.

VOCALIZATIONS When breeding, loud *cuck cuck cuck, cow cow, cowlp cowlp cowlp*. Chicks peep loudly when soliciting food.

OR (Lincoln County)—May · GREG GILLSON

Black-footed Albatross
Phoebastria nigripes

DESCRIPTION 32 in/81 cm, wingspan 84 in/213 cm. **Large** seabird with **long, narrow wings**; generally **dark-brown** body, wings, tail, head; pale face; variably white vent, uppertail coverts; blackish legs, feet. **Long grayish-pink bill** with dark tip. *Juvenile:* Dark bill; vent, rump dark brown (also dark on some adults).

SIMILAR SPECIES Long bill, large size diagnostic for albatross. Juvenile Short-tailed Albatross (p. 103) also all-dark, but larger with prodigious, bright-pink bill, grayish-pink feet. Laysan Albatross (p. 102), adult Short-tailed Albatross show white head, underparts.

STATUS & DISTRIBUTION Breeds Nov–Jun on small islands in Hawaiian chain, mostly Midway Atoll, Laysan; a few on islands off Japan. Forages throughout North Pacific, especially in Gulf of Alaska, along North American coast. In PNW, common off outer coast Apr to mid-Oct (slight peaks late Apr–May, Aug–Sep); irregularly uncommon to rare Nov–Mar. Rarely occurs closer than 15 mi/25 km from shore, but occasional in Strait of Juan de Fuca, Hecate Strait. Seldom seen from land.

HABITAT ASSOCIATIONS Nests on flat, open sandy ground. Forages on open ocean, in PNW generally in deep water near continental shelf break. Flocks concentrate near fishing boats.

BEHAVIOR & FEEDING Soars dynamically on stiff wings. Forages at surface, primarily for squid, fish; often scavenges behind fishing boats, mixing with gulls, fulmars, other seabirds. Courts with bill clappering, elaborate dancing like other albatrosses; raises one chick. First breeds at 5–9 years.

VOCALIZATIONS Generally silent in PNW.

Laysan Albatross
Phoebastria immutabilis

DESCRIPTION 32 in/81 cm, wingspan 78 in/198 cm. **Large** seabird with **long, narrow wings**; white head, rump, underparts; blackish-gray back, tail, upper surface of wings. Underwings white with variably extensive black edging, other black markings. **Long pinkish bill**, dark smudge around dark eye. *Juvenile:* Bill more grayish.

SIMILAR SPECIES Plumage pattern gull-like, but albatross much larger, shows longer wings, dark tail, different flight style with wings held stiffly. Rare Short-tailed Albatross (p. 103) significantly larger with much heavier bill; adults have white back, dark-backed subadults show dark nape.

STATUS & DISTRIBUTION Breeds Nov–Jun on small islands in Hawaiian chain (principally Midway Atoll, Laysan); many fewer off Japan. Populations expanding after feather hunting caused declines; in recent decades has colonized Guadalupe, other Mexican islands. Forages throughout North Pacific, especially around Aleutians. In PNW, uncommon year-round off outer WA/OR coast (30 mi/48 km median); high counts Dec–Feb. Seen casually from land. BC observer coverage infrequent; reports rare.

HABITAT ASSOCIATIONS Nests colonially on flat, open ground near vegetation, forages on open ocean. In PNW, generally in areas of upwelling near continental shelf break.

BEHAVIOR & FEEDING Like other albatrosses, forages sitting on water. Primarily takes squid, fish eggs, fish; scavenges, following fishing boats. Soars dynamically in wind, flight labored in calm air. When nesting, feeds up to 1,000 mi/1,600 km from colony. First breeds at 7–10 years. Long-term monogamous pair raises one chick. Long lived; one banded individual nested at age 61.

VOCALIZATIONS Generally silent in PNW.

Japan (Tori shima)—Apr · NIGEL VOADEN

Juvenile · WA (Grays Harbor County)—Jul · RYAN SHAW

Short-tailed Albatross
Phoebastria albatrus

DESCRIPTION 36 in/91 cm, wingspan 87 in/221 cm. **Large, long-winged** seabird; **massive pink bill** with grayish tip. **Mostly white** with head, neck washed orange; **upperwing extensively black**. Tail black, underwing outlined black. *Juvenile:* **Dark brown** throughout (held several years). Transitions to adult plumage over ≥10 additional years—white on body, wings increases over time.

SIMILAR SPECIES Laysan Albatross (p. 102) smaller with less massive bill; dark back, upperwing surface; subadults show white nape. Black-footed Albatross (p. 101) smaller; shorter billed; subadult paler faced than Short-tailed, often shows narrow white rump.

STATUS & DISTRIBUTION Breeds Oct–Jun on small islands off Japan (recently nested at Midway Atoll). Forages throughout North Pacific, especially around Aleutians. Population once estimated in millions, brought to brink of extinction in late 19th century by systematic slaughter for feather trade; volcanic activity at remnant colony nearly effected coup de grâce. Nesting islands protected since 1950s, population slowly increasing (currently about 1,200 birds); long-line fishing continues to threaten recovery. In PNW, 1–4 singles recorded nearly annually since mid-1990s, primarily Mar–Oct.

HABITAT ASSOCIATIONS Nests on barren islands, forages on open ocean. In PNW, mostly in deep water near continental shelf break; historically also occurred inshore (one recent Puget Sound record).

BEHAVIOR & FEEDING Forages on surface, like other albatrosses. Scavenges behind fishing boats with other seabirds. Flight labored in calm, but soars high on stiff wings in strong wind. Long-term monogamous pair raises single chick; may not nest every year.

VOCALIZATIONS Generally silent in PNW.

Murphy's Petrel
Pterodroma ultima

DESCRIPTION 15 in/38 cm, wingspan 35 in/89 cm. **Dark gadfly petrel; stiffly held slender wings, whitish chin**, stubby black bill. Body grayish-brown, **wings gray above** with obscure, somewhat darker "M" pattern; silver flashes visible on lower surfaces of primaries. Head appears dark-hooded compared to paler gray back. All plumages similar; adults appear browner when worn.

SIMILAR SPECIES Sooty, Short-tailed Shearwaters (pp. 110–111) larger, heavier bodied; flight less buoyant, graceful; wings less pointed, held straighter in flight. Upperwings darker brown (less grayish), lack "M" pattern. Providence Petrel (not shown) extremely similar but larger with darker hood; single records WA (off Westport, Sep 1983), BC (off Tofino, Oct 2009).

STATUS & DISTRIBUTION Nests Mar–Dec on Pitcairn Islands, other south-central Pacific tropical islands; disperses post-breeding to northeastern Pacific. Recently recognized as irregular visitor to PNW pelagic waters, usually well offshore; status still poorly known. May occur year-round but most records Apr–May, concentrated off OR, fewer farther north. Near-threatened due to rat predation on nesting islands, limited breeding range.

HABITAT ASSOCIATIONS Open, mostly warmer seas, generally in deep water. Nests on rocky island cliffs.

BEHAVIOR & FEEDING Forages by picking squid, other invertebrates, fish from surface. Strong, graceful, buoyant flight, in free-wheeling arcs in strong wind; comes to land only for breeding. Pair nests in scrape amid vegetation, shares duties—one parent feeding up to 2,800 mi/4,500 km from nest while mate assumes incubation shift.

VOCALIZATIONS Generally silent in PNW. Accelerating soft hooting near nest.

New Caledonia—Oct · ED McVICKER

New Caledonia—Oct · ED McVICKER

Mottled Petrel
Pterodroma inexpectata

DESCRIPTION 14 in/36 cm, wingspan 32 in/81 cm. **Stocky, gray gadfly petrel** with thick black bill, **dark-gray belly, flanks**, contrasting with white face, vent. Upperwing has dark M-shaped pattern, silver-gray trailing edge; **underwing white with bold black bars**.

SIMILAR SPECIES Smaller than Northern Fulmar, Pink-footed Shearwater. Several seabirds with somewhat similar upper- or underwing patterns lack contrasting dark belly—Buller's Shearwater (p. 107), immature kittiwakes (p. 210), other *Pterodroma* petrels such as Cook's, Hawaiian (neither shown; both casual in PNW).

STATUS & DISTRIBUTION Nests Dec–May on small islands in southern New Zealand. Ranges throughout Pacific, disperses north to near Aleutians May–Oct to exploit rich feeding grounds. Established by recent fieldwork as uncommon in PNW pelagic waters, usually well offshore. Mostly recorded migrating north (late Feb–Apr) or returning south to colonies (Oct–Dec). Considered near-threatened due primarily to introduction of non-native species on nesting islands.

HABITAT ASSOCIATIONS Open ocean; generally deep, cooler waters. Possibly more common in PNW during cold-water years (La Niña).

BEHAVIOR & FEEDING Feeds on small fish, squid, crustaceans, taken on or just below sea surface. Powerful flight, like other gadfly petrels. Long-term monogamous pair digs nest burrow in vegetated areas, often in mixed colonies with Sooty Shearwaters. During nesting, one parent may feed as far away as Antarctica while mate assumes incubation shift. Like many seabirds, arrives/departs from nest nocturnally.

VOCALIZATIONS Generally silent in PNW. While nesting, offers diverse calls including complex, far-carrying *ti ti ti*.

Light morph · *OR (Lincoln County)—Oct* · GREG GILLSON

Dark morph · *OR (Lincoln County)—Oct* · GREG GILLSON

Northern Fulmar
Fulmarus glacialis

DESCRIPTION 18 in/46 cm, wingspan 42 in/107 cm. **Stocky** seabird with **stiffly held wings** showing **pale flashes at base of primaries**. Thick, pale-yellow or pinkish bill with prominent nostril tube on top, strongly hooked tip. Two morphs. Most individuals in region gray or brownish gray throughout; minority have white head, breast, belly with gray wings, back, rump.

SIMILAR SPECIES Gulls less stocky; similar plumage but slender bill, longer wings, flight less stiff winged. Shearwaters (pp. 107–112) thinner bodied with slender bill, longer wings. Smaller *Pterodroma* petrels (pp. 104–105) show dark, shorter bills; wings longer, more pointed (strongly patterned in Mottled); flight more powerful. Jaegers (pp. 195–197) flight falcon-like.

STATUS & DISTRIBUTION Breeds Jun–Sep on islands throughout northern oceans; in Pacific, almost entirely on Aleutians, Pribilofs; winters at sea from ice-free Arctic south to Japan, Baja, North Carolina, France. Common Jul–Mar off PNW coast (but few reported BC Dec–Feb); casual Salish Sea after storms. Uncommon/rare Apr–Jun. Possibly breeds Triangle Island, BC.

HABITAT ASSOCIATIONS Pelagic, generally in deep water near continental shelf break; often closer to shore in storms. Pacific population nests at steep vegetated sites.

BEHAVIOR & FEEDING Forages on surface by picking, plunge-diving, or seizing from water surface; diet includes squid, fish, offal. Scavenges behind fishing boats with gulls, other seabirds. Flies close to water with shallow wingbeats. Monogamous pair raises single offspring in scrape in densely packed colony shared with kitti-wakes, other seabirds.

VOCALIZATIONS Flocks may cackle or grunt; harsh stuttered rhythmic croaks near nest.

OR (Lincoln County)—Oct · GREG GILLSON

WA (Grays Harbor County)—Aug · RYAN MERRILL

Buller's Shearwater
Puffinus bulleri

DESCRIPTION 17 in/43 cm, wingspan 39 in/99 cm. Fairly large seabird; **light gray above with bold blackish M-shaped marking across spread wings, mantle;** dark cap, white underparts, white underwings with dark edging. Blackish bill.

SIMILAR SPECIES Pink-footed Shearwater (p. 108) larger, lacks bold dorsal markings, shows heavy pinkish bill. Other possible confusion species smaller. Rare Manx Shearwater's (p. 112) wings evenly dark above. Even rarer Mottled Petrel (p. 105) shows similar dorsal markings, but with dark belly, bold underwing markings, heavier bill. Immature Black-legged Kittiwake (p. 210), Bonaparte's Gull (p. 212) have similar dorsal markings but fly with deeper wingbeats.

STATUS & DISTRIBUTION Breeds Nov–Mar on islands off northern New Zealand; post-breeding dispersal across Pacific, then northward as far as Aleutians. In PNW, rare/uncommon (occasionally fairly common) well offshore late Aug–Oct, mainly mid-Sep through mid-Oct; very small numbers Jun–early Aug. Nearly unrecorded in region until 1930s; increased dramatically throughout range subsequent to feral swine eradication on breeding grounds.

HABITAT ASSOCIATIONS In PNW, usually associated with warmer waters from continental shelf edge into deeper waters. Breeds on craggy, forested islands.

BEHAVIOR & FEEDING Typical shearwater flight, alternating glides with shallow wingbeats; more acrobatic while picking small fish, jellyfish, krill, other invertebrates off surface. Does not dive. Gregarious; often in large single-species rafts in migration, but in PNW typically flocks with other shearwaters, mixed seabird assemblages. Nests in burrows or rock crevices within foliage.

VOCALIZATIONS Generally silent in region.

BC (off Ucluelet)—Sep · RALPH HOCKEN

OR (Lincoln County)—May · GREG GILLSON

Pink-footed Shearwater
Puffinus creatopus

DESCRIPTION 19 in/48 cm, wingspan 43 in/109 cm. **Large** seabird; dark brown above, **white below**; brownish face, flanks. Primaries, secondaries brownish; wing linings white with variable amount of brown mottling. **Pinkish bill** with dark tip. Very rare dark morph shows grayish-brown upperparts, underparts. *Juvenile:* Appears fresh plumaged May–Jul, when adults molting.

SIMILAR SPECIES Buller's Shearwater shows dark cap, bill; strongly patterned upperparts. Other common PNW shearwaters have dark bellies; rarer species with white bellies (e.g., Manx Shearwater, p. 112) much smaller. Dark morph almost identical to Flesh-footed Shearwater (p. 109), but Pink-footed grayer brown above, duller bill, broader wings. Immature gulls lack contrast between dark-brown back, white belly; flight less stiff winged.

STATUS & DISTRIBUTION Breeds Nov–May on three islands off coast of Chile; most disperse post-breeding north to Mexico, US. In PNW, fairly common to common Jul–Oct off outer coast, uncommon (or farther offshore) Apr–Jun, rare Nov–Mar. Irregularly uncommon Strait of Juan de Fuca, Hecate Strait; rarely observed from land.

HABITAT ASSOCIATIONS In PNW, prefers warmer currents offshore over continental shelf. Nests at lightly forested sites to mid-elevation on islands with soil soft enough for burrow digging.

BEHAVIOR & FEEDING Feeds in loose flocks, taking small fish, squid, other organisms while sitting on water surface or with shallow dives, swimming underwater with wings. Frequently flocks with other seabirds, scavenges around fishing boats. Alternates glides on bowed wings with flapping, like other shearwaters.

VOCALIZATIONS Various nasal calls given during foraging, near nests.

Flesh-footed Shearwater
Puffinus carneipes

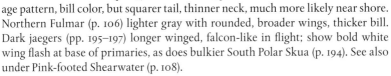

DESCRIPTION 19 in/48 cm, wingspan 44 in/112 cm. **Large, dark-brown** seabird. **Bright-pinkish bill** with dark tip.

SIMILAR SPECIES Gulls' flight style less stiff winged. Immature Heermann's (p. 215) similar in size, plumage pattern, bill color, but squarer tail, thinner neck, much more likely near shore. Northern Fulmar (p. 106) lighter gray with rounded, broader wings, thicker bill. Dark jaegers (pp. 195–197) longer winged, falcon-like in flight; show bold white wing flash at base of primaries, as does bulkier South Polar Skua (p. 194). See also under Pink-footed Shearwater (p. 108).

STATUS & DISTRIBUTION Breeds Nov–Apr on islands in Indian, southwestern Pacific Oceans including Australia, New Zealand. Disperses post-breeding throughout Pacific, generally moving northward, then south before Nov; migration pattern likely clockwise, as with Pink-footed, Sooty, Buller's Shearwaters. In PNW, rare off outer coast, casual Hecate Strait; most seen May, Jul–Oct, but few in OR waters before Aug. Casual north to WA Nov–Mar.

HABITAT ASSOCIATIONS In PNW, found well offshore over deeper waters, preferring warmer currents. Nests on vegetated islands.

BEHAVIOR & FEEDING Much like those of Pink-footed, its close relative. Forages on small fish, other marine organisms, follows fishing boats; may dive more frequently for prey (recorded at depths >40 ft/12 m near breeding grounds). In PNW, small numbers mix with flocks of other shearwaters. Pairs nest in burrows, raise single offspring, share duties. Like other seabirds, shows strong site fidelity.

VOCALIZATIONS Nasal calls given during foraging; more varied repertoire near nests.

Sooty Shearwater
Puffinus griseus

DESCRIPTION 17 in/43 cm, wingspan 40 in/102 cm. Fairly large seabird; head, body, tail, **upperwings dark chocolate brown; underwings show conspicuous silver panel**. Sloping forehead; fairly long, blackish bill. In flight, feet seldom project beyond tip of tail.

SIMILAR SPECIES Short-tailed Shearwater (p. 111) a bit smaller—shorter tail, slighter body, less barrel chested; underwing generally more uniformly dark, not showing conspicuous silver panel. Steeper forehead, shorter bill; in flight, feet often project beyond tip of tail. See also under Short-tailed Shearwater.

STATUS & DISTRIBUTION Breeds Nov–Apr on islands off southern tip of South America, southeastern Australia, New Zealand; disperses across open sea throughout Atlantic, Pacific north to Alaska, Greenland. In PNW, common offshore migrant May–early Oct, uncommon Mar–Apr, late Oct; rare Nov–Feb. Uncommon Salish Sea, mostly Aug–Oct. Flocks of hundreds of thousands observed Aug–Sep from beaches along WA/OR coast, fewer into estuaries (e.g., Willapa Bay).

HABITAT ASSOCIATIONS In PNW, concentrates near continental shelf edge, especially over cool upwellings but often just offshore, unlike other shearwaters. Nests in crevices, soil burrows.

BEHAVIOR & FEEDING Typical shearwater flight, alternating wingbeats, glides on stiffly held wings; glides straight, low in calm conditions, but towers high in strong winds. Takes mostly fish by diving; attains depths of 230 ft/70 m near breeding grounds. Feeds with other seabirds, but nearshore migrant flocks often single-species. Monogamous pair takes turns attending single chick, alternating multi-day foraging flights to Antarctic with local feeding bouts.

VOCALIZATIONS Generally silent in PNW; whines near nest.

Short-tailed Shearwater
Puffinus tenuirostris

DESCRIPTION 16 in/41 cm, wingspan 37 in/94 cm. Fairly large seabird; head, body, tail, upperwings **dark chocolate brown**, underwings mottled brown; pale panel on underwing often muted—if whitish, contrasts most with bases of secondaries. **Steep forehead**; blackish **small, slender bill**. In flight, feet usually project beyond tip of tail.

SIMILAR SPECIES Sooty Shearwater (p. 110) slightly larger, more robust, barrel chested, with longer bill, more sloping forehead, extensive silver underwing panels; less likely in PNW Nov–Mar than Short-tailed. Rare Flesh-footed Shearwater (p. 109) larger with conspicuous pink bill. Dark-morph Northern Fulmar (p. 106) generally paler, grayer with broader wings, tail; large pale bill usually obvious. Rare Murphy's Petrel (p. 104) smaller with proportionately large head, grayer above with dark "M" pattern across upperwings.

STATUS & DISTRIBUTION Breeds Nov–Apr on islands off southeastern Australia, disperses through North Pacific to Arctic waters. In PNW, occurs irregularly year-round, mostly offshore: common to uncommon Oct–Feb, uncommon to rare Mar–Sep. Rare Salish Sea, mostly Oct–Jan; sporadically fairly common when driven close to land by late-fall storms. True seasonal status obscured by identification confusion with Sooty Shearwater.

HABITAT ASSOCIATIONS Pelagic, concentrating over continental shelf, especially near upwellings of cool water; breeds at open grassy sites.

BEHAVIOR & FEEDING Often flocks with Sooty Shearwater, other seabirds while diving for fish, marine invertebrates. Feeding, breeding behavior, flight style similar to Sooty's but flies more buoyantly with snappier wingbeats.

VOCALIZATIONS Generally silent in region; screeched calls near nest.

WA (Clallam County)—Jul · RYAN MERRILL

WA (Clallam County)—Jul · RYAN MERRILL

Manx Shearwater
Puffinus puffinus

DESCRIPTION 13 in/33 cm, wingspan 31 in/79 cm. **Small** shearwater; head, body **brownish black above, white below**, curving upward behind auriculars. White wing linings contrast with dark trailing edge formed by flight feathers. Blackish, relatively long bill. *Juvenile:* Fresh plumaged Sep–Dec, when adults molting.

SIMILAR SPECIES Buller's Shearwater (p. 107) larger, but could be mistaken for Manx when sitting on water. In flight, Buller's shows conspicuous dark "M" pattern across gray wings (versus uniformly dark upperwings of Manx). Black-vented Shearwater (not shown; casual in PNW) has dark undertail coverts, less-contrasting dorsal coloration.

STATUS & DISTRIBUTION Breeds on islands in North Atlantic. In PNW, rare but increasingly regular visitor to all offshore waters; may breed BC (Triangle Island), WA (Destruction, Alexander Islands). Frequent just off suspected breeding islands or within Sooty Shearwater flocks off beaches. Most sightings Mar–Nov, casual Dec–Feb (more regular in fall off OR/WA than off BC). Casual in Salish Sea.

HABITAT ASSOCIATIONS Pelagic, but frequently sighted from land; occurs to continental shelf edge, especially in upwellings of cool water. Nests on open islands, often with dense ground foliage.

BEHAVIOR & FEEDING Rapid flight low over water; bursts of wingbeats alternating with short glides; often wheels in high arcs in strong winds. Forages mostly for fish in shallow dives from water surface. Like other shearwaters, exhibits delayed maturation, strong site fidelity, shared care of young, nocturnal arrival/departure from nesting burrow in colonial breeding area.

VOCALIZATIONS On breeding islands gives rhythmic, moaning calls.

OR (Lincoln County)—May · GREG GILLSON

WA (Grays Harbor County)—Jul · MICHAEL WOODRUFF

Fork-tailed Storm-Petrel
Oceanodroma furcata

DESCRIPTION 8.5 in/22 cm. Small **gray** seabird with forked tail, dark smudge around eye, **blackish underwing coverts**. Tail feathers gray with whitish outer webs; **pale carpal bar** on upperwing contrasts with dark forewing. Distinctive, swallow-like flight, fluttering interspersed with short glides.

SIMILAR SPECIES Leach's Storm-Petrel (p. 114), although also fork tailed, has dark body, white rump. Red Phalarope (p. 193) shows similar gray plumage, wing pattern, but smaller headed, lacks forked tail, flight less fluttery.

STATUS & DISTRIBUTION Breeds on small islands from Aleutians south to Kuril Islands, northern California; disperses throughout North Pacific. In PNW, *O.f. plumbea* fairly common local breeder Apr–Oct on outer-coastal islands; larger, paler northern subspecies *O.f. furcata* breeds west through Aleutians, recorded to WA in winter; both forms rare Nov–Mar. Widespread breeder BC, fewer WA (outer Olympic Peninsula coast), OR (Tillamook, Curry Counties). Generally rare in protected waters (e.g., Salish Sea) but thousands appeared in Puget Sound Oct 1997; accidental inland western WA, OR.

HABITAT ASSOCIATIONS Pelagic, foraging over cool waters, concentrating near continental shelf break; may move farther offshore Oct–Mar. Nests in rock crevices or burrows.

BEHAVIOR & FEEDING Forages singly or in small groups, usually flying low into wind. Drops to water surface (often with feet extended) to feed on tiny fish, invertebrates, offal; may raft up in thousands, also follows fishing boats. Monogamous pair raises one chick. Colonies range from a few pairs to many thousands. Arrives/departs nocturnally from nesting burrow.

VOCALIZATIONS Hoarse, screeching calls at night on breeding islands.

WA (Grays Harbor County)—May · DOUG SCHURMAN　　WA (Grays Harbor County)—Jul · RYAN SHAW

Leach's Storm-Petrel
Oceanodroma leucorhoa

DESCRIPTION 8 in/20 cm. Small, **dark-brown** seabird with moderately forked tail, **U-shaped white rump patch**. Pale carpal bar on upperwing contrasts with blackish flight feathers. Nighthawk-like flight with deep wingbeats. No PNW records of dark-rumped forms breeding off southern California, Baja.

SIMILAR SPECIES Fork-tailed Storm-Petrel (p. 113) pale gray, bulkier, with shorter, broader wings. Wilson's Storm-Petrel (not shown; casual but increasing in PNW) smaller with less pointed wings, more fluttery flight; feet extend beyond tail in flight.

STATUS & DISTRIBUTION Breeds on offshore islands in North Atlantic, North Pacific, winters to tropical seas. In PNW, fairly common to locally common breeder May–Oct on outer-coastal islands; generally forages well offshore even while nesting. Smaller numbers Mar–Apr, Sep–Oct; casually lingers Nov–Feb. Breeding colonies numerous in BC (peak abundance northern end Vancouver Island), fewer farther south (mostly northern WA; Curry County, OR). Leach's comprise less than one-tenth of storm-petrel sightings in region because of nocturnal foraging habits, preference for waters far offshore. Rarely recorded from land (Puget Sound, off Vancouver Island), usually Oct–Dec after strong storms. Accidental inland.

HABITAT ASSOCIATIONS Forages well offshore over warmer waters, often in association with albacore tuna. Nest sites range from unvegetated to forested.

BEHAVIOR & FEEDING Usually feeds nocturnally, primarily on crustaceans. Foraging flight often erratic, turning into wind, dropping to surface. Monogamous pair raises one chick in burrow or crevice, arriving/departing nocturnally.

VOCALIZATIONS Chuckling phrases in flight at breeding islands; churring calls from burrows at night.

Breeding · OR (Lincoln County)—Jun · ROY W. LOWE

Non-breeding · BC (Deep Bay)—Sep · MIKE YIP

Juvenile · California—Nov · ROBERT ROYSE

Brandt's Cormorant
Phalacrocorax penicillatus

DESCRIPTION 34 in/86 cm, wingspan 49 in/124 cm (males larger than females). Dark, round-headed, short-tailed diving bird; plumage reflects greenish. **Pale-buff chin; in flight, thick neck held fairly straight.** *Breeding:* **Bright-blue gular pouch**; head, neck show purplish sheen; irregular white plumes head to back. *Non-breeding:* Duller, loses plumes. *Juvenile:* Plain, tan breast; matures third year.

SIMILAR SPECIES Pelagic Cormorant (p. 117) thinner neck held straight in flight; tail longer; white flank patch in breeding. Double-crested Cormorant (p. 116) shows orange (versus blue or dark) gular pouch; longer wings, tail; neck held with more pronounced crook in flight.

STATUS & DISTRIBUTION Endemic to West Coast; breeds from southwestern BC to Baja California, north intermittently to southern Alaska. Post-breeding (Jul–Aug), disperses north to Kenai Peninsula, south to northwestern Mexico. In PNW, a few breeding sites BC (off southern Vancouver Island), WA (Cape Flattery, Cape Disappointment); many OR sites. Fairly common year-round throughout. Most frequent Columbia River mouth, Strait of Juan de Fuca; fewer interior Salish Sea, but locally abundant Aug–May (e.g., Active Pass, BC).

HABITAT ASSOCIATIONS Exclusively marine; avoids land except for nesting. Colonial breeder on promontories; bare, rocky coastal islands. Prefers areas of coastal upwelling, strong tidal currents; often near kelp beds, mostly inshore.

BEHAVIOR & FEEDING Captures fish, squid, other invertebrates by diving. Gregarious. Flies low over water, often in long lines, never far from surf. Southern breeders disperse northward to take advantage of abundant fisheries.

VOCALIZATIONS *Gwauk* given repeatedly at nest, otherwise silent.

Breeding · *WA (Whatcom County)—Apr* · DOUGLAS L. BROWN

Breeding · *California—Feb* · GREG GILLSON

Juvenile · *WA (Snohomish County)—Apr* · DENNIS PAULSON

Double-crested Cormorant
Phalacrocorax auritus

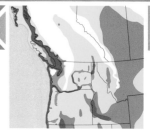

DESCRIPTION 34 in/86 cm, wingspan 53 in/134 cm. **Bulky**, dark diving bird; long tail, thick neck; **yellow-orange facial skin**, gular pouch. **In flight, neck held with pronounced crook**. *Breeding:* Plumage briefly held; white plumes behind eye. *Non-breeding:* Duller, loses plumes. *Juvenile:* Browner; orangish bill (versus grayish in adult); pale breast, neck; matures third year.

SIMILAR SPECIES Other PNW cormorants (pp. 115, 117) shorter winged, hold neck straighter in flight. Brandt's Cormorant (p. 115) shows buff chin. Pelagic Cormorant (p. 117) smaller; bill, head, neck much thinner.

STATUS & DISTRIBUTION Common resident along North American coasts Alaska, Newfoundland to Baja California, Cuba; nests locally across interior. Northern populations move south Sep–Oct. In PNW, widespread lowland resident; common coastally (nests north to southwestern BC), expanding inland (most breeders Klamath, Harney Basins; major rivers, northwestern MT). Regional movements poorly understood. Generally increases Feb–Apr, Aug–Nov; coastal migrants peak Sep–Oct. Interior birds retreat to ice-free waters.

HABITAT ASSOCIATIONS Freshwater, saltwater habitats. On coast remains well inshore.

BEHAVIOR & FEEDING Prefers shallow water. Often dives to bottom; takes mostly fish, some amphibians inland. Swims low in water, head tilted upward; requires running start to fly from surface. Colonial breeder, nesting in trees or on ground. Roosts on wires, sandbars, man-made structures; perches with wings open to dry them. Migrants fly high in V-formations; large movements occur with favorable winds. Piscivorous diet leads to conflicts with commercial, recreational interests, pressure for population control.

VOCALIZATIONS Grunts, but seldom heard away from nest.

Breeding · OR (Lincoln County)—Apr · MATT T. LEE

Non-breeding · WA (Snohomish County)—Mar · DENNIS PAULSON

Breeding · WA (Whatcom County)—Apr · MIKE D. BAILEY

Pelagic Cormorant
Phalacrocorax pelagicus

DESCRIPTION 27 in/69 cm, wingspan 40 in/102 cm. **Smallest** PNW cormorant; dark with greenish iridescence. **Slender neck**; slight head barely thicker than neck, often appears crested. Dark **pencil-thin bill**. *Breeding:* Plumage held Feb–Jul. **White flank patch**, purplish glow on neck. Gular pouch, bare skin around eye become red; brownish-orange bill base. *Non-breeding:* Duller, loses flank patch. *Juvenile:* Uniformly dark brown, lacks crest; matures second year.

SIMILAR SPECIES Brandt's Cormorant (p. 115) bulky with larger head, buff chin, thick bill, thicker neck held slightly crooked in flight. Double-crested Cormorant (p. 116) larger; orangish gular pouch; neck held with pronounced crook in flight. Red-faced Cormorant (not shown; casual along coast south to Strait of Juan de Fuca) larger, yellowish bill; thicker neck, brighter red facial skin extends across forehead.

STATUS & DISTRIBUTION Resident along Pacific coasts from Arctic to China, northern Baja California; in winter, some northern breeders withdraw southward. In PNW, common, widespread resident in marine habitats; less common southern Puget Sound, north coast BC.

HABITAT ASSOCIATIONS Strictly salt water; a few stray into lower Columbia River, other coastal rivers, lakes. "Pelagic" moniker inaccurate; stays within sight of shore.

BEHAVIOR & FEEDING Least gregarious of PNW cormorants. Dives deep to capture fish, crustaceans, often in waters over rocky substrates. Unlike most cormorants, takes flight quickly from water surface. Pairs breed colonially or alone. Nest built of vegetation on island, steep bluff, piling, bridge, other site inaccessible to predators.

VOCALIZATIONS Grunts, hisses near nest; otherwise silent.

OR (Washington County)—Nov · GREG GILLSON

WA (Asotin County)—Apr · KEITH CARLSON

American White Pelican
Pelecanus erythrorhynchos

DESCRIPTION 62 in/157 cm, wingspan 108 in/274 cm. **Large white** water bird; **capacious yellowish-orange bill**, legs, feet. **Black outer flight feathers** visible on spread wing. In flight, neck pulled flat against back. *Breeding (Feb–May):* Bare parts orange; laterally compressed "horn" toward bill tip; modest crest. *Non-breeding:* No crest; crown gray Jun–Jul. Bill duller, loses horn. *Juvenile:* Bare parts grayish; head, flight feathers dusky.

SIMILAR SPECIES Brown Pelican (p. 119) gray or brown, smaller (half the weight).

STATUS & DISTRIBUTION Nests locally interior West from Northwest Territories to northern Mexico; winters south to Florida, El Salvador. Occurs year-round in PNW (except winter BC/northwestern MT); major increase Feb–Oct. Scattered colonies central BC (Stum Lake), south-central WA (Columbia Plateau), south-central OR (Malheur-Harney Basin), south-central, southeastern ID (Minidoka NWR, Blackfoot Reservoir); fairly low site tenacity. Non-breeding flocks wander widely during summer throughout interior, south along major rivers into western OR interior valleys; rare but increasing on westside (recent breeding colony Columbia River mouth).

HABITAT ASSOCIATIONS Breeds on islands in freshwater lakes, marshes, rivers. At other seasons, major rivers, open marsh, shallow marine estuaries.

BEHAVIOR & FEEDING Nests in large, densely packed colonies. Gregarious year-round, rides thermals in squadron-like flocks. Scoops fish while swimming, throws back head to swallow. May herd schooling fish synchronously. Takes mostly rough fish; sometimes feeds far from colony. Group courtship includes bowing, strutting; both sexes scrape nest in gravel, near water; young fed regurgitated fish from pouch.

VOCALIZATIONS Grunts, croaks; otherwise silent.

Juvenile · *WA (Grays Harbor County)—Jul* · GREGG THOMPSON

Non-breeding · *WA (Grays Harbor County)—Oct* · GREGG THOMPSON

Brown Pelican
Pelecanus occidentalis

DESCRIPTION 49 in/124 cm, wingspan 82 in/208 cm. **Brownish gray** with dark-brown flight feathers, **pouched bill**. Flies with neck pulled in against back. Adult plumage acquired at 3–5 years after complex series of molts. ***Breeding:*** Proximal section of pouch bright red; whitish head, brown neck, blackish belly. ***Non-breeding:*** Whitish-yellow head, whitish neck. ***Juvenile:*** Evenly brown with white belly.

SIMILAR SPECIES Much larger American White Pelican (p. 118) white. Cormorants smaller with shorter bills.

STATUS & DISTRIBUTION Western subspecies *P.o. californicus* breeds on offshore islands along Pacific Coast, southern California to Baja California; other subspecies East Coast, West Indies, South America. Disperses widely post-breeding, ranging up coast rarely to Alaska. In PNW, common OR/WA outer coast Jul–Oct, uncommon to Vancouver Island, Salish Sea, tapering off into Nov as birds retreat southward. Rare but increasing in recent years Dec–Mar, uncommon Apr–Jun. Casual in fresh water west of Cascades, accidental in interior.

HABITAT ASSOCIATIONS Marine coasts; feeds in fairly warm, shallow waters.

BEHAVIOR & FEEDING Gregarious at all seasons. Moves north to exploit fisheries associated with West Coast upwellings. Plunge-dives for schooling fish up to 3 ft/1 m below surface; less frequently, scoops fish while swimming. Keeps inshore, rarely forages over 12 mi/20 km from land. Follows fishing boats, takes offal. Kleptoparasitized by Heermann's Gull, which has similar post-breeding dispersal. Nesting colonies number to thousands. Male gathers materials, female builds nest on ground or in tree, lays 2–3 eggs; 1–2 young fledge.

VOCALIZATIONS Mostly silent.

American Bittern
Botaurus lentiginosus

DESCRIPTION 28 in/71 cm, wingspan 43 in/109 cm. Fairly short-legged, stocky **brownish** wader, heavily streaked below, finely vermiculated above; long, black malar stripe on thick neck. **Greenish legs**; long, stout horn-colored bill; hidden whitish shoulder plumes visible during aggressive encounters. In flight, neck pulled in, shows **pointed wings with contrasting dark flight feathers**. *Juvenile:* Duller; less black on neck.

SIMILAR SPECIES Green Heron (p. 126) smaller, greenish above; brownish immature has shorter wings, orange-yellowish legs. Immature Black-crowned Night-Heron (p. 127) has rounder wings, lacks contrasting primaries.

STATUS & DISTRIBUTION Breeds central BC to Newfoundland, south to central California, New Mexico, Virginia; winters mostly near coast southwestern BC, Louisiana, New Jersey south to Panama. Declining across much of range. In PNW, uncommon resident (rare ID, western WY), mostly in lowlands; east of Cascades/BC Coast Range, leaves before winter except for a few in WA, OR; west of crest, resident south from southwestern BC with numbers reduced Dec–Mar.

HABITAT ASSOCIATIONS Nests in large, open freshwater marshes; in winter, frequents brackish marsh. Migrants may use smaller wetlands.

BEHAVIOR & FEEDING Secretive; mostly crepuscular habits, cryptic coloration hamper detection. Most conspicuous during territorial squabbles, aerial chases in spring. Solitary; hunts deliberately, walking with downward-facing eyes; strikes, grabs vertebrate or invertebrate prey. Flies with fast, powerful wingbeats; when alarmed, mimics marsh grasses by freezing, swaying with neck extended, bill pointed skyward. Mostly monogamous, minimal pair bond; nests on ground in marsh.

VOCALIZATIONS Resounding pump-like *bump ahh lunnk*; deep nasal squawk in alarm.

Least Bittern
Ixobrychus exilis

DESCRIPTION 13 in/33 cm, wingspan 20 in/52 cm. **Blackbird-sized** buff-colored heron with **dark crown, back**; fairly long yellow-green legs; long yellowish bill; paler, vaguely streaked below. In flight, neck pulled in; trailing legs, **prominent buff upperwing coverts** visible. *Male:* Greenish-black back, cap. *Female:* Purplish-brown back, cap. *Immature:* Paler; more streaked below.

SIMILAR SPECIES Green Heron (p. 126) larger, lacks buff wing patches; other herons much larger.

STATUS & DISTRIBUTION North American subspecies (*I.e. exilis*) breeds from southern Manitoba, New Brunswick, to West Indies, Mexico, Central America, in West locally, discontinuously from south-central OR to Baja California; partial migrant to frost-free wintering grounds. Other races to South America. In PNW, rare breeder south-central OR (Klamath, Harney Basins); casual BC, southwestern OR; accidental May–Jul in ID, northwestern MT, western WY.

HABITAT ASSOCIATIONS Nests in open freshwater or brackish marshes with stable water levels, approximately half covered by dense emergent plants; strongly associated with cattails. On wintering grounds, frequents saline, brackish marshes.

BEHAVIOR & FEEDING Takes small fish, other vertebrates, various invertebrates. May build feeding platform; also hunts while grasping stalks of emergent plants with long claws. Walks slowly in crouch, sometimes uses wing flicks to flush prey. When alarmed, freezes or burrows off through stalks; flies rarely, weakly. Builds elevated platform nest in marsh; pair attends young together. Probably monogamous, but secretive behavior, dense habitat impede field study.

VOCALIZATIONS Varied repertoire; territorial call low, frequently repeated *oowh oowh oowh*; also rail-like tics, alarmed *nank* when flushed.

Juvenile · Utah—Feb · JOHN CRAWLEY

Breeding · OR (Washington County)—Jan · GREG GILLSON

Great Blue Heron
Ardea herodias

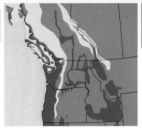

DESCRIPTION 48 in/122 cm, wingspan 74 in/188 cm. **Huge**, long-necked, long-legged wader; large **dagger-like bill**. Light **gray above**, brownish neck streaked whitish ventrally; rusty bend of wing, thighs; white face, crown with blackish plumes. Flies with broad wings cupped, trailing legs visible; neck usually pulled in. *Juvenile:* Duller; grayer neck, lacks plumes.

SIMILAR SPECIES Great Egret (p. 123), smaller Snowy Egret (p. 124) all-white, more lightly built; other long-legged waders occurring regularly in PNW smaller, shorter necked. Sandhill Crane (p. 149) has shorter bill, red crown, flies with neck extended.

STATUS & DISTRIBUTION Breeds mostly lowlands south-central Alaska to Nova Scotia, south to northern South America. In PNW, breeds throughout, but in BC only southwestern lowlands, interior valleys, with isolated nesting north to Haida Gwaii. Most common west of Cascades/BC Coast Range, where resident year-round; largest coastal colonies near major river deltas. In interior fairly common, becomes locally rare Dec–Jan, moving to ice-free areas; departs western WY.

HABITAT ASSOCIATIONS Adaptable, feeds in diverse shallow marine, freshwater habitats, also agricultural fields (particularly in winter). Prefers to breed at open freshwater marsh with tall trees for nest sites.

BEHAVIOR & FEEDING Stands or walks slowly on land, in water; grasps or spears small animals including mammals, birds. Flies with slow, powerful wingbeats. Monogamous, nesting mostly colonially; elaborate displays near nest, also defends feeding territories. Bald Eagle nest predation sometimes forces colonies to relocate.

VOCALIZATIONS Raspy *frahhhnnk* often given when flushed; other calls at colony.

Great Egret
Ardea alba

DESCRIPTION 38 in/97 cm, wingspan 58 in/147 cm. Lanky, long-necked **white** wader; **long yellow bill; black feet**, legs. In flight, trailing legs prominent, neck usually pulled in. Acquires long, wispy back plumes (aigrettes) Feb–Jul; yellow lores turn green during nesting.

SIMILAR SPECIES Great Blue Heron (p. 122) larger, grayish. Two smaller egrets rare or local in PNW: Snowy (p. 124) has black bill, yellow feet; Cattle (p. 125) stocky, shorter necked with short yellowish bill.

STATUS & DISTRIBUTION Cosmopolitan across temperate, tropical zones. North American populations still recovering from plume hunting; breeding distribution patchy north to southwestern WA, New England; continental interior, Northeastern breeders winter southward. In PNW interior, locally common breeder OR (Harney Basin), WA (Potholes), uncommon southern ID; most depart by Oct, rarely winter. West of crest, resident south from southwestern WA (numbers peak Sep–Mar); breeds WA (Kalama, Ridgefield NWR), western OR (rare but increasing at coast). Disperses widely throughout region (mostly late Jul–Sep); rare northwestern MT, southern BC, western WY, Idaho Panhandle, accidental Haida Gwaii.

HABITAT ASSOCIATIONS Lowlands. Nests near fresh, salt water; feeds in shallow wetland marshes, floodplains, wet fields, mud flats, ditches.

BEHAVIOR & FEEDING Hunts predominantly by slow stalking, in aggregations or alone; impales or grabs fish, also invertebrates, other vertebrate prey. Flies buoyantly, frequently disperses northward in PNW; often roosts in trees. Gregarious. Nests colonially in shrubs, trees, often with other waders; male displays vigorously near nest.

VOCALIZATIONS Low *kraaak* sometimes uttered when flushed; varied repertoire at nests.

Snowy Egret
Egretta thula

DESCRIPTION 24 in/61 cm, wingspan 40 in/102 cm. Long-necked **white** wader; long **black bill** with **yellow lores**; black legs, **yellow feet**; flies with neck pulled in. Nuptial back plumes (aigrettes) Feb–Jul; lores brighten to red during nesting. *Juvenile:* No plumes; legs yellowish green, bill often pale; lores grayish through winter.

SIMILAR SPECIES Great Egret (p. 123) larger; yellow bill. Cattle Egret (p. 125) stocky; short yellowish bill. Little Blue Heron (not shown; casual in PNW) immature has thicker, bicolored bill; may show dark primary tips.

STATUS & DISTRIBUTION Breeds locally from OR to New England south to Costa Rica, predominantly along East Coast; winters mostly coastally from central California, New Jersey to Caribbean, South America. In PNW, uncommon to locally fairly common breeder in southern interior OR (e.g., Upper Klamath Lake, Malheur NWR), southern ID (mostly in Snake River Plain), also just east of region in WY. Most breeders leave by Sep. Casual late Apr–Nov north to Idaho Panhandle, WA, southern BC.

HABITAT ASSOCIATIONS Breeds lowland wetlands, e.g., willow-lined canals, reservoirs, marshes, lakes, often on islands; winters primarily to estuaries, brackish marsh; migrants in diverse wetlands.

BEHAVIOR & FEEDING Forages frantically in shallows, flushing prey with brightly colored feet, wing flicks; seizes fish, crustaceans, other small aquatic creatures. Highly social, nesting colonially with other waders on low trees, bushes. Defends nest, foraging territory with aggressive displays. Nestling mortalities linked to pesticides in recent years.

VOCALIZATIONS High-pitched nasal *graaah* when flushed; various calls near nests.

Breeding · ID (Nez Perce County)—May · KEITH CARLSON

Non-breeding · WA (Clallam County)—Nov · DOUG SCHURMAN

Cattle Egret
Bubulcus ibis

DESCRIPTION 20 in/51 cm, wingspan 37 in/94 cm. Compact **white** wader; **stout yellow bill**; short, dark legs usually greenish; flies with short neck pulled in. From Mar–Jul, **buff-colored nuptial plumes** on crown, back, chest; lores, bill, iris, legs brighten to reddish. *Juvenile:* No plumes, bill blackish into fall.

SIMILAR SPECIES Other egrets larger with longer bill, neck; Great Egret (p. 123) has blackish legs; Snowy Egret (p. 124) blackish bill, yellow feet.

STATUS & DISTRIBUTION Cosmopolitan breeder except in extreme climates; first settled in New World in South America, reached Florida in 1941, Vancouver Island by 1969. Breeds widely across southern US, scattered north to southeastern OR, southern Saskatchewan, Massachusetts; very local in West. Interior breeders migrate south. In PNW, breeds rarely OR (Harney Basin) May–Sep, regularly southeastern ID (e.g., Oxford Slough, Bear Lake); spring migrants casual rest of region. Prone to long-distance vagrancy. Irregularly rare Oct–Dec in post-breeding dispersal throughout lowlands north to Haida Gwaii, central interior BC (casual northwestern MT). Most disappear by winter, a few survive to spring (coastal OR).

HABITAT ASSOCIATIONS Nests near wetlands in native heronries; forages in open lowlands (deltas, floodplains, agricultural fields), rarely disperses to high elevation, marine shorelines.

BEHAVIOR & FEEDING Gregarious. Grazes in association with livestock, rarely tractors. Takes mostly orthopterans, other invertebrates, fewer frogs, seldom fish. Hunts prey disturbed by cattle, defending feeding territories around chosen animal from conspecifics. Flies to colonial tree-roosts with constant flapping.

VOCALIZATIONS Fairly quiet; croaks, squawks near nest.

Juvenile · OR (Washington County)—Jul · GREG GILLSON

Juvenile · OR (Washington County)—Sep · GREG GILLSON

Adult · OR (Washington County)—Dec · NAGI ABOULENEIN

Green Heron
Butorides virescens

DESCRIPTION 18 in/46 cm, wingspan 27 in/69 cm. Stocky, short-legged, crested wader; dark **greenish above**, purplish-brown neck, white streak down breast center, **orange legs**. *Juvenile:* Browner; streaked breast, neck; buff-tipped upperwing coverts; yellowish-green legs; transitions to adult plumage over second summer.

SIMILAR SPECIES American Bittern (p. 120) larger, browner, wings more pointed in flight. Least Bittern (p. 121) shows buffy wing patches.

STATUS & DISTRIBUTION Western subspecies (*B.v. anthonyi*) breeds down coast from southwestern BC to Baja; smaller eastern forms range from Dakotas, Nova Scotia south to West Indies, Panama. Most winter south from central California, South Carolina. PNW range expanding northward; arrived WA 1939, BC 1953. West of Cascades/BC Coast Range, uncommon Apr–Sep, rare Nov–Mar; breeds northward in BC to Campbell River, Whistler. Rare interior OR (has bred Klamath Basin), eastern WA (regular Klickitat County); casual western Vancouver Island, interior BC, southern ID; accidental northern ID, northwestern MT, western WY.

HABITAT ASSOCIATIONS Lowlands, rarely middle elevations; sheltered fresh water (riparian growth, swampy thickets, shoreline beneath trees); also coastal ditches, stagnant pools. Nest sites vary: thickets, deciduous trees away from water, open marsh sites.

BEHAVIOR & FEEDING Secretive, patient; still-hunts or walks slowly, sometimes uses bait (twigs, feathers) to lure fish within range; also takes other animal prey with quick, darting stroke, rarely launching off perch. While perched, often flicks tail, raises crest nervously. Solitary nester, site often high in deciduous trees; only rarely forms colonies.

VOCALIZATIONS Forceful *skeeoww* uttered in flight or alarm.

Breeding · OR (Harney County)—May · MATT T. LEE   Juvenile · BC (Delta)—Sep · GREGG THOMPSON

Black-crowned Night-Heron
Nycticorax nycticorax

DESCRIPTION 25 in/64 cm, wingspan 44 in/112 cm. Short-necked, **stocky wader**; red eye, short yellow legs, **stout black bill**; rounded, even-colored wing in flight. *Adult:* Pale gray, whiter ventrally; **black back, cap**; long white head plume. *Juvenile:* Pale lower mandible. **Streaked** overall; white-spotted upperwing coverts through first year; adult pattern second year, but streaked below.

SIMILAR SPECIES American Bittern (p. 120) wings pointed, contrasting dark primaries; Green Heron (p. 126) smaller with long thin bill. Great Blue Heron (p. 122) larger; much longer bill, neck.

STATUS & DISTRIBUTION Widespread, breeding over much of Africa, Americas, southeastern Eurasia temperate, tropical zones; in North America north to WA, Saskatchewan, southern Quebec. Winters mostly coastally or along major rivers. In PNW, locally common lowland breeder east of Cascades/BC Coast Range from central WA, OR, southern ID, to western WY, rarely northwestern MT; disperses northward post-breeding (casual to Clearwater Lake, BC); migrates to ice-free areas within breeding range in winter (Snake, Columbia Basins). West of crest generally rare (uncommon OR); most frequent during Jul–Sep dispersal. Winter roosts, isolated breeding north to Salish Sea deltas (Stillaguamish, Skagit in WA; Fraser in BC).

HABITAT ASSOCIATIONS Diverse lowland wetlands for nesting, roosting sites; migrates coastally or along river valleys.

BEHAVIOR & FEEDING Nocturnal; nests, roosts diurnally in trees. Still-hunts opportunistically, taking varied invertebrate, vertebrate prey. Powerful flyer, also sometimes glides. Subject to vagrancy. Nests colonially near shallow water for foraging. Monogamous; defends nesting, feeding territories.

VOCALIZATIONS Barked, oft-repeated *quork* when leaving roosts.

Breeding · *Alberta—May* · GERALD ROMANCHUK

Immature · *Texas—Feb* · DENNIS PAULSON

Breeding · *OR (Harney County)—May* · KEN ARCHER

White-faced Ibis
Plegadis chihi

DESCRIPTION 23 in/58 cm, wingspan 38 in/97 cm. Gracile wader; **long, decurved bill**, reddish legs, red eye; bronzy-**purplish iridescent** plumage. Flies with neck extended, feet trailing beyond tail. *Breeding:* Purplish-chestnut head, body; greenish-brown wings; prominent **thin white line encircles bare facial skin**, eye. *Non-breeding:* Duller; white facial feathers turn grayish. *Juvenile:* Brownish eye, legs; neck, head variably streaked white; otherwise resembles non-breeding.

SIMILAR SPECIES Other large wading birds of PNW lack decurved bill. Long-billed Curlew (p. 171) smaller bodied, streaked brown; cormorants (pp. 115–117) similar in flight but shorter billed.

STATUS & DISTRIBUTION Locally common breeder Great Basin, irregularly north to southern Alberta, Dakotas, south to central Mexico, Florida Panhandle, also disjunctly South America; winters southern California, Gulf Coast, south to El Salvador. In PNW interior, uncommon May–Jul north to central WA, western WY, casual to BC, northwestern MT; rare west of Cascade crest predominantly May–Jul; a few late fall coastally to southwestern BC. Local nester OR (Lake, Harney Counties), southeastern ID (e.g., Camas NWR), southwestern WY at edge of region.

HABITAT ASSOCIATIONS Nests, feeds in shallow lowland marshes with emergent vegetation; forages on flooded fields, mud flats.

BEHAVIOR & FEEDING Probes shallow water, mud, mostly for invertebrates located by tactile or visual means. Flies with rapid wingbeats, periods of gliding. Nomadic; shifts nesting locations in response to drought, reduced water levels. Colonial breeder, often in dense marsh vegetation; pair shares all duties.

VOCALIZATIONS Nasal *ern ern ern* when flushed; *oink*, other varied calls near nest.

WA (Asotin County)—May · KEITH CARLSON

OR (Lincoln County)—Sep · GREG GILLSON

Turkey Vulture
Cathartes aura

DESCRIPTION 26 in/66 cm, wingspan 66 in/168 cm. Blackish long-tailed raptor with **bare red head**; appears plump when perched. Long, broad wings in **strong dihedral** during **tilting, unsteady soaring**; **light-gray undersides of flight feathers** contrast prominently with dark body. *Juvenile:* Grayish head.

SIMILAR SPECIES Aloft, Golden Eagle (p. 144) larger, wing pattern different, flight steadier. Northern Harrier (p. 133) has longer tail, white rump; dark-morph Ferruginous, Swainson's Hawks (pp. 139, 143) heads appear larger—latter with dark flight feathers. Other raptors soar with wings held flatter.

STATUS & DISTRIBUTION Ranges southern Canada to South America, breeding range discontinuous across Great Basin, Plains states. In PNW, fairly common late Feb–Oct north to south-central BC (Apr arrival in north), scarce in Blue Mountains, Columbia Plateau; breeds locally, mostly mid-elevation (e.g., southeastern Vancouver Island, BC interior valleys, OR/WA Cascades, ID/MT/WY Rockies); Nov–Feb rare southern Vancouver Island, San Juan Islands, uncommon Willamette Valley southward. Migrants concentrate in hundreds late Sep–early Oct southern Vancouver Island, northern Olympic coast, southeastern OR (Malheur NWR); spring numbers lower (Mar–Apr).

HABITAT ASSOCIATIONS Forages over grassland, other open areas near hills with updrafts; boulder fields, outcrops, cliffs for nesting.

BEHAVIOR & FEEDING Soars with little flapping, searching for carrion by sight, smell; gregarious, roosting in tall trees, often perching with wings spread. Relies on thermals when migrating; reluctantly crosses water bodies, waiting for favorable winds. Monogamous, possibly long-term; nests in caves, rocks, abandoned buildings away from humans.

VOCALIZATIONS Grunts, hisses (seldom heard).

Family Cathartidae—NEW WORLD VULTURES **129**

ID (Nez Perce County)—Aug · KEITH CARLSON

Nest · BC (Mission)—Jul · DAMON CALDERWOOD

Osprey
Pandion haliaetus

DESCRIPTION 24 in/61 cm, wingspan 64 in/163 cm (averages; females larger than males). **Large** raptor; **blackish wings, back, mask**; white crown, underparts. In flight, from below, banded flight feathers contrast with white body; **wings slightly angled**, almost gull-like. Older feathers often appear bleached, faded. *Juvenile:* Similar, with light dorsal feather edging.

SIMILAR SPECIES Faded third-year Bald Eagle (p. 132) may show dark mask, white belly, but larger with dark chest; gulls with different plumage, wings more pointed in flight.

STATUS & DISTRIBUTION Nearly cosmopolitan. Holarctic breeders winter south to tropics; Australasian race sedentary. In North America, breeds across boreal zone, also south in western mountains, along coasts. In PNW, fairly common Mar–Oct at low-to-moderate elevation but nearly absent southeastern OR, Columbia Plateau. Migrants generally return late Mar–Apr (vanguard arrives OR/WA late Feb). Post-breeding, departs southward Jul–Sep, lingers very rarely Nov–Jan. Breeding concentrations Flathead River/Lake, Kootenay Lake, Pend Oreille, Willamette, Columbia Rivers, Snohomish River estuary.

HABITAT ASSOCIATIONS Rivers, lakes, estuaries in proximity to shallow fish-rich waters.

BEHAVIOR & FEEDING Feeds on live fish, hovering, plunging feet first, catching prey up to 3 ft/1 m below surface; rarely aquatic birds, reptiles. Migrants readily cross large water bodies, arid expanses. Often remains on wintering grounds until second spring. Generally monogamous, high mate fidelity; up to three young raised in bulky stick nest on broken treetop, power tower, or provided platform, usually near water; sometimes colonial.

VOCALIZATIONS Highly vocal; diverse whistled notes.

Juvenile · *California—Jun* · MIKE DANZENBAKER

WA (Pacific County)—date unknown · VIRGINIA & DANIEL POLESCHOOK

WA (Pacific County)—date unknown · VIRGINIA & DANIEL POLESCHOOK

White-tailed Kite
Elanus leucurus

DESCRIPTION 15 in/38 cm, wingspan 39 in/99 cm. Graceful falcon-like raptor; **light gray** above; **black shoulder, carpel patches. White underparts**, head, long tail; reddish eye; long, dark primaries. **Hovers frequently**, soars with wings in dihedral. *Juvenile:* Brownish, scalloped back, rufous-streaked breast fade to adult plumage by winter.

SIMILAR SPECIES Male Northern Harrier (p. 133) has black wingtips, darker tail, white rump. Gulls, terns lack shoulder patches, shaped differently. Similar-sized falcons (pp. 282–284) show banded flight feathers, lack white underparts.

STATUS & DISTRIBUTION Ranges WA to Baja California; southern Florida, Gulf Coast, Mexico to South America; US breeders mostly in California, Texas. Once persecuted as pest, nearly extirpated; range expanded after 1950, recently may be retracting again. In PNW, uncommon Aug–Mar in lowlands west of Cascades north to southwestern WA (Nisqually NWR), casual southwestern BC; highest numbers Sep–Feb augmented by northward post-breeding dispersal. Casual southern OR east of Cascade crest; accidental northwestern MT (Nov, Mar). Uncommon breeder Rogue Valley; rare elsewhere Apr–Jul, breeding casually north to southwestern WA.

HABITAT ASSOCIATIONS Open areas with scattered trees—prairie, fallow fields, coastal dunes, marsh along river valleys.

BEHAVIOR & FEEDING Perches prominently in open; gregarious especially in fall, winter, roosting communally. Hunts rodents from extended stationary hover; rarely insects, birds, lizards. Monogamous, builds nest in small treetop; may breed in loose colony defending small territory with flutter flights, leg-hanging, talon-grappling; also antagonistic toward larger raptors. Sometimes two broods per year.

VOCALIZATIONS Whistled *kewp*; grating calls less frequent.

First-year · WA (Pierce County)—Mar
GREGG THOMPSON

BC (Deep Bay)—Mar · RALPH HOCKEN

Subadult · BC (Fraser Valley)—Nov
LIRON GERSTMAN

Bald Eagle
Haliaeetus leucocephalus

DESCRIPTION 33 in/84 cm, wingspan 82 in/208 cm (averages; female larger than male). Bulky; **long head, short tail projection**; soars on long, broad, flat wings. Dark brown; **white head, tail**; yellow feet, iris, bill. *First-year:* Dark head, tail, bill, iris. *Subadult:* Four-year transition to adult plumage; **underwing coverts whitish** throughout. Bleached feathers may give white-bellied, white-backed appearance through third summer.

SIMILAR SPECIES In flight, Golden Eagle (p. 144) head projection shorter than tail, wings pinch in at body; subadult underwing white at base of primaries; dark coverts; tail shows abrupt white base, dark tip. Other raptors smaller, wings shorter.

STATUS & DISTRIBUTION Ranges Alaska to Labrador, south to northwestern Mexico. In PNW, common breeder west of Cascades/BC Coast Range, uncommon east; nearly absent Columbia Plateau, southeastern OR, but fairly common northern interior BC, northwestern MT; disperses northward late Aug–early Oct to salmon runs, e.g., Haida Gwaii, southeastern Alaska. Fairly common near ice-free waters Nov–Mar; concentrates into thousands southwestern BC (Harrison, Cheakamus, Squamish Rivers), hundreds at Klamath Basin, OR.

HABITAT ASSOCIATIONS Usually near water: coastline, lakes, rivers; mostly lowlands, migrants range to high elevation.

BEHAVIOR & FEEDING Feeds opportunistically, mostly on fish along coast, water birds in interior, carrion; steals food from smaller raptors; concentrates at fish spawns, forages on coastal flats. Gregarious in fall, winter, roosting in tall trees. Monogamous, long-term bond, returns to territory Oct–Jan; eggs laid Mar in huge nest within tree crown, young fledge Jul–Aug.

VOCALIZATIONS Series of chirping whistles, piercing screams.

Female · OR (Washington County)—Apr · GREG GILLSON

Male · WA (Skagit County)—Dec · GREGG THOMPSON

Female · WA (Skagit County)—Dec · GREGG THOMPSON

First-year · WA (Skagit County)—Apr · GREGG THOMPSON

Northern Harrier
Circus cyaneus

DESCRIPTION 19 in/48cm, wingspan 44 in/112 cm (averages; female larger than male). Long winged, lanky; **white rump,** long banded tail, strong dihedral in flight, **owl-like face.** *Male:* **Light gray,** paler below, black wingtips visible in flight; may take three years to attain adult plumage. *Female:* Brown above, brown-streaked buff below. *First-year:* Female-like; mostly unstreaked **reddish-brown breast**.

SIMILAR SPECIES Other hawks in PNW lack white rump. Rough-legged (p. 142) tail base white; some Swainson's (p. 139) show white "U" on rump, but tail finely banded; smaller Cooper's (p. 135) sometimes fluffs white undertail around rump in display flight. Short-eared Owl (p. 251) wings broader, head larger, flight moth-like.

STATUS & DISTRIBUTION Holarctic; winters temperate zone to northern tropics. In North America, breeds north to northern Alaska, Labrador. In PNW, local nester in lowlands—common east of Cascades/BC Coast Range, uncommon west of crest from southwestern BC southward. Fairly common westside Aug–Mar, less common in interior; concentrates Nov–Feb at areas of high prey density (e.g., Fraser Delta, Samish Flats, Columbia Plateau).

HABITAT ASSOCIATIONS Marshes, fields, grasslands; also mountains Jul–Sep in migration.

BEHAVIOR & FEEDING While hunting, courses low in erratic flight. Uses vision, hearing, catching mostly small mammals, some birds; migrants fly higher. In winter, often roosts communally on ground. Courting pairs perform spectacular roller-coaster flights with midair prey transfers. Nests on ground; up to five young fledge. Male often polygamous—provisions most food to 2–5 nests.

VOCALIZATIONS Piercing whistles, chattered *kek kek kek*.

BC (Surrey)—Jan · ROY PRIEST

First-year · WA (Whatcom County)—Feb
DOUGLAS L. BROWN

First-year · ID (Jefferson County)
Feb · DARREN CLARK

Sharp-shinned Hawk
Accipiter striatus

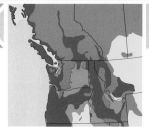

DESCRIPTION 12 in/30 cm, wingspan 22 in/56 cm (averages; female significantly larger than male). **Short winged**; long thin yellow legs, petite bill; broadly banded **long square-tipped tail**. Eye appears large on small rounded head; **red iris**. Grayish above, finely barred reddish brown below (male darker). When soaring, wrists held forward, nearly even with head projection. *First-year:* Brownish above, whitish below, brown breast streaks grade to belly blotches; **yellow iris**.

SIMILAR SPECIES Cooper's Hawk (p. 135) larger, square headed, less buoyant in flight; leading edge of wing straight while soaring; tail longer, rounder; adult appears capped due to brownish nape; first-year, lower breast usually lightly streaked. American Kestrel (p. 280), Merlin (p. 281) have dark iris, pointed wings.

STATUS & DISTRIBUTION Ranges, in numerous races, from Arctic treeline to Argentina. Northern populations breed central Alaska, Labrador, south to Mexico; withdraw from northern forests, higher elevations in winter. In PNW, fairly common forest breeder, mostly in mountains; widespread migrant throughout, common along ridges Aug–Oct; fairly common Nov–Mar at lower elevations.

HABITAT ASSOCIATIONS Most breed in dense conifers in younger mixed forests; at other seasons, woodland edge, farmyards, suburbs.

BEHAVIOR & FEEDING Like other accipiters, ambushes birds in low, rapid flight—mostly songbirds, also (by larger female) up to dove size; takes some mammals while nesting. In sustained flight, alternates rapid flapping with glides; thermals assist travel. Shadows migrant flocks, patrols feeders in winter; secretive but pugnacious near concealed nest.

VOCALIZATIONS Squeals, chips near nest, high-pitched *kik kik kik* at other times.

WA (King County)—Jun · GREGG THOMPSON

First-year · WA (Asotin County)—Jul · KEITH CARLSON

Cooper's Hawk
Accipiter cooperii

DESCRIPTION 17 in/43 cm, wingspan 32 in/81 cm (averages; female larger than male). Lanky, short wings, **crow-sized**; long, thin yellow legs; **long, broadly banded, round-tipped tail**. Finely barred reddish brown below; grayish cap, back; **brownish nape**, reddish iris. Male bluish gray, redder below. Soars with wings held straight across. *First-year:* Brown back; white, brown-streaked underparts; **yellow iris.**

SIMILAR SPECIES Sharp-shinned Hawk (p. 164) smaller, but female close to male Cooper's size; legs thinner, head rounder, tail square at tip; soars with wrists held forward. Adult lacks capped appearance, first-year breast usually more heavily marked. Northern Goshawk (p. 136) larger with broader tail, adult grayish below, first-year heavily streaked to undertail. Peregrine Falcon (p. 282) has dark iris, pointed wings. Buteos' (pp. 137–143) tails broad, shorter.

STATUS & DISTRIBUTION Breeds across continent, southern Canada to Mexico, Florida; winters southern BC, Wisconsin, Maine south to Guatemala. In PNW, fairly common breeder lowlands to higher elevations west of Cascades/BC Coast Range; uncommon to fairly common east of crest (rarely in desert areas). Increasingly in urban areas in recent years. Migrants widespread; withdraws from higher elevations in winter.

HABITAT ASSOCIATIONS Nests in open or fragmented forest; also uses farms, neighborhoods.

BEHAVIOR & FEEDING Catches birds, mammals, some reptiles ambushed with rapid burst; also cruises, stakes out feeders. Prefers robin-, pigeon-sized birds. Typical accipiter flight; flapping alternates with gliding. Monogamous, fairly secretive nester in tree crown. Migratory, but may remain year-round in territory.

VOCALIZATIONS Varied calls include repeated *kek*, nasal *whaew*. Young beg with rising whistle.

First-year · MT (Ravalli County)—Dec · KATE DAVIS

BC (Vancouver)—Dec · MIKE YIP

Northern Goshawk
Accipiter gentilis

DESCRIPTION 20 in/51 cm, wingspan 42 in/107 cm (averages; female larger than male). Stocky forest hawk; **conspicuous white supercilium**, yellow legs, **long broad tail**; wings long, pointed for an accipiter. **Gray** upperparts, lighter ventrally with fine vermiculations, fluffy white undertail; reddish iris; tail broadly banded or slate gray. *First-year:* Blotchy brownish dorsally with underparts heavily **streaked to undertail**; buff secondary coverts; **wavy tail bands** dark with thin white edging. Adult plumage attained over two years.

SIMILAR SPECIES Cooper's Hawk (p. 135) smaller; first-year undertail usually unstreaked, tail banding even, supercilium less pronounced. Buteos' (pp. 137–143) tails shorter, broader; Gyrfalcon (p. 284) wings more pointed, eye blackish.

STATUS & DISTRIBUTION Holarctic. In North America, breeds from Arctic treeline south in mountains to Mexico, Virginia. In PNW, uncommon breeder, mostly mid-to-high elevation east of Cascades/BC Coast Range. Rare breeder Olympics, OR Coast Range; historically also westside lowlands, now mostly extirpated. Some dispersal Oct–Feb into lowlands throughout. Smaller *A.g. laingi* (Haida Gwaii, Vancouver Island) now classified "imperiled."

HABITAT ASSOCIATIONS Breeds older forests, preferring conifers in PNW; forest edge, rural areas at other seasons.

BEHAVIOR & FEEDING Reclusive, seldom perching in open; catches jay-, grouse-sized birds or mammals (especially snowshoe hare) in seemingly reckless flight, cruising below trees or from perch. Alternates stiff wingbeats with short glides. Monogamous; soars, displays above territory. Aggressively attacks intruders near nest; pair often maintains alternate nest sites within territory.

VOCALIZATIONS Loud *kyke kyke kyke*, also wails near nest; juvenile begs with whistles.

First-year · WA (Pierce County)—Nov · GREGG THOMPSON

WA (Cowlitz County)—Nov · DOUG SCHURMAN

First-year · WA (Pierce County)—Nov · GREGG THOMPSON

Red-shouldered Hawk
Buteo lineatus

DESCRIPTION 17 in/43 cm, wingspan 39 in/99 cm (averages; female larger than male). Broad winged, fairly **long tailed**; barred reddish ventrally, adult breast solid rusty orange; **black tail with 4–5 white bands**. Wings checkered black-and-white; translucent **transverse crescent near wingtip** in flight. Rusty head, underwing, shoulders; dark-brown iris. *First-year:* Browner; **evenly mottled** underparts, narrower tail bands, yellowish-brown iris.

SIMILAR SPECIES First-year Red-tailed Hawk (pp. 140–141) shows patagial bar in flight, finely banded tail, unstreaked whitish upper breast. Broad-winged Hawk (p. 138) smaller; adult's tail blackish with broad white band, first-year's with dark, narrow bands (subterminal band wider). Accipiters (pp. 134–136) show long tails with broad bands.

STATUS & DISTRIBUTION Western subspecies (*B.l. elegans*) breeds southwestern OR to northern Baja. In PNW west of Cascades, uncommon breeder lowland OR; rare north to WA in post-breeding dispersal (Aug–Mar), casual Apr–Jul. East of crest, uncommon resident south-central OR (breeding suspected), casual north to Tri-Cities, WA (Aug–Mar). Declining California populations have rebounded in recent decades, accompanied by northward push. Other subspecies from Minnesota, Maine, to northeastern Mexico, Florida.

HABITAT ASSOCIATIONS Nests in moist forest, woodlands; in California, has successfully adapted to nesting in suburban eucalyptus groves. Outside breeding, wooded wetlands, riparian bottomland with wet meadows.

BEHAVIOR & FEEDING Perches within trees. Highly vocal all seasons, frequently detected by voice. Flight accipiter-like with rapid flaps, gliding. Captures amphibians, mammals, birds predominantly by still-hunting. Monogamous pair builds stick nest in crotch near trunk, reuses for years.

VOCALIZATIONS Loud drawn-out *keyeeer keyeeer keyeer.*

Alberta—Jun · GERALD ROMANCHUK

BC (Kootenays)—Sep · GORDON F. BROWN

First-year · ID (Boise County)—Sep
JERRY LIGUORI

Broad-winged Hawk
Buteo platypterus

DESCRIPTION 15 in/38 cm, wingspan 34 in/86 cm (averages; female larger than male). **Stocky**; in flight, broad, fairly pointed, **dark-tipped wings** with black trailing edge show little contrast between coverts, flight feathers. Grayish-brown upperparts, rich brown ventral barring; white-tipped **black tail with broad white band**, thinner band near base. *Dark Morph:* Dark-brown body, wing, tail coverts. *First-year:* Longer tail; brown upperparts, white ventrally with blotchy streaks; **narrow tail bands (terminal band widest)**; some dark morphs show tawny-streaked breast.

SIMILAR SPECIES Red-shouldered Hawk (p. 137) larger, 4–5 even white tail bands, checkered upperwing coverts, translucent crescents near wingtip. Red-tailed Hawk (pp. 140–141) larger, shows patagial bar in flight. Swainson's Hawk (p. 139) longer winged with dark flight feathers. Accipiters (pp. 134–136) longer tailed, shorter winged.

STATUS & DISTRIBUTION Breeds from eastern BC to Labrador, south to Texas, northern Florida, Cuba; winters southern Florida, Mexico to Brazil; most migration east of Rockies. In PNW, rare migrant throughout (Apr–early Jun, Aug–early Oct), majority May or Sep in interior mountains, extreme southern Vancouver Island. Recent western range expansion; local breeder in BC south to near Golden. Dark morph rare range-wide; more frequent in West.

HABITAT ASSOCIATIONS Forest breeder; migrates along ridges, river valleys.

BEHAVIOR & FEEDING Captures small vertebrates, insects, mostly hunting from perch. Highly migratory. Thousands use thermals to kettle to great height, then glide for miles; mass movements concentrated mid-Apr, mid-Sep; some (mostly yearlings) move May–Jun. Secretive breeder; monogamous pair displays over territory.

VOCALIZATIONS High, thin whistle.

Light morph · WA (Yakima County)—Jun
JOE SWEENEY

Dark morph · ID (Madison County)—May
DARREN CLARK

Intermediate morph · ID (Nez Perce County)—Sep · KEITH CARLSON

First-year · ID (Jefferson County)—Aug
DARREN CLARK

Swainson's Hawk
Buteo swainsoni

DESCRIPTION 19 in/48 cm, wingspan 51 in/130 cm (averages; female larger than male). Slim; broad, **long pointed wings** with **dark flight feathers**; finely banded tail (terminal band wider). Soars with wings in dihedral. Polymorphic; adult plumage attained over 2–3 years. *Light Morph:* Grayish-brown upperparts, white ventrally with brown bib, white wing linings. *Dark Morph:* Dark body plumage, pale undertail, rufous-tinged wing linings. In PNW, many adults intermediate, with variably rufous underparts. *First-year (morphs vary):* Pale-edged dark-brown upperparts, paler ventrally with streaks, blotches; light supercilium; **dark eyeline**, malar, central throat streak; flight feathers paler than adult. Molts through summer, migration, shows bleached head feathers.

SIMILAR SPECIES Other buteos lack dark flight feathers; Northern Harrier (p. 133) tail longer, entire rump white.

STATUS & DISTRIBUTION Breeds in interior West—BC (disjunctly to eastern Alaska), Minnesota south to northern Mexico; winters to Argentina, a few in southern Florida, central California. In PNW, breeds in open landscapes east of Cascades/BC Coast Range excluding northern ID; north of Columbia Plateau, majority from Okanagan. Rare west of crest in spring migration; casual fall. Returns late Apr–May, mass exodus Aug–Sep. Barely casual anywhere Nov–Mar.

HABITAT ASSOCIATIONS Breeds prairies, fields with nesting trees; in BC grasslands adjacent to fragmented forests. Winters agricultural areas.

BEHAVIOR & FEEDING Captures rodents, other vertebrates, insects by perch-hunting, ground chases. Migrants gregarious, exploit thermals; subadult flocks feed at orthopteran concentrations. Long-term monogamous pair perches conspicuously, often nests in shelterbelts near humans.

VOCALIZATIONS Shrill, weak *queeeoh.*

"Western" Rufous morph
WA (Yakima County)—May
DOUG SCHURMAN

"Western" Light morph First-year · WA
(Skagit County)—Mar · GREGG THOMPSON

"Western" Light morph · OR (Washington County)
Mar · GREG GILLSON

"Western" Dark morph · BC (Penticton)—Feb
LAURE W. NEISH

Red-tailed Hawk
Buteo jamaicensis

DESCRIPTION 19 in/48 cm, wingspan 49 in/124 cm (averages; females larger than males). Bulky **dark-headed** buteo; broad wings held relatively flat in flight. **Red tail**, black-bordered underwing attained in second summer (generally also dark iris). Two polymorphic types in PNW. **"Western":** Light morph brownish dorsally with **pale scapular patches**; belly band of dark streaks on creamy rufous underparts; **dark patagial bar** visible in flight on leading edge of underwing. Dark morph dark brown (many individuals show rusty underparts, recognized as rufous morph by some authorities); in flight, pale remiges contrast with dark underwing coverts. *First-year:* Finely banded brownish tail, breast whiter than adult's, yellow iris. **"Harlan's":** Prevalent dark morph **blackish** with **whitish tail**, sometimes variably grayish, rufous tinged, or banded. In rare light morph, white dominates plumage; intermediate morphs show white-flecked head, breast.

SIMILAR SPECIES Other buteos lack patagial bar. Rough-legged Hawk (p. 142), Ferruginous Hawk (p. 143) longer winged with feathered tarsi, soar in dihedral. In light morph, Rough-legged shows white tail with black tip, whitish head, dark carpal patches on pale underwing; Ferruginous shows rufous upperparts, large flatter head with prominent yellow gape, mostly white tail. Dark morphs of both generally warmer toned than "Harlan's"—best distinguished by shape. Northern Harrier (p. 133) appears lanky, long tailed with white rump. Eagles much larger with longer wings. See also under Swainson's Hawk (p. 139).

STATUS & DISTRIBUTION Breeds in numerous races from central Alaska to Labrador, south to Caribbean, Costa Rica; winters within range, withdrawing from north. Most familiar PNW raptor, "Western" (*B.j. calurus*, along with smaller but otherwise similar *B.j. alascensis* in coastal BC) fairly common breeder throughout, but nearly all leave northern BC Dec–Feb; dark-morph individuals more common east of Cascades. Northern-breeding "Harlan's" (*B.j. harlani*) rare but widespread Oct–Mar, majority reported from southwestern BC, northwestern WA. "Eastern" (*B.j. borealis*), "Krider's" (*B.j. krideri*) occur only east of PNW.

"Harlan's" Light morph First-year · OR
(Jefferson County)—Nov · TOM CRABTREE

"Western" Dark morph · MT
(Flathead County)—Feb
KURT LINDSAY

"Harlan's" Dark morph · Utah—Dec
JERRY LIGUORI

"Harlan's" Dark morph First-year
Alaska—Aug · RON HORN

"Western"

"Harlan's"

HABITAT ASSOCIATIONS Open habitats with isolated tree stands, wooded edges—often clear-cuts, along freeways; also alpine meadows in migration. Shuns dense forest.

BEHAVIOR & FEEDING Highly adaptable; takes mammals, snakes, other prey from perch, kiting, or cruising flight. Long-term monogamous pair builds several bulky stick nests within territory located high in tree or on cliff ledge, protected with flight displays year-round. Average clutch of 2–3, raised by both parents.

VOCALIZATIONS Rasping drawn-out *keeee arrr* directed at intruders; courting pair offers sharp repeated *kwirk*. Young beg with repeated *ple uk*.

First-year Light morph · WA (Whatcom County)—Nov
DOUGLAS L. BROWN

Light morph Male · MT (Flathead County)—Dec · KURT LINDSAY

First-year Dark morph · ID (Jefferson County)—Dec · DARREN CLARK

Light morph · WA (Clark County)—Jan · ROGER WINDEMUTH

Rough-legged Hawk
Buteo lagopus

DESCRIPTION 20 in/51 cm, wingspan 53 in/135 cm (averages; female larger than male). Broad winged, bulky, **small-billed** buteo; soars with wings in dihedral. **Feathered tarsi**, dark iris, small feet. Variable, often rust-tinged adult plumage attained over two years. First-year has pale iris, white dorsal primary panel; tail tip diffuse blackish. *Light Morph:* **Whitish breast, head**; dark eyeline, belly; pale underwing with **dark carpal patch**; white tail with black tip. Male often lacks black belly, tail shows several bands. *Dark Morph:* **Blackish with white flight feathers**; tail base often dark.

SIMILAR SPECIES First-year Red-tailed Hawk's (pp. 140–141) wings held flatter, show patagial bar; light-morph Ferruginous Hawk's (p. 143) tail all-white, dark morph shows white crescent within carpal patch; "Harlan's" Hawk's (pp. 140–141) tarsi unfeathered; Northern Harrier's (p. 133) rump white.

STATUS & DISTRIBUTION Holarctic breeder across taiga, tundra; winters temperate latitudes. Dark morph less common. In PNW, locally common in interior Nov–Apr south from southern BC (Okanagan Valley, Creston); on westside, locally common in lowlands (e.g., Fraser Valley, Samish Flats) Sep–Apr, occasionally May, uncommon elsewhere. Casual Jun–Jul (BC).

HABITAT ASSOCIATIONS Breeds tundra, stunted boreal forest; winters open lowlands to mid-elevation; migrants may use mountain ridges.

BEHAVIOR & FEEDING Small-rodent specialist, hunting from stationary hover or perch; also scavenges; conspicuous in open, often perched on twigs appearing small for its bulk. Migrants may flock, aggregate at prey-rich sites, roost communally; males typically winter farther south. Pair builds nest on cliff, ground, rarely tree.

VOCALIZATIONS Squealed *keeearr* seldom heard in south.

Dark morph · *OR (Harney County) —May* · GREG GILLSON

Light morph · *Utah—Nov* · DARREN CLARK

Light morph · *OR (Crook County)—Jan* TOM CRABTREE

Ferruginous Hawk
Buteo regalis

DESCRIPTION 22 in/56 cm, wingspan 56 in/142 cm (averages; female larger than male). Largest PNW buteo; large head, **prominent yellow gape**; feathered tarsi. Aloft, holds broad, **long, pointed wings in strong dihedral**; shows pale flight feathers, **whitish tail**, light dorsal patch formed by white-based primaries. *Light Morph:* Pale grayish head; **rufous** back, leg feathering, wing linings; white breast, belly. *Dark Morph:* Dark, often rufous-tinged body plumage with darker tail; distal wing linings show white crescent. *First-year:* Vaguely banded tail; light morph lacks rufous ventrally.

SIMILAR SPECIES Other buteos have smaller heads, bills: Rough-legged Hawk's (p. 142) tail black-tipped, carpal patch darker; "Harlan's" Hawk (pp. 140–141), Swainson's Hawk (p. 139) tarsi unfeathered, latter with darker flight feathers. Eagles larger; longer winged in flight.

STATUS & DISTRIBUTION Breeds southern Alberta, North Dakota to southwestern states; winters in southern breeding range, northern Mexico. In PNW, declining due to habitat degradation (threatened WA, endangered OR). Rare, local breeder late Feb–Jul east of Cascades (casual BC, absent northern ID, northwestern MT); migrates Feb–Apr, Jul–Oct; winters rarely. Casual western OR (winters Rogue Valley). High frequency of dark morphs WA, OR.

HABITAT ASSOCIATIONS Breeds prairie, shrub-steppe habitats; hunts in agricultural areas.

BEHAVIOR & FEEDING Hunts from perch or stationary hover. Prefers rabbits, gophers, ground squirrels; also captures snakes, birds, insects. Migrants aggregate at prey-rich winter or stopover sites outside PNW. Monogamous pair builds large nest with twigs, bones, dung on cliff, pinnacle, infrequently tree, artificial structure.

VOCALIZATIONS Weak, downslurred *quee arr.*

MT (Flathead County)—Oct · KEN ARCHER

First-year · BC (Boundary Bay)—Jan · GREGG THOMPSON

Golden Eagle
Aquila chrysaetos

DESCRIPTION 32 in/81 cm, wingspan 82 in/208 cm (averages; female larger than male). Brown, buteo-like; **small bill, head**; golden nape, long tail, **feathered tarsi**; soars in dihedral on long wings that bulge at secondaries. Tail, wings evenly dark with variable gray banding. Bleached feathers may give patchy blond appearance. *First-year:* **White patch at base of flight feathers**; white tail with broad dark terminal band. Transitions to adult plumage over 6–7 years.

SIMILAR SPECIES Subadult Bald Eagle (p. 132) larger bill; flat winged in flight, shows whitish underwing coverts; larger head projects farther than tail. Turkey Vulture (p. 129) has featherless head, teetering flight. Other PNW raptors smaller.

STATUS & DISTRIBUTION Holarctic breeder, withdraws from north in winter. In North America, nests Alaska to Mexico, northeastern Canada. In PNW, decreasing due to declining prey, lead poisoning; still widespread but uncommon resident east of Cascades/BC Coast Range (rare northern ID). Rare westside resident (e.g., Vancouver Island, San Juan Islands, Olympics, southwestern OR). Rare Oct–Apr in westside lowlands, Columbia Plateau. Fairly common migrant northwestern MT.

HABITAT ASSOCIATIONS Breeds mountains, canyons; hunts open forest, shrub-steppe, tundra, other treeless habitats, occasionally over lakes.

BEHAVIOR & FEEDING Maneuverable for its size. Hunts rabbits, large rodents, small ungulates, waterfowl from perch or flight; also eats carrion. Most migrants observed Sep–Nov, Mar–Apr. In PNW, long-term monogamous pair maintains territory year-round, builds massive nest on cliff, sometimes tree.

VOCALIZATIONS Weak repeated *chee up* in alarm, other muted calls; juvenile begs with hissing.

California—Jan · DAVID E. QUADY

Texas—Mar · DAVE KRUEPER

Yellow Rail
Coturnicops noveboracensis

DESCRIPTION 7.25 in/18.5 cm. **Small**, ultra-secretive marsh bird. Dark cap, facial patch; **clear buffy-yellow breast, upper belly**. Upperparts feathers dark brown with two thin, white transverse bands toward tip, broad buffy margins, creating appearance of **longitudinal yellow stripes on white-flecked dark back**. Primaries, underwing coverts light gray; **white secondaries** form prominent patch visible in flight. *Chick:* Black, fluffy (like other rails), **unbanded pink bill**. *Immature:* Darker, less yellowish.

SIMILAR SPECIES Immature Sora (p. 147) larger, darker, back not striped buffy, pale (versus dark) undertail coverts.

STATUS & DISTRIBUTION Breeds boreal Canada, northern tier of states east of Rockies, but highly local; small disjunct populations south-central OR, northeastern California. Winters coastal marshes of Southeast. Rarely seen in migration. In PNW, breeds late Apr–early Sep in BC (near Anahim Lake on northwestern Chilcotin Plateau, casually Rockies), south-central OR (e.g., Klamath Marsh NWR); non-breeders accidental elsewhere in region.

HABITAT ASSOCIATIONS Breeds wet sedge meadows.

BEHAVIOR & FEEDING Migrates at night. In daytime, may fly short distances barely above marsh vegetation, legs dangling. Otherwise walks or runs, keeping under cover. Diet insects, small snails, other aquatic invertebrates, seeds. Female builds concealed ground nest of woven grasses/sedges, incubates (mean clutch eight eggs). Chicks leave nest after two days; transition to feeding independently in three weeks, after which no longer brooded by female.

VOCALIZATIONS Male's territorial call repeated sets of clicks in twos, threes, mostly at night. Response readily elicited by tapping pebbles together, but birds adept at staying hidden.

WA (King County)—Apr • GREGG THOMPSON

Virginia Rail
Rallus limicola

DESCRIPTION 9.5 in/24 cm. Long-legged marsh bird with **long, thin, slightly down-curved red bill**. Brownish upperparts mottled black-and-buffy, **brownish-orange breast**, gray face; banded black-and-white flanks, undertail. Short tail often cocked upward. *Chick:* Downy black with **black band on bill**. *Immature:* Duskier than adult; blackish face, breast, bill; white throat.

SIMILAR SPECIES Sora (p. 147) has shorter, thicker yellowish bill, yellow-green (versus reddish) legs; adult shows gray breast, black face mask.

STATUS & DISTRIBUTION Breeds across North America from southern Canada south, except for lower Great Plains, Southeast; winters along coasts, in Mexico. Also resident South America. Summer resident low to middle elevations throughout PNW, but local—fairly common southwestern, south-central BC, WA, OR, southern ID; uncommon southeastern BC, northern ID, northwestern MT, western WY. Most leave Sep–Oct, return Apr–May. Winter resident in ice-free lowland marshes—rare/casual ID, northwestern MT, southeastern BC, uncommon to fairly common farther west, especially along coast.

HABITAT ASSOCIATIONS Densely vegetated wetlands—ponds, estuaries, marshes (freshwater or brackish), wet meadows, even drainage ditches. Needs shallow standing water, emergent vegetation, edges for foraging.

BEHAVIOR & FEEDING Mostly runs or walks, staying well hidden. Inefficient flyer; migrates at night, flying low. Largely animal diet, from insects to small fish; secondarily seeds (opposite of Sora, lessening competition in shared habitat). Woven basket nest at water level in deep vegetation. Large brood of precocial young, tended by both parents.

VOCALIZATIONS Calls include *kiddik kiddik kiddik* in breeding season; quacking grunts throughout year, often in descending series.

Chick · OR (Harney County)—Jul · DAMON CALDERWOOD

WA (Clark County)—May · ROGER WINDEMUTH

Immature · WA (Snohomish County)—Jul · GEORGE PAGOS

Sora
Porzana carolina

DESCRIPTION 9 in/23 cm. Reclusive marsh bird with **chicken-like yellow bill, black mask on face**. Olive-brownish upperparts flecked black, white. **Gray breast**, cheeks, neck sides; barred brown-and-white sides, flanks; pale undertail coverts. Short tail often cocked upward. **Chick:** Downy black with **orange chin bristles**. **Immature:** Browner; pale throat, breast; lacks black mask.

SIMILAR SPECIES Virginia Rail (p. 146) has long, decurved bill; adult legs, bill red, breast brownish-orange. Yellow Rail (p. 145) smaller, prominent yellowish back stripes, dark undertail coverts, white secondaries.

STATUS & DISTRIBUTION Breeds across continent from subarctic south to Great Lakes, northern Great Plains, Southwest; winters along both coasts, throughout Central America, West Indies to Guyana, Peru. Summer resident, migrant, throughout PNW from sea level to mountain lakes, but local; common OR, fairly common ID, eastern WA, central, southern interior BC; uncommon western WA (Puget Trough), southwestern BC, western WY, northwestern MT. Most leave Aug–Oct, return Apr–May. Rare winter resident in lowlands of southwestern BC, western WA, western OR; casual farther east.

HABITAT ASSOCIATIONS Wet meadows (especially sedge), freshwater emergent marshes (cattails, tules); less often ponds, lakes, coastal salt marshes, fields.

BEHAVIOR & FEEDING Reluctant flier in breeding marshes but migrates long distances, flying at night. Proficient, willing swimmer. Diet predominantly seeds, some invertebrates. Nest hidden in vegetation at water level; large brood of precocial young. Parents share familial duties.

VOCALIZATIONS Territorial call loud, descending whinny (both sexes). Rising *ter ee* given independently but also ahead of whinny. Often vocalizes at night.

Juvenile · WA (Pierce County)—Aug
JOHN RIEGSECKER

Adult with chicks · WA (King County)—Jul · GREGG THOMPSON

WA (Clark County)—Jan · KEN ARCHER

American Coot
Fulica americana

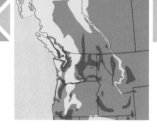

DESCRIPTION 15 in/38 cm, wingspan 26 in/66 cm. Rotund aquatic rail, sits high in water. **Dark gray**; black head, neck; white outer undertail coverts. Pointed **white bill with band near tip, white facial shield** (dark red on forehead). **Red iris**, greenish or yellowish legs, **long lobed toes**. *Chick:* Downy black; **bare red crown, bill**; yellow-orange facial bristles. *Juvenile:* Paler; gray legs, no red on forehead.

SIMILAR SPECIES Pied-billed Grebe (p. 100) brown. Common Gallinule (not shown; casual southern OR, southern ID) slimmer; brownish back, narrow white horizontal line on flanks, yellow-tipped red bill, red forehead shield.

STATUS & DISTRIBUTION Breeds mostly western half North America, Midwest, to northern South America; winters warmer parts of breeding range to Panama. In PNW, locally common breeder, migrant (Mar–May, Sep–Nov), winter resident; east of Cascades, winter freeze-up concentrates birds on large bodies of open water.

HABITAT ASSOCIATIONS Breeds in diverse freshwater wetlands with mixture of emergent vegetation, open water, mostly at lower elevations. On passage, also large lakes, reservoirs, saltwater bays, estuaries. Additionally in winter, city parks, golf courses, agricultural lands adjacent to water.

BEHAVIOR & FEEDING Forages in water, on surface, tipping up, diving; also on land. Diet mostly plant matter; some insects, other small animals. Requires long take-off run, splashing water with wings, feet. Platform nest over water, large brood of precocial young. Territorial, combative in nesting season, but forms cooperative flocks in migration, winter.

VOCALIZATIONS Noisy squawks, cackles, grunts; *puck* notes singly or in series.

BC (Delta)—Sep · DOUGLAS L. BROWN

WA (Grant County)—Mar · JOSEPH V. HIGBEE

Sandhill Crane
Grus canadensis

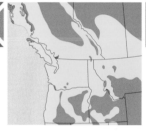

DESCRIPTION 40–45 in/102–114 cm, wingspan 72–76 in/183–193 cm (Arctic-breeding birds smaller than those breeding in PNW). Tall, long-legged, long-necked inhabitant of open wetlands. Overall **gray with red crown**, **white cheeks**, dark, straight bill; plumage often stained rusty. Ornamental inner **wing feathers overhang short tail**, forming distinctive "bustle." *Juvenile*: Brownish gray, lacks red crown.

SIMILAR SPECIES Great Blue Heron (p. 122) lacks bustle, flies with neck folded back.

STATUS & DISTRIBUTION Summer resident northeastern Siberia, Alaska, northern Canada, through Great Lakes region to New England (rare), discontinuously western Canada to northern Colorado; winters Southwest, Texas, Gulf Coast, Mexico. Also year-round resident southeastern states, Cuba. Three distinct populations breed in PNW: 1) uncommon to fairly common ID, uncommon northwestern MT, western WY, winters southwestern US, northwestern Mexico; 2) uncommon interior BC, rare south-central WA, fairly common OR (Cascades east), winters Central Valley of California; 3) uncommon BC mainland coast, coastal islands, migrating through lower Columbia River bottomlands (southwestern WA, northwestern OR) where some winter, others continue to Central Valley of California. Populations breeding farther north migrate through much of PNW in large numbers (peak movement Apr, Oct).

HABITAT ASSOCIATIONS Wet meadows, parklands, river valleys, flooded pastures; may forage in agricultural fields, clear-cuts.

BEHAVIOR & FEEDING Omnivorous. Walks, rarely runs. Flies with neck extended. Forms lifelong pair bond. Leaping, bowing courtship dance inaugurates breeding season. Nests near water in emergent vegetation. Usually single chick raised to adulthood, remains with parents until spring.

VOCALIZATIONS Far-carrying, bugling rattle, often in flight.

Black-necked Stilt
Himantopus mexicanus

DESCRIPTION 14.5 in/37 cm, wingspan 29 in/74 cm. Graceful wader; **black dorsally** with **white underparts**, forehead, rump, tail, spot above eye; **long, bright-pink legs**; needle-like black bill, black underwings. *Male:* Glossy black plumage; pinkish wash on breast in breeding plumage. *Female:* Back, nape brownish, less glossy. *Chick:* Downy, mottled brownish. *Juvenile:* Grayish black, less glossy than adult, pale legs.

SIMILAR SPECIES American Avocet (p. 151) stouter; bluish legs, upturned bill; in flight, broad white stripes on wings, back.

STATUS & DISTRIBUTION Breeds locally, disjunctly, from southern BC, Alberta, Delaware south to Mexico, West Indies, Brazil; withdraws in winter from colder parts of range to California, southern Florida, Mexico; also resident Hawaii (endangered subspecies). Increasing summer resident in PNW. Arrives beginning Mar, rarely lingers to Oct. Breeds east of Cascades north to WA (Okanogan, Pend Oreille Counties), irregularly BC (Kamloops, Okanagan, East Kootenay); fairly common south-central WA, southeastern OR, uncommon southern ID, western WY, northwestern MT. West of crest, very rare breeder Willamette Valley, occasionally north to southwestern BC (Saanich). Migrant overshoots rare Apr–May, mostly Puget Sound, also to Idaho Panhandle, BC (southwestern coast, interior).

HABITAT ASSOCIATIONS Nests shallow wetlands with emergent vegetation including sewage ponds, alkaline lakeshore, flooded pasture.

BEHAVIOR & FEEDING Forages visually in shallows, picking insects, crustaceans, other invertebrates from water surface, sometimes from air or below surface; individuals spread apart to feed. Monogamous pairs nest semi-colonially; aggressively defend nest, precocial chicks.

VOCALIZATIONS Strident, variable *wrek*, repeated incessantly in alarm; juveniles emit quieter *peek*.

Breeding Male · OR (Harney County)—May · KURT LINDSAY

Non-breeding Female · WY (Park County)—Aug
DOUG SCHURMAN

American Avocet
Recurvirostra americana

DESCRIPTION 18 in/46 cm, wingspan 29 in/74 cm. Elegant wader; mostly white underparts, tail, back; black primaries, secondary coverts, inner scapulars form **dorsal chevron pattern** in flight; long bluish legs. **Thin black upward-curved bill**; female's more sharply curved. *Breeding:* **Rusty head, neck, breast** Feb–Jul. *Non-breeding:* Rusty areas turn pale gray. *Chick:* Downy, mottled cinnamon. *Juvenile:* Duller than adult; buffy head, nape.

SIMILAR SPECIES No other large shorebird shares distinctive back pattern. Black-necked Stilt (p. 150) slighter, legs pink.

STATUS & DISTRIBUTION Breeds regularly from south-central BC, southwestern Manitoba south disjunctly to southwestern states, also California coast, Central Valley, locally on coast Virginia to northeastern Mexico; winters California, southern Florida, Mexico south to Guatemala. Summer breeding resident locally in PNW; population expanding. Common Mar–Nov central WA, southeastern OR, southern ID, western WY; common to uncommon Apr–Aug south-central BC (Kelowna, southern Cariboo Plateau); irregularly uncommon to casual elsewhere east of Cascades/BC Coast Range. Migrants rare west of crest, mostly May–Jun (has nested Salish Sea lowlands, southern Willamette Valley). Casual coastally Aug–Feb, mostly OR.

HABITAT ASSOCIATIONS Nests open wetland, alkaline shoreline, mud flats; at other seasons, flooded fields, tidal mud flats, brackish impoundments.

BEHAVIOR & FEEDING Forages mostly by touch in shallows or mud for invertebrates, small fish, seeds; uses scything technique, wading or swimming depending on water depth. Frequently feeds, roosts in tight flocks. Monogamous pairs form during winter or migration, may nest semi-colonially. Courtship includes crossed-bill dance. Aggressively defends nest, precocial chicks.

VOCALIZATIONS High whistled *queep*.

Chick · *BC (Vancouver)—Jul* · GREGG THOMPSON   *OR (Lincoln County)—Mar* · GREG GILLSON

Black Oystercatcher
Haematopus bachmani

DESCRIPTION 17.5 in/45 cm, wingspan 32 in/81 cm. Chunky, **all-black** shorebird with **long, chisel-like, bright-red bill**, eye-ring; relatively short pinkish legs; golden eye. Shows long, broad wings in flight. *Chick:* Mottled grayish. *Juvenile:* Dark-tipped, reddish-yellow bill.

SIMILAR SPECIES Unique. Other shorebirds less bulky, lack bright-red bill. Pigeon Guillemot (p. 204) has shorter, black bill, white wing patch.

STATUS & DISTRIBUTION Breeds along coast, Aleutians to Baja California (hybridizes with American Oystercatcher in Baja, where ranges overlap). In PNW, common resident Haida Gwaii south along rocky outer coast to OR; rare on sandy shorelines, with transients using rock jetties. In Salish Sea, common BC, uncommon WA south to Skagit County, rare farther south.

HABITAT ASSOCIATIONS Strictly marine; accidental to inland WA (King, Yakima Counties). Prefers to breed on open rocky islets, also headlands, gravelly shore; feeds along rocky intertidal shoreline, rarely open seaside uplands; loafs on jetties, breakwaters.

BEHAVIOR & FEEDING Forages for mollusks, crustaceans, polychaetes, other organisms when tide low; uses laterally compressed bill to pry shells apart. Usually in pairs or family groups, often roosts with bill tucked under wing. Walks deliberately, flies with stiff wingbeats. Not classically migratory, but disperses; forms flocks numbering up to a hundred (primarily subadults) Oct–Mar, may concentrate at herring spawns. Monogamous pair forms long-term bond, displays vigorously in hunchback posture, carefully guards precocial chicks.

VOCALIZATIONS Highly vocal; loud repeated yelps—*keee* or *keeyah*; piped series in display, rapid *kli kli kli klidew* in alarm.

Non-breeding · WA (Jefferson County)—Jan · JOSEPH V. HIGBEE

Juvenile · BC (Campbell River)—Sep · MIKE VIP

Breeding · BC (Comox)—Apr · TERRY THORMIN

Molting Adults · WA (Whatcom County)—Aug · DOUGLAS L. BROWN

Black-bellied Plover
Pluvialis squatarola

DESCRIPTION 11 in/28 cm, wingspan 29 in/74 cm. Plump with **short thick bill**, fairly short dark legs, **white rump**, wing stripe; **black axillaries** visible in flight. *Breeding:* Black face, breast, belly; white crown, nape, undertail; spangled back. Female flecked white ventrally, dusky crown, browner back. *Non-breeding:* Dingy whitish ventrally; brownish-gray, speckled upperparts; head plain with vague, pale supercilium. *Juvenile:* Back darker with buff spotting, breast finely streaked, legs grayer.

SIMILAR SPECIES Golden-Plovers (pp. 154–155) smaller, more finely built, lack black axillaries, white rump; in non-breeding plumage, show stronger facial markings with dark cap, broad pale supercilium. Bills longer in other large shorebirds.

STATUS & DISTRIBUTION Holarctic tundra breeder except Scandinavia, Greenland; winters along coasts southwestern BC, Massachusetts, Britain, southern Japan to southern continents. In PNW, common late Jul–May along outer coast, also Fraser, Samish Deltas; locally uncommon farther south in westside lowlands. Locally uncommon east of Cascades/BC Coast Range Sep–Nov, rare May–early Jun—e.g., WA (Coulee Lakes), OR (Klamath, Harney Basins). A few summer, mostly on outer coast.

HABITAT ASSOCIATIONS Nests on tundra, at other seasons mostly coastal—mud flats, mowed or plowed fields, beaches, alkaline lakeshores.

BEHAVIOR & FEEDING Forages visually by running, stopping, picking; takes mostly worms, insects, marine organisms. Flocks spread out to feed with tide out, roost tightly at high tide, often on high beach. Usually flocks with Dunlins, also knots, dowitchers. Most adults migrate Jul–Aug, juveniles Sep–Nov. Monogamous breeder.

VOCALIZATIONS Very vocal; mostly forlorn, whistled *plee o weee*.

Family Charadriidae—PLOVERS **153**

Breeding · *Alaska—Jun* · GREGG THOMPSON   Juvenile · *WA (Grays Harbor County)—Sep* · GREGG THOMPSON

American Golden-Plover
Pluvialis dominica

DESCRIPTION 10 in/26 cm, wingspan 27 in/66 cm. Slim with short thin bill, fairly short dark legs; **dark crown**, upperparts spangled with golden; **four primaries generally project beyond tertials**. *Breeding:* Black underparts; thick white band extends across forehead over eye to bend of wings; often molting during spring migration. Female duller. *Non-breeding:* Dingy-gray underparts, conspicuous supercilium. *Juvenile:* Similar to adult non-breeding with crisp back spotting, **whitish supercilium**, vaguely barred breast.

SIMILAR SPECIES Pacific Golden-Plover (p. 155) barely smaller; shorter primary projection; in breeding plumage, white continues down sides to undertail; juvenile supercilium yellowish. Black-bellied Plover (p. 153) larger with black axillaries, white rump; white crown, undertail in breeding plumage.

STATUS & DISTRIBUTION Breeds regularly from Bering Strait east to Baffin Island, south to northern BC, northern Manitoba; winters to South America. Most migrants use Mississippi Valley northbound, fly down East Coast in fall. In PNW, uncommon westside Jul–Oct (primarily outer coast), rare spring (mostly May); east of crest rare Sep–Oct; otherwise casual. Juveniles predominate Sep–Nov. Recently documented breeding central BC (Itcha/Ilgachuz Mountains).

HABITAT ASSOCIATIONS Nests sparse, open tundra to mid-elevation, winters on pampas. Migrants use pasture, mowed or plowed fields, mud flats, beaches.

BEHAVIOR & FEEDING Forages visually by running, stopping, picking; eats insects, other invertebrates, some seeds, berries; may probe for worms. Powerful flier; flocks with other shorebirds, especially *Pluvialis*. Monogamous; site-faithful male displays in flight near nest, shares nesting duties.

VOCALIZATIONS Whistled *QUEE dle* in flight; other calls near nest.

Juvenile · WA (Grays Harbor County)—Sep · GREGG THOMPSON   Breeding · Midway Island—Apr · LEE BARNES

Pacific Golden-Plover
Pluvialis fulva

DESCRIPTION 9.75 in/25 cm, wingspan 24 in/61 cm. Slim with short bill, dark legs; **dark crown**, upperparts spangled with golden; **three or fewer primaries project beyond tertials**. *Breeding:* Black face, breast, belly; white band extends across forehead over eye, below folded wing to undertail; female duller. *Non-breeding:* **Overall golden hued**; conspicuous supercilium. *Juvenile:* Similar to adult non-breeding; crisp golden spotting, barred breast; **yellowish face, supercilium.**

SIMILAR SPECIES American Golden-Plover (p. 154) slimmer; proportionately shorter bill, legs, longer wings; in breeding plumage, entirely black below (use care identifying molting spring migrants); juvenile supercilium whitish. Larger Black-bellied Plover (p. 153) shows black axillaries, white rump; white crown in breeding plumage.

STATUS & DISTRIBUTION Breeds western Siberia to Alaska Peninsula, winters coastally—mostly southern Asia, Pacific islands, a few to southern California. In PNW, uncommon Jul–Nov west of Cascades/BC Coast Range (mostly outer coast); rare late Apr–May, casual/rare Jun, Dec–Mar; casual east of crest (WA, OR, ID) Sep–Oct.

HABITAT ASSOCIATIONS Nests moist or dry tundra; outside breeding, *Salicornia* marsh, pasture, tilled fields, flats, beaches; lawns, mid-elevation slopes in Hawaii.

BEHAVIOR & FEEDING Feeding similar to American Golden-Plover; takes small vertebrates more often. Flocks with other shorebirds, feeds with other *Pluvialis*; most PNW migrants in small flocks, adults Jul–Aug, juveniles predominate Sep–Oct. Powerful flyer, makes non-stop ocean crossings. Monogamous pair may form before spring arrival; male displays in flight, provides nest scrape, shares duties.

VOCALIZATIONS Whistled *chu WEET* in flight; other calls near nest.

Snowy Plover
Charadrius nivosus

DESCRIPTION 6.25 in/16 cm. **Plain sandy brown with short thin blackish bill,** fairly long grayish legs; white underparts, hindneck collar; wing stripe visible in flight. *Breeding:* Male has **black bars on foreneck sides, forehead, behind eye**; female has browner bars. *Non-breeding:* Similar to adult female; no forehead bar. *Chick:* Downy; spotted brownish dorsally. *Juvenile:* Pale feather edging.

SIMILAR SPECIES Semipalmated Plover (p. 157) larger with blackish neck-ring, yellow-orange legs. Killdeer (p. 158) chick fuzzy with breast band. Small sandpipers show longer bills.

STATUS & DISTRIBUTION Breeds along coast from southern WA disjunctly to Chile; also scattered Great Basin to interior Mexico, Gulf Coast to West Indies; withdraws from interior in winter. In PNW, threatened coastal population resident WA (rare Pacific County, casual Grays Harbor County), OR (rare Heceta Head to Cape Blanco, casual Tillamook, Clatsop Counties). Nests southern interior OR (Klamath to Harney Counties), strays north in ID to American Falls. Vagrants (mostly May–Jun) casual north to southwestern BC, accidental to MT.

HABITAT ASSOCIATIONS Nests at extensive beaches, alkaline lakeshore, evaporation ponds; coastal at other times.

BEHAVIOR & FEEDING Forages visually like other plovers, taking insects, other invertebrates; also probes, foot-trembles. Gregarious, but flocks only infrequently with other shorebirds. Usually runs when disturbed. Territorial pair nests in open scrape. Monogamous, although female often deserts brood, re-pairs; sex ratio skewed to males. Anthropogenic coastal disturbance reduces nesting success; beach closures have increased production.

VOCALIZATIONS Whistled *too WHEEJT*, husky *prurt* in flight.

Breeding · WA (Pacific County)—May · GREGG THOMPSON   Juvenile · ID (Nez Perce County)—Aug · KEITH CARLSON

Semipalmated Plover
Charadrius semipalmatus

DESCRIPTION 7 in/18 cm. Plain brownish upperparts with **white collar**, white ventrally with blackish breast band; **short stout bill**; **yellowish legs**; wing stripe visible on long wings in flight. **Breeding:** Proximal half of bill orange; black forecrown, cheek. **Non-breeding:** Blackish bill, white supercilium more pronounced, breast band sometimes partial. **Juvenile:** Like non-breeding, with light dorsal edging.

SIMILAR SPECIES Snowy Plover (p. 156) smaller, thin billed, partial breast band, gray legs; Killdeer (p. 158) larger with double breast band, chick fuzzy with single band.

STATUS & DISTRIBUTION Breeds across American Arctic south to Haida Gwaii, Nova Scotia; winters coastally from WA, Virginia to Patagonia. In PNW, common Apr–May, Jul–Sep on outer coast, locally around Salish Sea; uncommon Oct–Mar, local southern WA/OR outer coast, rare farther north. Rare Apr–May east of Cascades/BC Coast Range, locally uncommon Aug–Nov. Migrates in lowlands, rarely in mountains. Breeds regularly Haida Gwaii, casually mainland BC (Chilcotin, Iona), WA (Grays Harbor), OR (Coos Bay, Malheur NWR); casual Jun elsewhere.

HABITAT ASSOCIATIONS Nests at open gravel areas; at other seasons, uses mud flats, tidal estuaries, beaches, alkaline lakes, sewage lagoons.

BEHAVIOR & FEEDING Forages visually like other plovers, takes mostly insects, other invertebrates from mud, shallow water; also probes, foot-trembles. Gregarious; spreads out to feed when tide out, roosts on beaches, flocks with other shorebirds. Monogamous; male forms nest scrape, pair shares parental care. Most adults migrate Jul–Aug, juveniles late Aug–Oct.

VOCALIZATIONS Rising whistled *chu weet* most frequent.

Family Charadriidae—PLOVERS **157**

Chick · *OR (Harney County)—Jun*
DAMON CALDERWOOD

BC (Parksville)—May · RALPH HOCKEN

Killdeer
Charadrius vociferus

DESCRIPTION 10 in/25 cm, wingspan 24 in/61 cm. Plain brown upperparts with white collar, white ventrally with **two black breast bands**; white forehead, eyebrow; **short dark bill**, fairly short pale legs; **rusty rump**, tail; white wing stripe visible in flight. *Chick:* Downy; single breast band.

SIMILAR SPECIES Semipalmated Plover (p. 157) smaller, single breast band, short bill, gray rump. Mountain Plover (p. 159) lacks breast bands; Ruddy Turnstone (p. 172) smaller, chunky with white back, tail base.

STATUS & DISTRIBUTION Breeds Alaska to Newfoundland south to South America; winters south from BC, Kansas, Maine. In PNW, common resident west of Cascades/BC Coast Range, except uncommon BC north from Knight Inlet; some withdraw from north Jan–Feb. Common Mar–Oct throughout east of crest; uncommon to rare Nov–Feb, when absent western WY. Congregates by hundreds at favorable locales (e.g., Boundary Bay, Willamette Valley), mostly Oct–Dec.

HABITAT ASSOCIATIONS Wide-open sites mostly in lowlands, also valleys to moderate elevation; uses shoreline, lawns, tilled fields, beaches, road edges, lots, flat rooftops.

BEHAVIOR & FEEDING Forages visually day or night by running, stopping, picking, taking mostly insects, other invertebrates, some seeds, small vertebrates; also probes, foot-trembles. Secretive at nest but feigns broken wing as distraction display when discovered. Monogamous pair forms scrape nest in bare gravel, shares care of precocial young. Bond sometimes long-term, may double-brood. Flocks in PNW concentrate in farm fields Jul–Feb.

VOCALIZATIONS Highly vocal. Strident calls include *kill deeah, dee eh*; gives rapid trill when nervous.

Juvenile · *WA (Grays Harbor County)—Jan* · GREGG THOMPSON

Breeding · *Utah—Apr* · PAUL HIGGINS

Mountain Plover
Charadrius montanus

DESCRIPTION 8.75 in/22 cm. **Plain** rufous-tinged brown upperparts, dingy whitish ventrally; bull headed with short, thin, dark bill; white wing stripe, **gray tail with subterminal black band** visible in flight. *Breeding:* **Black forehead patch, loral line**. *Non-breeding:* Plain, without black facial markings; browner breast. *Juvenile:* Like non-breeding, with rusty dorsal feather edging (diminished by wear), darker cap.

SIMILAR SPECIES Killdeer (p. 158) slimmer with double breast band; non-breeding Black-bellied Plover (p. 153) shows black axillaries in flight; golden-plovers (pp. 154–155) slimmer, spangled golden above, lack black tail band.

STATUS & DISTRIBUTION Breeds disjunctly in declining numbers on western Great Plains from extreme southeastern Alberta, MT to Nuevo León; winters central California to southern Arizona, southern Texas, northern Mexico. In MT, WY, widespread breeder east of Continental Divide. In PNW, has bred western WY (Sublette County); migrants casual elsewhere (mostly WA/OR outer coast, Willamette Valley), generally Oct–Feb; away from WY, few spring records east of Cascades.

HABITAT ASSOCIATIONS Breeds on flat, bare ground in native grasslands grazed by livestock, prairie dogs, bison, or pronghorn, also tilled fields; at other seasons, agricultural fields, alkaline flats, beaches.

BEHAVIOR & FEEDING Forages visually, mostly for insects, by running, stopping; also foot-trembles to flush prey. Migrates in small flocks, concentrating in larger groups in favorable habitat. Monogamous pairs loosely colonial but highly territorial, nesting in ground scrape, often among prairie dogs. Exhibits multi-clutch strategy, producing two clutches incubated by both sexes; some polyandry documented.

VOCALIZATIONS Fairly quiet. Whistled, rapid *we we we we*; harsh *grrip* in flight.

Family Charadriidae—PLOVERS **159**

Juvenile · ID (Nez Perce County)—Jul · KEITH CARLSON   Breeding · WA (Okanogan County)—Jun · RYAN SHAW

Spotted Sandpiper
Actitis macularius

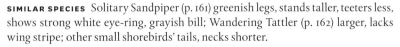

DESCRIPTION 8 in/20 cm. Short yellowish legs, white supercilium, **constant teetering** motion; **wing stripe visible in flight**. *Breeding:* Dark spots on white underparts, faint dorsal barring, **reddish bill**. *Non-breeding:* Plain grayish brown dorsally; dusky neck; **white underparts extend in wedge anterior to folded wing**; pale bill. *Juvenile:* Similar to non-breeding adult but with dorsal barring.

SIMILAR SPECIES Solitary Sandpiper (p. 161) greenish legs, stands taller, teeters less, shows strong white eye-ring, grayish bill; Wandering Tattler (p. 162) larger, lacks wing stripe; other small shorebirds' tails, necks shorter.

STATUS & DISTRIBUTION Widespread breeder across North America, Arctic treeline south to central California, Virginia; winters southwestern BC, Carolinas to South America. In PNW, fairly common, nearly ubiquitous resident Apr–Sep from coast to timberline. Highly migratory; arrives Apr–Jun, departs Jul–Oct. From Nov–Mar, rare west of Cascades, mostly Salish Sea with fewer on outer coast; casual east of crest, but increasing; most records from OR/WA.

HABITAT ASSOCIATIONS Nests in open or wooded sites along ponds, rivers, streams, wet fields, riparian shrub-steppe. At other seasons, anywhere near water, including marine sites.

BEHAVIOR & FEEDING Forages visually for various invertebrates, tiny fish, rarely carrion. Flies distinctively low over water, alternating stiff, shallow wingbeats with glides on bowed wings; territorial year-round; does not flock. Female generally polyandrous; breeding territory often includes more than one male. Nests on ground in vegetation near water. Sexes share parental care but male primary incubator. Young precocial.

VOCALIZATIONS Low-pitched whistled *twee tweet twee twee* in flight or alarm.

Breeding · BC (Chetwynd)—Jun · GARY S. DAVIDSON

Juvenile · WA (King County)—Aug · GREGG THOMPSON

Juvenile *T.s. cinnamomea* · WA (King County)—Aug
GREGG THOMPSON

Breeding · Yukon Territory—May · JUKKA JANTUNEN

Solitary Sandpiper
Tringa solitaria

DESCRIPTION 8.75 in/22 cm. Finely built with thin grayish bill, prominent **white eye-ring, greenish legs**; dark upperparts with fine spotting; whitish belly; dark breast, underwing. **Black-barred white outer tail feathers** visible in flight. *Breeding:* Finely striped breast; molts on wintering grounds. *Juvenile:* Back spotting white in subspecies *solitaria*, cinnamon tinged in *cinnamomea*.

SIMILAR SPECIES Spotted Sandpiper (p. 160) less tall; yellow legs, dark eyeline; teeters constantly. Lesser Yellowlegs (p. 165) larger; white rump, yellow legs.

STATUS & DISTRIBUTION Breeds Alaska to Labrador, winters Gulf of Mexico to Argentina. Two subspecies in PNW, usually separable in juvenal plumage: *T.s. cinnamomea* breeds west of Rockies central Alaska to central BC, *T.s. solitaria* east of Rockies. In PNW, *cinnamomea* widespread breeder interior BC at higher elevations north from Okanagan; territorial behavior rare south to OR, northwestern MT, but nesting only confirmed once (Idaho Panhandle). Migrants uncommon in interior mid-Apr to mid-May, Jul–early Oct (more frequent southbound); less numerous west of crest, rare at coast. Both subspecies migrate through interior but proportions unclear.

HABITAT ASSOCIATIONS Nests forested boreal ponds, bogs; at other seasons, shallow fresh water including muddy ditches, stagnant pools. Shuns marine habitats.

BEHAVIOR & FEEDING Picks larvae, other invertebrates, tiny vertebrates from water, foot-trembles to flush prey; walks deliberately, often bobs foreparts while standing. Seldom flocks, but gathers at preferred habitats. When flushed, may tower to great height, calling frequently. Breeds in old passerine nest in conifer; young precocial.

VOCALIZATIONS Sharp rising whistled *peet WHEET*; near nest, sings with series of whistles.

Juvenile · BC (Nanaimo)—Aug · RALPH HOCKEN

Breeding · WA (Grays Harbor County)—Aug · RYAN SHAW

Wandering Tattler
Tringa incana

DESCRIPTION 11 in/28 cm, wingspan 22 in/56 cm. Sturdy; attenuated shape, **horizontal posture**. Plain grayish overall with dark loral stripe. Long blackish bill, **short greenish-yellow legs**; in flight, **all-dark wings**. *Breeding:* Heavily barred whitish below. *Non-breeding:* Gray breast, white belly. *Juvenile:* Similar to non-breeding; pale fringes on coverts.

SIMILAR SPECIES Spotted Sandpiper (p. 160) smaller, browner, wing stripe visible in flight; shorter, yellowish bill. Willet (p. 163) larger with longer legs. Lesser Yellowlegs (p. 165) longer legged, more gracile. Surfbird (p. 174) has short bill; white tail base, wing stripe visible in flight.

STATUS & DISTRIBUTION Breeds from northeastern Siberia to Alaska, northwestern Canada; winters coastally from California to Peru, throughout Pacific islands to Australia. Migrant in PNW (late Apr–early Jun, Jul–early Oct); common Haida Gwaii; fairly common locally along outer coast; uncommon (Strait of Georgia) to casual (southern Puget Sound) in Salish Sea; casual inland (BC, WA, OR). Rare Nov–Mar, mostly OR.

HABITAT ASSOCIATIONS Nests along gravelly rivers, lakes, braided creeks from coastal to montane habitats. Winters primarily on wave-washed, rocky marine shore, especially jetties; rare on sand or at fresh water.

BEHAVIOR & FEEDING Bobs frequently while foraging alone for invertebrates. Away from breeding grounds, searches among boulders in intertidal zone, picking mollusks, other invertebrates, fish. Territorial at all seasons, but migrants converge at favored sites; loosely associates with other rocky shorebirds. Strong flight, nesting likely monogamous.

VOCALIZATIONS "Tattles" with whistled *lidididididi* when flushed; other piping calls near nest.

Breeding · OR (Harney County)—May · GREG GILLSON

Breeding · ID (Jefferson County)—Apr · NETTA SMITH

Non-breeding · WA (Pacific County)—Aug · GREGG THOMPSON

Willet
Tringa semipalmata

DESCRIPTION 15 in/38 cm, wingspan 26 in/66 cm. **Sturdy.** Plain looking, grayish. White belly, rump; long **bluish-gray legs**; long stout grayish bill. **Wings flash bold black-and-white pattern** in flight. ***Breeding:*** Browner; lightly barred underparts. ***Non-breeding:*** Uniform grayish upperparts, breast. ***Juvenile:*** Browner; dark bars, pale edging on dorsal feathers.

SIMILAR SPECIES Greater Yellowlegs (p. 164) smaller, slender; yellow legs, thinner bill. Godwits (pp. 167–169) have long, noticeably upturned bills; wing stripe less bold or absent; Hudsonian tail black tipped.

STATUS & DISTRIBUTION Western subspecies *T.s. inornatus* breeds from Prairie Provinces to Nebraska, Colorado, Great Basin; winters coastally to South America. In PNW, fairly common breeder eastern OR (Klamath, Malheur Counties north to Crook, Grant Counties), southern ID, western WY. Migrants rare elsewhere, mostly interior overshoots late Apr–May or coastal transients Jul–Sep; casual to southern BC. Winters locally on coast in BC (Tsawwassen), WA (Tokeland), OR (Newport Bay, Coos Bay, Bandon). Atlantic Coast subspecies (*T.s. semipalmata*) not recorded PNW.

HABITAT ASSOCIATIONS Nests grasslands, shrub-steppe, saltbrush flats adjacent to alkaline lakes, freshwater wetlands; may feed in cultivated fields; winters to coastal estuaries.

BEHAVIOR & FEEDING Forages visually or by touch on marsh or beach by probing, picking, searching under debris for insects, crustaceans, worms, other organisms; outside breeding season, flocks with godwits, Whimbrel; may defend winter feeding territory. Monogamous; adjacent nesting pairs mutually provide defense against predators. Precocial young often abandoned early by parents, left to fend for themselves.

VOCALIZATIONS Varied calls include *pill will willet* song, loud *klilililili* in flight.

Juvenile · ID (Nez Perce County)—Aug · KEITH CARLSON

Breeding · BC (French Creek)—Jul · RALPH HOCKEN

Juvenile · WA (King County)—Aug · GREGG THOMPSON

Greater Yellowlegs
Tringa melanoleuca

DESCRIPTION 13.5 in/34 cm, wingspan 28 in/71 cm. Elegant grayish wader; long bright-**yellow legs**; long slightly **upturned gray-based dark bill**; upperparts speckled whitish, belly white; **plain wings, white rump** visible in flight. *Breeding:* Breast, flanks barred; some back feathers black. *Non-breeding:* Fewer dark feathers. *Juvenile:* Browner; crisp dorsal spotting.

SIMILAR SPECIES Lesser Yellowlegs (p. 165) delicate appearing; all-dark bill straight, shorter—in profile, equal to width of head. Willet (p. 163) stocky, thicker bill, grayish legs. Ruff (p. 179) appears potbellied, drooping bill shorter.

STATUS & DISTRIBUTION Widespread breeder from central Alaska across boreal Canada to Labrador; winters mostly coastally from southwestern BC, Connecticut south to Chile. In PNW, breeds BC, mostly east of Coast Range from Okanagan northward, also Haida Gwaii, northern Vancouver Island; bred 1983–1986 at high elevation in OR (Wallowa County). Migrants fairly common region-wide Mar–May (linger casually through Jun), southbound late Jun–Nov (juveniles peak Sep). Uncommon western lowlands Dec–Feb, but hundreds sometimes converge coastal OR, WA; rarely winters east of crest (south-central WA, casually ID).

HABITAT ASSOCIATIONS Nests bogs, muskeg, boreal ridges; at other seasons, shallow open water, mostly lowlands, often estuaries, tidal flats.

BEHAVIOR & FEEDING Wades in shallows, swings bill side to side, runs to capture mostly insects, small fish. Strong flier; gregarious away from nest, often flocking with other shorebirds. Monogamous pair nests on ground, vigilantly perches in trees, guards precocial young.

VOCALIZATIONS Ringing *tew*, repeated 3–4 times, continuous in alarm; rolling *tee wee* in courtship.

Lesser Yellowlegs
Tringa flavipes

DESCRIPTION 10 in/25 cm, wingspan 24 in/61 cm. **Delicate** grayish wader; long bright-**yellow legs**, fairly **short, straight dark bill**; speckled whitish upperparts, white belly; **plain wings, white rump** visible in flight. ***Breeding:*** Breast finely streaked. ***Nonbreeding:*** Duller. ***Juvenile:*** Crisp dorsal spotting.

SIMILAR SPECIES Greater Yellowlegs (p. 164) more robust; slightly upturned pale-based bill, longer—in profile, 1.5 times width of head. Solitary Sandpiper (p. 161) legs greenish, eye-ring more prominent; Stilt Sandpiper (p. 181) legs greenish, bill tip droops; female Ruff (p. 179) scalloped dorsally, bill droops slightly.

STATUS & DISTRIBUTION Breeds Alaska across Canada to Hudson Bay, south to south-central Alberta; winters central California, southern New Jersey coastally to Caribbean, Mexico, Chile. In PNW, rare breeder BC north from Chilcotin Plateau. Migrates throughout. Uncommon Apr–May, fairly common late Jun–Oct (adults peak Jul; juveniles begin arriving mid-Jul, peak Aug–Sep). Dec–Feb, rare on westside (mainly outer coast, casual southwestern BC); casual east of Cascades (OR/WA/ID). Generally outnumbers Greater Yellowlegs on eastside in fall migration.

HABITAT ASSOCIATIONS Nests open boreal forest, tundra edge; at other seasons, lowland shallow waters including flooded fields. Less likely on tidal flats in PNW than Greater Yellowlegs.

BEHAVIOR & FEEDING Wades, scythes in shallows, taking mostly invertebrates, some fish with bill jabs; snatches insects from air; forms larger flocks than Greater Yellowlegs, but both gather with other shorebirds. Monogamous ground-nesting pair secretive; young precocial.

VOCALIZATIONS Whistled *tew* or *tew tew*, repeated in alarm; rolling *pilee wee* in courtship.

Alberta—Jul · TERRY THORMIN

Upland Sandpiper
Bartramia longicauda

DESCRIPTION 12 in/30 cm, wingspan 27 in/69 cm. Slim, long tailed, with **large dark eye**, yellow legs, brownish dorsal streaking, white belly. **Short yellowish bill** droops slightly; long thin neck gives **pinhead appearance**. In flight, shows **evenly darkish upperparts**, white outermost primary. *Juvenile:* Pale dorsal edging.

SIMILAR SPECIES Long-billed Curlew (p. 171) juvenile with growing bill similar but appears downy; Whimbrel (p. 170) bill longer, strongly decurved; Buff-breasted Sandpiper (p. 180) short necked with black bill. Pectoral Sandpiper (p. 183) eye smaller, lower edge of dark breast sharply defined.

STATUS & DISTRIBUTION Breeds regularly east of Rockies from BC, Maritimes south to northern Oklahoma, New Jersey; fewer Alaska to western Northwest Territories. Winters South America. Once very local PNW breeder; current range uncertain, much contracted; confirmed Lincoln County (MT) 2007, adjacent BC (Grasmere) 2004. Bred into 1990s at Riske Creek (BC), near Spokane/Coeur d'Alene (WA/ID), Valley County (ID), Grant, Umatilla, Union Counties (OR)—all with more recent reports, but no confirmed nesting. Migrants casual throughout—mostly interior May–Jul, coast Jul–Sep.

HABITAT ASSOCIATIONS Nests prairie, heath, upland tundra, airfields, blueberry barrens; winters to pampas. Migrants use open areas.

BEHAVIOR & FEEDING Forages visually, plover-like, in upland fields for invertebrates, some seeds; frequently flocks—feeds communally, nests colonially. Strong migrant, but summering-ground flight stiff winged with shallow strokes. Perches on fence posts; when alighting, often raises wings above back. Monogamous, ground nesting; frequently displays with fluttering wing stroke.

VOCALIZATIONS Hollow gurgled "wolf whistle" in display; ethereal *qui dee dee* in flight.

Breeding Male · BC (Delta)—Sep · DOUGLAS L. BROWN   Juvenile · WA (Skagit County)—Aug · RYAN MERRILL

Hudsonian Godwit
Limosa haemastica

DESCRIPTION 16 in/41 cm, wingspan 30 in/76 cm. Smallest godwit; elegant with **long, upturned pink-based bill**, dark legs, white supercilium, **white-based black tail**; contrasting **black underwing linings**, white wing stripe visible in flight. **Breeding:** Grayish upper-parts, pale head, variably barred rusty breast; females duller, larger. **Non-breeding:** Plain gray with lighter belly. **Juvenile:** Grayish with rusty dorsal edging, white undertail.

SIMILAR SPECIES Bar-tailed Godwit (p. 168) legs shorter, tail finely barred, under-wing grayish brown; Marbled Godwit (p. 169) larger, evenly cinnamon toned; dowitchers (pp. 188–189) smaller, bills straight.

STATUS & DISTRIBUTION Breeds sparingly at widely disjunct sites, northern Alaska to Hudson Bay; winters to South America. Main migration elliptical—northbound through eastern Great Plains, southbound off East Coast in multi-day, non-stop flight over Atlantic. In PNW, southbound migration almost entirely coastal; juveniles rare mid-Aug–early Nov, adults less frequent Jul–Nov. Northbound, casual May, most from east of Cascades/BC Coast Range (predominantly south-central BC, WA Columbia Plateau).

HABITAT ASSOCIATIONS Nests in sedge-dominated tundra, bogs, muskeg inter-spersed with boreal forest; at other seasons, frequents coastal mud flats, freshwater wetland, grassy fields, rocky beaches, estuaries. In PNW, recorded mostly from coastal sites preferred by Marbled Godwits.

BEHAVIOR & FEEDING Probes for food, walking belly deep in water. Takes animal, plant materials including worms, other invertebrates, berries; tubers especially important on southbound migration. Flocks with yellowlegs, dowitchers, Stilt Sandpipers, other shorebirds. Monogamous pair forms on territory; males display, perch vigilantly in trees.

VOCALIZATIONS Quiet when not nesting; sharp rising *toe WHIT* when flushed.

Breeding Female · WA (Pacific County)—Sep · GREGG THOMPSON

Non-breeding · WA (Pacific County)—Oct · DENNIS PAULSON

Juvenile · WA (Pacific County)—Oct · MARV BREECE

Bar-tailed Godwit
Limosa lapponica

DESCRIPTION 16 in/41 cm, wingspan 31 in/79 cm. Elegant. Darkly streaked upperparts; long, upturned pink-based bill, light supercilium, grayish legs; **finely barred tail**, dorsal dark carpal patch, **even-toned underwing** visible in flight. *Breeding:* **Clean rufous underparts**; females larger, much paler. Southbound migrants often tattered (molt on wintering grounds). *Non-breeding:* Black-streaked grayish upperparts, white belly to undertail. *Juvenile:* Darker, crisply patterned back.

SIMILAR SPECIES Hudsonian Godwit (p. 167) smaller with white-based black tail, black underwing linings. Marbled Godwit (p. 169) overall cinnamon (caution needed with faded adults). Curlews (pp. 170–171) show decurved bills.

STATUS & DISTRIBUTION Breeds Scandinavia east to Alaska, winters coastally Britain, China to South Africa, Australasia. Dark-rumped subspecies *L.l. baueri* nests eastern Russia, western Alaska; winters Australia, New Zealand, a few along West Coast to Baja. In PNW, casual May–early Jun, rare Jul–Nov, predominantly WA/OR outer coast, fewer northern Olympic Peninsula coast, southwestern BC; casually lingers through winter. Juvenile vanguard appears late Aug, both age classes occur thereafter. One record of white-rumped Eurasian subspecies from northwestern WA in 2002.

HABITAT ASSOCIATIONS Nests on tundra; at other seasons, uses coastal mud flats, salt marshes.

BEHAVIOR & FEEDING Forages while walking, probing for invertebrates; grazes for berries in north. Flocks into thousands in Eurasia. In PNW, usually found as singles with Marbled Godwits, Black-bellied Plovers, other shorebirds. Non-stop migratory flight from Alaska to southern hemisphere among longest recorded for any bird. Monogamous pair forms on territory; males display, aggressively attack intruders.

VOCALIZATIONS Quiet away from breeding grounds; nasal *kurk kik kew* in flight.

Breeding · *WA (Grays Harbor County)—Apr* · GREGG THOMPSON

WA (Whatcom County)—Apr · GREGG THOMPSON

Marbled Godwit
Limosa fedoa

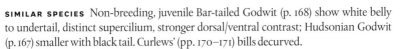

DESCRIPTION 18 in/45 cm, wingspan 30 in/76 cm. Largest godwit; **overall cinnamon toned** with long **upturned mostly pinkish bill**, dark legs. Upperparts darker, heavily marked; **cinnamon underwing** visible in flight. *Breeding:* Underparts darkly barred. *Non-breeding:* Underparts variably fade to pale buff. *Juvenile:* Crisper wing-covert patterning than adult non-breeding but difficult to separate.

SIMILAR SPECIES Non-breeding, juvenile Bar-tailed Godwit (p. 168) show white belly to undertail, distinct supercilium, stronger dorsal/ventral contrast; Hudsonian Godwit (p. 167) smaller with black tail. Curlews' (pp. 170–171) bills decurved.

STATUS & DISTRIBUTION Breeds central Alberta to western Ontario, Montana, South Dakota; also James Bay, Alaska Peninsula; winters coastally from WA, North Carolina to Panama. In PNW, locally common Jul–May outer coast north to Willapa Bay (where over a thousand winter); fairly common in migration north to Haida Gwaii; uncommon/rare northern Olympic coast to southwestern BC (Blackie Spit). A few remain through Jun, mostly outer coast. Irregularly winters southwestern OR (Coos Bay southward); rare/casual elsewhere in western lowlands. In interior, migrants rare late Apr–early Jun, Jul–Sep, but flocks >100 annual Aug–Sep southeastern ID.

HABITAT ASSOCIATIONS Nests shortgrass prairie adjacent to wetland; also upland grassland. James Bay population uses tundra, open taiga. At other seasons, mud flats, beach, pasture, wetlands, mostly at or near coast.

BEHAVIOR & FEEDING Probes for worms, other invertebrates, picks insects, takes some plant materials. Often feeds in belly-deep water. Large winter flocks roost in tight mass, tolerate close proximity while foraging. Monogamous pair defends large territory.

VOCALIZATIONS Raucous; hoarsely whistled *kar WEK*, rolled during interactions.

Whimbrel
Numenius phaeopus

DESCRIPTION 16.5 in/42 cm, wingspan 33 in/84 cm. Godwit-sized curlew, brownish overall with white belly, streaked upperparts, barred underwings. Grayish legs, long decurved bill, dark line through eye; dark crown shows buff median stripe. *Juvenile:* Bolder dorsal spotting, head stripes less distinct.

SIMILAR SPECIES Long-billed Curlew (p. 171) larger, longer billed, with cinnamon underwings, plain crown. Godwits (pp. 167–169) show upturned bills.

STATUS & DISTRIBUTION Holarctic tundra breeder; winters coastally to tropics. In PNW west of Cascades/BC Coast Range, North American subspecies (*N.p. hudsonicus*) common at outer coast mid-Apr–May, Jul–early Aug, also Salish Sea river floodplains on spring migration; uncommon elsewhere. Remains fairly common locally through Jun—e.g., Grays Harbor, Willapa Bay; becomes uncommon Sep–Oct, then rare Nov–Mar (late records coastal). Rare east of crest (mostly May), barely casual Aug–Sep. White-rumped Eurasian form (presumably Siberian subspecies *N.p. variegatus*) accidental WA/OR coast.

HABITAT ASSOCIATIONS Nests tundra, taiga; migrants use tilled fields, heaths, salt marsh, rocky shore, flats; winters in coastal habitats.

BEHAVIOR & FEEDING Forages while walking. Diet varied; picks, probes mostly for crabs, worms, other invertebrates, berries, other plant material. Flocks into hundreds use plowed fields in spring, estuaries (often with godwits) in early summer. Flies strongly, high over land. Spreads out to feed at low tide, often on drier mud, dunes; roosts on beaches, jetties. Juvenile migrants scarce—most overfly PNW. Monogamous pairs nest on ground.

VOCALIZATIONS Varied; whistled, rapidly repeated *whi wi* in flight, also other low whistles.

Male · *WA (Pacific County)—Apr* · GREGG THOMPSON

Breeding Male · *MT (Madison County)—Jul* · KEITH CARLSON

Long-billed Curlew
Numenius americanus

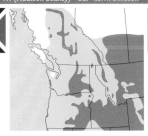

DESCRIPTION 23 in/59 cm, wingspan 36 in/91 cm. **Largest** North American shorebird; streaky brownish dorsally with buff-toned underparts, **finely streaked crown**, grayish legs, extremely **long pink-based sickle-like bill**. In flight, shows **cinnamon underwings**, remiges. *Female:* Bill significantly longer. *Juvenile:* Similar to adult; richer cinnamon, growing bill may be shorter.

SIMILAR SPECIES Smaller Whimbrel (p. 170) grayish brown, shorter billed, with barred underwings, prominent dark head stripes. Marbled Godwit (p. 169) bill upturned.

STATUS & DISTRIBUTION Breeds central BC, Saskatchewan to northeastern California, New Mexico; winters down Pacific, Gulf Coasts to interior Mexico, Costa Rica. In PNW, fairly common local breeder Mar–Jul east of Cascades/BC Coast Range, north in BC to Cariboo–Chilcotin; generally declining, although increasing at northern edge of range. Lingers rarely in south to Oct. Uncommon locally year-round along outer coast north to Grays Harbor, rare to southwestern BC (Blackie Spit). Westside migrants peak Apr but rarely detected—most frequent Willamette Valley, Puget Trough.

HABITAT ASSOCIATIONS Nests shortgrass prairie, large pastures; cultivated fields, especially in north. Winters tidal flats; fields, lakes, lagoons in interior.

BEHAVIOR & FEEDING Forages visually—also by touch, probing burrows. Takes grasshoppers, worms, other invertebrates. May run toward prey. At coast, defends feeding territory, takes mostly crustaceans, some fish; flocks with Whimbrels, godwits, feeding on flats, roosting on beach, marsh, coastal pasture. Strong flight alternates with glides. Monogamous pair nests on ground, defends large breeding territory with flight displays. Male provides most brood care.

VOCALIZATIONS Loud whistled, rising *cur leee ew.*

*Family Scolopacidae—*SANDPIPERS, SNIPES, AND PHALAROPES **171**

Juvenile · WA (Grays Harbor County)—Aug · GREGG THOMPSON

Breeding Male · WA (Grays Harbor County)—May · GREGG THOMPSON

Ruddy Turnstone
Arenaria interpres

DESCRIPTION 9.5 in/24 cm. Stocky with short **orangish legs**, dark chisel-like bill, black tail with white base; **white throat**, underwing. **White back**, inner wing, wing stripe impart **pied impression in flight**. *Breeding:* Harlequin-like with rufous scapulars; marbled black-and-white head, secondary coverts. Females duller. ***Non-breeding:*** Dull brown replaces rufous; brown head. *Juvenile:* Plainer than adult.

SIMILAR SPECIES Black Turnstone (p. 173) legs brownish, throat dark, less white at bend of wing; lacks rufous tones. Larger Surfbird (p. 174) lacks white back patches.

STATUS & DISTRIBUTION Circumpolar, mostly coastal breeder in High Arctic; winters coastally, in Americas mostly from California, Massachusetts to Tierra del Fuego. In PNW west of Cascades/BC Coast Range, fairly common late Apr–mid May on outer coast, uncommon in protected waters, irregularly to inland valleys; Jul–Sep fairly common OR coast, uncommon along coast farther north; rare Oct–Mar. Casual east of crest May, Jul–Sep.

HABITAT ASSOCIATIONS Nests rocky coast, tundra; outside of breeding season, uses marine flats, pebbly beaches, jetties, log booms; rarely plowed fields, freshwater wetland.

BEHAVIOR & FEEDING Forages opportunistically. Pries mussels, turns debris, raids bird nests for eggs, captures arthropods, marine organisms with bill; takes carrion, plant material, also horseshoe crab eggs (East Coast). Often flocks with other shorebirds but defends feeding territory. Long-term pair bond probable; male guards female, nest site tenaciously against conspecifics. Pair builds ground nest; female provides most nest attendance.

VOCALIZATIONS Noisy with chattering, low nasal rattles in alarm; offers more complex calls while nesting.

WA (Grays Harbor County)—Aug · DOUGLAS L. BROWN

Breeding · WA (Grays Harbor County)—Apr · RYAN SHAW

Juvenile · WA (Grays Harbor County)—Aug · GREGG THOMPSON

Black Turnstone
Arenaria melanocephala

DESCRIPTION 9.25 in/23 cm. Stocky with **brownish legs**, chisel-like bill, **dark throat**, black tail with white base. White back, underwing, inner wing, wing stripe all impart **pied impression in flight**. *Breeding:* Black dorsally; white patches above, below eye. *Non-breeding:* Browner, face fairly plain. *Juvenile:* Duller, olive tinged.

SIMILAR SPECIES Ruddy Turnstone (p. 172) has orangish legs, white throat, white at bend of wing prominent; upperparts show rufous-toned edging. Larger Surfbird (p. 174) lacks white on back.

STATUS & DISTRIBUTION Breeds almost entirely on Alaskan coastal tundra, Cape Hope south to Alaskan Peninsula; winters along coast Kodiak Island to Baja California. In PNW, common in preferred marine habitat Jul–early May (uncommon southern Puget Sound); a few stragglers summer rarely. Casual east of Cascades/BC Coast Range (OR, WA, northwestern MT, BC), also inland OR west of crest. Largest flocks (low thousands in BC) occur at peak northward movement Apr–early May. Southbound vanguard arrives Jun (Haida Gwaii); migration protracted to Nov.

HABITAT ASSOCIATIONS Nests coastal tundra, scarce in uplands; at other seasons, rocky coastline, jetties, log booms, pebbly beaches, fewer on mud flats; rare in plowed fields, uplands.

BEHAVIOR & FEEDING Takes insects, other invertebrates, seeds, birds' eggs, carrion, intertidal organisms pried from substrate or exposed by turning debris. Flocks frequently with Surfbirds, Rock Sandpipers; acts as de facto sentinel with alarm calls. Mate, site fidelity high; pair builds ground nest, male provides most brood attendance.

VOCALIZATIONS Highly vocal; shrill chatter, high prolonged rattle when flushed.

Non-breeding · OR (Tillamook County)—Jan · GREG GILLSON

Juvenile · WA (King County)—Sep · GREGG THOMPSON

Breeding · WA (Grays Harbor County)—Apr · RYAN SHAW

Surfbird
Calidris virgata

DESCRIPTION 10 in/25 cm, wingspan 26 in/66 cm. Stocky; grayish with white belly, **yellow legs**, **stout yellow-based dark bill**; broad wing stripe, **white-based black tail** visible in flight. **Breeding:** Dark ventral chevrons; streaky-whitish head, neck; variably rufous scapulars (bleached pale by summer). **Non-breeding:** Plain grayish; white belly with fine flecks. **Juvenile:** Browner with pale wing-covert edging.

SIMILAR SPECIES Turnstones (pp. 172–173) smaller, white visible on back in flight; Wandering Tattler (p. 162) has long bill, plain gray wings, tail; Rock Sandpiper (p. 175) smaller with longer, drooping bill, dark rump.

STATUS & DISTRIBUTION Breeds Alaska, Yukon on alpine tundra; winters Kodiak Island south along coast to Chile. In PNW, fairly common in preferred coastal habitat Jul–early May, except rare Puget Sound south of Seattle; lingers casually to Jun. Flocks number to 2,000 (BC), smaller farther south. Juveniles join faded adults by Aug.

HABITAT ASSOCIATIONS Nests middle to high elevation on rocky alpine tundra; outside breeding season, rocky coasts, jetties, log booms; less frequently sand, mud flats.

BEHAVIOR & FEEDING Appears rather sluggish, often allowing close approach. Takes insects in mountains while breeding; at other seasons, forages on rocks, using whole body to pry bivalves, barnacles from substrate; pokes under seaweed for other invertebrates, fish roe; eats some algae. Flocks frequently with turnstones, Rock Sandpipers, but defends feeding territory. Little studied on remote breeding grounds; presumed monogamous, but often sociable, weakly territorial near nests.

VOCALIZATIONS Seldom heard. Aggressive squeaks while feeding; near nest, harsh, repeated calls, "laughs."

Non-breeding · WA (Grays Harbor County)—Jan · RYAN SHAW   Breeding · WA (Grays Harbor County)—May · GREGG THOMPSON

Rock Sandpiper
Calidris ptilocnemis

DESCRIPTION 8.5 in/22 cm. **Portly**; relatively **short drooping bill**, short yellowish legs; wing stripe visible in flight. **Breeding:** Whitish face, dark auriculars, variably rufous upperparts, lower **breast blackish**, dark legs. **Non-breeding:** Grayish upperparts; white ventrally, dark spots breast to flanks; **yellowish bill base**. **Juvenile:** Dorsal pale edging, rufous scapulars (rarely seen south of BC). Larger subspecies *C.p. ptilocnemis* paler in non-breeding plumage; brighter, Dunlin-like in breeding.

SIMILAR SPECIES Dunlin (p. 176) less paunchy; longer bill, legs. Turnstones, Surfbird (pp. 172–174) have short bills, white tail bases.

STATUS & DISTRIBUTION Pacific counterpart of Purple Sandpiper of eastern North America, western Europe—similar, sometimes considered conspecific. Breeds along coast from Russian Far East, Seward Peninsula, Bering Sea islands, Aleutians, to Alaska Peninsula, Kodiak Island; winters coastally Aleutians to Japan, northern California. In PNW, Oct–early May locally fairly common BC, uncommon WA outer coast, rare to locally common Puget Sound, OR; uncommon Aug–Sep in north (Haida Gwaii, Prince Rupert). Pribilof-breeding *C.p. ptilocnemis* accidental.

HABITAT ASSOCIATIONS Nests coastal tundra; rarely montane tundra, disturbed areas; limited to rocky shore, jetties in PNW, but also uses tidal flats in Alaska outside of breeding.

BEHAVIOR & FEEDING Picks sluggishly, scythes through algae for marine invertebrates in intertidal habitat, usually within spray zone. Tight flocks number to thousands in north, <50 in PNW. Flocks with other rocky shorebirds, feeding when tide drops; eats insects while nesting. Nests in ground scrape; monogamous pair shares parental care.

VOCALIZATIONS Squeaky *chert*; complex trills near nest.

Breeding · BC (Delta)—May · LEE BARNES

Non-breeding · BC (Victoria)—Apr · GERALD ROMANCHUK

Dunlin
Calidris alpina

DESCRIPTION 8 in/20 cm. Hunched appearance. Short neck, dark legs, long **dark bill with drooping tip**; wing stripe visible in flight. *Breeding:* Plumage attained Apr; mostly **rufous upperparts** with **black belly,** whitish face, breast. *Non-breeding:* **Plain brownish gray** with white belly, faint supercilium. *Juvenile:* Browner with light feather edging, blackish belly (plumage not seen in PNW).

SIMILAR SPECIES Larger, plainer gray with longer bill than "peeps" (pp. 184–185, 187). Stilt Sandpiper's (p. 181) bill droops only slightly; greenish, longer legs. Non-breeding Curlew Sandpiper (not shown; casual in PNW) looks longer legged with white rump, evenly drooping bill. Baird's Sandpiper (p. 186) smaller with straight bill; folded wings extend beyond tail.

STATUS & DISTRIBUTION Circumpolar; nests to Arctic, winters south to subtropics. Subspecies *C.a. pacifica* nests southwestern Alaska, winters coastally BC to Baja California—majority in PNW. Common Oct–May west of Cascades/BC Coast Range with flocks into tens of thousands at outer coast, Fraser Delta, northern Puget Sound, Willamette Valley; east of crest, flocks to hundreds, uncommon Oct–Apr (rare in small numbers BC). A few remain Jun–Sep, mostly on outer coast.

HABITAT ASSOCIATIONS Nests moist tundra; at other seasons, beaches, tidal flats; lowland lakeshores, muddy fields, estuaries.

BEHAVIOR & FEEDING Picks or probes mud for invertebrates, some plant material. Feeds at low tide, forms huge roosts. Tight, swirling flocks appear smokelike in distant views. Monogamous pair defends tundra territory; male provides more parental care, rarely maintains second female.

VOCALIZATIONS In flight emits harsh *kreev*; trills, whinnies near nest.

Juvenile · WA (Grays Harbor County)—Sep · GREGG THOMPSON

Non-breeding · WA (Whatcom County)—Apr · DOUGLAS L. BROWN

Breeding · WA (Grays Harbor County)—May · GREGG THOMPSON

Sanderling
Calidris alba

DESCRIPTION 7.5 in/19 cm. Thick necked, stout with straight **blunt-tipped black bill**, white underparts; **broad white wing stripe** visible in flight. Black legs, feet without hind toe. *Breeding:* Mottled-rufous head, neck, upper breast, back. *Non-breeding:* **Pale-gray upperparts.** *Juvenile:* Spangled blackish dorsally, black bend of wing; buff breast in fresh plumage.

SIMILAR SPECIES Other small sandpipers (pp. 184–187) have hind toe, darker non-breeding plumage. Breeding Red-necked, Little Stints (not shown; casual in PNW) rufous washed, but smaller with thinner bills. Semipalmated Sandpiper (p. 184) smaller, less bull necked, lacks black at bend of wing.

STATUS & DISTRIBUTION Circumpolar High Arctic breeder; winters coastally throughout temperate, tropical latitudes (in Americas, southeastern Alaska, Maritimes to Tierra del Fuego). In PNW, locally common along coasts Jul–May (rare Jun). Common on outer coastal beaches (highest reported densities in North America), spottily distributed Salish Sea, rocky BC central coast; rare western lowlands away from coast. Rare May–early Jun east of Cascades/BC Coast Range, locally uncommon Jul–Oct with counts over a hundred possible from Potholes (WA), Harney Lake (OR).

HABITAT ASSOCIATIONS Nests tundra ridges, migrates to sandy beaches; also mud flats, alkaline lakeshore, rocky shore.

BEHAVIOR & FEEDING Forages on beach above incoming waves, running like windup toy. Picks, repeatedly probes, for invertebrates; takes insects while nesting. Post-breeding, roosts, feeds in flocks, often with other shorebirds; raises back feathers while defending feeding territory. On breeding grounds, females may mate sequentially with more than one male.

VOCALIZATIONS Noisy, sharp *kwip*, rapid twitter on beaches; complex variety near nest.

Breeding · *WA (Grays Harbor County)—May* · GREGG THOMPSON | Juvenile molting to Non-breeding · *WA (Pacific County)—Nov* · RYAN

Red Knot
Calidris canutus

DESCRIPTION 10 in/25 cm, wingspan 24 in/61 cm. **Chunky**, pot bellied with horizontal posture, long wings, fairly **short blackish bill**; shows **pale rump**, wing stripe, gray tail in flight. *Breeding:* Striking **pinkish-rust head to belly**; bluish-gray crown, mottled black/rust upperparts. *Non-breeding:* Gray; white supercilium, belly. *Juvenile:* Like non-breeding, with neatly fringed upperparts.

SIMILAR SPECIES Black-bellied Plover (p. 153) larger; short bill, black axillaries. Sanderling (p. 177) mostly white ventrally in breeding plumage, pale in non-breeding. Breeding dowitchers (pp. 188–189) less pinkish; long bill. Dunlin's (p. 176) longer bill droops at tip.

STATUS & DISTRIBUTION Breeds High Arctic, central Siberia east to Greenland. Winters locally temperate, tropical latitudes on coast—North American breeders California, Massachusetts, Britain to Chile. Irregular in PNW. Along outer coast, uncommon (OR) to sometimes common late Apr–early Jun (mid-May peaks of thousands Willapa Bay to Grays Harbor); many fewer Jul–Nov, casual Dec–Mar north to southwestern BC. Rare May, Aug–Sep Fraser Delta, Puget Sound. Casual inland.

HABITAT ASSOCIATIONS Nests elevated tundra; stages, winters on tidal inlets, mud flats, beaches; rarely rocky shore, inland lakeshore, tilled fields.

BEHAVIOR & FEEDING Relaxed demeanor while foraging at low tide for marine invertebrates; roosts at high tide, often with other shorebirds—in PNW, especially Black-bellied Plover, dowitchers. Swift, powerful flier; makes long, non-stop movements over water between food-rich stopovers. Monogamous pair eats terrestrial invertebrates, nests on ground; male provides brood care.

VOCALIZATIONS Whistles near nest in display, otherwise quiet; soft *ker rit* in flight.

Juvenile · OR (Washington County)—Oct
GREG GILLSON

Juvenile · WA (Grays Harbor County)—Sep · GREGG THOMPSON

Breeding Male · Romania—Apr · CRISTIAN MIHAI

Ruff
Calidris pugnax

DESCRIPTION 12 in/30 cm, wingspan 21 in/53 cm (averages; female significantly smaller than male). **Stocky** with small head, **short slightly drooping bill**, adult legs yellowish to pinkish or orangish; white U-shaped rump, weak wing stripe visible in flight. ***Breeding:*** Male has black, reddish or whitish **decorative ruff, facial warts**, black breast; bill usually orangish, black tipped. Female ("reeve") breast variably blackish, black bill (base sometimes red). ***Non-breeding:*** Dark upperparts with pale scalloping, whitish underparts; dark bill. ***Juvenile:*** Buffy head to breast, **upperparts evenly scalloped with buff**; white belly, dark bill, dull-**greenish legs**.

SIMILAR SPECIES Buff-breasted Sandpiper (p. 180) smaller, straight billed, dark rumped. Yellowlegs (pp. 164–165) more gracile, bills thinner, legs bright yellow. Sharp-tailed Sandpiper (p. 182) has bold supercilium.

STATUS & DISTRIBUTION Breeds across Eurasian boreal zone, England to Siberia; winters Ireland east to Australia (mostly Africa); regular vagrant to North American coasts. In PNW, appears almost any month: rare Aug–early Oct (mostly juveniles), casual Nov–Jul. Highest numbers in western lowlands, especially near coast; casual east of Cascades/BC Coast Range to ID (most records from south-central WA).

HABITAT ASSOCIATIONS Nests moist tundra, grassy marsh; at other seasons uses mud flats, coastal marsh, flooded fields, sewage ponds.

BEHAVIOR & FEEDING Picks while wading for invertebrates, tiny vertebrates, seeds. Migrants flock by thousands in Old World. In PNW, usually found as singles or in small groups with yellowlegs. Breeding males dance at leks. Breeding system complex; no pair bond, females provide parental care.

VOCALIZATIONS Quiet; low, grunted calls.

Juvenile · *WA (Grays Harbor County)—Aug* · GREGG THOMPSON

Buff-breasted Sandpiper
Calidris subruficollis

DESCRIPTION 8 in/20 cm. Sleek, small headed with thin neck, upright posture, **short black bill**, **yellow legs**, plain face, white underwing; upperparts appear dark in flight. *Adult:* Buffy head to belly with white vent, **buffy dorsal fringing**; underwing flight feathers darkly mottled. Breeding/non-breeding similar. *Juvenile:* Dorsal fringing whiter, underwing plainer.

SIMILAR SPECIES Ruff (p. 179) larger with drooping bill, contrasting white uppertail coverts in flight. Baird's Sandpiper (p. 186) less upright, longer bill, dark legs. Upland Sandpiper (p. 166) larger, yellow billed, with dark ventral markings.

STATUS & DISTRIBUTION High Arctic breeder, Wrangel Island east to Baffin Bay; winters Paraguay to Argentina. Adults migrate almost entirely through center of continent. In PNW, juveniles rare Aug–early Oct, vast majority outer coast late Aug–early Sep; less frequent westside lowlands away from coast; casual east of Cascades/BC Coast Range. Adults accidental Apr–May.

HABITAT ASSOCIATIONS Breeds drier tundra ridges, winters cattle-grazed pampas, coastal marsh; in migration, often far from water on open short-grass habitats including turf farms, pasture, *Salicornia*, high beach, drying lake margins.

BEHAVIOR & FEEDING Forages with high-stepping gait, also runs, stops to pick prey, plover-like. Takes arthropods, other invertebrates, seeds. Defends feeding territory in migration. In PNW, small groups or individuals the norm, sometimes associating with Killdeer, other plovers. Breeding males gather at expansive leks, display by raising one or both wings; may mate with several females. No pair bond formed. Females nest, rear young alone.

VOCALIZATIONS Quiet, reedy *breeet* in flight; males *tick* repeatedly in display.

Juvenile · WA (Grays Harbor County)—Sep · GREGG THOMPSON | Breeding · Alberta—May · TERRY THORMIN

Stilt Sandpiper
Calidris himantopus

DESCRIPTION 9 in/23 cm. Graceful, long necked; long **greenish-yellow legs**, long dark **bill with drooping tip**; whitish supercilium; **plain wings, white rump** visible in flight. ***Breeding:*** Darkly mottled upperparts, dark ventral barring; rufous in crown, auriculars. ***Non-breeding:*** Plain gray above, whitish below. ***Juvenile:*** Upperparts crisply fringed, underparts variably peach toned fading to whitish.

SIMILAR SPECIES Lesser Yellowlegs (p. 165) straight billed, bright-yellow legs; dowitchers (pp. 188–189) larger with longer, straight bill; Curlew Sandpiper (not shown; casual in PNW) thinner with shorter, black legs, more strongly drooping bill; Dunlin (p. 176) legs shorter, dark.

STATUS & DISTRIBUTION Breeds from northern Alaska disjunctly along Arctic coast to James Bay; winters south from extreme southern US, Mexico (majority to South America). Migrates mostly Great Plains eastward, many overflying Gulf/Caribbean. In PNW, juveniles rare (BC) to irregularly uncommon Aug–Oct both sides of Cascades (especially WA); double-digit counts occasional at mid-Aug peak. Adults casual May–Aug, predominantly east of crest.

HABITAT ASSOCIATIONS Nests on open sedge-dominated tundra; at other seasons, fresh water including sewage ponds, muddy fields, flooded pasture, pond margins. Rare in marine habitat.

BEHAVIOR & FEEDING Forages deliberately, walking belly deep in water like dowitcher but bill probing closer to body, tail held higher, head frequently submerged; takes mostly insects, some invertebrates, seeds. Monogamous bond forms on territory in conjunction with male displays, may last through several seasons. Pair nests on ground; female deserts young soon after hatch.

VOCALIZATIONS Quiet *tew* in flight; buzzy trills, "laughs" near nest.

Juvenile • *WA (Skagit County)—Sep* • RYAN MERRILL

Sharp-tailed Sandpiper
Calidris acuminata

DESCRIPTION 8.25 in/21 cm. Plump, brownish. Dark, slightly drooping bill, **fairly long pale legs**, weak wing stripe in flight; **white eye-ring, supercilium contrast with rufous cap.** *Breeding:* Bold spots, chevrons, breast to undertail (duller non-breeding plumage not seen in PNW). *Juvenile:* Colorful (intensity varies); well-delineated reddish cap, white "braces" down back, **unstreaked rufous upper breast.**

SIMILAR SPECIES Pectoral Sandpiper's (p. 183) streaked upper breast contrasts with white belly; shorter legs, pale bill. Baird's Sandpiper (p. 186) smaller with blackish legs, folded wings extending beyond tail. Dowitchers (pp. 188–189) much longer billed.

STATUS & DISTRIBUTION Asian species; breeds northern Siberia, winters Melanesia to Australasia. Adults migrate directly to/from wintering grounds; juveniles fly east to Pacific (many stage at Yukon-Kuskokwim Delta), continue south over ocean. In PNW, juveniles rare Sep–Nov (accidental Dec) with peak in early Oct; aggregations rarely number to double digits—most from BC (Haida Gwaii, Fraser Delta, southeastern Vancouver Island), WA (Port Susan, Grays Harbor, Dungeness), OR (Bandon, Willamette Valley); many fewer east of Cascades/BC Coast Range, mostly from south-central WA; accidental to ID, northwestern MT. Adults casual/accidental late Apr–May, Jul–Aug.

HABITAT ASSOCIATIONS Nests on tundra; when sharing habitat with Pectoral Sandpiper, prefers drier nest sites; at other seasons, marine or freshwater grassy marshes, muddy fields, mud flats.

BEHAVIOR & FEEDING Picks, probes for invertebrates; crouches to avoid detection. In PNW, often with Pectoral Sandpipers, dowitchers. Breeding males provide no parental care, leave territory before females.

VOCALIZATIONS Soft whistled *tu wheet* repeated in flight.

Breeding · *Alaska—Jun* · GREGG THOMPSON | Juvenile · *WA (Snohomish County)—Sep* · GREGG THOMPSON

Pectoral Sandpiper
Calidris melanotos

DESCRIPTION 8.5 in/22 cm. Bulky, brownish. Fairly **heavy drooping bill, yellowish legs**; densely **streaked breast abruptly contrasts with white belly**. Wings show weak stripe in flight. *Breeding:* Brown breast, streaks fairly heavy (duller non-breeding plumage not seen in PNW). *Juvenile:* Brighter. Buffy breast, finely streaked; crisply marked upperparts with white "braces" down back; crown streaked rufous, light supercilium prominent.

SIMILAR SPECIES Sharp-tailed Sandpiper (p. 182) juvenile has distinct reddish cap, unstreaked buffy breast; adult has dark chevrons ventrally. Least Sandpiper (p. 187) much smaller, breast border less distinct.

STATUS & DISTRIBUTION Breeds on Arctic tundra from Russia (Taymyr Peninsula) east to Hudson Bay; winters Peru to southern Argentina, fewer to South Pacific islands. In PNW, uncommon Jul–Aug (mostly adults), fairly common Sep–early Nov (mostly juveniles), evenly distributed both sides Cascades/BC Coast Range. Irregular but generally rare on spring passage (May), preponderantly near coast.

HABITAT ASSOCIATIONS Nests flat, marshy tundra; migrants often away from water, using sedge-filled ditches, grassy puddles, tilled fields, pasture, *Salicornia*, mud flats, pond margins; winters grassy fields, wetlands.

BEHAVIOR & FEEDING Forages for aquatic, terrestrial invertebrates, some plant materials; crouches when aerial predators approach. PNW flocks usually small, tame, difficult to detect. Strong flier; bulk of population makes marathon migratory flights through Great Plains in single-species flocks. May join other shorebirds while fattening up at stopovers. Larger, promiscuous male develops bulging chest sac, defends large territory, leaves parental care to females.

VOCALIZATIONS Flight call *drrrit*, complex song. Male displays with low hooting.

Juvenile · WA (King County)—Aug · GREGG THOMPSON | Breeding · ID (Jefferson County)—May · DARREN CLARK

Semipalmated Sandpiper
Calidris pusilla

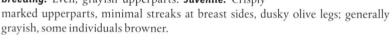

DESCRIPTION 5.75 in/15 cm. Grayish with short, **straight blunt-tipped bill**, blackish legs, whitish supercilium; white wing stripe visible in flight. *Breeding:* Fairly drab; black-centered scapulars, **minimal rufous** on mantle, **ventral streaking limited** to upper breast. *Non-breeding:* Even, grayish upperparts. *Juvenile:* Crisply marked upperparts, minimal streaks at breast sides, dusky olive legs; generally grayish, some individuals browner.

SIMILAR SPECIES Western Sandpiper (p. 185) has fine-tipped drooping bill; breeding shows bright rufous upperparts, black chevrons breast to flanks; juvenile has rufous scapulars. Least Sandpiper (p. 187) smaller, slighter; yellowish legs, dusky breast. Baird's Sandpiper (p. 186) has thinner bill; folded wings extend beyond tail. Sanderling (p. 177) larger without hind toe.

STATUS & DISTRIBUTION Breeds northeastern Siberia across northern Canada to Labrador; most winter coastally southern Mexico, Hispaniola to South America. Main migration east of Rockies. In PNW, locally uncommon throughout late Jun–Sep, rare May (peak early in month). Most numerous BC (Fraser Delta, Boundary Bay, Victoria), WA (Port Susan, Whidbey Island, Grant County), rare OR. Juvenile passage begins mid-Jul.

HABITAT ASSOCIATIONS Nests shrubby tundra, sedge marsh. At other seasons, soft mud flats, pond margins, beaches; prefers fresh water in PNW.

BEHAVIOR & FEEDING Picks, probes for aquatic invertebrates in mud. While nesting, takes terrestrial prey, some seeds. Staging East Coast migrants take horseshoe crab eggs; fewer use marine microhabitats in PNW. Flocks with other shorebirds. Males arrive first on breeding grounds, supply multiple nest scrapes, most parental care.

VOCALIZATIONS In flight, thin *cheet*, husky *chert*; complex calls while nesting.

Non-breeding · WA (Grant County)—Aug · RYAN SHAW

Breeding · WA (Grays Harbor County)—May · GREGG THOMPSON

Juvenile · WA (Grays Harbor County)—Aug · RYAN SHAW

Western Sandpiper
Calidris mauri

DESCRIPTION 6.25 in/16 cm. Small with **fairly long, fine-tipped drooping bill**, blackish legs, whitish supercilium; white wing stripe visible in flight. *Breeding:* Rufous on face, crown, upperparts; **black chevrons breast to flanks**. *Non-breeding:* Grayish upperparts, white underparts. *Juvenile:* Browner; **even row of rufous-fringed scapulars**, pale covert edging, olive-tinged legs.

SIMILAR SPECIES Least Sandpiper (p. 187) smaller; finer bill, yellowish legs, dusky breast. Semipalmated Sandpiper (p. 184) has short, straight, blunt-tipped bill; smaller head, neck; juvenile lacks rufous scapulars. Baird's Sandpiper (p. 186) larger; straight bill; folded wings extend beyond tail. Non-breeding Dunlin (p. 176) larger, plainer with longer bill.

STATUS & DISTRIBUTION Breeds eastern Siberia to western Alaska, disjunctly northern coast; winters coastally southwestern BC, New Jersey to South America, also interior Mexico. Most numerous shorebird in PNW. Common in western lowlands Apr–May, late Jun–Nov; rare early Jun. Dec–Mar, uncommon outer coast, rare Salish Sea, Willamette Valley. East of Cascades/BC Coast Range fairly common late Jun–Oct, uncommon (OR) to rare (BC) Apr–May, accidental Nov–Mar.

HABITAT ASSOCIATIONS Lowlands to mid-elevation. Nests wet tundra; at other seasons beaches, mud flats, pond margins, marshes.

BEHAVIOR & FEEDING Probes, picks invertebrates, microbes, other organic material from mud while wading, walking. Flocks into hundreds of thousands on migration, often with Dunlin, dowitchers. Roosts tightly at high tide above most other shorebirds on beach. Male arrives first on breeding grounds, supplies nest scrapes, shares parental care.

VOCALIZATIONS In flight, squeaked *dcheet*; twitters in aggression; scratchy trills near nest.

Family Scolopacidae—SANDPIPERS, SNIPES, AND PHALAROPES **185**

Baird's Sandpiper
Calidris bairdii

DESCRIPTION 7.5 in/18 cm. Brownish with **thin straight bill**, blackish legs, dusky upper breast, diffuse pale supercilium; wing stripe visible in flight. **Folded wings extend beyond tail.** *Breeding:* Grayer with black-centered scapulars. *Non-breeding:* Brownish gray with light dorsal edging. *Juvenile:* Buffy breast, **upperparts broadly scalloped** with whitish edging.

SIMILAR SPECIES Folded wings on smaller PNW sandpipers do not extend beyond tail. Least Sandpiper (p. 187) has yellowish legs; Western Sandpiper's (p. 185) bill droops; Semipalmated Sandpiper (p. 184) short bill with blunt tip. Sharp-tailed, Pectoral Sandpipers (pp. 182–183) larger, bulky with yellowish legs.

STATUS & DISTRIBUTION Breeds in High Arctic, eastern Siberia east to Greenland; winters in lowlands, mountains south from Ecuador. Most adults make long, speedy migration through interior North America, overflying much of temperate latitudes. In PNW, more frequent east of Cascades/BC Coast Range, increasingly toward WY; preponderance of westside records from outer coast. Juveniles uncommon Aug–Oct (locally common Aug BC, northwestern MT), adults rare Apr–May, Jul–Aug (uncommon BC), accidental Nov–Jan. Migrants regular in subalpine Aug–early Sep.

HABITAT ASSOCIATIONS Nests dry tundra, lowlands to mountain ridges; other seasons drying mud flats, lake margins, marshes, wet fields, alpine runoff zones, beaches.

BEHAVIOR & FEEDING Captures insects, some spiders, crustaceans, walking primarily on higher ground. In PNW, flocks usually number fewer than a hundred; often feeds with other shorebirds but higher on beaches, shorelines. Monogamous pair forms scrape nest in gravel, male supplies most parental care.

VOCALIZATIONS Flight call grating, rolled *creeep*; more complex calls near nest.

Non-breeding · BC (Delta)—Sep · JOHN GORDON

Breeding · WA (King County)—Apr · GREGG THOMPSON

Juvenile · BC (Sidney)—Sep · TED ARDLEY

Least Sandpiper
Calidris minutilla

DESCRIPTION 5 in/13 cm. Smallest sandpiper; brownish with short wings, short **fine-tipped drooping bill**, **yellowish legs**, whitish supercilium; **dusky upper breast**, whitish belly. Wing stripe visible in flight. ***Breeding:*** Dark; black-centered scapulars, upperwing coverts. ***Non-breeding:*** Grayish-brown upperparts. ***Juvenile:*** Rufous toned; crisply marked upperparts, white "braces" down back.

SIMILAR SPECIES Western Sandpiper (p. 185) larger with longer bill, dark legs; Semipalmated Sandpiper (p. 184) blunt-tipped bill, cleaner breast, dark legs; Pectoral Sandpiper (p. 183) much larger, proportionately longer legs. Larger Baird's Sandpiper (p. 186) has straight bill, dark legs; folded wings extend beyond tail.

STATUS & DISTRIBUTION Breeds Alaska to Labrador, south to northern BC, Nova Scotia; winters south from southwestern BC, Carolinas to interior southern US, South America. In PNW, breeds locally BC (Haida Gwaii, Chilcotin Plateau); rare elsewhere during Jun. Widespread, common Mar–May, Jul–Oct. Fairly common outer coast Nov–Feb, uncommon Salish Sea, Willamette Valley, casual north to Haida Gwaii, rare east of Cascades.

HABITAT ASSOCIATIONS Nests boggy tundra, boreal sedge meadow; at other seasons, mud flats, pond edge, coastal marsh, beaches, muddy fields.

BEHAVIOR & FEEDING Pecks or probes for insects, other small invertebrates; frequently in small groups but occurs in thousands at migration peaks (in PNW, adults early Jul, juveniles late Aug). Habitually not shy—crouches alertly but allows close approach. Roosts at high tide at upper edge of shorebird flocks on beach. Male arrives first on breeding grounds, supplies nest scrape, most parental care.

VOCALIZATIONS Flight call *pree eet*; complex song, calls near nest.

Non-breeding · *Texas—Dec* · DENNIS PAULSON

Juvenile · *OR (Coos County)—Aug* · GREG GILLSON

Breeding "Pacific" · *WA (Grays Harbor County)—May* · JOSEPH V. HIGBEE

Short-billed Dowitcher
Limnodromus griseus

DESCRIPTION 11 in/28 cm, wingspan 19 in/48 cm. Chunky with **long straight bill,** finely banded tail, greenish legs, whitish supercilium; pale secondaries, **white wedge on lower back** visible in flight. *Breeding:* "Pacific" subspecies upperparts mottled black/rufous; **rufous breast, white lower belly, heavily barred flanks.** "Prairie" subspecies rufous ventrally to undertail; brighter than "Pacific" dorsally. *Non-breeding:* Grayish; white belly. *Juvenile:* Rusty cap, breast; coverts fringed rufous, **tertials show rusty markings**.

SIMILAR SPECIES Long-billed Dowitcher's (p. 189) back rounder; breeding adult solid rufous ventrally, juvenal tertials gray, plain. Wilson's Snipe's (p. 190) head, back white striped. Stilt Sandpiper (p. 181) smaller with longer legs.

STATUS & DISTRIBUTION Nests southern Alaska to Labrador, winters coastally US to South America. "Pacific" (*L.g. caurinus*) nests Kodiak Island to southern Yukon, Haida Gwaii; "Prairie" (*L.g. hendersoni*) nests central Alberta to northern Ontario. In PNW west of Cascades/BC Coast Range, "Pacific" common coastally, uncommon inland valleys (late Mar–mid-May, late Jun–Oct, rarely to Dec); has bred BC (Masset). East of crest uncommon Aug–Sep (primarily juveniles), rare May–Jul (adults). "Prairie" rarely reported; "Atlantic" (*L.g. griseus*) unrecorded.

HABITAT ASSOCIATIONS Nests taiga; at other seasons, prefers salt water, tidal flats, beaches, marsh, wet fields.

BEHAVIOR & FEEDING Probes in shallows like sewing machine for invertebrates, some plant material; flocks with other shorebirds, numbering to tens of thousands at Grays Harbor. Monogamous, but remains social while nesting; frequently perches on trees on territory; males provide most chick attendance.

VOCALIZATIONS Rapidly whistled *tlu tu tu tu* most frequent.

Breeding · ID (Jefferson County)—May · DARREN CLARK

Juveniles · ID (Nez Perce County)—Oct · KEITH CARLSON

Juvenile · WA (Snohomish County)—Sep · GREGG THOMPSON

Juvenile molting to Non-breeding · WA (Grays Harbor County)
Oct · RYAN SHAW

Long-billed Dowitcher
Limnodromus scolopaceus

DESCRIPTION 11.5 in/29 cm, wingspan 19 in/48 cm. Chunky with **long straight bill**, finely banded tail, greenish legs, whitish supercilium; pale secondaries, **white wedge on lower back** visible in flight. *Breeding:* Upperparts darkly mottled; **rusty ventrally to undertail**, subtle barring at sides of upper breast. *Non-breeding:* Grayish; white belly. *Juvenile:* Browner than non-breeding adult, with buffy breast, pale dorsal edging.

SIMILAR SPECIES Short-billed Dowitcher (p. 188) smaller with flatter back, wider white tail-barring, shorter bill on average. In breeding plumage, sides of upper breast finely spotted (versus barred), belly whitish (versus rufous) to undertail, barred flanks. Juvenile brighter with internal tertial markings.

STATUS & DISTRIBUTION Breeds High Arctic coastal plain, Taymyr Peninsula (Russia) east to western Northwest Territories; winters southwestern BC, Carolinas south to El Salvador. In PNW, west of Cascades/BC Coast Range, fairly common Apr–May, Jul–Nov; uncommon Dec–Mar (mostly WA, OR). East of crest, common May, Jul–Nov; rarely lingers Dec–Mar in OR, south-central WA. Highest counts thousands (adults), tens of thousands (juveniles) from Lake, Harney Counties (OR). A few linger through Jun throughout PNW.

HABITAT ASSOCIATIONS Nests grassy tundra; at other seasons, prefers fresh water, mud flats, marshes, alkaline lake margins, muddy fields; rarely marine in PNW.

BEHAVIOR & FEEDING Like Short-billed Dowitcher, but mostly freshwater habitats; takes invertebrates, some seeds by probing. In PNW, flocks with Dunlin, Black-bellied Plover in winter. Presumed monogamous breeder but apparently more social than Short-billed.

VOCALIZATIONS Sharp *keek*, sometimes in rapid series; more vocal than Short-billed.

ID (Nez Perce County)—Sep · KEITH CARLSON

Courtship · WA (Clark County)—Mar · ROGER WINDEMUTH

Wilson's Snipe
Gallinago delicata

DESCRIPTION 10.5 in/27 cm, wingspan 18 in/46 cm. Stocky; brownish with **whitish dorsal striping**, **long straight bill**, short greenish legs, dark wings, **rusty tail**; in flight, white belly set off by streaked upper breast, barred flanks, underwings. Plumage generally similar throughout year. ***Breeding:*** Fresh scapulars contrast with duller coverts. ***Juvenile:*** Darker (plumage briefly held).

SIMILAR SPECIES Proportionately longer bill than other shorebirds except dowitchers (pp. 188–189), which show white back wedge, lack whitish head stripes.

STATUS & DISTRIBUTION Breeds Aleutians east to Labrador, south to central California, western Pennsylvania; winters from Kodiak Island, Iowa, Nova Scotia south to Colombia. In PNW, common breeder east of Cascades/BC Coast Range up to subalpine elevations (Apr–Aug); migrants swell numbers locally Sep–early Nov; becomes uncommon, local Dec–early Mar, increasingly rare eastward to WY. West of crest uncommon, local breeder (e.g., Haida Gwaii, southeastern Vancouver Island, northern Olympic Peninsula, lower Columbia River floodplain, Willamette Valley, OR Coast Range); becomes fairly common with migrant influx Jul–Mar.

HABITAT ASSOCIATIONS Nests sedge-dominated boggy meadows; non-breeding, flooded fields, pond margins, brackish marsh, ditches.

BEHAVIOR & FEEDING Mostly crepuscular; probes secretively for insects, worms, other invertebrates; flushes explosively when discovered. Concentrates into hundreds during migration at productive feeding locales. Male flies high in display, diving with vibrating tail feathers to produce hollow "winnowing" sound; monogamously paired females also winnow. Pair partitions brood to share parental care.

VOCALIZATIONS Rasped *skresh* when flushed; repeated, nasal *jick* from exposed perch near nest.

Wilson's Phalarope
Phalaropus tricolor

DESCRIPTION 9 in/23 cm. Plump, long necked with dark legs, **black needle-like bill**; plain wings, **white rump** visible in flight. *Breeding:* Female **pale-gray crown to nape**; dark rufous-black stripe through eye to scapulars; grayish upperparts, white belly; male duller. *Non-breeding:* Pale gray dorsally, **white face, gray post-ocular line**. *Juvenile:* Browner with buff edging, yellow legs.

SIMILAR SPECIES Red-necked Phalarope (p. 192) shows wing stripe in flight; blackish-gray head in breeding plumage, black eyeline in non-breeding. Lesser Yellowlegs (p. 165) has gray face, breast. Other phalaropes (pp. 192–193) show white wing stripe in flight, bold, black post-ocular line in non-breeding—Red much stockier with thick bill; breeding Red-necked has blackish-gray head.

STATUS & DISTRIBUTION Breeds primarily in interior—BC, Manitoba south to California, Colorado, disjunctly north to Yukon, east to New Brunswick; winters to South America. In PNW, fairly common breeder May–Aug, mostly lowlands east of Cascades/BC Coast Range; stages in tens of thousands at Lake, Harney Counties (OR) by Aug, rarely lingers to Sep. Uncommon but increasing westside breeder north to southwestern BC, most frequently Willamette Valley; rarely nests near outer coast.

HABITAT ASSOCIATIONS Breeds at freshwater marsh, lake margins; migrants use alkaline ponds, sewage ponds, flooded fields; winters mainly at saline mountain lakes.

BEHAVIOR & FEEDING Spins in water, creating feeding vortex to pick tiny invertebrates from surface; also feeds in association with ducks, avocets in disturbed water, takes insects from land—the most terrestrial phalarope. Pairs court during migration. Sexual roles reversed (male incubates, raises young). Females exhibit polyandry if males available, then depart for staging.

VOCALIZATIONS Low nasal *ennf.*

Family Scolopacidae—SANDPIPERS, SNIPES, AND PHALAROPES **191**

Breeding Female · WA (Pacific County)—May · GREGG THOMPSON

Juvenile · WA (Pacific County)—Aug · RYAN SHAW

Red-necked Phalarope
Phalaropus lobatus

DESCRIPTION 7.5 in/19 cm. Compact with small head, thin neck, **thin straight black bill**, short legs; **white wing stripe** visible in flight. *Breeding:* Female has **dark-gray head**, white chin, reddish neck, rust-striped mantle, white underparts; male duller. *Non-breeding:* White-streaked gray upperparts, white neck, white head with **thick black post-ocular line**. *Juvenile:* Darker ventrally with gold-striped mantle.

SIMILAR SPECIES Red Phalarope (p. 193) bulky; stout bill usually pale at base; back evenly gray in non-breeding plumage. Wilson's Phalarope (p. 191) has thinner bill, white rump; in breeding plumage, shows dark stripe from bill down neck side; lacks wing stripe.

STATUS & DISTRIBUTION Circumpolar breeder south to Aleutians, northern BC, James Bay; winters principally to tropical oceans, with most migration pelagic. In PNW, common at sea, fairly common inland May, Jul–Sep; rare Jun, late Oct–Nov. Inland counts highest on southbound movement east of Cascades; spring numbers at sea average higher (to tens of thousands). Most frequent in lowlands; rarely to subalpine.

HABITAT ASSOCIATIONS Nests tundra, taiga. Migrants use sewage ponds, flooded fields, lakes, tidal upwellings, rarely land.

BEHAVIOR & FEEDING Paddles lobed toes to spin, create upward vortex, bringing tiny invertebrates to surface for visual capture. Gregarious, forming loose migrant flocks at sea, sometimes with Red Phalarope. May travel overland at night, individuals flocking with other shorebirds. Pairs form at breeding grounds; often monogamous, polyandry infrequent. Sexual roles reversed with males choosing mate, incubating, providing brood care.

VOCALIZATIONS Frequent *kit kit*, also twitter, cluck near nest.

Non-breeding · OR (Lincoln County)—Oct · GREG GILLSON

Breeding Female · Alaska—Jun · GREGG THOMPSON

Non-breeding · WA (Pacific County)—Nov · RYAN MERRILL

Red Phalarope
Phalaropus fulicarius

DESCRIPTION 8.25 in/21 cm. Stout, thick necked with straight **sturdy bill**, short legs; wing stripe visible in flight. ***Breeding:*** Female has yellowish bill, black head, white face, **rufous underparts**, white underwing, rust-streaked upperparts; male duller. ***Non-breeding:*** Plain pale-gray mantle, white underparts, thick black post-ocular line, **pale-based black bill**. ***Juvenile:*** Similar with buff dorsal edging, peachy-buff breast in fresh plumage.

SIMILAR SPECIES Red-necked Phalarope (p. 192) smaller with thin all-dark bill; white dorsal streaking in non-breeding plumage (golden in juvenal plumage). Sanderling (p. 177) less erratic flight, does not swim, lacks black eyeline. Wilson's Phalarope (p. 191) thinner bill, white rump, lacks wing stripe.

STATUS & DISTRIBUTION Circumpolar breeder across High Arctic, winters to subtropical oceans; migration routes pelagic. In PNW, common Hecate Strait, throughout pelagic waters, mostly May, Aug–Sep, but irregular year-round with periodic windblown "wrecks" Oct–Jan along outer coast, Strait of Juan de Fuca; otherwise rare Salish Sea, Willamette Valley; rarer eastward (barely casual ID, accidental western WY, northwestern MT).

HABITAT ASSOCIATIONS Breeds on tundra; at other seasons, pelagic, rarely inshore waters, sewage ponds, lakes.

BEHAVIOR & FEEDING Generally on land only to nest. Spins in water with lobed toes like other phalaropes but also upends for small crustaceans at marine upwellings, takes aquatic insects while nesting. Gregarious; sometimes with greater numbers of Red-necked Phalarope; frequently feeds commensally with whales, other birds. Polyandry frequent but monogamous pair more usual; sex roles reversed as with other phalaropes. Non-territorial while nesting.

VOCALIZATIONS Repeated high-pitched *pikk*; also twitters, buzzy screams while nesting.

OR (Lincoln County)—Sep • GREG GILLSON

South Polar Skua
Stercorarius maccormicki

DESCRIPTION 21 in/53 cm, wingspan 52 in/132 cm. **Heavy-bodied**, thick-necked, gull-like seabird; **broad, dark wings** with **white flash at base of primaries**; short wedge-shaped tail. *Adult:* Brownish gray without warm tones; hooked bill, black legs. Three morphs (dark, light, intermediate) vary clinally, also with age, bleaching. All show **contrasting lighter nape**; head, underparts also pale in lighter morphs. *Juvenile:* Plainer, grayer; bluish bill, legs.

SIMILAR SPECIES Pomarine Jaeger (p. 195) less bulky, longer tail, smaller bill, upperwing flashes more obscure. Large first-year gulls thinner necked, wingtips more attenuated, lack white primary flashes.

STATUS & DISTRIBUTION Antarctic breeder; pelagic at other seasons, moving north before Apr as far as Alaska, Greenland (more common Pacific than Atlantic). In PNW, postulated clockwise migration around Pacific delays arrival—uncommon in pelagic waters Jun–Oct, rare May, Nov–Dec; most records juveniles. Counts peak over continental shelf Sep–Oct, but recent surveys farther offshore have also recorded high Jun numbers. Avoids inshore waters.

HABITAT ASSOCIATIONS Nests on open ground; pelagic at other seasons.

BEHAVIOR & FEEDING Feeds on fish, penguin chicks, eggs, carrion near nest; fish, krill outside of breeding. Menacing flight with slow, steady wingbeats—often attacks shearwaters, other seabirds, forcing food disgorgement; also dives for fish, feeds on surface offal. Some molt while in PNW; rapid loss of primaries imparts ratty appearance. Begins breeding aged 5–6 years; long-term monogamous pair shows high site fidelity, displays raucously near nest.

VOCALIZATIONS Generally silent in North Pacific; near nest, harsh, gull-like long-call.

Juvenile · *California—Sep* · BILL SCHMOKER

Subadult · *OR (Lincoln County)—Aug* · GREG GILLSON

Adult Light morph · *WA (Grays Harbor County)—Jul* · RYAN SHAW

Pomarine Jaeger
Stercorarius pomarinus

DESCRIPTION 19 in/48 cm (adult 23 in/58 cm with tail), wingspan 50 in/127 cm. Dark-mantled, full-bodied, gull-like seabird; like other jaegers, transitions to adult plumage over four years. Dark pointed wings with **white flash at base of primaries**, heavy **bicolored bill**. *Adult:* Dark legs; central rectrices form elongated, **rounded tail streamers** (lacking in non-breeding plumage). Light morph has dark cap, underwing coverts; yellowish neck, white belly; often shows dark breast band. Dark morph blackish. *Subadult:* Barred underwing coverts, streamers shorter. *Juvenile:* Strongly banded undertail, underwing; no streamers, bluish legs.

SIMILAR SPECIES Parasitic Jaeger (p. 196) shows pointed central rectrices, smaller bill, narrower wings; adult cap smaller, juvenile nape streaked. South Polar Skua (p. 194) larger, cold gray with short tail; juvenile Long-tailed Jaeger (p. 197) slender; head, bill smaller.

STATUS & DISTRIBUTION Nearly circumpolar, irregular breeder south to central Alaska (absent Europe, Greenland); winters to tropical seas. Population 10 percent dark morph. In PNW, fairly common Jul–Nov, uncommon Dec–Jun, in pelagic waters; migrants rare but regular inshore off outer coast, BC/WA protected waters; casual inland.

HABITAT ASSOCIATIONS Nests lowland Arctic tundra; at other seasons, pelagic.

BEHAVIOR & FEEDING At sea, primarily pirates fish in midair from terns, gulls, other seabirds, with swift flight; follows fishing boats for bycatch. Highly migratory. Forms small flocks, migrates in waves, but usually observed singly. Nesting dependent on brown lemming cycle, resulting in nomadic lifestyle; also eats other small mammals, birds. Presumably monogamous; pair cooperatively feeds lemmings to young.

VOCALIZATIONS Nasal long-call at nest. Rarely utters yelps outside of breeding.

Juvenile Light morph · *WA (Grays Harbor County)—Sep*
BOB KOTHENBEUTEL

Adult Light morph · *Manitoba—Jun* · DEBRA HERST

Juvenile Dark morph · *Utah—Aug* · PAUL HIGGINS

Adult Dark morph · *Alaska—Jun* · ZAK POHLEN

Parasitic Jaeger
Stercorarius parasiticus

DESCRIPTION 17 in/43 cm (adult 20 in/51 cm with tail), wingspan 45 in/114 cm. **Falcon-like** seabird with dark upperparts, pointed wings with **white flash at base of primaries**. *Adult:* Dark legs, **elongated, pointed tail streamers** (lacking in non-breeding plumage). Light morph has small dark cap, indistinct breast band, yellowish neck, white belly; dark morph blackish overall. Most birds intermediate. *Subadult:* Variable, often unevenly patterned; tail shorter. *Juvenile:* **Warm brownish**, no streamers, pale legs; streaked neck; barred back, undertail, belly, underwing.

SIMILAR SPECIES Pomarine Jaeger (p. 195) blunt central rectrices; bicolored heavy bill; light-morph adult breast band darker, cap more extensive. In PNW, dark-morph jaegers far more frequently prove to be Parasitic than Pomarine. Long-tailed Jaeger (p. 197) wings narrower, shafts of outer primaries white; light dorsal coverts contrast with dark flight feathers on adult; juvenile cold grayish. Heermann's Gull (p. 215) less falcon-like, lacks white primary bases.

STATUS & DISTRIBUTION Circumpolar breeder south to Alaska Peninsula, Hudson Bay, Scotland, Kamchatka Peninsula; winters to tropical oceans. In PNW, fairly common Salish Sea to far beyond continental shelf May, Jul–Oct, rare Mar–Apr, Jun, lingers casually to Dec. East of Cascades/BC Coast Range, rare Aug–Oct at time of peak oceanic movement.

HABITAT ASSOCIATIONS Nests tundra; at other seasons, mostly pelagic; inland migrants use rivers, larger lakes.

BEHAVIOR & FEEDING Pirates food from gulls, terns in acrobatic flight: Bonaparte's Gull, Common Tern frequent PNW targets. Nesting pairs take small birds, eggs, small mammals cooperatively, steal food deliveries from colonial seabirds.

VOCALIZATIONS Quiet at sea (rarely utters *weeet*); varied calls near nest.

Adult · *Alaska—Jun* · GREGG THOMPSON

Juvenile Light morph · *BC (Hecate Strait)—Aug* · LIRON GERSTMAN

Subadult Light morph · *WA (Grays Harbor County)—Aug* · RYAN SHAW

Long-tailed Jaeger
Stercorarius longicaudus

DESCRIPTION 15 in/38 cm (adult 22 in/56 cm with tail), wingspan 42 in/107 cm. Graceful. Long attenuated wings, **shafts of outer primaries white**; stubby bill, **tail length always greater than wing width**. *Adult:* Tail streamers extremely long if unbroken. Dark legs, cap; white neck, breast; gray belly to vent; **gray mantle contrasts with dark flight feathers**. Non-breeding variably banded, often lacks streamers. *Subadult:* Barred underwing coverts (versus uniform in adult); tail shorter. *Juvenile:* Polymorphic, ranging from blackish to light gray with white head. Extensively barred; short, blunt tail projection; pale legs.

SIMILAR SPECIES Parasitic Jaeger (p. 196) wings broader; juvenile warm brownish; light-morph adult generally shows breast band. Juvenile Pomarine Jaeger (p. 195) has larger head, bill.

STATUS & DISTRIBUTION Circumpolar High Arctic breeder (above latitude 60°N in North America); winters to southern-hemisphere temperate seas. In PNW, rare well offshore late Apr–May, fairly common late Jul–Oct (peak late Aug); rare inshore Aug–Oct. Casual inland Jun–Dec, mostly east of Cascades/BC Coast Range.

HABITAT ASSOCIATIONS Nests on tundra; highly pelagic at other seasons; interior vagrants use large rivers, lakes.

BEHAVIOR & FEEDING Buoyant flyer, kleptoparasitizing small seabirds; also scavenges, follows fishing boats. In PNW, targets Sabine's Gull, Arctic Tern, stealing food in midair almost playfully. Lemming specialist on tundra, often hunting kestrel-like from hover or perch; supplements diet with fledgling birds, fish. Unlike other jaegers, hawks insects, eats berries. Monogamous pair defends territory against all other jaegers.

VOCALIZATIONS Quiet in south. Breeding calls include rattled *krr krr krit*.

Non-breeding · WA (Jefferson County) —Dec
DENNIS PAULSON

Breeding · WA (Jefferson County) —Jul · GREGG THOMPSON

Common Murre
Uria aalge

DESCRIPTION 16 in/41 cm, wingspan 27 in/69 cm. Large auk, **brownish-black upperparts, white underparts. Long narrow all-black bill**. *Breeding:* Head, neck entirely black, meeting white breast in smooth line (plumage held for much of winter). *Non-breeding:* White throat, lower face, cheek; **dark, downcurved post-ocular line**. *Immature:* Resembles non-breeding (plumage attained by half-sized chick at fledging time).

SIMILAR SPECIES Caution: fledged murre chicks resemble small auk species. See also under Thick-billed Murre (p. 199).

STATUS & DISTRIBUTION Breeds along Pacific, Atlantic coastlines from Low Arctic south to Japan, California, Maritimes, Portugal; winters south of sea ice close to breeding range. In PNW, nests locally along outer coast (most abundantly OR). Numbers increase late summer as birds move north, south to winter off southwestern Vancouver Island, WA, northern OR; many also to Salish Sea.

HABITAT ASSOCIATIONS Strictly marine. Breeds coastal islands, frequently in association with other seabirds (storm-petrels, cormorants, Glaucous-winged Gull, Western Gull, puffins, other auks). Winters at sea over continental shelf, also inland marine waters.

BEHAVIOR & FEEDING Dives for fish, marine invertebrates. Flies in lines low to water with rapid wingbeats; walks upright, clumsily. Nests in dense colonies on bare rock. Nest sites average just 75–80 in² (500 cm²) per pair. Parents incubate upright, settling onto single egg tucked between feet, take turns foraging at sea. Chick fledges at 3–4 weeks, leaping into water or rolling down cliff, finishes growth at sea attended by male parent.

VOCALIZATIONS Various guttural alarm, recognition calls. Highly vocal on colonies.

Thick-billed Murre
Uria lomvia

DESCRIPTION 17 in/43 cm, wingspan 29 in/74 cm. **Stocky** auk, **black upperparts, white underparts**. Fairly long, deep, **black bill**; culmen strongly downcurved toward tip. ***Breeding:*** Face, neck slightly more brownish (less black) than back; white of breast extends up onto neck in sharp point. Bold **white line along cutting edge of upper mandible**. ***Non-breeding:*** White throat, foreneck; white mandibular streak fainter or absent. ***Immature:*** Resembles non-breeding, smaller bill.

SIMILAR SPECIES Common Murre (p. 198) slimmer with lighter-colored upperparts (more brownish); narrower, straighter bill lacks white line. In breeding plumage, white of breast meets dark throat in gentle curve; non-breeding has more white on face, blackish post-ocular line. Pigeon Guillemot (p. 204) has white in wing. Murrelets (pp. 200–203) smaller, shorter billed.

STATUS & DISTRIBUTION Circumpolar. Breeds Arctic coastlines, south in Pacific to BC, Kuril Islands, in Atlantic to Newfoundland, Iceland. Winters south of sea ice, generally within breeding range. In PNW, several pairs nest on Triangle Island, BC. Migrants rare BC to WA (most fall/winter) on pelagic, inland marine waters; casual OR.

HABITAT ASSOCIATIONS Similar to Common Murre. Considerable breeding-range overlap in Pacific, often share same breeding sites.

BEHAVIOR & FEEDING Thick-billed sometimes forages in deeper water than Common Murre, often nests on narrower ledges, but biology closely similar. Both among most abundant auks in world, yet also leading victims of oil spills, bycatch in fishing nets, nesting-colony predation by Bald Eagles, gulls, ravens.

VOCALIZATIONS Vocal array much as Common Murre.

Non-breeding · *WA (Whatcom County)—Dec* · douglas l. brown

Breeding · *BC (Campbell River)—Jun* · terry thormin

Marbled Murrelet
Brachyramphus marmoratus

DESCRIPTION 10 in/25 cm, wingspan 16 in/41 cm. Small, **compact** auk. **Short black bill**. In flight, wings longer, narrower, more pointed than other auks. *Breeding:* Brown upperparts with rusty scaling, reddish scapulars; **mottled lighter-brown underparts, throat**. *Non-breeding:* **Blackish upperparts**, crown; **white underparts, scapulars, partial collar**. *Juvenile:* Smudgy version of non-breeding adult.

SIMILAR SPECIES Two other *Brachyramphus* murrelets casual in PNW (neither shown). Long-billed Murrelet has broken white eye-ring; in breeding plumage, back more solidly brown, throat pale; non-breeding lacks white collar. Breeding Kittlitz's Murrelet has pale (versus dusky) undertail, back speckled yellowish; in non-breeding, white extends above eye. Other black-and-white PNW auks lack white scapulars.

STATUS & DISTRIBUTION Breeds coastally, Aleutians to California; winters generally within breeding range. PNW populations severely declining with loss of nesting habitat. Still common locally BC; uncommon, fragmented WA/OR. Densest populations Haida Gwaii, BC's mid-coast, southwestern Vancouver Island; winter concentrations Strait of Juan de Fuca, Strait of Georgia as birds move from outer coast.

HABITAT ASSOCIATIONS In PNW, breeds moist, mature forest with layered canopy, usually <30 mi/50 km from coast; forages, winters inshore marine waters.

BEHAVIOR & FEEDING Rapid flight. Often seen in pairs. Diet fish, small crustaceans, squid, taken by diving to sea floor or by underwater pursuit. Lays single egg on moss-covered limb in old-growth conifer. Parents share incubation, chick-raising, commute to sea to forage. Chick flies to sea, lives independently, at age 4–6 weeks.

VOCALIZATIONS Most common call loud *keer keer keer* in flight at nest near dawn.

Non-breeding · WA (Island County)—Jul · GREGG THOMPSON

Breeding · WA (Jefferson County)—May · RYAN MERRILL

Ancient Murrelet
Synthliboramphus antiquus

DESCRIPTION 10 in/25 cm, wingspan 17 in/43 cm. Small, **chubby** auk; **gray back, black head, nape, throat; white neck sides**, eye arcs, underparts; short grayish-yellow bill. *Breeding:* Prominent white streaking on crown; black throat more extensive.

SIMILAR SPECIES Non-breeding Marbled Murrelet (p. 200) has white scapulars, dark (versus white) underwing. Scripps's, Guadalupe Murrelets (pp. 202–203) show white throat, black back. Murres (pp. 198–199) larger, heavier billed.

STATUS & DISTRIBUTION Breeds Pacific Rim from Korea, Aleutians to BC. Winters ice-free parts of breeding range south to California, Taiwan. Half of world population nests Haida Gwaii; limited breeding also suspected northern WA. Uncommon off outer coast Aug–Feb, rarer Mar–May; fairly common Nov–Jan eastern Strait of Juan de Fuca, locally Strait of Georgia, uncommon/rare Salish Sea farther south. Casual vagrant to interior, mostly Aug–Dec.

HABITAT ASSOCIATIONS Breeds forested island slopes adjacent to shore. At sea, favors strong upwelling, tidal mixing.

BEHAVIOR & FEEDING Swift, assured flight, usually in small groups; typically dive or belly-flop synchronously into water from flight. Diet zooplankton, small fish, taken in relatively short, shallow dives or at surface. Colonial burrow nester under roots, logs. Two eggs incubated by both parents. Chicks not fed at nest, walk to shore at night aged 1–3 days; parents fly ahead, wait in water. Family groups reunite by vocal recognition, remain together at sea until chicks fully grown.

VOCALIZATIONS Basic adult call *chirrup* nocturnally at nest site, also at sea; additionally, various chips, rattles, whistles. Hatchling call *wee wee*.

WA (Grays Harbor County)—Sep · RYAN SHAW

California—Aug · MIKE DANZENBAKER

Scripps's Murrelet
Synthliboramphus scrippsi

DESCRIPTION 9.5 in/24 cm. **Small** auk; **black upperparts; white underparts**, underwing coverts. Thin black bill. Side of **face dark** to below eye, **white arcs around eye**.

SIMILAR SPECIES Former "Xantus's" Murrelet species split in 2012 into Scripps's, Guadalupe (p. 203). Latter very similar but with white extending up on side of face in front of eye, onto auriculars. See also discussion of other similar species under Guadalupe Murrelet.

STATUS & DISTRIBUTION Breeds at islands off Pacific coast of southern California, Baja California (but not Guadalupe Island). Post-breeding dispersal to pelagic waters, Baja to BC. In PNW, rare but regular late Jun–early Dec on outer continental shelf, slope, typically 25–50 mi/40–85 km offshore. Rarely seen from land.

HABITAT ASSOCIATIONS Nests on immediate coast on bare cliffs, steep scree slopes, or under low vegetation. At sea, mostly in waters ≥650 ft/200 m deep, often much deeper.

BEHAVIOR & FEEDING Almost always seen in pairs. Strong flier but maneuvers with difficulty. Can leap directly into flight from water. Diet, feeding habits incompletely known; in breeding season, eats mostly larval fish, small adult fish, krill caught by swimming underwater. Strong pair bond, nest-site fidelity; lays two eggs in rock cavity or under dense vegetation. Sexes share incubation. Young leave nest after 1–2 days (peak Apr–May), follow parents to sea, raised far from land.

VOCALIZATIONS Nocturnal twitter calls around nesting islands. In PNW, no vocalizations described.

California—Sep · GLEN TEPKE

Guadalupe Murrelet
Synthliboramphus hypoleucus

DESCRIPTION 9.5 in/24 cm. **Small** auk; **black upperparts; white underparts**, underwing coverts. Thin black bill. **White extends up in front of eye** (often above), onto auriculars.

SIMILAR SPECIES Former "Xantus's" Murrelet species split in 2012 into Guadalupe, Scripps's (p. 202). Latter very similar, but with side of face dark to below eye, white arcs around eye. Ancient Murrelet (p. 201) has gray back, black throat, stubby yellow bill. Non-breeding Marbled Murrelet (p. 200) has white scapulars, dark underwing. Murres (pp. 198–199) much larger with heavier bill, no white around eye.

STATUS & DISTRIBUTION Breeds at Guadalupe Island, small numbers irregularly other islands, off Pacific coast of Baja California (casually north to southern California). Post-breeding dispersal Baja to BC, usually far offshore. Irregular in PNW, far scarcer than Scripps's Murrelet. Rare/casual OR/WA (accidental to Haida Gwaii) Jun–early Dec on oceanic waters off continental shelf, typically ≥55 mi/90 km offshore. Population small (<5,000 birds).

HABITAT ASSOCIATIONS Nests in crevices on bare seaside cliffs, steep slopes with sparse vegetation—at Guadalupe Island, mostly offshore islets free of feral cats. At sea, prefers deep waters (≥6,500 ft/2,000 m).

BEHAVIOR & FEEDING Not systematically studied; thought to be generally similar to those of Scripps's Murrelet—i.e., diet of larval fishes, small adult fishes, krill during nesting season. Like Scripps's, almost always seen in pairs, young raised at sea. Post-breeding diet unknown.

VOCALIZATIONS Need study. Vocalizes from water at night near nesting sites. In PNW, no vocalizations described.

Non-breeding · WA (Whatcom County)—Dec · DOUGLAS L. BROWN

Breeding · WA (Snohomish County)—Apr · DOUG SCHURMAN

Breeding · WA (Grays Harbor County)—Apr · GREGG THOMPSON

Pigeon Guillemot
Cepphus columba

DESCRIPTION 13 in/33 cm, wingspan 23 in/58 cm. Medium-sized auk with thin straight black bill. **Vermilion-red legs, mouth lining.** In flight, wings more rounded than other auks. **Breeding:** **Dark blackish-brown body**; large **white upperwing patch** with brown slash. **Non-breeding:** **Mostly whitish** with mottled-gray back, dark line behind eye; white wing patch, dark wingtips retained. ***Juvenile:*** Resembles non-breeding adult, but duskier.

SIMILAR SPECIES Wing patch distinguishes from other PNW auks in all plumages. Much larger White-winged Scoter (p. 63) shows white secondaries (versus upperwing coverts) in flight.

STATUS & DISTRIBUTION Resident along both coasts of Pacific from Bering Strait to California, Kuril Islands; some pushed south in winter by sea ice. In PNW, fairly common breeder on entire coastline. Winter numbers swell in sheltered marine waters (WA, BC), drop precipitously along exposed outer coast.

HABITAT ASSOCIATIONS Breeds along rocky or bluff-lined coastlines, occasionally ventures out to edge of continental shelf. Protected inshore waters in winter.

BEHAVIOR & FEEDING Feeds inshore on small fish, invertebrates, usually by probing on rocky bottom (depth ≤100 ft/30 m). Uses feet, wings for underwater propulsion —other auks use only wings. Walks proficiently on land. Sometimes breeds as isolated pairs, more commonly small colonies, using pre-existing nesting cavities (cliffs, rock jetties, beached logs, piers, bridges, outfall pipes) or excavating burrows in sandy banks. Lifelong pair bond, strong nest-site fidelity, shared parental duties. Clutch 1–2 eggs; young independent at 5–6 weeks.

VOCALIZATIONS Trills, screams, whistles given near nest.

Alaska—Jun · ROBERT ROYSE

Alaska—May · STEVEN G. MLODINOW

Parakeet Auklet
Aethia psittacula

DESCRIPTION 9.5 in/24 cm. **Small, stout** auk, gray-black upperparts, **white underparts**, white iris, line of narrow white plumes curving down behind eye. Round, **red-orange bill**, lower mandible tip curves up. In flight, wings appear long, paddle shaped; dark underwing. *Juvenile:* Like adult but dusky bill, iris; plumes shorter.

SIMILAR SPECIES Distinctive if seen well. Cassin's Auklet (p. 206), most likely confusion species in PNW, has grayer underparts, dark, pointed bill, no facial plumes; wingbeats more rapid.

STATUS & DISTRIBUTION Breeds islands, mainland coast, from Gulf of Alaska, Bering Sea to Sea of Okhotsk. Winters open ocean south of breeding range, widely scattered south to Japan, California, casually Hawaii. In PNW, rare to irregularly uncommon Oct–Apr well offshore.

HABITAT ASSOCIATIONS Nests cliff crevices, boulder piles on beaches, talus slopes, sometimes with low vegetative cover. When feeding, avoids strong surface currents, upwellings.

BEHAVIOR & FEEDING Not a highly gregarious species. Nests in small colonies; at sea, usually seen as singles or small groups. Winter diet unknown. Near breeding sites, specialized in feeding on various types of jellyfish, also takes small crustaceans, larval fish; diving depths not recorded. Does not excavate nest but may use abandoned burrows of other species. Single egg; both parents incubate, brood. Chick left alone after first week as parents forage, flies from nest fully fledged when three-fourths grown (about five weeks of age), lives independently at sea.

VOCALIZATIONS Silent in PNW. Loud, vibrating whistle ("whinny") main call in breeding season.

Juvenile · WA (Grays Harbor County)—Aug · GEORGE PAGOS

Adult · California—Apr · GLEN TEPKE

Cassin's Auklet
Ptychoramphus aleuticus

DESCRIPTION 9 in/23 cm. Small, plump **gray** auk with **white arc above eye** (sometimes also below), **white iris** (dark brown in juvenile); whitish belly, undertail. Short, black chisel-like bill; base of lower mandible pale. Short, broad-based wings.

SIMILAR SPECIES Rhinoceros Auklet (p. 207) much larger, heavier billed.

STATUS & DISTRIBUTION Breeds Aleutians, coastal islands, south to central Baja California. Most winter offshore, southern BC to southern Baja. In PNW, common breeder BC (northern mainland coast, west coast Vancouver Island, ≥1 million Haida Gwaii), WA (northern outer coast); several small colonies OR. Common May–Oct outer coastal waters, western Strait of Juan de Fuca; uncommon to rare inner marine waters. Major southbound migration offshore starting Jul (peak Sep–Oct), presumably breeders from farther north. In winter, uncommon to fairly common off western Vancouver Island; common off WA, OR; rare Salish Sea.

HABITAT ASSOCIATIONS Forages mostly over continental shelf, slope, far from land. Nests sited on level to fairly steep terrain with ferns, grasses, forbs, or sometimes trees—predominantly Sitka spruce with grass, moss, shrub understory.

BEHAVIOR & FEEDING Rarely seen from shore. At sea, usually in singles or pairs. Diet zooplankton, secondarily juvenile fish, taken while swimming underwater. Nests colonially in excavated burrows. Single egg; parents forage by day, return to feed chick at night. Fledges, lives at sea independently at 6–7 weeks.

VOCALIZATIONS Impressive at night on breeding colony. Principal call *kreek*, likened to reluctant iron gate, often in chorus described as pigs squealing. Seldom heard at sea.

Breeding · WA (Clallam County)—May · KEN ARCHER

Non-breeding · WA (Snohomish County)—Dec · DENNIS PAULSON

Juvenile · WA (Snohomish County)—Mar · NICK DEAN

Rhinoceros Auklet
Cerorhinca monocerata

DESCRIPTION 15 in/38 cm, wingspan 22 in/56 cm. Medium-sized, **gray-brown** auk with **heavy yellow bill.** Upperparts darker than underparts; dirty-whitish belly visible in flight. *Breeding:* Narrow **white plumes** curve back from eye, base of gape; **vertical "horn"** at base of upper mandible. *Non-breeding:* Slightly smaller, paler bill; facial plumes, horn mostly or completely absent. *Juvenile:* Smaller, grayer bill; lacks horn, facial plumes.

SIMILAR SPECIES Juvenile Tufted Puffin (p. 209) much heavier with huge bill, round-headed appearance. Cassin's Auklet (p. 206) tiny by comparison, uniform gray with dark bill.

STATUS & DISTRIBUTION Breeds along both sides of Pacific from Aleutians south to Japan, California, shifting southward in winter. In PNW, common breeder on outer coast of BC, northern WA, locally northern Salish Sea; several small colonies OR coast. Large migratory movements off outer coast (peaks Apr, Sep). Winters off outer coast (rare BC, uncommon to fairly common WA, OR), in Salish Sea (fairly common but local).

HABITAT ASSOCIATIONS Nests upslope on vegetated islands with deep, loose soil for burrows; forages in open marine waters out to continental shelf break, mainly at tidal rips, other areas of upwelling.

BEHAVIOR & FEEDING Strong flier, close to water surface. Typically feeds cooperatively, diving to fairly shallow depths, herding schools of prey fish. Single egg in burrow nest. Parents forage by day, visit nest usually at night. Chick leaves nest for sea before fully grown.

VOCALIZATIONS Among other calls, series of *mooo* notes at nest at night. Seldom heard at sea.

Horned Puffin
Fratercula corniculata

DESCRIPTION 15 in/38 cm, wingspan 23 in/58 cm. **Chunky, large-billed** auk. **Black upperparts**, underwing; **white underparts**. *Breeding:* Deep, laterally compressed **yellow bill with red tip**. Black crown, neck, throat surround **white face**. Small, dark "horn" of bare skin projects above eye. *Non-breeding:* Horn absent, gray face; duller, smaller bill. *Juvenile:* Resembles non-breeding adult; gray bill, in profile much narrower.

SIMILAR SPECIES Tufted Puffin (p. 209) has black underparts (dusky in juvenile). Murres (pp. 198–199) have thinner, black bills, white underwing coverts. Other black-and-white auks in PNW smaller.

STATUS & DISTRIBUTION Breeds on islands, mainland coasts from northeastern Russia, Alaska, south to BC, Sakhalin Island. A few winter south of sea ice in breeding range; most disperse widely across central Pacific south to latitude of Japan, California. In BC, small numbers nest May–Sep (Haida Gwaii, Scott Islands); otherwise rare but regular (deep oceanic waters) to casual (nearshore/continental shelf waters) off all coasts in PNW, including Salish Sea.

HABITAT ASSOCIATIONS Nests colonially in rock crevices on cliffs, boulder piles on beaches, rarely soil burrows. Forages mostly over continental shelf while breeding; non-breeders, post-breeders inhabit open ocean much farther offshore (>100 mi/ 160 km).

BEHAVIOR & FEEDING Flies fast, neck pulled in. Walks comfortably on land. Forages underwater at relatively shallow depths for fish, invertebrates. Single egg. Chick fed fish by day by both parents, abandons nest for sea when less than fully grown.

VOCALIZATIONS Low, growling notes given singly or in combination at nest. Rarely heard at sea.

Breeding · WA (Jefferson County)—Jul · GREGG THOMPSON

Non-breeding · WA (Grays Harbor County)—Aug · RYAN SHAW

Tufted Puffin
Fratercula cirrhata

DESCRIPTION 16 in/40 cm, wingspan 25 in/64 cm. Heavy-set, **large-billed, black** auk. *Breeding:* Deep, laterally compressed **orange bill. White face**; long **blond plumes** trail down neck behind eye. *Non-breeding:* Dark-gray face, plumes absent; smaller duller bill. *Juvenile:* Gray face, breast; underparts gray to whitish. Bill smaller than adult, yellowish gray. No plumes.

SIMILAR SPECIES Size, all-dark body distinctive. Juvenile Rhinoceros Auklet (p. 207) smaller than juvenile Tufted Puffin, with smaller bill, flatter head profile.

STATUS & DISTRIBUTION Breeds along coastline, offshore islands, from Chukchi Sea to southern California, northern Japan. Winters south of sea ice, widely dispersed across North Pacific south to latitude 35°N. In PNW, locally common breeder Apr–Sep on Pacific coastline (half of regional population at Triangle Island, BC), northern Salish Sea. Rarely seen in winter except open ocean far offshore.

HABITAT ASSOCIATIONS Requires sites with herbaceous vegetation, loose soils, for excavating burrows. When nesting, forages on outer continental shelf, deeper inshore waters. Highly pelagic in winter (subadults year-round).

BEHAVIOR & FEEDING Rapid flight, neck pulled in; steers, lands inexpertly. Often nests in large colonies. May forage in small, mixed-species seabird flocks; at sea, usually seen singly or in pairs. Dives, swims underwater, usually <200 ft/60 m deep. Forages, feeds chicks fish by day. Adult diet fish plus invertebrates (squid, crustaceans). Single egg in burrow nest. Chick attended by both parents, leaves nest upon fledging, lives independently at sea ≥2 years before returning to breed.

VOCALIZATIONS Various groans at nest site.

Non-breeding · OR (Lincoln County)—Feb · GREG GILLSON

First-year · WA (Grays Harbor County)—Jan · RYAN SHAW

Breeding · Alaska—Jun · GLENN BARTLEY

Black-legged Kittiwake
Rissa tridactyla

DESCRIPTION 16 in/41 cm, wingspan 38 in/97 cm. Medium-sized gull; transitions to adult plumage over three years. Thick neck, stubby bill, **short black legs**; long wings slightly sickle shaped in flight. *Breeding:* Medium-gray mantle, yellow bill, white head, tail, underparts; **solid black wingtips c**ontrast with **pale-gray primaries**. *Non-breeding:* Dark auricular spot, dusky nape, greenish bill. *First-year:* **Black collar, auricular patch,** tail tip. In flight, blackish outer primaries, carpal bars form "M" across upperwings.

SIMILAR SPECIES Bonaparte's Gull (p. 212) lacks black primaries. Juvenile Little Gull (p. 213) comparably tiny. Tern-like Sabine's Gull (p. 211) lacks black "M." Red-legged Kittiwake (not shown; casual Dec–Aug in PNW) smaller; red legs, darker mantle; first-year lacks carpal bar, tail band. Other adult gulls show white markings in black wingtips.

STATUS & DISTRIBUTION Circumpolar coastal breeder south to Kuril Islands, southern Alaska, Maritimes, Portugal; winters at sea, subarctic to subtropical zones. In PNW, fairly common Aug–Mar in pelagic waters, uncommon inshore; uncommon Apr–Jul, except subadults common Mar–Oct BC outer coast. Rare Salish Sea; casual/rare inland, mostly Columbia River (accidental to northwestern MT). Nesting recently near Prince Rupert, BC.

HABITAT ASSOCIATIONS Cliff nester, preferring rugged islands; at other seasons, pelagic over continental shelf, rare on beaches, jetties; sometimes wrecked to fresh water after severe storms.

BEHAVIOR & FEEDING Feeds in mixed-species aggregations over upwellings, picking or surface-plunging for fish, invertebrates. Powerful, buoyant flight; shears fulmar-like with stiff wingbeats. Nests in tight colonies.

VOCALIZATIONS Nasal yodeled *kitty weeek* while nesting.

First-year · BC (Penticton)—Sep · LAURE W. NEISH

First-year · OR (Washington County)—Sep · GREG GILLSON

Breeding · WA (Grays Harbor County)—Aug · RYAN MERRILL

Sabine's Gull
Xema sabini

DESCRIPTION 13 in/33 cm, wingspan 37 in/94 cm. Small, distinctive gull; transitions to adult plumage over two years. Tern-like with weakly forked tail; on upperwing, in flight, **black outer primaries**, gray coverts contrast strikingly with wedge of **white inner remiges**. *Breeding:* **Grayish-black hood**, yellow-tipped black bill, gray mantle, white tail, underparts. *Non-breeding:* Partial hood. *First-year:* **Grayish-brown upperparts**, black tail tip.

SIMILAR SPECIES Upperwing pattern unique among PNW gulls. Black-legged Kittiwake (p. 210) larger; immature has black carpal bar, dorsal collar. First-year Franklin's Gull (p. 214) shows blackish half-hood; upperwings mostly grayish in flight.

STATUS & DISTRIBUTION Circumpolar breeder across High Arctic south to Alaska Peninsula; winters to tropical oceans. Migration routes primarily pelagic. In PNW, common in pelagic waters Apr–May, Aug–Oct, casual nearly year-round; numbers generally higher while southbound, but spikes irregularly recorded in spring. Fairly rare elsewhere in region, with infrequent large flocks late May–early Jun in protected marine waters or east of WA Cascades; generally rare inland late Aug–Oct (uncommon WA Columbia Plateau in Sep).

HABITAT ASSOCIATIONS Breeds on moist tundra. At other seasons pelagic, rarely uses inshore waters, major rivers, lakes.

BEHAVIOR & FEEDING Flight tern-like. Takes insects, other invertebrates, fish while nesting; surface-dips at sea for zooplankton, small fish, offal, often over upwellings; forms tight flocks frequently, feeding with other species. Grazes mud flats at inland sites. Loosely colonial, often nesting on islands. Pairs apparently monogamous, share parental duties.

VOCALIZATIONS Buzzy tern-like calls; mostly quiet outside of breeding.

Non-breeding · WA (Pierce County)—Sep · GREGG THOMPSON

Breeding · BC (Richmond)—Jun · LIRON GERSTMAN

Juvenile · BC (Sechelt)—Aug · PENNY HALL

Juvenile · BC (Parksville)—Aug · RALPH HOCKEN

Bonaparte's Gull
Chroicocephalus philadelphia

DESCRIPTION 13 in/33 cm, wingspan 34 in/86 cm. Small gull; transitions to adult plumage over two years. Dainty, **tern-like** with short pinkish legs, blackish bill, square tail; primaries form **broad white leading edge**, black trailing edge in flight. *Breeding:* Pearl-gray mantle, white underparts; **black hood, white nape**, eye crescents. *Non-breeding:* White head; **black auricular spot**. *First-year:* Black carpal bar, tail tip. Juvenile browner.

SIMILAR SPECIES Franklin's Gull (p. 214) larger, mantle darker; dark half-hood in non-breeding plumage. Small terns (pp. 230–232) black-capped, strongly forked tails. Little Gull (p. 213) tiny bill, dark underwing; black nape in breeding; immature shows blackish cap. Black-headed Gull (not shown; casual PNW) underside of primaries dark; red bill, yellowish in immature.

STATUS & DISTRIBUTION Breeds across boreal zone, Alaska to Quebec; winters southwestern BC, Maine, south to Mexico. In PNW, breeds interior BC north from Bridge Lake. Common year-round southern Strait of Georgia, northern Puget Sound; migrants peak Mar–Apr, Aug–Oct; subadults linger May–Jul, juveniles arrive Aug. Uncommon, local, often irregular elsewhere west of Cascades/BC Coast Range; in OR, movement mostly over ocean. Uncommon east of crest with later migration peaks, near-complete withdrawal Dec–Mar.

HABITAT ASSOCIATIONS Breeds boreal wetlands; outside breeding, found mostly along inshore marine waters, also lakes, marshes; concentrates at sewage ponds.

BEHAVIOR & FEEDING Dives, pecks, spins phalarope-like for fish, invertebrates; hawks insects in buoyant flight, takes fish roe; thousands congregate at tidal rips. Monogamous pair builds nest in conifer.

VOCALIZATIONS Low buzzy *geerr*; quiet *tchew*.

Breeding · *Manitoba—Jun* · GLENN BARTLEY

First-year · *Utah—Nov* · PAUL HIGGINS

Non-breeding · *Utah—Nov* · RICK FRIDELL

Little Gull
Hydrocoloeus minutus

DESCRIPTION 11 in/28 cm, wingspan 28 in/71 cm. Smallest gull; transitions to adult plumage over two years. **Diminutive** with short black bill, pearl-gray mantle, short white tail, reddish legs; wings appear fairly rounded in flight. **Breeding:** Head black to nape; in flight, **wings gray above, black below.** **Non-breeding:** White head with black cap, auricular spot. **First-year:** **Black cap**, tail tip; in flight, upperparts show dark "M" pattern, black carpal bar; pale underwing; blackish mantle until Nov.

SIMILAR SPECIES Breeding-plumaged Bonaparte's Gull (p. 212), Black-headed Gull (not shown; casual in PNW) have white eye crescents, white nape, lack black underwing. Juvenile Black-legged Kittiwake (p. 210) larger; wings more pointed, lacks black cap.

STATUS & DISTRIBUTION Breeds primarily Germany east to China. In North America, has bred around Great Lakes, Hudson/James Bays; winters coastally, also Great Lakes. In PNW, rare year-round northern Puget Sound, casual elsewhere west of Cascades/BC Coast Range (peaks Mar–Apr, Sep–Nov); accidental east of Cascades to BC, MT, ID.

HABITAT ASSOCIATIONS Nests at fresh or brackish wetlands, also on river islets; at other seasons, lakes, beaches, sewage ponds, inshore marine waters.

BEHAVIOR & FEEDING Surface-dips, pecks surface in fluttery tern-like flight, capturing tiny fish, invertebrates; may hover, upend, wade; hawks insects, mostly while nesting. In PNW, usually found with Bonaparte's Gulls at tidal rips. Monogamous pair nests on ground, usually in colonies, often with other gulls, terns; shares nesting duties.

VOCALIZATIONS Nasal *keck* in flight; displays with long series.

Breeding · ID (Jefferson County)—May · JOSEPH V. HIGBEE

First-year · WA (King County)—Aug · RYAN MERRILL

Breeding · OR (Harney County)—Apr · KEN ARCHER

Franklin's Gull
Leucophaeus pipixcan

DESCRIPTION 15 in/38 cm, wingspan 38 in/97 cm. Fairly small, handsome gull; transitions to adult plumage over three years. Dark legs, dark-gray mantle, hooded appearance; **prominent white eye-crescents**; wings somewhat rounded in flight. *Breeding:* **Red bill, black head**, rose-tinged whitish underparts, white tail; in flight, white band separates black wingtips from rest of wing. *Non-breeding:* **Blackish half-hood**, bill. *First-year:* Tail tip broadly banded, black except for outermost rectrices; mantle brownish until Sep.

SIMILAR SPECIES Bonaparte's Gull (p. 212) has lighter-gray upperparts; Sabine's Gull (p. 211) smaller with striking wing pattern.

STATUS & DISTRIBUTION Breeds northern Alberta to Minnesota, south disjunctly to Nevada; winters to western coastal South America. In PNW, nests southeastern OR (Malheur NWR), southeastern ID (~40,000 at Grays Lake). Transients uncommon mid-Apr–Oct west of Cascades north to Vancouver Island, rare east of BC Coast Range. Migrant non-breeders (sometimes in small flocks) peak May–Jun outside of breeding areas; juvenile dispersal begins late Jul. Most transients found Aug–Oct as singles within flocks of smaller gulls. Accidental Dec–Mar western OR (coast, interior valleys), northwestern MT (Flathead Lake).

HABITAT ASSOCIATIONS Nests freshwater marshes with emergent vegetation. Migrants use lakes, sewage ponds, cultivated fields, major rivers, coastline; range to higher elevations outside PNW. Winters coastally (sometimes pelagic).

BEHAVIOR & FEEDING Gregarious, foraging in large, dense flocks for fish, invertebrates, rodents on water, land. Monogamous pairs colonial, build nests on floating debris.

VOCALIZATIONS Loud *meowi* in flight; long-call more nasal than that of larger gulls.

Breeding in molt · WA (Grays Harbor County)—Jul
GREGG THOMPSON

First-year · BC (Ucluelet)—Sep · GERALD ROMANCHUK

Non-breeding · WA (Grays Harbor County)—Sep · RYAN SHAW

Heermann's Gull
Larus heermanni

DESCRIPTION 19 in/48 cm, wingspan 51 in/130 cm. Medium-sized gull; transitions to adult plumage over three years. Distinctive, with **dark underparts, blackish tail**. *Breeding:* Velvety gray, darker dorsally with white head, pale rump, **dark-tipped red bill**, white tail tip. *Non-breeding:* Grayish head. *First-year:* **Uniform dark brown** (with pale dorsal edging until Sep); yellowish bill.

SIMILAR SPECIES Other adult gulls show white underparts, subadults have streaks or mottling; dark-morph jaegers (pp. 195–197) fly falcon-like with white flash at base of primaries or strongly barred undertail (rarely, aberrant Heermann's Gulls show white upperwing coverts).

STATUS & DISTRIBUTION Breeds on islands, western Mexico to central California; post-breeding, disperses coastally to BC, Guatemala; most winter Mexico. In PNW, common late Jun–Nov along coast north to southwestern BC; rare Dec–Mar, uncommon Apr–May (unseasonal reports largely from OR). Casual inland west-side (mostly OR valleys), accidental east of Cascades (WA, OR, ID).

HABITAT ASSOCIATIONS Strictly coastal; nests on Isla Raza in Gulf of California, other arid islands. In PNW, disperses along outer-coast intertidal zone, fewer to Salish Sea, rarely pelagic waters (≤35 mi/60 km offshore).

BEHAVIOR & FEEDING Forages over ocean, surface-plunging for fish, crustaceans; joins mixed flocks picking herring from surface. Frequently kleptoparasitizes pelicans, other seabirds. Also takes eggs, lizards from land. Highly gregarious; colonies of monogamous pairs number to tens of thousands, migrate en masse after nesting. PNW arrival date varies year to year.

VOCALIZATIONS *Yow aow* in flight; long-call hollower than that of other gulls.

First-year · WA (King County) — Jan · DENNIS PAULSON

Non-breeding · OR (Washington County) — Nov · GREG GILLSON

Breeding · WA (Whatcom County) — Apr · NICK DEAN

Mew Gull
Larus canus

DESCRIPTION 16 in/41 cm, wingspan 45 in/114 cm. Medium-sized gull; transitions to adult plumage over three years. Long winged with **dove-like head**, dusky iris, **slender yellowish bill**. *Breeding:* White head, tail, underparts; yellowish legs, medium-gray mantle; **black wingtips with large white spots** near tip. *Non-breeding:* Heavily streaked head, chest; greener bill with faint ring. *First-year:* Neatly scaled grayish-brown upperparts, dark tail band, pinkish legs, dark-tipped bill; back gray by Dec.

SIMILAR SPECIES Ring-billed Gull (p. 217) has less round head, adult lighter gray with bold ring on bill, less white in wingtips. California Gull (p. 218) larger with long, stout bill.

STATUS & DISTRIBUTION Breeds from Iceland across Eurasia to central Canada; North American subspecies (*L.c. brachyrhynchus*, sometimes considered separate species) nests Alaska to northern Saskatchewan, winters coastally Kodiak Island to Baja California. In PNW, breeds BC (mostly west of Coast Range) south to Harrison Lake, southern Vancouver Island. Common western lowlands Oct–early May, rare Jun–Jul, uncommon Aug–Sep; rare eastside Sep–May, except uncommon Columbia Plateau, accidental western WY.

HABITAT ASSOCIATIONS Adapted to varied freshwater, nearshore marine habitats. In PNW, nests at lakes; at other seasons, uses sewage ponds, coastal habitats, rivers, agricultural fields.

BEHAVIOR & FEEDING Forages on land, water for fish, other vertebrates, invertebrates, offal; plunge-dives, hawks insects. Gregarious; flocks into thousands, mixes with other gulls, especially Ring-billed, on westside river deltas. Long-term monogamous pair nests on ground or trees, sometimes colonially; high nesting-site tenacity.

VOCALIZATIONS Nasal mewed calls, higher than other gulls.

First-year · OR (Lincoln County)—Aug · GREG GILLSON

Breeding · WA (Grant County)—Apr · DENNIS PAULSON

Breeding · ID (Jefferson County)—Mar · DARREN CLARK

Ring-billed Gull
Larus delawarensis

DESCRIPTION 17 in/43 cm, wingspan 48 in/122 cm. Medium-sized gull; transitions to adult plumage over three years. *Breeding:* **Pearl-gray upperparts**; white head, underparts, tail; wingtips extensively black with white near tip. **Yellow bill with black ring** near tip; **yellow iris, legs.** *Non-breeding:* Streaked head. *First-year:* Mottled grayish-brown upperparts, dark tail band, pink legs; develops sharply bicolored bill, gray back by Dec.

SIMILAR SPECIES Mew Gull (p. 216) round headed, smaller billed; adult darker gray with larger white wingtip spots; juvenile has neatly scalloped upperparts. California Gull (p. 218) adult has bolder white tertial tips; bill has black-and-red spot. Other large gulls have heavier bills, broader wings.

STATUS & DISTRIBUTION Breeds from interior PNW to Labrador, Great Slave Lake south to northern California; winters from southern BC across US south to Mexico, Caribbean. In PNW, breeds locally east of Cascades/BC Coast Range; thousands concentrate on Columbia Plateau (OR/WA), non-breeders summer throughout. Becomes uncommon Nov–Feb (locally common Okanagan, Flathead Valleys), withdrawing from western WY. Common year-round west of crest (peak numbers Oct–Dec), nesting rarely recorded at WA coast.

HABITAT ASSOCIATIONS Mostly at low elevation near fresh water, tilled fields, urban parking lots; locally in marine habitats.

BEHAVIOR & FEEDING Adaptable, opportunistic, omnivorous, taking refuse, fish, other organisms from land or water, worms in fields; hawks termites, other insects; steals food from other birds. Gregarious; often flocks, nests with other gulls. Generally monogamous, but female/female pairs formed when males in short supply.

VOCALIZATIONS Typical for gull; wheezy long-call.

Family Laridae—GULLS AND TERNS **217**

First-year · OR (Lincoln County)—Sep · GREG GILLSON

Non-breeding · OR (Washington County)—Nov · GREG GILLSON

Breeding · WA (Spokane County)—Mar · JON ISACOFF

California Gull
Larus californicus

DESCRIPTION 20 in/51 cm, wingspan 53 in/135 cm. Fairly large gull; transitions to adult plumage over four years. ***Breeding:*** White head, underparts, tail; medium-gray mantle; wingtips extensively black with white near tip; evenly **thin yellow bill with black-and-red spot** near tip, dark iris, **yellow or greenish-yellow legs**. ***Non-breeding:*** Streaked head, greenish legs. ***First-year:*** White-fringed upperparts, dingy underparts, dark tail, **bluish-pink legs**; develops bicolored bill, mottled back by Dec.

SIMILAR SPECIES Adult bill distinctive. First-year gulls differ as follows: Herring (p. 219) larger, wings shorter, bill mostly blackish; Ring-billed (p. 217), Mew (p. 216) have smaller bills, paler plumage; Lesser Black-backed (p. 226) bill dark, rump whiter.

STATUS & DISTRIBUTION Breeds interior California to Northwest Territories, east to Dakotas; winters southern BC to Mexico. In interior PNW, subspecies *L.c. californicus* locally common breeder (uncommon BC). Common/fairly common Sep–Apr eastern WA, ID, south-central BC (Okanagan); elsewhere in interior, uncommon (migration) to rare (Nov–Feb). Migrates westward for winter, joined by larger, lighter-mantled *L.c. albertaensis* from northern Prairie Provinces (intergrades exist). Common Jul–Nov outer coast, ranging to 30 mi/50 km offshore. Lesser numbers remain west of crest year-round.

HABITAT ASSOCIATIONS Island breeder in arid habitats; at other seasons, varied urban, agricultural, marine settings.

BEHAVIOR & FEEDING Opportunistic, omnivorous on land, water; takes insects, other invertebrates, vegetable matter, also fish, bird eggs, refuse. Nests in colonies of hundreds to tens of thousands, in PNW often with Ring-billed Gulls. Monogamous pair shares duties.

VOCALIZATIONS Typical for gull; harsh long-call.

Non-breeding · OR (Lincoln County)—Mar · GREG GILLSON

First-year · BC (Penticton)—Oct · LAURE W. NEISH

Herring Gull
Larus argentatus

DESCRIPTION 23 in/58 cm, wingspan 57 in/145 cm. Large gull; transitions to adult plumage over four years. Large head with sloping forehead, fairly large, straight-edged bill; **pink legs.** *Breeding:* White head, underparts, tail; pearl-gray mantle, **black wingtips** tipped white, yellow bill with red spot, **pale yellow iris.** *Non-breeding:* **Coarsely streaked head, neck.** *First-year:* Variably mottled; black wingtips, dark iris; bill base usually pale.

SIMILAR SPECIES Thayer's Gull (p. 220) has rounder head, smaller bill, most with dark iris; adult wingtips grayish (versus black) ventrally. California Gull (p. 218) slimmer, wings longer, adult legs yellowish; "Olympic" Gull (p. 223) has heavier bill, lighter primaries, dark iris.

STATUS & DISTRIBUTION Holarctic breeder, sub-boreal to Arctic. Taxonomy unsettled—several races often considered separate species. North American *L.a. smithsonianus* nests central Alaska to Labrador, winters ice-free northern waters to Panama. In PNW, breeds central interior BC, also near Prince Rupert; rare/absent Jun–Aug elsewhere. East of Cascades/BC Coast Range, locally fairly common/common Sep–May (rare/casual southeastern OR, western WY). On westside, common migrant along outer coast to edge of continental shelf, uncommon inland; winters in variable numbers. Darker Siberian *L.a. vegae* recorded PNW Dec–Mar (status unclear).

HABITAT ASSOCIATIONS Nests freshwater islands, barrier beaches. At other seasons, majority in PNW offshore or on interior lakes/major rivers.

BEHAVIOR & FEEDING Opportunistic predator; takes mostly fish, marine invertebrates; often pelagic; scavenges carrion, refuse in cities. Flocks with other gulls, roosting in tight groups. Long-term monogamous pairs nest colonially or alone, sharing parental care.

VOCALIZATIONS Typical for gull; clear, bugled long-call.

Family Laridae—GULLS AND TERNS **219**

Non-breeding (light-eyed) · WA (Pacific County)—Feb
DENNIS PAULSON

Non-breeding · WA (Island County)—Jan · DENNIS PAULSON

First-year · OR (Washington County)—Jan · GREG GILLSON

Near-breeding · BC (Parksville)—Apr · GERALD ROMANCHUK

Thayer's Gull
Larus thayeri

DESCRIPTION 21 in/53 cm, wingspan 54 in/137 cm. Fairly large gull; transitions to adult plumage over four years. **Round head with dark iris** (rarely amber), **small bill**; pink legs. *Breeding:* White head, underparts, tail; medium-gray mantle, yellow bill with red spot. **Wingtips black with white tips dorsally, grayish ventrally.** *Non-breeding:* Heavily streaked head, neck. *First-year:* Checkered brownish; darker wingtips show pale inner webs, tertials mostly solid grayish brown. Black bill; tail has dark band.

SIMILAR SPECIES Herring Gull's (p. 219) bill larger, forehead sloping; adult iris lighter yellow. "Kumlien's" Gull's (p. 221) wingtips grayish white, head more dove-like, first-year tertials finely patterned. "Olympic" Gull (p. 223) bulbous billed with sloping forehead. California Gull (p. 218) shows variable leg color, but never clear pink.

STATUS & DISTRIBUTION High Arctic coastal breeder, Northwest Territories to western Greenland; most winter along Pacific Coast. In PNW, locally common Oct–Mar in westside lowlands. Concentrates in protected waters—e.g., Victoria, Qualicum Bay (BC); Tacoma, Elwha River mouth (WA); northern Willamette Valley. Lingers farther north to May, rarely Jun–Aug. On eastside, rare north to Thompson/Shuswap/Golden (BC), uncommon Okanagan, Flathead Valleys.

HABITAT ASSOCIATIONS Nests remote island cliffs. At other seasons, lakes, fields, parks, landfills, buildings, river mouths, beaches.

BEHAVIOR & FEEDING Forages in marine/estuarine environments, less commonly fresh water, taking primarily fish, some invertebrates; also plunders nests, scavenges carrion, refuse in cities. Flocks with other gulls (often species smaller than itself). Colonial nester, presumed monogamous but breeding biology little known.

VOCALIZATIONS Typical for gull.

First-year · BC (Penticton)—Mar · LAURE W. NEISH

Non-breeding · BC (Comox)—Mar · JUKKA JANTUNEN

Non-breeding · WA (Clallam County)—Oct · STEVEN G. MLODINOW

"Kumlien's" (Iceland) Gull
Larus glaucoides kumlieni

DESCRIPTION 21 in/53 cm, wingspan 54 in/137 cm. Fairly large gull; transitions to adult plumage over four years. **Dove-like head** with **small bill**; pink legs. *Breeding:* White head, underparts, tail; pearl-gray mantle, **whitish wingtips**, yellow iris. Yellow bill with red spot. *Non-breeding:* Streaked head, neck. *First-year:* **Whitish overall** with variably brownish flecking, primary tips; **finely patterned tertials**; dark bill, iris.

SIMILAR SPECIES First-year Thayer's (p. 220) has grayish-brown primaries with pale inner webs, mostly solid brownish-gray tertials, darker tail; some individuals appear intermediate, probably inseparable from "Kumlien's." Small *barrovianus* race of Glaucous (p. 222) stout billed with sloping forehead; first-year shows sharply bicolored bill. Beware of bleached or leucistic individuals of other gull species.

STATUS & DISTRIBUTION "Kumlien's" often treated as separate species, at other times lumped with Iceland (as at present) or Thayer's. High Arctic coastal breeder from mouth of Hudson Bay to Baffin Island; winters primarily Greenland, northeastern North America. Annual overall in PNW Oct–Apr; casual/rare BC (reports increasing), elsewhere casual/accidental state by state. Greenland-breeding *L.g. glaucoides* accidental in region.

HABITAT ASSOCIATIONS Nests on steep rocky cliffs, many winter in North near gaps in sea ice. In PNW, uses varied interior, coastal habitats—lakes, beaches, muddy fields, landfills, sewage ponds.

BEHAVIOR & FEEDING Forages mostly for fish, marine invertebrates, offal by pecking, surface-plunging in marine environments. Opportunistic; takes eggs or chicks from nesting alcids. Flocks of hundreds common in core range; in PNW, singles flock with other gulls. Breeding biology at inaccessible colonial cliffs understudied.

VOCALIZATIONS Typical for gull, but rarely heard in PNW.

Glaucous Gull
Larus hyperboreus

DESCRIPTION 25 in/64 cm, wingspan 60 in/152 cm. Large gull; transitions to adult plumage over four years. Bulky, broad winged with **stout bill**, **white wingtips**, pinkish legs; appears **flat headed**, small eyed. *Breeding:* White head, underparts, tail; light-gray mantle, yellow bill with red spot; yellow iris. *Non-breeding:* Blotchy head, neck.
First-year: **Whitish overall** with fine brownish markings; **pink-based bill sharply bicolored**, dark iris. Alaska-breeding *L.h. barrovianus* less bulky, smaller bill.

SIMILAR SPECIES "Kumlien's" Gull (p. 221) has round head; first-year has small black bill. First-year Thayer's Gull (p. 220) smaller billed; grayish wingtips. Glaucous-winged Gull (p. 223) has grayish wingtips, bill never sharply bicolored.

STATUS & DISTRIBUTION Circumpolar breeder north from subarctic; in North America, winters sparsely south to OR, Virginia along coasts, major rivers, Great Lakes. In PNW, uncommon Nov–Apr west of Cascades/BC Coast Range, progressively less common southward (unrecorded Rogue, Umpqua Valleys). East of crest, uncommon WA, rare OR, ID, northwestern MT, south-central BC (mostly Okanagan). Casual Jun–Oct, mostly WA/BC outer coasts.

HABITAT ASSOCIATIONS Coastal breeder on cliffs, tundra, ponds, shelf ice; outside of breeding season, mostly coastal, occasionally pelagic; also fresh water, landfills, farm fields, sewage ponds, parking lots.

BEHAVIOR & FEEDING Opportunistic predator, taking various birds, small mammals, eggs, fish, invertebrates; eats some vegetation. Scavenges tidal areas, kleptoparasitizes other species. Gregarious, flocks into hundreds; in PNW, usually one or two with other gulls. Monogamous pairs nest mostly colonially, often joining other seabirds. Infrequently hybridizes with Glaucous-winged or Herring Gulls.

VOCALIZATIONS Typical for gull; long-call deep toned.

Non-breeding · OR (Lincoln County)—Mar · GREG GILLSON

First-year · OR (Washington County)—Feb · GREG GILLSON

Glaucous-winged Gull
Larus glaucescens

DESCRIPTION 25 in/64 cm, wingspan 59 in/150 cm. Large gull; transitions to adult plumage over four years. Bulky; appears broad winged with **grayish wingtips**, pinkish legs, dark iris, **heavy bulbous-tipped bill**. *Breeding:* White head, underparts, tail; medium-gray mantle; wings with broad white trailing edge, white spots near tip. Yellow bill with red spot; red orbital ring. *Non-breeding:* Head, neck darkly smudged. *First-year:* **Uniform brownish gray including wingtips**; black bill.

SIMILAR SPECIES Most large gulls show darker wingtips. Smaller Thayer's (p. 220) bill evenly thin; adult wingtips blackish dorsally. Glaucous (p. 222) wingtips white; adult has yellow eye, first-year has sharply bicolored bill. "Olympic" (see below and p. 224) has darker wingtips.

STATUS & DISTRIBUTION Breeds along coast from Kamchatka, Aleutians, to OR; winters from Bering Sea coastally to Baja California, Japan. In PNW, common year-round resident, breeder westside lowlands, mostly near coasts, south in OR to Lane County; also Columbia estuary, rarely east to Tri-Cities. Outside breeding, disperses to south-central BC (fairly common Okanagan, uncommon Shuswap), ID, southern OR (Klamath Basin), rarely northwestern MT. In PNW, interbreeds extensively, indiscriminately with Western Gull, producing variable hybrid swarm ("Olympic" Gull).

HABITAT ASSOCIATIONS Salt water (inshore, pelagic), lowland freshwater habitats, including beaches, mud flats, lakes, rivers, fields, cities. Historically nested on rocky islets, headlands; now adapted to buildings, piers, pilings, other structures.

BEHAVIOR & FEEDING Omnivorous; takes fish, varied invertebrates, carrion, landfill refuse. Flocks into thousands with other gulls. Long-term monogamous pairs nest colonially or semi-colonially.

VOCALIZATIONS Include bugled long-call, staccato *ca ca ca* in alarm.

First-year · OR (Coos County)—Aug · GREG GILLSON

Breeding · OR (Lincoln County)—Mar · GREG GILLSON

Western Gull
Larus occidentalis

DESCRIPTION 24 in/61 cm, wingspan 58 in/147 cm. Large gull; transitions to adult plumage over four years. Bulky, broad winged with **massive bill**, pinkish legs, dark iris. *Breeding:* White head, underparts, tail; **dark-gray mantle**, yellow bill with red spot; white-tipped black primaries, broad white trailing edge visible on wing in flight. *Non-breeding:* **Unstreaked head**. *First-year:* Dark with light mottling; black wingtips, bill.

SIMILAR SPECIES Slaty-backed Gull (p. 225) appears potbellied, thinner billed; adult has pale iris, streaked head (Aug–Mar), string of white ventral spots on wingtips, blackish-gray mantle—darker than Western Gull race of PNW. Lesser Black-backed Gull (p. 226) slim, long winged, thinner bill, adult has yellow legs. Adult head in "Olympic" Gull (see below) streaked in non-breeding; first-year wingtips lighter.

STATUS & DISTRIBUTION Breeds along coast, WA to Baja California; range extends slightly in winter. In PNW, common breeder, year-round resident north to Destruction Island (WA). Non-breeders uncommon to Vancouver Island, Puget Sound, mostly Aug–Feb; rare inland along Columbia River, Willamette Valley; casual/accidental south-central, southeastern OR, ID, interior BC. In PNW, interbreeds extensively, indiscriminately with Glaucous-winged Gull (p. 223), producing variable hybrid swarm ("Olympic" Gull).

HABITAT ASSOCIATIONS Nests islands, piers, buoys. Feeds primarily on salt water, coast to 25 mi/40 km offshore; also adjacent fresh water, landfills, fields.

BEHAVIOR & FEEDING Opportunistic; predator or scavenger. Diet mostly fish, some carrion, other organisms, refuse. Gregarious, highly social; nests colonially, often with other seabirds. Generally monogamous but female/female pairs form when sex ratios skewed.

VOCALIZATIONS Typical gull with loud, trumpeted long-call.

Breeding · WA (Pierce County)—Apr · DOUG SCHURMAN

Breeding · WA (Pierce County)—Apr · GEORGE PAGOS

Non-breeding · BC (Qualicum)—Mar · MIKE YIP

First-year · California—Jan · TODD B. EASTERLA

Slaty-backed Gull
Larus schistisagus

DESCRIPTION 24 in/61 cm, wingspan 58 in/147 cm. Large gull; transitions to adult plumage over four years. **Pot-bellied appearance** with stout, straight-edged bill, **pink legs**. *Breeding:* White tail, head, underparts; **dark slate-gray mantle**, black wingtips with prominent white "string of pearls" on underside of outer primaries; **yellow iris**, yellow bill with red spot. *Non-breeding:* Head **streaking darkly concentrated around eye**. *First-year:* Darkly mottled, but quickly bleaches whitish; black bill, dark iris.

SIMILAR SPECIES Western Gull (p. 224) has heavier bill; adult iris dark, less white on ventral wingtips; Lesser Black-backed Gull (p. 226) slim, thinner bill, adult legs yellow; first-year Herring Gull (p. 219) has thinner bill with pale base.

STATUS & DISTRIBUTION Asian species. Breeds coastally Kamchatka Peninsula to northern Japan, winters mostly Japan to Hong Kong; recorded with increasing frequency in North America (has bred at Aniktun Island, Alaska). In PNW, rare Nov–Apr west of Cascades/BC Coast Range, with most from southwestern BC, Puget Trough, Willamette Valley; accidental east of crest.

HABITAT ASSOCIATIONS Nests on rocky cliffs along rugged ocean shores. Outside of breeding, uses landfills, shoreline, estuaries; in PNW, often in agricultural fields, urbanized coastal settings.

BEHAVIOR & FEEDING Opportunistic, foraging on water or land by surface-dipping, scavenging, grazing for carrion, invertebrates, fish, other small vertebrates, alcid eggs, or nestlings. Flocks with other gulls; prone to long-range vagrancy, appearing on wrong side of world more often recently; apparently monogamous, nesting in growing numbers thanks to increasing availability of refuse near colonies.

VOCALIZATIONS Typical for gull; long-call loud, slow.

Breeding · WA (Pacific County)—Aug · RYAN MERRILL

Molting to second-winter · WA (Grant County)—Oct
TOM MUNSON

First-year · Colorado—Dec · STEVEN G. MLODINOW

Lesser Black-backed Gull
Larus fuscus

DESCRIPTION 21 in/53 cm, wingspan 55 in/140 cm. Fairly large gull; transitions to adult plumage over four years. Long wings; fairly long, **straight-edged bill**. *Breeding:* White head, underparts, tail; **dark slate-gray mantle**, black wingtips with white tips, yellow bill with red spot; **yellow iris, legs**. *Non-breeding:* Streaked head, neck. *First-year:* Upperparts usually neatly checkered; lightly streaked breast, whitish head, rump; blackish bill, wings, iris.

SIMILAR SPECIES Western Gull's (p. 224) bill heavier; adult has pink legs, dark iris; mantle sometimes appears lighter. Smaller California Gull's (p. 218) adult mantle medium-gray, iris dark. Slaty-backed Gull (p. 225) appears pot-bellied; stouter bill, adult legs pink. First-year Herring Gull (p. 219) evenly mottled with pale inner primaries.

STATUS & DISTRIBUTION Native to Old World. Subspecies *L.f. graellsii* (breeds northwestern Europe, winters to western Africa) rapidly increasing visitor to eastern North America. Rare in PNW, first recorded 1989 on Columbia River in BC; since 2000, annual Oct–Apr east of Cascades/BC Coast Range in BC, WA, ID (accidental OR, northwestern MT). Casual west of crest.

HABITAT ASSOCIATIONS Breeds on islands, tundra, barrier beaches, buildings; at other seasons, mostly marine; also frequents landfills, urban areas, tilled fields. In PNW, often at alkaline lakes, major rivers.

BEHAVIOR & FEEDING Opportunistic, foraging on water or land for invertebrates, fish, other small vertebrates, refuse, eggs, carrion. Flocks with other large gulls; nests in colonies within core breeding range; recently recorded nesting in Maine, paired with Herring Gull.

VOCALIZATIONS Typical gull voice; deeper long-call.

Breeding · ID (Jefferson County)—May · DARREN CLARK

Juvenile · BC (Fairwinds)—Aug · RALPH HOCKEN

Breeding · WA (Okanogan County)—Jun · RYAN SHAW

Black Tern
Chlidonias niger

DESCRIPTION 10 in/25 cm, wingspan 26 in/66 cm. Diminutive; gray mantle, thin black bill, short square tail, fairly short broad wings, gray underwing. *Breeding:* **Black head, breast**; white from legs to undertail. *Non-breeding:* White underparts, nape; **black cap extends to auricular patch**; prominent **dark blotch on side** anterior to wing. *Juvenile:* Similar; back scalloped brownish.

SIMILAR SPECIES Common, Arctic, Forster's Terns (pp. 230–232) have forked tails, lighter mantles; non-breeding lack hooded appearance, side blotch. In flight, Common Nighthawk (p. 254) shows long tail, less attenuated wingtip, white primary bar (visible in closer view).

STATUS & DISTRIBUTION Declining local breeder eastward from central California across northern temperate, boreal zones to western Siberia; winters to tropical seas. In PNW, locally common breeder mid-May–mid-Aug east of Cascades/BC Coast Range—south-central, southeastern OR; north-central, northeastern WA; central, southeastern BC; northern, southeastern ID; northwestern MT (migration extremes Apr, Nov). West of crest, rare lowland migrant late May–early Jun, along coasts Aug–Oct; rare breeder, e.g., Willamette Valley; Ridgefield NWR (WA); Pitt Lake, Iona Island (BC).

HABITAT ASSOCIATIONS Breeds freshwater marshes, ponds; migrants also use inshore marine waters. Winters coastally.

BEHAVIOR & FEEDING Forages with erratic, fluttering flight, frequently swooping to water while hawking insects. Also takes tiny fish, frogs; diet principally piscivorous at sea. Gregarious; migration probably nocturnal in part. Concentrates into hundreds at marine staging areas before flight to tropics. Monogamous pairs nest in fairly small colonies; low site fidelity.

VOCALIZATIONS Calls sharp *kip*; harsh *keeef* in alarm.

Caspian Tern
Hydroprogne caspia

DESCRIPTION 20 in/51 cm, wingspan 51 in/130 cm. **Largest tern**; white underparts, pearl gray dorsally with **large, thick red bill**, dark cap, weakly forked white tail, long pointed wings with **dark primary undersurface**. *Breeding:* Deep-red bill with darker tip, solid black cap. *Non-breeding:* Streaked crown, whitish forehead. *Juvenile:* Like non-breeding; brownish-tinged back, reddish-orange bill.

SIMILAR SPECIES Common, Arctic, Forster's Terns (pp. 230–232) much smaller, thin billed, less black on underwing. Elegant Tern (p. 229) smaller with slender yellowish-orange bill. Large gulls' wings less pointed.

STATUS & DISTRIBUTION Breeds nearly worldwide in temperate, tropical zones, north in North America to southern Alaska, Northwest Territories, Labrador; winters coastally southward from southern California, North Carolina. In PNW, rapid population increase since 1950s; now locally common Mar–Sep with stragglers into early Nov; casual Dec–Feb (OR/WA). Local breeder in interior (WA, OR, ID, northwestern MT, western WY); on westside from Fraser Delta (rarely) southward in Salish Sea, along outer coast to Columbia mouth (≤10,000 nesting pairs at dredge-spoil islands in Columbia estuary in recent years). Concentrates outer coast Jul–Aug; transients widespread.

HABITAT ASSOCIATIONS Breeds on islands, barrier beaches, rooftops, lots; outside breeding season, uses coastal habitats, rivers, lakes.

BEHAVIOR & FEEDING Forages high over water, plunge-diving for fish; carries fish long distances in bill for courtship activities or feeding young at nest. Usually nests colonially at open sites, sometimes with gulls; locations shift year to year depending on water levels, human disturbance.

VOCALIZATIONS Harsh, screeched *kaa yarrr*; juveniles beg with whistle.

Non-breeding · *California—Dec* · GANESH JAYARAMAN

Non-breeding · *OR (Clatsop County)—Oct* · ART CLAUSING

Elegant Tern
Thalasseus elegans

DESCRIPTION 16 in/41 cm, wingspan 35 in/89 cm. Large headed with **bushy black crest**; long, **thin yellowish-orange bill**, white underparts, pearl-gray mantle, white shallowly forked tail, **long wings with dark wedge at tip**, legs generally dark. *Breeding:* Bill becomes redder. *Non-breeding:* White forehead. *Juvenile:* Resembles non-breeding; mantle brownish in fresh plumage.

SIMILAR SPECIES Caspian Tern (p. 228) larger, stocky, with thick red bill. Forster's Tern (p. 232) smaller; bill shorter, broad based, dark tipped; lacks dark primaries. Other PNW terns appear smaller with rounder heads; shorter, straight bills.

STATUS & DISTRIBUTION Breeds southern California–northwestern Mexico, with most in Gulf of California (Isla Raza); disperses post-breeding along coast, irregularly north to WA, southwestern BC; winters Mexico to Chile. In PNW, occurs erratically Jul–early Nov in inshore marine waters during El Niño years, mostly outer coast—first recorded 1983, up to 1,000 at Willapa Bay 1992; rarely to Victoria area, Boundary Bay, Puget Sound; fewer in recent years, often reaching only to OR on northward dispersal.

HABITAT ASSOCIATIONS Nests on arid islands, other open sites including dredge spoils; stays inshore in protected marine waters; roosts on beaches, mud flats, piers, jetties.

BEHAVIOR & FEEDING Flies strongly with rapid wingbeats. Hovers, plunge-dives mostly for small fish, following favored anchovies northward. Gregarious; nests colonially in tight groups at open sites among Heermann's Gulls, Caspian Terns for colony defense. Carries fish in bill in courtship like other terns; vagrants may hybridize with other large terns.

VOCALIZATIONS Calls include grating *kerrick*, higher *seep*.

Juvenile · ID (Nez Perce County)—Sep · KEITH CARLSON

Breeding · BC (Richmond)—Sep · LIRON GERSTMAN

Common Tern
Sterna hirundo

DESCRIPTION 13 in/33 cm, wingspan 32 in/81 cm. Sleek; light below with pearl-gray mantle, thin bill. Strongly **forked tail white with dark edges**; pointed wingtips show **dark wedge on primaries dorsally**, dark tips ventrally. *Breeding:* Black cap, **dark-tipped red bill**, red legs. *Non-breeding:* Black bill, white forehead, dark carpal bar. *Juvenile:* Like non-breeding, with buff-edged scapulars, pale bill base.

SIMILAR SPECIES Arctic Tern's (p. 231) legs shorter, head smaller, wings narrower, paler; black trailing edge on underside of primaries thinner; in breeding plumage, longer tail, all-red bill. Forster's Tern (p. 232) whiter ventrally, evenly pale upperwing; reddish-orange bill, feet; gray tail on breeding adult; non-breeding shows black mask. Caspian Tern (p. 228) comparatively huge, thick billed. Wing patterns variable on molting terns.

STATUS & DISTRIBUTION Nearly Holarctic breeder south to temperate zone; winters to tropics, subtropics. In PNW, rare May–early Jun east of Cascades/BC Coast Range; has bred northwestern MT, southeastern ID, otherwise casual Jun–Jul; uncommon Aug–early Oct, primarily on major rivers, lakes (BC numbers higher). West of crest, declining but still numerous migrant. Common outer coast late Apr into May, rare late May–early Jun; fairly common Aug–Oct, mostly Salish Sea. Rare western lowlands away from sea; apparently declining on marine waters.

HABITAT ASSOCIATIONS Nests colonially on islands, beaches; at other seasons, uses predominantly inshore marine waters, rivers, lakes.

BEHAVIOR & FEEDING In PNW, flies low over tidal rips, hovers, plunge-dives for fish. Gregarious, roosting on beaches, floating debris. Carries fish to court mate, feed young.

VOCALIZATIONS Calls include slurred *kee uhrr*, sharp *kip*.

Juvenile · *OR (Multnomah County)—Aug* · ART CLAUSING

Breeding · *Alaska—Jul* · DONALD W. NELSON

Breeding · *Alaska—Jul* · DONALD W. NELSON

Arctic Tern
Sterna paradisaea

DESCRIPTION 13 in/33 cm, wingspan 32 in/81 cm. Slim with pearl-gray upperparts, deeply forked white tail, **ghostly-white wings** with **narrow black trailing edge** on primary undersurface; **rounded head** appears neckless; very short legs. *Breeding:* Black cap; white cheek contrasts with grayish underparts. **Red bill**, legs. *Non-breeding:* Black bill, white forehead. *Juvenile:* Like non-breeding with dark dorsal edging.

SIMILAR SPECIES Common Tern (p. 230) has longer legs, flatter head, whiter underparts, primaries show dark wedge across upper surface, wider ventral tips; in breeding plumage, black-tipped red bill, shorter tail streamers. Forster's Tern (p. 232) larger, flat headed; breeding-plumage bill, feet reddish orange; shows mask in non-breeding plumage.

STATUS & DISTRIBUTION Circumpolar breeder from High Arctic south to WA, Massachusetts, Britain, Russian Far East; winters to Antarctica. In PNW, has bred BC (Chilcotin Plateau), WA (Everett, Dungeness); uncommon in pelagic waters late Apr–Nov (peaks early May, mid-Aug); rare away from breeding sites both inshore, east of Cascades/BC Coast Range, but status obscured by identification difficulties.

HABITAT ASSOCIATIONS Breeds tundra, open beach near fresh or salt water; winters at sea, migrants mostly pelagic.

BEHAVIOR & FEEDING Flies with snappy wingbeats, more buoyant than Common Tern. Hovers, dips, plunge-dives for fish, insects, other invertebrates; carries fish to court mate, feed young. Gregarious; roosts on beaches, floating debris; joins other seabirds in pelagic waters at disturbances associated with marine predators; in PNW, sometimes nests within Caspian Tern colony. Monogamous pair shares duties.

VOCALIZATIONS Calls include *kip*, squeaked descending *kee uhrr*.

Breeding · OR (Klamath County)—Jul · DONALD W. NELSON

Breeding · ID (Jefferson County)—May · DARREN CLARK

Juvenile · Utah—Aug · PAUL HIGGINS

Non-breeding · Mexico (Yucatán)—Dec · RYAN SHAW

Forster's Tern
Sterna forsteri

DESCRIPTION 14 in/36 cm, wingspan 32 in/81 cm. Somewhat **long billed**; white ventrally with **uniform pearl-gray upperparts**, strongly forked **gray tail with white edges**. *Breeding:* Black cap, black-tipped reddish-orange bill; white forehead in second summer. *Non-breeding:* Appears **masked** with dark auriculars, whitish crown, nape; black bill. *Juvenile:* Like non-breeding, with mottled-brown upperparts.

SIMILAR SPECIES Common Tern (p. 230) smaller, redder bill; shorter legs, longer wings, non-breeding crown black. Smaller-bodied Arctic Tern (p. 231) shows rounder head, short legs, bill; non-breeding crown black. Larger Caspian Tern (p. 228) thick billed with darker wingtips.

STATUS & DISTRIBUTION Breeds disjunctly from central Alberta to southern California, Delaware, northern Mexico; winters northern California, Delaware south to Honduras. In PNW, very local breeder, fairly common Apr–Sep from south-central WA, Klamath Basin east to WY; rare southern BC (Creston), northwestern MT. Rare transient May–Jun west of Cascades—mostly Rogue, Willamette Valleys, Ridgefield NWR (WA)—or along coast late Aug–Oct (casual OR to Dec).

HABITAT ASSOCIATIONS Nests in large freshwater, saltwater, brackish marshes with tall emergent stands; at other seasons, lakes, coastal habitats.

BEHAVIOR & FEEDING Graceful flier. Forages mostly on small fish by plunge-diving; also hawks insects; less gregarious than Common, Arctic Terns, but roosts, flocks with gulls, other terns. Nests in small colonies, less frequently in isolated pairs on island, floating vegetation, or mammal lodge near cattails, other emergents; in courtship, male "parades" with fish around female.

VOCALIZATIONS Calls include harsh *kehrrp*; *chik chik chik* in alarm.

Rock Pigeon
Columba livia

DESCRIPTION 13 in/33 cm, wingspan 28 in/71 cm. Familiar domestic pigeon; selective breeding has produced wide variation in color, patterning. Most common ("wild") form gray with **dark bill**, pinkish legs; dark head, neck; iridescent feathers on neck, two black bars across wing, **black terminal tail band. Whitish rump, white underwings**.

SIMILAR SPECIES Band-tailed Pigeon (p. 234) has black-tipped yellow bill, yellow legs, white bar on nape, broad gray tail band; gray rump, underwing. Eurasian Collared-Dove (p. 235) pale grayish buff with black bar on nape, tail tipped white.

STATUS & DISTRIBUTION Original range Eurasia, Africa; domesticated for thousands of years, introduced worldwide. Arrival in PNW not documented—first feral populations seemingly established by about 1940. Now locally common, widespread, perhaps still increasing, almost always closely tied to human-influenced landscapes.

HABITAT ASSOCIATIONS Cities, towns, farms, ranches, using human structures for roosting, nesting; less frequently, cliffs within commuting distance (10 mi/16 km) of foraging opportunities. Absent from extensive forest, higher elevations.

BEHAVIOR & FEEDING Strong, fast flier. Glides with wings in "V." Nests any time of year, typically colonially; often two or more broods. Nest of twigs, other plant fibers, droppings on flat surface beneath overhang. Usually two eggs. Parents feed hatchlings "milk" generated in crop, begin transition to adult food after about one week. Diet mostly waste grain, weed seeds from ground; occasionally trees, shrubs for ripe fruit. Also human discards/handouts such as bread.

VOCALIZATIONS Territorial, courtship song rolling, low-pitched *coo* notes in various combinations. Vocal year-round.

WA (Whatcom County)—Apr · BRIAN STECH

WA (Pierce County)—May · JOSEPH V. HIGBEE

Band-tailed Pigeon
Patagioenas fasciata

DESCRIPTION 14 in/36 cm, wingspan 26 in/66 cm. Overall gray with purplish head, pinkish breast; broad, **pale-gray terminal band on tail**, iridescent feathers below **white hindneck crescent; yellow legs, bill** (tipped black). *Juvenile:* Plain gray head, breast; lacks neck crescent.

SIMILAR SPECIES See under Rock Pigeon (p. 233).

STATUS & DISTRIBUTION Western North America to Argentina. Pacific population breeds moist forest zones of coastal mountains, Cascades, Sierra Nevada from southeastern Alaska to northern Baja; substantial movement to southern California for winter. In PNW, locally fairly common summer resident from tidewater to Cascade crest, both slopes BC Coast Range; casual visitor farther inland, mostly Apr–Jun (some possibly from Colorado/Utah populations). Most migrate south Sep–Oct, return starting late Feb. Highly local, generally uncommon winter resident (nearly absent from interior).

HABITAT ASSOCIATIONS Coniferous, mixed forest; well-treed parks, residential neighborhoods, rural areas. May forage on agricultural fields, tidal flats, other open habitats; in winter, semi-open lowlands, edge habitats, with nearby food resource. Visits mineral springs in nesting season.

BEHAVIOR & FEEDING Gregarious year-round. Diet principally fruit, seeds, flowers of native, ornamental trees, shrubs, in season—madrone (*Arbutus*), Garry oak particularly favored; also spilled grain, seed from feeders. In distinctive flap-and-glide territorial display, male circles at treetop height, chirping, with wings, tail spread. Flimsy platform nest on large limb (Douglas-fir widely used), usually single egg. Squab fed crop milk, moving to adult diet by fledging time.

VOCALIZATIONS Song low *woot woo*, usually repeated in series of five from high in tree.

BC (Oliver)—Nov • LAURE W. NEISH

WA (King County)—Jun • BOB KOTHENBEUTEL

Eurasian Collared-Dove
Streptopelia decaocto

DESCRIPTION 12 in/30 cm, wingspan 22 in/56 cm. **Bulky, pale**-grayish-buff dove. Lightly flushed pinkish head, breast; narrow, white-edged **black collar** on nape. **Blunt, white-tipped tail**. Black bill, rose-pink legs. *Juvenile:* Brown iris (red in adult), collar not fully developed, light-reddish edging on body, wing feathers.

SIMILAR SPECIES African Collared-Dove (also called Ringed Turtle-Dove; not shown, occurs in PNW as escaped cage bird) smaller, paler, with white (versus gray) undertail, two-syllable *coo crrrooo* song. Mourning Dove (p. 237) browner, more slender; pointed tail, no collar.

STATUS & DISTRIBUTION Native to South Asia, introduced or expanded naturally into much of Old World. Released in Bahamas in 1972, quickly spread across North America, reaching PNW (OR) in 1999. Now resident locally throughout, increasing steadily.

HABITAT ASSOCIATIONS Prairies, croplands, cattle-feeding operations, grain elevators, small woodlots, semi-rural residential tracts, towns. Often seen on overhead wires, power poles, buildings. Requires dependable grain supply, including feeders, with nearby trees for nesting, roosting. Avoids dense forest, urban core.

BEHAVIOR & FEEDING Like other doves/pigeons, strong flier, bobs head while walking, drinks by suction without lifting head. Gregarious. Diet principally seeds, cereal grains, taken on ground. Little data on breeding in PNW. Elsewhere, nests any time of year but mostly spring/summer, often two or more broods; usually two eggs in stick nest in tree. Parental care similar to other pigeons/doves.

VOCALIZATIONS Male advertising song *coo COO coop*, repeated in series from high perch; female version shorter, higher pitched, quieter. Also gutteral *waaah* when alighting.

California—Apr · GREG GILLSON

Arizona—May · JIM BURNS

White-winged Dove
Zenaida asiatica

DESCRIPTION 11 in/28 cm, wingspan 19 in/48 cm. Robust, **square tailed**. Gray brown, including underwing. Outer tail feathers tipped white. **White wing patch** on secondary (greater) coverts visible in flight, contrasting with black upper surface of flight feathers; shows on perched bird as white line below folded wing. Black dash on lower cheek, bare blue skin around eye, red-orange iris. Dark bill; reddish legs, feet. *Juvenile:* Brown legs, feet; light-brown iris, reduced cheek marking.

SIMILAR SPECIES White wing patch diagnostic. Mourning Dove (p. 237) slimmer with graduated, pointed tail. Eurasian Collared-Dove (p. 235) pale with dark hindneck collar.

STATUS & DISTRIBUTION Resident from southern US to Central America, West Indies; bulk of northern breeders withdraw southward or to coasts in winter. Range expanding northward since 1980s. Only five records in PNW prior to 1994; since then, average of three per year, mostly single-day, scattered across whole of region (May–Jan). Annual in OR in recent years (majority along coast).

HABITAT ASSOCIATIONS Undetermined in PNW. Closest resident populations in cactus/palo verde/ocotillo deserts, thorn forest, riparian deciduous trees, often interspersed with sources of agricultural grain; also urban parks, gardens, residential neighborhoods. Adaptable across its large range, from coastal mangroves to mountain pine-oak forests.

BEHAVIOR & FEEDING Diet not studied in PNW. Elsewhere, seeds, nuts, fruit according to availability. Breeding unknown in PNW. In primary range, breeding biology similar to other pigeons/doves.

VOCALIZATIONS Advertising, territorial song *WHO COOKS for YOUuu*; also longer variant, series of accented hoots, coos. Neither likely to be heard in PNW.

OR (Benton County)—Nov • MATT T. LEE

BC (Osoyoos)—Jul • JUKKA JANTUNEN

Mourning Dove
Zenaida macroura

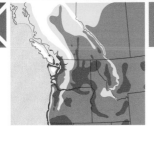

DESCRIPTION 12 in/30 cm, wingspan 18 in/46 cm. **Slender**, small headed; **long, pointed tail**, white tips of outer tail feathers visible in flight. Grayish brown above, buffy below; pinkish hue to breast, bluish crown (more pronounced in male). Small, thin, dark-gray bill; dark-brown iris, blue skin around eye (adult). Vivid pink legs, feet. *Juvenile:* Dusky facial markings; buffy feather edging gives lightly scalloped look.

SIMILAR SPECIES Eurasian Collared-Dove (p. 235) paler with blunt-tipped tail, black collar on nape. White wing patches readily distinguish rare White-winged Dove (p. 236).

STATUS & DISTRIBUTION Continent-wide, southern Canada to Central America, West Indies. Summer resident in PNW, uncommon/fairly common west of Cascades (rare/casual north of Campbell River), common in interior (uncommon north of Williams Lake). Partially migratory; most migrants leave Aug–early Oct, winter southwestern US, western, north-central Mexico, return Mar–May. Highly local winter resident, fairly common OR, eastern WA, southern interior BC, northwestern MT; uncommon ID, western WA, southwestern BC.

HABITAT ASSOCIATIONS Avoids closed forest, alpine areas. Frequents open habitats with available water, food source, e.g., shrub-steppe, rangeland, agricultural fields, woodlands/forest edges, shelterbelts, orchards, suburban neighborhoods. In migration or winter, concentrates near feeders, feedlots, grain storage/transport facilities.

BEHAVIOR & FEEDING Swift flier. Diet almost exclusively cultivated cereal crops, wild seeds, taken on open ground. Loose platform nest in/on tree, shrub, human-made structure, ground. Usually two eggs, often two or more broods. Parental care similar to other pigeons/doves.

VOCALIZATIONS Song slow, mournful cooing: *ooo AAA ooo ooo ooo.*

Yellow-billed Cuckoo
Coccyzus americanus

DESCRIPTION 11 in/28 cm, wingspan 18 in/46 cm. Slender with long, pointed wings; **long, graduated tail**. Grayish above, white below; **bright cinnamon-rufous primaries, secondaries** obvious in flight; black rectrices with broad white tips, forming appearance of **white tail spots** when seen from below. Fairly heavy, pointed, slightly curved **yellow bill**; yellow orbital ring. *Juvenile:* Rectrices gray instead of black.

SIMILAR SPECIES Black-billed Cuckoo (not shown; casual southern interior BC, accidental elsewhere in PNW) has black bill, smaller white tail spots, lacks rufous in wings.

STATUS & DISTRIBUTION Breeds east of Rockies in extreme southern Canada, US, south through Mexico, West Indies; historic breeding range west of Rockies now severely contracted (rare, local ID, southwestern states). Winters primarily South America. In PNW, irregular, rare breeder west of Cascades north to southwestern BC into early 20th century; presently casual region-wide except rare in southeastern ID (breeding confirmed). Interior historical status poorly documented, but majority of recent reports from southern BC (mid-May–Oct); US records show clear Jun–Jul peak.

HABITAT ASSOCIATIONS Riparian woodlands, thickets, rural gardens.

BEHAVIOR & FEEDING Skulks in thick vegetation, searching for insects, particularly caterpillars. Flight direct with deep wingbeats. Recent tracking data indicate frequent, nearly year-round movements. Pair builds flimsy nest, shares parental care; young fledge less than three weeks after eggs laid. May also "dump" eggs in other species' nests.

VOCALIZATIONS Song throaty, wooden series, slowing at end: *kakakakowkow kowp kowp kowp*. Also hard, knocking *kok kok kok kok kok*; series of hollow *coo* notes.

OR (Multnomah County)—Oct · DOUG SCHURMAN

BC (Delta)—Mar · JOHN GORDON

Barn Owl
Tyto alba

DESCRIPTION 16 in/41 cm, wingspan 42 in/107 cm. *Adult:* **Medium-sized** owl with **heart-shaped** face; **white or buff below** with small spots, **golden buff above**. Broad wings, short tail, relatively long legs. Males tend to be whiter ventrally, with fewer dark markings. *Juvenile:* Nestlings covered in fluffy white down; flying subadults similar to adults.

SIMILAR SPECIES Some individuals nearly pure white below; can be confused with Snowy Owl (p. 243) when seen in flight, especially at night; otherwise distinctive.

STATUS & DISTRIBUTION Ranges on all continents (except Antarctica) wherever there is no significant winter snowfall. In PNW, rare to locally fairly common resident at low to middle elevations from southern coastal BC, southern Okanagan Valley south through WA, ID, northwestern MT, western WY, OR. Accidental north to Peace River lowlands.

HABITAT ASSOCIATIONS Most common in old pastures, fields with abundant source of meadow voles; also found in urban, suburban situations, any open agricultural, grassland habitat; shuns contiguous forest. Nests in old barns, other buildings or structures that provide cover, privacy, shelf for nesting; also in hollow trees, small caves in cliffs, large nest boxes, holes in haystacks.

BEHAVIOR & FEEDING Forages at night, coursing low over fields, listening for mice. Some individuals target locally abundant prey such as roosting starlings. Breeds year-round during peaks in prey populations, sometimes rearing multiple broods, but in PNW nests primarily Mar–Jul; occasionally flocks at winter roosts (frequently dense conifers). Juveniles may disperse far beyond natal territory.

VOCALIZATIONS Hissing shrieks, high-pitched twitter.

BC (Penticton)—Jun • DICK CANNINGS   BC (Penticton)—Jun • DICK CANNINGS

Flammulated Owl
Psiloscops flammeolus

DESCRIPTION 6.75 in/17 cm. **Tiny** owl, size of small coffee cup; grayish with rufous highlights to face, back; distinct silver "V" pattern in feathers between eyes; dark vermiculated striping on breast, belly. **Dark eyes**, unfeathered toes; small feathered "ear" tufts, sometimes not visible. *Juvenile:* Downy; pale gray barred with darker gray.

SIMILAR SPECIES Other small owls show yellow eyes (caution: can appear dark in some situations). Western Screech-Owl (p. 241) has feathered toes; Northern Saw-whet Owl's (p. 253) head larger, ventral striping different; Northern Pygmy-Owl (p. 245) has relatively long tail, different facial pattern.

STATUS & DISTRIBUTION Breeds mostly in interior, south-central BC to southern California, in mountains to Oaxaca; winters central Mexico to El Salvador. In PNW, locally common mid-elevation breeder east of Cascades/BC Coast Range south from Williams Lake, Radium Hot Springs (rare western WY); spills over crest in southwestern OR to Josephine County. Highly migratory; returns May, leaves for wintering grounds Sep–Oct.

HABITAT ASSOCIATIONS Drier forests of mature Douglas-fir or mixed conifers (ponderosa pine increasingly southward) with grassy openings, aspen, at middle to higher elevations. Requires snags with cavities for nesting.

BEHAVIOR & FEEDING Forages almost entirely on large insects (crickets, beetles, moths), taken from large trees, shrubs. Secondary cavity-nester, prefers flicker nest holes, readily uses appropriate nest boxes. Nests May–Aug, rarely seen after young fledge in Jul or Aug.

VOCALIZATIONS Call soft, hollow *boop* or *boodo BOOP*; rarely heard after Jun. Female gives mewing call; juveniles, rasping *khah* begging call.

ID (Bingham County)—Feb · DARREN CLARK

BC (Okanagan)—Jan · JOHN GORDON

Western Screech-Owl
Otus kennicottii

DESCRIPTION 8.5 in/22 cm. **Small** owl, grayish brown (reddish brown in some coastal individuals), with **"ear" tufts**; dark vermiculated striping on breast, belly; **yellow eyes**. *Juvenile:* Downy; pale gray barred with darker gray.

SIMILAR SPECIES Flammulated Owl (p. 240) much smaller, has dark eyes. Northern Saw-whet Owl (p. 253), Northern Pygmy-Owl (p. 245) smaller, lack "ear" tufts; ventral striping different.

STATUS & DISTRIBUTION Ranges southeastern Alaska to northwestern Mexico. In PNW, uncommon sedentary resident nearly throughout; absent Haida Gwaii. West of Cascades/BC Coast Range, populations (especially urban) declining, possibly correlated with Barred Owl arrival. In interior, inhabits intermontane valleys south from BC (Lillooet, Kamloops, Vernon, Kootenay Lake, Cranbrook) but virtually absent from Columbia Plateau, other arid landscapes, away from riparian areas.

HABITAT ASSOCIATIONS Open forests, woodlands, usually near water. In interior, black cottonwood, water birch, aspen, generally below 3,000 ft/900 m; on coast, coniferous, mixed forests, often associated with bigleaf maple or oak, typically <1,000 ft/300 m but ≥4,000 ft/1,200 m in southern OR.

BEHAVIOR & FEEDING Highly nocturnal. Feeds on wide variety of small prey: rodents, birds, lizards, frogs, fishes, crayfish, large insects, worms. Secondary cavity nester, readily uses appropriate nest boxes. Nests Apr–Jun, family groups stay together until mid-Aug.

VOCALIZATIONS Calls (given by both sexes, females higher pitched) include bouncing-ball pattern of whistled hoots—speeding up, descending in pitch toward end; also short trill immediately followed by longer trill. Females, juveniles give descending *de de do* begging calls. Note: Screech-owls do not screech.

Interior • WA (Spokane County)—Nov • JON ISACOFF

Coastal • BC (Victoria)—May • TED ARDLEY

Great Horned Owl
Bubo virginianus

DESCRIPTION 22 in/56 cm, wingspan 44 in/111 cm. **Very large** owl with **distinct "horns"** (feather tufts); grayish brown (coastal birds darker), barred on breast, belly; **yellow eyes.** *Juvenile:* Downy; buffy gray with dark ventral barring; lacks horns.

SIMILAR SPECIES Long-eared Owl (p. 250) smaller, slimmer; horns longer, placed more toward center of head. Great Gray Owl (p. 247) has larger head, lacks horns.

STATUS & DISTRIBUTION Ranges in New World from Arctic treeline to Patagonia, except West Indies. Fairly common resident breeder throughout PNW but absent Haida Gwaii. Generally sedentary, but some individuals disperse long distances in fall.

HABITAT ASSOCIATIONS Found in almost all habitats including open forests, grasslands, farmlands, residential suburbs, cities (has disappeared as nester in Seattle in recent years for unknown reasons). Generally absent from tundra, scarce in contiguous dense, wet coniferous forest. Often roosts in barns, hay sheds, abandoned buildings during winter.

BEHAVIOR & FEEDING Feeds on variety of prey but prefers mid-sized birds, mammals (hares, cottontails, jackrabbits, muskrat, rats, grouse). Nests Jan–May in stick nests built by other species such as ravens, crows, hawks; also on towers, cliff ledges, bridge supports, or other suitable platforms. Young remain dependent on adults until fall. Primarily nocturnal but active day or night, especially while feeding young.

VOCALIZATIONS Call (given by both sexes, females higher-pitched) series of 4–7 low hoots, e.g., *hoo hoohoo HOO hoo.* Females give nasal *hwaay* during courtship. Juveniles beg for food with loud, rising screech *rrrheeeik* (often misidentified as "screech owl").

Snowy Owl
Bubo scandiacus

DESCRIPTION 23 in/58 cm, wingspan 52 in/132 cm. **Very large** owl, predominantly **white** with varying amounts of black spotting, barring; females more heavily marked than males. Yellow eyes, no conspicuous "ear" tufts. *Subadult:* First-winter duskier than respective adult, male becomes nearly all-white by fourth year.

SIMILAR SPECIES Barn Owl (p. 239) sometimes essentially white below, but smaller with buffy upperparts, black eyes.

STATUS & DISTRIBUTION Circumpolar, nomadic breeder on Arctic tundra in northern Canada, northern Alaska, northern Eurasia. Rare to irregularly uncommon Oct–Apr throughout PNW south to central OR, southeastern ID, infrequently southern OR; generally more often seen on coast such as at Fraser, Skagit, Nisqually Deltas, Grays Harbor, Columbia estuary. East of Cascades, annual south to central WA (Lincoln, Grant Counties), northwestern MT (Flathead Lake area). Numbers spike (primarily immatures) during periodic southbound irruptions, the timing of which remains somewhat mysterious. Accidental May–Sep.

HABITAT ASSOCIATIONS In PNW, open habitats including agricultural fields, pastures, airports, marshes, mud flats. On coast, majority seen near concentrations of waterfowl; in interior, most often in grain fields, where concentrations occur during irruptions.

BEHAVIOR & FEEDING Active day or night but often crepuscular, taking wide variety of prey with falcon-like flight. In PNW, prefers mid-sized mammals, birds, including rats, voles, ducks, grebes; on breeding grounds, lemmings, ptarmigan. Nests on ground on open tundra. Male establishes territory; female selects nest site, tends nestlings, provisioned by male. Gregarious in irruptions.

VOCALIZATIONS Mostly silent in PNW; on breeding grounds, gives series of low hoots.

Northern Hawk Owl
Surnia ulula

DESCRIPTION 16 in/41 cm, wingspan 28 in/71 cm. **Medium-sized** owl; **long-tailed**, brownish gray above, heavily spotted with white (spots finer on crown); white below with fine, dark, horizontal barring. Prominent **black framing around white face**; yellow eyes. *Juvenile:* Downy, short tailed; face, crown pattern similar to adult.

SIMILAR SPECIES Boreal Owl (p. 252) has similar facial, dorsal patterns, but underparts show vertical streaks; much shorter tailed.

STATUS & DISTRIBUTION Circumpolar, breeding in subarctic, subalpine forests in Canada, Alaska, northern Eurasia. In PNW, rare to uncommon montane breeder south to central ID, north-central WA, northwestern MT; more often seen in winter. Individuals may set up territory Nov–Mar at lower-elevation sites east of Cascades/BC Coast Range, rarely south to central WA; casual farther south or on westside in US. Nomadic; often breeds at particular site for 1–2 years, then gone.

HABITAT ASSOCIATIONS In summer prefers meadows in burned subalpine or plateau forests with abundant snags; wintering birds use varied open habitats, often with old fields, pastures, where voles common.

BEHAVIOR & FEEDING Unlike most other owls, active primarily during day; perches conspicuously in open while hunting. Feeds on wide variety of small mammals, birds, but generally settles at sites with abundant voles. Nests in large cavities in snags, or hollowed tops of snags. Male establishes breeding territory with circling display flights; provisions brooding female.

VOCALIZATIONS Falcon-like series of yelping notes; on breeding grounds, gives rarely heard territorial song—long, resonant, screech-owl-like trill.

Northern Pygmy-Owl
Glaucidium gnoma

DESCRIPTION 6.75 in/17 cm. *Adult:* **Tiny** owl with **small, round head**, crown spotted with white; gray-brown upperparts, white underparts with dark streaks. Relatively **long tail** has whitish bars. "False eyes" on nape black ringed with white. *Juvenile:* Crown, nape generally unspotted.

SIMILAR SPECIES Northern Saw-whet Owl (p. 253) has shorter tail, larger head; warmer brown rather than gray brown. Call-notes faster. Flammulated Owl (p. 240) has "ear" tufts, shorter tail, dark (versus yellow) eyes, different call.

STATUS & DISTRIBUTION Ranges northern BC, southern Alaska south in mountains to Honduras. Breeding resident throughout PNW except Haida Gwaii, Columbia Plateau, southeastern OR, southwestern ID; mostly extirpated throughout urbanized Puget Trough, Willamette Valley. Generally uncommon; rare BC northern mainland coast, western WY. Considered resident, but appearances at nonbreeding locations Oct–Apr indicate some migration or downslope movement.

HABITAT ASSOCIATIONS Breeds in wide variety of coniferous forests, often at high elevations; some move into valley-bottom agricultural or suburban habitats in winter.

BEHAVIOR & FEEDING Unlike most other owls, more active during daytime than at night. Preys on voles, mice, shrews, small birds, insects. Nests Apr–Jun in tree cavities, usually excavated by mid-sized woodpeckers such as Hairy Woodpecker.

VOCALIZATIONS Call slow series of whistled toots, one every two seconds: *kook . . . kook . . . kook . . .* ; replaced occasionally by very rapid series of lower notes when bird is agitated. Imitations of tooting call will often bring in mobs of various small, agitated birds—occasionally a pygmy-owl as well.

WA (Franklin County)—May · RYAN SHAW

Juveniles at nest · **WA (Adams County)—May** · GREGG THOMPSON

Burrowing Owl
Athene cunicularia

DESCRIPTION 9.5 in/24 cm. **Small** owl; **long legs**. Brown above spotted with white; white below, barred with brown flecks. Yellow eyes. **Juvenile:** Fluffier with buffy belly, brown collar across upper breast.

SIMILAR SPECIES Short-eared Owl (p. 251) larger; shorter legs, vertical brown streaks on breast, belly. Other small owls lack long, nearly bare tarsi.

STATUS & DISTRIBUTION Breeds in West from south-central BC to Baja, southern Mexico, winters primarily California to Honduras; also resident southern Florida, West Indies, much of South America. In PNW, local breeder in dry grasslands east of Cascades/BC Coast Range south from near Kamloops. Uncommon Mar–Sep WA, OR, southern ID; rare western WY, casual Idaho Panhandle, northwestern MT. Extirpated as breeder in BC by 1980 with conversion of prairies to cropland; continuing reintroductions since 1991 maintain small, local population. Rare Oct–Feb, mostly WA Columbia Plateau, Willamette Valley, fewer northern Salish Sea, OR coast; formerly nested rarely in open habitats west of Cascades.

HABITAT ASSOCIATIONS Breeds in dry native grasslands; in winter occasionally uses coastal shoreline habitats, agricultural fields, airports.

BEHAVIOR & FEEDING Feeds on variety of small mammals, large insects, birds—notably pocket mice in spring/early summer, crickets, beetles in late summer. Migratory; pairs form after spring arrival. Nests, roosts in underground burrows dug by badgers, ground squirrels, other mammals; often loosely colonial. Provision of artificial "burrows" (e.g., buried pipes) by conservationists, wildlife managers boosts productivity in areas of disturbed habitat.

VOCALIZATIONS Common contact call rough *keee ki ki kik*; male territorial call accented *CU coooo*.

Great Gray Owl
Strix nebulosa

DESCRIPTION 27 in/69 cm, wingspan 52 in/132 cm. **Very large** gray owl with **huge round head**, face marked with fine darker concentric circles; black chin, white "bowtie"; **yellow eyes**, bill. *Juvenile:* Face darker, lacks concentric rings; head, breast, belly downy through summer.

SIMILAR SPECIES Barred Owl (p. 249) smaller; blackish eyes, lacks bowtie. Great Horned Owl (p. 242) similar size; smaller head, prominent "horns," black bill; heavier with larger feet for killing large prey.

STATUS & DISTRIBUTION Circumpolar; in North America, breeds central Alaska to Quebec; in West, disjunctly south to Yosemite. Winters irregularly south to Massachusetts. In PNW, rare to uncommon resident in forested mountains, plateaus east of Cascades/BC Coast Range; status poorly understood south of Canada—more local, rare, except uncommon ID. On westside, breeds in OR (Siskiyous, Willamette NF); casual Nov–Mar in lowlands, including coast, resulting from downslope or southward movements (e.g., out of BC interior down Fraser Valley).

HABITAT ASSOCIATIONS Forest edges with meadows, often pastures in woodland matrix, mostly at higher elevations (above 3,000 ft/900 m); lower in Siskiyous.

BEHAVIOR & FEEDING Nomadic, may not breed when prey scarce. Feeds almost entirely on voles, pocket gophers; large facial disk efficient at gathering sound, so can locate prey under deep snow or even under shallow soil layer. Nests in old stick nest of hawk or on open snags, mistletoe platforms.

VOCALIZATIONS Territorial call series of low, hollow hoots, descending in pitch toward end. Young beg with harsh squawk.

OR (Jackson County)—Jun • PETER J. THIEMANN

Spotted Owl
Strix occidentalis

DESCRIPTION 17.5 in/44 cm, wingspan 40 in/102 cm. **Large** owl, brown with white-spotted upperparts, round face, **no "horns"**; breast, belly heavily **barred** with brown flecks. **Dark eyes.** *Juvenile:* Spotting less distinct.

SIMILAR SPECIES Barred Owl (p. 249) closely similar but grayer overall; vertical brown belly streaking (versus horizontal barring); call less monotone with different cadence, often more complex.

STATUS & DISTRIBUTION "Northern" Spotted Owl (*S.o. caurina*) resident in mature forests from southwestern BC south through mountains to northern California. In PNW, found locally, sparsely from extreme southwestern mainland BC south through Olympics, WA/OR Cascades, OR Coast Range, Siskiyous. Populations declining throughout region due to habitat loss from extensive logging, competition from invasive Barred Owl. Nearing extirpation in Canada, threatened in US (annual declines nearing 7 percent). Remaining strongholds include forested southwestern OR, higher-elevation eastside WA Cascades. Difficult to find anywhere; nest-site information closely guarded to protect owls' welfare. Recovery plans controversial, highly contested by landowners, timber interests. Two other subspecies resident southern California, southwestern states to central Mexico.

HABITAT ASSOCIATIONS Principally extensive old-growth, structurally complex coniferous forest; on east slope of Cascades, often steep, open sites dominated by Douglas-fir or ponderosa pine.

BEHAVIOR & FEEDING Feeds primarily on wood rats, flying squirrels; also other small mammals, large insects. Most birds nest less than annually, use preexisting site such as cavity, snag, mistletoe platform.

VOCALIZATIONS Common call loud, throaty three- or four-note *hoo hoohoo hoooo* (first note sometimes missing). Female call higher pitched; also clear, rising whistle. Young beg with hissing.

Juvenile · BC (Port Coquitlam)—May · DAMON CALDERWOOD | Pair · WA (Snohomish County)—Mar · GREGG THOMPSON

Barred Owl
Strix varia

DESCRIPTION 21 in/53 cm, wingspan 42 in/107 cm. **Large** owl; gray brown with white-spotted upperparts, **no "horns"**; concentric whitish circles on round face, **dark eyes**. Upper breast barred brown; lower breast, belly, white with prominent **vertical brown streaks**. *Juvenile:* Blotchy underparts obscure belly streaks.

SIMILAR SPECIES Spotted Owl (p. 248) closely similar; browner overall with horizontal brown belly spotting; call shorter, more monotone, rhythm different. Great Gray Owl (p. 247) larger, yellow eyes, shows white "bow tie."

STATUS & DISTRIBUTION Originally limited to eastern North America, expanded in early 1900s across boreal forest to southeastern Alaska; since 1950s, steadily extending southward toward central California. In PNW, increasing resident in well-forested areas throughout except Haida Gwaii, western WY. Fairly common BC, WA, western OR; uncommon Idaho Panhandle, northwestern MT, eastern OR; rare wanderer in fall/winter (Aug–Feb) southern ID, OR high desert, open westside agricultural areas. Disjunct population in central Mexico may be separate species.

HABITAT ASSOCIATIONS Dense forests with large old trees for nesting; often associated with wet river-bottom forest, flourishes in large westside city parks.

BEHAVIOR & FEEDING Usually nocturnal; feeds on small mammals including mice, squirrels; also other vertebrates, invertebrates. Nests annually Mar–Jun, usually in large cavity; fledglings dependent until Aug. Aggressive; outcompetes, occasionally interbreeds with Spotted Owl, possibly impacts other PNW owls. Humans sometimes attacked, primarily in fall.

VOCALIZATIONS Loud, accented *who cooks for you, who cooks for YOUaalll* by both sexes, often call-and-response. Female higher pitched; also gives rough, rising whistle; young beg with rising hiss.

BC (Boundary Bay)—Jan · GREGG THOMPSON

WA (Snohomish County)—Jan · GREGG THOMPSON

Long-eared Owl
Asio otus

DESCRIPTION 15 in/38 cm, wingspan 36 in/91 cm. **Medium-sized** owl; **long "ear" tufts** atop head, orange facial disk, long wings with dark carpal patch. Brownish-gray upperparts; pale breast, belly with dark, rust-flecked stripes, bars. *Juvenile:* Downy; blackish face, shorter ear tufts.

SIMILAR SPECIES Great Horned Owl (p. 242) much larger, bulkier, ear tufts more on corners of head. Short-eared Owl (p. 251) similar wings, flight style (Long-eared rarely seen in flight during day) but buffier, less gray, lacks long ear tufts.

STATUS & DISTRIBUTION Holarctic across southern boreal, temperate latitudes in open country; in North America, breeds BC, Maritimes south to Baja, Virginia; withdraws southward in winter, ranging to central Mexico. In PNW, widespread resident but easily overlooked—rare to locally fairly common east of Cascades/BC Coast Range, rare on westside; some upslope dispersal to subalpine Aug–Oct. Concentrates in lowlands Oct–Feb at group roosts near abundant prey (mostly interior); rare on coastal plain.

HABITAT ASSOCIATIONS Grasslands, pastures, with copses of trees (e.g., aspen, birch, alder, Russian olive), open forests, forest edges with meadows.

BEHAVIOR & FEEDING Feeds mostly on voles; forages exclusively at night, flying over meadows or through open forests. Nests in old stick nests of hawks, crows, magpies, or on mistletoe platforms. Territorial males produce loud wing-clap, striking wings together under body while in flight. Roosts in trees.

VOCALIZATIONS Territorial call series of widely spaced hollow hoots: *oooo oooo oooo*. Females give variety of nasal barks, wails, when agitated.

Short-eared Owl
Asio flammeus

DESCRIPTION 15 in/38 cm, wingspan 38 in/97 cm. **Medium-sized** owl; slender, round headed with barely visible "ear" tufts above yellow eyes. Brownish-buff upperparts; **pale, brown-striped breast, belly**. Long wings show **dark carpal patch** dorsally, ventrally. *Juvenile:* Downy; face dark, eyes browner.

SIMILAR SPECIES Long-eared Owl (p. 250) similar in size, shape, wing markings, but grayer above with evenly patterned underparts, long ear tufts; highly nocturnal. Barn Owl (p. 239) has rounder wings, heart-shaped face; unstreaked below.

STATUS & DISTRIBUTION Nearly cosmopolitan; in North America, breeds northern Alaska to Newfoundland, south to California, West Indies but critically imperiled or extirpated in eastern US. In PNW, declining, nomadic breeder in open habitats; uncommon locally across interior; nearly extirpated west of Cascades/BC Coast Range (possible nesting recently at Boundary Bay, Samish Flats, Willamette Valley). Migrants widespread, locally common Oct–May; concentrated Nov–Feb mostly at coastal deltas, other westside lowland marsh (e.g., Ridgefield NWR, Samish Flats, Finley NWR), fewer at eastside locations where voles abundant.

HABITAT ASSOCIATIONS Grasslands, marshes, old fields; migrants sometimes use alpine tundra.

BEHAVIOR & FEEDING Feeds almost entirely on voles, foraging mostly early morning or late afternoon by coursing back and forth over fields with slow, deep wingbeats in buoyant, moth-like flight. Territorial male produces wing-claps by striking wings together under body while in flight. Nests, roosts communally on ground in low vegetation; young develop quickly, fledge on foot within two weeks.

VOCALIZATIONS Male territorial call rapid series of short hoots; both sexes give nasal barks when agitated.

Juvenile · WA (Pierce County)—Aug · DOUG SCHURMAN   Alberta—Jan · TERRY THORMIN

Boreal Owl
Aegolius funereus

DESCRIPTION 10 in/25 cm, wingspan 21 in/53 cm. **Small owl; large head, short tail**; dark brown above, spotted white; white breast, belly, broadly streaked with brown. **Black crown, finely spotted with white**; yellow eyes (appear dark under certain conditions). **White facial disk** boldly outlined in black, **charcoal-gray cheek patches**. *Juvenile:* Dark brown with contrasting white eyebrows, chin markings; wings spotted white.

SIMILAR SPECIES Northern Saw-whet Owl (p. 253) much smaller, browner, with brownish facial disk; crown streaked (versus spotted) with white. Juvenile eyebrows join to form triangle.

STATUS & DISTRIBUTION Found in boreal, subalpine forests throughout northern hemisphere. In PNW, rare to uncommon resident from just west of Cascade/BC Coast Range crest eastward in subalpine forests, south to OR Cascades, western WY. Seasonal movements little understood; casual in winter on Fraser Delta, migrants accidental in open interior.

HABITAT ASSOCIATIONS Prefers older forests of subalpine fir, spruce, especially those with small meadows; rarer in lodgepole pine forests. Will nest at more moderate elevations in Douglas-fir, ponderosa pine, if nest sites unavailable in higher-elevation foraging habitat.

BEHAVIOR & FEEDING Nocturnal; preys on small mammals (especially voles) but also small birds. Nests Apr–Jun in tree cavities (especially Pileated Woodpecker, Northern Flicker holes); frequently uses aspens. Roosts against tree trunk in dense forest.

VOCALIZATIONS Male's courtship song rapid series of hollow whistles that increases in volume, pitch, lasts about two seconds, very similar to sound of winnowing snipe. Contact call nasal *mooo a*; agitated call sharp, barking *skiew*.

A.a. brooksi · BC (Haida Gwaii) —Aug · JOHN BURRILL

BC (Victoria)—Oct · LIAM SINGH

Juvenile · Alberta—May · TERRY THORMIN

Northern Saw-whet Owl
Aegolius acadicus

DESCRIPTION 8 in/20 cm. **Tiny** owl with **large head, short tail**; brown above, spotted with white; white breast; belly broadly streaked with brown; yellow eyes (can appear dark under certain conditions). White areas replaced by buff on endemic Haida Gwaii subspecies (*A.a. brooksi*). ***Juvenile:*** Similar to adult but rich buff brown below.

SIMILAR SPECIES Northern Pygmy-Owl (p. 245) smaller, with proportionately smaller head, longer tail; call-notes similar but pygmy-owl call much slower. Boreal Owl (p. 252) larger; white facial disk outlined in black.

STATUS & DISTRIBUTION Found across southern Canada, northern US, south in mountains to southern Mexico. In PNW, fairly common but inconspicuous breeding resident in forested habitats east of Cascades/BC Coast Ranges throughout; uncommon in coastal forests. Quite migratory; northern breeders augment low-elevation southerly populations in winter, especially on coast. Hundreds of migrants trapped, banded each fall at Rocky Point (southern Vancouver Island), Boise Ridge (southwestern ID).

HABITAT ASSOCIATIONS Forests of all types, especially older low- to mid-elevation forests. Generally replaced by Boreal Owl in subalpine forest, but can be common at high elevations in years of high prey populations.

BEHAVIOR & FEEDING Highly nocturnal, roosts during day in thick vegetation; preys on small mammals (especially deer mice), fewer birds. Nests in tree cavities, particularly Northern Flicker holes.

VOCALIZATIONS Male's courtship song long monotonous series of whistled toots at rate of about two per second (one per two seconds for pygmy-owl). Contact call nasal, catlike whine; agitated call rapid series of three short metallic squeals.

ID (Jefferson County)—Aug · DARREN CLARK

WA (Adams County)—May · KEN ARCHER

Common Nighthawk
Chordeiles minor

DESCRIPTION 9 in/23 cm. **Cryptic** plumage, mottled brown, black, gray, buffy, white; underparts narrowly barred brown. **Large flat head, large eyes, short bill, wide gape.** Throat white (male), buffy (female, juvenile). Short legs. **Long, narrow wings; white bar on prima-ries** prominent in flight, shows as white patch on folded wing. Long, barred tail, shallowly notched, with white subterminal band on underside (male only).

SIMILAR SPECIES Common Poorwill (p. 255) distinguished by light tail corners, absence of white wing-bar, different call, perch-based nocturnal foraging habits. Shorter wings, tail lend roosting bird compact appearance.

STATUS & DISTRIBUTION Breeds across continent from subarctic Canada to Central America; winters South America. Summer resident in PNW. Fairly common/locally common Cascades eastward, on westside rare/locally uncommon, declining; casual/rare BC northern mainland coast. Highly migratory. Returns late May–early Jun, departs late Jul–early Oct (peak mid-Aug through mid-Sep).

HABITAT ASSOCIATIONS Shrub-steppe, fields, dunes, scablands, stony ridges, open forest, clear-cuts, burns. Rare in cities (formerly common).

BEHAVIOR & FEEDING Takes insects in extended, erratic, buoyant flight from just above ground/water level up to 800 ft (250 m), mostly near dawn, dusk but also broad daylight, nighttime at outdoor lighting. Skims drinking water from surface in flight. Male produces booming sound with wings in mating display dive. Two eggs laid directly on ground, occasionally gravel roofs. Roosts on ground, limbs, other horizontal surfaces. Often flocks in fall migration.

VOCALIZATIONS Nasal *peent* call, given repeatedly in flight. Hisses at intruders near nest.

WA (Kittitas County)—May · GREGG THOMPSON

Common Poorwill
Phalaenoptilus nuttallii

DESCRIPTION 8 in/20 cm. **Cryptic** plumage, mottled browns, grays, buffy, black, white; lighter underparts. **Large, flat head; large eyes, short bill, wide gape edged by bristles**. White throat feathering (buffy in juvenile) extends across upper breast. Short legs, small feet. **Broad, short, rounded wings**. Short, rounded **tail with whitish corners**.

SIMILAR SPECIES See under Common Nighthawk (p. 254).

STATUS & DISTRIBUTION Breeds Great Plains westward, southernmost Canada to northern Mexico; winters US–Mexico borderlands southward within breeding range. In PNW, fairly common, often local summer resident southern interior BC (mainly Okanagan Valley but north to Riske Creek), eastern WA (especially Cascades lower eastern slope), eastern/southwestern OR, southern ID, western WY. Rare northwestern MT, Idaho Panhandle. Accidental western lowlands, coast. Highly migratory in PNW. Most return late Apr–mid-May, depart by mid-Sep (extremes Mar–Nov).

HABITAT ASSOCIATIONS Low to middle elevations in dry, open shrublands, grasslands, often on rocky slopes with ponderosa pine, Douglas-fir, juniper, near streambeds or unpaved roads. Also (southwestern OR) chaparral, oaks.

BEHAVIOR & FEEDING Nocturnal. Roosts tight on ground by day, well camouflaged. Most active dawn, sunset, moonlit nights. Takes flying insects pursued in low, short sallies from ground in noiseless, flapping, moth-like flight. Often rests on gravel roads between sallies; red eye shine reveals location. Ground nesting; two eggs in shallow scrape. May flock in migration. Survives cold, prey scarcity by entering torpor.

VOCALIZATIONS Whistled *POOR WILL up* (second note higher; lower third note inaudible at distance), given repeatedly from perch. Hisses if disturbed.

California—Jul
MIKE DANZENBAKER

Nest · ID (Shoshone County)—Jul · DARREN CLARK

Black Swift
Cypseloides niger

DESCRIPTION 7 in/18 cm. Fleet, aerial insectivore, appears **overall black**; usually seen foraging overhead on **long, pointed, backward-curving wings**, with flickering wingbeats, long glides on wings held below horizontal. **Long, wide tail**, square when folded, often shallowly notched when fanned.

SIMILAR SPECIES Vaux's Swift (p. 257) smaller, shorter tailed, wings have narrower base; wingbeats more rapid, glides less often; pale breast, throat noticeable at close range. White-throated Swift (p. 258) has contrasting black-and-white plumage; narrower, notched tail, sharply pointed when folded. Swallows' wingbeats less stiff; wings proportionately shorter, broader, less swept back.

STATUS & DISTRIBUTION Summer resident discontinuously from southeastern Alaska, BC, through western states to Costa Rica, West Indies; most winter South America. In PNW, common BC westward from Coast Ranges (but absent Haida Gwaii), rare to fairly common interior; fairly common northern WA Cascades, uncommon Olympic Peninsula; locally uncommon Idaho Panhandle, northwestern MT; in OR, only confirmed breeding Lane County, migrants (mostly spring) uncommon coastally, rare interior valleys. Migrants return mid-May–early Jun, depart late Aug–early Oct.

HABITAT ASSOCIATIONS Nests damp, shaded ledges, recesses on sheer cliffs from seacoast to 8,500 ft (2,600 m) in mountains, frequently at waterfalls. Forages above mountains, lowlands, often far from nest sites.

BEHAVIOR & FEEDING Semi-colonial nester. Cup nest of moss, single egg. On wing all day, returning once or twice to feed chick. Seeks swarms, hatches, of flying insects above land, water, from near ground level to sometimes great heights. Flocks in migration.

VOCALIZATIONS Chip notes in twittering series, in flight.

Vaux's Swift
Chaetura vauxi

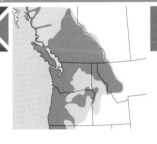

DESCRIPTION 4.25 in/11 cm. **Small, short bodied,** tapering toward ends; long, pointed, backswept wings. **Short tail** rounded when fanned, disappears when folded, giving bird "winged cigar" look. Blackish-brown upperparts; rump, uppertail coverts lighter. Grayish-brown underparts with **upper breast, throat noticeably paler.** Tiny black bill, wide gape like other swifts.

SIMILAR SPECIES Black Swift (p. 256), White-throated Swift (p. 258) larger, longer tailed; coloration of underparts diagnostic but sometimes difficult to discern in field. See also under Violet-green Swallow (p. 325).

STATUS & DISTRIBUTION Summer resident from southeastern Alaska, BC to western MT, central California. Year-round resident central Mexico to Panama, coastal Venezuela. Northern migrants winter Mexico, Honduras, in range of southern residents. As breeder in PNW, fairly common to common BC's south coast, Vancouver Island, uncommon/rare farther north (absent Haida Gwaii); uncommon/fairly common southern interior BC; fairly common forested parts WA, OR; fairly common west-central ID, Panhandle; uncommon/fairly common northwestern MT. Locally common migrant (rare southeastern OR, casual southern ID, western WY). Most return first half May, depart first half Sep (extremes late Mar–late Oct).

HABITAT ASSOCIATIONS Coniferous, mixed forest zones, including cities. Forages over forest, water, occasionally grasslands.

BEHAVIOR & FEEDING Nests, roosts semi-colonially inside hollow trees, snags, chimneys, also nest boxes high in trees. Takes small insects in fast, erratic, agile flight, returning frequently to feed young. Nest cemented to wall with saliva; usually six eggs. Migrants stage at communal roosts, often spectacular numbers in tall chimneys.

VOCALIZATIONS Rapid, insect-like series of high-pitched chips.

BC (Naramata)—Apr • LAURE W. NEISH

BC (Penticton)—Jun • GLENN BARTLEY

White-throated Swift
Aeronautes saxatalis

DESCRIPTION 6.5 in/16.5 cm. **Black with contrasting white** throat, breast, midline of belly, flank patches, trailing edge of secondaries, tertials. **Long, narrow, deeply notched tail, pointed when closed.** Wings narrow, pointed, swept back in flight, like other swifts. *Juvenile:* Dark feathering paler.

SIMILAR SPECIES See under broader-winged Black Swift (p. 256); smaller, slower-flying Vaux's Swift (p. 257).

STATUS & DISTRIBUTION Year-round resident California, southwestern US to Honduras; summer resident north to MT, southern BC. In PNW, range expanding for last 100 years. Locally fairly common south-central, southeastern BC (mostly Okanagan, but north to Williams Lake); eastern WA (mostly along Columbia River, tributaries); central, eastern OR (especially Malheur County); rare southwestern OR (possibly breeds). Uncommon central, southern ID, rare Panhandle; uncommon northwestern MT; fairly common western WY. Non-breeders accidental west of Cascades/BC Coast Range in WA, BC. Casual/irregular migrant western OR. Most return Apr–early May, leave late Aug–Sep (extremes early Mar–mid-Oct).

HABITAT ASSOCIATIONS Nests cliffs, rimrock in canyons, coulees, mountains, from low-elevation sagebrush flats, forested hills to alpine snowfields (Steens Mountain, OR); also bridges, other human-built structures. Usually forages fairly close to nest site.

BEHAVIOR & FEEDING Small feet used only to clamber, cling at nest, roost, like other swifts. Fast flight, instantaneous course adjustments in pursuit of insects. Nests semi-colonially, often near Cliff, Violet-green Swallows. Saucer nest inside crevice, 3–6 eggs. Forages all day in groups, with frequent returns to feed young.

VOCALIZATIONS Long, high, staccato *ji ji ji jir jir jir jiizh jiiizh*, in flight.

Male · ID (Jefferson County)—May · DARREN CLARK

Male · BC (Okanagan)—Jun · GLENN BARTLEY

Female · ID (Nez Perce County)—Aug · KEITH CARLSON

Black-chinned Hummingbird
Archilochus alexandri

DESCRIPTION 3.5 in/9 cm. **Slender** with **long, straight black bill**, metallic greenish-gray upperparts, grayish-white underparts, greenish flanks. *Male:* Matte **black chin, throat bordered by iridescent violet below**; dark tail. *Female:* **Clean whitish chin, throat**; tail green or black with three outer rectrices tipped white. *Immature:* Resembles adult female; narrow buffy margins on head, nape, back feathers disappear with wear.

SIMILAR SPECIES Primary PNW range overlaps Calliope (p. 263), Broad-tailed (p. 262), Rufous (p. 264). Males of these three distinctive; females, immatures show some buffy or rufous on underparts. Calliope tiny, short billed. See also under Anna's (p. 260).

STATUS & DISTRIBUTION Breeds in much of West from southern BC to central Mexico; winters mostly southern Texas to southwestern Mexico. In PNW, uncommon to locally fairly common summer resident south-central, southeastern interior BC (rare north of Kamloops), eastern WA (largely absent Columbia Plateau agricultural lands), eastern OR (greatest density northeastern valleys, foothills), ID, northwestern MT; rare western WY, casual Pacific slope. Returns mid-Apr through May; departs mid-Jun through early Sep, males preceding females, immatures. No reliable winter records.

HABITAT ASSOCIATIONS Lower elevations. Riparian communities, scrub, canyons, open woodlands, orchards, gardens, towns.

BEHAVIOR & FEEDING Takes nectar from variety of flowers, sugar water from feeders, vigorously pumping, spreading tail while hovering. Also small insects, spiders. In display dive, male's wings produce trill in shallow, back-and-forth arc. Female builds cup nest, incubates eggs (usually two), tends young alone.

VOCALIZATIONS Calls include clipped chip, often in chattering series. Song weak, rarely heard.

Anna's Hummingbird
Calypte anna

DESCRIPTION 3.75 in/9.5 cm. **Largest** hummingbird in PNW. Relatively short, straight bill. Iridescent-green upperparts, **dull-gray underparts tinged greenish**. White around eye. *Male:* **Iridescent rose-red crown**, gorget; dark tail. *Female:* Usually some rose feathers on chin, throat. Outer three rectrices tipped white. *Immature:* Resembles adult female; rose feathering begins to appear with age.

SIMILAR SPECIES Adult male Anna's distinctive in good light. Rufous (p. 264), Allen's (p. 265) smaller with rufous coloration on flanks, tail in all plumages. Black-chinned (p. 259) more slender, whiter underparts, proportionately longer billed; pumps tail repeatedly while hovering.

STATUS & DISTRIBUTION Historical range Baja to San Francisco Bay Area; expanding rapidly since 1960s, now resident along Pacific slope to southeastern Alaska, inland into deserts of Southwest. In PNW, uncommon/locally common resident western OR, western WA, southwestern BC, rare farther north in coastal BC; rare/locally uncommon southern interior BC, eastern WA, eastern OR; rare southwestern, northern ID, northwestern MT. Only hummingbird wintering regularly in PNW.

HABITAT ASSOCIATIONS In PNW, nearly exclusively tied to human-modified landscapes—parks, gardens, homes with feeders; a few breed in natural riparian habitats.

BEHAVIOR & FEEDING Can enter torpor to survive cold weather. Takes flower nectar, sugar water from feeders, small insects, sap. Hovers with tail straight, motionless. Male J-shaped territorial dive with loud noise produced in front of intruder. Nests as early as Jan on branch (two eggs); brood rearing strictly by female.

VOCALIZATIONS Male song buzzes, sputters, squeaks, trills from high perch. Main call rather forceful chip. Many other vocalizations.

Immature Male · Mexico (Baja California Sur)—May · DAN CORDELL

Male · Arizona—Mar · ROGER WINDEMUTH

Female · California—Mar · LIRON GERSTMAN

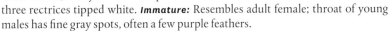

Costa's Hummingbird
Calypte costae

DESCRIPTION 3.25 in/8 cm. **Small**, compact, **short-tailed** hummingbird; bill relatively long, downcurved. Bronzy-green upperparts, whitish underparts. *Male:* **Iridescent purple head, elongated gorget feathers**; flanks tinged greenish. Dark tail. *Female:* Plain white throat, rarely with small spot of violet. Outer three rectrices tipped white. *Immature:* Resembles adult female; throat of young males has fine gray spots, often a few purple feathers.

SIMILAR SPECIES Does not typically co-occur with Black-chinned (p. 259), Broad-tailed (p. 262) in PNW. Anna's (p. 260) larger with duskier underparts; does not pump tail while hovering. Bill less curved, proportionately shorter. Male's head, gorget rose-red; shorter gorget corners. Calliope (p. 263) tiny, bill shorter; female, immature have buffy underparts; male has green crown, flaring magenta gorget. Rufous (p. 264), Allen's (p. 265) show rufous on flanks, tail in all plumages.

STATUS & DISTRIBUTION Breeds southwestern US, northwestern Mexico; winters mostly southern part of breeding range south to Sinaloa. Regular vagrant northward along Pacific Coast. In PNW, rare westside visitor, casual/rare lower eastern slope Cascades/BC Coast Range, accidental farther east. Records in all months, but great majority Apr–Jun.

HABITAT ASSOCIATIONS Undetermined in PNW, where most often observed at sugar-water feeders. In primary range, hot deserts, other dry scrub, chaparral.

BEHAVIOR & FEEDING Commonly pumps tail while hovering. Breeding biology in core range generally as for other regional hummingbirds. Male display dive multiple loops with penetrating whistle.

VOCALIZATIONS Male song continuous high, faint, modulated whistle. Usual call soft *tic*, sometimes in series (both sexes).

Female · Colorado—Aug · BILL SCHMOKER

Female · Arizona—Jul · BILL SCHMOKER

Male · ID (Jefferson County)—May · DARREN CLARK

Broad-tailed Hummingbird
Selasphorus platycercus

DESCRIPTION 3.75 in/9.5 cm. **Large** hummingbird; iridescent-green upperparts, crown; **long, broad tail**. Straight, relatively short bill. *Male:* **Iridescent rose-red gorget**. Whitish underparts; greenish flanks, sides (sometimes with buffy). *Female:* **Underparts washed buffy/pale rufous**; white eye-ring; throat usually with a few small rose feathers on background of fine spots. **Outer tail feathers have rufous base**, white tips. *Immature:* Resembles female, but tail base less extensively rufous.

SIMILAR SPECIES Male: Anna's (p. 260) entire head rose-red; gorget has elongated corners. Calliope (p. 263) has gorget of individual rays. Female/immature: Rufous (p. 264) very similar but tail shorter, less broad, with rufous base on most (not just outer) tail feathers. Calliope smaller; shorter tail with little or no rufous.

STATUS & DISTRIBUTION Breeds mountains of interior West from central Rockies to Guatemala; winters central Mexico southward within breeding range. In PNW, fairly common breeder western WY, southern ID; rare summer visitor, possible breeder, central ID, northwestern MT, eastern OR; casual northern ID, southeastern WA; accidental southeastern, south-central BC. Most return May, depart Jul–Aug (extremes Apr–Sep). Accidental west of Cascades summit.

HABITAT ASSOCIATIONS Riparian corridors, aspen groves, open conifer forests with shrubby edges; in valleys, mountains up to subalpine meadows.

BEHAVIOR & FEEDING Readily enters nocturnal torpor to survive cold high-mountain temperatures. Feeding habits, breeding biology similar to other PNW hummingbirds. Loud, diagnostic wing trill—buzzy, whistling, insect-like—produced in male's territorial dive display, aggressive flights.

VOCALIZATIONS Main call clear chip, often paired or in short series. No song.

Female · *Colorado—Aug* · BILL SCHMOKER

Male · *WA (Yakima County)—Jun* · TOM KOGUT

Calliope Hummingbird
Selasphorus calliope

DESCRIPTION 3 in/7.5 cm. **Smallest** hummingbird in PNW. Short, straight bill; **short tail**. Greenish upperparts with bronze gloss. Tail base often has minor amounts of rufous feather edging. *Male:* Grayish underparts, orangish-buff flanks with bronzy-green sheen. When flared, **elongated magenta-red gorget feathers stand out separately** against white throat. *Female:* Underparts broadly washed orangish buff. White throat with small green spots. Tail extensively black, outer three rectrices tipped white. *Immature:* Resembles female; young male shows some throat color before migrating south.

SIMILAR SPECIES Male unmistakable. Female, immature Broad-tailed (p. 262), Rufous (p. 264), Allen's (p. 265) larger, longer-billed, with obvious rufous tail base; tail of perched bird projects beyond wingtips. Other PNW hummingbirds lack buffy on underparts.

STATUS & DISTRIBUTION Breeds mountains of interior West from central BC to Utah, central California, disjunctly northern Baja. Winters western Mexico south to Oaxaca. In PNW, common/fairly common summer resident east of Cascades/BC Coast Range summit (also southwestern OR), uncommon north of Kamloops; rare spring migrant west of crest. Most return Apr–May, depart late Jun through Aug (adult males first).

HABITAT ASSOCIATIONS Open forest, shrubby growth, edge habitat, orchards, gardens. Foothills to mountain meadows, often along streams; more common at low to middle elevations.

BEHAVIOR & FEEDING Takes flower nectar, small insects, sap, sugar water at feeders. Two male displays: deep, U-shaped dive; also hovers in front of female with buzzing wings, flared gorget. Breeding biology similar to other PNW hummingbirds.

VOCALIZATIONS Unremarkable high, soft chip notes. Soft *ptzinng* at bottom of display dive.

Rufous Hummingbird
Selasphorus rufus

DESCRIPTION 3.5 in/8.5 cm. *Male:* **Rufous crown, back, rump**; in small percentage of individuals, back may have varying amounts of green. **Iridescent orange-red gorget**. Upper breast white, underparts rufous. Tail rufous with green tip. *Female:* Upperparts green. Throat plain white or streaked with greenish dots; orange-red feathering varies from none to solid spot. Underparts whitish, **rufous sides. Rufous tail base**; outer rectrices have white tips. *Immature:* Resembles female.

SIMILAR SPECIES Treated under Allen's Hummingbird (p. 265).

STATUS & DISTRIBUTION Breeds southern Alaska to OR, ID; winters mostly central Mexico. Regular vagrant across continent. In PNW, common coastal-slope breeder (including Haida Gwaii); fairly common to common interior BC, eastern WA; fairly common northeastern OR, central ID/Panhandle, northwestern MT; uncommon eastern slope OR Cascades; rare breeder central, southeastern OR, southern ID, western WY. Northbound migration coastal, peaks Mar–early Apr, with birds reaching interior destinations by May. Post-breeding dispersal to higher elevations begins Jun (males first). Southbound departure Jul–Sep, mainly in mountains (common WY Rockies). Accidental western lowlands winter.

HABITAT ASSOCIATIONS Open, semi-open forests, thickets, riparian corridors, shrubby edges, orchards, farms, parks/gardens, often near water; montane meadows in summer, fall migration. Generally absent from arid interior south of BC.

BEHAVIOR & FEEDING Feeding preferences, breeding biology similar to other PNW hummingbirds. Lowland arrival exploits early-blooming shrubs. Tail held upward while hovering. Male territorial display series of high, J-shaped dives, with several short, emphatic notes followed by rasping buzz emitted at bottom of arc.

VOCALIZATIONS Chips, other warning notes. No song.

Male · *California—Mar* · MIKE DANZENBAKER

Allen's Hummingbird
Selasphorus sasin

DESCRIPTION 3.5 in/8.5 cm. *Male:* Resembles typical male Rufous Hummingbird (p. 264) but **crown, back, rump green**; in some individuals, rump may be more or less rufous. *Female/immature:* Indistinguishable from Rufous in field.

SIMILAR SPECIES Consult technical manuals for distinguishing Allen's from Rufous by subtle differences of measurements within age, sex classes. Green-backed, rufous-rumped males could be either species; hybrids exist. Male territorial display (described below) usually diagnostic within small area of range overlap. Female Broad-tailed (p. 262) has narrow, complete eye-ring; longer tail, broader than female Rufous/Allen's, with rufous base on outer (versus all) tail feathers. Calliope (p. 263) smaller than either; shorter tail with little or no rufous.

STATUS & DISTRIBUTION Breeds coastally, southwestern OR–southern California; winters small area central Mexico (population in Los Angeles County, Channel Islands sedentary). In PNW, fairly common summer resident southwestern OR coastal strip north to Bandon, uncommon/rare to Coos Bay, inland river valleys; accidental north to Seattle. Returns late Feb–Mar; timing of departure uncertain due to identification difficulties, but probably mostly Jul. Breeding documented only for coastal Curry County; post-breeders may disperse upslope to Siskiyous, overlapping Rufous breeding range.

HABITAT ASSOCIATIONS Coastal scrub, adjacent forest; poorly understood for OR.

BEHAVIOR & FEEDING Generally like Rufous, including tail held pointed upward while hovering. In distinctively different territorial display, male weaves back and forth at height of subject before climbing to begin J-shaped dive, producing short, continuous, modulated whine at bottom of arc.

VOCALIZATIONS Similar to those of Rufous.

Family Trochilidae—HUMMINGBIRDS **265**

Female · WA (Whatcom County)—Jan · DOUGLAS L. BROWN

Male · WA (King County)—Nov · DOUG SCHURMAN

Male · WA (King County)—Oct · DOUG SCHURMAN

Belted Kingfisher
Megaceryle alcyon

DESCRIPTION 13 in/33 cm, wingspan 20 in/51 cm. **Large-headed, shaggy-crested, stout-billed** fishing bird, mostly **slate blue** with **white** underparts, collar, wide slate-blue breast band. *Male:* Lacks rufous markings. *Female:* Rufous flanks, additional rufous band across lower breast. *Juvenile:* Rufous flanks, single dark breast band. Bill shorter than that of adult.

SIMILAR SPECIES None in PNW.

STATUS & DISTRIBUTION Summer resident across continent south of Arctic, north of arid Southwest. Abandons coldest parts at freeze-up; winters Pacific Coast (south of Aleutians), most of US, Mexico, Caribbean (a few farther south). In PNW, fairly common western lowlands year-round; in interior, fairly common summer, rare to locally uncommon winter near open water.

HABITAT ASSOCIATIONS Variety of coastal, estuarine, freshwater locations at low, middle elevations, including dune belts, protected marine waters, wetlands, streams, lakes, ponds. Needs soft banks for nest burrows in proximity to clear, relatively still water for foraging.

BEHAVIOR & FEEDING Perches, or hovers, above water to search for prey—primarily various fish, but also some insects, mollusks, crustaceans, other animals. Captures prey in bill in shallow plunge, returns to perch to swallow it; regurgitates undigested bones, scales, shells as pellets. May take some berries in winter. Both sexes excavate nest burrow, usually 3–6 ft (1–2 m) deep in stream bank, seaside bluff, but also occasionally in road cuts, gravel pits, sawdust piles. Commonly 6–7 eggs (extremes 2–8). Eggs incubated, young tended by both parents.

VOCALIZATIONS Main call loud, ratchet-like rattle, given year-round (often in flight).

"Red-shafted" Female · BC (Penticton)—Feb · LAURE W. NEISH

"Yellow-shafted" Female *(right)* with juvenile Male · Alberta—Jun · GERALD ROMANCHUK

"Red-shafted" Male · OR (Washington County)—Mar · GREG GILLSON

Northern Flicker
Colaptes auratus

DESCRIPTION 12 in/30 cm, wingspan 20 in/51 cm. Robust woodpecker; brownish with **black bib, white rump**, long bill, stiff tail; barred black above, **spotted black below** with brightly colored feather shafts in wings. *"Red-shafted":* Brown cap, gray face, red shafts, **red moustache mark** (male). *"Yellow-shafted":* Gray crown, brown face, yellow shafts, **red nape crescent, black moustache mark** (male). Intergrades show intermediate characters, e.g., orange or mixed-color remiges.

SIMILAR SPECIES Williamson's Sapsucker female (p. 270) smaller with black breast, yellow belly, gray underwing.

STATUS & DISTRIBUTION Breeds throughout most of North America south to Nicaragua, Caribbean; withdraws from boreal habitats Nov–Mar. Two forms common in PNW: "Red-shafted" (*C. a. cafer*) breeds most of region, overlapping, intergrading with "Yellow-shafted" (*C. a. luteus*) in north (roughly, Cariboo–Chilcotin northward), extra-regionally along eastern slope of Rockies. Northern, high-mountain breeders (both forms) move south, downslope Sep–Apr, joining year-round resident "Red-shafted"; "Yellow-shafted" present then, although intergrades far outnumber pure phenotypes. Some flickers nesting south to western WA show red napes.

HABITAT ASSOCIATIONS Nearly ubiquitous, timberline to shrub-steppe; woodlands, open landscapes, urban areas, old-growth forest.

BEHAVIOR & FEEDING Forages for ants, beetles, other invertebrates, mostly on ground, less frequently in trees; fruits, other plant material most important Aug–Mar. Highly conspicuous with boisterous interactions, vocalizations, evenly spaced drumming. Undulating flight, tree-clinging behavior, like other woodpeckers; also may perch upright. Migrants flock loosely. Pair excavates cavity in live or dead wood; monogamous, with some polyandry recorded.

VOCALIZATIONS Calls include *woika woika woika*, long series of *kuk* notes, piercing *keeww*.

Lewis's Woodpecker
Melanerpes lewis

DESCRIPTION 10.5 in/27 cm, wingspan 21 in/53 cm. Long, straight bill, **dark iridescent greenish-black upperparts**, stiff pointed rectrices. *Adult:* Blackish crown, **red face**, **pinkish-red belly**; gray upper breast, collar. *Juvenile:* Duller; brownish face, minimally pink breast, weakly marked collar.

SIMILAR SPECIES Acorn Woodpecker (p. 269) white on face, rump, primary bases; sapsuckers (pp. 270–273) smaller with dorsal black-and-white barring, whitish rump; crows in flight appear surprisingly similar, but larger.

STATUS & DISTRIBUTION Breeds in interior, south-central BC to western South Dakota, south to New Mexico, rarely western Oklahoma; winters south-central WA, south irregularly to northern Mexico. In PNW, local, uncommon, declining breeder east of Cascades/BC Coast Range; winters north to WA (Yakima County), irregularly BC (southern Okanagan). Nested historically west of crest (southern BC, WA), rarely but more recently OR (Jackson County). Migrants uncommon east of Cascades, rare westside, mostly OR (Willamette, Rogue Valleys), casual north to Haida Gwaii.

HABITAT ASSOCIATIONS Breeds in ponderosa pine, Garry-oak zones, black cottonwood woodlands, often near shrub-steppe; also burns, formerly including westside. Winters open oak forest, orchards, rarely suburbs; migrants occur throughout to subalpine, rare in coastal habitats.

BEHAVIOR & FEEDING Tree clinging, hole nesting like other woodpeckers, but differs in non-undulating flight, preference for foraging by flycatching rather than excavating. Also takes fruits, acorns, other seeds. Migrants form flocks, remain gregarious Aug–Mar, protecting stored nuts. Nests May–Jul in rotting wood (often cottonwood); frequently reuses old cavities.

VOCALIZATIONS Fairly quiet. *Churrr*, squeaky chatter while nesting; shrill alarm note.

Acorn Woodpecker
Melanerpes formicivorus

DESCRIPTION 9 in/23 cm. Black upperparts, **clown-like face**, chisel-like bill, stiff pointed rectrices. **Red crown; white iris, forehead, wing patches**, rump. Black breast grades to vertical streaks on white belly. *Female:* Top of crown black, red limited to rear of crown.

SIMILAR SPECIES Other woodpeckers of PNW show dark iris. Lewis's Woodpecker (p. 268) lacks wing patches, white on face; White-headed Woodpecker (p. 278) face entirely white. Male Williamson's Sapsucker (p. 270) shows white facial stripes.

STATUS & DISTRIBUTION Breeds south-central WA through California, south disjunctly to Colombia. In PNW, resident north to WA (Klickitat County); in OR, west of Cascades throughout Willamette Valley, adjacent hills, also south from Douglas County to coast, Klamath River Canyon. Accidental during acorn shortages east to western WY; casual north to south-central BC.

HABITAT ASSOCIATIONS Open oak forest, tanoak stands bordering clear-cuts, mixed oak-conifer woodlands, adjacent riparian strips.

BEHAVIOR & FEEDING Flycatches with steep vertical forays from high perch, rarely probes for wood borers. Mostly eats acorns, insects; also takes other plant material, drinks sap. Exhibits typical woodpecker tree-clinging behavior, undulating flight. Breeds cooperatively with complex social system that may include polygyny or polyandry; groups average 4–5 individuals. Acorns stored in drilled holes (often in dead limbs) of granary tree; colony vigorously defends cache, nesting cavities from other birds. Nests Apr–Sep, frequently reusing nests that may accommodate several egg layers. Excavated nest sites also used for group roosts.

VOCALIZATIONS Raucous *wicka wicka*; other harsh, nasal calls, chatter.

Female · BC (Merritt)—Jun · BRIAN STECH

Male · WA (Yakima County)—Jun · GREGG THOMPSON

Williamson's Sapsucker
Sphyrapicus thyroideus

DESCRIPTION 9 in/23 cm. Chisel-like bill, stiff pointed rectrices. Adults have yellow belly, black breast, white rump. Strongly dimorphic. *Male:* **Mostly black** (back, tail, head); red throat (white in juvenile); **white facial stripes, wing patch**. *Female:* **Fine horizontal barring, no wing patch, plain brown head**. *Juvenile:* Lacks yellow belly (both sexes), black breast (female).

SIMILAR SPECIES Other sapsuckers (pp. 271–273) both sexes have white-mottled back, white wing patch; none have plain brown head of female Williamson's. Northern Flicker (p. 267) larger with spotted underparts.

STATUS & DISTRIBUTION Mountain breeder disjunctly from southern interior BC to northern Baja California, New Mexico; winters mostly southwestern US, Mexico. In PNW, fairly common local breeder south from BC (Thompson-Okanagan, East Kootenay), east from Cascades/BC Coast Range, with spillover to southwestern OR (Jackson County). Casually winters north to south-central WA. Migrants rarely detected (Mar–Apr, Aug–Oct), casual west of crest.

HABITAT ASSOCIATIONS Nests open coniferous forest, mixed riparian woods at higher elevation; often associated with western larch, ponderosa pine, quaking aspen, Douglas-fir; in winter uses more hardwoods.

BEHAVIOR & FEEDING Drills evenly spaced holes in live trees (usually Douglas-fir or pine), drinking sap year-round; switches primarily to insects while nesting; berries, other fruit, plant fibers also important, especially in winter. Maintains foraging routes. Typical woodpecker tree-clinging behavior, undulating flight; drums irregularly like other sapsuckers but with longer pauses. Monogamous pair excavates nest hole (frequently in live larch), territorial toward all sapsuckers.

VOCALIZATIONS Slightly nasal *churr*; chattered flicker-like long-call; female offers harsh *sheeer*.

Male · *Alberta—May*
TERRY THORMIN

Female · *Manitoba—Jun* · DENNIS PAULSON

Juvenile · *Utah—Feb* · RICK FRIDELL

Yellow-bellied Sapsucker
Sphyrapicus varius

DESCRIPTION 8.5 in/22 cm. Pied black-and-white with facial stripes, black breast, white-mottled back. Chisel-like bill, stiff pointed rectrices, red crown, pale-yellow belly; **white secondary coverts** form prominent elongate white wing patch. *Male:* **Red throat** bordered by black. *Female:* White throat. *Juvenile:* Lacks red; mottled white, black, brown with white moustache, eyeline, wing patch; **adult characters attained gradually** through first year.

SIMILAR SPECIES Other sapsuckers molt to adult plumage by first fall. Red-naped (p. 272) has back mottling in two vertical rows; more extensively red on throat, black border below white moustache less distinct; red nape (Yellow-bellied rarely shows a few red feathers). Female Williamson's (p. 270) shows fine, even barring, plain brown head, lacks wing patch.

STATUS & DISTRIBUTION Breeds central Alaska to Newfoundland, south in East to North Carolina; winters Massachusetts, Kansas, south to Panama. In PNW, uncommon breeder Apr–Aug only in Prince George vicinity, otherwise casual Sep–May except accidental western WY, northwestern MT; casual Jun–Aug in BC away from breeding sites.

HABITAT ASSOCIATIONS Nests in poplars, mixed conifers; at other seasons, various woodlands, scrub, orchards.

BEHAVIOR & FEEDING Quietly drills evenly spaced sap wells in live trees, drinks sap year-round, also eats berries, other fruit, tree tissues; highly insectivorous while nesting, taking mostly ants. Typical woodpecker tree-clinging habits, undulating flight. Strongly migratory, males arriving by Apr to establish drumming posts, begin nest-cavity excavation. Drums irregularly, as other sapsuckers. Monogamous pair mostly uses live aspens for nesting; may hybridize with other sapsuckers at range periphery.

VOCALIZATIONS Loud nasal mews, repeated *wicka*.

Red-naped x Red-breasted · WA (Kittitas County) —Jun · GREGG THOMPSON

Male · MT (Flathead County)—Apr · KURT LINDSAY

Red-naped Sapsucker
Sphyrapicus nuchalis

DESCRIPTION 8.5 in/22 cm. Pied black-and-white with facial stripes, **black breast**, white-mottled back. Chisel-like bill, stiff pointed rectrices, pale-yellow belly; **red crown, nape, throat**; secondary coverts form prominent **elongate white wing patch**. *Female:* White chin. *Juvenile:* Like adult but lacks red; molts to adult plumage by Aug.

SIMILAR SPECIES Yellow-bellied Sapsucker (p. 271) shows bolder black border below white moustache, lacks red nape; mottling more evenly distributed across back. Red-breasted Sapsucker (p. 273) lacks white facial lines, black bib. Female Williamson's Sapsucker (p. 270) finely barred; plain brown head, lacks wing patch.

STATUS & DISTRIBUTION Breeds in interior from central BC to New Mexico, east to western South Dakota; winters southern Utah to central Mexico. In PNW, common mid- to high-elevation breeder east from Cascades/BC Coast Range excluding Columbia Plateau, southeastern OR; spills into westside subalpine in north, mixed needleleaf–broadleaf in south. Migrants uncommon across eastside lowlands Mar–May, Aug–Oct; rare Pacific slope, mostly Puget Trough. Essentially entire population leaves by Oct. Hybridizes with Red-breasted Sapsucker from southwestern BC to OR, extensively in WA (Puget Sound nearly to Columbia River).

HABITAT ASSOCIATIONS Nests in deciduous, mixed coniferous forest often containing aspen or willow; at other seasons, varied woodland, scrub.

BEHAVIOR & FEEDING Drills, maintains sap wells, defending against other birds. Drinks sap year-round; also eats fruit, tree tissues, but during nesting mostly gleans or flycatches for insects. Usual tree-clinging, undulating-flight woodpecker behaviors, irregular drumming like other sapsuckers. Monogamous; nests in live or dead tree, often aspen; frequently reuses cavities.

VOCALIZATIONS Nasal mews, repeated *wicka*.

Red-breasted Sapsucker
Sphyrapicus ruber

DESCRIPTION 8.75 in/22 cm. Colorful. **Red breast, head** except vague white moustache; yellow belly; black back mottled white; secondary coverts form **elongate white wing patch**. Chisel-like bill, stiff pointed rectrices. *Juvenile:* Dark unpatterned head quickly molts to red. Hybrids with Red-naped Sapsucker intermediate—e.g., may show hint of white facial lines, red breast bleeding to black bib, black facial marks obscured by red.

SIMILAR SPECIES Other sapsuckers (pp. 270–272) show white facial lines, lack red below throat. Lewis's Woodpecker (p. 268) has gray collar, plain greenish-black upperparts.

STATUS & DISTRIBUTION Nests southeastern Alaska to California, winters coastally Haida Gwaii to Baja. Fairly common breeder in PNW west of Cascades/BC Coast Range in OR/WA/southern BC (spilling over locally onto east slope); farther north, in central BC across province to Rockies. Northern interior breeders abandon breeding grounds for Pacific slope in winter (Oct–Feb). Non-breeders casual year-round in interior BC/WA/OR, accidental ID. Hybridizes with Red-naped Sapsucker where ranges overlap.

HABITAT ASSOCIATIONS Breeds coniferous forest, preferring mature cedar/hemlock/spruce; more frequent in mixed woods in south. Moves downslope below heavy snow to winter in parks, suburbs, riparian woodlands.

BEHAVIOR & FEEDING Quietly drills sap wells in live trees, revisiting stations on regular route; drinks sap, eats berries, tree tissues, gleans for insects. Typical woodpecker tree-clinging behavior, undulating flight, irregular sapsucker drumming. Monogamous pair excavates nest in soft wood, shares parental care. Rarely if ever reuses cavities, excavating new hole in same snag instead.

VOCALIZATIONS Nasal *chuur*; scratchy repeated *wicka*.

Male *P.p. gairdnerii* · *WA (Whatcom County)—Mar* · MIKE D. BAILEY

Female · *BC (Osoyoos)—Apr* · LAURE W. NEISH

Juvenile · *BC (Richmond)—Jul* · KATHERIN

Downy Woodpecker
Picoides pubescens

DESCRIPTION 6.75 in/17 cm. **White back**, underparts, supercilium, moustache mark; black bars on white outer rectrices; black-and-white **checkered wings**. Stiff, pointed tail; chisel-like **bill half as long as distance from bill base to back of head**. *Male:* Red spot on nape. *Juvenile:* Red forecrown. Birds resident west of Cascade crest in southwestern BC, WA, OR (subspecies *P.p. gairdnerii*) show white areas replaced with dingy brownish gray; upperwing coverts, secondaries mostly black.

SIMILAR SPECIES Hairy Woodpecker (p. 275) nearly identical; larger with bill length equal to distance from bill base to back of head. Sapsuckers (pp. 270–273) show elongate white wing patch at rest as well as in flight.

STATUS & DISTRIBUTION Resident from Alaska to Labrador, south to Florida, California. In most of PNW, common lowland resident, fewer at higher elevations; uncommon in BC west of Coast Range north of Campbell River, essentially absent as breeder western Vancouver Island, casual Haida Gwaii. Clean-white interior birds uncommon west of Cascade crest, usually outside breeding season.

HABITAT ASSOCIATIONS Mostly deciduous woodlands, parks, suburbs; riparian, agricultural habitats.

BEHAVIOR & FEEDING Probes dead limbs, twigs, weed stalks for insects, other arthropods; also takes fruits, seeds; common at suet feeders. Males forage higher on smaller twigs; typical woodpecker tree-clinging behavior, undulating flight. Territorial drumming slow, even. Generally sedentary, with some female dispersal. Breeds later in spring than Hairy Woodpecker. Monogamous pair excavates cavity, usually in dead stub of live or dead tree; fledgling-care period often lengthy.

VOCALIZATIONS Calls include descending rattle-like whinny, flat *pik*.

Hairy Woodpecker
Picoides villosus

DESCRIPTION 9.5 in/24 cm. **White back**, underparts, supercilium, moustache mark; checkered black-and-white wings. Stiff, pointed tail; chisel-like bill. **Bill length equal to distance from bill base to back of head.** *Male:* Red spot on nape. *Juvenile:* Red fore-crown. In Pacific-slope populations, white replaced with dingy grayish, upperwing coverts mostly black; subspecies *P.v. picoideus*, endemic to Haida Gwaii, shows black barring on back, flanks, outer rectrices.

SIMILAR SPECIES Downy Woodpecker (p. 274) smaller, shorter bill (only half as long as distance from bill base to back of head). Black-backed Woodpecker (p. 277) shows glossy, entirely black upperparts. American Three-toed Woodpecker (p. 276) shorter billed, barred heavily on flanks; male has yellow forecrown (as does Black-backed).

STATUS & DISTRIBUTION Resident Alaska to Newfoundland south to Panama, Bahamas; highly variable across broad range with many races described. In PNW, common resident in intact forest habitats throughout; absent Columbia Plateau, drier parts of OR, southwestern ID, except uncommon in migration. White-breasted races resident east from Cascades/BC Coast Range, but some individuals appear in westside lowlands, especially Oct–Apr.

HABITAT ASSOCIATIONS Prefers coniferous forest in PNW, also uses mixed woods.

BEHAVIOR & FEEDING Probes for insects, also eats fruits, seeds; frequents bird feeders; typical woodpecker tree-clinging posture, undulating flight. Territorial drumming rapid, slows at end. Mostly sedentary, some disperse in fall; avoids urbanized areas. Courtship occurs in winter. Monogamous pair excavates nest in living tree, shares parental duties, often partitioning brood for fledgling care.

VOCALIZATIONS Calls include rapid whinny; sharp, loud *piik*; sputtered alarm notes.

Female *P.d. dorsalis* · ID (Fremont County)—Jun · DARREN CLARK Male *P.d. fasciatus* · WA (Okanogan County)—Mar · GREGG THOMPSON

American Three-toed Woodpecker
Picoides dorsalis

DESCRIPTION 8.75 in/22 cm. **Stocky.** Three toes, chisel-like bill, stiff tail; black wings barred white. White breast, supercilium, moustache mark; **black-barred white back, flanks, sides.** *Male:* **Yellow crown** patch. *Juvenile:* Duller; small yellow crown patch. Larger, longer-billed *P.d. dorsalis* sides, flanks less evenly barred, sometimes streaked; lacks barring across white back.

SIMILAR SPECIES Hairy Woodpecker's (p. 275) bill longer, sides lack heavy barring; male has red nape spot. Black-backed Woodpecker's (p. 277) upperparts entirely black. Sapsuckers show elongate white wing patch.

STATUS & DISTRIBUTION Transcontinental in northern forests. Three subspecies: *P.d. fasciatus* resident Alaska, northwestern Canada south to OR; *P.d. dorsalis* in Rockies, northwestern MT to New Mexico; *P.d. bacatus* in East. In PNW, uncommon, mostly sedentary at high elevation from Cascades/BC Coast Range eastward (rare eastern Vancouver Island, Olympics)—*fasciatus* in BC, WA, OR, northern/central ID; *dorsalis* in southeastern ID, western WY. Both occur northwestern MT (intergrade Flathead County); some individuals show *dorsalis* characteristics west to northeastern WA (Ferry County). Black-backed population with much-reduced white barring in southeastern BC may reflect contact with *bacatus*.

HABITAT ASSOCIATIONS Subalpine forests, usually dominated by spruce, fir, larch, or lodgepole pine.

BEHAVIOR & FEEDING Flakes bark, probes for bark-beetle larvae, other insects; rarely takes plant material. Often concentrates in coniferous stands disturbed by beetle infestations or burns. Typical woodpecker tree-clinging posture, undulating flight; territorial drumming slow, accelerating. Monogamous pair excavates nest cavity in dead or living tree, shares parental duties.

VOCALIZATIONS Calls include hollow *pik*, shrill rattle-like whinny.

Female · WA (Yakima County)—Oct · GREGG THOMPSON | Male · WA (Yakima County)—May · TOM KOGUT

Black-backed Woodpecker
Picoides arcticus

DESCRIPTION 9.75 in/25 cm. Sleek. Long chisel-like bill, stiff tail, three toes, **glossy-black upperparts**, wings with white-barred remiges. White underparts, moustache mark; flanks, **sides finely barred** with black. *Male:* **Yellow crown patch**. *Juvenile:* Duller; small yellow crown patch.

SIMILAR SPECIES Hairy Woodpecker (p. 275) has white supercilium, back; most lack barred sides. American Three-toed Woodpecker (p. 276) squatter with white on back. Male Williamson's Sapsucker (p. 270) shows white wing patch, black breast.

STATUS & DISTRIBUTION Resident central Alaska to Newfoundland south to central California, upstate New York. In PNW, presence strongly localized by habitat preferences. Uncommon mid- to high-elevation resident east of Cascades/BC Coast Range; rarely breeds Pacific slope of WA/OR Cascades west to upper Clackamas drainage; also into Siskiyous. Declining Oregon Cascades/Sierra Nevada population genetically distinct, considered threatened (fewer than 1,000 pairs).

HABITAT ASSOCIATIONS Prefers burns, infestation-killed old-growth conifers from subalpine down to ponderosa pine zone, also clear-cut edges.

BEHAVIOR & FEEDING Exploits wood-boring beetle infestations by flaking bark from dying trees, fallen snags, then probing, mostly for larvae; also takes bark beetles, other insects. Typical woodpecker tree-clinging posture, undulating flight. Drumming slow, long, accelerating. Irruptive due to unpredictable availability of food supply, but western populations generally remain sedentary within montane habitats. Concentrates, nests by preference in extensive, relatively recent burns. Monogamous pair excavates nest cavity in living or dead tree, often very close to ground, sharing parental care by partitioning fledglings.

VOCALIZATIONS Calls include abrupt *pkkk*, harsh buzzy whinny.

Female · WA (Chelan County)—May · GREGG THOMPSON

Male · WA (Okanogan County)—Jun · RYAN SHAW

White-headed Woodpecker
Picoides albolarvatus

DESCRIPTION 9.5 in/24 cm. **Black** with **white head**, diffuse **white primary patch** visible at rest or in flight; chisel-like bill, stiff tail. *Male:* Red spot at back of head. *Juvenile:* Duller; briefly retained reddish crown.

SIMILAR SPECIES Acorn Woodpecker (p. 269) has black face; white iris, rump. Pileated Woodpecker (p. 279) much larger with large red crest.

STATUS & DISTRIBUTION Resident in interior from south-central BC to southern California, east to western ID. In PNW, uncommon east of Cascades at higher elevations; in BC, historically uncommon, now breeds in extremely low numbers in Okanagan north to Naramata; has also declined in OR/WA due to past logging practices. West of Cascades, nests locally in OR (Siskiyous, upper northern Umpqua drainage). Casual vagrant to range periphery, e.g., BC (Falkland, Golden), OR (Malheur NWR, coastal sites), WA (Orcas Island, Nisqually NWR), northwestern MT (Lincoln, Flathead Counties), western WY (Grand Teton, Yellowstone NPs).

HABITAT ASSOCIATIONS East of Cascades, mature, open ponderosa pine forest, rarely mixed-conifer stands; west of crest true fir/Engelmann spruce forest. Frequents recent burns.

BEHAVIOR & FEEDING Probes or chips bark for ants, wood-boring or scale insects; also eats seeds of ponderosa, sugar pines, other trees. Clings to trees; flight undulating, like other woodpeckers; long territorial drumming at moderate speed. Monogamous pair remains together year-round, excavates nest cavity fairly close to ground, often in large-diameter stump; shares parental duties including partitioning brood for fledgling care.

VOCALIZATIONS Calls include *piik* usually doubled or tripled, extended into rattle.

Female · BC (Kelowna)—Feb
LAURE W. NEISH

Male · WA (King County)—Feb
GREGG THOMPSON

Female · WA (Jefferson County)—Apr
TOM MICHALSKI

Pileated Woodpecker
Dryocopus pileatus

DESCRIPTION 16 in/41 cm, wingspan 29 in/74 cm. Lanky, with **large crimson crest**, stout chisel-like bill, long stiff tail. **Black overall** with **white wing patch**, neck stripe, facial markings, wing linings. *Male:* Red malar mark.

SIMILAR SPECIES Crows (pp. 318–319) lack white markings, red crest. Other woodpeckers in region much smaller, lack crest.

STATUS & DISTRIBUTION Resident BC to Newfoundland south to central California, Florida, excluding most of interior West. In PNW, limited to forested habitats. Fairly common west of Cascades/BC Coast Range but absent Haida Gwaii, coastal BC north of Bella Coola; uncommon east of crest excluding Columbia Plateau, eastern OR (excepting Blue Mountains), southern ID; casual western WY. Partially migratory; most leave northern edge of PNW in winter, may move downslope.

HABITAT ASSOCIATIONS Mature coniferous forests, mixed woodlands including urban parks, neighborhoods with ample snags, decaying logs for nesting/foraging.

BEHAVIOR & FEEDING Excavates large deep oval or rectangular holes in trees, pries apart rotting logs, searching for ants, beetle larvae, other insects; chisels through healthy-looking hemlock to access insect-damaged heartwood. Eats fruits, other plant materials when available. Flight less undulating than other woodpeckers, but clings to trees in typical fashion. Often secretive; hides behind tree trunks, but calls conspicuously in flight above or within canopy. Drumming loud, slow, hollow, accelerating. Monogamous pair may mate for life. Male chooses, begins excavation of nest cavity each year in dead tree; pair shares parental duties.

VOCALIZATIONS Long series of wild, hollow *kuk* notes with irregular rhythm, abrupt ending.

Male · WA (Clark County)—Jan
ROGER WINDEMUTH

Female · OR (Benton County)—Feb
MATT.T. LEE

Female · WA (Yakima County)—Apr · DOUG SCHURMAN

American Kestrel
Falco sparverius

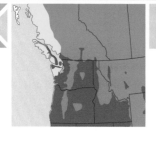

DESCRIPTION 10 in/25 cm, wingspan 21 in/53 cm (averages; female larger than male). **Delicate**, long-tailed falcon with **two black stripes on white face**, barred rufous back; pointed wings, blackish iris. *Male:* Blue-gray wings, solid **russet tail** with broad black subterminal band. Breast rusty in adult, streaked in first-year. *Female:* Russet wings, buffy breast with dark streaks, russet tail with fine banding.

SIMILAR SPECIES Merlin (p. 281) more compact, darkly streaked below, broadly banded tail; vague single malar stripe; flight more powerful.

STATUS & DISTRIBUTION Breeds throughout Americas south from central Alaska, Labrador; winters south from southern BC, New England. In PNW west of Cascades/BC Coast Range, rare breeder southeastern Vancouver Island, Fraser Lowlands, northwestern WA; locally common Tacoma prairies southward through OR. Numbers augmented by migrants Aug–Mar but always rare along entire outer coast; casual Haida Gwaii. East of crest, common/fairly common migrant, breeder to subalpine; withdraws from mountains, northern breeding grounds in winter, uncommon in lowlands Oct–Feb.

HABITAT ASSOCIATIONS Open areas near edge or coulee; farmland, grasslands, shrub-steppe, alpine meadows, clear-cuts.

BEHAVIOR & FEEDING Perches prominently in open, often bobbing tail. Flies buoyantly; captures mostly rodents, insects, flying from perch or stationary hover; rarely takes birds, lizards. Most PNW breeders migrate south, replaced by others arriving from north; resident males winter in greater numbers than females. Monogamous pair defends territory, raises up to six young in cavity nest in tree, cliff, silt bluff, or nest box.

VOCALIZATIONS Rapidly repeated piercing *kli.*

Merlin
Falco columbarius

DESCRIPTION 11 in/28 cm, wingspan 23 in/58 cm. Swift-flying falcon; ventral streaking, banded tail, faint malar, **blackish iris**, pointed wings, barred underwing. Adult male grayish dorsally; female, first-year brownish. Races separable but intergrades frequent. *"Taiga"*: **Black tail with 3–4 grayish bands**; male medium gray. *"Black"*: **Dark ventrally**; reduced tail bands, underwing spots; hooded appearance; dark slate gray dorsally (sexes similar). *"Prairie"*: Light ventrally; reduced malar, whitish supercilium; 4–5 broad, bluish-white tail bands; **male light bluish gray**.

SIMILAR SPECIES Peregrine, Prairie Falcons (pp. 282–283) larger; prominent malar. American Kestrel (p. 280) dainty; buoyant flight, strong facial markings. Accipiters (pp. 134–136) lack facial markings; wings short, rounded; iris red or yellow; tail of perched bird extends well beyond wingtips.

STATUS & DISTRIBUTION Holarctic. In New World, "Taiga" (*F.c. columbarius*) breeds continent-wide, Arctic treeline to northern states; winters to Venezuela; in much of PNW, formerly rare, now locally common breeder, increasing in cities, towns; fairly common westside Aug–May, uncommon east. "Black" (*F.c. suckleyi*) breeds coastal forests Alaska to WA; in PNW, uncommon resident Pacific slope, rare migrant east. "Prairie" (*F.c. richardsoni*) breeds northern Great Plains; in PNW, rare Sep–Apr, mostly east of Cascades.

HABITAT ASSOCIATIONS Breeds at conifer-forest edge, well-treed neighborhoods; hunts open areas, winters lowlands.

BEHAVIOR & FEEDING Diet nearly exclusively small birds captured in dashing flight. Rarely soars; perches high, aggressive toward larger raptors. Co-opts old tree nests, mostly from corvids; male courts female with spectacular, noisy displays.

VOCALIZATIONS Intense *ki ki ki ki ki*, other calls near nest.

First-year · *WA (Skagit County)—Dec* · GREGG THOMPSON

Adult "Anatum" · *WA (Skagit County)—Feb* · GREGG THOMPSON

Peregrine Falcon
Falco peregrinus

DESCRIPTION 16 in/41 cm, wingspan 41 in/104 cm (averages; female larger than male). Sleek with **thick malar**; dark gray above, **black barring below**, light bib; **long, pointed wings reach tail tip** when perched. First-year browner with heavy ventral streaks, blue (versus yellow) facial skin. Plumage varies with race. **"Anatum":** Mostly unmarked buff bib. **"Peale's":** Larger; white, heavily streaked bib; first-year grayish. **"Tundra":** Smaller; white bib unstreaked, malar narrow; first-year, buffy crown, pale supercilium.

SIMILAR SPECIES Merlin (p. 281) smaller; less distinct malar. Prairie Falcon (p. 283) browner with black axillaries. Gyrfalcon (p. 284) larger; malar obscure; wings broader, fall short of tail tip when falcon perched. Cooper's Hawk (p. 135) has rounded wings, no malar; iris red or yellow (versus blackish).

STATUS & DISTRIBUTION Cosmopolitan, polytypic; most nest northern hemisphere; in North America winters south from Aleutians, Nova Scotia. In PNW, "Anatum" (*F.p. anatum*), "Peale's" (*F.p. pealei*) fairly common Pacific slope residents, the latter coastal (BC/WA). "Anatum" uncommon resident in interior, withdraws from mountain aeries Sep–Feb. "Tundra" (*F.p. tundrius*) breeds across North American Arctic; in PNW, uncommon outer coast Sep–Oct, Apr–May traveling to/from Chilean winter quarters.

HABITAT ASSOCIATIONS Nests cliffs, coastal mountains, near water; bridges, urban skyscrapers; at other seasons, hunts open lowlands, tidal flats, marsh, beaches.

BEHAVIOR & FEEDING Fastest-flying bird, boldly captures avian prey up to duck-size with stoops up to 200 mph/320 km/h; favors pigeons, shorebirds, rarely mammals, carrion. Long-term monogamous pair defends nest against intruders, conspecifics; exhibits high nest-site fidelity.

VOCALIZATIONS Harsh, repeated *rehk rehk rehk*, other calls.

WA (Adams County)—May · BOB KOTHENBEUTEL

WA (Yakima County)—Jun · DOUG SCHURMAN

Prairie Falcon
Falco mexicanus

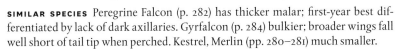

DESCRIPTION 16 in/41 cm, wingspan 40 in/102 cm (averages; female larger than male). **Thin dark malar**, white supercilium, pale nape patches; pointed wings nearly reach tip of rufous-tinged tail. **Brownish** upperparts, white ventrally with dark spots; dark iris; **blackish axillaries, underwing coverts** revealed in flight. *First-year:* Thin streaks ventrally.

SIMILAR SPECIES Peregrine Falcon (p. 282) has thicker malar; first-year best differentiated by lack of dark axillaries. Gyrfalcon (p. 284) bulkier; broader wings fall well short of tail tip when perched. Kestrel, Merlin (pp. 280–281) much smaller.

STATUS & DISTRIBUTION Breeds in interior West from southern BC, southern Saskatchewan south to Mexico; in winter, numbers reduced in north, extends range to coast, Mississippi River. In PNW, mostly uncommon resident east of Cascades from WA southward, but common Snake River Canyon in ID (highest density range-wide); rare southern interior BC. Some move up mountains or outside of region to higher prey densities or cooler habitats Jul–Oct. Rare westside lowlands Sep–Apr (casual southeastern Vancouver Island). Has bred southwestern OR (Jackson County).

HABITAT ASSOCIATIONS Nests arid, open areas on escarpments, bluffs, river canyons; hunts adjacent agricultural lands; migrants use open alpine habitats, may winter to coastal flats.

BEHAVIOR & FEEDING Hunts on wing, soaring or hugging contour, or from perch; takes prey in low stoop or tail-chase. Eats mostly ground squirrels, larks, meadowlarks, gallinaceous birds, lizards. Nests ledges, rock cavities, often at high density at favored locations; monogamous with low mate fidelity.

VOCALIZATIONS Repeated *kak*, more shrill than peregrine.

First-year Gray morph · *Alaska—Jul* · BRYCE W. ROBINSON

Adult Gray morph · *WA (Snohomish County)—Feb* · GREGG THOMPSON

Adult Gray morph · *WA (Snohomish County)—Jan* · BOB KOTHENBEUTEL

Gyrfalcon
Falco rusticolus

DESCRIPTION 22 in/56 cm, wingspan 50 in/127 cm (averages; female larger than male). Powerful; broad, pointed wings, **vague malar**, dark iris, yellow facial skin; when bird perched, **wings fall well short of tip of long, finely-banded tail**. Most PNW birds gray morph: grayish upperparts, whitish ventrally with dark breast spots; bars, heart shapes on flanks. In white, dark morphs, white or black dominate plumage. *First-year:* Heavily streaked ventrally, facial skin bluish; gray morph brownish. Adult plumage attained over 2–3 years.

SIMILAR SPECIES Other falcons smaller, wings more pointed; Peregrine (p. 282) has prominent malar; aloft, Prairie (p. 283) shows blackish axillaries, underwing coverts. Northern Goshawk (p. 136) has rounded wings, broadly banded tail, red or yellow iris.

STATUS & DISTRIBUTION Circumpolar Arctic breeder south through Norway, Kamchatka, extreme northwestern BC; winters to northern temperate zone, withdrawing only from Far North. In PNW, generally rare Oct–Apr but locally uncommon WA (Samish Flats, Waterville Plateau), BC (Boundary Bay); casual southern OR, western WY. Casual region-wide May, Aug–Sep. Females predominate in PNW; dark morph infrequent (most BC), white morph accidental.

HABITAT ASSOCIATIONS Nests rocky coasts, tundra. Migrates along coastlines; winters coastal marsh, agricultural flats, river valleys.

BEHAVIOR & FEEDING Ptarmigan diet mainstay; in PNW, primarily waterfowl, fewer gallinaceous birds, mammals; also kleptoparasitizes, scavenges. Hunts by soaring, cruising, or perching; flies rapidly, hugging contour for concealment; tail-chases or stoops to force prey to ground. Monogamous pair lays eggs on cliff, appropriated nests. Individuals maintain winter territories.

VOCALIZATIONS Gruff repeated *kak*, rarely heard.

Olive-sided Flycatcher
Contopus cooperi

DESCRIPTION 7.5 in/19 cm. **Relatively large** flycatcher; olive green above, **white throat, breast, belly** contrast with **dark vest** formed by gray-green flanks, sides. Olive undertail coverts. White patches at top of flanks often show above wing on lower back. Large, dark, slightly peaked head; large, dark bill with pale base. Long, pointed wings; faint wing-bars. *Juvenile:* Like adult.

SIMILAR SPECIES Western Wood-Pewee (p. 286) smaller, grayish below, vest less contrasting; wing-bars prominent. Vocalizations completely different.

STATUS & DISTRIBUTION Breeds across boreal North America, south in mountains to southwestern states, Baja; populations declining in some areas. Winters primarily in Andes, uncommonly north to Mexico. Uncommon to locally fairly common breeder throughout forested PNW (but absent Haida Gwaii). Arrives May (occasionally late Apr on westside), most sightings mid-May through mid-Aug. Late migrants arrive Jun at lower-elevation riparian areas east of Cascades. Fall migration Aug–early Sep.

HABITAT ASSOCIATIONS Breeds in all westside forests, especially fragmented older growth; Douglas-fir, subalpine forests in interior. Favors openings such as old burns, clear-cuts with scattered trees, wetland edges, urban parks, light-density neighborhoods. Winters in similarly structured forests; migrants less particular, use arid riparian sites.

BEHAVIOR & FEEDING Perches conspicuously atop snags or treetops, sallying out to catch large flying insects such as bees, wasps, beetles, often returning to same perch. Bulky nest constructed by female on upper branch surface, usually in conifer; pair highly aggressive toward intruders.

VOCALIZATIONS Male territorial song loud *quick THREE beers*. Both sexes offer softer series of three notes: *pip pip pip*.

BC (Penticton)—Jun · LAURE W. NEISH

WA (Spokane County)—May · MICHAEL WOODRUFF

Western Wood-Pewee
Contopus sordidulus

DESCRIPTION 6.25 in/16 cm. **Drab** flycatcher; olive gray above, paler below; appears "vested" due to darker sides. Dark face, **no eye-ring, somewhat peaked head**; long, pointed blackish wings with **pale wing-bars**; dark bill has pale-orange base to lower mandible. *Juvenile:* Lower mandible more extensively pale.

SIMILAR SPECIES Willow Flycatcher (p. 289) less pointed wings; whiter throat, belly. Other *Empidonax* show obvious white eye-rings. Calls distinctive.

STATUS & DISTRIBUTION Breeds southern Alaska to Manitoba, south in mountains to Honduras; winters from Costa Rica to Bolivia. Common in drier, open forests throughout PNW; absent from Haida Gwaii, rare along BC coast except drier forests around Strait of Georgia. Rare in dense coastal forest of WA/OR. Arrives May, most leave by Aug, a few into Sep; casual Oct. Declining in urban areas as habitat changes.

HABITAT ASSOCIATIONS East of Cascades/BC Coast Range, breeds in dry ponderosa pine or Douglas-fir forests at low to moderate elevations, also cottonwood/aspen riparian zones; local at higher-elevation clear-cuts. In coastal forests, restricted to riparian woodlands. Migrants widespread. Winters in tropical forest.

BEHAVIOR & FEEDING Forages for flying insects by sallying out from high perches; resettles onto perch with fluttering wings. Female builds nest of soft plant material atop fork of open branch—usually in cottonwood, aspen, ponderosa pine. Pair shares feeding duties.

VOCALIZATIONS Common song burry *PEEE urr*, descending in pitch; alternated in early morning with *PEE pipip* song. Other calls include rough *bsew*, rising *breeeh*.

Alberta—Jun • GERALD ROMANCHUK

Yellow-bellied Flycatcher
Empidonax flaviventris

DESCRIPTION 5.5 in/14 cm. **Large headed** with conspicuous yellowish-white eye-ring; relatively bright greenish above, yellow green below with **yellow throat. Short blackish tail**; blackish wings fairly short with prominent white wing-bars. Short broad-based bill, black above, orange below. *Juvenile:* Wing-bars tinged buff.

SIMILAR SPECIES Pacific-slope, Cordilleran Flycatchers (pp. 294–295) teardrop-shaped eye-rings (more pointed at rear). Other *Empidonax* have white or grayish throats; vocalizations distinctive. Note restricted range of Yellow-bellied Flycatcher in PNW.

STATUS & DISTRIBUTION Breeds across boreal forests of Canada, north-central, northeastern US; winters eastern Mexico to Panama. Rare to locally uncommon breeder in BC at far northeastern corner of PNW—e.g., east of Prince George (Bowron River), around Mackenzie, very locally in Rocky Mountain Trench south to Golden. Migrates east of Great Plains (nearly unrecorded as migrant in PNW).

HABITAT ASSOCIATIONS Breeds in spruce or regenerating lodgepole pine forest with mossy understory, often boggy; less often balsam poplar, white birch, willow stands. Winters in low-elevation tropical forest. Migrants use diverse habitats.

BEHAVIOR & FEEDING Usually sings from prominent perch, often tops of trees. Forages at lower levels in forest, catching insects in mid-air or gleaning them from vegetation in short flights. Mossy nest built on ground in moss or other depression by female; male assists with parental care.

VOCALIZATIONS Song repeated *chebunk*, somewhat similar to *chebek* of Least Flycatcher but less emphatic, repeated at slower pace. Rising *purwee* call (lower pitched, more plaintive than *su weep* of Pacific-slope Flycatcher); also short *psik*, *brrt* notes.

Alberta—Jun • TERRY THORMIN

BC (Prince George)—Jul • GREG DROZDA

Alder Flycatcher
Empidonax alnorum

DESCRIPTION 5.75 in/14.5 cm. Fairly large *Empidonax* with **narrow white eye-ring**; greenish above, **white throat, dusky chest**, pale yellow belly. Tail appears long; dark wings show long primary projection, prominent white wing-bars. Relatively long bill, black above, all-orange below. *Juvenile:* Wing-bars tinged buff.

SIMILAR SPECIES Willow Flycatcher (p. 289) browner above with less conspicuous eye-ring; essentially identical in field; best separated by song (Alder strongly accented on middle syllable, Willow more on first syllable). Note range. Other *Empidonax* show more-prominent eye-rings; songs differ.

STATUS & DISTRIBUTION Breeds across northern forests of Alaska, Canada, north-central, northeastern US; winters primarily in northwestern South America. Migrates east of Great Plains. In PNW, breeds in central interior BC south to Shuswap Highlands, Thompson Plateau around Nicola Valley; replaced by Willow Flycatcher at lower elevations at south end of range. Rare in BC Rockies south of Golden, casual northwestern MT (breeding suspected; confirmed breeding just east of Continental Divide in Teton County, MT). Migrants casual west to BC coast, fewer across northern WA, accidental in remainder of region. Arrives late May, gone by early Sep.

HABITAT ASSOCIATIONS Nests in alder, willow, other shrubby stands around wetlands. In migration, various open or edge habitats.

BEHAVIOR & FEEDING Forages for insects by capturing in midair or by gleaning from vegetation; eats some berries. Female builds nest close to ground in crotch of deciduous (occasionally coniferous) vegetation; pair shares parental care.

VOCALIZATIONS Song burry *way BEE o*. Call *pip*, somewhat thinner than Willow's *whit*.

OR (Washington County)—Jun · GREG GILLSON

WA (King County)—Jun · GREGG THOMPSON

Willow Flycatcher
Empidonax traillii

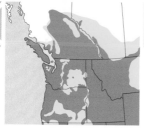

DESCRIPTION 5.75 in/14.5 cm. Drab with **inconspic-uous white eye-ring**; **brownish** above, **whitish throat, dusky chest**, pale-yellow belly. Fairly long tail; dark wings show prominent white wing-bars. Relatively long bill, black above, all-orange below. *Juvenile:* Brownish-buff wing-bars.

SIMILAR SPECIES Alder Flycatcher (p. 288) brighter; greener above, narrow eye-ring more conspicuous, primary projection longer; however, essentially identical; best separation by song (Willow's strongly accented on first syllable, Alder's on second syllable). Other *Empidonax* eye-rings much more prominent; songs differ.

STATUS & DISTRIBUTION Breeds from southern BC across southern Canada to Quebec (locally Maritimes); through northern Great Plains south to Georgia; in West south to Arizona (rare California). Winters coasts of southern Central America to northern Andes. In PNW, nests from BC (Cariboo–Chilcotin, usually at lower elevations; Mt. Robson Provincial Park) south through region except northern coast BC, Columbia Plateau, treeless areas of OR. Rare western Vancouver Island, outer coasts of WA/OR. Arrives late May (earlier on westside), gone before Oct.

HABITAT ASSOCIATIONS Breeds in alder, willow stands around wetlands, occasionally upland rose/snowberry (northwestern MT); west of Cascades from central OR northward, also regenerating clear-cuts, clearings with broom, bracken.

BEHAVIOR & FEEDING Generally similar to Alder Flycatcher; tends to nest higher in deciduous shrub (usually willow) than that species. Late broods may fledge just before Sep.

VOCALIZATIONS Burry *FITZ bew* song, strongly accented on first syllable; occasionally shortened to *Fbew*. Calls include rich *whit*, thicker than Alder's *pip*; throaty *zweeo*, suggestive of Alder.

WA (Skagit County)—Jun · DOUG SCHURMAN

WA (Skagit County)—Jun · DOUG SCHURMAN

Least Flycatcher
Empidonax minimus

DESCRIPTION 5.25 in/13.5 cm. **Smallest PNW flycatcher**, compact with conspicuous white eye-ring; greenish-brown above, pale below, dusky wash to breast. **Relatively short tail**; blackish wings show bold white wing-bars, short primary projection. Broad-based **short bill**, black above, orange below. *Juvenile:* Buffy wing-bars.

SIMILAR SPECIES Other *Empidonax* longer billed (except Hammond's), larger overall; best identified by song. Hammond's (p. 291) also small but lower mandible blackish, primary extension longer, eye-ring less symmetrical. Ruby-crowned Kinglet (p. 351), Hutton's Vireo (p. 310) perch with more horizontal posture.

STATUS & DISTRIBUTION Breeds across forests of Canada, northern US; winters primarily in Central America. Migrates east of Rockies. In PNW, breeds east of Coast/Cascade mountains throughout BC (common central BC, local, uncommon in south); locally eastern WA (primarily northeastern), eastern OR (Grant County), ID, northwestern MT, western WY but breeding status poorly known. Arrives mid-May, gone by early Sep. Migrants casual/rare on westside (primarily spring overshoots); annual in western WA in recent years.

HABITAT ASSOCIATIONS Breeds deciduous groves, woodlands, especially quaking aspen, cottonwood, birch; varied habitats at other seasons.

BEHAVIOR & FEEDING Forages aerially for insects, also gleans from vegetation, takes berries in fall. Female constructs compact nest in mid-canopy crotch of deciduous tree (often aspen, willow, alder), rarely in shrub. Female broods, incubates; male shares feeding duties.

VOCALIZATIONS Characteristic song emphatic, snappy, rapidly repeated *chebec*, often offered continuously for long periods. Yellow-bellied Flycatcher's *chebunk* similar but less emphatic, not in rapid series. Call soft *wit*, occasionally sharper if given in alarm.

Hammond's Flycatcher
Empidonax hammondii

DESCRIPTION 5.5 in/14 cm. Active, large-headed *Empidonax* with somewhat asymmetrical white eye-ring. Short bill, tail, give bird "cute" appearance. Grayish green above, **grayer head**; gray throat, chest; pale-yellow belly. Blackish tail appears short; dark wings show **long primary projection**, white wing-bars. **Short, narrow bill mostly blackish below.** Habitually flicks tail rapidly upward, flicks wings. *Juvenile:* Buffy wing-bars.

SIMILAR SPECIES Dusky Flycatcher (p. 293) has shorter wings, longer tail, longer bill with paler coloration; southbound adults typically disheveled looking (molt only after arriving in tropics). Gray Flycatcher (p. 292) pumps tail gently downward. Least Flycatcher (p. 290) has broad bill with orange lower mandible; shorter wings.

STATUS & DISTRIBUTION Breeds across forests of West, winters Central America. In PNW, common breeder in coniferous forests (casual Haida Gwaii, uncommon along WA/OR coasts). First arrivals mid- to late Apr; most arrive May, depart Aug–Sep. Rarely lingers to mid-Oct.

HABITAT ASSOCIATIONS Prefers rather dense stands of older conifers; also mature coastal red-alder forests, mixed riparian woodlands east of Cascades/BC Coast Range. Winters in montane forest; migrants appear anywhere.

BEHAVIOR & FEEDING Foraging behavior similar to other *Empidonax*. Female constructs nest at moderate height on horizontal conifer branch, male helps feed young.

VOCALIZATIONS Three-part song, *seepik seezrrt bzrrt* (often only one or two segments given). Similar to Dusky Flycatcher's, but has two different buzzy parts, lacks Dusky's characteristic upslurred *tsweet* element. Call sharp *pip* (like Pygmy Nuthatch), quite different from soft *wit* of Dusky. Uncommonly gives *peeew prip* call (first part downslurred).

WA (King County)—May · GREGG THOMPSON

Nest · OR (Harney County)—Jun · DAMON CALDERWOOD

Gray Flycatcher
Empidonax wrightii

DESCRIPTION 6 in/15 cm. Slim with **even white eye-ring**; dull gray above; gray throat, breast; pale-yellow belly. Blackish-gray tail; fairly short dark wings have white wing-bars. **Long, narrow bill**; lower mandible orange at base, often tipped with black as if dipped in ink. Habitually **pumps long tail downward**. *Juvenile:* Brighter-yellowish belly.

SIMILAR SPECIES Often appears slimmer, duller, grayer than other PNW *Empidonax*. Note bill shape, eye-ring, tail-dipping habit, vocalizations.

STATUS & DISTRIBUTION Breeds in interior West from southern BC to Arizona, New Mexico; winters in Mexico. Recent immigrant to northern portions of PNW; first recorded 1970 (WA), 1984 (BC). Presently fairly common to common breeder locally in southern ID, eastern OR, eastern WA, south-central BC (Okanagan Valley); migrants rare in western OR (Rogue Valley, Detroit Flats), rare to casual elsewhere in westside OR, WA. Arrives late Apr, departs Aug–Sep, casual Oct in OR.

HABITAT ASSOCIATIONS In BC, WA, mostly breeds in open stands of ponderosa pine with grass or sagebrush/bitterbrush understory, rarely open shrub-steppe. In OR, southern ID, western WY, uses sagebrush-juniper woodland. Winters in arid scrub. Migrants often recorded in riparian migrant traps.

BEHAVIOR & FEEDING Feeds primarily by flying to ground from low perch, gleaning insects from plants or on ground. Loose cup nest of grasses usually placed in low crotch of branch (often against trunk) in ponderosa pine, juniper, sagebrush.

VOCALIZATIONS Song rich *chelep chelep, chelep sweet*. Call *whit*, similar to Dusky, Willow Flycatchers.

ID (Jefferson County)—May · DARREN CLARK

BC (Peachland)—May · LAURE W. NEISH

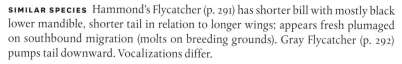

Dusky Flycatcher
Empidonax oberholseri

DESCRIPTION 5.75 in/14.5 cm. Medium-sized, typical *Empidonax*; eye-ring somewhat teardrop-shaped like Hammond's. **Tail long** in relation to **short wings**. Often flicks tail upward. **Relatively long, narrow bill; lower mandible has pale base**. Molt occurs on wintering grounds, so adults appear worn, drab, dull grayish after breeding. *Juvenile:* Broader off-white wing-bars, yellower below.

SIMILAR SPECIES Hammond's Flycatcher (p. 291) has shorter bill with mostly black lower mandible, shorter tail in relation to longer wings; appears fresh plumaged on southbound migration (molts on breeding grounds). Gray Flycatcher (p. 292) pumps tail downward. Vocalizations differ.

STATUS & DISTRIBUTION Breeds across montane forests of western North America, winters in Mexico, Guatemala. In PNW, uncommon to common breeder east of Cascades/BC Coast Range, also mountains of southwestern OR. Rare on upper western slope of Cascades; migrants rare in western lowlands. Vanguard arrives mid- to late Apr, majority in May; fall migration in Aug–Sep, casual Oct.

HABITAT ASSOCIATIONS Breeds dry, open ponderosa pine/Douglas-fir forests with scattered tall shrubs, also shrubby clear-cuts within subalpine forests; winters in similar habitats. Migrants frequent in shady riparian areas.

BEHAVIOR & FEEDING Forages aerially for insects; also gleans or pounces on prey. Nest built by female in crotch of tall shrub. Male feeds incubating female, assists with fledglings.

VOCALIZATIONS Song three-part *seept szree tsweet* (final syllable upslurred); often only one or two segments given. Call soft *wit*. Gives lazy *du du duhic* (with *hic* higher-pitched) in late morning or afternoon. See also under Hammond's Flycatcher.

OR (Harney County)—May · DENNIS PAULSON

BC (Comox)—Jul · TERRY THORMIN

Pacific-slope Flycatcher
Empidonax difficilis

DESCRIPTION 5.5 in/14 cm. Brightly colored *Empidonax* with broad yellow-white **eye-ring narrowing to point behind eye**; greenish above, yellowish throat, darker chest, yellow belly. Shows **slightly peaked rear crown**, dark wings with prominent white wing-bars; tail appears long. **Broad bill; lower mandible entirely orange.** *Juvenile:* Less yellowish underparts, broader buff wing-bars.

SIMILAR SPECIES Cordilleran Flycatcher (p. 295) essentially identical; best distinguished by voice. Yellow-bellied Flycatcher (p. 287) shows rounder head, shorter tail, brighter green dorsally, eye-ring much less teardrop shaped; limited to eastern BC.

STATUS & DISTRIBUTION Breeds from Baja California to Alaska east through OR/WA Cascades, across interior BC, northern WA possibly to northern ID, northwestern MT. Winters Pacific coast of Mexico. In PNW, common in coastal forests; status east of Cascades/BC Coast Range confused by extensive intergradation with Cordilleran Flycatcher, but most authorities contend Pacific-slope breeds uncommonly east at least to eastern BC/northeastern OR. Arrives mid- to late Apr on coast, late Apr–late May in interior. Departs late Aug–Sep.

HABITAT ASSOCIATIONS Breeds in westside mature forests, especially along streams, ravines. Interior populations closely tied to riparian habitats along shady creeks, also lakeshores in wetter coniferous forests, well-treed gardens. Winters diverse tropical forest habitats; migrants prefer shady stopovers.

BEHAVIOR & FEEDING Primarily insectivorous; makes forays from perch. Mossy nest placed on ledge of road or stream bank, rock bluff, upturned roots, under eaves, bridges. Female provides most parental care; male helps feed young.

VOCALIZATIONS Song high-pitched, three-part *pseet ptik seet*. Call upslurred *suweet*, often inserted into song.

ID (Jefferson County)—Aug · DARREN CLARK

Arizona—May · GLENN BARTLEY

Cordilleran Flycatcher
Empidonax occidentalis

DESCRIPTION 5.5 in/14 cm. Visually indistinguishable in field from Pacific-slope Flycatcher (p. 294).

SIMILAR SPECIES See under Pacific-slope Flycatcher. Essentially identical to that species although, on average, Cordilleran larger with greener upperparts; calls distinctive in core ranges, but separation problematic in northern part of intermountain PNW.

STATUS & DISTRIBUTION Formerly lumped with Pacific-slope Flycatcher into single species, "Western" Flycatcher; split in 1989. Cordilleran breeds in mountains from southern Mexico north through Rockies to Alberta; winters southern Mexico within breeding range. In PNW, arrives late Apr–late May, departs late Aug–Sep. Locally uncommon to common breeder in western WY, southern ID, southeastern OR; unclear how far northward, westward through Rockies breeding range extends. "Western" Flycatchers reported as Cordilleran uncommon northwestern MT, northern ID, rare southeastern WA, northeastern OR, but status confused by apparent co-occurrence or intergradation with Pacific-slope. One study recorded intermediate vocalizations from BC Cascades east to Rocky Mountain foothills of Alberta, south to southeastern WA. More recent genetic work indicates admixing east to South Dakota, northern Colorado. Many ornithologists believe further fieldwork may prove "Western" Flycatcher split untenable.

HABITAT ASSOCIATIONS Breeders closely tied to montane riparian habitats along shady creeks, especially those with mossy cliffs; less common in open mid- to higher-elevation forests (WY).

BEHAVIOR & FEEDING Similar to Pacific-slope Flycatcher.

VOCALIZATIONS Song three-part *sweea tipit seet*. Call unslurred, rising, two-part *we seet*, often inserted into song. "Western" Flycatcher calls intermediate between Pacific-slope/Cordilleran, or individual birds giving calls of both species, documented regularly in areas of range overlap.

Juvenile · WA (King County)—Jul · DOUG SCHURMAN

WA (King County)—Apr · JOSEPH V. HIGBEE

Black Phoebe
Sayornis nigricans

DESCRIPTION 7 in/18 cm. Medium-sized flycatcher, **black with white belly,** tail shows white outer edge. *Juvenile:* Browner above with cinnamon wing-bars.

SIMILAR SPECIES Eastern Kingbird (p. 302) larger with white underparts, white band across tip of tail. Other phoebes (pp. 297–298) similar in size, habits, but quite different in plumage (Say's rusty below, Eastern olive-gray).

STATUS & DISTRIBUTION Resident from southwestern WA south through Central, South America. In PNW, highest numbers occur in southern OR west of Cascades; uncommon to locally common resident at low elevations in Rogue, Applegate, Illinois Valleys, coastal lowlands north to Coquille River, Coos Bay; rare Umpqua Valley. Range expansion in recent years north through Willamette Valley. Since 2000, reported annually along lower Columbia River in WA (predominantly Sep–Apr); breeding confirmed there, also north to Thurston County in 2012. Rare Klamath Basin, coastal WA, Puget Trough to Lower Mainland BC, mainly winter; accidental southern ID.

HABITAT ASSOCIATIONS Closely tied to habitats near water: slow-moving rivers, ditches, ponds, lakes.

BEHAVIOR & FEEDING Perches upright like other flycatchers; pumps tail regularly, often while calling. Non-migratory, but exhibits post-breeding dispersal principally during late fall/winter. Primarily takes fairly large flying insects by making forays from perch; often hovers while searching for prey. Nest cemented with mud onto rock face, boulder, dirt bank, bridge, culvert, or other sheltered location; pair shares parental duties, often produces two broods. Monogamous pair bond may last several years.

VOCALIZATIONS Song alternating *pitee, pitew* notes; call sharp *tsip.*

WA (Whitman County)—Jun · TOM MUNSON

Eastern Phoebe
Sayornis phoebe

DESCRIPTION 7 in/18 cm. Medium-sized, drably colored flycatcher; **dark head**, brownish-gray back, wings, tail; dingy-whitish breast, belly; some gray on sides. **Habitually pumps tail** gently downward. Generally appears **round headed**; does not show strong wing-bars. *Juvenile:* Pale feather edging forms faint wing-bars; pale-yellow belly.

SIMILAR SPECIES Other phoebes (pp. 296, 298) similar in size, habits, but plumage much different; Western Wood-Pewee (p. 286) smaller, more slender, grayer below, shows strong wing-bars, peaked crown. *Empidonax* flycatchers (pp. 287–295) smaller with prominent wing-bars; do not pump tail except for Gray Flycatcher, which is paler gray with eye-ring.

STATUS & DISTRIBUTION Breeds from extreme southeastern Yukon across southern Canada to Maritimes, south to Texas, Alabama. Migrates mostly from Great Plains eastward, winters south from New Jersey to central Mexico. Vagrant in PNW; records scattered throughout, nearly year-round but with prominent May–Jun peak. BC records concentrated near coast during spring; most US records from east of Cascades in OR/WA/ID, although equally likely either side of crest in OR. Recently confirmed breeding in central BC.

HABITAT ASSOCIATIONS Often breeds near water, also woodland edge, farms, light-density residential neighborhoods; winters, migrates through diverse habitats.

BEHAVIOR & FEEDING Forages aerially from perch for flying insects, takes some berries outside of nesting season. Nests mostly on human-made structures (under eaves, bridges, culverts), rarely rock faces, dirt banks; female builds nest, male assists with defense, feeding young. Often double-broods.

VOCALIZATIONS Song drawn-out burry, whistled *phee bree* or *phee bridip*; call sharp *tsip*.

WA (King County)—Mar • GREGG THOMPSON

Say's Phoebe
Sayornis saya

DESCRIPTION 7.5 in/19 cm. Flycatcher with **cinnamon-orange breast, belly; gray head**, diffuse blackish eyeline; **black tail** contrasts with brownish-gray back, wings. *Juvenile:* Rusty edges to wing feathers.

SIMILAR SPECIES Western Kingbird (p. 301) may look similar in poor lighting; larger, yellow below, white outer tail feathers. Eastern Phoebe (p. 297) gray-and-white below, dips tail more frequently. Black Phoebe (p. 296) distinctly black-and-white.

STATUS & DISTRIBUTION Breeds from Alaska, Yukon south through western North America to central Mexico; winters mostly California, Utah south through breeding range. In PNW east of Cascades, common breeder, migrant; arrives mid-Feb–Apr, departs late Aug–Sep. West of crest, rare spring migrant, mostly Willamette Valley, Puget lowlands north to Greater Vancouver; casual but more widespread in fall. Regular but rare resident Nov–Jan in Rogue Valley; casual in winter elsewhere in OR, ID, WA, southern BC.

HABITAT ASSOCIATIONS Breeds in open habitats, especially dry grasslands, desert edge, often near barns, cliffs; rarely in wetter landscapes (e.g., northwestern MT); north of PNW, uses alpine tundra. Favors similar habitats outside breeding; also coastlines, farmland, mountain meadows.

BEHAVIOR & FEEDING Perches upright. Primarily insectivorous; forages closer to ground than Eastern Phoebe, hovering frequently, sometimes stalking prey on foot; early-returning individuals may walk on ice to catch insects near open water. Female builds nest under eaves, inside outbuildings, under bridges, or in cliff crevices. Male provides defense, feeds young. Pair often raises two broods.

VOCALIZATIONS Song alternating *pideer, pedreep* notes; call clear, plaintive, descending *peeer.*

Flying from nest · OR (Jackson County)—Jul · DAMON CALDERWOOD

WA (Yakima County)—Jun · DOUG SCHURMAN

Ash-throated Flycatcher
Myiarchus cinerascens

DESCRIPTION 8.5 in/22 cm. Elegant looking with gray-brown head, **puffy crest**; pale-gray throat, breast; **very pale-yellow belly. Flight feathers, including rectrices, extensively rufous**; whitish wing-bars, relatively **heavy black bill**. *Juvenile:* Wings edged buff; lacks gray tips to tail feathers.

SIMILAR SPECIES Other PNW flycatchers lack rufous in wing, tail. Willow (p. 289) smaller, lower mandible yellow. Western Wood-Pewee (p. 286) smaller, no yellow below. Western Kingbird (p. 301) larger, less slender, tail black with white edges; appears round headed (versus high crested).

STATUS & DISTRIBUTION Breeds from south-central WA through mountains of West to central Mexico; winters at low to mid-elevations from extreme southeastern California, southwestern Arizona to El Salvador. In PNW, fairly common breeder locally in OR (southwestern interior valleys, east of Cascades), south-central WA (most along Columbia River from White Salmon to Rock Creek, rare north to Wenatchee); rare southern ID. Arrives May (earlier on westside), departs Jul–Aug. Away from breeding areas, migrants rare to casual Apr–Nov to southwestern BC, western WY (accidental northwestern MT).

HABITAT ASSOCIATIONS Breeds in oak or juniper woodlands, chaparral, other arid riparian habitats.

BEHAVIOR & FEEDING Forages for flying insects, moving perch to perch. Rarely takes fruit, small vertebrates. Nests in tree cavities; also uses nest boxes (often intended for bluebirds), pipes, crates, great variety of other artificial cavities. Incorporates hair, snakeskin, debris into nest. Female incubates, male defends nest.

VOCALIZATIONS Common calls include *pik, ha wheer, br ik, ka brik*; song repetitive series of *ha wheer* notes, other calls.

BC (Balaklava Island)—Oct · IVAN DUBINSKY

WA (Whatcom County)—Nov · GREGG THOMPSON

Tropical Kingbird
Tyrannus melancholicus

DESCRIPTION 9 in/23 cm. Robust flycatcher with gray-green back, **bright-yellow underparts**; gray head, whitish throat, upper breast washed with pale gray; dark-brown tail, central rectrices shorter than outer ones. Black **bill relatively long, heavy.** Like other kingbirds, has narrow orange crown stripe (almost always concealed). *Juvenile:* More-distinct pale edging to upperwing coverts.

SIMILAR SPECIES Western Kingbird (p. 301) has uniform-length black tail with white edges, grayer back; yellow of belly does not extend to upper breast.

STATUS & DISTRIBUTION Resident throughout New World tropics from equatorial region north to central Mexico, rare breeder north to southern Texas, southeastern Arizona. Also migrates south in austral summer to breed in subtropical Brazil, Bolivia, Argentina. In PNW, increasingly frequent with nearly all records along coast Oct–Nov during post-breeding dispersal—now uncommon OR, rare WA, casual north to southwestern BC. A few late Sep, Dec records, one from Feb. Nearly unrecorded away from westside lowlands (accidental ID).

HABITAT ASSOCIATIONS Breeds in wide variety of open habitats—agricultural fields, riversides, parks, gardens, partially cleared forest, other human-modified sites. In PNW, almost always found near coast in similar habitats.

BEHAVIOR & FEEDING Sallies from open perches to catch insects in air. Also eats berries, other small fruits. Bulky nest built by female on branch in open situations, also on utility poles, other structures. Male assists with feeding young.

VOCALIZATIONS Distinctive call high twitter: *tze ze ze ze ze ze zeip.* Dawn song combination of short notes, trills: *pt prrrrr pt pt prrrr pt.*

BC (Penticton)—Jul · LAURE W. NEISH

Western Kingbird
Tyrannus verticalis

DESCRIPTION 9 in/23 cm. Greenish-gray back, black bill, **yellow belly**; pale-gray head with hint of dark mask; pale-gray throat, breast. **White-edged black tail**; black bill. *Juvenile:* Paler-yellow belly.

SIMILAR SPECIES Tropical Kingbird (p. 300) larger bill, greener back; brighter yellow of belly extends up onto breast; tail lacks white edging, may appear notched. Calls differ. Smaller-billed Cassin's Kingbird (not shown; casual ID/OR) shows pale tail tip, darker-gray throat contrasting with white malar. See also under Ash-throated Flycatcher (p. 299), Say's Phoebe (p. 298).

STATUS & DISTRIBUTION Breeds southwestern Canada, western US, northwestern Mexico; winters Pacific slope from Mexico to Costa Rica, also southern Florida. In PNW, common breeder east of Cascades southward from south-central BC (Quesnel). Rare, local breeder west of Cascades in BC, WA. In western OR, fairly common breeder Rogue, Umpqua Valleys, uncommon Willamette Valley, rare on southwestern coast. Uncommon (OR) to rare (farther north) migrant on coast. Arrives mid-Apr in western OR, late Apr–May elsewhere; westside migrants continue through Jun. Departure begins early Jul, most gone by mid-Aug, rare by mid-Sep; casual Oct/Nov.

HABITAT ASSOCIATIONS Breeds low, middle elevations in semi-arid grasslands, open agricultural habitats with scattered trees or utility poles. Similar habitats at other seasons.

BEHAVIOR & FEEDING Sallies out from conspicuous perches to catch flying insects, rarely gleans, eats berries. Pair selects site, female constructs untidy nest on open branches or utility pole. Both sexes exhibit extreme aggression toward intruders.

VOCALIZATIONS Characteristic calls short, nasal *bik, bidik, weekadu.*

Eastern Kingbird
Tyrannus tyrannus

DESCRIPTION 8.5 in/21 cm. Large bicolored flycatcher; dark gray above, black head, white underparts, breast washed grayish. **Black tail with conspicuous white terminal band**. Like other kingbirds, narrow orange-red crown stripe almost always concealed. *Juvenile:* Narrower tail band, pale wing edging more conspicuous.

SIMILAR SPECIES Fork-tailed Flycatcher (not shown; casual PNW) slighter bodied with white (versus gray-washed) breast, lighter gray back contrasting with dark cap. Tail much longer (but beware broken or molting tails), strongly forked, lacks white tip.

STATUS & DISTRIBUTION Breeds throughout most of southern Canada, US, except Pacific Coast, arid Southwest; winters in South America. In PNW, common breeder east of Cascades/BC Coast Range (local in southeastern OR). Locally uncommon to rare in westside lowlands of BC (Fraser Valley west to Pitt Meadows), WA (Skagit, Snohomish Valleys), OR (Sandy River near Portland); migrants rarer toward outer coast. Arrives mid-May, leaves Aug–early Sep, accidental Oct–Nov.

HABITAT ASSOCIATIONS Breeds low/middle elevation in open habitats, e.g., riparian woodland edge, orchards, other agricultural landscapes, dry grasslands where perches available; migrants sometimes concentrate near fruiting trees. Winters at forest edge.

BEHAVIOR & FEEDING Insectivorous in spring, early summer; also takes berries in late summer. Sallies out from conspicuous perches to catch flying insects in typical kingbird fashion. Territorial birds aggressively defend nest area. Nest built on open branches of trees, large shrubs, occasionally utility poles (BC). Pair feeds young for weeks after fledging. Gregarious during fall migration, winter.

VOCALIZATIONS Sputtering, twittered *d d d d* ZEER, *d*ZEE *d*ZEE *d*ZEE.

Oklahoma—Apr · BOB KOTHENBEUTEL

Oklahoma—Apr · BOB KOTHENBEUTEL

Scissor-tailed Flycatcher
Tyrannus forficatus

DESCRIPTION 10–15 in/25–38 cm. Whitish with pale-gray back, blackish wings; **pale, salmon-pink belly**, sides; dark eyeline. **Deeply forked, very long black-and-white tail**. Scarlet underwing coverts. Narrow orange crown stripe almost always concealed. *Juvenile:* Paler, tail shorter, lacks pink coloration below.

SIMILAR SPECIES Distinctive. Northern Mockingbird (p. 363) somewhat resembles short-tailed immature but overall grayer, shows white patches in wings. Black-billed Magpie (p. 317) long tailed, but much larger with black head. Fork-tailed Flycatcher (not shown; casual PNW) has black cap, lacks pink-tinged plumage.

STATUS & DISTRIBUTION Breeds south-central US (mostly Kansas, Oklahoma, Texas) south into northeastern Mexico; winters southern Mexico to Panama. In PNW, rare, rather irregular vagrant May–Nov; distribution of records predominantly May–Jun in westside lowlands, fewer from interior—indicative of spring dispersal northward along coast.

HABITAT ASSOCIATIONS Breeds in variety of open habitats with scattered trees, e.g., prairies, savannas, towns, pastures, golf courses. At other seasons, uses similar areas including airports; may winter in second-growth tropical scrub.

BEHAVIOR & FEEDING Makes foraging flights to capture grasshoppers, beetles, other large invertebrates, gleaned from vegetation or plucked from air. Flight straight, tail folded, often making sharp turns with flared tail. Migrants, wintering birds gregarious—may flock into hundreds—but in PNW recorded as singles. Nests in isolated tree; female builds bulky structure, provides most parental care; male assists by feeding young.

VOCALIZATIONS Pre-dawn song repeated *pup, perdeep*. Chattering calls reminiscent of Western Kingbird, often paired with zigzag flights, flared tail feathers.

Loggerhead Shrike
Lanius ludovicianus

DESCRIPTION 9 in/23 cm. Large-headed songbird; stubby black bill with sharp, slightly hooked upper mandible. **White primary bases, outer rectrices, throat.** *Adult:* Grayish (darker on back); **black wings, tail, broad mask**. *Juvenile:* Indistinct breast scaling.

SIMILAR SPECIES Northern Shrike (p. 305) larger; longer, more sharply hooked bill with pale base to lower mandible; adult lighter gray with white rump, narrow mask; immature browner with indistinct mask. Northern Mockingbird (p. 363) more slender, longer billed, lacks mask; slower wingbeats.

STATUS & DISTRIBUTION Breeds central WA, central Alberta disjunctly to western Quebec, south through Florida, Mexico (extirpated from former New England nesting range over last 50 years). Withdraws southward in winter. In PNW east of Cascades, uncommon, declining breeder at lower elevations OR, southern ID, western WY, central WA; migrants rare to northwestern MT, casual south-central BC (southern Okanagan). Winters mostly to south except rare, local Oct–Jan southern ID, OR north to south-central WA. On westside, migrants rare north to northwestern WA, mostly Mar–Apr. Recorded year-round western OR.

HABITAT ASSOCIATIONS Breeds grasslands, shrublands; migrants use any open area.

BEHAVIOR & FEEDING Perches raptor-like at top of shrub, hunting grassy areas for insects, also birds, reptiles, rodents. Flight similar to Northern Shrike but less undulating. Captures prey with bill, hovering briefly in open areas; impales food on thorn or barbed wire for feeding or storage. Open-cup nest constructed in low shrub; female may re-pair with second male after fledging first brood.

VOCALIZATIONS Piercing, squeaked *ju SSSKK*; also warbled song, harsh buzzes.

Juvenile · *WA (Snohomish County)* — *Nov* · GREGG THOMPSON | *WA (Skagit County)* — *Mar* · GREGG THOMPSON

Northern Shrike
Lanius excubitor

DESCRIPTION 9.75 in/25 cm. Large-headed, long-tailed songbird; **large bill** with sharply hooked upper mandible. **White on primary bases, outer rectrices**; breast has indistinct scaling. *Adult:* Mostly pearl gray. White rump; **black wings, tail, thin mask**. *Juvenile:* Variably brownish gray; adult black areas dark brownish (often indistinct).

SIMILAR SPECIES Loggerhead Shrike (p. 304) smaller; adult mantle darker, including rump; broader mask crosses shorter, black bill (Northern bill often pale). Northern Mockingbird (p. 363) bill thinner, lacks mask.

STATUS & DISTRIBUTION Holarctic breeder across taiga, tundra; also grassy scrub in Old World. In North America, winters taiga to temperate zone, regularly to northern California, Massachusetts, rarely to southern US. In PNW, fairly common Oct–Apr throughout southward from eastern, southwestern BC, rarely arriving Sep (may breed in central BC mountains); irregular southwestern OR. Transients rare western Vancouver Island, north of Campbell River.

HABITAT ASSOCIATIONS Open areas with scattered trees from lowlands to foothills; most frequent in agriculture, shrublands, coastal habitat. Migrants also use mountains.

BEHAVIOR & FEEDING Perches upright prominently, often at top of shrub when searching for prey. Flight undulating with rapid flapping, halting pauses. Swoops to dispatch victim with bill; also pursues by clambering through bushes, hovering. Takes rodents, insects, rarely reptiles; birds to dove-size in winter. Impales prey on thorn or barbed wire in sheltered location for feeding or storage. PNW numbers irruptive dependent on reproductive success, food supply on breeding grounds, where presumed monogamous.

VOCALIZATIONS Usually quiet outside breeding; occasionally offers warbled phrases (possibly to lure songbird quarry).

Warbling Vireo
Vireo gilvus

DESCRIPTION 5.25 in/13.5 cm. Fairly **nondescript** with **light supercilium**, faint eyeline; plain greenish-tinged gray upperparts, gray crown, whitish underparts. *Juvenile:* Brighter with more ventral yellow, particularly near flanks.

SIMILAR SPECIES Red-eyed Vireo (p. 307) larger, longer billed, greener above with black line above white supercilium. Philadelphia Vireo (not shown; casual PNW) yellow upper breast, dark eyeline extends through lores. Other PNW vireos show prominent wing-bars. Adult Tennessee Warbler (p. 374) greener dorsally with thin, pointed bill.

STATUS & DISTRIBUTION Breeds Yukon to Nova Scotia south to Mississippi, Mexico; winters Mexico to Nicaragua. In PNW, common breeder late Apr–Aug, sea level to subalpine except Haida Gwaii, Columbia Plateau, parts of central, southeastern OR; generally uncommon west of BC Coast Range. Migrants widespread, remain casually to late Oct. Populations breeding west, east of Rockies genetically distinct, may constitute separate species, but dubiously separable in field; PNW status of eastern form unclear.

HABITAT ASSOCIATIONS Mixed forests—deciduous, frequently riparian, often surrounded by coniferous.

BEHAVIOR & FEEDING Gleans insects, other arthropods from canopy; takes some berries Aug–Apr. Joins mixed flocks in migration. Upon arrival, sings nearly constantly, but inconspicuous due to slow foraging style. Monogamous pair usually in close proximity. May erect crest, utter alarm notes in excitement; weaves basket nest suspended from horizontal forks like other vireos, shares parental care. Most PNW adults migrate to northwestern Mexico before Aug to complete molt.

VOCALIZATIONS Song languid, rambling Purple Finch–like warble, unlike other vireos; calls include extended mewing.

WA (King County)—Jun · GREGG THOMPSON

Red-eyed Vireo
Vireo olivaceus

DESCRIPTION 6 in/15 cm. Bulky, short tailed, with **flat-looking head**, heavy bill. **Plain green upperparts** with gray cap, whitish below; white **supercilium bordered with black** line above, another below through red eye. *Juvenile:* Brown eye.

SIMILAR SPECIES Warbling Vireo (p. 306) smaller with shorter bill; lacks black line above supercilium. Other regularly occurring PNW vireos show wing-bars. Adult Tennessee Warbler (p. 374) smaller with thin, pointed bill.

STATUS & DISTRIBUTION Breeds southwestern Yukon to Newfoundland, south to Texas, Florida; winters Amazon Basin; also resident in South America. In PNW, locally common breeder interior BC south locally to northwestern MT, southwestern ID, WA/OR Blue Mountains. West of Cascades/BC Coast Range, common but very local from southwestern BC to Willamette Valley, mostly along rivers; casual south to Rogue Valley. Arrives late May–Jun, most depart Aug. Migrants widespread but uncommonly seen except at breeding sites.

HABITAT ASSOCIATIONS Breeds mature deciduous forest, especially riparian cottonwood, maple; migrants less particular.

BEHAVIOR & FEEDING Forages mostly in canopy, primarily on insects; takes high percentage of small fruit in fall, continues fruit-based diet on winter grounds. Migrates nocturnally, arriving in PNW from east, returning eastward in fall before long southward trek. Erects crest, fans tail in excitement or alarm. Pair monogamous. Female assumes most nest building, incubation, all brooding duties while male sings, defends territory. Frequent victim of cowbird brood parasitism.

VOCALIZATIONS Song repetitive, continuous series of whistled phrases, sweeter, more complex than other, similar vireo songs. Mewed *zerrr, ny EEAH* given in alarm.

ID (Oneida County)—Jul · DARREN CLARK

ID (Oneida County)—Jun · DARREN CLARK

Plumbeous Vireo
Vireo plumbeus

DESCRIPTION 5.5 in/14 cm. Compact with heavy bill. Predominantly grayish with whitish underparts, grayish flanks, **white wing-bars**; **bold white eye-ring, lores give appearance of "spectacles."** First-year (Aug–Mar) may show pale-yellow wash on vent.

SIMILAR SPECIES Smaller Cassin's Vireo (p. 309) has thinner bill, yellow on flanks; gray of upperparts usually somewhat greenish in tone. Song sweeter, less burry.

STATUS & DISTRIBUTION North American population breeds disjunctly from southeastern MT, southwestern South Dakota, eastern California through interior Southwest to Oaxaca; most winter western, central, southwestern Mexico. In PNW, locally common breeder mid-May to early Sep in southeastern ID; otherwise rare peripherally in southwestern ID, southeastern OR (Harney, Lake Counties; nesting attempt reported near Lakeview). Reported rarely western WY, casually northern OR (Multnomah, Wallowa Counties). Difficulty of separating Plumbeous from Cassin's in field may obscure PNW distribution of these species, particularly during migration.

HABITAT ASSOCIATIONS Over most of range, breeds in pine or oak/juniper forest; also uses arid riparian willow/cottonwood woodland.

BEHAVIOR & FEEDING Forages deliberately, sluggishly, by gleaning, probing for insects; also eats fruits outside of breeding season. May join mixed flocks in migration. Male selects nest site, begins construction usually at low height, rarely higher in canopy. Monogamous pair weaves basket-like nest on horizontal fork with spiderweb silk, grasses; decorates outside with paper, moss; shares parental duties. Frequently subjected to cowbird parasitism.

VOCALIZATIONS Loud, simple, low-pitched, burry whistles with long pauses, sung year-round; series of harsh *cheb* notes in alarm.

BC (Saanich)—Jun · GLENN BARTLEY

Nest · OR (Harney County)—May · GREG GILLSON

Cassin's Vireo
Vireo cassinii

DESCRIPTION 5.25 in/13.5 cm. Compact with short stout bill, grayish-green upperparts, grayish head, **white wing-bars**, whitish underparts, yellowish flanks; **white eye-ring, lores form bold "spectacles."** Worn adults (Apr–Jul) may lack yellow tones.

SIMILAR SPECIES Hutton's Vireo (p. 310) smaller; diffuse white eye-ring broken at top. Larger Plumbeous Vireo (p. 308) more purely gray (versus greenish gray) with heavier bill; lacks yellow on flanks. Blue-headed Vireo (not shown; casual in PNW) brighter; gray head abruptly contrasts with greenish back, white throat.

STATUS & DISTRIBUTION Breeds from BC, southwestern Alberta to Baja California; most winter Mexico. In PNW, present Apr–Oct; fairly common breeder except Columbia Plateau, WA outer coast, southeastern OR, southern ID, western WY; in BC, rare north of Campbell River west of Coast Range, absent Haida Gwaii. Cassin's, Blue-headed, Plumbeous quite similar in appearance, vocalizations, long lumped as "Solitary" Vireo; field identification, species limits, PNW distribution in confusion since 1997 split into three species.

HABITAT ASSOCIATIONS Low- to mid-elevation forest breeder, most frequent in open, mixed conifers east of Cascades/BC Coast Range; migrants also use subalpine, urban, shrub-steppe, riparian sites.

BEHAVIOR & FEEDING Forages sluggishly in upper canopy for insects; fruits important in fall/winter. Inconspicuous unless singing. Joins mixed flocks in migration. Monogamous pair weaves basket-like nest on horizontal fork, often at low height, decorated with paper, moss, leaves; may raise two broods.

VOCALIZATIONS Loud song of simple, slurred, burry whistles with long pauses; falling series of harsh *shep* notes in alarm.

WA (Clallam County)—Nov • RYAN SHAW

Hutton's Vireo
Vireo huttoni

DESCRIPTION 5 in/12.5 cm. Stocky. **Large round head**, stubby bill, pale lores, prominent **diffuse white eye-ring broken above eye**. Greenish gray overall with lighter underparts, white wing-bars, **bluish-gray feet**. Endemic Vancouver Island subspecies *V.h. insularis* darker, richer green on average.

SIMILAR SPECIES Ruby-crowned Kinglet (p. 351) closely similar at first glance, but smaller with thin bill, yellowish feet, black below lower wing-bar; male has red crown (frequently hidden); restless forager, flicks wings more often. Larger Cassin's Vireo (p. 309) has longer bill, well-defined "spectacles"; head less round.

STATUS & DISTRIBUTION Resident from southwestern BC down coast to Baja California, also mountains from southeastern Arizona to Guatemala. In PNW, fairly common but often overlooked resident west of Cascades/BC Coast Range north to northern Vancouver Island; east of crest rare (Klickitat County) to casual (Yakima, Benton Counties) in WA; casual OR (Malheur NWR). Generally sedentary with some Aug–Dec dispersal.

HABITAT ASSOCIATIONS In PNW, mixed woodlands dominated by Douglas-fir, Sitka spruce, cedar; partial to oaks in south. Interior populations prefer other conifers.

BEHAVIOR & FEEDING Forages from canopy to understory, gleaning insects, other arthropods; rarely takes plant material. Inconspicuous except Feb–Mar, when males sing nearly constantly. May join mixed flocks with chickadees, kinglets, or warblers outside of breeding. Usually found in pairs, indicating that monogamous bond may be long-term. Establishes territory early. Pair weaves basket-like nest on horizontal fork like other vireos, shares parental care.

VOCALIZATIONS Song slurred, whistled *zweep*, repeated monotonously; calls include rising *bree dee dee*, harsh mewing.

Interior mountains · WA (Okanogan County)—Mar
GREGG THOMPSON

Cascades to coast · OR (Washington County)—May · GREG GILLSON

Juvenile · BC (Mount Washington)—Jun · TERRY THORMIN

Gray Jay
Perisoreus canadensis

DESCRIPTION 11.5 in/29 cm, wingspan 19 in/48 cm. Small billed with **gray upperparts**, pale underparts. **White forehead**; amount of white or dark on rest of head varies clinally from east to west. Populations in Rockies, Blue Mountains white crowned with dark on head limited to post-ocular stripe, nape; those from Cascades/BC Coast Range westward dark crowned with white auriculars. *Juvenile:* Overall **dark gray** with whitish malar.

SIMILAR SPECIES Larger Clark's Nutcracker (p. 316) shows longer bill, shorter tail with white outer rectrices. Crested Steller's Jay (p. 314) may appear round headed when molting.

STATUS & DISTRIBUTION Resident from Alaska to Newfoundland, south to northwestern Vermont, disjunctly to New Mexico. In PNW, fairly common in higher-elevation mountains (except south-central ID); also locally in lesser numbers down to coastline from BC Coast Range, Vancouver Island, Olympic Peninsula south to OR (Douglas County); absent Haida Gwaii.

HABITAT ASSOCIATIONS Extensive coniferous forests, less commonly mixed woods; prefers spruce, fir, mountain hemlock, lodgepole pine. Degradation of lowland forest has reduced range region-wide.

BEHAVIOR & FEEDING Omnivorous, foraging flexibly; scavenges, takes seeds, berries, arthropods, nestling birds, rodents. "Whiskey Jack" shows curiosity, begging from humans, stealing food; caches items in trees for winter with specialized sticky saliva, carrying heavier parcels with feet. Sedentary monogamous pair assisted by at least one (often unrelated) non-breeder for nestling provision, territory defense; less dominant juveniles expelled from territory by fall, dominant ones allowed to remain.

VOCALIZATIONS Subdued for corvid; whistled *weeo*, hoarse chatter, twitters, warbling; also mimics other birds.

OR (Lake County)—Aug · DONALD W. NELSON

Pinyon Jay
Gymnorhinus cyanocephalus

DESCRIPTION 10.5 in/27 cm, wingspan 19 in/48 cm. **Dull blue** overall with **short tail**, white throat streaks, long spike-like bill; bluest on head, but appears dark in poor light. *Juvenile:* Grayer; blue mostly on wings, tail.

SIMILAR SPECIES Mountain Bluebird (p. 353) smaller with short bill, white undertail. Clark's Nutcracker (p. 316) gray-and-black with white in tail, secondaries.

STATUS & DISTRIBUTION Resident in interior from south-central OR to western South Dakota, south to Baja California, New Mexico. In PNW, uncommon breeder OR from Ochoco Mountains south to Lake County, rare Klamath Basin; uncommon southeastern ID (Cassia to Caribou Counties). Wanders widely Sep–Apr; vagrants casual to southwestern OR, south-central WA, western WY, northwestern MT, recently southeastern BC (Lister).

HABITAT ASSOCIATIONS Juniper woodlands, ponderosa-pine edge; also uses shrub-steppe, oak woodland.

BEHAVIOR & FEEDING Highly gregarious year-round with nomadic flocks into hundreds. Inquisitive forager, mostly on seeds, primarily adapted to harvest pinyon-pine mast; also takes other seeds, fruit, invertebrates, lizards, nestling birds. Gathers, transports, then hides seeds up to 6 mi/10 km away from harvest site; individuals cache up to 2,500 seeds each fall. Incredible memory capacity facilitates recovery during winter/spring. Noisy flocks assemble in tight mass before vacating feeding area for long flight. Monogamous pairs mate for life, build nests colonially in synchrony; subadult male offspring often help provision young, defend nest.

VOCALIZATIONS Nasal, gull-like calls include *hwoaa*, varied chatters. California Quail–like *kweahh kwa kwa* offered at dawn.

312 *Family Corvidae*—CROWS AND JAYS

"Woodhouse's" · ID (Bannock County)—Jan · DARREN CLARK

"California" · WA (Clark County)—May · GEORGE PAGOS

Western Scrub-Jay
Aphelocoma californica

DESCRIPTION 11.5 in/29 cm, wingspan 16 in/41 cm. **Long tailed without crest**; blue dorsally with drab back, white supercilium, dark cheek. "California" has **partial blue breast band**, brightly contrasting whitish underparts. "Woodhouse's" **duller**; gray (versus brown) back, grayish underparts, **vague breast band** (often absent), reduced supercilium, **smaller bill.** *Juvenile:* Duller; gray head.

SIMILAR SPECIES Pinyon Jay (p. 312) evenly colored with very short tail. Blue Jay (p. 315) crested with white in wings, tail.

STATUS & DISTRIBUTION Two distinctive forms: "California" resident Cascades to coast, southwestern WA to Baja; "Woodhouse's," Great Basin, central Rockies to central Mexico. In PNW, "California" slowly expanding for century northward through Willamette Valley, now common resident to southern Puget Sound, fairly common Seattle, casual to southwestern BC. Also increasing on OR/WA coast, up Columbia to The Dalles. Casual east of WA Cascades away from Columbia Plateau. "Woodhouse's" breeds uncommonly south-central ID south of Snake River; accidental vagrant farther north. Both forms reported regularly south-central OR but true status unclear.

HABITAT ASSOCIATIONS Deciduous woodland, semi-open scrub, neighborhoods, often near oaks ("California"), juniper woodlands ("Woodhouse's"); rare at higher elevations.

BEHAVIOR & FEEDING Omnivorous; forages on arthropods, fruits, seeds (mostly acorns for "California," conifer seeds for "Woodhouse's"); frequents feeders, opportunistically robs nests; buries thousands of seeds for future retrieval. Some dispersal outside range (mostly Oct–Jan); irruptive movements often result from acorn shortages. Somewhat gregarious, but monogamous pair territorial when nesting; female incubates, broods.

VOCALIZATIONS Noisy, harsh, high-pitched rising *sheeeenk* most frequent; also rapidly repeated *weink*.

N. Rockies—BC (Bijoux Falls PP)
—Sep · JUKKA JANTUNEN

C.s. carlottae—BC (Haida Gwaii)—Oct · JOHN BURRILL

WA (Kitsap County)—Jun · KEN ARCHER

Steller's Jay
Cyanocitta stelleri

DESCRIPTION 11.5 in/29 cm, wingspan 19 in/48 cm. Long tailed, **mostly blue**, blackish upper body with **prominent crest**, fine black banding on tail, wings; fine blue streaks on forehead. *Juvenile:* Grayish head, back. Northern Rocky Mountain populations show white above, below eye; birds from forested intermontane PNW westward darker, lack white head markings—larger endemic Haida Gwaii subspecies *C.s. carlottae* shows jet-black head, slate-gray back; may lack tail bands.

SIMILAR SPECIES Blue Jay (p. 315) has whitish underparts, white wing-bar, black necklace; other PNW jays lack crest. Scrub-Jay (p. 313) gray ventrally.

STATUS & DISTRIBUTION Resident forest zones of West from southern Alaska to Nicaragua, in numerous geographic races. In PNW, fairly common resident to treeline except Columbia Plateau, arid eastern OR, southern ID. Poorly understood southward or downslope fall migration may swell urban populations. Post-breeding movements (mostly Aug–Oct) rarely result in appearances in ID, WA of southern Rocky Mountain race (prominent white streaks on forehead), as well as northward intrusion of lighter-blue birds from montane southern OR, Nevada, California. Provincial bird of BC.

HABITAT ASSOCIATIONS Coniferous, mixed forests including suburbs; migrants move along coast, rarely into open arid habitats.

BEHAVIOR & FEEDING Omnivorous; adaptable, foraging on ground or trees for conifer seeds, acorns, some arthropods. Frequents feeders, robs nests, kills small vertebrates; garrulous, gregarious, frequently mobbing predators. Migrants reluctant to cross water bodies, make repeated tentative forays. Socially complex but monogamous; possible long-term bond; behaves secretively around bulky stick nest.

VOCALIZATIONS Harsh *shaark*, rapid repeated *wek*; also warbles, whistles, mimics.

MT (Flathead County)—Oct · JAN L. WASSINK

Blue Jay
Cyanocitta cristata

DESCRIPTION 11 in/28 cm, wingspan 18 in/46 cm. **Crested**, long tailed. Blue upperparts, whitish underparts, **black necklace, white wing-bar**; tail, wings thinly banded black. *Juvenile:* Slightly duller blue.

SIMILAR SPECIES Western Scrub-Jay (p. 313) lacks crest, wing-bar. Steller's Jay (p. 314) upper body blackish; lacks wing-bar, whitish underparts.

STATUS & DISTRIBUTION Resident across eastern North America from Newfoundland south to Florida, west to northeastern BC, eastern Colorado. In PNW, expanding westward. Rare resident in southeastern BC (Kootenays), with suspected breeding also noted in northwestern MT (where now common resident), Idaho Panhandle, northeastern OR, southeastern WA. Transients occur throughout northward to southern BC, mostly Oct–May, rarely linger to Jun; rare west of Cascades/BC Coast Range; more frequent on eastside, nearing uncommon status on WA Columbia Plateau.

HABITAT ASSOCIATIONS Deciduous, mixed forests, including suburbs.

BEHAVIOR & FEEDING Omnivorous, but mostly takes acorns, other mast; also eats fruits, arthropods, small vertebrates including nestling birds. Hammers large items with bill while holding them with feet; frequents feeders. Some percentage of population latitudinally migratory late Apr–May, Sep–Oct; diurnal movement conspicuous, small flocks flying with prevailing winds. Mobs predators garrulously, frequently. Monogamous pair forms long-term bond. Secretive near nest. Female incubates, broods while fed by male, raises young in bulky stick nest. In PNW, transients may remain at one location through winter, associating with local jays.

VOCALIZATIONS Noisy; diverse calls include sharp *jaaay*, musical whistles, conversational chatter, rusty pump-like squeal, nasal whining; also mimics local raptors.

BC (Penticton)—Oct · LAURE W. NEISH

Clark's Nutcracker
Nucifraga columbiana

DESCRIPTION 12 in/30 cm, wingspan 23 in/58 cm. Stout, medium gray; **long spike-like bill**, whitish face; black wings with **white secondaries, black tail with white outer rectrices**, both conspicuous in flight. *Juvenile:* Brownish gray; smaller bill.

SIMILAR SPECIES Pinyon Jay (p. 312) similar shape but plain, uniform blue; smaller Gray Jay (p. 311) has longer tail, lacks white in flight feathers.

STATUS & DISTRIBUTION Resident in interior from north-central BC to southern California, Colorado, New Mexico; two tiny disjunct populations in northern Mexico. In PNW, locally common resident near timberline in most mountains east from Cascades/BC Coast Range; descends lower when exploiting ponderosa pine. Irruptive movements result rarely in fluctuating numbers to lowlands. Rare on westside at high elevations including Vancouver Island, Siskiyous; irregularly casual OR Coast Range to sea level; uncommon breeder in drier eastern Olympics. Introduced blister rust, presently decimating whitebark pine, may threaten populations.

HABITAT ASSOCIATIONS High-elevation whitebark pine communities, less frequent to ponderosa or fir zones.

BEHAVIOR & FEEDING Distinctive corvid, specialized to extract seeds from pine cones. Transports seeds in sublingual pouch, buries tens of thousands annually for future retrieval; unrecovered seeds important in regeneration of high-elevation forests. Opportunistic; also feeds on arthropods, small vertebrates, carrion, handouts from hikers. Flight strong, slightly undulating; usually flocks when not nesting. Long-term monogamous pair shares parental care. Builds nest near food caches by late winter, feeds stored seeds to young; families move upslope by spring.

VOCALIZATIONS Noisy with harsh, raspy *karrrgk*, descending *taaarr*, low rattles.

Nest · BC (Okanagan Falls)—Jun · DAMON CALDERWOOD

Alberta—Nov · GERALD ROMANCHUK

Black-billed Magpie
Pica hudsonia

DESCRIPTION 19 in/48 cm, wingspan 25 in/64 cm. **Long tail**; pied with **white belly**, scapulars, primaries; folded wings, tail iridescent blue but appear blackish in poor light; stout bill. *Juvenile:* Shorter tail.

SIMILAR SPECIES Blue Jay (p. 315) crested with shorter tail. Other PNW corvids lack white belly.

STATUS & DISTRIBUTION Resident from southern Alaska to northwestern BC, also throughout interior West from northern Saskatchewan to northern New Mexico, east to northwestern Minnesota. In PNW, increasingly common resident east of Cascades/BC Coast Range, most frequent Columbia, Okanagan/Okanogan, Snake Valleys, other arid lowlands, but often disperses post-breeding to higher elevation. On westside, casual in lowlands (mostly Aug–Mar), accidental north to Haida Gwaii; breeds uncommonly only in Rogue Valley.

HABITAT ASSOCIATIONS Breeds in shrub-steppe, suburban ranchland, agricultural landscapes, open woodland; prefers to nest in riparian thickets (often Russian olive). Outside of breeding, uses open conifer, mixed forest.

BEHAVIOR & FEEDING Omnivorous. Forages cleverly, opportunistically exploiting arthropods, seeds, fruits, carrion, cervid ectoparasites, other food sources. May cooperatively kill larger prey or harass predators to steal prey; takes more seeds Nov–Mar. Agile flyer. Forms large post-breeding flocks, sometimes makes extensive movements, gathers at communal roosts. Gregarious; remains social year-round with complex behaviors such as "funeral" gatherings upon discovery of dead conspecific. Monogamous pair forms long-term bond, builds bulky domed nest; female incubates, broods while male feeds; pair shares fledgling care before juveniles join dispersing flocks.

VOCALIZATIONS Noisy; repeated nasal, high-pitched, barked *jaerk*, other squeals, chatter.

Alberta—Apr · GERALD ROMANCHUK   OR (Tillamook County)—Jun · ART CLAUSING

American Crow
Corvus brachyrhynchos

DESCRIPTION 17 in/43 cm, wingspan 37 in/94 cm. Chunky; completely **black** with stout bill, short **fan-shaped tail**; broad wings, variable flight shape dependent on behavior. *Juvenile:* Brownish black with red mouth lining.

SIMILAR SPECIES Northwestern Crow (p. 319) more or less inseparable; slightly smaller, voice more nasal. Common Raven (p. 320) larger with wedge-shaped tail, longer bill; soars frequently, croaks.

STATUS & DISTRIBUTION Breeds across North America from southern Northwest Territories, Labrador south to northern Baja California, Florida; withdraws partially from northern range in winter. In PNW, common westside resident in WA/OR, abundant in cities; common, increasing, eastward from Cascades/BC Coast Range to WY (historically not present in shrub-steppe, extensive forest). Withdraws from much of eastern OR, southern ID in winter. American Crow has genetically swamped coastal Northwestern Crow in broad, ill-defined hybrid zone around Puget Sound, where these two forms now customarily considered indistinguishable north to US/Canada border.

HABITAT ASSOCIATIONS Cities, suburbs, agricultural areas with scattered trees, woodlands.

BEHAVIOR & FEEDING Omnivorous, foraging (for example) on refuse, roadkill, crops, fruit, seeds, arthropods. Frequent nest robber, fledgling predator. Intelligent, highly gregarious; post-breeding, forms huge night roosts, often in cities where safe from most predators. Long-term monogamous pair often protects territory year-round, raises one brood per season in stick nest. Adjacent pairs cooperate to harass raptors, ravens, other threats, with assistance from peripheral non-breeding helpers.

VOCALIZATIONS Raucous, with varied complex communication; calls include *caaww*, hollow rattles; intensity modified to impart specific meanings. Juveniles beg with high, hoarse *cahh*.

BC (Haida Gwaii) — Nov • JUKKA JANTUNEN

Northwestern Crow
Corvus caurinus

DESCRIPTION 16 in/41 cm, wingspan 34 in/86 cm. Chunky; completely **black** with stout bill, short **fan-shaped tail**; broad wings, variable flight shape dependent on behavior. *Juvenile:* Brownish black with red mouth lining.

SIMILAR SPECIES American Crow (p. 318) more or less inseparable; larger on average, voice higher pitched, less nasal. Common Raven (p. 320) larger with wedge-shaped tail, longer bill; croaks deeply.

STATUS & DISTRIBUTION Resident coastally from Kodiak Island south to WA. In PNW, common western BC, San Juans, northwestern Olympic Peninsula. Brought into contact by land clearance, Northwestern, American Crows have interbred freely around Puget Sound for over 100 years; now effectively indistinguishable there. Northwestern customarily regarded as only crow along Pacific slope northward from US/Canada border.

HABITAT ASSOCIATIONS Seashores, cities, suburbs, agricultural areas with scattered trees, woodlands.

BEHAVIOR & FEEDING Omnivorous, inquisitively foraging at coastlines, fields, or urban areas; diet similar to American Crow but takes more marine organisms. Caches food, like other corvids. Intelligent, highly gregarious, many even nesting in loose colonies; forms post-breeding communal night roosts, largest in urban areas. Complex social structure; dominance established by various displays; groups cooperate to harass potential predators during diurnal hours. Long-term monogamous pair returns to territory late winter to raise brood in stick nest, often with assistance from previous year's offspring; secretive before young fledge. Frequently nests on ground in island settings. Female incubates, broods.

VOCALIZATIONS Noisy with complex communications including nasal *caaww*, guttural clucks; intensity modified to impart specific meanings. Juveniles beg with higher-pitched *cahh*.

WA (Clallam County)—Mar · NETTA SMITH

Alberta—Feb · GERALD ROMANCHUK

Common Raven
Corvus corax

DESCRIPTION 24 in/61 cm, wingspan 52 in/132 cm. Largest songbird; entirely **glossy black** with long wings, long **wedge-shaped tail**, long, formidable bill. **Puffy throat**, head feathers erected in display impart even larger look. *Juvenile:* Brownish black with red mouth lining.

SIMILAR SPECIES Crows (pp. 318–319) much smaller with shorter bill, fan-shaped tail, rounder wings, different voice.

STATUS & DISTRIBUTION Holarctic resident to North Africa; in New World, nests from High Arctic to Nicaragua, scarce in eastern states except along Appalachians. In PNW, fairly common, historically including urbanized Puget Sound, northern Willamette Valley, where now mostly extirpated; recovery apparently slowed due to exclusion by increasing crow density. Highest numbers southern BC mountains, across interior east of Cascades.

HABITAT ASSOCIATIONS Adapted to all habitats providing elevated nest sites, except tropical forest.

BEHAVIOR & FEEDING Omnivorous. Feeds primarily by scavenging but also takes rodents, arthropods, fruits, other plant materials. Intelligent; remarkably adept at finding, robbing nests, including those of other corvids; follows predators or hunters to exploit leftovers but always cautious, harassing competitors mercilessly. Caches food when abundant resource located. Frequently cavorts with playful aerial acrobatics; post-breeding night roosts number into hundreds. Establishes dominance hierarchies to minimize confrontations, particularly among gregarious subadults. Long-term monogamous pair builds stick nest on cliff, tree, or structure, often adjacent to raptors on favored cliffs; clutches average five eggs.

VOCALIZATIONS Complex, varied calls include low, hoarse croak, higher-pitched *kraaah* given in series when excited, rattles, liquid bell-like tones; garrulous juveniles beg with screamed *aayah*.

England—Jun · GARY VAUSE

BC (Central Saanich)—Mar · MIKE YIP

Sky Lark
Alauda arvensis

DESCRIPTION 7 in/18 cm. Ground-dwelling songbird. Brown back with blackish streaking; buff **breast with short black streaks**; brown auriculars framed by white eyebrow; dark malar. Buff flanks with faint brown streaks. **Short dark tail**, white outer webs on outer tail feathers. **Crown feathers often raised** to form short, blunt crest. Pale legs. *Juvenile:* Dark back feathers edged buff to form scaly pattern.

SIMILAR SPECIES American Pipit (p. 365) longer tailed, lacks crest. Lapland Longspur (p. 368) has heavier, shorter bill, reddish-brown upperwing coverts. Savannah Sparrow (p. 408) often with yellowish eyebrow; lacks white tail edges. Juvenile Horned Lark (p. 322) appears longer tailed.

STATUS & DISTRIBUTION Native to Eurasia, introduced Hawaii, New Zealand, Australia. In PNW, very local, introduced resident on Saanich Peninsula north of Victoria. Formerly more widespread on eastern Vancouver Island (e.g., Comox until 1953), San Juan Island, WA (until 2000). Handful of Nov–Feb records from nearby mainland (Fraser Delta; Sequim, WA), possibly vagrants from northeastern Asian populations.

HABITAT ASSOCIATIONS Throughout range, variety of treeless habitats including cultivated land, pastures, dunes, moorland, airports, playing fields. On Saanich Peninsula, found on mowed grass (Victoria airport), farm fields.

BEHAVIOR & FEEDING Forages on ground, eating seeds, grain, green plant material; in breeding season, also eats beetles, caterpillars, other invertebrates. Gregarious outside breeding season.

VOCALIZATIONS Long loud warbling song lasting 2–3 minutes or more in high flight, shorter when given from ground; occasionally includes mimicked calls of other species. Common call liquid *chirrup*.

E.a. strigata · WA (Grays Harbor County)—Mar · CHARLIE WRIGHT

E.a. merrilli · WA (Grant County) – Jun · GREGG THOMPSON

Juvenile (E.a. strigata) · WA (Pacific County)—Aug
DENNY GRANSTRAND

E.a. arcticola · BC (Fanny Bay)—Sep · RALPH HOCKEN

Horned Lark
Eremophila alpestris

DESCRIPTION 7 in/18 cm. Ground-dwelling songbird, size of large sparrow. Brownish above, white below; **blackish breast band, mask, forehead**; black feathers protrude from sides of crown behind eyes, often raised to form tiny "horns." **Blackish tail** with pale webs on outer feathers. Yellow or white throat, eyebrow. Sexes similarly marked (females generally paler). Coastal subspecies *E.a.strigata* has bright-yellow breast, boldly black-streaked back. *Juvenile (all races):* Lacks adult facial pattern; dark-brown back spangled with gold flecks; dusky, mottled breast.

SIMILAR SPECIES American Pipit (p. 365) lacks blackish facial, breast patterning; longspurs (pp. 368–369) have stouter bill, different face pattern.

STATUS & DISTRIBUTION Circumpolar. In North America, widespread in open landscapes from Arctic to central Mexico. Locally common in PNW. White-throated races breed on alpine tundra BC Coast Range (*E.a. arcticola*) to WA Cascades, Olympics, winter in lowlands. Other geographic races, mostly yellow-throated (e.g., *E.a. merrilli*), breed in arid interior. Some individuals overwinter, others migrate south; migrant flocks peak Mar–Apr, Sep–Oct. Westside *E.a. strigata* now extirpated southwestern BC, nearly so WA; declining but still fairly common locally in Willamette Valley.

HABITAT ASSOCIATIONS Wide variety of treeless habitats; in PNW, particularly alpine tundra, steppe, agricultural land, airports, coastal prairies.

BEHAVIOR & FEEDING Forages on ground. Eats seeds much of year; in breeding season, also variety of insects, other arthropods, alpine berries. Walks, does not hop. Flight undulating.

VOCALIZATIONS Flight call thin, goldfinch-like *seedidi* or *seleet*. Song weak, tinkling series, falling then rising at end, given in high, circling flight or from elevated perch on ground; often rambling, lasting less than one minute.

Male *(right)* and Female · WA *(King County)—Jun* · GEORGE PAGOS

Female · WA *(Snohomish County)—Aug* · GREGG THOMPSON

Purple Martin
Progne subis

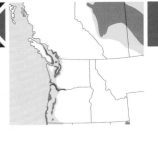

DESCRIPTION 8 in/20 cm. Large swallow; tail shallowly notched. *Male:* **Entirely bluish-black body** with dull-black wings, tail. *Female:* **Grayish-white collar, forehead,** underparts; dull-bluish-black back; dull-black wings, tail. *Juvenile:* Like female, with white, finely streaked belly, vent; dull-black back, crown. First-summer male shows variable number of dark-blue adult feathers on juvenal plumage.

SIMILAR SPECIES Other PNW swallows significantly smaller, bellies clean-white or buff. European Starling (p. 364) in flight shows shorter wings, short, square tail. Black Swift's (p. 256) wings narrow, swept back; does not perch upright.

STATUS & DISTRIBUTION Breeds across much of southeastern Canada, eastern US, locally in West south to northwestern Mexico; winters South America. In PNW, uncommon, local breeder along protected coastlines (e.g., Salish Sea, Willapa Bay), also lower Columbia River, Willamette Valley, OR Coast Range/Cascade valleys, foothills; rarely Tacoma prairies. Migrants more widespread, arrive OR early Apr, BC by late Apr–early May; accidental ID, northwestern MT. Flocks gather late Jul–early Aug, depart by mid-Sep. Casual Oct.

HABITAT ASSOCIATIONS Most PNW martins breed in estuaries with suitable nest sites; also inland sites associated with lakes, marshes.

BEHAVIOR & FEEDING Forages for insects, from low over ground to higher than 300 ft/100 m overhead. Nests in cavities. Unlike in East, where reliant on "apartment" birdhouses, PNW martins primarily nest on pilings over water, either in woodpecker cavities or in human-provided gourds or boxes. Tree-cavity nests, formerly common, now rare in PNW.

VOCALIZATIONS Rich, burry *cheedr* calls; musical chirruping song.

One-year-old Female · *WA (King County)—Apr*
DOUG SCHURMAN

BC (Nanaimo)—Apr · RALPH HOCKEN

Tree Swallow
Tachycineta bicolor

DESCRIPTION 5.75 in/14.5 cm. Medium-sized swallow; **metallic blue-black** upperparts, including rump, face above eyes; **white underparts**. Slightly notched tail, relatively broad wings. *Female:* One-year-old often dark grayish above. *Juvenile:* Dark-gray upperparts, often tinged brownish; pale-gray breast band.

SIMILAR SPECIES Violet-green Swallow (p. 325) has narrower wings, white face, rump patches; in good light, glosses purple and green (versus metallic blue). Northern Rough-winged Swallow (p. 326) resembles juvenile, but warmer brown with dingy-brown throat. Bank Swallow (p. 327) smaller; breast band dark brown, contrasting, rather than pale gray, indistinct.

STATUS & DISTRIBUTION Breeds Alaska to Labrador south to California, northern Georgia; most winter south of breeding range to Panama. Common but local breeder throughout PNW. Arrives late Feb on coast, warmer parts of interior (earlier in south, a few late Jan in OR); Mar–Apr rest of region. Departs late Jul–Aug, most gone by Oct; rare Nov–Jan in westside lowlands, casual elsewhere.

HABITAT ASSOCIATIONS Breeds around wetlands, open grasslands, pastures. Less likely to nest in backyard habitats than Violet-green Swallow. Generally absent from forests, subalpine/alpine habitats. Common in migration over lakes, reservoirs, large rivers.

BEHAVIOR & FEEDING Forages aerially for insects, often over pastures, water. Nests in tree cavities (e.g., flicker nest holes), readily accepts nest boxes. Pairs up after arrival. Female makes nest with grass, copiously lined with feathers; male shares feeding duties for single brood of 4–7. Often forms large flocks in migration.

VOCALIZATIONS Liquid chirps; agitated birds give harsher chattering calls.

Female · BC (Parksville)—Jun · RALPH HOCKEN

Male · BC (Victoria)—Jun · TERRY THORMIN

Male · OR (Deschutes County)—Apr · TOM CRABTREE

Violet-green Swallow
Tachycineta thalassina

DESCRIPTION 5.25 in/13.5 cm. Small swallow; metallic-green upperparts; purple **rump flanked by large white patches** extending to **white underparts**. Face **white above eyes**. *Female:* Duller; dusky face in first year. *Juvenile:* Brownish-gray upperparts, including face.

SIMILAR SPECIES Tree Swallow (p. 324) broader winged, metallic blue above including rump, upper part of face; call-notes more liquid. Juveniles even-toned dorsally (Violet-green's face, rump distinctly paler). Swifts show narrow pointed wings, more fluttery flight; Vaux's (p. 257) shows gray underparts; White-throated (p. 258) has longer wings, black-and-white underparts.

STATUS & DISTRIBUTION Breeds in West from Alaska to Mexico; most winter Baja south to Nicaragua. Nests throughout PNW other than Haida Gwaii (where casual transient). Common except in open areas (Cariboo–Chilcotin, Columbia Plateau, Klamath Basin), where restricted to human settlements or cliffs along rivers, coulees. Migrants return to coastal areas, low-elevation valleys late Feb, elsewhere Mar; migration peaks Mar–Apr. Fall peak Aug–Sep with single-species flocks reaching thousands, continuing through Oct in westside lowlands; casual Nov–Jan, mostly western OR.

HABITAT ASSOCIATIONS Breeds rocky cliffs, also urban, rural habitats. Common in migration over lakes, reservoirs, large rivers, including higher elevations.

BEHAVIOR & FEEDING Forages aerially for insects, often over water. Frequently migrates in large flocks. Nests singly or colonially in cavities, often rock crevices, but also in buildings, snags, nest boxes. Generally lays single clutch of 4–6 eggs; male assists with parental care.

VOCALIZATIONS Call more musical than Tree Swallow's. Boisterous high-pitched finch-like chirps, chatters offered predawn.

Northern Rough-winged Swallow
Stelgidopteryx serripennis

DESCRIPTION 5.5 in/14 cm. Medium-sized swallow with short, square tail. **Warm-brown upperparts**, white underparts except for **dirty-brown throat**. *Juvenile:* Like adult but with cinnamon wing-bars.

SIMILAR SPECIES Bank Swallow (p. 327) smaller with proportionately longer, notched tail; grayer brown above, shows contrasting pale-brown rump, dark-brown collar, white throat. Forages in small groups. Juvenile Tree Swallow (p. 324) appears brownish above, but lacks brownish throat.

STATUS & DISTRIBUTION Breeds coast to coast from BC, Maine south to Costa Rica; most winter south from southern California, Gulf Coast to western Panama. Uncommon to locally common breeder throughout PNW at low to moderate elevation, except absent from Haida Gwaii. Locally common in migration, usually in small groups (occasionally flocks of hundreds). Migrants arrive late Mar–Apr (late Apr–early May in cooler locations); stage mid-Jul, most gone by late Aug, a few stragglers after Sep. Accidental Nov–Feb.

HABITAT ASSOCIATIONS Nests in dirt banks along roads, streams, lakes; occasionally in open pipes, cavities in rock cliffs. Migrates over wetlands, lakes, reservoirs, large rivers, but also away from water.

BEHAVIOR & FEEDING Forages aerially for insects, often over water, frequently near ground. Flies with smoother, more powerful wingbeats than other swallows. Pairs breed singly or in small, loose colonies; reuse nest holes dug by Bank Swallow, Belted Kingfisher, other species. Female provides most care for single brood.

VOCALIZATIONS Short, liquid buzzy call *bzzrp*—reminiscent of Bank Swallow but lower, softer in tone, not rapidly repeated.

BC (Oliver)—May · LAURE W. NEISH

WA (Adams County)—May · GREGG THOMPSON

Bank Swallow
Riparia riparia

DESCRIPTION 5.25 in/13 cm. Small swallow; **grayish-brown upperparts**, **noticeably paler rump**; white underparts except for **dark brown collar**. Relatively long, slim, notched tail.

SIMILAR SPECIES Northern Rough-winged Swallow (p. 326) larger with dingy-brown throat, shorter, squarer tail; warmer brown above without contrasting pale rump. Juvenile Tree Swallow (p. 324) brownish above, often shows dusky breast band, but larger, lacks distinct dark collar.

STATUS & DISTRIBUTION Holarctic breeder, in New World from Alaska to Labrador south to central US, disjunctly northeastern Mexico; majority winter across temperate southern hemisphere with fewer north to western Mexico, northern Africa. In PNW, common but local breeder east of Cascades/BC Coast Range. Fairly common but local west of crest—mostly WA, where colonization first noted in 1990s continues to expand along Skagit, Toutle, Green, Snoqualmie, other westside rivers. Arrives late to colonies (Apr–May). Fall migration underway late Jul–early Aug; most gone by late Aug, but large single-species flocks often linger in interior (e.g., Columbia Plateau). Rare migrant Aug–Sep near coast.

HABITAT ASSOCIATIONS Breeds colonially (tens to hundreds of nests), mostly at low elevation, in holes dug into dirt banks along roads, rivers, lakes, also in sand piles; often uses gravel pits. Flocks in migration over wetlands, lakes, reservoirs, large rivers.

BEHAVIOR & FEEDING Aerial insectivore, like other swallows. Tends to forage fairly close to ground, often over water. Pairs excavate burrows using specially adapted bill, share parental duties.

VOCALIZATIONS Chattering series of buzzy calls: *bzz bzz bzz zz zz*.

Cliff Swallow
Petrochelidon pyrrhonota

DESCRIPTION 5.5 in/14 cm. **Square tailed** with **pale orange-buff rump**; gray-black back, tail, crown, upperwings; gray collar, **white forehead**, chestnut cheeks, blackish throat. Grayish-white underside. *Juvenile:* Like adult, but with dusky head, facial markings; throat sometimes paler.

SIMILAR SPECIES Other PNW swallows lack pale rump strongly contrasting with dark back.

STATUS & DISTRIBUTION Breeds Alaska to Nova Scotia south to Oaxaca, absent from most of southeastern US; winters in South America. Common but local breeder throughout PNW, more numerous east of Cascades/BC Coast Range than on westside; generally absent from BC coast other than Strait of Georgia. Arrives late Mar (in south) to Apr (May in cooler locations). Large flocks gather Jul; migration continues Aug–early Sep, some seen through Oct. Casual Nov–early Dec.

HABITAT ASSOCIATIONS Nests around rimrock cliffs, but now more commonly in open barns, eaves of buildings, culverts, or under bridges. Nest sites usually adjacent to foraging habitat of pastures, grasslands, lakes, marshes. Uncommon in urban habitats, absent from extensive forests.

BEHAVIOR & FEEDING Forages for insects, usually fairly high above ground. Nests colonially, building enclosed, feather-lined nests of dry mud attached to flat surface with tubular front entrance at top, frequently reused in successive years. In spring, often seen gathering mud at puddles, fluttering wings above back to ward off unwanted copulation attempts. Monogamous pair shares nest building, parental care duties; average 3–4 young fledged.

VOCALIZATIONS Song series of creaking, scratchy notes; calls include soft *err* or *peew*.

BC (Nanaimo)—Jul · RALPH HOCKEN

Alberta—Jun · GERALD ROMANCHUK

Barn Swallow
Hirundo rustica

DESCRIPTION 6.75 in/17 cm. Elegant swallow with **long, forked tail**. Metallic blue-black upperparts; **orange-brown throat**, forehead; buff breast, belly, often paler in female. *Juvenile:* Shorter tail, paler below.

SIMILAR SPECIES Long, forked tail diagnostic in PNW. Cliff Swallow (p. 328) also has orange-brown face, but white forehead, dark throat, pale buff rump, short, square tail.

STATUS & DISTRIBUTION Nearly cosmopolitan; most breed northern hemisphere. In New World, widespread breeder southern Alaska to Newfoundland south to central Mexico; majority winter in South America. Common breeder throughout PNW from sea level to subalpine (more numerous at lower elevations). Arrives Apr–May (late Mar OR). Large flocks form late Jul, most gone by late Sep, uncommon to rare Oct–Nov. Rare in recent years Dec–Feb (most numerous midwinter swallow), primarily along coasts.

HABITAT ASSOCIATIONS Most common in rural habitats, but possible almost anywhere. In urban areas, limited to locations with open foraging habitat, nest sites such as bridges, accessible buildings.

BEHAVIOR & FEEDING Forages close to ground for insects, swooping low over lawns, pastures, water. Loosely colonial, socially monogamous, but extra-pair copulations common. Pair builds bowl-shaped mud nest lined with feathers on ledge or vertical surface inside barn, outbuilding, covered porch, culvert, or under bridges, eaves—frequently reused multiple years. Lays 4–6 eggs, often double-broods; young may fledge into Sep in PNW. Formerly nested in caves, mine shafts, but now only rarely.

VOCALIZATIONS Scratchy, squeaky song; call soft *vid*, or (when alarmed) louder *vid veep*.

Pacific slope · OR (Washington County) —Dec · GREG GILLSON | Interior · WA (Okanogan County)—Mar · RYAN SHAW

Black-capped Chickadee
Poecile atricapillus

DESCRIPTION 5.25 in/13.5 cm. **Small thin bill**, white belly, variably buff-tinged sides; gray wings, tail, back. **White cheek** divides black cap from **black bib**. Pacific-slope birds duskier pinkish-brown ventrally. *Juvenile:* Yellow gape briefly held.

SIMILAR SPECIES Mountain Chickadee (p. 331) shows white supercilium; flanks usually whiter. Smaller Chestnut-backed Chickadee (p. 332) has sooty-brown cap, chestnut sides, back. Boreal Chickadee (p. 333) has brownish cap; appears richly orange brown ventrally.

STATUS & DISTRIBUTION Resident Alaska to Newfoundland, south to northern New Mexico, Tennessee. In PNW, common low- to mid-elevation resident, ranges to high elevation in Blue Mountains but absent west of BC Coast Range north of Sunshine Coast. Also rare San Juan, Gulf Islands, high Cascades.

HABITAT ASSOCIATIONS Prefers deciduous woodlands, thickets, suburbs; scarce in dense conifers, absent from arid steppe away from major drainages.

BEHAVIOR & FEEDING Forages in trees for arthropods, often hangs on small branches or bark; also eats seeds, visits feeders, caching seeds nearby; while nesting, takes nearly all animal material. Highly sociable; forms flocks outside of breeding, acts as nuclear species for mixed flocks. Alarm calls reflect level of danger by increasing number of high "*dee*"s. Considered resident, but juveniles flock, irrupt from low-mast areas, migrate diurnally. Uses shallow hypothermia (torpor) overnight to survive northern winters. Monogamous pair excavates cavity in rotten wood, also uses existing holes, nest boxes.

VOCALIZATIONS Song clear, whistled *feee beee* (second note lower); Puget Sound dialect differs: *bee beee beee beee*. Calls include *chick a dee dee dee*, lispy *tsick*.

Mountain Chickadee
Poecile gambeli

DESCRIPTION 5.25 in/13.5 cm. Small thin bill, **white supercilum**, grayish-white underparts (faintly buff in some populations); grayish wings, tail, back. **White cheek** divides dark cap from **black bib**. *Juvenile:* Yellow gape briefly held.

SIMILAR SPECIES Other chickadees lack white supercilium, generally show buffy or brownish flanks.

STATUS & DISTRIBUTION Resident southern Yukon disjunctly to northern Baja California, western Texas. In PNW, common mountain resident from just west of Cascades/BC Coast Range crest eastward; also Siskiyous west to extreme southwestern OR Coast Range. Irregularly irrupts into lowlands Oct–Apr, rarely reaching westward across Puget Sound, even to WA outer coast. Rare hybrids with Black-capped Chickadee show intermediate characteristics.

HABITAT ASSOCIATIONS Coniferous forest up to treeline; in PNW, mostly ponderosa, lodgepole pine, spruce-fir (juniper in southern ID, eastern OR); also uses aspen stands.

BEHAVIOR & FEEDING Gleans for arthropods from small branches, mostly high in conifers. Eats seeds (especially Sep–Mar), frequently caching them for later recovery. Gregarious outside of breeding; often forms small mixed flocks with nuthatches, other chickadees, warblers. Generally sedentary with some downslope movement Sep–Nov, but juveniles flock up irregularly, irrupt from areas with depleted mast, migrating diurnally. Survives harsh winters by using nocturnal shallow hypothermia; on hot summer days, becomes inactive after early morning. Long-term monogamous pair selects existing hole or nest box together, shares parental duties, with female incubating.

VOCALIZATIONS Thin whistled *feee beee beee*; calls include hoarse *chick dee dee dee*, lispy, harsh *chi ti ti ti ti ti.*

Chestnut-backed Chickadee
Poecile rufescens

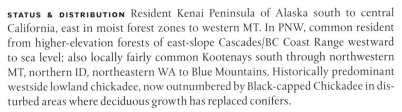

DESCRIPTION 4.75 in/12 cm. Tiny bill, sooty-brown cap; grayish wings, tail; **rich-chestnut sides, back**; whitish belly. **White cheek** divides cap from **black bib**. *Juvenile:* Yellow gape briefly held.

SIMILAR SPECIES Other chickadees larger, lack rich chestnut on back, sides.

STATUS & DISTRIBUTION Resident Kenai Peninsula of Alaska south to central California, east in moist forest zones to western MT. In PNW, common resident from higher-elevation forests of east-slope Cascades/BC Coast Range westward to sea level; also locally fairly common Kootenays south through northwestern MT, northern ID, northeastern WA to Blue Mountains. Historically predominant westside lowland chickadee, now outnumbered by Black-capped Chickadee in disturbed areas where deciduous growth has replaced conifers.

HABITAT ASSOCIATIONS Moist coniferous forest; mixed forest dominated by conifers, including urbanized habitats. Dispersing birds wander to deciduous lowlands.

BEHAVIOR & FEEDING Gleans arthropods from twigs, small branches, mostly high in trees; also eats seeds, other plant material, especially Oct–Apr; regular at feeders, caching seeds nearby. Gregarious. Forms larger post-breeding flocks than other chickadees, also joins mixed groups with nuthatches, kinglets, Townsend's Warblers, other chickadees. Generally sedentary but may wander upslope diurnally Aug–Oct, sometimes above treeline; rarely irrupts greater distances to arid lowlands when mast dwindles. Likely enters torpor on cold nights, as other chickadees, but undocumented. Monogamous pair excavates cavity in soft wood or uses nest box or existing cavity.

VOCALIZATIONS Lacks whistled song of other chickadees; series of husky chips may serve same function. *Chick zhee zhee* call high, hoarse.

Alberta—Dec · GERALD ROMANCHUK

Boreal Chickadee
Poecile hudsonicus

DESCRIPTION 5.25 in/13.5 cm. Small bill, **orange-brown sides**, whitish belly; **grayish-brown cap,** back; gray wings, tail. Somewhat **obscure whitish cheek** divides cap from black bib. *Juvenile:* Yellow gape when young.

SIMILAR SPECIES Black-capped Chickadee (p. 330) has black cap, lacks extensive richly colored sides. Smaller Chestnut-backed Chickadee (p. 332) has chestnut back, larger white cheek patch. Mountain Chickadee (p. 331) whiter ventrally, shows white supercilium.

STATUS & DISTRIBUTION Resident from central Alaska across boreal zone to Newfoundland. In PNW, resident east from BC Coast Range, northern Cascades, mostly >5,000 ft/1,500 m elevation. Widespread but uncommon in BC; rare in US along international border from Cascades to Rockies (breeds WA, northern Idaho Panhandle, northwestern MT). Shows some downslope post-breeding movement in BC, where casual Dec–Feb to Fraser Lowlands, Greater Vancouver.

HABITAT ASSOCIATIONS Subalpine coniferous forests; in PNW, mostly Engelmann spruce, subalpine fir, larch, whitebark or lodgepole pine.

BEHAVIOR & FEEDING Gleans arthropods from conifer branches at middle to upper levels; eats seeds from cones, also other plant material; carries, stores food in caches sometimes secured with plant down or saliva. Less gregarious than other chicka-dees; forms small flocks post-breeding, often with nuthatches, kinglets, other chickadees. Mostly sedentary in PNW, more irruptive in eastern North America; likely uses torpor as other chickadees to survive extreme cold. Monogamous pair excavates cavity in rotten wood; female incubates, broods young.

VOCALIZATIONS Territorial whistled song of other chickadees replaced by trilled gargle; *zhee, chick a dee*; other calls wheezy, drawled.

Family Paridae—CHICKADEES AND TITS **333**

OR (Jackson County)—Apr · PETER J. THIEMANN

Oak Titmouse
Baeolophus inornatus

DESCRIPTION 5.5 in/14 cm. Prominently **crested**; over-all **plain grayish brown** with lighter underparts, plain gray face, stubby bill, bluish feet. *Juvenile:* Crest less well developed; briefly held yellow gape.

SIMILAR SPECIES Juniper Titmouse (p. 335) nearly identical but slightly larger, grayer, with lower-pitched voice. Other small, plain passerines lack crest.

STATUS & DISTRIBUTION Resident from extreme southwestern interior OR through California, disjunctly to southern Baja. In PNW, resident only in southwestern OR; breeds commonly at lower elevations in Rogue Valley, rarely in Illinois, Umpqua Valleys; uncommon in Klamath Basin. Formerly treated as single species, "Plain" Titmouse, with mostly allopatric Juniper Titmouse; split into two in 1996.

HABITAT ASSOCIATIONS Oak forests, oak-pine woodlands; in OR, often oak groves mixed with madrone (*Arbutus*), Douglas-fir, ponderosa pine, other conifers; also uses open riparian strips with oak component, spacious suburbs with indigenous scrub.

BEHAVIOR & FEEDING Feeds mostly on acorns, seeds, other plant materials; arthropods taken more while breeding. Forages on ground, branches, bark, using heavy bill to flake, pry, or tear; visits feeders, caches frequently; often hammers open seeds held in feet. Highly sedentary. Sociable only within family groups—shuns larger flocks. Long-term monogamous pair defends territory year-round; uses existing hole, old woodpecker nest or nest box, preferring natural cavities. Female incubates, broods while male assists with feeding, defense, shepherding of young. Vigorously mobs predators such as small owls.

VOCALIZATIONS Warbled *ti ti ti teeww* song offered Dec–May; also whistled *shue shue shue shue*. Scolds with harsh *shci schi*.

ID (Madison County)—May · DARREN CLARK

Juniper Titmouse
Baeolophus ridgwayi

DESCRIPTION 5.5 in/14 cm. Prominently **crested**; overall **plain grayish** with lighter underparts, plain face, stubby bill, bluish feet. *Juvenile:* Crest less developed; yellow gape when young.

SIMILAR SPECIES Oak Titmouse (p. 334) nearly identical but slightly smaller, browner, with higher-pitched voice. Other small songbirds lack crest.

STATUS & DISTRIBUTION Resident in interior West from southeastern OR to western Oklahoma Panhandle, south to southeastern Arizona. In PNW, uncommon resident in southeastern OR—mostly Lake County, casual to Harney County (Klamath County reports probably attributable to Oak Titmouse). Common southeastern ID from Cassia to Bonneville Counties; rare, local southwestern ID (North Fork Owyhee River). Increasingly reported since 2005 from around Idaho Falls to northwestern WY (Teton, Park Counties).

HABITAT ASSOCIATIONS Mid-elevation mature juniper forests, adjacent sagebrush.

BEHAVIOR & FEEDING Omnivorous, like Oak Titmouse. Takes plant material (especially juniper seeds), with more arthropods captured in breeding season. Forages mostly in trees, sometimes on ground, using heavy bill to flake bark. Caches or hammers open seeds held in feet. Highly sedentary, but more prone to form winter flocks than Oak Titmouse; family group may accompany mixed flocks of chickadees, other passerines. Long-term monogamous pair highly territorial; typically nests in existing hole in mature juniper trunk, also other cavities, nest boxes. Pair adds grasses, bark strips, feathers; female incubates alone, fed by male. Often reuses nest cavity year to year.

VOCALIZATIONS Low-pitched, burry, whistled *shue shue shue shue*; also even-pitched *scjidji scjidiji scjidiji*, more-rapid rattled calls.

Male "Lead-colored" · OR (Harney County)—May
GREG GILLSON

Female "Pacific" · WA (King County)—Mar · GREGG THOMPSON

Bushtit
Psaltriparus minimus

DESCRIPTION 4.25 in/11 cm. Smallest North American passerine by weight. **Plain grayish**, nondescript; paler ventrally with **long tail**, tiny bill. *Male:* Dark iris. *Female:* White iris. *Juvenile:* Like male; female eye lightens within weeks. Two forms: "Pacific" grayish brown with brown cap, "Lead-colored" grayer with gray crown.

SIMILAR SPECIES Chickadees (pp. 330–333) show white cheek patches. Blue-gray Gnatcatcher (p. 347) has white outer rectrices. Pudgy kinglets (pp. 350–351) show wing-bars, shorter tails.

STATUS & DISTRIBUTION "Pacific" form (several subspecies) resident from southwestern BC to Baja, "Lead-colored" form (*P.m. plumbeus*) in interior West from Great Basin to Mexico. In PNW, "Pacific" common lowland resident west of Cascades southward from Fraser Delta plain, southeastern Vancouver Island, eastward in southwestern OR to Klamath Basin; range extended in last 70 years to south-central OR (Deschutes, Lake Counties), south-central WA (Klickitat, Yakima, Kittitas Counties), eastern Vancouver Island, locally to western shore. "Lead-colored" expanded in last century to north-central OR, recently central WA (Grant County).

HABITAT ASSOCIATIONS Lowlands with open deciduous or mixed woods, edges; towns, parks, urban residential areas. In interior, arid brush.

BEHAVIOR & FEEDING Forages in flocks nearly year-round, moving tree to tree in tight groups of up to 50 birds, often in single file, gleaning from foliage. Takes mostly arthropods, also some plant material. Pairs form in spring; may exhibit cooperative breeding, polygyny, or polyandry. Long, hanging nest with top entrance, concealed low in canopy or understory; densely woven with moss, lichen, spider web.

VOCALIZATIONS Calls include *tsip*, trilled alarm call.

White-breasted Nuthatch
Sitta carolinensis

DESCRIPTION 6 in/15 cm. **Stub tailed** with thin chisel-like bill. **Medium-gray** mantle, dark cap extending to nape; **white face, underparts**; rusty undertail. *Male:* Black cap. *Female:* Slate-gray cap. *Juvenile:* Duller. "Slender-billed" form paler gray; breast sides, flanks browner on average; thinner bill; calls differ.

SIMILAR SPECIES Red-breasted Nuthatch (p. 338) rusty ventrally with prominent black eyeline. Much larger Downy Woodpecker (p. 274) shows white on back, hitches up trees.

STATUS & DISTRIBUTION Resident central BC to Nova Scotia, south to Oaxaca. Two forms resident in PNW: *S.c. tenuissima/nelsoni* fairly common east of Cascades/ BC Coast Range north through central BC (Thompson-Okanagan), uncommon farther north in interior valleys, mostly absent Columbia Plateau, southeastern OR, southern ID; west of crest, *S.c. aculeata* ("Slender-billed" Nuthatch) fairly common southwestern OR; uncommon lowland valleys north to southwestern WA (Cowlitz County), historically to Puget Sound, where extirpated due to loss of preferred habitat. Transients remain casual throughout westside lowlands.

HABITAT ASSOCIATIONS Ponderosa pine, mixed woods in interior; also commonly found in burns. "Slender-billed" form prefers Garry-oak stands; also uses cottonwood.

BEHAVIOR & FEEDING Eats seeds year-round; frequently caches. Takes arthropods while nesting, walking up or down limbs. Generally sedentary but migrates from harsher climates, casually irrupts southward; joins mixed flocks. Maintains territory throughout year. Dominant male forms long-term monogamous bond with female; pair nests in natural cavity or old woodpecker nest.

VOCALIZATIONS Harsh, nasal *ena ena ena*; rapid trilled, whistled notes. "Slender-billed" higher pitched, gives series of clear courtship whistles.

Red-breasted Nuthatch
Sitta canadensis

DESCRIPTION 4.25 in/11 cm. **Stubby tailed** with straight, chisel-like bill. Blue-gray mantle, **rusty underparts**; white supercilium separates black cap from **black eyeline**. *Male:* Black crown, nape. *Female:* Grayer nape, eyeline. *Juvenile:* Duller.

SIMILAR SPECIES Pygmy Nuthatch (p. 339) smaller, lacks white supercilium. Larger White-breasted Nuthatch (p. 337) has white breast, lacks eyeline. Chickadees (pp. 330–333) show longer tail, black bib.

STATUS & DISTRIBUTION Resident from Kodiak Island across Canada to Newfoundland, south in West to southeastern Arizona, in Appalachians to North Carolina; migrants irregular to Florida, Texas. In PNW, common forest resident, except uncommon west of BC Coast Range north of Sunshine Coast. Numbers variable throughout, especially in urban areas.

HABITAT ASSOCIATIONS Mature coniferous forest, treeline to coast; also mixed woodlands, well-treed cities. Transients range to shrub-steppe riparian thickets.

BEHAVIOR & FEEDING Forages acrobatically up or down limbs. Conifer seeds major diet component year-long; also frequents feeders; takes more arthropods while breeding. Often joins mixed flocks for foraging or nocturnal migration. Populations from high elevation or boreal latitudes regularly migrate (Aug–Nov), irrupting southward every few years; lowland birds partially migratory, abandoning areas with inadequate mast; return movement (Mar–May) less obvious. Some winter nomads remain at food-rich sites in marginal habitats for breeding. Monogamous pair excavates nest cavity in rotten wood, often smearing conifer sap around nest hole to deter predators; highly territorial males provide defense.

VOCALIZATIONS Calls include nasal *enk* given in series, rapid repeated *en en en en en* when agitated.

BC (Oliver)—May • GERALD ROMANCHUK

Pygmy Nuthatch
Sitta pygmaea

DESCRIPTION 4 in/10 cm. **Stubby** with straight, chisel-like bill. **Brown cap extends to nape**, blending into darker eyeline. **Bluish-gray mantle**; underparts variably peachy buff with gray flanks. *Juvenile:* Evenly grayish above.

SIMILAR SPECIES Red-breasted Nuthatch (p. 338) shows richly rusty underparts, white supercilium. Larger White-breasted Nuthatch (p. 337) shows white face extending above eye. Chickadees (pp. 330–333) longer tailed with black bib.

STATUS & DISTRIBUTION Resident in habitat-specific patches in interior West from south-central BC to western Nebraska, south to Mexican Volcanic Belt; also along central California coast. In PNW, locally fairly common resident in mid-elevation ponderosa pine zone east of Cascades/BC Coast Range southward from south-central BC (Okanagan, Similkameen Valleys), northwestern MT; absent from much of ID, eastern OR, eastern WA; casual vagrant as far as outer coast. PNW populations declining due to loss of old-growth ponderosa stands.

HABITAT ASSOCIATIONS Mature ponderosa pine, rarely mixed conifers.

BEHAVIOR & FEEDING Forages frenetically up or down small limbs, twigs, cones, needles, primarily for arthropods, also taking small amounts of plant materials. Highly gregarious. Flock size may grow to a hundred individuals by Feb; also joins mixed-species flocks. Uses cavities year-round for nesting, roosting. Often roosts packed together in formations, entering shallow hypothermia to minimize heat loss. Cooperative breeder with some pairs employing helpers, although apparently monogamous; nests in cavity excavated in rotten wood, natural hole, or nest box; sometimes raises two broods. Female broods, incubates while male feeds her.

VOCALIZATIONS Frequent loud, sharp peeping; also chips, squeaks.

Brown Creeper
Certhia americana

DESCRIPTION 5.25 in/13.5 cm. Slim. **Long stiff tail**; thin, decurved bill, white supercilium. **Streaked grayish brown** dorsally, rump plain rusty; **underparts white** with buffy undertail. Light wing stripe visible in flight. *Juvenile:* Spotted buff dorsally, supercilium less distinct.

SIMILAR SPECIES Nuthatches (pp. 337–339) lack streaking, decurved bill. Bewick's Wren (p. 341) unstreaked with freewheeling tail. Larger Downy Woodpecker (p. 274) shows white back.

STATUS & DISTRIBUTION Breeds from Kodiak Island disjunctly to central Alaska, east to Newfoundland, south in western mountains to Nicaragua, in Appalachians to West Virginia; winters south to Gulf of Mexico, withdrawing from northernmost range. In PNW, fairly common breeder except rare west-central BC, absent Columbia Plateau, southeastern OR; winters throughout forested areas, with fewer remaining at high elevation; rare in shrub-steppe riparian thickets, mostly Oct–Apr.

HABITAT ASSOCIATIONS Coniferous or mixed forest, preferring mature stands.

BEHAVIOR & FEEDING Forages for arthropods, probing bark crevices while hitching up tree trunk using tail as brace; white breast may provoke prey movement, aiding detection. Flies down to base of next tree to begin climbing again. Often joins mixed-species flocks outside of breeding season. Apparently monogamous. Nests under sheet of loose bark on trunk of dying tree, rarely in bark crevices of very large tree. Nest constructed with twigs, moss, feathers, grass, spider silk, primarily by female, who also incubates, broods.

VOCALIZATIONS Calls include high, thin *tseee*; song extremely high pitched, composed of rising, falling notes ending on high note.

Bewick's Wren
Thryomanes bewickii

DESCRIPTION 5.25 in/13.5 cm. Slim; **plain brown** with bold **white supercilium**, slightly decurved **thin bill**, grayish underparts, white throat; tail finely banded brown with black-and-white ventral edging. *Juvenile:* Yellowish gape.

SIMILAR SPECIES Marsh Wren (p. 346) smaller with white back streaks, juvenile plain with indistinct supercilium. Other PNW wrens (pp. 342–345) lack white supercilium.

STATUS & DISTRIBUTION Resident southwestern BC to Baja California, Utah to Missouri south to Mexico (summer resident north to southern WY); remnant declining populations east of Mississippi River. In PNW, common west of Cascades/BC Coast Range, mostly in lowlands, north to southeastern Vancouver Island, southwestern mainland BC; east of crest, rare at low to middle elevation north to south-central BC (southern Okanagan), but locally fairly common along major drainages, following significant expansion over last 50 years; casual southeastern OR, western WY; accidental northwestern MT.

HABITAT ASSOCIATIONS Forest edge, thickets, hedgerows, riparian vegetation; flourishes in urban backyards, parks.

BEHAVIOR & FEEDING Forages for arthropods, gleaning dense undergrowth, probing bark crevices, often flicking tail side to side; eats little plant material. Resident, with some post-breeding dispersal; often joins mixed flocks, mostly Oct–Jan when pairs may separate. Nest generally placed low in thicket, cavity, nest box, or other man-made object. Male sings, defends territory, sometimes mates with second female. Incubating, brooding done by female; often raises two broods.

VOCALIZATIONS Song extremely variable series of warbles, trills, beginning with inhalation-like buzz; confused easily with Song Sparrow. Calls include scolds, harsh buzzes, sharp *jik*.

Rock Wren
Salpinctes obsoletus

DESCRIPTION 6 in/15 cm. Squat. Brownish-gray upperparts speckled white; **buff supercilium**, slightly decurved bill, **buff-tipped tail**. Underparts show variable streaking on whitish breast, **peachy flanks**; undertail coverts banded black. *Juvenile:* Buffy with dorsal barring.

SIMILAR SPECIES Canyon Wren (p. 343) longer billed; white breast sharply contrasts with rufous belly. Other PNW wrens smaller with shorter bills.

STATUS & DISTRIBUTION Breeds in interior West from southern BC to Dakotas, south disjunctly to Costa Rica; also central California coast to southern Baja; winters mostly south from California, Oklahoma. In PNW, fairly common breeder east of Cascades/BC Coast Range where appropriate habitat exists, expanding northward into central interior BC over last century. Rare westside breeder on bare ridge outcroppings, except uncommon OR in Siskiyous west to Curry County. Winters (Nov–Mar) uncommonly north to eastern WA, casual to BC (Okanagan); also rare western lowlands to coast, where individuals rarely remain into summer.

HABITAT ASSOCIATIONS Arid rocky areas, often with loose scree, from low desert to above treeline; migrants use man-made breakwaters, agricultural areas.

BEHAVIOR & FEEDING Forages on ground for orthopterans, other arthropods, running beneath vegetation; also eats some plant material. Frequently bobs when challenging intruders. In PNW, moves downslope Aug–Oct, concentrating at lower-elevation, warmer sites (e.g., Columbia River), where occasionally winters; migrants return by May. Monogamous pair nests in rock crevice, uses flat stones to "pave" walkway to nest, often raises two broods.

VOCALIZATIONS Remarkably variable song includes repeated ringing trills, warbles; buzzy *pid zeeee* in alarm.

Canyon Wren
Catherpes mexicanus

DESCRIPTION 5.75 in/14.5 cm. Fairly slim with **long thin, decurved bill**; finely banded long tail. Mostly **bright rufous brown**, with tiny white flecks on upperparts. Gray head to nape; **clean-white throat, breast** contrast strongly with rufous belly. *Juvenile:* Duller brown, fewer flecks.

SIMILAR SPECIES Rock Wren (p. 342) has shorter bill; buff supercilium, tail tip. Other PNW wrens smaller with shorter bill, lack rufous tail.

STATUS & DISTRIBUTION Resident from south-central BC disjunctly to western South Dakota, south through Mexico. In PNW, highly local resident east of Cascades—fairly common southward from central WA, central ID, uncommon to rare BC (Okanagan, West Kootenay), northwestern MT, western WY. Rare Pacific slope of OR/WA Cascades (more frequent in south), also Rogue Valley. Some post-breeding dispersal Aug–Oct with possible downslope movement; casual vagrant to outer coast.

HABITAT ASSOCIATIONS Sheer cliffs, canyon walls, talus slopes, associated woodland edge; may use abandoned buildings.

BEHAVIOR & FEEDING Forages for arthropods by probing crevices or gleaning on rock; large feet, short legs facilitate climbing or descending vertical surfaces. Detection difficult Nov–Feb due to reticent behavior, inaccessible habitat; easily noted by frequent song while breeding, but rarely sings in winter months. Nesting information limited. Apparently monogamous with long-term pair bond; carries material into small cavern or crevice where female incubates, broods young; may raise two broods.

VOCALIZATIONS Song descending series of liquid whistles ending on burry notes; calls include *geeet* during typical wren bobbing display, buzzy *jeenk*.

BC (Parksville)—Jun • RALPH HOCKEN

House Wren
Troglodytes aedon

DESCRIPTION 5 in/12.5 cm. Nondescript **plain brown**; pale underparts, vague eyeline, **light eye-ring**, thin bill; **finely banded wings**, tail. Cocks tail, as other wrens. *Juvenile:* Yellowish gape.

SIMILAR SPECIES Bewick's Wren (p. 341) shows white supercilium. Smaller Pacific Wren (p. 345) stubby tailed, looks darker. Marsh Wren (p. 346) has whitish supercilium, streaked back; juvenal upperwing coverts plain (versus barred), lacks eye-ring.

STATUS & DISTRIBUTION Northern form breeds south of boreal forests across Canada, most of US to Baja California, northern Georgia; winters from northern California, Carolinas to Mexico. Expected in PNW Apr–Oct; common east of Cascades/BC Coast Range south from central BC (Thompson Valley); uncommon, local on westside south from BC Sunshine Coast, but fairly common southeastern Vancouver Island, San Juan Islands, southwestern WA (Ridgefield NWR) south through OR; casual in recent years Nov–Mar. Other races resident Caribbean, Middle, South America often considered separate species.

HABITAT ASSOCIATIONS Drier forest edge, open woodland, clear-cuts, suburbs; transients use weedy fields.

BEHAVIOR & FEEDING Forages low for arthropods; perches up aggressively but also furtive. May migrate upslope Aug–Sep before departure. Migration primarily nocturnal. Cavity nester. Male fills several prospective holes with materials, vigorously protects territory with constant singing, physical combat against conspecifics, other cavity nesters, including Bewick's Wren; often destroys eggs or kills bluebirds during cavity competition. Female chooses male, lays in one cavity, incubates, broods; often double-broods. Male sometimes mates with second female.

VOCALIZATIONS Song exuberant with trills, whistles, rattles in rapid series. Calls include rapid nasal chatter, mewing, sharp *jick*.

WA (King County)—Mar · GREGG THOMPSON

BC (Haida Gwaii)—Oct · JUKKA JANTUNEN

Pacific Wren
Troglodytes pacificus

DESCRIPTION 4 in/10 cm. **Round**; tiny. **Chocolate brown** with **rufous-brown breast**, thin bill, pale supercilium; finely banded wings, belly, **stubby tail** (invariably held cocked). *Juvenile:* Yellowish gape.

SIMILAR SPECIES House Wren (p. 344) paler breasted with eye-ring, longer tail. Larger Bewick's Wren (p. 341) shows bold white supercilium. Marsh Wren (p. 346) has whitish supercilium, streaked back.

STATUS & DISTRIBUTION Breeds west of Rockies from Aleutians to central California, northeastern OR, central ID; winters mostly in breeding range, withdrawing where snowpack high. Split from Winter Wren in 2010 based on genetics, vocalizations; both species nest sympatrically on lower eastern slope of Rockies in northeastern BC (Peace River region). In PNW, fairly common resident to mid-elevation west of Cascades/BC Coast Range; downslope movement swells lowland numbers Oct–Mar. Uncommon breeder eastward in mountains to northwestern MT (rare central BC, eastern ID). Migrants uncommon in eastside lowland riparian thickets Sep–Nov, Mar–Apr; rare Dec–Feb.

HABITAT ASSOCIATIONS Nests wet coniferous forest; uses tangles, urban areas in winter, migration.

BEHAVIOR & FEEDING Forages erratically, mouse-like, in undergrowth for arthropods, some snails, seeds. Curious; investigates intruders from open perch, bobbing like other wrens. Winters close to open water in colder climates. Male maintains territory (often year-round), sings mostly Feb–Aug, builds multiple domed nests of mosses in upturned roots or cavity near ground; often polygynous in optimal habitat. Female chooses nest, incubates, broods, sometimes raising two clutches.

VOCALIZATIONS Song complex, lengthy series of tinkling trills, warbles. Calls include *chit chit*, rapid, staccato series of chips.

Marsh Wren
Cistothorus palustris

DESCRIPTION 5 in/13 cm. Pudgy, long legged; reddish brownish with darker **white-streaked back**, brownish-gray underparts, thin bill; finely banded tail invariably cocked up. **Dark cap** sets off **whitish supercilium**. *Juvenile:* Dull, almost plain brown with vague supercilium.

SIMILAR SPECIES Bewick's Wren (p. 341) has bolder supercilium. House Wren (p. 344) shows eye-ring, banded upperwing coverts. Pacific Wren (p. 345) darker, lacks back streaks.

STATUS & DISTRIBUTION Breeds locally from BC to Maritimes, Atlantic, Gulf Coasts, south to US–Mexico border but excluding most of southeastern, southwestern interior US (disjunct population central Mexico); winters south from southwestern BC, Nebraska, New Jersey to northern Oaxaca, northern Veracruz. In PNW, breeds fairly commonly in lowlands, rarely western Vancouver Island, BC mainland coast; absent Haida Gwaii. Withdraws from interior Oct to mid-Mar, lingering rarely during milder years. Populations west of Great Plains differ genetically, vocally from eastern populations, presently under study for split into separate species.

HABITAT ASSOCIATIONS Open freshwater or brackish marsh with dense emergent vegetation, often cattails; also salt marsh, wet fields, adjacent scrub.

BEHAVIOR & FEEDING Forages mouse-like for arthropods in marsh vegetation. Secretive but curious; perches up, often straddling across two stalks with long legs. Highly territorial, competitive. Often destroys eggs of other species; frequent target of blackbird aggression. Male maintains territory, singing day or night, weaves multiple spherical nests amid emergent stalks; female chooses nest, incubates, broods, sometime raises two clutches. Polygyny frequent.

VOCALIZATIONS Song mechanical but musical rattled trill begun with a few call-notes. Call distinctive *tik*.

Breeding Male · ID (Jefferson County) — May · DARREN CLARK

Non-breeding · WA (Grays Harbor County) — Oct · RYAN SHAW

Nest with cowbird chick · OR (Jackson County) — Jul
DAMON CALDERWOOD

Blue-gray Gnatcatcher
Polioptila caerulea

DESCRIPTION 4.5 in/11.5 cm. Slender; **bluish-gray** upperparts, whitish-gray underparts, prominent **white eye-ring**, long black tail with **white outer rectrices**; thin pale bill. *Male:* Shows black supraloral line Jan–Aug. *Juvenile:* Browner upperparts.

SIMILAR SPECIES *Oreothlypis* warblers (pp. 374–377) shorter tailed, lack white rectrices; first-year Virginia's Warbler shows yellowish rump. Much larger Northern Mockingbird (p. 363) shows white in wings, dark eyeline. Ruby-crowned Kinglet (p. 351) greenish gray with short tail, wing-bars.

STATUS & DISTRIBUTION Breeds from southwestern OR to southern Maine, south to Bahamas, Guatemala, excluding most of Great Plains; winters south along coasts from central California, Virginia to Cuba, through Mexico to Honduras. In PNW, fairly common low-elevation breeder Apr–Aug in Rogue Valley, rare elsewhere southern OR, uncommon southeastern ID. Reports increasing farther north in recent years—now casual west of Cascades to southwestern BC (mostly reverse migrants Oct–Nov, sometimes remaining into winter); fewer east of crest (mostly May–Jul migrant overshoots) casual to south-central WA (Yakima County), rare northwestern WY (Teton, Park Counties).

HABITAT ASSOCIATIONS Various woodlands, generally preferring oak; in PNW, arid, scrubby areas, often along riparian strips, also juniper woodlands.

BEHAVIOR & FEEDING Flips tail constantly while foraging actively in small branches, gleaning or hover-gleaning arthropods from foliage. Outside of breeding, often joins mixed flocks. Migration probably diurnal. Monogamous nesting pair defends territory with song, aggressive displays; constructs open-cup nest in outer limbs, shares parental care. Frequent victim of cowbird brood parasitism.

VOCALIZATIONS Song of wheezy notes, sharp chips in series; calls with buzzy mewing.

OR (Douglas County)—May • DENNIS PAULSON

OR (Lincoln County)—Jul • GREG GILLSON

Wrentit
Chamaea fasciata

DESCRIPTION 6.5 in/16.5 cm. Drab; large headed with **long, rounded tail**; thin bill, **white iris**, hint of pale supercilium. **Pink-tinged breast** obscurely streaked. In OR, varies from chestnut brown in moist habitats to grayish-mantled at drier sites.

SIMILAR SPECIES Bushtit (p. 336) tiny, small headed, usually in flocks. Wrens (pp. 341–346) show proportionately shorter tail, dark iris; Bewick's also has white supercilium.

STATUS & DISTRIBUTION Resident from western OR to northern Baja California; sedentary, with limited post-breeding dispersal. In PNW, historically found only in southwestern OR. Extended range steadily northward in last century to Columbia River; now fairly common from coastline to edges of Willamette Valley, expanding eastward into Cascade foothills north to Clackamas County; rare north of Yamhill County, except along coast. In south, uncommon eastward in Siskiyous to moderate elevation (~4,000 ft/1,200 m).

HABITAT ASSOCIATIONS Breeds in dense thickets of salal, huckleberry, blackberry, other broadleaf shrubs; also open woodland understory, riparian corridors, regenerating clear-cuts.

BEHAVIOR & FEEDING Forages mostly near ground, frequently holding tail cocked. Gleans arthropods from bark or foliage; also eats fruits, other plant material. Often heard, rarely seen due to proclivity to remain in thick brush. Commonly holds larger food items in foot while dissecting or dismembering; also feeds hanging upside down. Pairs form long-term monogamous bond, roost together, build tidy open-cup nest with spider silk, bark strips; share territory defense, all parental duties.

VOCALIZATIONS Both sexes sing year-round—male a few clear whistles accelerating to descending trill, female evenly repeated *churr*; calls include buzzy rattle.

OR (Klamath County)—Feb · GREG GILLSON

Juvenile · BC (Parksville)—Sep · RALPH HOCKEN

American Dipper
Cinclus mexicanus

DESCRIPTION 7.5 in/19 cm. **Stout**, chunky, **uniform slate gray** with **short tail**, thin dark bill, grayish-pink legs. Shape, bobbing motions suggest large wren. Often flashes white eyelids. *Juvenile:* Paler underparts; pinkish-yellow legs, bill.

SIMILAR SPECIES All PNW wrens (pp. 341–346) much smaller; mimic-thrushes' (pp. 360–363) songs similar but generally lower pitched.

STATUS & DISTRIBUTION Resident in West from Aleutians east to western South Dakota, south to Panama; restricted to higher elevations in southern range. In PNW, uncommon resident along streams in foothills, mountains to treeline, also down to forested coasts; moves downstream extensively (Aug–Nov) to major rivers, estuaries to winter at ice-free elevations; latitudinal migrants also increase winter densities in southwestern BC. Rare on Snake, Okanagan Rivers, other major drainages in arid habitats; otherwise absent away from mountains east of Cascades/BC Coast Range.

HABITAT ASSOCIATIONS Nests on rushing streams or rivers, rarely pond margins; uses stream mouths, urbanized areas, salmon runs in larger rivers at other seasons.

BEHAVIOR & FEEDING Truly aquatic songbird. Forages by swimming or walking on stream bottom in pursuit of caddisfly, other aquatic larvae, small fish, roe; "flies" penguin-like underwater. Bobs on streamside rocks while investigating intruders or protecting territory. Mostly monogamous, rarely polygynous; pair builds bulky domed nest at streamside attached to rocks, overhanging wood, or under bridge. Female incubates, broods; first clutch often fledged by March; may also raise second brood.

VOCALIZATIONS Song series of loud, piercing musical whistles, chatter; calls include buzzy *bzzeet zeet zeet*.

Golden-crowned Kinglet
Regulus satrapa

DESCRIPTION 3.75 in/9.5 cm. Tiny; olive gray with whitish underparts, **short notched tail**, thin bill. Shows **broad white supercilium** bordered black, dark wings with **bold wing-bar**, golden-green edging. *Male:* Black crown with orange-and-yellow center. *Female:* No orange in crown. *Juvenile:* Duller; crown gray.

SIMILAR SPECIES Warblers (pp. 371–394) larger, longer tailed. Ruby-crowned Kinglet (p. 351) greener with eye-ring, lacks head stripes.

STATUS & DISTRIBUTION Breeds across continent from Kodiak Island to Newfoundland, south in mountains disjunctly to Guatemala; winters in breeding range except Canadian interior, also south across US to northern Mexico, northern Florida. In PNW, common resident sea level to mountain passes, lowland numbers augmented Oct–Mar by migrant influx. East of Cascades/BC Coast Range, breeds above ponderosa pine zone; uncommon late Aug–May in scrub or plantations Columbia Plateau, southeastern OR, other arid areas.

HABITAT ASSOCIATIONS Breeds mostly in mature conifers, including urban stands (prefers spruce-fir in PNW). Winters woodlands, using deciduous thickets more than in breeding season. Migrants appear anywhere.

BEHAVIOR & FEEDING Eats arthropods year-round. Forages constantly from tips of branches by gleaning or hover-gleaning, ceaselessly flicking wings. Gregarious when not nesting; joins mixed flocks. Roosts along branch, tightly packed to withstand extreme cold. Monogamous. Nesting pair remains high, constructs hammock-like nest under conifer twigs with moss, bark, spider silk, feathers, hair; female lays second clutch (up to nine eggs) while male raises first brood.

VOCALIZATIONS Song begins with three high, thin notes, ends with tumbling chatter. Call *tsee tsee tsee* or *tsee.*

Ruby-crowned Kinglet
Regulus calendula

DESCRIPTION 4 in/10.5 cm. Plump, short tailed; thin bill, **yellow feet**. Overall grayish green with paler underparts, diffuse **white eye-ring**, **white wing-bars** with black patch behind lower bar. *Male:* Red crown, only exposed in excitement. *Juvenile:* Lacks red crown (both sexes).

SIMILAR SPECIES Golden-crowned Kinglet (p. 350) has white supercilium, lacks eye-ring. Larger Hutton's Vireo (p. 310) thicker billed, feet bluish; lacks black behind lower wing-bar. Nashville Warbler (p. 376) breast yellow, lacks wing-bars.

STATUS & DISTRIBUTION Breeds below northern treeline from Alaska to Labrador, south to northern Vermont, in western mountains to Arizona; winters south from southwestern BC, Kansas, Connecticut to Guatemala. In PNW, common breeder at high elevations from just west of Cascades crest eastward; also Olympics, uncommonly to lower-elevation western BC. In winter, fairly common in westside lowlands south from Campbell River, rare/casual in interior south from Okanagan, Kootenays, northwestern MT. Migrants nearly ubiquitous Mar–May, Sep–Oct.

HABITAT ASSOCIATIONS Breeds in mature conifers, also aspens; winters in woodlands, suburbs, hedgerows.

BEHAVIOR & FEEDING Gleans or hover-gleans arthropods from foliage, branches, flicking wings constantly; outside nesting season, also takes plant material, joins mixed flocks. Congregates in attractive habitats, especially while migrating. Territorial in wintering quarters; sings Feb–May. Monogamous; female builds globular nest high in conifer with moss, bark, spider silk, twigs; incubates up to nine eggs, broods while male provisions.

VOCALIZATIONS Sings rolling series of trills, twitters, repeated phrases; calls include husky *jidi dit*, repeated *jditt* in alarm near nest.

Female · WA (Yakima County)—Apr · GREGG THOMPSON

Male · WA (Kittitas County)—Apr · GREGG THOMPSON

Juvenile · BC (Penticton)—Jul · LAURE W. NEISH

Western Bluebird
Sialia mexicana

DESCRIPTION 7 in/18 cm. Small **upright-perching** thrush; blue wings, tail; short thin bill. *Male:* **Dark purplish-blue** head, back, wings, tail; **rusty-brown breast**, shoulders; grayish-blue belly. *Female:* **Duller, less blue; grayish** back, head; paler rust breast. *Juvenile:* Like female but with white eye-ring; spotted breast, back.

SIMILAR SPECIES Mountain Bluebird (p. 353) brilliant sky blue; thinner bill; longer legs, wings; male without rust, female gray or slightly rusty on breast, flanks always grayish.

STATUS & DISTRIBUTION Ranges in West from southern BC to Mexico. In PNW, locally common breeder east of Cascades; less frequent west of crest, but still locally common, e.g., Tacoma prairies (WA); Willamette, Rogue, Umpqua Valleys, eastern slope Coast Range (OR). Mostly absent from coast, low, hot, open interior. Winters in much lower numbers; migrants return Feb–Mar. Population decline in last century largely due to habitat alteration, House Sparrow competition. Nest-box programs have aided recovery locally.

HABITAT ASSOCIATIONS Open ponderosa pine woodlands, meadows, low-elevation clear-cuts, burns; prairie with aspen copses, snags.

BEHAVIOR & FEEDING Forages mostly on insects, hunting from low perch over short grass; eats some berries. Secondary cavity nester, partial to nest boxes mounted at open sites near ground. Nests Apr–Aug, may lay two clutches. Flocks when not nesting; concentrates near mistletoe, junipers in winter; migrants more common in mountains, rare in lowlands away from breeding sites.

VOCALIZATIONS Seldom sings; low, whistled *chwer* often given in flight by flocking birds. Calls somewhat harsher than those of Mountain Bluebird, include chattering.

Male · WA (King County)—Mar · GREGG THOMPSON

Female · WA (Skagit County)—Mar · RYAN MERRILL

Mountain Bluebird
Sialia currucoides

DESCRIPTION 7 in/18 cm. Small **upright-perching** thrush; short, thin bill; **brilliant blue wings, tail**. *Male:* Intense **sky blue above**, paler on breast; white undertail. *Female:* Blue limited to wings, tail. **Grayish head, body**, may show some rust on breast; white eye-ring. *Juvenile:* Similar to female; spotted breast, back.

SIMILAR SPECIES Western Bluebird (p. 352) almost purplish blue; rusty below, bill heavier, wings shorter, female rusty to flanks. Pinyon Jay (p. 312) much larger, duller, shows blue to undertail.

STATUS & DISTRIBUTION Breeds central Alaska east to Manitoba, south to southwestern US; winters to Mexico. Fairly common breeder in PNW from subalpine zone of Cascades/BC Coast Range eastward. Widespread in ID, where honored as state bird. Mostly absent from lower Columbia Plateau. Winters OR, southern ID, rarely southern WA, casually southern BC. Migrants depart by Oct, return Feb–Mar. Rare, regular migrant through western lowlands, especially Mar–May.

HABITAT ASSOCIATIONS Prefers dry, open country, including bunchgrass prairie, shrub-steppe, agricultural meadows, burns, forest edge, subalpine parkland. Nest-box projects in otherwise inhospitable areas offset loss of natural habitat caused by fire suppression.

BEHAVIOR & FEEDING Forages mostly on insects; also eats berries (important in winter). Hovers more than Western Bluebird, often hunts from wires. Secondary cavity nester, preferring flicker-sized holes in trees, stubs; also uses nest boxes, rock crevices, buildings, rarely Cliff Swallow nests. Large flocks form by Aug.

VOCALIZATIONS Song sequence of burry warbled whistles. Thin *fwer* often given by flocking birds; other calls include nasal *chak*.

Juvenile · Utah—Aug · PAUL HIGGINS   BC (Victoria)—Apr · TED ARDLEY

Townsend's Solitaire
Myadestes townsendi

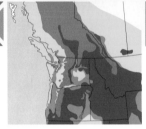

DESCRIPTION 9 in/23 cm. **Slender** thrush, upright perching; short, stubby bill. Warm gray overall, white lower wing-bar, **bold white eye-ring. Tail long, black-ish; outer feathers white**. Rusty white in flight feathers forms wing stripe in flight. *Juvenile:* Similar; body feathers broadly buff spotted.

SIMILAR SPECIES Juvenile bluebirds (pp. 352–353) smaller, flight feathers blue. Flycatchers (pp. 285–303) have proportionately larger heads.

STATUS & DISTRIBUTION Breeds central Alaska to northwestern Mexico, east to Rocky Mountain foothills. Withdraws from colder parts of range in winter, moving downslope, south. In PNW, fairly common montane breeder, except rare to absent in wet coastal forests. Downslope movement by Sep. Migrants fairly common throughout (fewer west), return late Mar–May. Uncommon Nov–Mar east of Cascades, mostly OR to WY; a few remain north to BC interior valleys; rare in westside lowlands.

HABITAT ASSOCIATIONS Breeds near openings in drier coniferous forests up to subalpine zone. Prefers rugged terrain, steep banks; partial to burns, clear-cuts. Winters near junipers, other fruit sources. Migrants use varied habitats, often moving along ridges.

BEHAVIOR & FEEDING Nests Apr–Jul, almost always on ground, at open site in road-cut, dirt bank, or among roots; female incubates, broods; both parents provision young. In nesting season, diet insects, some fruit. Flycatches above canopy, gleans larger insects while hovering. Shifts to berries post-breeding. In winter, maintains feeding territories centered on productive junipers.

VOCALIZATIONS Lengthy, elaborate, richly warbled finch-like song given infrequently. Calls include squeaky *kree eek* while nesting, year-round whistled *twee*, reminiscent of pygmy-owl.

WA (Ferry County)—Jun · BRIAN STECH

Veery
Catharus fuscescens

DESCRIPTION 7.25 in/18.5 cm. **Plain** thrush; elegant *Catharus* shape. **Rich, evenly rust-brown upperparts**; buff-washed upper breast with **indistinct blurry spots** grades to grayish belly. Wing stripe visible from below in flight. *Juvenile:* Plumage held briefly, buff edges on body feathers.

SIMILAR SPECIES Breast markings less distinct than other *Catharus* thrushes (pp. 356–357); Hermit has contrasting rufous tail; Swainson's, prominent buffy eye-ring. Vocalizations differ.

STATUS & DISTRIBUTION Ranges from central BC to Newfoundland, south in Appalachians to North Carolina, in Rockies disjunctly to New Mexico. Winters southern Brazil. Locally common breeder in PNW in lower montane zone eastward from Cascades/BC Coast Range, rarely west. Widespread south-central, southeastern BC, eastern WA to northwestern MT (where in sharp decline); uncommon south to western WY. Absent OR, except uncommon lower Blue Mountains, southwest locally to Crook County. Migrants rarely observed; return mid-May, depart apparently Aug.

HABITAT ASSOCIATIONS In PNW, breeds strictly in riparian habitats. Frequents alder, willow stands with red-osier dogwood, wild rose, other low growth in understory. Migrants rarely recorded outside appropriate habitat.

BEHAVIOR & FEEDING Monogamous pair nests on or near ground Jun–Jul, well concealed. Forages close to ground, mostly for insects while breeding, later shifts to berries, other small fruits. Rarely takes small amphibians. Furtively hops through dense vegetation where difficult to see. Best detected by voice. Departure difficult to pinpoint once singing ceases.

VOCALIZATIONS Ethereal advertising song given mostly near dawn, dusk: descending series of 3–5 low, flute-like notes. *Veeyeer* call uttered when disturbed; harsher alarm notes.

"Olive-backed" · *Alberta—Jul* · GERALD ROMANCHUK

"Russet-backed" · *WA (King County)—May* · GREGG THOMPSON

Swainson's Thrush
Catharus ustulatus

DESCRIPTION 7 in/18 cm. Typical *Catharus* thrush. Brownish upperparts; distinctly spotted, buff-washed upper breast; whitish belly. **Buffy, spectacle-like eye-ring,** wing stripe visible from below in flight. Two forms: "Olive-backed" **drab olive above**; "Russet-backed" **warm, rusty brown,** breast spots more diffuse. *Juvenile:* Buff-edged upperparts.

SIMILAR SPECIES Separated by vocalizations from other *Catharus* thrushes (pp. 355, 357). Veery shows less distinct breast markings; Hermit, contrasting rufous tail, thin white eye-ring.

STATUS & DISTRIBUTION Breeds Alaska to Newfoundland, south to southern California, in mountains to northern New Mexico, West Virginia. Leaves breeding range before Nov, winters Mexico to South America. In PNW, migrants arrive May, secretive but widespread. Locally common breeder throughout—"Russet-backed" (*C.u. ustulatus/phillipsi*) Cascades/BC Coast Range west to sea level, "Olive-backed" (*C.u. swainsoni*) east across rest of region except arid steppe. Some interbreeding where ranges meet in northern WA, BC.

HABITAT ASSOCIATIONS Moist, shady mixed forest, lowlands to subalpine zone (in Rockies); generally above Veery, below Hermit Thrush elevation ranges, but may overlap either. Prefers dense understory in mature forest, often riparian. "Russet-backed" partial to salmonberry thickets.

BEHAVIOR & FEEDING Forages on ground or in trees. Takes invertebrates while breeding, increasingly fruits later. Nests Jun–Jul, on or near ground. Furtive, best detected by voice. Transients join mixed flocks, stay near cover.

VOCALIZATIONS Song series of nasal whistles spiraling upward. Calls include whistled *whit*, whines, grating alarm chatter, clear *queep* in flight. "Russet-backed" song more nasal, complex; "Olive-backed" *whit* more emphatic. Hundreds detected per evening by nocturnal flight calls.

Hermit Thrush
Catharus guttatus

DESCRIPTION 6.75 in/17 cm. Grayest *Catharus* thrush in PNW; olive brown above, sharply **contrasting reddish-brown tail.** Breast buffy white, **dark spotted**; flanks gray. Thin bill, **thin white eye-ring**, brownish face. Wing stripe visible from below in flight. At least five subspecies in PNW, differing in size, head color (grayish to brown). *Juvenile:* Plumage held briefly, buff edges on body feathers.

SIMILAR SPECIES Told from other *Catharus* thrushes (pp. 355–356) by vocalizations. Veery breast markings blurry; Swainson's shows distinct buffy spectacles, non-contrasting tail, seldom cocked. Fox Sparrow (pp. 412–413) heavily marked ventrally, bill conical.

STATUS & DISTRIBUTION Nests across Canada below tundra edge, south locally in mountains to Baja California, Pennsylvania; winters southwestern BC, Middle Atlantic states to Guatemala. Common forest breeder throughout PNW at higher elevations, usually above Swainson's Thrush (however, both nest to sea level in north of region). Migrants common, widespread throughout region Apr–May, Sep–Nov. Winters uncommonly in lowlands, mostly west, rarely interior north to southern BC.

HABITAT ASSOCIATIONS Prefers drier coniferous, mixed forests, regenerating clearcuts. Winters thickets, woodland edge, suburbs.

BEHAVIOR & FEEDING Forages close to ground, eats insects, fruit. Picks berries off low shrubs, more in fall, winter. Diagnostically cocks, then lowers, tail while pumping wings. Seldom flocks, but nocturnal migrants sometimes dense. Nests low, May–Aug, open cup typically in small shrub; possibly two broods.

VOCALIZATIONS Song clear whistle followed by ethereal spiraling whistles at different pitches. Calls include rising *zhweeee*, muffled *chup*—less rich, shorter than Varied Thrush call.

American Robin
Turdus migratorius

DESCRIPTION 10 in/25 cm, wingspan 17 in/43 cm. **Bulky** thrush, solid-grayish back, fairly upright stance. Long, stout **yellow bill**; dark stripes on white throat, **dull-orange breast**, white undertail; white marks above, below eye. *Male:* Crown blackish, colors more vibrant. *Female:* Duller; breast lighter orange. *Juvenile:* Dark-spotted breast, white-spotted upperparts.

SIMILAR SPECIES Varied Thrush (p. 359) more squat with dark mask. Spotted Towhee (p. 397) smaller with dark hood, white belly. *Catharus* thrushes (pp. 355–357) smaller, lack orange breast.

STATUS & DISTRIBUTION Breeds across Canada, US except southernmost states, south in mountains of Mexico. Facultative migrant; driven south by cold, returning north when temperature allows; winters from coastal PNW across southern Canada, most of US, south to Guatemala. Widespread, common resident throughout PNW.

HABITAT ASSOCIATIONS Ubiquitous; backyards to treeline to shrub-steppe. Prefers semi-open areas; uses broken forest, cities, desert edges. Breeds wherever trees, other structures available for nest placement, mud for construction. Winter congregations often found near fruit-bearing thickets, water sources.

BEHAVIOR & FEEDING Drawn to lawns. Runs on ground or stands still searching for worms, insects, other invertebrates. Takes fruit from ground, shrubs, more in fall, winter. Roosts communally at night in dense vegetation after breeding season; winter flocks can number in thousands. Monogamous pair produces two or more broods per year.

VOCALIZATIONS Song lengthy, rich caroling with discrete rising, falling phrases offered from high perch. Calls include *tuk tuk tuk*, sharp *piik* given when perturbed; high, thin *sreep* flight call.

Female · WA (Snohomish County)—Feb · GREGG THOMPSON   Male · WA (Snohomish County) – Mar · BOB KOTHENBEUTEL

Varied Thrush
Ixoreus naevius

DESCRIPTION 9.5 in/24 cm. Stocky, short tailed. **Dark breast band, mask**, bill; **orange eyebrow**, breast, throat, wing patches, wing-bars. Light wing stripe visible in flight. **Male:** Bluish-gray cap, back, tail; black breast band, mask. **Female:** Dark areas brownish-gray, breast band indistinct; eyebrow sometimes whitish. **Juvenile:** Breast mottled, lacks breast band.

SIMILAR SPECIES American Robin (p. 358) tail longer, no breast band. Black-headed Grosbeak (p. 421) has huge conical bill.

STATUS & DISTRIBUTION Breeds Alaska, Yukon to northern California; vacates northern part of range to winter as far south as southern California. Widespread, fairly common breeder in PNW in extensive coniferous forest, more numerous Cascades/BC Coast Range westward. Mostly extirpated from lowlands as breeder due to forest fragmentation, except on Haida Gwaii, western Vancouver Island, outer Olympic Peninsula. Moves downslope below heavy snow in fall/winter. Widespread migrants arrive lowlands Sep, fairly common to Apr.

HABITAT ASSOCIATIONS Moist, mature coniferous forests with dense understory. Winters thickets, forest edge, well-treed parks, suburbs; never far from fruit source.

BEHAVIOR & FEEDING Forages on ground, less often in trees, for insects, fruit; in winter, often congregates near *Arbutus* (madrone), ornamentals, feeding on fruit. Flocks less than robins; maintains winter feeding territory, but gregarious in migration. Female builds bulky nest, often on or near old nests.

VOCALIZATIONS Male sings year-round from high perch, increasingly with approach of spring—long, trilled whistle on single pitch, repeated at different pitches after long pauses. Calls include rich *chup*; also thin *zipf*, raspy mobbing chatter.

BC (Pitt Meadows)—Jun · MIKE D. BAILEY

Nest · BC (Okanagan Falls)—Jul · DAMON CALDERWOOD

Gray Catbird
Dumetella carolinensis

DESCRIPTION 9 in/23 cm. Slim; **slate grayish** overall with **black cap**, chestnut undertail; long tail, blackish **thin bill**. *Juvenile:* Slightly browner; chestnut undertail less evident.

SIMILAR SPECIES Sage Thrasher (p. 362) lighter gray with brown-streaked white underparts. Northern Mockingbird (p. 363) shows white patches in wings, tail.

STATUS & DISTRIBUTION Breeds eastward from southwestern BC, northwestern Arizona to Nova Scotia, northern Florida. In PNW, uncommon breeder May–Sep east of Cascades/BC Coast Range from central BC (Williams Lake) to northeastern OR (rarely south to Deschutes County), southern ID, western WY; locally common, notably south-central BC (Okanagan Valley), north-central to northeastern WA, northwestern MT. Except as migrant, mostly absent from Columbia Plateau, southeastern OR. Rare/casual summer visitor west of Cascades from southwestern BC (regular breeder Pitt Meadows) to southern OR (has bred Newport, OR, possibly Skagit County, WA). Accidental in winter throughout.

HABITAT ASSOCIATIONS Prefers deciduous habitats at low to moderate elevation, often riparian, including thickets, tangles, open woodland, agricultural edge.

BEHAVIOR & FEEDING Forages mostly in low shrubs or on ground, taking arthropods, small fruit, with more of the latter after nesting season. Remains close to cover but may sing from exposed perch; furtive when not singing. Monogamous pair raises young in open-cup nest concealed within shrub—sometimes two broods. Migrants in PNW continue well into Jun, often use marginal habitats including riparian strips within shrub-steppe of Columbia Plateau.

VOCALIZATIONS Sings with continuous series of squeaky notes including mimicry of other species; also cat-like *meewwha*, harsh *kek kekgh*.

ID (Blaine County)—Sep • DAVE LAWRENCE

Male singing • Alberta—May • GLENN BARTLEY

Brown Thrasher
Toxostoma rufum

DESCRIPTION 11 in/28 cm, wingspan 14 in/35 cm. Slim, **long tailed**; rich **rufous dorsally** with white wing-bars; **white underparts show heavy dark-brown streaks**; pale-orange iris; long, thin, slightly decurved bill. *Juvenile:* Bluish iris; lightly streaked upperparts.

SIMILAR SPECIES Sage Thrasher (p. 362) gray dorsally with shorter tail. Northern Mockingbird (p. 363) gray, shows white in wings, tail. *Catharus* thrushes (pp. 355–357) much smaller, shorter tailed, spotted beneath rather than streaked.

STATUS & DISTRIBUTION Breeds central Alberta to New Brunswick, south through Florida; winters in southeastern US from southern Indiana, Connecticut southward, also disjunctly to Arizona. In PNW, casual year-round throughout region but increases to rare May–Jun. Many OR records occur during winter. Breeds just east of Continental Divide in MT.

HABITAT ASSOCIATIONS Riparian thickets or other early-successional growth including dense brush, tangles, scrub.

BEHAVIOR & FEEDING Forages by scratching through fallen leaves on ground searching for arthropods, small vertebrates, seeds, berries; never far from thick brush; heavy flight, close to ground with uneven wingbeats. Monogamous pair builds bulky nest concealed near ground in dense cover, shares parental care, often raises two broods per year. Migrants tend to be solitary, rarely joining sparrow flocks; usually found alone in PNW.

VOCALIZATIONS Male sings from prominent perch with tail pointing downward, sometimes at top of tree. Song diverse repertoire of continuous musical notes with identical phrases repeated twice; generally exhibits little mimicry of other species. Call-note very loud *chack!*

Sage Thrasher
Oreoscoptes montanus

DESCRIPTION 8.5 in/22 cm. Slender; **pale grayish** dorsally with faint white wing-bars, **streaked below with brownish chevrons** on white breast; buffy flanks, pale iris, thin bill. Faded birds show less streaking, lack wing-bars. *Juvenile:* Wing-bars bolder, back streaked.

SIMILAR SPECIES Northern Mockingbird (p. 363) longer tailed with white flashes in wing, tail. Brown Thrasher (p. 361) larger, rufous brown dorsally. All PNW streaked-breasted sparrows (pp. 395–419) show conical bill.

STATUS & DISTRIBUTION Breeds in interior West from south-central BC, southwestern Saskatchewan south to eastern California, northern New Mexico; most winter south of breeding range to Mexico. In PNW, locally fairly common east of Cascades mid-Mar–Sep, except common across southern ID, barely rare northwestern MT, casual Idaho Panhandle; in BC, rare breeder southern Okanagan Valley. Occurs rarely Apr–May in lowlands west of Cascades, where casual through Nov; casual Oct–Feb in areas of high breeding densities, mostly OR.

HABITAT ASSOCIATIONS Breeds low- to mid-elevation sagebrush-dominated shrub-steppe.

BEHAVIOR & FEEDING Highly terrestrial; forages primarily by running on ground after arthropods, eats some plant material. Sings from perch atop sage or other shrub; male displays with undulating flight, wing flaps. Pair builds nest on ground or in shrub, shares parental duties, single brood or sometimes two (ID). After breeding, may form loose flocks before departure southward.

VOCALIZATIONS Sings with continuous low-volume series of warbles or musical notes that run on with very few pauses, little mimicry of other species; alarm notes include *chup*, harsh scolding.

Northern Mockingbird
Mimus polyglottos

DESCRIPTION 10.5 in/27 cm, wingspan 14 in/36 cm. Lanky, **long tailed**, with pale iris, dark, **thin bill**; pale gray dorsally, dingy whitish below with **bold white wing patches**, outer rectrices. *Juvenile:* Dark iris, streaked breast.

SIMILAR SPECIES Northern Shrike (p. 305) larger headed with thicker, hooked bill; juvenile brownish, adult shows dark mask. Loggerhead Shrike (p. 304) darker gray with black mask, thicker bill. Sage Thrasher (p. 362) lacks white in flight feathers.

STATUS & DISTRIBUTION Common resident California to southern Maine, south into Mexico; occurs irregularly north to southern BC, Nova Scotia. Rare resident in PNW; migrates regularly northward Apr–Jun to as far as Haida Gwaii, where accidental. Disperses principally along outer coast but appears throughout region, with a few nesting records mostly from Rogue Valley (OR) or east of Cascades. Occurrence in PNW continues to increase concurrent with northward spread in California.

HABITAT ASSOCIATIONS Desert scrub, agricultural lands, suburbs, other semi-open areas; often associates with power lines in PNW.

BEHAVIOR & FEEDING Tends to fly with slow, steady wingbeats. Forages on ground or in shrubs, taking arthropods or plant material; often winters near multi-flora rose. Frequently flashes open wings while walking. Monogamous pair uses open-cup nest concealed in shrubs—may double-brood. Perches conspicuously, aggressively defending territory against all intruders, including humans.

VOCALIZATIONS Sings with continuous diverse series of notes, whistles, mimicked calls of other species, repeating phrases many times; also offers sharp *chack*, harsh raspy *hew* in alarm.

Breeding · OR (Washington County)—Apr · GREG GILLSON

Non-breeding · BC (Delta)—Nov · MIKE D. BAILEY

Juvenile · BC (Surrey)—Jun · ROY PRIEST

European Starling
Sturnus vulgaris

DESCRIPTION 8.5 in/21.5 cm. Chunky, **short tailed**; long, **thin bill**. *Breeding:* Iridescent blackish with greenish sheen, buff-brown feather tips, **yellow bill**. *Non-breeding:* **White spotting** throughout body plumage, prominent brown edging on wings; dark bill. *Juvenile:* Plain grayish brown; dark bill.

SIMILAR SPECIES Western Meadowlark (p. 428) glides between halting wingbeats, shows white outer rectrices, yellow breast. Brown-headed Cowbird (p. 434), other small PNW blackbirds (pp. 426–427, 429–431) undulate in flight; tails longer, bills conical. Purple Martin (p. 323) has longer wings, shorter bill.

STATUS & DISTRIBUTION Native to Eurasia, introduced to North America in New York City in 1890. Now resident south-central Alaska to Newfoundland south to Jamaica, northern Mexico, wintering south to Yucatan. In PNW, reached western WY, northwestern MT, ID by 1941; Willamette Valley by 1947; Puget Sound, coastal BC in 1950s; populations expanded to millions, now apparently leveling off. Widespread common resident but scarce in mountains, contiguous forest, desert habitats away from cities.

HABITAT ASSOCIATIONS Cities, woodlands, farms.

BEHAVIOR & FEEDING Probes ground for insect larvae, worms; drawn to lawns, where males guard females closely. Also flycatches, plucks fruit from trees, searches feedlots, cities for refuse. Flight strong with straight trajectory; flocks often "ball up" in response to avian predators. Highly social; thousands aggregate Aug–Feb at noisy evening roosts. Usually monogamous, rarely polygamous. Competes with native species for nest cavities; two or more broods per year.

VOCALIZATIONS Sings year-round with series of squeaks, gurgles, whistles, mimicry of other species; calls include *che che che*.

American Pipit
Anthus rubescens

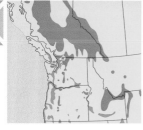

DESCRIPTION 6.5 in/16.5 cm. Slender; **thin bill**, long dark tail with **white outer rectrices**. Plain brownish-gray mantle, unstreaked throat; buffy underparts usually streaked. Supercilium, eye-ring, malar, **wing-bars whitish**. *Breeding:* Breast strongly buffy, heavily to lightly streaked (rarely unstreaked). *Non-breeding:* Whiter breast, heavier streaking. *Juvenile:* Faint supercilium.

SIMILAR SPECIES Sky Lark (p. 321) shorter tailed, streaked back, crested appearance. Warblers smaller; Palm (p. 387) also pumps tail, frequently feeds on ground, but has bright-yellow undertail coverts; Yellow-rumped (pp. 388–389) shows yellow rump in flight. Sparrows (pp. 395–419) have conical bills.

STATUS & DISTRIBUTION Breeds on Arctic, alpine tundra from Labrador to Siberia, south in mountains to New Hampshire, Arizona; winters New Jersey, southwestern BC, southern interior US, to El Salvador. In PNW, fairly common breeder above treeline south to northwestern WY, southeastern OR (Steens Mountain). Widespread migrant away from urban areas (Sep–Oct, mid-Apr–early May); spring flocks may exceed a thousand. Uncommon Nov–Mar in lowlands west of Cascades south from Fraser Delta, mostly along coasts; rarely winters farther east, mostly southern ID, Columbia Plateau (OR/WA).

HABITAT ASSOCIATIONS Breeds on tundra, high-elevation meadows; at other seasons open, often moist habitats—plowed fields, pond margins, mud flats, beaches.

BEHAVIOR & FEEDING Bobs tail constantly while walking, searching for seeds, arthropods. Forms flocks except while nesting. Migrants nearly always perch on ground, occasionally on wires. Often approachable, but flushes when alarm given. Lays single clutch. Female broods, incubates; male assists feeding.

VOCALIZATIONS Sharp *pi pit* call frequent in flight.

WA (King County)—Nov · GREGG THOMPSON

Bohemian Waxwing
Bombycilla garrulus

DESCRIPTION 8.25 in/21 cm. Chunky; **silky brownish gray** overall with **wispy crest**, black mask, white wing markings, **chestnut undertail**; waxy yellow on tips of primaries, **short tail**; secondaries variably red tipped. *Male:* Glossy black throat. *Female:* Black limited, more diffuse. *Juvenile:* Dull with ventral streaking, whitish throat.

SIMILAR SPECIES Cedar Waxwing (p. 367) smaller, more yellowish, undertail white. European Starling (p. 364) flight more direct; larger, longer billed, lacks silky plumage.

STATUS & DISTRIBUTION Holarctic. In New World, breeds Alaska to Hudson Bay, south in mountains to southern BC; winters southern coastal Alaska to Labrador, south to Colorado, Massachusetts, irregularly irrupting farther south. In PNW, breeds rarely southern BC, casually Idaho Panhandle, north-central WA, possibly northwestern MT; one isolated record OR (Clatsop County). Locally common Nov–early Apr east of Cascades/BC Coast Range south to western WY, northern OR (uncommon Oct, late Apr–May, rare farther south); occasional large irruptions west of crest, but rare most years.

HABITAT ASSOCIATIONS Breeds open conifer-dominated forest, restricted to mountains in PNW; post-breeding, wanders to wherever fruit is concentrated.

BEHAVIOR & FEEDING Forages for small fruit year-round, sallies for aerial insects during summer. Highly gregarious, flocking even during nesting season. Wanderers descend on ripe fruit in tight, swirling masses; usually eat fruit whole, sometimes passing berries back and forth. Monogamous pairs form in winter, nest Jun–Jul; male guards female, but shows no territoriality. Female incubates, broods young.

VOCALIZATIONS Calls frequently in flight or from perch with thin, trilled *sreeee*, lower pitched than Cedar Waxwing.

WA (King County)—Nov · GREGG THOMPSON

Juvenile · WA (Skagit County)—Oct · NICK DEAN

Cedar Waxwing
Bombycilla cedrorum

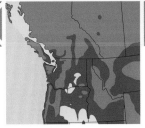

DESCRIPTION 7.5 in/19 cm. Sleek with **wispy crest**, black mask, **yellow belly**, **white undertail**; brownish back grades to gray rump. Plain gray wings show waxy red secondary tips (larger with age); short, dark tail yellow tipped. *Male:* Glossy black throat. *Female:* Diffuse dark chin. *Juvenile:* Dull, **streaked ventrally**.

SIMILAR SPECIES Bohemian Waxwing (p. 366) larger, grayer, with chestnut undertail, white wing-bar. European Starling (p. 364) larger; flies in direct line, non-undulating.

STATUS & DISTRIBUTION Breeds across southern Canada, south to northern California, northern Alabama; winters southern BC, Maine, south to Caribbean, Panama. In PNW, common breeder except rare Haida Gwaii, BC northern mainland coast. Migrants (late May–early Jun, late Aug–Oct) common, widespread but rarely visit extensive coniferous or treeless habitats; uncommon to rare Dec–Feb southern BC (lower Fraser, Okanagan Valleys; Kootenays) southward.

HABITAT ASSOCIATIONS Breeds along forest edges, riparian strips, other early successional habitats; winters in similar areas including suburbs with ornamental plantings.

BEHAVIOR & FEEDING Forages for small fruit year-round, sallies for insects during summer. Late nesting cycle coincides with availability of ripe fruit; loosely colonial, tending to flock even while nesting. Migrants descend on fruiting trees en masse, eating fruits whole; southbound movements irregular, determined by resource availability. Tight, swirling flocks display undulation in flight, often number into hundreds. Monogamous pairs form in migration, may produce two broods per year, showing little territoriality; female incubates, broods young.

VOCALIZATIONS Gives thin *sreeee* mostly in flight, similar to Bohemian Waxwing but higher pitched.

First-winter · WA (Whatcom County)—Sep
DOUGLAS L. BROWN

Breeding Male · BC (Victoria)—May · TED ARDLEY

Lapland Longspur
Calcarius lapponicus

DESCRIPTION 6.25 in/16 cm. Compact, long winged with **pale stout bill**, dorsal streaking, white outer rectrices; upperwing coverts form **rufous wing panel between white wing-bars**. *Breeding male:* White belly, **black face** separated from **rufous nape** by broad white band (plumage attained by wear). *Non-breeding male:* Most black obscured by brownish feather tips; breast smudged blackish, flanks streaked, **auricular outline** visible. *Female:* Averages duller than non-breeding male. *First-winter:* Like non-breeding but buffier, with less rufous in nape.

SIMILAR SPECIES Chestnut-collared Longspur (p. 369) smaller billed, shorter tailed, shows much more white in tail. Vesper Sparrow (p. 402) shows white eye-ring. American Pipit (p. 365), larks (pp. 321–322) have thin bills.

STATUS & DISTRIBUTION Holarctic. In North America, breeds south to James Bay, Kodiak Island; winters Newfoundland, southwestern BC to southern US. Uncommon in PNW (except rare/casual ID, western WY), most frequent Sep–Oct on southbound passage along outer coast, or Nov–Apr mixed with Snow Bunting/Horned Lark flocks east of Cascades/BC Coast Range. Rare Mar–May on northbound return, mostly on outer coast, fewer in Willamette Valley.

HABITAT ASSOCIATIONS Breeds on moist tundra; at other seasons, open ground with sparse vegetation, grassy fields, rarely alpine tundra.

BEHAVIOR & FEEDING Forages for grass seeds by walking on ground; switches to arthropods while breeding. Males establish territory, mate with one or more females; females provide all parental care. Highly gregarious outside breeding, often flocking with Horned Larks, Snow Buntings, other longspurs.

VOCALIZATIONS Calls include rich *chewlup*; flight call dry rattle. Song jumbled warbles, trills.

First-winter · BC (Victoria)—Oct · AZIZA COOPER

Non-breeding Male · Utah—Dec · PAUL HIGGINS

Breeding Male · Alberta—May · GERALD ROMANCHUK

Chestnut-collared Longspur
Calcarius ornatus

DESCRIPTION 6 in/15 cm. **Short winged** with stubby **grayish bill**, dorsal streaking, short **white tail with central black triangle**. *Breeding male:* **Black belly**, chestnut nape, black cap, creamy face bisected by black post-ocular bar (plumage attained by wear). *Non-breeding male:* Less adorned; plain faced with auricular spot, unstreaked dusky underparts. *Female:* Similar to non-breeding male, with colors more muted. *First-winter:* Like non-breeding; whitish wing-bars, obscure ventral streaks.

SIMILAR SPECIES Lapland Longspur (p. 368) has bolder auricular outline, less white in tail. Snow Bunting (p. 370) shows white inner wing at rest or in flight. No sparrow (pp. 395–419) shows mostly white tail.

STATUS & DISTRIBUTION Breeds from southern Alberta to eastern Minnesota, disjunctly south to northeastern Colorado; winters from Kansas, Arizona to central Mexico. Rare vagrant in PNW, barely annual with most records Oct–Nov from coastal OR, fewer from interior OR, WA outer coast; casual late Apr–Jul mostly in BC/WA.

HABITAT ASSOCIATIONS Breeds in short-grass prairie. At other seasons, uses similar habitats including pasture, scrubby beach.

BEHAVIOR & FEEDING Quietly forages by walking among grasses, taking mostly seeds, occasionally chasing flying insects. Switches primarily to arthropods while breeding. Flight undulating. Gathers into flocks in migration but stragglers reaching PNW are often alone. Males defend territory with song in flight or from perch. Monogamous pair nests on ground, may produce more than one clutch, with female providing most brooding of young.

VOCALIZATIONS Calls include *ki dell*, soft rattle in flight, gurgled conversational phrases; sings rich, sweet warbled series.

Snow Bunting
Plectrophenax nivalis

DESCRIPTION 6.75 in/17 cm. Long winged, **stubby bill**, unstreaked underparts, black tail with white edging; inner **wing shows large white patch** at rest or in flight; outer wing black. *Breeding male:* Black bill, back; white head, underparts (plumage attained by wear). *Non-breeding male:* Orange-yellow bill; head, back mottled brownish. *Female:* Similar to male, except breeding plumage mottled with gray; non-breeding browner. *Juvenile:* Light gray dorsally, brownish by Sep.

SIMILAR SPECIES Longspurs (pp. 368–369) lack extensive white wing patch. McKay's Bunting (not shown; casual winter in PNW along coast) wings, tail more extensively white, male's back white.

STATUS & DISTRIBUTION Holarctic breeder north of treeline. In North America, winters south from coastal Alaska, Labrador to Colorado, Virginia, rarely northern Florida. In PNW east of Cascades/BC Coast Range, common Oct–Mar south irregularly to northeastern OR (Wallowa County), southeastern ID; rare farther south. West of crest, rare inland, uncommon along outer coast (rare Apr–May) south to Tillamook. Accidental Jun Haida Gwaii.

HABITAT ASSOCIATIONS Nests on rocky tundra; winters on beaches, open lots, plains, stubble fields; frequents villages on northward migration.

BEHAVIOR & FEEDING Walks or runs on ground taking seeds, arthropods (more of the latter while nesting). Post-breeding flocks numbering into thousands move restlessly over open landscapes, rarely perching on wires, trees; mix with longspurs, larks, other ground species in migration. Pairs monogamous, nest in rocky crevices. Male arrives weeks before female, defends territory; female provides nest care.

VOCALIZATIONS Calls include thin *peep*, twitters, husky rattles; song rich warbled series.

OR (Multnomah County)—Jan · JACK WILLIAMSON

Ovenbird
Seiurus aurocapilla

DESCRIPTION 6 in/15 cm. **Thrush-like** warbler; white **underparts heavily streaked** with blackish; plain brownish-green upperparts with **orange crown bordered by dark stripes**, white eye-ring; stout bill, pinkish legs. *Juvenile:* Head pattern indistinct; browner with rust feather edging, pale wing-bars.

SIMILAR SPECIES Northern Waterthrush (p. 372) browner with bold whitish supercilium. *Catharus* thrushes (pp. 355–357) larger with rounder, less bold breast markings; lack crown pattern.

STATUS & DISTRIBUTION Breeds from southeastern Yukon, Newfoundland south to WY, northern Georgia; winters from Florida, West Indies to Panama. In PNW, possibly breeds eastern BC near northeastern edge of region. Migrants rare but regular May–Jul, fewer Aug–Nov; most numerous eastern OR, southern ID, but barely casual western BC, coastal WA, northwestern MT. Accidental in winter western OR, western WA.

HABITAT ASSOCIATIONS Breeds in mature deciduous, mixed forest with sparse understory, winters in tropical forest. Uses varied habitats in migration; in PNW, generally occurs in woodland dominated by deciduous growth similar to nesting localities.

BEHAVIOR & FEEDING Forages for arthropods by walking on ground, also eats some seeds; becomes more frugivorous during migration. Maintains winter territory. On breeding range, male sings from sub-canopy perch, establishes territory upon arrival. Pairs usually monogamous; may raise two broods in south. Female builds domed oven-like nest on ground at open site in thick leaf litter, provides nest care; male shares feeding duties.

VOCALIZATIONS Sings while perched but also sometimes in flight—loud, ringing, rapid *TEEcha TEEcha TEEcha* series, rarely with rambling introduction. Calls include smacked *chep*, sharp *tink*.

Utah—May · JOSEPH V. HIGBEE

Northern Waterthrush
Parkesia noveboracensis

DESCRIPTION 6 in/15 cm. Long-bodied, short-tailed warbler with stout bill, pale legs; **plain grayish brown dorsally**; bold **whitish supercilium** extends to nape; white **underparts darkly streaked** chin to flanks. *Juvenile:* Underparts more buffy, pale wing-bars, dorsal feathers with rusty edging.

SIMILAR SPECIES Ovenbird (p. 371) greener with striped crown; lacks supercilium. Sparrows show conical bill. *Catharus* thrushes (pp. 355–357) lack supercilium.

STATUS & DISTRIBUTION Breeds from Alaska, Newfoundland south to Virginia, disjunctly to OR; winters Florida, Caribbean, south to Peru; rarely lingers north to southwestern BC, Massachusetts. In PNW, uncommon to locally fairly common breeder Apr–Aug eastward across BC from Cascades/Coast Range, a few summering west to Prince Rupert; eastward from Okanogan Valley across north-central, northeastern WA, northern ID to western MT, northwestern WY. Small, local populations may nest in south-central, northeastern OR, west-central ID. Main migration east of Rockies. In PNW, rare throughout Aug–Oct; rare, local Nov–Mar, mostly western lowlands.

HABITAT ASSOCIATIONS Breeds dense wooded swamp, bogs, along alder-lined rivers; winters in mangrove, other wet tropical habitats; migrants often near muddy shoreline.

BEHAVIOR & FEEDING Forages for invertebrates while walking on mud, rarely takes fish, seeds; eats berries during migration. Perches horizontally, constantly bobs rear of body up and down. Maintains territories year-round; on breeding grounds, male establishes territory, attracts female. Nest often built in deadfall root mass; female provides nest care, male assists feeding young.

VOCALIZATIONS Song ringing series of loud chirps accelerating toward finish; calls include metallic *tchink*, soft *bzzz*.

Female · ID (Jefferson County)—May · DARREN CLARK

Breeding Male · Alberta—May · TERRY THORMIN

Black-and-white Warbler
Mniotilta varia

DESCRIPTION 5.25 in/13.5 cm. Distinctive; pied with **black-and-white streaks over entire body**; dark legs; thin, slightly decurved bill. *Male:* **Black auriculars, throat**; boldly streaked flanks. *Female:* Whitish auriculars, throat; underparts more buff or pinkish, less distinctly streaked. *Juvenile:* Browner upperparts; both sexes resemble adult female by first fall.

SIMILAR SPECIES Black-throated Gray Warbler (p. 392) gray backed with no white streaking; lacks eye-ring, median crown stripe. Adult Blackpoll Warbler (p. 385) has yellow legs, lacks head stripes; male shows black cap, white cheek; female upperparts tinged olive.

STATUS & DISTRIBUTION Breeds east of Rockies from southeastern Yukon, northeastern BC to Labrador, disjunctly south to Texas; winters south from Baja, coastal South Carolina through Caribbean to Colombia. In PNW, rare annual migrant throughout, most frequent southeastern OR, ID; records peak Apr–Jun, Aug–Nov, casual Jul, Dec–Mar. Isolated pairs recorded south to south-central BC (Lillooet), but breeding unconfirmed.

HABITAT ASSOCIATIONS Breeds deciduous, mixed forests, often associated with wetland; varied habitats in winter; migrants appear anywhere, often follow watercourses.

BEHAVIOR & FEEDING Creeps nuthatch-like along trunks, large limbs, probing for arthropods; unlike Brown Creeper, does not use tail for support. On migration, takes berries, joins mixed flocks, often exhibiting aggression toward other species. Males frequently sing en route, arrive before most other warblers on breeding grounds, claim territory, impress female with wing-fluttering display. Pair nests on ground at base of tree.

VOCALIZATIONS Song high-pitched series of evenly spaced *wee see* notes, like squeaky wheel; calls include sharp *chick*.

First-winter · ID (Jefferson County)—Oct
DARREN CLARK

Breeding Male · Manitoba—Jun · GLENN BARTLEY

Tennessee Warbler
Oreothlypis peregrina

DESCRIPTION 4.75 in/12 cm. Stubby; **short tailed**, plain, with **whitish supercilium**, dark eyeline, **thin bill, white undertail**. *Breeding male:* Gray head contrasts with green back, wings; grayish-white underparts. *Non-breeding male:* More subdued with yellower underparts. *Female:* Similar to male but duller. *First-winter:* Yellow breast; fresh individuals show pale wing-bars.

SIMILAR SPECIES All forms of Orange-crowned Warbler (p. 375) show yellow undertail, longer tail, less distinct eyeline, shorter, narrower supercilium. Warbling Vireo (p. 306) bill much heavier, slightly hooked at tip; pale lores. Female Black-throated Blue Warbler (p. 386) bulkier with heavy bill, white wing patch (sometimes lacking in first-winter plumage).

STATUS & DISTRIBUTION Breeds Yukon to Newfoundland, south to northern Minnesota, northern Vermont; winters Mexico to northern Ecuador. Breeding range east of Rockies barely laps into PNW; uncommon near northern edge of region, rare eastern BC to northwestern MT. Migrants casual Aug–Nov western BC, western WA, rare eastern WA to WY (mostly early Sep), OR (most frequent mid-May–early Jun). A few winter casually in OR.

HABITAT ASSOCIATIONS Boreal forest breeder in riparian or shrubby deciduous edge; migrants use varied woodlands. Winters in second-growth tropical habitats.

BEHAVIOR & FEEDING Flits nervously in constant motion while gleaning arthropods in outer foliage; takes fruit in migration, highly nectivorous in tropics. Outside breeding, forms loose flocks, mixes with other passerines. Breeding pair nests on ground in boggy habitat; female provides nest care.

VOCALIZATIONS Loud song: long series of chips in three parts, most rapid at finish. Call sharp *tsik*.

O.c. orestera · BC (Summerland)—Sep · LAURE W. NEISH   O.c. lutescens · WA (Pierce County)—Nov · RYAN SHAW

Orange-crowned Warbler
Oreothlypis celata

DESCRIPTION 4.75 in/12 cm. **Plain** with obscure breast streaks, **thin bill**. Upperparts grayish green, underparts variably yellowish. Face shows vague **pale eye-arcs, indistinct eyeline**. Subspecies *O.c. lutescens* usually brighter with extensively yellow underparts, yellow facial markings, greener upperparts; *O.c. orestera* averages grayer, duller—gray headed in some plumages. *Male:* Dull-orange crown usually hidden. *Female:* Drabber.

SIMILAR SPECIES Tennessee Warbler's (p. 374) undertail white, tail shorter, supercilium more distinct. Yellow Warbler (p. 383) plain faced. MacGillivray's Warbler (p. 378) shows bold eye-arcs, gray hood extending onto upper breast.

STATUS & DISTRIBUTION Two Western subspecies breed southern Alaska, southwestern Yukon to southwestern US: *lutescens*, sea level to coastal ranges, Cascades, Sierra Nevada; *orestera*, intermountain region east through Rockies. Both winter to southwestern US, western Mexico. In PNW, *lutescens* common breeder on Pacific slope; migrates primarily coastally but also through interior; arrives Mar–Apr, most gone by Oct. *Orestera* common migrant (Apr–May), uncommon breeder (Jun–Jul) through interior; fall movement interior, coastal (Aug–Oct). Both forms rare in lowlands Nov–Feb north to southwestern BC, more frequent west. Taiga-breeding *O.c. celata* recorded in migration (especially fall), but identification confusion makes status unclear.

HABITAT ASSOCIATIONS Breeds brushy forest edges, including regenerating clearcuts; in PNW, blackberry thickets preferred Nov–Feb.

BEHAVIOR & FEEDING Forages mostly low for arthropods, plant material, including sap at sapsucker wells. Joins mixed flocks in migration. Monogamous pair nests near ground; female builds nest, broods young.

VOCALIZATIONS Song colorless trill dropping off at end; call high, sharp chip.

Family Parulidae—NEW WORLD WARBLERS   **375**

Nashville Warbler
Oreothlypis ruficapilla

DESCRIPTION 4.75 in/12 cm. Compact, thin billed; **grayish head** with prominent **white eye-ring**. Yellow throat, breast, flanks, undertail; belly variably whitish. **Plain green wings.** *Breeding male:* Yellow-green back sharply contrasts with blue-gray head; chestnut crown patch often concealed. *Non-breeding male:* Less dorsal contrast, more olive ventrally. *Female:* Duller; crown patch mostly absent.

SIMILAR SPECIES Longer-tailed Virginia's Warbler (p. 377) grayer dorsally; yellow confined to breast patch, undertail. Yellow Warbler (p. 383) lacks contrasting grayish head, shows larger bill. Magnolia Warbler (p. 382) shows white tail base, wing-bars.

STATUS & DISTRIBUTION Western subspecies *O.r. ridgwayi* ("Calaveras" Warbler) breeds southern BC to southern California, east to northwestern MT; winters western Mexico to Guatemala. In PNW, common low- to mid-elevation breeder mid-Apr–Sep interior BC north to Williams Lake, south along eastern slope of WA/OR Cascades; fairly common to uncommon northeastern WA, northern, central ID, northwestern MT, Blue Mountains of WA/OR. West of Cascade crest, fairly common breeder southwestern OR, rare north to WA (Whatcom County); casual Oct–Mar, mostly southwestern OR. Migrants widespread, except rare near coast; disperse up to treeline. Eastern subspecies *O.r. ruficapilla* casually reported, status unclear.

HABITAT ASSOCIATIONS Breeds shrubby edge, early-successional mixed forest; migrants more catholic in habitat preference.

BEHAVIOR & FEEDING Agile, frequently shifting tail while foraging actively for arthropods, often in understory foliage. Joins mixed flocks, feeding higher in canopy on spring passage. Monogamous pair nests on ground in dense growth.

VOCALIZATIONS Song series of sweet trills, faster *ti ti ti* at end; calls include sharp *chink*.

Juvenile molting to First-winter · *Utah—Aug* · PAUL HIGGINS

Breeding Male · *Utah—May* · JOHN CRAWLEY

Virginia's Warbler
Oreothlypis virginiae

DESCRIPTION 4.75 in/12 cm. Thin billed; **grayish** with **yellow undertail, rump, central breast patch**; bold **white eye-ring**. *Breeding male:* Bright yellow undertail, breast patch; chestnut crown patch usually visible. *Non-breeding male:* Buffier ventrally, browner dorsally; crown patch obscure. *Female:* Similar to corresponding male plumages but less bright; on immature, yellow often confined to undertail.

SIMILAR SPECIES Shorter-tailed Nashville Warbler (p. 376) yellowish green dorsally, mostly yellow ventrally. Blue-gray Gnatcatcher (p. 347) shows white outer rectrices, lacks yellow. Shorter-tailed Ruby-crowned Kinglet (p. 351) shows bold wing-bars.

STATUS & DISTRIBUTION Breeds disjunctly from east-central California to southwestern South Dakota, western Texas; winters western Mexico. In PNW, uncommon, local breeder southeastern ID (Twin Falls to Caribou Counties), May–Jul; a few linger to Aug. Casual vagrant May–Nov in OR, with most records from southeastern counties (breeding suspected southern Malheur).

HABITAT ASSOCIATIONS Breeds in mixed pinyon/juniper or oak forests with scrubby understory. In PNW, limited mostly to steep slopes dominated by mountain mahogany (*Cercocarpus*) thickets from middle to fairly high elevation; also riparian strips along sagebrush ecotone. Migrants may use grassy or brushy fields.

BEHAVIOR & FEEDING Forages for arthropods by hover-gleaning, probing foliage, flycatching. Frequently bobs tail up and down, often remains low in understory. Migrants may join mixed flocks. Monogamous pair nests on ground in dense dryland vegetation. Male returns early, defends territory, singing from elevated perches. Female provides most parental care.

VOCALIZATIONS Song series of slurred trills with rapid finish similar to Nashville Warbler's, but less consistently structured. Calls include sharp chip.

First-winter Female · BC (Kaleden)—Aug
LAURE W. NEISH

Breeding Male · BC (Victoria)—May · TED ARDLEY

MacGillivray's Warbler
Geothlypis tolmiei

DESCRIPTION 5.25 in/13.5 cm. Stout billed, **gray hooded**; bright **yellow belly to undertail**. Olive dorsally with **plain wings**, bold **white eye-arcs**. *Male:* Bluish-gray hood; variably black on lores, bib. *Female:* Duller with less distinct eye-arcs; lacks black areas. *Juvenile:* Similar to female but washed brownish, throat buffy.

SIMILAR SPECIES Gray-headed forms of Orange-crowned Warbler (p. 375) show dark eyeline, obscure eye-arcs, thin bill. Nashville Warbler (p. 376) has yellow throat, complete white eye-ring. Mourning Warbler (not shown; casual in PNW) first-winter female shows indistinct eye-arcs or thin eye-ring, yellow throat, only trace of gray hood on breast.

STATUS & DISTRIBUTION Breeds in West from southern Yukon to New Mexico, winters western Mexico to Panama; disjunct sedentary population northeastern Mexico. In PNW, fairly common breeder mid-Apr–Sep from sea level to near treeline, except Haida Gwaii, Columbia Plateau, southeastern OR, southwestern ID; uncommon urbanized lowlands, near coast. Migration peaks early May, late Aug; casual Nov–Mar, mostly west of Cascades.

HABITAT ASSOCIATIONS Breeds at forest edges in dense underbrush, prefers regenerating clear-cuts, burns, Scotch broom thickets; similar early-successional habitats at other seasons.

BEHAVIOR & FEEDING Skulks low in undergrowth foraging mostly for insects. Male often sings from fairly exposed elevated perch. Migrants secretive, difficult to detect; may join mixed flocks. Monogamous pair conceals nest near ground in dense deciduous growth, often in riparian area; female provides nest care, male assists with nest defense, feeding young.

VOCALIZATIONS Song rhythmic series of buzzy trills ending lower pitched; calls include loud, sharp *tsik*.

Breeding Male · BC (Surrey)—May · MIKE D. BAILEY

Female (dull individual) · BC (Richmond)—Jun · DEBRA HERST

Female · BC (Comox)—Sep · TERRY THORMIN

Common Yellowthroat
Geothlypis trichas

DESCRIPTION 5 in/13 cm. **Plain winged**, olive dorsally with whitish-gray belly, **yellow throat**, breast, undertail. *Male:* **Black mask** bordered white above (grayish, unbordered in first year). *Female:* Lacks mask; **pale throat contrasts with dark auriculars**; may show faint eye-ring. *Juvenile:* Browner; buff wing-bars; throat lacks yellow initially, remains grayer in some first-year females.

SIMILAR SPECIES Yellow Warbler (p. 383) lacks well-defined dark auriculars that contrast sharply with pale throat. Nashville Warbler (p. 376) shows gray head, prominent eye-ring, lacks grayish belly. Orange-crowned Warbler (p. 375) has dark eyeline, thin bill.

STATUS & DISTRIBUTION Breeds central Yukon to Newfoundland, south to Mexico; winters from California, North Carolina to West Indies, Panama. In PNW, generally fairly common low- to mid-elevation breeder, but rare western Vancouver Island, absent Haida Gwaii; rare, local southeastern WA. Migrates late Mar–May, late Aug–Oct. Nov–mid-Mar, rare, sporadic, west of Cascades north to Vancouver Island; casual east of crest.

HABITAT ASSOCIATIONS Breeds in dense wetland vegetation, often dominated by cattails; also brushy fields, clear-cuts. Found in similar habitat at other seasons.

BEHAVIOR & FEEDING Creeps furtively through vegetation foraging for arthropods. Aggressively investigates intruders; may join mixed flocks in migration. Male sings from elevated perch or while rising above marsh in fluttering flight display. Usually monogamous; female constructs nest near ground in dense growth, provides nest care; male assists feeding young. May raise two broods.

VOCALIZATIONS Primary song *witchety witchety witchety*; also series of musical chirps in flight. Calls include flat *chep, tchadt*, buzzy rattle.

Female · *Manitoba—Jun* · DEBRA HERST

Subadult Male · *BC (Prince George)—Jul* · GREG DROZDA

Adult Male · *BC (Mt. Revelstoke NP)—May* · LAURE W. NEISH

American Redstart
Setophaga ruticilla

DESCRIPTION 5.25 in/13.5 cm. Long-tailed, plain-headed warbler with short bill. *Adult male:* **Black** with white belly, orange-red sides; **flashes orange-red base of primaries, base of outer rectrices** (plumage acquired second summer). *First-year male:* Gray/olive (versus black), orange yellow (versus orange red). *Female:* Head grayish, upperparts olive; **flashes yellow.**

SIMILAR SPECIES First-fall Magnolia Warbler (p. 382) shows yellow underparts; similar tail pattern but white (versus yellow) at base. Bullock's Oriole (p. 435) larger with white wing-bars.

STATUS & DISTRIBUTION Breeds southern Yukon to Newfoundland, disjunctly south to Arizona, Georgia; winters from southern California, southern Florida, Caribbean to Peru. In PNW, uncommon late May–Sep, accidental Oct–Dec. Low- to mid-elevation breeder east of Cascades/BC Coast Range, south to northern WA, northern ID, northwestern MT; rare locally to southeastern ID, northeastern OR, western WY; casual eastern slope OR Cascades. Breeds locally on westside from BC (Skeena Valley) to WA (Skagit Valley) south casually to OR (Rogue Valley); migrants rare throughout PNW.

HABITAT ASSOCIATIONS Breeds primarily deciduous forest; in PNW, prefers riparian corridors dominated by cottonwood, maple, alder, willow with shrubby understory. In migration, varied woodlands; diverse tropical sites in winter.

BEHAVIOR & FEEDING Forages flexibly, chiefly by rapidly gleaning insects from subcanopy while frequently flashing colored flight feathers; migrants eat some fruit. Defends territory year-round with calls, chases, or display, but joins mixed flocks. Monogamous (some males polygamous); female builds nest, often in sub-canopy, provides nest care; male shares feeding duties.

VOCALIZATIONS Song short, squeaky series with downslurred ending. Call rich, squeaked chip.

First-winter Female · *Utah—Jan* · RICK FRIDELL

Breeding Male · *Michigan—May* · ROBERT ROYSE

Northern Parula
Setophaga americana

DESCRIPTION 4.5 in/11.5 cm. Pudgy, short-tailed warbler; **blue gray dorsally** with yellow-green mantle patch, **white wing-bars, eye-arcs,** belly. **Yellow chin, breast.** *Male:* Blackish lores, variably dark breast band. *Female:* Duller; breast band indistinct (lacking in first-fall plumage).

SIMILAR SPECIES Smaller than other warblers with wing-bars. Additionally, Chestnut-sided (p. 384) lacks yellow underparts; fall Blackpoll (p. 385) shows faint streaking on breast, mantle; Magnolia (p. 382) has eye-ring, not eye-arcs, white band at tail base.

STATUS & DISTRIBUTION Breeds regularly from southeastern Manitoba to Maritimes, south disjunctly to Florida, eastern Texas; recently recorded breeding sporadically in coastal California, southwestern US. Winters Florida, West Indies, eastern Mexico south to Costa Rica. In PNW, rare but increasing Apr–Dec throughout region; annual primarily in OR. Records peak late May–Jun, secondarily Sep; in OR, most come from east of Cascades; in BC/WA, chiefly from coastal areas.

HABITAT ASSOCIATIONS Breeds in moderately aged to mature forest festooned with Spanish moss or *Usnea* (used for nest building); migrants use varied habitats. Winters in forested or early-successional tropical habitats.

BEHAVIOR & FEEDING Forages primarily in canopy for arthropods, gleaning or hover-gleaning from tips of branches; takes berries in migration; other plant materials, nectar in winter quarters. May forms flocks in migration; frequently joins mixed flocks. Male defends territory with song. Monogamous pair builds nest in epiphytes of canopy, shares parental care.

VOCALIZATIONS Sings rising, buzzy series terminating with sharp, clipped note or varied complex of buzzed calls; calls include sharp *cheep*.

First-winter · *Utah—Oct* · PAUL HIGGINS

Breeding Male · *Ontario—Jun* · GLENN BARTLEY

Magnolia Warbler
Setophaga magnolia

DESCRIPTION 5 in/12.5 cm. Striking ventrally; **white tail base**, undertail contrast sharply with dark tail tip, **yellow underparts.** Gray crown, **yellow rump**, white wing-bars. *Breeding male:* Black mantle, mask, necklace of blotchy breast streaks; white supercilium, wing panel. *Breeding female:* Duller than male; mask gray, back greenish. *Non-breeding (both sexes):* Mantle streaked greenish; loses wing panel, some of ventral streaking. Supercilium replaced with **white eye-ring.** *First-winter:* May lack ventral streaks.

SIMILAR SPECIES Undertail pattern eliminates other warblers. Additionally, Yellow-rumped (pp. 388–389), Chestnut-sided (p. 384) lack yellow underparts; Northern Parula (p. 381) shows eye-arcs, not eye-ring; Nashville (p. 376) lacks wing-bars.

STATUS & DISTRIBUTION Breeds southeastern Yukon to Newfoundland, south to southeastern BC, Great Smoky Mountains; winters Mexico, West Indies to Panama. In PNW, rare breeder in BC chiefly east of Coast Range south to Trout Lake; scattered summer records farther west may indicate breeding. Vagrants recorded annually across rest of region Apr–Dec, mostly east of Cascades, peaking May–early Jun (OR), Sep (elsewhere). A few summer away from breeding areas.

HABITAT ASSOCIATIONS Breeds in second-growth conifers; at other seasons, frequents diverse wooded habitats.

BEHAVIOR & FEEDING Forages by gleaning or hover-gleaning arthropods from outer branches; on migration, takes some fruit, joins mixed flocks. Male arrives early on breeding grounds, sings to attract female, delineate territory; pair builds nest in dense conifer close to trunk. Female provides nest care, pair shares feeding duties.

VOCALIZATIONS Song short, weak *sweet sweet sweeter*; calls with weak nasal *wenph*, atypical for warbler.

Yellow Warbler
Setophaga petechia

DESCRIPTION 5 in/12.5 cm. **Overall yellowish**; greener dorsally with yellow wing edging; **dark eye prominent on plain face**; yellow ventral tail spots. *Male:* Bright yellow with reddish-brown breast streaks. *Female:* Duller with **pale eye-ring**; lacks breast streaks. *Juvenile:* More grayish olive; whiter underparts; may remain drab into first winter.

SIMILAR SPECIES Orange-crowned Warbler (p. 375) has thinner bill, dark eyeline. Female Wilson's Warbler (p. 393) has dusky cap, longer tail without ventral spots. Nashville Warbler (p. 376) appears grayer dorsally with whiter eye-ring.

STATUS & DISTRIBUTION Breeds from Aleutians to northern Alaska, Newfoundland, south to Peru except most of southern US; northern races (including PNW) winter Mexico to northern South America. Common low- to mid-elevation breeder in PNW, widespread but local; on outer coast, mostly confined to river valleys, where uncommon (south) to rare (north); absent Haida Gwaii. Declined last 60 years due to cowbird parasitism, urbanization—nests scarce in cities. Migrants widespread late Apr–Jun, late Jul–Oct (peaks mid-May, early Sep).

HABITAT ASSOCIATIONS Breeds riparian woods (willow, cottonwood, alder), also shrubby edge; migrants prefer similar vegetation. Winters in diverse semi-open habitats.

BEHAVIOR & FEEDING Forages mostly in mid-canopy for arthropods by gleaning or hover-gleaning, takes some fruit. Joins mixed flocks in migration. Female builds nest, usually low, often exposed; provides nest care; when parasitized by cowbird, builds new nest atop old eggs, then lays fresh set. Male shares feeding duties.

VOCALIZATIONS Sings warbled *sweet sweet sweet I'm so sweet*; calls include thin *tsip*, loud musical chip.

Breeding Male · *BC (Vancouver)—Jul* · GREGG THOMPSON

First-winter · *Utah—Dec* · RICK FRIDELL

Chestnut-sided Warbler
Setophaga pensylvanica

DESCRIPTION 5 in/12.5 cm. Compact with stout bill, **bold wing-bars**; **white underparts**, outer rectrices. *Breeding male:* Chestnut sides, **golden cap**, streaked mantle, pied facial pattern. *Non-breeding male:* Dark-streaked, golden-green mantle, plain face, bold **white eye-ring**. *Female:* Duller, less prominently marked than comparable male plumages. *First-winter:* Lacks most streaking, chestnut; otherwise resembles non-breeding.

SIMILAR SPECIES Distinctive in all plumages. Non-breeding Magnolia Warbler (p. 382) yellow ventrally, white across tail base. Ruby-crowned Kinglet (p. 351) grayish green with whitish (not yellowish) wing-bars.

STATUS & DISTRIBUTION Breeds Alberta to Maritimes, south to Wisconsin, Pennsylvania, in Appalachians to northern Georgia; winters southern Mexico to Panama. In PNW, rare late May–Oct; records peak Jun, secondarily Sep, mostly east of Cascades/BC Coast Range, predominantly from OR, ID. Territorial birds recorded Jun–Jul in PNW, including one successful nesting at Puntchesakut Lake, BC, near northern edge of region.

HABITAT ASSOCIATIONS Breeds in shrubby areas at forest edge; migrants often use similar habitats. Winters in tropical gardens, other second-growth vegetation.

BEHAVIOR & FEEDING Distinctive posture with drooped wings, cocked tail. Forages, mostly low, for arthropods. Outside of breeding season, eats some fruit, accompanies mixed-species flocks. Male sings from elevated perch; defends territory against conspecifics, nearby Yellow Warblers. Monogamous; female builds nest in low bush, provides nest care, thwarts cowbirds by covering their eggs with nest material. Male assists with feeding young.

VOCALIZATIONS Song musical *please please please ta MEET CHA* with emphatic ending; call-note flat, low *chap.*

Breeding Male · *Alaska—Jun* · GLENN BARTLEY

First-winter · *California—Sep* · LAURE W. NEISH

Blackpoll Warbler
Setophaga striata

DESCRIPTION 5.5 in/14 cm. Bulky, short tailed. **White undertail**, streaked mantle, white wing-bars, white in outer rectrices. *Breeding male:* White underparts, black streaks on sides; **black cap, white cheek, nape; yellow legs, feet.** *Breeding female:* Like faded male; pale supercilium, dark eyeline; crown grayish, streaked. *Non-breeding (both sexes):* Streaky yellowish green; head pattern like breeding female, crown unstreaked; legs less yellow. *First-winter:* Resembles non-breeding; more vaguely streaked, often yellower.

SIMILAR SPECIES Yellow-rumped Warbler (pp. 388–389) longer tailed, yellow rump. Palm Warbler (p. 387) has yellow undertail, tail-wagging habit. Non-breeding Bay-breasted Warbler (not shown; casual in PNW) greener with dark legs, buffy undertail; often shows bay flanks.

STATUS & DISTRIBUTION Breeds across boreal zone from northern Alaska to Newfoundland, south to southeastern BC, New York; winters South America. In PNW, uncommon resident May–Sep in BC interior north from western Chilcotin, Yoho NP. Farther south in region (mostly east of Cascades/BC Coast Range), rare late Aug–Oct with first-year birds predominating; nearly absent northwestern MT, northern ID, western WY; casual late May–Jun.

HABITAT ASSOCIATIONS Breeds in wet, spruce-dominated boreal edge, often riparian willow/alder thickets; migrants use diverse wooded sites.

BEHAVIOR & FEEDING Appears comparatively sluggish while foraging for arthropods or berries. Joins mixed flocks in migration; often seen with Yellow-rumped Warblers in PNW. Bulk of population migrates to South America non-stop across Atlantic Ocean. Male often polygamous; pair may raise two broods, shares fledgling care.

VOCALIZATIONS Song rapid series of high *seet* notes, building in volume, then trailing off; calls with rich chip.

Female · BC (Penticton)—Dec · LAURE W. NEISH

Breeding Male · WA (King County)—Apr · MELISSA HAFTING

Black-throated Blue Warbler
Setophaga caerulescens

DESCRIPTION 5.25 in/13.5 cm. Unstreaked with **white patch at base of primaries** (absent on some first-winter females); highly dimorphic. ***Breeding male:*** **Dark blue dorsally** with **black mask**, throat, sides; snowy white underparts; shows white in outer rectrices. ***First-winter male:*** Veiled with green; throat feathers edged white. ***Female:*** Grayish green dorsally, olive-yellow underparts; face distinctive with **whitish malar, supercilium,** lower eye-arc.

SIMILAR SPECIES Other plain warblers distinguished from most females by lack of primary patch. Additionally, Orange-crowned (p. 375) has thinner bill, lacks whitish malar. Vireos have heavier bills, lack primary patch.

STATUS & DISTRIBUTION Breeds regularly from Great Lakes to Maritimes, south in Appalachians to northern Georgia, sporadically west to eastern Saskatchewan; winters West Indies, small numbers along Caribbean coast Mexico to Venezuela. In PNW, rare throughout, annual only in OR; appears nearly year-round with highest numbers in fall (peak Oct). Casual Jan–Aug; most winter records west of Cascades/BC Coast Range.

HABITAT ASSOCIATIONS Breeds in forest interior dominated by hardwoods; migrants appear at any wooded site; winters in dense secondary tropical forest.

BEHAVIOR & FEEDING Forages in lower strata, primarily gleaning arthropods, some fruit. Joins mixed flocks in migration; in PNW, vagrants may remain at feeding stations with suet. Male often sings from concealed perch. Monogamous pair frequently raises two broods; female builds nest near ground in dense shrub; pair bond strong, pairs often reunite following year.

VOCALIZATIONS Sings with buzzy *I'm so lay zeee* or more rapid series of rising buzzes. Call-notes sharp *chit*.

Breeding Male · *Saskatchewan—Jun* · GLENN BARTLEY

Non-breeding · *WA (King County)—Dec* · GREGG THOMPSON

Palm Warbler
Setophaga palmarum

DESCRIPTION 5.5 in/14 cm. Lanky, long tailed; flat head with **dark cap**, dark eyeline, **pale supercilium**. Obscurely streaked brownish mantle (often nearly plain); pale underparts lightly streaked. **Yellow undertail**, white tail spots. *Breeding:* Chestnut cap, yellow supercilium, throat; female duller. *Non-breeding:* Plainer; cap brown, yellow limited to undertail.

SIMILAR SPECIES Yellow-rumped Warbler (pp. 388–389) has yellow rump (versus undertail). Tail-bobbing American Pipit (p. 365) larger; undertail whitish/buffy. Sparrows show conical bill, lack yellow undertail.

STATUS & DISTRIBUTION Breeds eastern Yukon to Newfoundland, south to central Alberta, northern Wisconsin, Maine; most winter southeastern US, West Indies, Caribbean coast to Costa Rica, many fewer Pacific Coast, southwestern WA–California. In PNW, western subspecies (*S.p. palmarum*) uncommon Sep–Nov, rare Dec–May west of Cascades/BC Coast Range, primarily outer WA/OR coast; rare, widely scattered east of crest Sep–Oct, May. Casual throughout region Jun–Aug (mostly BC).

HABITAT ASSOCIATIONS Breeds in wet, semi-open, boggy areas dominated by stunted spruce; at other seasons open woodlands, weedy fields (often overrun by Scotch broom in PNW).

BEHAVIOR & FEEDING Incessantly wags tail, often walking on ground. Forages primarily for arthropods while nesting; more seeds, berries outside breeding. Forms small flocks, sometimes accompanying mixed flocks in migration; in PNW, may join Yellow-rumped Warblers or sparrows. Male sings from elevated perches on territory, infrequently in migration. Monogamous pair nests on ground in sphagnum, produces only one brood; female provides nest care.

VOCALIZATIONS Sings even-toned, buzzy trill of slurred notes; call-notes include sharp, loud *chik*.

"Audubon's" · WA (Klickitat County)—May · DAVID RENWALD

"Audubon's" Breeding Male · WA (King County)—Apr · GREGG THOMPS

"Myrtle" · Yukon Territory—May · JUKKA JANTUNEN

"Audubon's" Non-breeding · BC (Victoria)—Dec · MATTHEW CAMERON

Yellow-rumped Warbler
Setophaga coronata

DESCRIPTION 5.5 in/14 cm. **Yellow rump**, breast sides; **white tail spots**, eye-arcs; generally streaked overall with whitish belly. Juvenile heavily streaked, lacks yellow. First-winter usually browner, less streaked than adult. Two forms in PNW. *"Audubon's":* Breeding male bluish gray dorsally with black breast, **yellow throat,** whitish wing panel, yellow crown patch; female duller, plainer. Non-breeding (both sexes) brownish, plain faced except for eye-arcs. *"Myrtle":* Breeding male differs from "Audubon's" in having **black mask, white throat**, supercilium, white wing-bars (versus wing panel); female paler, less strongly marked. Non-breeding (both sexes) shows pale supercilium; **whitish throat extends below ear coverts.** Intergrades show intermediate traits (most noticeable in breeding plumage).

SIMILAR SPECIES Palm Warbler (p. 387) has yellow undertail. Townsend's Warbler (p. 390) shows yellow on face, not rump. Sparrows have stouter, conical bills, lack yellow rump. See also under Magnolia Warbler (p. 382).

STATUS & DISTRIBUTION "Audubon's" (*S.c. auduboni*) breeds from central BC, southwestern Alberta, south in mountains to southwestern US; winters to Honduras, withdrawing from coldest parts of breeding range. "Myrtle" (*S.c. coronata/hooveri*) breeds north, east of "Audubon's" from Alaska to Newfoundland, south along Appalachians to West Virginia; winters from Lower Midwest, Texas, coastally western BC, Massachusetts to Honduras. Two other sedentary races in Mexico, Guatemala. In PNW, "Audubon's" breeds commonly across forest zones (except Haida Gwaii, where rare transient); narrowly overlaps, intergrades with "Myrtle" in Rockies along both sides of crest south to about Kootenay NP. Both forms common in migration (late Mar–May, Sep–Nov); tend to move, flock separately, with most "Audubon's" gone by mid-Oct. Uncommon Dec–Feb, except "Myrtle" locally common on outer WA/OR coast; "Audubon's" fairly common but very local, e.g., central WA (Tri-Cities). Migrants showing mixed plumage reported rarely south of zone of interbreeding.

"Myrtle" Non-breeding (molting) · OR (Linn County) —Mar · MATT T. LEE

Juvenile · BC (Parksville)—Aug · MIKE YIP

"Myrtle" Breeding Male · BC (Nanaimo)—May
RALPH HOCKEN

"Myrtle" Female molting to Breeding · OR (Washington County) —Mar · RICHARD GRIFFIN

"Audubon's"

"Myrtle"

HABITAT ASSOCIATIONS Breeds primarily in mature conifers, less frequently mixed forest; at other seasons, prefers edge but uses various habitats.

BEHAVIOR & FEEDING Forages for arthropods or berries from ground to canopy, often flycatches or gleans invertebrates from foliage; in winter, principally takes fruit, in PNW preferring berries of California wax myrtle. Forms large, often single-species flocks when not breeding; fall "Audubon's" often migrates with Chipping Sparrows, Western Bluebirds. Female builds nest in conifer branches, provides nest care; male assists with feeding young.

VOCALIZATIONS Variable song, warbled two-part trill rising or falling at end. "Myrtle" call-note hard, flat *tup*; "Audubon's" weaker *chwit*. Both give rising *sip* in flight.

First-winter Female · WA (King County)—Oct · CRAIG KERNS

Breeding Male · WA (Pierce County)—Jan · GREGG THOMPSON

Hybrid Townsend's x Hermit Warbler · Arizona—Apr
JIM BURNS

Townsend's Warbler
Setophaga townsendi

DESCRIPTION 5 in/12.5 cm. Elegant; **black-and-yellow head pattern**, yellow breast with **dark side streaks**, greenish back, **white wing-bars**, whitish belly. *Male:* Black cap, cheek, bib separated by yellow. *Female:* Crown, cheek greener; bib reduced. *Juvenile:* Like female but veiled brownish; lacks bib.

SIMILAR SPECIES Black-throated Gray Warbler (p. 392) lacks yellow except pre-ocular spot. Hermit Warbler (p. 391) shows grayish mantle, unstreaked white below bib, plain yellow face—use caution with hybrids.

STATUS & DISTRIBUTION Breeds southern Alaska, Yukon to OR, western MT, ID; winters down coast from southwestern BC to Baja California, also southern Arizona to Costa Rica. In PNW, fairly common to locally common breeder in conifer-forest zones from BC south to WA, northeastern OR, central ID, northwestern MT; uncommon, local OR Cascades. In southwestern WA, western OR, replaced by Hermit Warbler, with which Townsend's frequently hybridizes in contact zones—especially eastern Olympics, southwestern WA Cascades. Migrants widespread late Apr–May, late Aug–Sep. Uncommon Oct–Mar on westside south from southwestern BC (Vancouver).

HABITAT ASSOCIATIONS Breeds in intact, relatively mature coniferous forest; absent from developed areas, arid interior, but migrants found nearly anywhere. Wintering birds often associate with cedars in PNW, montane forest in tropics.

BEHAVIOR & FEEDING Gleans or hover-gleans arthropods mostly high in conifers, rarely lower. Forms small flocks in migration; often accompanies chickadees, kinglets in mixed flocks. Pair nests on horizontal conifer branch.

VOCALIZATIONS Sings variable series of several buzzy, high, evenly pitched notes followed by thinner notes; call sharp *chip*.

Breeding Male · *WA (Thurston County)—Jul*
BOB KOTHENBEUTEL

Hybrid Hermit x Townsend's Warbler · *WA (Thurston County) Jun* · GREGG THOMPSON

Hybrid Hermit x Townsend's Warbler · *California—Dec*
GLEN TEPKE

First-winter Female · *California—Oct* · RICK FRIDELL

Hermit Warbler
Setophaga occidentalis

DESCRIPTION 5 in/12.5 cm. Plain **yellow face**, grayish mantle, white underparts, bold white wingbars. *Male:* **Black bib**, nape; throat border sharp. **Underparts plain white, mantle charcoal gray streaked black.** *Female:* Duller; tinged olive dorsally, buff ventrally; cheek duskier, bib reduced. *Juvenile:* Veiled brownish, bib absent; dull face molts to yellow by Sep.

SIMILAR SPECIES Townsend's Warbler (p. 390) with dark auriculars, streaked yellow breast, greenish back. Hybrid Hermit x Townsend's Warbler variable with mixed characters—usually Hermit-like, but breast yellowish or streaked; rarely shows dark auriculars.

STATUS & DISTRIBUTION Breeds western WA to southern California; winters central Mexico to Nicaragua, a few also coastal southern California. In PNW, breeds May–Aug west of Cascade crest: common OR, uncommon WA north to Olympics, southern Cascades. Migrants rare north of breeding range, mostly late Apr–May (casual to southwestern BC), rare east of WA/OR Cascades, casual to ID. Casual Oct–Mar in western OR. Out-of-range individuals likely to be hybrids—frequency of interbreeding with Townsend's Warbler prodigious at range interface.

HABITAT ASSOCIATIONS Breeds in mature coniferous forest; migrants use varied woodlands; winters tropical montane forest, conifers or oaks in California.

BEHAVIOR & FEEDING Forages primarily by gleaning arthropods in high conifers; may feed lower or take plant materials. Forms small flocks, often with Townsend's Warbler; also joins mixed flocks. Female builds nest in conifer, provides nest care.

VOCALIZATIONS Sings series of wheezy notes ending with pitch change, clearer than Townsend's Warbler, but some variations nearly indistinguishable; call sharp tip.

First-winter Female · BC (Sechelt)—Aug · PENNY HALL

Breeding Male · WA (Thurston County)—May · DENNIS PAULSON

Black-thoated Gray Warbler
Setophaga nigrescens

DESCRIPTION 5 in/12.5 cm. **Pied head pattern** with tiny **yellow pre-ocular spot**. White wing-bars, **gray back**; underparts show dark side streaks; tail white ventrally. *Male:* Black crown, cheek, extensive bib. *Female:* Crown, cheek grayer; throat white with bib reduced—similar to first-year male. *Juvenile:* Bib absent. Veiled brownish, buff ventrally; molts to grayer plumage by Sep.

SIMILAR SPECIES Townsend's Warbler (p. 390) yellow on face, breast; back greenish. Black-and-white Warbler (p. 373) shows white-streaked back, median crown stripe.

STATUS & DISTRIBUTION Two races, genetically divergent but similar in appearance; vocalizations differ. Coastal race breeds southwestern BC to northern California; Southwestern race southern California to southern WY, New Mexico. Winters southern California to Oaxaca. In PNW, coastal race fairly common breeder Apr–Sep west of Cascades/BC Coast Range north at least to Vancouver Island, mostly at low elevations. Uncommon, local breeder east of crest OR, southern WA to southern ID, at least partly Southwestern race but more study needed. Migrants linger to Oct, rare on eastside. Casual western lowlands Nov–Mar.

HABITAT ASSOCIATIONS Deciduous, mixed forest western WA, northern OR; oak woodlands, chaparral southwestern OR; juniper ridges southeastern OR, ID; many other habitats, including urban parks in migration.

BEHAVIOR & FEEDING Gleans, hover-gleans, sallies for insects in understory, lower canopy. Joins mixed flocks in migration. Pairs apparently monogamous; raise single brood.

VOCALIZATIONS Male delivers song from hidden or exposed perches—husky series of buzzy notes, often with emphatic ending. Calls include dull *chup*, rising *zipt* flight call.

Breeding Male · *WA (King County)—May* · GREGG THOMPSON

Female · *WA (King County)—May* · CRAIG KERNS

Wilson's Warbler
Cardellina pusilla

DESCRIPTION 4.75 in/12 cm. Brilliant; **yellow** ventrally with **plain face**, greenish dorsally with **plain wings**. Subspecies *C.p. chryseola* vivid golden yellow, forehead tinged ocher; *C.p. pileolata* averages paler. *Male:* Round **inky-black cap**. *Female:* Cap less distinct, less blackish.

SIMILAR SPECIES Yellow Warbler female (p. 383) has shorter tail, lacks contrasting dark cap. Orange-crowned Warbler (p. 375) bill thinner; shows dark eyeline, obscure breast streaks.

STATUS & DISTRIBUTION Two Western subspecies breed Alaska, Yukon to southwestern US: *chryseola* southwestern BC to southern California, tidewater to coastal ranges, Cascades, Sierra Nevada; *pileolata* Alaska south through intermountain region, Rockies. Both winter Mexico to Panama. In PNW, *chryseola* common westside breeder away from urban areas late Apr–Sep. *Pileolata* fairly common breeder interior BC, uncommon east of Cascades farther south, principally in moist, higher-elevation fir zones; common migrant (May–early Jun, late Aug–Sep) throughout. Rarely winters, but stragglers (subspecies undetermined) regular Oct–Dec. PNW status of eastern-breeding *C.p. pusilla* uncertain.

HABITAT ASSOCIATIONS Diverse-aged mixed moist forests with dense undergrowth, often riparian; migrants use all habitats; winters forest, less commonly edge habitats.

BEHAVIOR & FEEDING Flits through foliage at various heights, frequently flicking wings, tail; sallies, gleans twigs for arthropods, takes some plant material. Sings constantly in migration; may accompany mixed flocks. Usually monogamous. Female builds nest on or near ground in shrub, mossy depression, provides nest care; male assists feeding. Coastal race may double-brood.

VOCALIZATIONS Song emphatic series of slurred chips building in volume, speed; call nasal *timp*, atypical for warbler.

Yellow-breasted Chat
Icteria virens

DESCRIPTION 7.5 in/19 cm. Differs from typical warblers in many ways: oversized, long-tailed, **stout tanager-like bill**. Western subspecies (*I.v. auricollis*) plain grayish-green mantle; **bright yellow breast**, throat; **dark lores, white spectacles**, malar. White from belly to undertail. *Male:* Cheek blackish. *Female:* Cheek grayer.

SIMILAR SPECIES Common Yellowthroat (p. 379) smaller, bill thin; male with extensive black mask. Bullock's Oriole (p. 435) shows white wing-bars, no white on face.

STATUS & DISTRIBUTION Subspecies *auricollis* breeds scattered westward to Pacific from Saskatchewan, Plains states, west Texas, south to central Mexico; winters southern Baja California to Oaxaca. In PNW, arrives late Apr; locally common breeder in shrub-steppe/ponderosa pine ecotone eastward from Cascades in south-central BC, WA, central OR, becoming uncommon eastern OR, ID; rare, local northwestern MT. West of crest, rare in WA; uncommon (Willamette Valley) to fairly common (Rogue Valley) in OR. Migrants rare away from breeding localities, mostly in eastside riparian migrant traps (late Aug–Sep). Eastern-breeding *I.v. virens* not recorded PNW.

HABITAT ASSOCIATIONS Dense deciduous growth with open canopy, often riparian thickets.

BEHAVIOR & FEEDING Skulks in thick cover. Diet arthropods, fruits; sometimes holds food in feet. Male most visible during short, twisting, tail-pumping display flights, legs dangling, singing, often with exaggerated wingbeats. Generally monogamous; female builds bulky well-concealed nest near ground, provides nest care; male shares feeding duties.

VOCALIZATIONS Male sings day or night from concealed perch, remarkable series of squawks, rasping gurgles, rattles, whistles, interspersed with long pauses; female growls, scolds near nest.

Nest • OR (Jackson County)—Jul • DAMON CALDERWOOD

OR (Jackson County)—Feb • MATT T. LEE

California Towhee
Melozone crissalis

DESCRIPTION 9 in/23 cm. Stout. **Very long tail**, gray conical bill. **Plain grayish** overall with **cinnamon undertail**, eye-ring, facial wash; necklace of barely visible short streaks. *Juvenile:* Ventral streaking, rusty dorsal-feather edging.

SIMILAR SPECIES Wrentit (p. 348) smaller with thin bill, pale iris. Gray Catbird (p. 360) shows black cap, thin bill. All sparrows much shorter tailed. Other juvenile PNW towhees (pp. 396–397) heavily streaked, including upperparts.

STATUS & DISTRIBUTION Sedentary resident from southwestern OR to southern Baja California; disjunct northern population endemic to north-central California (Siskiyou, Modoc Counties), southwestern OR (Josephine, Jackson, Douglas, Klamath Counties). In PNW, fairly common resident in Rogue, Applegate, Illinois Valleys; uncommon Klamath Basin to Umpqua Valley.

HABITAT ASSOCIATIONS Arid upland (but not desert) sites, including chaparral, riparian, scrub-oak, sagebrush, low-density residential. In PNW, limited to low- to mid-elevation chaparral habitat; favors oak-chaparral ecotone rich with manzanita, ceanothus, or other scrubby plants.

BEHAVIOR & FEEDING Forages sluggishly, mostly on ground, predominantly for seeds, some fruit; takes more arthropods while nesting. Scratches ground with both feet, or gleans seeds from stalks. Generally does not flock. Monogamous pair forms lifelong bond. Male sings from elevated perches, abruptly ceasing with onset of nesting; female builds nest near ground in shrub or tree (often in poison oak), provides nest care. Pair often raises two broods per year.

VOCALIZATIONS Song accelerating series of sharp chips with warbled finish; calls include loud, rich *tchink*; thin buzzy *seeet*; pairs duet with squeals.

Green-tailed Towhee
Pipilo chlorurus

DESCRIPTION 7.25 in/18 cm. Slate-colored conical bill, **chestnut cap**; grayish overall with **golden-green highlights on wings, tail**; **white throat**, malar. *Juvenile:* Heavily streaked; flight feathers faintly olive greenish; lacks rufous cap.

SIMILAR SPECIES Spotted Towhee (p. 397) larger; lacks any trace of green. Larger California Towhee (p. 395) juvenile lacks bold streaking, greenish upperparts. All sparrows show proportionately shorter tails.

STATUS & DISTRIBUTION Interior breeder from southeastern WA, MT to northern Baja California, western Texas; winters southern California, central Texas to central Mexico. In PNW, locally fairly common May–Sep; breeds in mountains east of Cascades (eastern OR, southern, central ID, western WY; rare, local Blue Mountains of WA, absent northwestern MT), uncommonly on westside in OR (Umpqua NF, Siskiyous). Casual away from breeding sites (fall migrants, wintering individuals); spring overshoots casual (May–Jul) across region north to southern BC.

HABITAT ASSOCIATIONS Breeds in dense shrubs, disturbed montane forest edges, often at shrub-steppe ecotone, frequently on sloping terrain in PNW; at other seasons, uses any dense, brushy cover.

BEHAVIOR & FEEDING Forages by scratching ground with both feet or gleaning from low shrubs; takes predominantly seeds, insects; fewer fruits, other arthropods; may join mixed flocks for open-ground foraging. Male defends territory against other towhees, sympatric Fox Sparrows; female builds nest near ground in impenetrable shrub, provides nest care; male assists fledgling feeding, defense.

VOCALIZATIONS Sings rich, jumbled series—begins with slurred whistles, ends with trills; calls include ascending catlike *me oww*, high, sharp *tink* in alarm.

Juvenile · *BC (West Vancouver)—Aug* · ALICE SUN

Male Interior · *ID (Oneida County)—Jun* · DARREN CLARK

Female Pacific slope · *OR (Washington County)—Dec* · GREG GILLSON

Spotted Towhee
Pipilo maculatus

DESCRIPTION 8.25 in/21 cm. Dark conical bill, red eye; **dark hood, white-flecked dark upperparts** contrast with **rufous sides, white belly**; outer tail corners flash white in flight. Coastal forms duller; interior forms show heavy white dorsal flecks, larger tail spots. *Male:* Black hood, mantle. *Female:* Slate gray replaces black. *Juvenile:* Heavily streaked, lacks hood.

SIMILAR SPECIES Dark-eyed Junco (pp. 418–419) smaller, bill pinkish, lacks white flecking. Smaller juvenile Lark Sparrow (p. 403) shows faint facial pattern; white extends entire length of outer rectrices.

STATUS & DISTRIBUTION Breeds from southern BC to Saskatchewan, south to Guatemala; northern interior birds move south in winter. In PNW, common resident sea level to moderate elevation west of Cascades/BC Coast Range north to northern Vancouver Island. East of crest, fairly common locally Mar–Oct in brushy habitat north to central BC (Cariboo–Chilcotin), uncommon to northwestern MT; uncommon Nov–Feb (rarer northern, eastern parts of region). Interior form (three subspecies) intergrades with coastal form (two subspecies) in Cascades.

HABITAT ASSOCIATIONS Coastal form widespread breeder in overgrown fields, shrubby understory of open-canopy woodland including backyards; interior populations limited to riparian or deciduous thickets. Uses similar sites outside of breeding.

BEHAVIOR & FEEDING Forages by scratching vigorously with both feet on ground for seeds, arthropods, fruits; rarely takes lizards. Typically non-gregarious, but may accompany other emberizids. Female builds nest, provides nest care; male sings from treetop, partakes in fledgling care.

VOCALIZATIONS Sings variable buzzy trill; calls include *siee*, nasal *miahh*, rising *schreeee* in alarm.

BC (Richmond)—Mar • PAUL KUSMIN

WA (Grant County)—Nov • DOUG SCHURMAN

American Tree Sparrow
Spizelloides arborea

DESCRIPTION 6 in/15 cm. Fairly long tailed. **Colorful**; rusty cap, grayish face, rufous line through eye, **bicolored conical bill** yellowish below. Streaked mantle, **unstreaked breast with dark central spot**. *Juvenile:* Duller with blackish ventral streaking; lacks bold wingbars (plumage not seen in PNW).

SIMILAR SPECIES Chipping Sparrow (p. 399) smaller, duller; adult has blackish eyeline; lacks breast spot, bold white wing-bars, strongly bicolored bill. Immature White-crowned Sparrow (p. 416) larger; bill evenly pale, appears flat headed with pale median crown stripe.

STATUS & DISTRIBUTION Breeds from northern Alaska to Labrador, south to northern BC; winters from southern BC to Nova Scotia, south to northern Texas. In PNW, irregular migrant, winter visitor; uncommon late Oct–early Apr east of Cascades/BC Coast Range; rare south to OR (Malheur NWR); a few linger casually May–Sep (mostly BC). West of crest, rare south to Willamette Valley; occurs casually along coast south to OR (Curry County).

HABITAT ASSOCIATIONS Breeds in Arctic scrub, shrubby tundra. Migrants, wintering birds use thickets, overgrown fields, hedgerows, primarily lowlands to middle elevation.

BEHAVIOR & FEEDING Forages on ground, mostly for weed or grass seeds in PNW; more arthropods on taiga. Takes a few fruits, also gleans seeds off stalks. Forms large flocks, although PNW assemblages seldom exceed 20; also accompanies other sparrows. Female builds nest on or near ground, provides nest care.

VOCALIZATIONS Song complex musical jumble, seldom heard in PNW. Calls include *tsee* in flight; trilled *zidle dew*, resembling tinkling bells when given with many flock mates.

Breeding · BC (Champion Lakes)—May · GORDON F. BROWN

Breeding · BC (Richmond)—May · LIRON GERSTMAN

Juvenile · BC (Penticton)—Jul · LAURE W. NEISH

Non-breeding · WA (Spokane County)—Sep · TOM MUNSON

Chipping Sparrow
Spizella passerina

DESCRIPTION 5.5 in/14 cm. **Slim**, long tailed, with streaked mantle, gray rump, **unstreaked gray breast**, conical bill. ***Breeding:*** Chestnut cap, broad white supercilium, black **line through eye**; blackish bill. ***Non-breeding:*** Face duller, brownish-pink bill, brown eyeline; cap dull, streaked. ***Juvenile:*** Like non-breeding, with streaked breast.

SIMILAR SPECIES American Tree Sparrow (p. 398) colorful with central breast spot, rufous eyeline, bold white wing-bars. Clay-colored Sparrow (p. 400) shows pale lores, stronger facial pattern, brown (versus gray) rump, white median crown stripe. Brewer's Sparrow (p. 401) appears grayer with plainer face, pale lores, bold eye-ring.

STATUS & DISTRIBUTION Breeds from central Alaska to southern Newfoundland, south to Nicaragua; winters southward from Arizona, Virginia. In PNW, absent from closed-canopy forest; common breeder east of Cascades/BC Coast Range, except WA Columbia Plateau, other treeless zones; west of crest, more local—uncommon north to eastern Vancouver Island, most common in high-elevation open forests. Absent Haida Gwaii southward along outer coast to southern OR. Migrants ubiquitous, but scarce on westside; winters casually, mostly in western OR.

HABITAT ASSOCIATIONS Prefers drier, open grassy sites including urbanized areas, often associated with open conifers in interior, oaks in westside valleys (OR/WA).

BEHAVIOR & FEEDING Forages on or near ground for seeds, also arthropods, fruit. Gathers into large flocks outside of breeding season, often with bluebirds, warblers, other songbirds. Male arrives early to nesting territory; pair builds nest low in conifer, often with animal hair, shares duties.

VOCALIZATIONS Song mechanical extended trill on one pitch; calls include sharp *chip*, thin *seet*.

Clay-colored Sparrow
Spizella pallida

DESCRIPTION 5.25 in/13.5 cm. Slim, **long-tailed**, streaked-backed sparrow with **unstreaked grayish breast**, clean gray nape, pink conical bill. *Breeding:* Dark cap divided by **whitish crown stripe**; dark-bordered brown auriculars set off by **whitish malar**, white supercilium. *Non-breeding:* More buff colored. *Juvenile:* Like non-breeding; sparsely streaked breast molts to plain buff by Sep.

SIMILAR SPECIES Brewer's Sparrow (p. 401) shows bold eye-ring, lacks distinct central crown stripe, strong facial pattern. Chipping Sparrow (p. 399) appears shorter tailed with dark lores, gray (versus brown) rump; rear auricular border tends to be indistinct.

STATUS & DISTRIBUTION Breeds from central BC, Northwest Territories to New York, south to WY; most winter from Texas to Oaxaca. In PNW, range expanding; uncommon to rare year-round (migrant peak early Sep) but casual most of ID, eastern OR. Uncommon breeder May–Aug in eastern BC, locally fairly common northwestern MT, uncommon/rare northeastern WA, rare/casual Idaho Panhandle. Nov–Apr, rare west of Cascades, accidental in interior.

HABITAT ASSOCIATIONS Breeds in old fields, riparian scrubland, ponderosa pine savannah, other open sites; migrants use similar habitats. Desert scrub in winter range.

BEHAVIOR & FEEDING Forages on ground for seeds, insects. Forms flocks, often mixed with other sparrows—in westside PNW, frequently *Zonotrichia*. May hybridize with other *Spizella* at range periphery. Male sings persistently throughout hot days, rarely at night; also defends territory against other sparrow species. Female builds nest low in shrub, male assists with nest care.

VOCALIZATIONS Sings with series of 2–6 long, raspy, buzzing calls; calls include *tssip*, sharp, harder chip.

Brewer's Sparrow
Spizella breweri

DESCRIPTION 5.25 in/13.5 cm. **Slight**, long tailed, appears drab overall with streaked mantle, **unstreaked breast**; tiny, conical, pinkish bill; **white eye-ring**, white malar, grayish supercilium. "Timberline" subspecies larger, darker; shows stronger facial markings. *Juvenile:* Streaked breast molts to plain buff before Sep.

SIMILAR SPECIES Clay-colored Sparrow (p. 400) shows bold facial pattern, central crown stripe. Chipping Sparrow (p. 399) browner with dark lores; appears larger bodied. Larger Vesper Sparrow (p. 402) shows upper-breast streaking, white outer rectrices.

STATUS & DISTRIBUTION Breeds in interior from west-central Alaska disjunctly to southern California, east to southwestern Kansas; winters southern California to central Mexico. Two subspecies in PNW. Nominate *S.b. breweri* common breeder Apr–Sep east of Cascades/BC Coast Range in low- to mid-elevation sagebrush-dominated locales; west of Cascades, casual migrant south to OR. *S.b. taverneri* ("Timberline" Sparrow) breeds above treeline in Alberta Rockies, southeastern BC, northwestern MT (Glacier NP); migrants casual elsewhere. Subspecific identity of individuals rarely summering at high elevations farther south (to Rogue Valley) remains uncertain.

HABITAT ASSOCIATIONS Nominate race breeds moist, big-sagebrush-dominated shrub-steppe, usually above hottest valleys; "Timberline" race at grassy, shrub-dominated sites. Diverse steppe at other seasons.

BEHAVIOR & FEEDING Gleans arthropods from shrubs; takes more seeds in winter. Migrants form flocks, move to open sites, often accompany other sparrows. Males arrive first on nesting grounds, form densely packed territories in prime habitats. Nest built in shrub crown, pair shares duties.

VOCALIZATIONS Sings extended buzzy song; longer type with variously pitched trills, rasps. Calls include weak *tsip*.

Juvenile · WA (King County)—Oct · DOUG SCHURMAN | BC (Okanagan Falls)—Aug · LAURE W. NEISH

Vesper Sparrow
Pooecetes gramineus

DESCRIPTION 6 in/15 cm. Medium sized with pinkish bill, streaked mantle, often-hidden chestnut shoulder patch; ventral streaking mostly confined to upper breast. Long **notched tail**, dark with **white outer rectrices**. Distinctive facial pattern formed by brown auriculars, **white malar**, bold **white eye-ring**. Westside subspecies *P.g. affinis* smaller on average, shorter tailed. *Juvenile:* Lacks chestnut shoulder.

SIMILAR SPECIES Savannah Sparrow (p. 408) shorter tailed; crown stripe, supercilium prominent, often yellowish; lacks white rectrices. Sagebrush Sparrow (p. 405) adult grayer headed, breast plain with central spot; juvenile evenly streaked ventrally. Dark-eyed Junco (pp. 418–419) juveniles appear browner, plain faced.

STATUS & DISTRIBUTION Breeds from BC to Nova Scotia south to southern California, eastern Tennessee; winters California, South Carolina south to Oaxaca. In PNW, common Mar–Oct east of Cascades/BC Coast Range; breeds mid- to high elevations north to Vanderhoof, BC. Declining *P.g. affinis* uncommon lowlands-to-foothills breeder western OR—Rogue, Willamette Valleys, also along coast north to Bandon; rare, extremely local north to Vancouver Island (Nanaimo); state-endangered in WA, mostly extirpated as breeder south of Olympia. Rare westside migrant (less frequent fall), often to higher elevation; casual into winter north to southwestern BC.

HABITAT ASSOCIATIONS Breeds in semi-moist grassland, degraded shrub-steppe, other open areas; often at Christmas-tree farms (western OR).

BEHAVIOR & FEEDING Forages on ground for arthropods, seeds; flocks in migration. Male may sing long flight song. Female builds ground nest; male shares feeding duties. Pair sometimes raises two broods.

VOCALIZATIONS Musical song two long whistles followed by series of jumbled trills; calls include chip, rising *seeet*.

OR (Harney County)—May · KURT LINDSAY

First-winter · Alberta—Jul · CHRIS CHARLESWORTH

Lark Sparrow
Chondestes grammacus

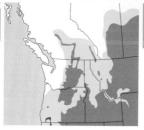

DESCRIPTION 6.5 in/16.5 cm. Robust; streaked mantle, pale wing-bars; **central spot on plain whitish-gray underparts;** long **rounded tail uniquely bordered with white;** grayish bill. **Complex head pattern** formed by chestnut auriculars, divided crown, lateral throat stripe. *Juvenile:* Streaked ventrally into Sep; head plumage dull through winter.

SIMILAR SPECIES Vesper Sparrow (p. 402) plainer headed; less white on notched tail. Sagebrush Sparrow (p. 405) auriculars gray, less white in tail. Clay-colored Sparrow (p. 400) smaller; lacks white in tail.

STATUS & DISTRIBUTION Breeds southern interior BC to Indiana, south to northern Mexico; winters from southwestern OR disjunctly to Oaxaca. In PNW, fairly common low- to moderate-elevation breeder east of Cascades/BC Coast Range north to south-central BC (Okanagan), rarely Cariboo–Chilcotin; uncommon, local northwestern MT. Occurs mostly May–Aug, arriving earlier OR. West of Cascades, fairly common Rogue Valley year-round resident; rarely nests north to Umpqua Valley; migrants rare OR, casual WA, BC. Casual in winter away from Rogue Valley.

HABITAT ASSOCIATIONS Breeds in degraded steppe, preferring cheatgrass-dominated grassland; fewer in woodland glades. Uses fallow fields, hedgerows at other seasons.

BEHAVIOR & FEEDING Forages on ground, primarily for seeds; takes insects while nesting. Often flushes high into air rather than diving to nearby cover. Gregarious even during nesting season; may accompany other sparrows in migration. Male arrives early to territory; courtship includes turkey-like strutting, twig passing. Female builds ground nest but pair may reuse old nests.

VOCALIZATIONS Sings choppy series of diverse trills often mixed with harsh *churr.* Calls include *tsip,* sharp *pink.*

Black-throated Sparrow
Amphispiza bilineata

DESCRIPTION 5.5 in/14 cm. Long tailed, with white in outer rectrices; **unstreaked** grayish mantle, lighter underparts; bluish-gray bill. **Black bib**, dark auriculars set off **white supercilium, malar**, to form elegant head pattern. *Juvenile:* Lacks bib; faintly streaked.

SIMILAR SPECIES No other PNW sparrow shows similar head pattern. Sagebrush Sparrow (p. 405) larger with central breast spot; supercilium less bold; lacks black bib.

STATUS & DISTRIBUTION Core breeding range extends from southeastern OR to central Mexico, irregularly north to south-central WA; winters southern Nevada southward through breeding range. Barely recorded in PNW through early 1900s (perhaps overlooked due to small numbers, absence some years); now uncommon breeder southwestern ID to southeastern OR (highly variable numbers Alvord, Warner Valley slopes); rare, irregular north to WA (central Columbia Plateau), seemingly expanding northward with breeding now suspected south-central BC (Osoyoos). Peak arrival late May, usually departs by Aug; overshoots casual west of Cascades May–early Jun, north to Vancouver Island. Accidental in winter.

HABITAT ASSOCIATIONS Breeds arid, rocky slopes; in PNW, often highly degraded shrub-steppe.

BEHAVIOR & FEEDING Forages on ground for seeds; eats insects in nesting season. Rarely drinks, thanks to specially adapted kidneys. Forms small migrant flocks, often arriving in groups to peripheral nesting areas; northward irruptions possibly tied to drought conditions in core range. Male sings from elevated perch, also during foraging. Pairs appear monogamous, build nest in low shrub; female provides nest care, male assists with fledglings.

VOCALIZATIONS Sings mechanical series of tinkled trills; calls include sharp *teep*, *chweep* in flight.

WA (Grant County)—Apr · GREGG THOMPSON

Sagebrush Sparrow
Artemisiospiza nevadensis

DESCRIPTION 6 in/15 cm. Plain **gray head**, streaked brownish mantle, bluish-gray bill, **plain whitish breast** with **dark central spot**; white supraloral, eye-ring, malar; long tail dark with white-edged outer rectrices. *Juvenile:* Similar but streaked brownish overall; buffy wing-bars.

SIMILAR SPECIES Black-throated Sparrow (p. 404) smaller with bold supercilium, lacks breast spot; adult shows bib. Lark Sparrow (p. 403) with complex facial pattern, more white in tail. Vesper Sparrow (p. 402) shows streaked breast, lacks gray head.

STATUS & DISTRIBUTION Breeds eastern WA, WY south to central California, northwestern New Mexico; winters southern Nevada to northern Mexico. Declining in PNW but locally common Feb–Oct east of Cascades in remaining appropriate habitat north to western WY, southern ID, central WA; casual Nov–Jan. Migrants rarely found away from breeding sites (casual north to south-central BC); casual vagrant Feb–Apr west of Cascades north to southwestern BC (Vancouver). In 2013, former "Sage" Sparrow split into Sagebrush Sparrow, Bell's Sparrow of coastal California, Baja.

HABITAT ASSOCIATIONS Breeds in semi-open areas; in PNW, big-sagebrush-dominated landscapes. Winters sagebrush, scrublands, grasslands; vagrants use open fields.

BEHAVIOR & FEEDING Forages on ground for seeds year-round, insects during nesting season; may form small flocks post-breeding. Monogamous pair arrives to territory together; male sings from elevated perches while female builds nest in shrub crown, rarely bunchgrass or on ground. Female provides nest care; male helps feed young.

VOCALIZATIONS Sings jumbled series of buzzy phrases reminiscent of subdued Western Meadowlark; calls include sharp *tink*.

First-winter Male · *Utah—Feb* · RICK FRIDELL

Female · *Colorado—May* · STEVEN G. MLODINOW

Breeding Male · *Alberta—Jun* · GERALD ROMANCHUK

Lark Bunting
Calamospiza melanocorys

DESCRIPTION 6.75 in/17 cm. Stocky sparrow with **large head**, short **white-tipped tail, robust bluish-gray bill**; white **wing patch** formed by coverts. *Male:* Breeding (Mar–Jul) black except white in wing, tail. Non-breeding blackish-brown dorsally, whitish underparts heavily streaked, often blotched blackish; whitish post-ocular stripe. *Female:* Browner than non-breeding male; lacks blotching. *Juvenile:* Resembles female; more buff overall, including wing patch; male attains some black plumage over first winter.

SIMILAR SPECIES Longspurs (pp. 368–369), other sparrows appear small headed, smaller billed; lack white wing patch. Purple Finch (p. 440) lacks wing patch. Male Bobolink (p. 425) shows white back, scapulars.

STATUS & DISTRIBUTION Breeds southern Prairie Provinces to northern Texas; winters Oklahoma Panhandle to central Mexico, Baja California. In PNW, periodically irrupts to western WY, southeastern ID, where breeding rare; otherwise casual vagrant—in interior predominantly May–Jul, on westside primarily Aug–Oct (most from WA/OR outer coast). Casual western OR in winter.

HABITAT ASSOCIATIONS Breeds in open grasslands, shrub-steppe, agricultural fields; uses similar areas at other seasons.

BEHAVIOR & FEEDING Forages on ground in open for arthropods, seeds, other plant materials. Highly gregarious; forms large flocks with southbound diurnal migration beginning by Jul, often over mountain passes. Breeds in loose colonies with multiple males performing aggressive flight displays while singing; male aggression diminishes greatly once territories established. Pairs usually monogamous but polygamy also occurs. Female selects site; pair builds nest, shares nesting duties.

VOCALIZATIONS Sings with repetitive liquid, whistled twittering; calls include low muffled *hewk*.

WA (Grant County)—Jun • GREGG THOMPSON

Juvenile • WA (Lincoln County)—Aug • TOM MUNSON

Grasshopper Sparrow
Ammodramus savannarum

DESCRIPTION 5 in/13 cm. **Flat headed** with large bill, short tail; mantle scalloped rufous, underparts plain buff. Ocher supraloral spot; **dark crown divided by white median stripe**. Vague post-ocular line, **white eye-ring** impart plain-faced look. *Juvenile:* Duller; breast streaked.

SIMILAR SPECIES Savannah Sparrow (p. 408) smaller billed, streaked more heavily than juvenile Grasshopper. Longer-tailed Clay-colored Sparrow (p. 400) shows bold face pattern. Lincoln's Sparrow (p. 410) shows strong eyeline, crisply streaked upper breast.

STATUS & DISTRIBUTION Breeds locally from southern BC to Maine, south disjunctly to Panama, Caribbean; winters southern California, Virginia, southward through breeding range. In PNW, fairly common but local breeder late Apr–Aug east of Cascades from south-central BC (Okanagan) to WA/OR Blue Mountains; irregular southeastern OR, rare ID, northwestern MT. Virtually unrecorded in migration. West of Cascades, breeds locally in Rogue, Willamette Valleys; territorial birds appear north casually to southwestern BC (Vancouver); accidental Oct–Jan.

HABITAT ASSOCIATIONS Breeds in open grasslands with sparse shrubs, bare ground—in PNW, mostly grassy, degraded shrub-steppe. Winters in diverse grasslands.

BEHAVIOR & FEEDING Feeds on ground, taking seeds, more insects in summer, including many grasshoppers. Often runs on ground; does not flock. PNW populations nomadic in response to rainfall or fire. Female builds domed ground nest, male sings from elevated perch or during flight display. Monogamous pair may be assisted by nest helpers; often raises two broods

VOCALIZATIONS Song opens *tik tik tik*, then very high, drawn-out, insect-like buzz; alternate song complex. Calls include trill, *tilik*, sharp *tik*.

Savannah Sparrow
Passerculus sandwichensis

DESCRIPTION 5.5 in/13.5 cm. PNW races small billed; **streaked overall** except white belly. **Short, notched tail**; whitish median crown stripe, **pale supercilium**; pinkish bill, legs. *Breeding:* Supercilium brighter—yellowish with bright-yellow supraloral. *Juvenile:* Buff-tinged breast; head pattern obscure.

SIMILAR SPECIES Lincoln's Sparrow (p. 410) gray headed with buff (versus white) malar, finer breast streaks. Song Sparrow (p. 409) larger with longer, rounded tail, heavier breast streaks, darker lateral throat stripe. Chipping Sparrow (p. 399) juvenile longer tailed; lacks dark throat stripe.

STATUS & DISTRIBUTION Breeds northern Alaska to Newfoundland, south in eastern US to northern Georgia, in mountains to Nicaragua; most winter California, Maryland southward through breeding range. In PNW, common breeder in appropriate habitat throughout except Haida Gwaii. Numbers decline Nov–Feb, when common westside only in Rogue Valley, uncommon OR/WA lowlands farther north, rare southwestern BC; casual east of Cascades north to Okanagan except rare/uncommon south-central WA, locally eastern OR; absent western WY. Migration prolonged (peaks late Apr–May, late Sep).

HABITAT ASSOCIATIONS Open grassland, agricultural fields, salt marsh at all seasons, but may occur out of habitat during migration (often on roadsides).

BEHAVIOR & FEEDING Walks on ground foraging for insects, seeds, other plant materials; less frequently feeds in branches. Migrants form post-breeding flocks numbering into hundreds. Can be monogamous or polygynous. Female builds concealed ground nest, provides nest care. Pair defends nest, feeds fledglings together; often raises second brood.

VOCALIZATIONS Variable song begins *ti ti ti*, ends with progressively lower-pitched buzzes. Calls include sharp *stik*, thin *tsew*.

Interior · *ID (Fremont County)—Jan* · DARREN CLARK

Pacific slope · *OR (Washington County)—Feb* · GREG GILLSON

Interior · *OR (Harney County)—May* · GREG GILLSON

Song Sparrow
Melospiza melodia

DESCRIPTION 6.25 in/16 cm. Streaked brownish overall with **long, rounded tail**; dark, **dense streaking** usually merges into central spot on whitish breast. Head pattern distinctive—wide, **gray supercilium**; dark eyeline, gray central crown stripe, heavy lateral throat stripe. Coastal forms darker, larger. *Juvenile:* Head stripes vague; shows eye-ring, buff-tinged breast.

SIMILAR SPECIES Fox Sparrow (pp. 412–413) bulky, plain headed; chevron-shaped ventral spots. Savannah Sparrow (p. 408) smaller; short, notched tail. Lincoln's Sparrow (p. 410) finely streaked with buff upper breast. Vesper Sparrow's (p. 402) outer rectrices white. Swamp Sparrow (p. 411) has vaguely streaked grayish underparts, bright rusty wings.

STATUS & DISTRIBUTION Breeds from Aleutians to Newfoundland, south to northwestern Mexico, northern Georgia; withdraws from northern interior in winter. In PNW, at least seven subspecies breed or winter. Common resident throughout to higher elevations; populations in mountains, northern areas migratory. Migration begins by Feb, southbound Aug–Oct; influx of northern migrants obscures status of year-round lowland residents.

HABITAT ASSOCIATIONS Breeds shrubs, thickets in wetter areas; uses diverse habitats including cities. Interior populations more concentrated into riparian habitats.

BEHAVIOR & FEEDING Adaptable omnivore, foraging on ground or foliage frequently near water, mostly for invertebrates, plant material. Pumps tail in flight; flocks in migration, often with other sparrows. Usually monogamous, sometimes polygamous. Westside nesting begins by late winter; female builds nest on or near ground, male provides most fledgling care while female starts second brood.

VOCALIZATIONS Song begins with clear notes followed by jumbled trill; calls include nasal *chimp*, thin *seet*.

OR (Jefferson County)—Sep · JACK WILLIAMSON

BC (Penticton)—Apr · LAURE W. NEISH

Lincoln's Sparrow
Melospiza lincolnii

DESCRIPTION 5.75 in/14.5 cm. Trim; fairly short tail, slender bill. Streaked dorsally; **finely streaked buffy breast** (may show central spot) ends abruptly at white belly. Brown crown divided by pale median stripe; **buff malar**, eye-ring; **grayish supercilium**. *Juvenile:* Supercilium obscured by dark streaks.

SIMILAR SPECIES Song Sparrow (p. 409) larger with coarse breast streaks. Savannah Sparrow (p. 408) shows whitish or yellowish supercilium. Swamp Sparrow (p. 411) has bright rusty upperwing coverts, lacks strong breast streaking.

STATUS & DISTRIBUTION Breeds from Alaska to Newfoundland south to Vermont, in mountains to southern California; winters from southwestern BC, Arkansas to Honduras. In PNW, fairly common breeder May–Sep; nests mostly at higher elevations but also in northwestern MT valleys, to sea level in BC. Migrants common (mid-Apr–May, late Aug–Oct) west of Cascades/BC Coast Range, fairly common east of crest; locally common Nov–Mar in westside lowlands, rare east to southwestern ID, casual eastern BC.

HABITAT ASSOCIATIONS Breeds willow-lined scrubby meadows, bogs; wet clearcuts, burns in BC; prefers open, wet, grassy places at all seasons, but spring migrants use woodlands.

BEHAVIOR & FEEDING Forages secretively, mostly on ground, often in thick cover; takes arthropods, fewer seeds. Flocks loosely in migration with other sparrows. Perches conspicuously when disturbed, often erecting crest. Monogamous pair nests on ground within dense shrub; male sings from exposed perch.

VOCALIZATIONS Song extended series of bubbly musical trills, offered only on nesting grounds; calls include sharp *chik*, thin *seeet*; buzzy chatter during territorial squabbles.

Swamp Sparrow
Melospiza georgiana

DESCRIPTION 5.75 in/14.5 cm. **Rufous wings**, black-streaked back, **grayish face**; white breast, nape, throat. Rounded tail; bill long, fairly thin, yellowish. ***Breeding:*** Rusty cap (male brighter), dark post-ocular line; **breast clean, pale gray.** ***Non-breeding:*** Cap brownish with median stripe; breast often vaguely streaked. ***Juvenile:*** Resembles non-breeding; cap blacker, face greener.

SIMILAR SPECIES Song Sparrow (p. 409) larger; breast heavily streaked. Tan-morph White-throated Sparrow (p. 414) larger; bill deeper based, grayer. Lincoln's Sparrow (p. 410) breast finely streaked. Chipping Sparrow (p. 399) slimmer, longer tailed; bold eyeline from bill to nape.

STATUS & DISTRIBUTION Breeds eastern Yukon to Newfoundland, south to Nebraska, West Virginia; winters mostly from Great Lakes, Massachusetts south to central Mexico, also from southwestern BC down West Coast. In PNW, rare breeder eastern BC northward from near Revelstoke; uncommon to rare Oct–Apr in westside lowlands north to Vancouver Island; accidental Haida Gwaii; rare east of Cascades/BC Coast Range, mostly in migration (casual northwestern MT, much of ID).

HABITAT ASSOCIATIONS Breeds in open marsh; winters wet semi-open areas, brushy thickets; migrants frequent weedy fields.

BEHAVIOR & FEEDING Forages on ground in wet places for invertebrates; more seeds taken in winter. Moves rail-like through emergent plants; often retreats back to cover on foot. Forms large, loose migratory flocks; in PNW, usually alone or in small groups, often with Song Sparrows. Usually monogamous. Female builds concealed nest near ground or water, provides nest care.

VOCALIZATIONS Song rich, even-toned trill fading at end; calls include sharp warbler-like *chip*, thin *seeet*.

"Sooty" · WA (Pacific County)—Oct · RYAN SHAW

"Red" · WA (Yakima County)—Jan · DENNY GRANSTRAND

"Sooty" · WA (Pierce County)—Apr · JOSEPH V. HIGBEE

P.i. altivagans · WA (Thurston County)—Mar · JOSEPH V. HIGBEE

Fox Sparrow
Passerella iliaca

DESCRIPTION 6.75 in/17 cm. Bulky, **plain-headed** sparrow; rufous tail, whitish breast with **chevron-shaped spots**; most show yellowish lower mandible. *Juvenile:* Duller. Numerous geographic races grouped into four types, all represented in PNW but often difficult to determine in field. Populations vary clinally in char-

"Sooty"

acteristics such as size, voice, mantle color, ventral spotting; intergrades exist. *"Sooty":* Variably chocolate to grayish brown dorsally; densely marked ventrally, **flanks dusky**, mantle plain. *"Thick-billed":* Gray head, back contrast with reddish tail; **chevrons small**, blackish; large **bill often grayish**. *"Slate-colored":* Usually brighter than "Thick-billed"; **gray back contrasts with rusty wings**; chevrons brownish. *"Red":* **Red auriculars**, white malar contrast with broad gray supercilium; chevrons rufous, flanks not dusky; shows **gray-streaked reddish back**, pale wing-bars. One "Slate-colored" subspecies, *P.i. altivagans*, similar to "Red" but with plainer head, browner upperparts.

SIMILAR SPECIES Song Sparrow (p. 409) has gray supercilium, brown head stripes. Hermit Thrush (p. 357) shows much thinner bill.

STATUS & DISTRIBUTION "Sooty" breeds coastally from Aleutians to WA, winters Haida Gwaii to northern Baja. "Thick-billed" breeds in mountains from California north into OR; winters California, northern Baja, mostly coastally. "Slate-colored" breeds in mountains from north-central BC south to Nevada, Colorado; winters western California to western Texas. "Red" breeds Alaska to Newfoundland south to New Hampshire; most winter east of Great Plains from Minnesota southward. In PNW, "Sooty" breeds uncommonly along coast, including islands, south to Point Grenville (WA); from Sep–Apr, common westside lowlands, uncommon farther inland along Columbia Gorge; rare migrant WA/OR east of crest, casual east to ID. "Thick-billed" fairly common breeder southwestern OR (Siskiyous), unclear how far north in Cascades interface with "Slate-colored" occurs; may breed to

"Thick-billed" · *California—May* · ROBERT ROYSE

"Slate-colored" · *BC (Kelowna)—Jun* · CHRIS CHARLESWORTH

"Thick-billed?" · *WA (Yakima County)—Jun* · TOM MANSFIELD

"Slate-colored?" · *OR (Lake County)—Aug* · DONALD W. NELSON

"Thick-billed"

"Slate-colored"

"Red"

southern WA. "Slate-colored" fairly common but local breeder from upper west slope Cascades/BC Coast Range across interior to Rockies (*P.i. altivagans* from central BC to southwestern Alberta). Extent of overlap with "Thick-billed" in Cascades of OR, southern WA undetermined. Rare Oct–Apr in lowlands (majority *altivagans*). "Red" casual migrant, primarily western WA.

HABITAT ASSOCIATIONS Breeds coastal scrub, open forest with thick undergrowth, subalpine brush; at other seasons frequents hedgerows, blackberry tangles, backyards.

BEHAVIOR & FEEDING Forages by scraping ground with both feet for invertebrates, plant materials; frequents birdfeeders. Often sings on migration, forms loose flocks. Pair builds nest on or near ground; breeding behavior little studied.

VOCALIZATIONS Complex, ringing, musical song varies with type; more buzzy in "Sooty," richest in "Red." Calls include loud smacking *chink*, thin *sisp*.

White morph First-winter · WA (King County)—Mar · GREGG THOMPSON

Tan morph · BC (Penticton)—Oct · LAURE W. NEISH

White-throated Sparrow
Zonotrichia albicollis

DESCRIPTION 6.25 in/16 cm. Chunky; grayish bill. **Unstreaked gray breast**, streaked brown mantle, white wing-bars. **White throat**, yellow supraloral. Pale supercilium, dark crown with pale median stripe give **striped-headed** appearance. Males brighter. *White morph:* Black-and-white head stripes (duller Aug–Mar). *Tan morph:* Buff-and-brown head stripes. *Juvenile:* Duller; dark ventral streaking; **blurry streaks** retained to spring.

SIMILAR SPECIES Swamp Sparrow (p. 411) thinner bill, grayer face, brighter rufous upperwing coverts. White-crowned Sparrow (p. 416) larger, grayer overall; lacks bold white throat. Song Sparrow (p. 409) heavily streaked breast, grayish supercilium.

STATUS & DISTRIBUTION Breeds from eastern Yukon to Newfoundland south to southern Alberta, Pennsylvania; winters mostly from southern Great Plains east to Maine, south to Texas, Florida, also southwestern BC to southern California. In PNW, increasingly common. Breeds in BC at northeastern corner of region; uncommon Sep–May in lowlands, predominantly west of Cascades south from southwestern BC; casual Jun–Aug away from breeding grounds. Rare east of crest, mainly from WA Columbia Plateau (most Sep–Oct, fewer Apr–May).

HABITAT ASSOCIATIONS Breeds near coniferous forest edge; at other seasons, scrubby woodland, backyards, hedgerows, weedy fields.

BEHAVIOR & FEEDING Diet mostly plant materials, more insects during breeding season; scrapes ground litter with both feet or feeds in shrubs. Flocks when not breeding; in PNW, usually small groups with other *Zonotrichia*. Monogamous; typically pairs with opposite morph. Female builds concealed nest on ground, usually double-broods.

VOCALIZATIONS Song piercing, whistled *oh see Canada Canada Canada*; calls include metallic *chink*, thin *seeep*.

First-winter · *WA (King County)—Jan* · GREGG THOMPSON   Breeding · *WA (King County)—May* · GREGG THOMPSON

Harris's Sparrow
Zonotrichia querula

DESCRIPTION 7 in/18 cm. **White breast,** wing-bars; streaked sides, mantle; lacks head stripes. Long tail, **large pink bill.** *Breeding:* Black of crown extends down around bill forming **bib**; gray face; females show less black. *Non-breeding:* Black reduced, face buffy. *Juvenile:* Streaked breast through Aug (plumage not seen in PNW); first-winter shows black-scaled crown, white throat, **black necklace** becoming full bib by spring.

SIMILAR SPECIES Other *Zonotrichia* (pp. 414, 416–417) gray breasted; immature White-crowned Sparrow shows head stripes. Lapland Longspur (p. 368) tail shorter with white outer rectrices. Male House Sparrow (p. 450) appears chunky; blackish bill, plain chestnut nape.

STATUS & DISTRIBUTION Canada's only endemic breeder; nests in Low Arctic from Northwest Territories to northwestern Ontario at Hudson Bay; winters principally southern South Dakota, eastern Colorado, western Missouri to Texas. Occurs irregularly in PNW in lowlands. Generally rare Oct–May; reports peak Jan–Apr (mostly immatures). Sometimes locally uncommon east of Cascades south from south-central BC (Okanagan), e.g., WA Columbia Plateau. Casual Jun–Sep.

HABITAT ASSOCIATIONS Breeds on shrubby tundra at boreal forest interface; at other seasons, woodland edge, hedgerows, weedy fields, backyard feeders.

BEHAVIOR & FEEDING Eats mostly plant materials, including spruce needles; more arthropods on nesting grounds. Forages on ground, also flycatches. Monogamous pair nests on ground. Forms small post-breeding flocks; intraflock dominance among males correlates with larger extent of black plumage. Often accompanies other sparrows—in PNW, usually other *Zonotrichia*.

VOCALIZATIONS Sings 2–3 even-pitched, clear whistles; calls include grating *cheenk*, high, raspy chatter.

Z.l. pugetensis · WA (King County)—Apr · GREGG THOMPSON

Juvenile *Z.l. pugetensis* OR (Washington County) —Jul · RICHARD GRIFFIN

Z.l. oriantha · Alberta—Jul
GERALD ROMANCHUK

First-winter *Z.l. gambelii* · WA (Douglas County)—Feb
RYAN SHAW

White-crowned Sparrow
Zonotrichia leucophrys

DESCRIPTION 6.75 in/17 cm. **Unstreaked gray breast**, bold **head stripes** (black-and-white in adults). Three subspecies in PNW: *Z.l. pugetensis* **yellowish bill**, black-and-tan-streaked back; *Z.l. gambelii, Z.l. oriantha* **pinkish-orange bill**, rufous-and-gray-streaked back; *oriantha* adult shows black (versus gray) lores. *Juvenile:* Streaked breast to Aug; brown-and-tan head stripes through spring.

SIMILAR SPECIES White-throated Sparrow (p. 414) browner, smaller, with bold white throat. Golden-crowned Sparrow (p. 417) has gold forehead, dusky bill; immature lacks well-defined head stripes. Chipping Sparrow (p. 399) much smaller, finely built, lacks broad buff median head stripe of immature.

STATUS & DISTRIBUTION Breeds across Alaska, northern Canada, south in West to California, New Mexico; winters southern BC, Lower Midwest to central Mexico. In PNW, *Z.l. pugetensis* common westside breeder (increasingly eastern slope WA Cascades), uncommon coastally Oct–Feb southwestern BC southward. *Z.l. gambelii* breeds southern interior BC northward; fairly common (westside) to common (east of crest) Sep–May southern BC southward (highly local Oct–Mar in interior). *Z.l. oriantha* fairly common breeder in interior mountains from southeastern BC to southern OR (Steens, Warner Mountains); rare migrant.

HABITAT ASSOCIATIONS Breeds in shrubby semi-open areas with bare ground, including westside cities; hedgerows, weedy fields at other seasons.

BEHAVIOR & FEEDING Forages on ground for plant material, arthropods; flocks into hundreds, often with other sparrows; flushes to cover when disturbed. Monogamous; female builds ground nest.

VOCALIZATIONS Songs vary. *Z.l. pugetensis* begins with whistles, then rhythmic series of trills ending with buzz; interior breeders richer, more musical. Calls include *bink*, thin *seet*.

Breeding · *WA (King County)—Apr* · GREGG THOMPSON | First-winter · *WA (Clallam County)—Nov* · RYAN SHAW

Golden-crowned Sparrow
Zonotrichia atricapilla

DESCRIPTION 6.75 in/17 cm. Even toned. **Unstreaked breast**, streaked mantle; long tail, **small dusky bill**. *Breeding:* Brighter; grayer face, breast; **black cap borders yellow central crown**. *Non-breeding:* Duller; crown less black. *Juvenile:* Streaked breast through Aug, **crown stripes lacking** through Apr; extent of yellow forehead variable.

SIMILAR SPECIES White-throated Sparrow (p. 414) browner, smaller, with bold white throat. White-crowned Sparrow (p. 416) grayer; pinkish or yellowish bill; bold head stripes. Harris's Sparrow (p. 415) larger; shows blackish necklace or bib on whitish breast. Hybrids among *Zonotrichia* recorded frequently.

STATUS & DISTRIBUTION Breeds Alaska down mountains to southern Alberta; winters along coast southwestern BC to northern Baja. In PNW, uncommon breeder northward in BC mountains from near international border in Cascades, Invermere in Rockies; absent near coast. Sep–May, common low to middle elevation west of Cascades/BC Coast Range; on eastside, locally fairly common central WA, central OR, rare elsewhere (accidental northwestern MT, western WY). Migrants most numerous Sep, May. Casual south of Canada Jun–Aug; out-of-range breeding recorded WA (Harts Pass), OR (Coos Bay).

HABITAT ASSOCIATIONS Breeds coniferous scrub, riparian thickets near treeline; at other seasons, hedgerows, moist brush, backyards. Migrants range to subalpine.

BEHAVIOR & FEEDING Forages on ground for seeds, arthropods, also in shrubs for blossoms, buds, fruits. Forms flocks, often with other *Zonotrichia*. Shows winter site fidelity; often sings away from breeding grounds. Monogamous pair nests on or near ground.

VOCALIZATIONS Song whistled, mournful *oh dear me*. Calls include weak *seeep*; rich, loud *bink*.

Family Emberizidae—NEW WORLD SPARROWS **417**

"Slate-colored" · BC (Sechelt)—Apr · PENNY HALL

"Cassiar" · BC (Penticton)—Apr · LAURE W. NEISH

"Oregon" Male · OR (Clatsop County)—Mar · RYAN SHAW

Dark-eyed Junco
Junco hyemalis

"Slate-colored"

DESCRIPTION 6 in/15 cm. Unstreaked sparrow; **pinkish bill**, **white outer rectrices**, white belly. Numerous geographic races grouped into several types; intergrades regular at range interfaces. *Juvenile:* Streaked overall. Four types occur in PNW. *"Slate-colored":* **Slate-gray upperparts** including breast; females show brownish mantle, flanks. *"Oregon":* Male shows **black hood**, brown mantle; female duller, gray hood. *"Pink-sided":* Similar to "Oregon" but head pale gray with contrasting black lores, ashy-white throat, flanks extensively pinkish, more white in tail. *"Gray-headed":* Grayish with **rufous back**, **blackish lores**.

SIMILAR SPECIES Vesper Sparrow (p. 402) also shows white outer rectrices, but streaked above, below with white eye-ring, malar mark. Black Phoebe (p. 296) perches upright, wags tail frequently; bill thin.

STATUS & DISTRIBUTION "Slate-colored" breeds in northern forests from Alaska to Newfoundland, south in Appalachians to Georgia; retreats from Alaska, most of Canada in winter, dispersing southward, largely east of Rockies. In PNW, breeders reach central BC along Rockies; uncommon across region Sep–Apr. "Oregon" breeds, winters much of West from southeastern Alaska to northern Baja, east to Alberta, Sierra Nevada, with some downslope or southward migration from snowier areas in winter. In PNW, common breeder in mountains (to sea level west of Cascades/BC Coast Range) except for southeast of region; increases throughout in lowlands Oct–Apr. Interbreeds commonly with "Slate-colored" in BC Rockies, producing intergrades frequently seen elsewhere in region in migration (e.g., "Cassiar" Junco). "Pink-sided" (often treated as part of "Oregon" complex) breeds southwestern Saskatchewan to WY, eastern ID; winters predominantly south of breeding range. Common breeder southeastern ID, western WY, where replaces "Oregon"; mostly absent in winter. "Gray-headed" resident in mountains of southwestern US, with some winter dispersal to California, northern Mexico. In PNW, uncommon to

"Oregon" Female · *WA (Walla Walla County)—Dec*
MICHAEL WOODRUFF

"Pink-sided" · *Arizona—Jan* · ROGER WINDEMUTH

Juvenile ("Oregon") · *WA (King County)—May* · CRAIG KERNS

"Gray-headed" · *Utah—Jan* · RICK FRIDELL

"Oregon"

"Pink-sided"

"Gray-headed"

rare local breeder southern ID, high-elevation south-eastern OR; accidental WA, western BC.

HABITAT ASSOCIATIONS Breeds in diverse woodlands, shrubby edges including neighborhoods; at other seasons, hedgerows, cropland, open woods.

BEHAVIOR & FEEDING Forages on ground or shrubs for seeds or fruit, often scratching with feet; frequent at feeders. Takes more arthropods during nesting season. Large flocks with stable hierarchies formed outside breeding season. Mixes with *Zonotrichia*, other sparrows in agricultural fields; flocks generally remain close to cover, frequently flying up to hedgerows or woodland edge. Monogamous pair usually nests on ground, less frequently in shrub. Male sings from high exposed perch, female provides nest care; lower-elevation pairs often raise two broods.

VOCALIZATIONS Sings even, musical trill; calls include sharp *tsip*, repeated *kew* series during interactions.

First-fall Male · ID (Blaine County)—Dec · DAVE LAWRENCE

Breeding Female · Alberta—Jul · GERALD ROMANCHUK

Breeding Male · Alberta—Jun · TERRY THORMIN

Rose-breasted Grosbeak
Pheucticus ludovicianus

DESCRIPTION 8 in/20 cm. Stocky; square tail, **heavy pinkish-white bill.** *Male:* Breeding-plumage head black, wings black with white patches, tail black with white outer rectrices; white rump, underparts. **Pinkish-red breast**, wing linings. Non-breeding similar with brownish-edged upperparts. *Female:* **Brown-and-white head stripes**, less white in flight feathers, yellow wing linings. Streaky brown mantle; whitish **coarsely streaked breast**. *Juvenile:* Like female; male distinguishable by fall, retains female-like head pattern to second spring.

SIMILAR SPECIES Black-headed Grosbeak (p. 421) bill bicolored (dark upper mandible); male wing linings yellow (versus pink); unstreaked, usually ochre central breast on female, immature male. Purple Finch (p. 440) female smaller, lacks median crown-stripe.

STATUS & DISTRIBUTION Breeds southeastern Yukon to Newfoundland, south to Kansas, northern Georgia; winters Mexico to Peru. In PNW, rare, increasing; most observed late May–Jun but recorded casually in all other months. Has bred interior BC. Casually pairs with Black-headed Grosbeak, producing hybrids.

HABITAT ASSOCIATIONS Breeds in moist, shrubby deciduous or mixed woods; at other seasons also uses gardens, more open habitats.

BEHAVIOR & FEEDING Gleans insects, plant materials mostly from canopy; rarely fly-catches, often visits feeders for sunflower seeds. Rapid, slightly undulating flight. Forms small flocks in migration; also joins mixed flocks, but in PNW usually found alone. Monogamous pair defends territory with song or chases of conspecifics; builds flimsy nest, most frequently in vertical crotch in upper canopy. Male shares nesting duties.

VOCALIZATIONS Both sexes sing slow series of rich, husky, whistled warbles; calls include metallic *chink*, clear *phee ur*.

First-winter Female · WA (Pierce County)—Aug · DEBRA HERST

Breeding Male · WA (King County)—May · GREGG THOMPSON

First-winter Male · BC (Okanagan Falls)—Aug · LAURE W. NEISH

Black-headed Grosbeak
Pheucticus melanocephalus

DESCRIPTION 8.25 in/21 cm. Plump; square tail, heavy bill with **grayish upper mandible.** *Male:* Breeding-plumage **head black**; black tail, wings with white patches; **tawny breast**, rump. Head pattern female-like through second spring. Non-breeding shows tawny supercilium. *Female:* Browner; streaked mantle, breast sides. **Brown-and-white head stripes**, less white in flight feathers. *Juvenile:* Like female; sexes distinguishable by fall.

SIMILAR SPECIES Rose-breasted Grosbeak (p. 420) shorter tail, pinkish-white bill; female coarsely streaked across entire (often whiter) breast. Evening Grosbeak (p. 449) male shows yellow supercilium; female plain headed. Purple Finch (p. 440) female smaller, lacks median crown stripe.

STATUS & DISTRIBUTION Breeds southern BC, southwestern Saskatchewan south to Oaxaca; winters Mexico. In PNW, breeds commonly sea level to moderate elevation southern BC southward, uncommonly but increasingly farther north. Migrants widespread, common late Apr–early Jun, Jul–Sep; casual north to southeastern Alaska. Nov–Mar casual at lowland feeders west of Cascades/BC Coast Range, accidental east of crest.

HABITAT ASSOCIATIONS Breeds deciduous forest with rich understory, also mixed or riparian woodland; found nearly anywhere in migration, winter.

BEHAVIOR & FEEDING Forages in canopy or understory for arthropods, fruits, seeds; frequents feeders, especially in spring. Flies rapidly with undulating wing-beats. Seldom flocks, but joins mixed-species groups, often moving upslope Jul–Sep. Monogamous; may arrive paired on nesting territory. Female generally builds nest in outer branches of canopy or understory; male shares nesting duties.

VOCALIZATIONS Both sexes sing long, melodious whistled warble, often includes phrase *whip wheeer*; calls include metallic *pik*, rising *phee oh*.

*Family Cardinalidae—*CARDINAL-GROSBEAKS **421**

Lazuli Bunting
Passerina amoena

DESCRIPTION 5.75 in/14.5 cm. Finch-like; fairly long tailed, bold **wing-bars**, grayish conical bill. *Male:* Adult shows blue upperparts, **azure head, throat**; blackish lores, **rusty breast**; white belly, wing-bars; veiled brownish Oct–Dec. First-year resembles adult blotched with brown or whitish. *Female:* Adult plain grayish-brown, blue-tinged upperparts, **plain cinnamon-buff breast**; wing-bars whitish buff (browner in first-year). *Juvenile:* Underparts variably streaked.

SIMILAR SPECIES Indigo Bunting (p. 423) smaller. Male blue. Female breast often streaked, olive-tinged; white throat, faint wing-bars. Western Bluebird (p. 352) larger, bill thinner; lacks wing-bars.

STATUS & DISTRIBUTION Breeds southern BC to southern Saskatchewan, south to northern Baja, northern New Mexico; winters southern Arizona to Oaxaca. In PNW, common breeder May–Aug east of Cascades/BC Coast Range (uncommon southeastern OR); uncommon westside north to southwestern mainland BC, except fairly common Rogue, Umpqua, southern Willamette Valleys; rare near coast north of Rogue River. Migrates through westside lowlands May–Jun, throughout region in rarely detected flocks Aug–early Sep. Casual western OR/western WA Oct–Mar.

HABITAT ASSOCIATIONS Breeds in brushy meadows, shrubby grassland, regenerating burns, Christmas-tree farms; at other seasons, roadsides, cultivation.

BEHAVIOR & FEEDING Forages on ground or foliage for arthropods, plant materials; frequently twitches tail. Migrants gregarious, rarely join mixed flocks. Males arrive first, establish territory, sing persistently until paired. Generally monogamous. Female builds nest low in thickets, provides most nest care. Molting strategies complex; adults depart by Jul to exploit Southwest monsoon season insect bonanza.

VOCALIZATIONS Sings jumble of sharp syllables, many often repeated; calls include buzzy *cheet*, dry *pik*.

Breeding Male · *WA (Clark County)—Jun* · GEORGE PAGOS

Female · *WA (King County)—Nov* · RYAN MERRILL

Indigo Bunting
Passerina cyanea

DESCRIPTION 5.5 in/14 cm. Finch-like with grayish conical bill, fairly long tail. *Male:* Adult **brilliant blue overall**; Oct–Mar veiled brownish. First-year duller, blotched heavily with brown. *Female:* Adult **plain rich brown**; bluish-tinged upperwing coverts, tail; whitish throat. **Breast vaguely streaked, olive toned**; duller brown first year. *Juvenile:* Resembles immature female; underparts more streaked, upperparts grayish edged. Hybrids with Lazuli Bunting show intermediate plumage.

SIMILAR SPECIES Lazuli Bunting (p. 422) larger; male breast rusty, belly white; female breast plain cinnamon buff, wing-bars bolder; grayer throat, rump; juvenile can show ventral streaking but wing-bars prominent. Mountain Bluebird (p. 353) larger, appears lighter blue; thin bill, whitish belly,

STATUS & DISTRIBUTION Breeds regularly from southern Manitoba, Texas east to Maine, Florida, west irregularly to California; winters southern Florida, Mexico to Panama. In PNW, rare but increasing May–Aug (most recorded late May–Jun); casual Nov–Apr OR, WA, ID. In PNW, usually with Lazuli Buntings; frequently pair, rarely producing hybrids.

HABITAT ASSOCIATIONS Nests in weedy fields, shrubby agricultural edge adjacent to forest away from development; outside of breeding, also marshes, other open sites.

BEHAVIOR & FEEDING Forages mostly in grass or foliage for small arthropods, seeds, berries; visits feeders. Often twitches tail to side. Migrants highly gregarious, sometimes join mixed flocks. Male arrives first, establishes territory, sings persistently throughout day. Forms pair bonds but extra-territorial matings common. Female builds nest low in deciduous growth, provides most nest care.

VOCALIZATIONS Sings short patterned series of repeated metallic chirps; calls include *tink*, dry *chik*.

Female (grayish) · WA (Okanogan County)—Jun
DOUGLAS L. BROWN

Female (yellowish) · BC (Mt. Robson PP)—Aug
MICHAEL WOODRUFF

Breeding Male · OR (Harney County)—May · NETTA SMITH

Western Tanager
Piranga ludoviciana

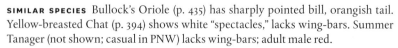

DESCRIPTION 7.25 in/18 cm. Compact with fairly **stout bill**. *Male:* Breeding plumage bright **yellow** with **scarlet face**, black wings with wing-bars (yellow upper, white lower); black back, tail. Back mottled olive through second year. Non-breeding duller; face less reddish. *Female:* Variably yellowish to grayish, often tinged olive; **wing-bars conspicuous**; lacks red face. *Juvenile:* Like female but browner.

SIMILAR SPECIES Bullock's Oriole (p. 435) has sharply pointed bill, orangish tail. Yellow-breasted Chat (p. 394) shows white "spectacles," lacks wing-bars. Summer Tanager (not shown; casual in PNW) lacks wing-bars; adult male red.

STATUS & DISTRIBUTION Breeds southeastern Alaska to Saskatchewan, south to Mexican borderlands; winters southern California to Panama. In PNW, common low- to mid-elevation forest breeder throughout, except Haida Gwaii; highest densities in dry forests east of Cascades/BC Coast Range. Rarely nests around cities or along BC outer coast. Migrants widespread, common late Apr–early Jun, Aug–Sep; casual Nov–Mar west of Cascades.

HABITAT ASSOCIATIONS Breeds open conifer-dominated forest; migrants use varied habitats including thickets in treeless landscapes.

BEHAVIOR & FEEDING Gleans large insects methodically from canopy, occasionally flycatches; also takes fruit, especially in fall. Migrants flock, also accompany mixed-species assemblages. During cold spring, often remains downslope awaiting mountain thaw; post-breeding adults may depart to Mexican molting grounds by Jul. Monogamous; female builds nest in open conifer, provides nest care; male defends territory, assists fledgling feeding.

VOCALIZATIONS Sings series of 5–7 husky phrases repeated after longer pause; calls include distinctive *pid er ick*, trilled rattle, clear *how ee*.

Breeding Female · *WA (Pend Oreille County)—Aug*
MICHAEL WOODRUFF

Breeding Male · *WA (Okanogan County)—Jun* · RYAN SHAW

Bobolink
Dolichonyx oryzivorus

DESCRIPTION 7 in/18 cm. Unique, long-winged blackbird; short **sparrow-like bill**. *Breeding male* (Apr–Jul): Head, bill, wings, **underparts black**; pale dorsally (buff on back of head, nape; rump, scapulars whitish). *Non-breeding male*: Overall **yellow buff**, streaked dorsally; mostly plain nape, underparts; **dark crown with buff median stripe**, pale lores, pinkish bill. *Female:* Smaller; like non-breeding male (less yellow May–Jul). *Juvenile:* Unstreaked flanks.

SIMILAR SPECIES Female Red-winged Blackbird (p. 426) larger; thinner bill, dense ventral streaks. Grasshopper Sparrow (p. 407) smaller; flat head, shorter tail, bold eye-ring. Western Meadowlark (p. 428) larger with long, thin bill.

STATUS & DISTRIBUTION Breeds southern BC to Labrador south disjunctly to Arizona, Kentucky; winters Bolivia to Argentina. In PNW, locally common breeder May–Aug at widely scattered locations east of Cascades/BC Coast Range north to south-central BC (Okanagan), south to southeastern OR (Malheur NWR), east to northwestern MT; uncommon at peripheral outposts in BC (Cariboo–Chilcotin), WA (Toppenish), OR (Klamath Basin). Migrants rare eastside through Sep; casual westside lowlands, mostly Sep–Oct on WA/OR outer coast; accidental to Dec.

HABITAT ASSOCIATIONS Breeds hayfields, wet meadows; fall migrants use open marsh for molting before flight to pampas.

BEHAVIOR & FEEDING Forages from ground, plant stems, for arthropods, seeds; takes mostly grain while layering fat for lengthy migration. Strongly polygamous. Male sings conspicuously from elevated perch or fluttering display. Female builds ground nest at leafy plant base, provides nest care; male assists with fledgling care.

VOCALIZATIONS Sings long, complex, bubbly series of warbles; calls include nasal *chuuk*, lively *bink*.

Family Icteridae—BLACKBIRDS AND ORIOLES **425**

Red-winged Blackbird
Agelaius phoeniceus

DESCRIPTION 8.75 in/22 cm. Stocky with fairly **stout, pointed bill. *Male:*** Glossy-black with **red epaulet bordered yellow**-buff; feathers edged brownish Aug–Mar. First-year epaulet indistinct; feathers white-streaked into second spring. ***Female:*** Smaller; dark brown, **white streaked**, washed rusty on chin; bold **buff supercilium**. First-year lacks rusty chin. ***Juvenile:*** Like first-year female but paler, more buff overall.

SIMILAR SPECIES European Starling (p. 364) shorter tail, thinner bill. Tricolored Blackbird (p. 427) plumage edged cold grayish (Aug–Mar); male epaulet white-bordered, female underparts blacker; other blackbirds lack epaulet. Rusty Blackbird (p. 430) has white eyes, lacks streaking. PNW sparrows show more-conical bills.

STATUS & DISTRIBUTION Breeds southern Alaska to Newfoundland south to Cuba, Costa Rica; withdraws from northern interior in winter. In PNW, resident except Haida Gwaii, common up to mountain passes, rare west of BC Coast Range north of Campbell River. Vacates high elevations, frozen interior Dec–Feb; moves south or shifts to agricultural areas.

HABITAT ASSOCIATIONS Breeds marshes, wet meadows, brushy edge; uses farms, feedlots in winter.

BEHAVIOR & FEEDING Adaptable omnivore, foraging mostly on ground or near water for grains, plant material (invertebrates while nesting); visits feeders. Undulating flight. Migrants gather into large flocks, often with other blackbirds. Highly polygynous; aggressive male deters intruders from territory with frequent song or attack. Female nest choice flexible; usually builds near ground in marsh, provides nest care; male may assist fledgling care.

VOCALIZATIONS Male sings *conk a reee*; numerous calls (some unique to each sex) include rattles, *chek*, varied alarm notes.

Female · WA (Adams County)—Apr · JOSEPH V. HIGBEE

Breeding Male · California—May · TODD B. EASTERLA

Tricolored Blackbird
Agelaius tricolor

DESCRIPTION 8.75 in/22 cm. Moderately stocky with pointed bill. *Male:* **Glossy blue black**; deep red **epaulet bordered white**; feathers **edged grayish** Aug–Mar. First-year epaulet indistinct; feathers streaked whitish. *Female:* Smaller, dark brown with whitish-buff supercilium; **mostly black underparts** streaked lightly with whitish. *Juvenile:* Like adult female but paler gray buff.

SIMILAR SPECIES Red-winged Blackbird (p. 426) thicker billed, plumage edged rufous (Aug–Mar); male epaulet orange red, bordered with yellow; female underparts lighter, washed rusty; other blackbirds lack epaulet.

STATUS & DISTRIBUTION Breeds mostly in California, northern Baja, disjunctly north to WA; most winter in California. In PNW, uncommon, intermittent breeder east of Cascades north to north-central OR (Umatilla County), central, southeastern WA (Grant to Whitman Counties); absent ID, western WY, northwestern MT; locally common OR (Klamath, southern Jackson Counties); irregular on westside north to Portland. Often shifts closer to central WA feedlots Aug–Feb when rare eastern OR, casual southwestern WA lowlands (Vancouver).

HABITAT ASSOCIATIONS Breeds cattail- or bulrush-dominated marsh, frequently near feedlots, dairies (also blackberry tangles in California); similar in winter.

BEHAVIOR & FEEDING Forages on ground or near water for invertebrates, seeds or livestock feed; often takes many grasshoppers. Typical blackbird undulating flight. Gathers with other blackbirds into large post-breeding flocks. Highly colonial. Males pair with 1–4 females, maintain densely packed territories; defend immediate nest area with familiar blackbird spread-winged singing display. Female builds nest, male shares fledgling care. Colony locations frequently shift year to year.

VOCALIZATIONS Male sings long, quiet growl; numerous calls include *chuk*, female chatter.

Western Meadowlark
Sturnella neglecta

DESCRIPTION 9.25 in/23.5 cm. Stout, short-tailed blackbird with **long, awl-like bill**. Upperparts, sides streaked; **crown striped** brown-and-buff, **outer rectrices white**. Black "V" on **yellow underparts** (pattern obscured with buff Aug–Jan). *Juvenile:* Buff throat, streaked breast; lacks "V."

SIMILAR SPECIES European Starling (p. 364) lacks yellow underparts, white outer rectrices. Female Bobolink (p. 425) smaller, bill sparrow-like, lacks white rectrices.

STATUS & DISTRIBUTION Breeds from southern BC to southeastern Ontario south through Great Plains to central Mexico; winter range shrinks in north, expands to southern Baja, northwestern Florida. In PNW, common breeder Apr–Aug east of Cascades/BC Coast Range north to central BC; Nov–Feb, withdraws from BC, becomes casual/rare (northwestern MT), rare (ID/WA) to uncommon (OR). Rapidly declining westside breeder south to northern Willamette Valley with urbanization of former agricultural lands; gone from southwestern BC, nearly extirpated western WA, remains fairly common OR south from Coburg, local to coast (Coos County), common Rogue Valley; fairly common Aug–Apr southwestern BC southward. State bird of MT, OR, WY.

HABITAT ASSOCIATIONS Breeds grasslands, shrub-steppe, prairies; coastal habitats, agricultural fields in winter.

BEHAVIOR & FEEDING Forages on ground for insects, seeds; probes soil, then opens gape (like other blackbirds). Flight alternating weak flapping, gliding. Forms sizable post-breeding flocks. Polygynous. Males often perch high, sing year-round; arrive on territory weeks before females. Well-concealed ground nest built by female; pair shares care of young.

VOCALIZATIONS Song gurgling series of flute-like notes; calls include *chupp*, rattle; thin *weeet* in flight.

Female · BC (Richmond)—May · PAUL KUSMIN

Breeding Male · WA (Adams County)—May · RYAN SHAW

First-winter Male · California—Sep · GLEN TEPKE

Yellow-headed Blackbird
Xanthocephalus xanthocephalus

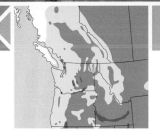

DESCRIPTION 9.5 in/24 cm. Bulky; stout billed, broad winged. *Male:* Black with **white upperwing patch**; head, **breast bright yellow**, tinged orange (head dusky Aug–Mar). First-year browner, wing patch reduced; crown, nape, face dark. *Female:* Smaller, browner; supercilium, **breast dull yellow**, streaked whitish. *Juvenile:* Rusty breast, head; buff wing-bars.

SIMILAR SPECIES Other PNW blackbirds lack combined yellow head, black belly; male Brown-headed Cowbird's (p. 434) head may appear tan but not yellow.

STATUS & DISTRIBUTION Largely interior breeder from BC, northern Baja to Lake Erie; most winter California to Mexico. In PNW, increasing, common breeder east of Cascades/BC Coast Range to moderate elevation; in recent years, thousands linger Oct–Mar, especially Columbia Plateau. Uncommon, local breeder in westside lowlands Apr–Sep from Willamette Valley (Fern Ridge Reservoir) north to southwestern BC (Fraser Lowlands); rare Oct–Mar in agricultural areas. Westside migrants peak late Apr–Jun.

HABITAT ASSOCIATIONS Breeds in open, deepwater bulrush- or cattail-dominated marsh; uses farm fields, feedlots at other seasons.

BEHAVIOR & FEEDING Forages mostly on ground or near water for aquatic insects, shifts to grains or seeds post-breeding; probes, then gapes, like other blackbirds. Highly colonial; flocks with other blackbirds. Polygynous male arrives early, establishes territory with flight displays; pairs with ≤6 females, dominates other sympatric blackbirds. Female weaves well-concealed open-cup nest over water in dead emergent stalks, provides nest care; male assists with care of older fledglings.

VOCALIZATIONS Song lengthy, mechanical, with unmusical croaks, buzzes, nasal wails; calls include rattles, liquid *keck*, female chatter.

Near-breeding Male · *Yukon Territory—May* · JUKKA JANTUNEN

Near-breeding Female · *Yukon Territory—May* · JUKKA JANTUNEN

Non-breeding Male · *BC (Victoria)—Dec* · TED ARDLEY

Rusty Blackbird
Euphagus carolinus

DESCRIPTION 9 in/23 cm. Round headed with **thin bill**, medium-long tail, **white iris**. *Male:* Breeding (Apr–Jul) **dull black** with little iridescence. Non-breeding shows pale supercilium, rusty-edged plumage. *Female:* Breeding plumage drab brownish gray; non-breeding **strongly edged rust** with grayish rump, buff underparts; pale supercilium contrasts with dark mask. *Juvenile* (seen only on breeding grounds): Slate gray with buff wing-bars, darker iris.

SIMILAR SPECIES Brewer's Blackbird (p. 431) deeper-based bill, lacks rust edging; molting male shows blotchy mixed-age plumage; female iris dark. Red-winged Blackbird's (p. 426) back streaked, iris dark. Grackles (pp. 432–433) larger, flat headed, longer tailed, with robust bills.

STATUS & DISTRIBUTION Declining breeder from Alaska to Newfoundland south to BC, Vermont; winters mostly southeastern US east of Great Plains. In PNW, uncommon, local breeder BC east of Coast Range; arrives Apr, departs from north by Sep. Rare Oct–Mar in southern BC (Okanagan), WA (mostly northern Puget Trough, Columbia Plateau); fewer western OR, ID, northwestern MT; casual western WY.

HABITAT ASSOCIATIONS Breeds in boreal bogs to northern treeline. At other seasons, wooded swamps, pond margins; in PNW, farm fields.

BEHAVIOR & FEEDING Forages on ground, often at water's edge, for insects, seeds, small vertebrates; takes more insects May–Jul, occasionally flycatching; rarely consumes other birds while wintering. Gregarious outside of breeding; flocks primarily with conspecifics but in PNW, singles associate with other blackbirds. Monogamous pair nests among tree branches over water; female provides nest care.

VOCALIZATIONS Lengthy song includes gurgle, then rising rusty hinge-like squeal. Calls include whistles, low *tchuk*.

Brewer's Blackbird
Euphagus cyanocephalus

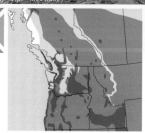

DESCRIPTION 9 in/23 cm. Slim with medium-long tail, relatively short, **fairly deep-based bill. *Male:* Glossy greenish black** with iridescent-purplish head, yellow iris. ***Female:* Drab** blackish-gray body plumage, browner Aug–Mar; **dark iris** (very rarely yellowish). ***Juvenile:*** Browner overall; male has dark iris into first Sep.

SIMILAR SPECIES Rusty Blackbird (p. 430) has thinner bill, shorter tail; Aug–Apr, shows dark mask, bold rust edging (including tertials). Red-winged Blackbird (p. 426) female streaked, male has red epaulet. Brown-headed Cowbird (p. 434) smaller; shows more-conical bill. Grackles (pp. 432–433) larger, bill heavier, tail often appears keel shaped.

STATUS & DISTRIBUTION Breeds BC to Great Lakes, south to northern Baja California; in winter, withdraws from northern interior, higher elevations, extends range southward to Gulf Coast, Oaxaca. In PNW, common resident sea level to mountains except rare western Vancouver Island, northern BC mainland coast, casual Haida Gwaii. East of Cascades/BC Coast Range, numbers peak Apr–Jul; locally common Aug–Mar in south. Declining in cities, expanding to sites where forests cleared (e.g., Olympic Mountains).

HABITAT ASSOCIATIONS Breeds in pastures, other open, human-modified habitats; at other seasons, prefers farms, feedlots, parking lots.

BEHAVIOR & FEEDING Forages on ground for invertebrates, seeds, rarely vertebrates; takes more insects Apr–Jul. Undulating flight. Migrants often flock with other blackbirds, starlings. In PNW, monogamous pair forms in winter. Colonial nester. Nest location flexible (usually on ground); female provides nest care, male assists with fledglings.

VOCALIZATIONS Sings buzzy *ka seee* or *schlruup*; calls include whistled *tsee ur*, nasal *chet*.

Common Grackle
Quiscalus quiscula

DESCRIPTION 12 in/30 cm, wingspan 17 in/43 cm. Burly, long tailed, blackish; **forehead slopes to long, deep-based bill**; adult iris yellow. *Male:* **Iridescent-purplish head contrasts sharply** with bronzy iridescence of body plumage. *Female:* Smaller, slightly duller. *Juvenile:* Browner without iridescence; brownish iris.

SIMILAR SPECIES Great-tailed Grackle (p. 433) larger; adult sports longer tail; male glosses purplish, lacks abrupt head/body color division; female head, breast buff brown. Less robust Brewer's Blackbird (p. 431) smaller billed, tail not held in keeled shape. Rusty Blackbird (p. 430) lacks purplish tone.

STATUS & DISTRIBUTION Breeds BC to Newfoundland south to Texas, Florida; withdraws in winter to southeastern breeding range. In PNW, western subspecies *Q.q. versicolor* breeds uncommonly southern ID, western WY, rarely interior BC, northwestern MT, casually eastern WA. Vagrants casual but increasing year-round throughout (most east of Cascades May–Jul); rarely remain through summer.

HABITAT ASSOCIATIONS Breeds moist woodland, diverse semi-open human-modified habitats; at other seasons, feedlots, agricultural fields near trees for roosting.

BEHAVIOR & FEEDING Varied foraging strategies primarily target seeds, grains, invertebrates; also eats refuse, vertebrates. Opens acorns with specially modified palate; sometimes robs nests of other species. Highly gregarious; flocks with conspecifics, other blackbirds, starlings, gathering in huge non-breeding roosts. Usually holds long tail in keeled shape, flies without undulation. Generally monogamous, often colonial; both sexes perform fluffed-out, spread-winged singing display. Nests in dense tree; female provides most nest care.

VOCALIZATIONS Sings harsh squeaked *kes er eeegh*; calls low, harsh *kek*, croaked *chi krrkk*.

Breeding Male · ID (Jefferson County)—Apr · DARREN CLARK

Female · Utah—May · PAUL HIGGINS

Great-tailed Grackle
Quiscalus mexicanus

DESCRIPTION 16 in/41 cm, wingspan 18 in/46 cm. **Lanky; long tail**, legs; flat head, yellow iris; long, robust bill. *Male:* Blackish with **purplish iridescence overall**, extremely long tail; duller with shorter tail through second winter. *Female:* Smaller, **grayish brown** with blackish flight feathers; buff brown into second year. *Juvenile:* Brown iris remains dark through first winter.

SIMILAR SPECIES Common Grackle (p. 432) smaller, sexes similar; purplish head contrasts with bronze body. Other PNW blackbirds much smaller; short legs, smaller bill, tail not held keeled.

STATUS & DISTRIBUTION Breeds primarily southern California to Kansas south to Peru; generally resident, some withdraw from north in winter. Range expanding since last century, now disjunct to OR, Iowa, Louisiana. In PNW, occurs year-round (peak Apr–Jul); rare OR, ID, WA, casual south-central BC (Okanagan), accidental north to Haida Gwaii; breeds rarely southeastern OR (Malheur NWR) to southeastern ID. Subspecies in PNW presumably larger *Q.m. monsoni* (rapidly expanding from Southwest).

HABITAT ASSOCIATIONS Breeds in parks, open human-modified habitats with scattered trees, water; also frequents farmland.

BEHAVIOR & FEEDING Forages in open grassy areas for plant materials, invertebrates, refuse, small vertebrates. Gregarious; flocks with other blackbirds, especially in winter. Flies without undulation. Male holds long tail in exaggerated keel shape, displays by fluffing head, other posturing; battles with feet. Colonial with complex polygyny; most females mate with dominant males. Female usually builds nest in small tree; provides all care for young.

VOCALIZATIONS Song outrageous cacophony of sharp whistles, mechanical hammering, sweeping sounds; calls include low *kuk*.

Juvenile · WA (Whatcom County)—Aug · DOUGLAS L. BROWN

Male · OR (Harney County)—May · GREG GILLSON

Female · WA (Pierce County)—Jun · NICK DEAN

Brown-headed Cowbird
Molothrus ater

DESCRIPTION 7.5 in/19 cm. Small blackbird; **conical bill**, relatively short tail. *Male:* **Black with brown head.** *Female:* Smaller, **plain brownish gray**; paler throat, vaguely streaked underparts. *Juvenile:* Resembles female; pale dorsal edging, yellow-buff underparts more distinctly streaked.

SIMILAR SPECIES Other PNW blackbirds (pp. 426–427, 429–431) larger, bill less conical; female Brewer's longer tailed. Female House Sparrow (p. 450) streaked dorsally, pale supercilium. Blue Grosbeak (not shown; casual OR, southern ID, western WY) larger bill, longer tail, warm plumage, brown wing-bars.

STATUS & DISTRIBUTION Historically endemic to Great Plains, now breeds BC, southern Yukon to Newfoundland, south to central Mexico, Florida; in winter, withdraws from northern interior, expands range southward through Baja. In PNW, common Apr–Oct except uncommon west of BC Coast Range north of Georgia Depression; breeds throughout except Haida Gwaii, where rare migrant. Uncommon Nov–Feb west of Cascades/BC Coast Range; in interior, locally uncommon WA Columbia Plateau, rare southeastern ID, casual elsewhere.

HABITAT ASSOCIATIONS Widespread breeder at woodland edges, suburbs, agricultural areas; in winter, frequents farmland (often feedlots in PNW); migrants use coastal dunes.

BEHAVIOR & FEEDING Forages mostly on ground for seeds, arthropods. Undulating flight. Migrants gather into flocks, roost, forage with other blackbirds. Brood parasite; female lays eggs furtively in other species' nests. Fledgling often monopolizes parental care, causing population declines in many songbird species. In spring, male groups court females with bows, toppling displays.

VOCALIZATIONS Male song whistle followed by gurgle. Flight call thin whistle. Female rattles; juvenile begs with *cheep*.

Adult Male · BC (Penticton)—May · LAURE W. NEISH

Subadult Male · OR (Harney County)—May · GREG GILLSON

Female · BC (Osoyoos)—May · JOHN GORDON

Bullock's Oriole
Icterus bullockii

DESCRIPTION 8.5 in/22 cm. Slim blackbird; long tail, **slender grayish bill, white wing-bars.** *Male:* **Orange** with black cap, back, wings, eyeline, narrow bib, central rectrices; large **white wing patch.** First-year less orange with olive cap, lacks wing patch; grayish back streaked black. *Female:* Grayish olive with whitish belly; orange wash on head, breast, tail. *Juvenile:* Like female.

SIMILAR SPECIES Western Tanager (p. 424) bill blunt, heavier; female lacks orange tones. Other orioles casual PNW (not shown). Scott's (breeds irregularly southeastern ID) lacks orange in all plumages. Male Baltimore black headed, Hooded orange hooded; both lack solid white wing patch. Females confusing: Hooded has longer tail, strongly decurved bill; Baltimore less grayish; Orchard smaller, yellower.

STATUS & DISTRIBUTION Breeds southern BC, western Dakotas to northern Mexico; most winter Mexico to Guatemala. In PNW, fairly common low- to mid-elevation breeder May–Jul east of Cascades/BC Coast Range north to central BC. On westside, fairly common southwestern OR to southwestern WA (Ridgefield NWR); uncommon but increasing northward to Vancouver Island (mostly river valleys); rare along entire outer coast.

HABITAT ASSOCIATIONS Open deciduous woodland, shelterbelts, riparian cotton-woods, parks, suburbs; uses adjacent shrub-steppe open spaces. Migrants may move upslope.

BEHAVIOR & FEEDING Forages in canopy for arthropods, later in season nearer ground; also takes fruits, nectar. Strong, direct flight. Migrants form small flocks; most depart to Southwest before Aug to molt. Monogamous. Female weaves hanging basket nest in outer branches of tree, provides nest care.

VOCALIZATIONS Sings bubbly rhythmic series of whistles, high-pitched squawks; calls include rolling chatter, harsh *zcheck*.

"Hepburn's" Non-breeding Male · BC (Kamloops)—Nov
CHRIS WENGER

"Hepburn's" Juvenile · WA (Whatcom County)—Jul
JON TIMMER

"Brown-cheeked" Breeding Male · MT (Glacier NP)—Jul
KURT LINDSAY

"Brown-cheeked" Non-breeding Female · OR (Benton County)
—Nov · MATT T. LEE

Gray-crowned Rosy-Finch
Leucosticte tephrocotis

DESCRIPTION 6.25 in/16 cm. Long winged with short black legs, notched tail. Evenly **conical yellow bill** turns blackish Apr–Jul. *Male:* "Hepburn's" **rich brown** with **pinkish edging** on wings, rump, belly; **head gray**, fore-crown blackish. "Brown-cheeked" similar with brown cheek (endemic Wallowas subspecies duskier). *Female:* Paler with yellowish-pink edging. *Juvenile:* Grayish brown with eye-ring, tan wing-bars; gray face acquired by Sep.

SIMILAR SPECIES Black Rosy-Finch (p. 437) blackish; lacks rich brownish tones; some immatures seem intermediate, possibly inseparable. *Haemorhous* finches (pp. 439–441) streaked dorsally; House Finch shows blurry ventral streaking, rounded culmen.

STATUS & DISTRIBUTION Breeds Alaska to western Montana, eastern California; winters southern BC to South Dakota, south to New Mexico; Aleutian, Pribilof populations sedentary. Two forms fairly common breeders in PNW above treeline: "Hepburn's" (*L.t. littoralis*) BC Coast Range south through Cascades; "Brown-cheeked" BC Rockies south to northwestern MT (*L.t. tephrocotis*), disjunctly northeastern OR (*L.t. wallowa*, endemic to Wallowas). Migrants widespread, winter locally in lowlands east of Cascades/BC Coast Range, also Mary's Peak in OR Coast Range; rarely recorded in western lowlands Oct–Apr, casual Haida Gwaii.

HABITAT ASSOCIATIONS Breeds in rocky clefts near tundra, glaciers; open rocky areas year-round.

BEHAVIOR & FEEDING Walks on ground or snow foraging for seeds, buds, insects; scrapes with bill, rarely flycatches. Gregarious year-round, nests in loose colonies; winter roost sites include Cliff Swallow colonies. In autumn, disperses downslope in undulating flight; post-breeding flocks may reach thousands. Sometimes visits feeders.

VOCALIZATIONS Song seldom heard; calls include chirped *tchew*.

Black Rosy-Finch
Leucosticte atrata

DESCRIPTION 6.25 in/16 cm. Long winged with short, black legs, notched tail. Evenly **conical yellow bill** turns blackish Apr–Jul. *Male:* Gray hindcrown; **pinkish on wings**, rump, belly contrasts with **overall black**, gray-edged plumage. *Female:* **Cold grayish brown**; orangish-pink edging. *Juvenile:* Like female, with eye-ring, cinnamon-buff wing-bars; gray hindcrown acquired Sep.

SIMILAR SPECIES Gray-crowned Rosy-Finch (p. 436) warmer brown (versus blackish), but some first-winter birds may be indistinguishable. Juvenile Brown-headed Cowbird (p. 434) larger; appears shorter winged, longer tailed. *Haemorhous* finches (pp. 439–441) streaked dorsally.

STATUS & DISTRIBUTION Scattered breeding sites stretch from MT to southeastern OR, Utah; winters within breeding range, also to eastern California, northern New Mexico. In PNW, rare local breeder above treeline in Rockies of northwestern MT, central ID, western WY; also southeastern OR (Steens Mountain), possibly northeastern OR (Wallowa Mountains). Migrants irregular in lowlands from general vicinity of breeding range to eastern OR, southern ID, western WY. Rare, local in winter from western WY across southern ID to southern OR (Alvord Desert, casual west to Lake County), but winter distribution poorly understood.

HABITAT ASSOCIATIONS Breeds in rocky clefts adjacent to alpine tundra, snowfields; at other seasons, high desert, other open, rocky areas.

BEHAVIOR & FEEDING Approachable, gregarious like other rosy-finches; may join these in large mixed flocks to visit feeders or to roost. Forages on ground for seeds, buds, insects. Apparently monogamous; female builds nest in rock crevice, provides nest care; male guards mate closely.

VOCALIZATIONS Series of chirps; calls include *tchew*, high-pitched note in alarm.

Female/First-year Male · BC (Vancouver)—Feb
LIRON GERSTMAN

Female/First-year Male *P.e. carlottae* · BC (Haida Gwaii)
—Oct · JUKKA JANTUNEN

Adult Male · MT (Flathead County)—Feb · KEN ARCHER

Pine Grosbeak
Pinicola enucleator

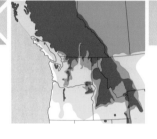

DESCRIPTION 9 in/23 cm. Plump, long-tailed finch; **rounded black bill**, thin eyeline, prominent **white wing-bars**. *Male:* Bright **pinkish-red** head, rump, upper breast; wings dark, back mottled grayish. Underparts gray (coastal races more extensively reddish). First-year like female (through second summer). *Female:* Mostly **grayish**; head, rump golden russet. *Juvenile:* Brownish overall; buff wing-bars.

SIMILAR SPECIES White-winged Crossbill (p. 443) smaller, shorter tailed with crossed mandibles. *Haemorhous* finches (pp. 439–441) smaller; lack bold wing-bars. Bohemian Waxwing (p. 366) short tailed with crest.

STATUS & DISTRIBUTION Holarctic. In New World, breeds across taiga, boreal zones northern Alaska to Atlantic Canada, Maine, south in western mountains to California, New Mexico; winters irregularly south to Ohio. In PNW, uncommon, local, possibly irregular high-elevation breeder in mountains of BC, WA, OR (Wallowas, hypothetically in Cascades), northern, central ID, northwestern MT, western WY. Post-breeding, periodically irrupts into lowlands east of Cascades/BC Coast Range; rarely descends to westside lowlands. Smaller, darker subspecies *P.e. carlottae* endemic to Haida Gwaii.

HABITAT ASSOCIATIONS Breeds in open, subalpine coniferous forests (lower elevations in Haida Gwaii); outside of breeding, frequents human-modified habitats supporting favored foods.

BEHAVIOR & FEEDING Forages mostly in trees for fruit, other plant material; more arthropods while breeding. Gregarious post-breeding; small flocks wander widely to find preferred foods (e.g., mountain ash, crabapple). Seldom joins mixed flocks. Monogamous; female builds bulky, concealed nest on limb low in conifer, provides nest care; male shares fledgling care.

VOCALIZATIONS Sings appealing series of whistled warbles; calls include whistled *pu deep* or *plit er eek*.

Female · MT (Flathead County)—Nov · JAN L. WASSINK   Male · WA (Pierce County)—Nov · RYAN SHAW

House Finch
Haemorhous mexicanus

DESCRIPTION 6 in/15 cm. **Small head,** short wings, streaked brownish-gray mantle; **short, rounded bill;** slightly notched long tail. **Blurry, dark streaking on whitish underparts.** *Male:* Red (sometimes yellowish) crown, breast, rump, wash on back. *Female:* **Plain head,** without red. *Juvenile:* Like female.

SIMILAR SPECIES Other *Haemorhous* finches have shorter tail, straighter culmen; females show broad white supercilium; adult males lack belly streaks. Purple Finch (p. 440) has large head; male purplish red. Cassin's Finch (p. 441) shows whitish eye-ring; female crisp ventral streaking. PNW sparrows lack female's plain head.

STATUS & DISTRIBUTION Breeds southeastern Alaska to maritime Quebec south to Florida, Chiapas. Historically native to southwestern US, Mexico; expanded rapidly northwestward in last century; introduced to New York in 1940, now widespread in eastern North America. In PNW, first BC record 1935, not widespread in WA until 1980s; now common low- to mid-elevation resident nearly throughout (casual west of Coast Range north of Vancouver Island; on steppe, limited principally to irrigated areas). Partial migrant, but movements poorly understood; decreases near coast Dec–Feb.

HABITAT ASSOCIATIONS Farms, cities; desert, grassland, woodland edge; shuns dense forest.

BEHAVIOR & FEEDING Forages on ground or foliage for fruit, seeds, buds; visits feeders; takes more insects while nesting. Undulating flight. Flocks gregariously year-round, sometimes joining mixed flocks. Monogamous; may pair during winter. Males minimally territorial. Nest usually constructed low in evergreen or on structure; female often relinquishes fledgling care to male, begins second brood.

VOCALIZATIONS Sings hoarse warbled series ending harshly; calls include sharp *cheep.*

"Eastern" Female · BC (Prince George)—May
GREG DROZDA

"Pacific" Female · BC (Sechelt)—Apr · PENNY HALL

"Pacific" Male · WA (Whatcom County)—Jan · DOUGLAS L. BROWN

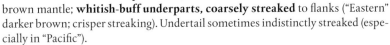

Purple Finch
Haemorhous purpureus

H.p purpureus

H.p californicus

DESCRIPTION 6 in/15 cm. Stocky; **large head**, notched tail, stout conical bill. *Male:* Unstreaked belly. **Raspberry red** of head, breast washes onto flanks, infuses brown back (brighter in "Eastern" subspecies). First-year like female; attains red over second summer. *Female:* **Broad white supercilium**, streaked olive-brown mantle; **whitish-buff underparts, coarsely streaked** to flanks ("Eastern" darker brown; crisper streaking). Undertail sometimes indistinctly streaked (especially in "Pacific").

SIMILAR SPECIES House Finch (p. 439) slimmer, small headed; male more orange red, belly streaked; female head plain. Cassin's Finch (p. 441) shows whitish eye-ring, more evenly conical bill; male's scarlet crown contrasts with pink head; female crisply streaked to undertail.

STATUS & DISTRIBUTION Two subspecies (no intergradation described). "Pacific" (*H.p. californicus*) resident, short-distance migrant western BC to California. In PNW, fairly common breeder from coast across Cascades/BC Coast Range to upper edge of ponderosa pine zone, north to Vancouver Island, Lillooet; rare eastern OR mountains. "Eastern" (*H.p. purpureus*) breeds Yukon to Newfoundland south to Virginia, winters to southeastern US. In PNW, fairly common breeder interior BC south to East Kootenay; most depart Oct–Feb, migrating east of Rockies. Reported casually elsewhere in PNW.

HABITAT ASSOCIATIONS Breeds moist coniferous forest, mixed woods; at other seasons, semi-open areas with fruiting trees.

BEHAVIOR & FEEDING Forages in trees for fruits, buds, some insects; visits feeders, takes grit from ground; flocks with other finches outside nesting season. Monogamous pair builds nest concealed on conifer branch, shares duties.

VOCALIZATIONS Sings warbled series without harsh ending; calls include slurred Cassin's Vireo–like whistle, sharp *bink*.

Female · BC (Penticton)—Apr · LAURE W. NEISH   Male · BC (Penticton)—Apr · LAURE W. NEISH

Cassin's Finch
Haemorhous cassinii

DESCRIPTION 6.25 in/16 cm. Stocky with notched tail, **evenly conical bill**, whitish **eye-ring**; crown often appears peaked. *Male:* **Scarlet crown**, head to breast reddish pink; upperparts washed pinkish; underparts unstreaked. First-year like female; attains red, loses ventral streaking over second summer. *Female:* Olive-brown-streaked upperparts, white supercilium; white ventrally with **crisp streaking to undertail**. *Juvenile:* Like female.

SIMILAR SPECIES Purple Finch (p. 440) culmen slightly rounded. Male more purplish-red; female ventral streaking blurry, undertail generally unstreaked. House Finch (p. 439) round headed with decurved culmen; male belly streaked; female head plain.

STATUS & DISTRIBUTION Breeds southern interior BC to western South Dakota, south to northern Baja California, northern New Mexico; winters mostly within breeding range, also south to central Mexico (Guanajuato). In PNW, fairly common breeder in mountains east from Cascades/BC Coast Range, north in BC to Williams Lake; moves irregularly to lowlands Sep–May. On westside, uncommon breeder near Cascade crest, rare Siskiyous; casual in lowlands; accidental near coast at any season. Most withdraw from WA, BC Oct–Mar.

HABITAT ASSOCIATIONS Mid- to high-elevation open coniferous forests—frequently pine, in PNW often ponderosa.

BEHAVIOR & FEEDING Forages in canopy or on ground, mostly for seeds, buds, some insects; visits feeders. Flies with undulation like other finches; flocks year-round, nesting in loose colonies. Migration irregular, poorly understood. Monogamous pair builds nest on conifer limb out from trunk.

VOCALIZATIONS Sings complex, bubbly warbled series; mimics other species. Calls include *chi di yip* in flight, burry *twey oh*.

Female · WA (King County)—May · GREGG THOMPSON

Juvenile · BC (Penticton)—Aug · LAURE W. NEISH

Male · WA (King County)—May · GREGG THOMPSON

Red Crossbill
Loxia curvirostra

DESCRIPTION 6.25 in/16 cm. Chunky, **large-headed** finch; blackish wings, **short notched tail**. Heavy **bill with crossed tips**. *Male:* Generally brick red, rarely yellowish; brownish auriculars, whitish undertail with dark chevrons. *Female:* Olive yellow. *Juvenile:* Greenish brown, white ventrally; heavily **streaked** overall; sexes distinguishable by winter.

SIMILAR SPECIES White-winged Crossbill (p. 443) shows bold white wing-bars; male more pinkish red. Smaller *Haemorhous* finches (pp. 439–441) show longer tail, conical bill. Smaller Pine Siskin (p. 448) slender billed, shows yellow wing flashes.

STATUS & DISTRIBUTION Holarctic coniferous-forest breeder south to Vietnam, Algeria, Nicaragua; North America hosts ten "types" distinguished by size, call-note, bill shape. In PNW, eight types occur as fairly common irregular residents. Highly erratic, nomadic breeder. Movements most apparent Apr–early Jun, Oct–Nov. Abundance varies with mast availability—most frequently uses spruce, hemlock, Douglas-fir, pine. Rarely wanders to WA Columbia Plateau, treeless areas of OR/ID. Sedentary "South Hills" type endemic to southern ID.

HABITAT ASSOCIATIONS Mature coniferous forest, rarely mixed woods; in migration, even through cities.

BEHAVIOR & FEEDING Conifer-seed specialist; also takes other mast, buds, insects, minerals from ground; rarely visits feeders. Bills of each type have evolved to extract seeds from cones of different tree species. Highly gregarious while seeking or leaving productive trees; flocks swirl synchronously, calling loudly in undulating flight. Breeds Dec–Sep, tailored to food availability. Monogamous. Pairs often nest semi-colonially. Nest concealed in conifer; female provides nest care.

VOCALIZATIONS Sings varied series of chirps, warbles; calls include *toop, kip kip*.

WA (Adams County)—Feb · DENNY GRANSTRAND

Male · WY (Yellowstone NP)—May · KATIE LASALLE-LOWERY

White-winged Crossbill
Loxia leucoptera

DESCRIPTION 6.5 in/16.5 cm. Stout, short-tailed finch; black wings, **broad white wing-bars**, slender **bill with crossed tips**. *Male:* **Pinkish red**; black tail, post-auricular spot; dark chevrons on white undertail. *Female:* Brownish yellow; dusky ventral streaking. *Juvenile:* Grayish brown, white ventrally; **heavily streaked** overall; sexes distinguishable by fall.

SIMILAR SPECIES Red Crossbill (p. 442) lacks bold wing-bars; male duller red (less pinkish). Larger Pine Grosbeak's (p. 438) bill stubby; appears much longer tailed.

STATUS & DISTRIBUTION Holarctic coniferous-forest breeder—in North America, south to northern New Mexico, Michigan, Vermont, rarely irrupting to Kansas, Kentucky. In PNW, nomadic, irregular presumed breeder (rarely confirmed)—sporadically common interior BC, uncommon northwestern MT, mostly rare western BC, northeastern WA, northeastern OR (Wallowa Mountains), Idaho Panhandle, western WY. Rarely irrupts along Cascades at any season (most likely Jul–Dec) south to OR (Douglas County); occurs casually in westside lowlands year-round, even to outer coast.

HABITAT ASSOCIATIONS Mature boreal/subalpine forest; rarely wanders to various other habitats during irruptions.

BEHAVIOR & FEEDING Forages on spruce or larch mast using crossed bill to open cones; rarely takes buds, other seeds, arthropods; sometimes visits feeders. Highly gregarious, flocking year-round; often joined by other finches in mixed flocks. Calls loudly during undulating flight. Nests in conifer during any month, contingent on adequate food supply. Monogamous pair bond may extend beyond nesting period, but male-skewed sex ratio sometimes results in female leaving fledgling care to male.

VOCALIZATIONS Lengthy song combines staccato trills, chattering chips; calls include dry *jit jit jit.*

Female · BC (Prince George)—Mar · GREG DROZDA

Male · BC (Penticton)—Jan · LAURE W. NEISH

Common Redpoll
Acanthis flammea

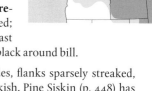

DESCRIPTION 5.25 in/13.5 cm. Compact finch; short **yellow conical bill**, deeply notched tail. Brownish-gray upperparts streaked black; white ventrally, sides streaked dark to undertail; white wing-bars; **red fore-crown, blackish around bill.** *Male:* Breast pinkish red; immature more streaked, less reddish. *Female:* Breast lacks red, streaking heavier. *Juvenile:* Lacks red cap, black around bill.

SIMILAR SPECIES Hoary Redpoll (p. 445) whiter; sides, flanks sparsely streaked, rump, undertail plain white; male barely tinged pinkish. Pine Siskin (p. 448) has thinner bill, darkly streaked breast; yellow in wings, tail. Larger *Haemorhous* finches (pp. 439–441) show grayish bills; lack black on face.

STATUS & DISTRIBUTION Holarctic across tundra, taiga; in North America, breeds south to northern BC, Newfoundland; winters to WY, Massachusetts, irregularly to southern US. In PNW, irregular, highly local Oct–Apr, mostly in lowlands. Periodically common east of Cascades/BC Coast Range south to northeastern OR (casually Malheur NWR); rare ID. On westside, sometimes fairly common BC, except casual western Vancouver Island, Haida Gwaii; rare south to Willamette Valley (casually Medford). Irruption-year breeding extends southward almost to PNW. Casual BC year-round.

HABITAT ASSOCIATIONS Breeds shrubby boreal forest edge; in PNW, often found near alders, birch.

BEHAVIOR & FEEDING Gregarious. Flits through scrub, forages acrobatically, hanging on outer branches, weed stalks, taking primarily tiny seeds. Picks grit from ground, arthropods while nesting; visits feeders. Migrant flocks into thousands swirl with undulating flight. Builds nest low, often raises two broods.

VOCALIZATIONS Sings series of chatter, trills; calls include *chjit chjit chjit*, rising *swee*.

Hoary Redpoll
Acanthis hornemanni

DESCRIPTION 5.5 in/14 cm. Plump, stout-necked finch; **red forecrown**, broad white wing-bars, notched tail, **stubby yellow bill** surrounded by black. **Whitish-gray upperparts** streaked black; white ventrally, sides sparsely streaked; **rump, undertail plain white**. Winter birds buffier overall. *Male:* Back frosty, breast pinkish tinged; immature less pink. *Female:* Breast lacks pink; undertail may show ≤2 thin streaks. *Juvenile:* More streaked, lacks red cap, black around bill.

SIMILAR SPECIES Common Redpoll (p. 444) bill averages longer, face appears less "pushed-in"; browner mantle, streaked to tail; ventral streaking heavier, extending onto undertail; male breast reddish. Separation difficult; photographic documentation desirable.

STATUS & DISTRIBUTION Holarctic tundra breeder, in North America across High Arctic; regularly winters south to Alaska Peninsula, New Brunswick, erratically to WY, Pennsylvania. In PNW, subspecies *A.h. exilipes* occurs Oct–Apr (peak Dec–Jan) principally in lowlands—east of Cascades/BC Coast Range rare, irregular BC, WA, northwestern MT, casual ID, accidental OR, western WY. West of crest casual (Fraser Lowlands) to accidental (Haida Gwaii, Puget Lowlands). North Atlantic-breeding *A.h. hornemanni* not recorded in PNW.

HABITAT ASSOCIATIONS Open tundra with scrubby brush, thickets of dwarf trees; in PNW, often alder, birch, or willow edge.

BEHAVIOR & FEEDING Gregarious. In PNW, always found with wintering flocks of Common Redpolls, exhibiting similar undulating flight, foraging strategies, diet. Single-species flocks on breeding grounds smaller than those of Common Redpoll, with which it often breeds sympatrically. Apparently monogamous; builds nest in dwarf shrub.

VOCALIZATIONS Similar to Common Redpoll; *chjit chjit chjit* in flight.

Female · ID (Nez Perce County)—Jan · RYAN SHAW

Juvenile · WA (Pierce County)—Aug · RYAN SHAW

Male · OR (Washington County)—Mar · RICHARD GRIFFIN

Lesser Goldfinch
Spinus psaltria

DESCRIPTION 4.5 in/11.5 cm. Petite with stubby, dusky conical bill, pale wing-bars, notched tail. **Yellowish ventrally**, throat to undertail; **white primary bases**. *Male:* **Black crown**, wings; greenish, obscurely streaked back. Tail appears mostly white with black tip in flight. First-fall crown greenish. *Female:* Lacks black crown, white in tail; some individuals more grayish. *Juvenile:* Browner; buff wing-bars. Only green-backed form (*S.p. hesperophila*) occurs in PNW.

SIMILAR SPECIES Larger, longer-tailed American Goldfinch (p. 447) shows white (versus yellowish) undertail, bolder wing-bars on darker wing, pinkish bill Mar–Sep. Male black cap limited to forecrown; white extends to tail tip. Pine Siskin (p. 448) heavily streaked. Warblers show thinner bills.

STATUS & DISTRIBUTION Resident southern WA east to Colorado, Texas, south to Panama. In PNW, uncommon resident southern WA along Columbia, Snake Rivers (Clark to Asotin Counties); in OR, fairly common Rogue, southern Willamette Valleys; rare on coast south from Lincoln County; common Klamath Basin May–Sep. Northward, eastward expansion of last century continues; now rare across southern OR, southern ID; casual northward across WA to southwestern BC, northwestern MT. Some withdrawal in winter.

HABITAT ASSOCIATIONS Resident in riparian scrub, oak woodland, thickets, suburbs.

BEHAVIOR & FEEDING Gregarious year-round (less in breeding season). Forages on weed stalks primarily for seeds; frequents feeders, associates with other finches. Undulating flight. Monogamous; female assumes most nesting duties; male assists by also feeding regurgitated seeds to young.

VOCALIZATIONS Sings rich, lengthy, twittered series including mimicked phrases; calls include *te leeee, tsweee ee*.

Non-breeding Female · BC (Summerland)—Aug · LAURE W. NEISH

Breeding Male · WA (Snohomish County)—Jun · RYAN SHAW

Breeding Female · OR (Linn County)—May · MATT T. LEE

American Goldfinch
Spinus tristis

DESCRIPTION 5 in/13 cm. **Unstreaked**; prominent **wing-bars**, white undertail, short conical bill, notched tail. *Male:* Breeding (Mar–Sep) bright **yellow** with **black forecrown**, wings, tail; pinkish bill. Non-breeding olive brown, face washed yellowish; dark bill. *Female:* Breeding duller than breeding male, greenish back. Non-breeding less yellow than male. *Juvenile:* Browner; buff wing-bars.

SIMILAR SPECIES Lesser Goldfinch (p. 446) has yellowish undertail, dusky bill, white primary bases; male's entire crown black, tail has prominent white patches, black tip; female's wing contrasts less with body. Pine Siskin (p. 448) streaked overall, bill thinner. Warblers show thinner bill.

STATUS & DISTRIBUTION Breeds BC to southern Newfoundland, south to Nevada, Georgia; in winter, more localized in northern interior, range expands to northern Mexico. In PNW, numbers fluctuate locally throughout year. Generally common lower-elevation breeder north to Prince George, casual to Haida Gwaii; nearly absent west of BC Coast Range north of Campbell River. Oct–Mar, locally common east of Cascades/BC Coast Range, common westside lowlands Willamette Valley southward, uncommon farther north. Washington's state bird.

HABITAT ASSOCIATIONS Open weedy areas near dense roosting cover.

BEHAVIOR & FEEDING Forages mostly on seeds; fond of thistle, alder; visits feeders. Flocks year-round, often with other finches; flight undulates. Usually nests after summer solstice low in open shrub. Monogamous, but female may re-nest, leaving care of first-brood fledglings to male. Young fed regurgitated seeds.

VOCALIZATIONS Jumbled song of repeated twitters, phrases; calls include *tee di di di*, thin *twi eee*.

Juvenile · BC (Penticton)—Sep · LAURE W. NEISH

Juvenile · OR (Linn County)—Oct · MATT T. LEE

WA (Snohomish County)—Jun · NICK DEAN

Pine Siskin
Spinus pinus

DESCRIPTION 5 in/13 cm. Dainty finch. Brownish, streaked; underparts lighter, flight feathers variably yellowish. Short notched tail, **thin conical bill.** *Male:* **Broad yellow wing-bars**; yellow wing stripe, tail flash visible mostly in flight. Ventral streaking variable. *Female:* Duller; yellow reduced, wing-bars white. *Juvenile:* Buffy wing-bars.

SIMILAR SPECIES Other finches lack yellow wing flashes; *Haemorhous* finches (pp. 439–441) larger, thicker billed, longer tailed. Goldfinches (pp. 446–447) unstreaked, shorter billed. Redpolls (pp. 444–445) show stubby yellow bill surrounded by black; juvenile appears paler from below. Juvenile Yellow-rumped Warbler (pp. 388–389) thinner billed, longer tailed.

STATUS & DISTRIBUTION Breeds Alaska to Newfoundland, south through western US to Guatemala; in winter, withdraws from northern interior, extends range into southeastern US. In PNW, common resident of forest zones, irregular due to nomadic lifestyle; uncommon transient Aug–early Jun on WA Columbia Plateau, steppe areas of OR, ID. May be widespread or locally absent dependent upon mast supply; most consistent at higher elevations.

HABITAT ASSOCIATIONS Breeds primarily in coniferous forest, also mixed woods; at other times, woodland edges, alder forest, weedy areas.

BEHAVIOR & FEEDING Gregarious year-round. Forages on outer branches, weed stalks for small seeds, other plant material, arthropods; defends feeders ferociously. Swirls in tight flocks, undulating flight, often with other finches. Pairs form during winter, nest in loose colonies, sometimes by late Feb. Female builds nest on conifer limb at moderate height away from trunk, provides nest care.

VOCALIZATIONS Sings jumble of husky twitters, trills; calls include rising *zreeee*, sharp *chi di di.*

Breeding Female · OR (Washington County)—May
GREG GILLSON

Breeding Male · BC (Penticton)—May · LAURE W. NEISH

Evening Grosbeak
Coccothraustes vespertinus

DESCRIPTION 8 in/20 cm. **Chunky**, short-tailed finch with black tail, wings; **white patches on secondaries**; massive conical bill greenish in spring, whitish in winter. *Male:* **Bright-yellow supercilium**; dusky-brown head grades to yellow belly, back. *Female:* Grayish brown washed with yellowish; white in tail, primaries. *Juvenile:* Browner than adult female with darker bill; male brighter, shows more yellow.

SIMILAR SPECIES Black-headed Grosbeak (p. 421) male has black head; female shows prominent white supercilium.

STATUS & DISTRIBUTION Breeds across southern Canada south to New England, in Western mountains to central Mexico; irregular in winter to Texas. Irruptive, nomadic. In PNW, fairly common but irregular mid-elevation breeder locally in forested habitats—populations fluctuate with cone-crop abundance, possibly declining region-wide. Usually stays within breeding habitat but May, Aug–Oct movements can produce incursions into urban lowlands or open arid areas (e.g., Columbia Plateau). Winter distribution tends to be unpredictable.

HABITAT ASSOCIATIONS Primarily coniferous forest; also mixed woods, human-modified habitats.

BEHAVIOR & FEEDING Gregarious year-round. Loosely colonial while nesting; flocks may number over a hundred outside of breeding. Forages in trees on seeds, buds; prefers maple, ash, pine, but voraciously devours sunflower seeds at bird feeders; also takes caterpillars such as spruce budworm, other forest pests. Propensity for taking gravel or salt along roadsides leads to traffic mortality. Undulating flight, loud flight calls diagnostic overhead. Female constructs flimsy nest in mid-canopy, watched over by male.

VOCALIZATIONS Song series of boisterous repeated whistles, warbles; noisy calls include strident, ringing *tcheew*, also rattles, clicks, chattering.

House Sparrow
Passer domesticus

DESCRIPTION 6.25 in/16 cm. **Stout**, short tailed; **unstreaked** dingy-gray breast, brown-streaked upper-parts; pale conical bill shows **rounded culmen.** *Male:* Gray crown, plain chestnut nape, **black bib** from lores to breast. Duller Aug–Feb, brightening through feather wear; bill turns black Mar–Jul. *Female:* Duller; pale supercilium; lacks black, chestnut. *Juvenile:* Like female.

SIMILAR SPECIES Native sparrows less compact. Harris's (p. 415) lacks chestnut nape; White-throated (p. 414) dark crown shows prominent stripes. *Haemorhous* finches (pp. 439–441) show ventral streaking.

STATUS & DISTRIBUTION Native Eurasia to North Africa, introduced nearly world-wide. Breeds across North America, southern Canada to central Mexico, irregularly north to Alaska, Newfoundland, south to West Indies, Panama. Arrived late 1800s in PNW, now common near human habitation except uncommon western BC north of Georgia Depression, absent Haida Gwaii. Some withdraw in winter.

HABITAT ASSOCIATIONS Cities, suburbs, agricultural areas; shuns contiguous forest, seldom found at higher elevations.

BEHAVIOR & FEEDING Highly gregarious year-round. Feeds primarily on ground for grains, seeds, refuse; also takes arthropods, other plant material; regular at feeders. At food-rich sites, may reside inside buildings during colder weather. Gathers in nocturnal roosts in dense bushes; presence revealed by predawn chorus of chirping notes. Long-term monogamous pair builds sloppy globular nest within cavity, crevice, or previously used nest to produce several broods Feb–Aug; shares duties. Outcompetes, sometimes kills native species in nest-site disputes.

VOCALIZATIONS Sings with repeated *chir rup* notes. Calls include *cheep*, with multiple calling birds creating noisy din; rattles in excitement.

REFERENCES

Status, distribution, and natural history information in this book is drawn from many print publications and on-line resources. We list here a selection of fundamental reference works covering individual states and provinces or, in a few cases, the whole North American continent. These are the ones we consulted most often and that we recommend as good places to begin for readers seeking to deepen their understanding of the birds of the Pacific Northwest.

Alderfer, Jonathan (ed.). 2014. *National Geographic Complete Birds of North America* (2nd edition). National Geographic Society.

Atlas of the Breeding Birds of British Columbia. Bird Studies Canada. birdatlas.bc.ca.

Birds of North America Online. Cornell Lab of Ornithology. bna.birds.cornell.edu.

BirdWeb: Seattle Audubon's Guide to the Birds of Washington State. Seattle Audubon Society. birdweb.org.

Burleigh, Thomas D. 1971. *Birds of Idaho.* Caxton Printers.

Campbell, R. Wayne, et al. 1990–2001. *The Birds of British Columbia.* 4 vols. Royal British Columbia Museum; University of British Columbia Press.

Cannings, Russell, and Richard Cannings. 2013. *Birdfinding in British Columbia.* Greystone Books.

Christmas Bird Count. National Audubon Society. audubon.org/conservation/science/christmas-bird-count.

eBird. Cornell Lab of Ornithology. ebird.org/content/ebird/.

Evanich, Joseph E., Jr. 1990. *The Birder's Guide to Oregon.* Portland Audubon Society.

Faulkner, Douglas W. 2010. *Birds of Wyoming.* Roberts and Company.

Hadley, Jane (ed.). 2015. *A Birder's Guide to Washington.* 2nd edition. American Birding Association.

Herlyn, Hendrik G., and Alan L. Contreras. 2009. *Handbook of Oregon Birds: A Field Companion to Birds of Oregon.* Oregon State University Press.

Idaho Bird Distribution: Mapping by Latilong. Idaho Museum of Natural History; Idaho Fish and Game; Idaho Audubon Council. idahobirds.net/distribution/dist_index.html.

Marshall, David B., Matthew G. Hunter, and Alan L. Contreras (eds.). 2003. *Birds of Oregon: A General Reference*. Oregon State University Press.

Montana Bird Distribution Committee. 2012. P.D. *Skaar's Montana Bird Distribution*. 7th edition. Montana Natural Heritage Program.

Montana Field Guides. Montana Natural Heritage Program; Montana Fish, Wildlife & Parks. fieldguide.mt.gov/displayOrders.aspx?class=Aves.

Orabona, A., et al. 2012. *Atlas of Birds, Mammals, Amphibians, and Reptiles in Wyoming*. Wyoming Game and Fish Department (PDF).

Scott, Oliver K. 1993. *A Birder's Guide to Wyoming*. American Birding Association.

Semenchuk, Glen P. 1992. *The Atlas of Breeding Birds of Alberta*. Federation of Alberta Naturalists.

Smith, Michael R., Philip W. Mattocks, Jr., and Kelly M. Cassidy. 1997. *Breeding Birds of Washington State: Location Data and Predicted Distributions*. Seattle Audubon Society.

Svingen, Dan, and Kas Dumroese. 2004. *The Idaho Bird Guide: What, Where, When*. 2nd edition. Backeddy Books.

Wahl, Terence R., Bill Tweit, and Steven G. Mlodinow (eds.). 2005. *Birds of Washington: Status and Distribution*. Oregon State University Press.

INDEX

The Index provides page-number references for mentions of common (English) names of species in the Species Accounts. **Boldfaced** numbers indicate primary accounts.

About the Authors

Born in Boston, **TOM AVERSA** relocated to Seattle in 1996 to work as a zookeeper, avian trainer, and educator presenting birds of prey in free-flight programs at the Woodland Park Zoo. His lifelong curiosity about the natural world focuses on bird behavior, status, and distribution, which led to service on the Washington Bird Records Committee and ultimately co-authoring four books on Pacific Northwest birds including *Birds of Southwestern British Columbia* (with Richard Cannings and Hal Opperman). Tom and his wife, Cheryl, recently relocated to Maine, where he teaches about wildlife and captive-wildlife care as an adjunct instructor at Unity College. He also works to conserve land for the Sebasticook Regional Land Trust.

RICHARD CANNINGS was born and raised in the Okanagan Valley of BC and worked for most of his career as a biologist. He curated the Cowan Vertebrate Museum at the University of British Columbia for 17 years, then worked with Bird Studies Canada for 16 years, coordinating Canadian Christmas Bird Counts, the eBird program, and the British Columbia Owl Survey. He was a founding director of the Okanagan Similkameen Conservation Alliance and has also served as a board member for the Nature Conservancy of Canada. Richard has written over a dozen books on the natural history of British Columbia, including *Birds of Interior BC and the Rockies*. In 2015 he moved from biology to politics and now serves as a Member of Parliament in Ottawa.

A longtime student of bird life, **HAL OPPERMAN** has authored, co-authored, edited, and contributed to numerous publications and online resources on birds and birding, including *BirdWeb* and the *Sound to Sage* breeding bird atlas, both hosted by the Seattle Audubon Society, and *Birds of Southwestern British Columbia* (with Richard Cannings and Tom Aversa). Hal received his B.A. in biology from Knox College and his Ph.D. in art history from the University of Chicago. He is now Professor Emeritus of Art History at the University of Washington, where he taught from 1967 until his retirement. His core research area is animals and nature in art.